November 3, 2019

AD 2036 Is The End

Dear Pastor Lundblom,

I hope you enjoy this book that I wrote in 2006. Christ will surely return. Blessed is the Lord our God.

Sincerely,

Daniel S. Hafpe...

AD 2036 Is The End

The Truth About the Second Coming of Christ and the Meaning of Life

Christian T. Jacobsen

iUniverse, Inc.

New York   Bloomington   Shanghai

AD 2036 Is The End
The Truth About the Second Coming of Christ and the Meaning of Life

iUniverse books may be ordered through booksellers or by contacting:

iUniverse
1663 Liberty Drive
Bloomington, IN 47403
www.iuniverse.com
1-800-Authors (1-800-288-4677)

Because of the dynamic nature of the Internet, any Web addresses or links contained in this book may have changed since publication and may no longer be valid.

All names and stories in this book are fabricated. Any resemblance to real persons and events is purely coincidental. The dialog, and every scene and situation, is fictitious.

ISBN: 978-0-595-43798-6 (pbk)
ISBN: 978-0-595-88128-4 (ebk)

Printed in the United States of America

For those that contend with God, and prevail.

Contents

List of Figures and Tables

Foreword

Congratulations. You have now begun to read the second most important book in the world.

That is a bold statement, but it would be false modesty for me to proceed without making it. God has given me a profound insight: I have deciphered the End Times prophecies and related them to the sweep of human history; I have related them to the very meaning of life. The only thing that is more important than that is the Bible itself.

An ancient Persian apothegm instructs:

> He who knows not, and knows not he knows not—
> he is a fool, shun him;
> He who knows not, and knows that he knows not—
> he is a pupil, teach him;
> He who knows and knows not he knows—
> he is asleep, wake him;
> He who knows and knows he knows—
> he is wise, follow him.[1]

I know that what I know about the Second Coming of Jesus Christ is the truth. You will do well to heed the apothegm and show due deference to he who has been granted wisdom.

It is the Holy Spirit that has given me this undeserved word of knowledge. And the Holy Spirit has guided me as I presented the information according to my literary style. One of my proof-readers observed that most pastoral anecdotes involve innocuous and transparent tales, such as stealing from the cookie jar. But, he said, my anecdotes are coarser, my language is saltier, and my methodology is not-at-first discernable. So be it. I am not a prude, and I have never been one to sacrifice one word that God has given me to say for the sake of propriety or convention.

The revelation has been given to me—it has not been given to you except through me. With that revelation has come responsibility and prerogative. In this book I say what needs to be said about what is going on in the world, and I say it from my heart.

You cannot critique Michelangelo with, "Why did you paint God the Father as an old bearded Caucasian touching the finger of Adam on the ceiling of the Sistine Chapel? The Heavenly Father is a Spirit and has no human form. You have misrepresented Him for the sake of your art." Nor can you goad the Renaissance master with, "It was really very wrong of you to paint your own face into the flayed skin of the Apostle Bartholomew. There is no way to be certain that he looked like you. This shows that you are vain and have a martyr's complex."

These are the comments of a self-righteous imbecile, not of a Christian.

So, likewise, do not complain of my prose, nor cast dispersions upon my dialog. This book is a work of truth in the form of art. If you cannot appreciate the art—if you view it as simply a series of polemical invectives—then you are not worthy of the truth that it conveys.

But beware because Christ cautioned us not to be taken by surprise when He returns.

> *Remember, therefore, what you have received and heard; hold it fast, and repent. But if you do not wake up, I will come like a thief, and you will not know at what time I will come to you. [Revelation 3:3 TNIV]*

Therefore, wake up and hold fast to what you receive through my writing. It is the truth about the Second Coming, and it is all-of-a-piece. If you end up accepting the title, then you will be bound to accept every major concept. There can be no common-cause between the idea that the world shall end in less than three decades and the idea that the world is billions of years old. You must choose between the two. Similarly, you cannot force any marriage of ideas between my teachings and those, say, of the late Dispensationalist, Dr. J. Vernon McGee (AD 1904–AD 1988). The only thing that he and I agree upon is that the Lord Jesus is coming back in the very near-term—on the particulars, either he is dead wrong, or I am dead wrong. You'll see the truth of the matter as you read through my book: the Word of God vindicates me beautifully, and it indicts the Dispensationalists (see Appendix II for a detailed definition of Dispensationalism).

The ideas that I present herein are entirely new to eschatological publishing, and they are inarguable for anyone that maintains that the Bible is inerrant. I have proven my case through the perfect harmony of the biblical timelines (Appendix III). That necessarily means that everyone that has previously written about the Second Coming has been in error—though some have been much more erroneous than others. And I may, in fact, be wrong about this-or-that inconsequential detail. That would be embarrassing, but not the end of the world (pardon the pun). Nevertheless, in terms of the outline and the timeline and the paradigm, I pledge to you before God that what I have written is the truth about the Second Coming of Christ and the meaning of life. I am not claiming infallibility, but I am claiming that God has favored me above all other post–apostolic authors.

I tell you all of this as preparation for what follows. Most books about the Second Coming of Christ are myopic—even obsessive—with talk of:

- the establishment and expansion of the modern State of Israel;
- the appearance of a spotless and pampered red heifer within Palestine;
- the Rapture of naked Born-Again Christians seven years before the end of the world;
- a European Union despot that will arise from the Israelite Tribe of Dan, and the brief and terrible reign of his one-world government;
- a new universal currency that will be implanted into the right hand;
- the construction of a new Jewish temple;
- the bodily, thousand-year, reign of Christ from this earth's Jerusalem;
- and a horrendous seven-year Tribulation, and Armageddon.

Many American Evangelicals adhere to these myths as closely as they adhere to the Gospel itself. Some even commingle their false End Times interpretations with Christ's Gospel—declaring that a Christian that does not particularly care about modern-day Jews living in modern-day Israel (at least 'not care' in the spiritual-sense) is an apostate to the Christian faith and is under God's wrath. They tend to be the type of people that frown when one enjoys a cold, tall, beer, or that close their eyes when they see snakes coming out of a skull in a special effects movie.

I maintain the radical position that it is only those that do not particularly care about the Lordship of Jesus Christ that are under God's wrath.

> *No one who has faith in God's Son will be condemned. But everyone who doesn't have faith in him has already been condemned ... [John 3:18 CEV]*

And how did the Lord Jesus describe those that embrace lies about the Way to salvation, and yet nitpick about the behavior of others?

> *Blind guides, who strain out a gnat and swallow a camel! [Matthew 23:24 NKJV]*

You will, therefore, not find me writing about the Dispensationalist topics itemized above except in a manner that mocks the goofballs that espouse them. When I am not debunking, I expend my pages trying to convince you that the entire reality of planet Earth is akin to a movie, or a dream, that will abruptly end one day. I explain that the only surety for what lies afterward is to be found in entrusting your soul to the God-man, Jesus Christ. I relate biographical episodes from my personal walk with Jesus, and lore that has been handed down to me from other Christians about God's keen interest in our souls. I go into some detail about world history and Church history. I describe the various christological formulations, and expose the disastrous results of deviation from the Bible's teaching about Jesus Christ. I unmask the Antichrist religion, the cultural Great Harlot, and the scientific False Prophet. And, as a man of science, I cannot refrain from expounding upon the latter argument to include a short treatise on the inanity of evolutionary theory.

What does any of this have to do with the Second Coming of Christ? A great deal. What has been going on in the world is God's history. He is in control, and He has a plan. His Second Coming is contextual to all other affairs. It is not an aberration, but a promised derivative of the mess that we have made of things, for,

> … where sin abounded, grace did much more abound:
> That as sin hath reigned unto death, even so might
> grace reign through righteousness unto eternal life by
> Jesus Christ our Lord. [Romans 5:20–21 KJV]

Now read! Read with fervor! This is about what God has done for you, and what God is going to do for you within this generation.

It is God's history. Trust in Christ and make God's history into your hope.

Christian T. Jacobsen, Ph.D.
December 2007

Preface

This book is a true and faithful interpretation of Biblical End Times prophecy and teaching. It provides an approximation, or a time-window, for the Second Coming of Jesus Christ. It explains the meaning of various events that the Bible associates with His final judgment upon the world. But this book is as much about metaphysics as it is about eschatology. I simply stumbled upon the latter during meditations on the meaning of life, the utility of science, and the creation of the physical world. I did not realize it until recently, but the subject of the end of the world draws logically from these things. Because of this, the book is set out as a sequential series of vignettes, sermonettes, and allegories. Each is prefaced by a Bible verse from which the ideas are drawn. I have also peppered the text with supporting Bible citations. The informed reader will know where to find even more biblical confirmation on any particular point.

Christianity is all about the meaning of life. It tells us that all things have been created by one Supreme Being.

> *All things were created through Him and for Him.*
> *[Colossians 1:16 NKJV]*

We are to enjoy them and to use them to glorify Him.

> *Therefore, whether you eat or drink, or whatever you*
> *do, do all to the glory of God. [1 Corinthians 10:31*
> *NKJV]*

Christianity also tells us that something has gone horribly wrong with God's original plan for us.[2] The fault lies with a spiritual saboteur, and with humanity's free-will acquiescence to his deviation.

> *The thief comes only to steal and kill and destroy.*
> *[John 10:10 ESV]*

Christianity tells us that the penalty for each of us would have been eternal separation from God, except for the fact that He is love. In grace, He chose to forgive us. God therefore set out upon a cosmic rescue mission in which He took human form at a particular calendar date in human history.

> *And his name will be the hope of all the world.*
> *[Matthew 12:21 NLT]*

At a time without flush toilets or air conditioners or hot showers—a time when human life was not worth a plugged nickel—Jesus Christ came into this miserable world and lived a perfect life. He taught and prophesied and healed, and then allowed Himself to be killed in order to conquer death's hold over us. It was a well-planned and flawlessly-executed operation. Any person that accepts this gift in the quiet of his or her own heart is guaranteed eternal life.

> *How great is the love the Father has lavished on us,*
> *that we should be called children of God! And that is*
> *what we are! [1 John 3:1 NIV]*

Central to God's plan is a compilation of sixty-six books and letters that we know as the Holy Bible. It is a written representation of the character of the God-man, Jesus. Both the Bible and Jesus are therefore referred to as the 'Word of God.' The Bible foretold of Jesus' ministry, and then recorded His birth, life, death, resurrection, and ascension. It tells the story of His early Church. It instructs those that entrust their souls to Jesus to spread His message, called the Gospel, or Good News, throughout the world. And it promises that when that task is done, Jesus will come from the sky to give us incorruptible bodies and to build a new Heaven and new Earth.

> *... the mystery of God will be accomplished, just as he*
> *announced to his servants the prophets. [Revelation*
> *10:7 TNIV]*

This final promise is about to be fulfilled.

Let us not think that the coming of Christ is far off;
let us look up … let us expect …

Dr. Martin Luther

Matthew 13:39 [NKJV]
... the harvest is the end of the age ...

1. A Day of Finality

A day of finality is approaching. It is a day when human history will end, and the entirety of mankind will be divided into two parts. The division will not be by race, language, timeline epoch, or the religion that you were born into; the distinction will be, rather, between those that trust that God loved us enough to become a human being, and those that do not.

What does this trust really mean? It means to accept that God has existed for eternity, that He is all powerful, and all knowing, and all present, and that He cares infinitely about each human soul. It means to accept that He is love, and that He has come to earth as the historical figure, Jesus of Nazareth.

He came once to die; He is coming again to reign.

There will be no more delay! [Revelation 10:6 TNIV]

Do you believe that God became a man in order to save you from spiritual death? You should. It is true, and a day of finality is rapidly approaching. It is a day of His choosing. He will come to remake all things for those that trust in Him.

John 15:1,4–6,8 [NIV]
I am the true vine, and my Father is the gardener ... Remain in me, and I will remain in you. No branch can bear fruit by itself; it must remain in the vine. Neither can you bear fruit unless you remain in me. I am the vine; you are the branches. If a man remains in me and I in him, he will bear much fruit; apart from me you can do nothing. If anyone does not remain in me, he is like a branch that is thrown away and withers; such branches are picked up, thrown into the fire and burned ... This is to my Father's glory, that you bear much fruit, showing yourselves to be my disciples.

2. Mr. Shepherdson's Hubbard Squash

My friend, Shepi Shepherdson, was the greatest farmer in the Empire State. He didn't have the largest plot of land, and he didn't turn the greatest profit per acre, but he was able to do things with plants that others could not do. He was a little old man with thick round glasses, but he was strong and wise.

Shepi grew vegetables, nuts, fruits, and he kept bees. One of his favorite crops was the Hubbard squash. It is like a pumpkin, except bigger and uglier. His heirloom variety was pale blue, with lots of bumps on it. They could get to be enormous in his fertile Hudson River Valley soil. It was Shepi's hobby to see how big he could grow the Hubbard squash.

One springtime, many years ago, he planted a squash seed. It sprouted and spread across his soil like a vine does. It produced a flower; the flower turned into a baby Hubbard squash. It grew and grew. Soon Shepi realized that he had a winner. It promised to be the biggest one that he had ever grown. Everyday he would check on the squash. He watered it, fertilized it, and weeded around it. June and July passed; things looked good.

Now, Hubbards are top-heavy—like a big egg. One night the squash fell over and, from its weight, ripped itself away from the mother plant. It was forever separated from the living part of the vine.

When Shepi went for his morning constitutional, he saw the damage. "Oh no! My prized squash!" he said. Then he spoke to the squash, "Why did you fall away, Hubbard? You were so young! When the sun comes up, your part of the vine will wilt, and then you shall rot because you are only half ripe. Now you are as good as dead …"

He considered throwing it into the compost pile, but he loved his squash. He wanted to save it. He saw that the mother plant was giving sap at the point of the break; it was falling to the ground because there was no place for it to go. An idea came to him.

He brought the two broken ends of the vine close to each other, and tied them in place. Then he cut some tendrils off the tips of the vine, and inserted the back of them into the juicy part of mother plant's vine and the top of them into the fleshy part of the breakaway's vine. He hoped that the juice would flow across the tendril conduit.

It worked! The broken vine came back to life that very day, and the squash continued to grow.

A week later, I visited. When he saw my car, he excitedly pointed toward the fields, "Come here! Come along! I want to show you something!"

We stood over his handiwork, and he beamed, "My Hubbard was dead and I brought it back to life."

I marveled, "Mr. Shepherdson, you're a genius! How did you think of such a thing?"

He smiled benignly, "Because it's mine. I had to try."

August and September passed, and he harvested a gigantic Hubbard squash. He was famous in his town, and the principal of the elementary school invited him at the beginning of each school year to teach farming techniques. He secured the squash in his flatbed and drove over to tell the children the story.

Then he brought the squash home, and put it in a cornucopia near his hearth.

~~~~~~~~~~~~~~~~~~~~~~~~

You and I are a lot like the Hubbard squash. When we are young we are foolish, and when we get old we become ugly, pale, and have warts. And we are top-heavy; we are squash-heads, really.

Humanity was growing in perfect harmony in God's garden until we fell into sin. We fell so far that we even separated ourselves from the love of God. He could have said, "Agh! Look what happened to my prized human beings! They fell into sin and are good for nothing. They're going to die. I might as well throw them away." But God loved us with a determined love. And instead of letting us rot, God decided to sacrifice the most tender part of Himself—His beloved Son, Jesus Christ. He sent Him to live with us, and He cut Him off on Good Friday. Then He brought Him back to life on Easter Sunday, and made Him the conduit of life between Himself and His people.

> *... to all who received him, to those who believed in*
> *his name, he gave the right to become children of*
> *God ... [John 1:12 NIV]*

It is only through Jesus that we can become children of God. What if Mr. Shepherdson had used a dry stick that he had found on the ground, or a plastic straw, to bridge the gap? It would not have worked. It had to be part of the living plant. So God used the Son of God and the Son of Man to breathe life back into us. He who was fully God and fully man said,

> *... whoever drinks of the water that I shall give him*
> *will never thirst. But the water that I shall give him*
> *will become in him a fountain of water springing up*
> *into everlasting life. [John 4:14 NKJV]*

When a person comes to salvation, God becomes excited and has a party in Heaven, and the angels tell him, "Lord God, you are a genius!" And when the time comes for Christians to leave this earth, God picks us up and carries us into His house as His prized possession.

Become part of the one and only Life-Giving Force in the universe. Pray in this way:

*Dear Heavenly Father, I know that I have fallen into
sin and that I am separated from You. I am helpless and
can do nothing to save myself. But I say to the devil
today, 'Enough from you! In the name of the Lord, go
away!' And I ask that from Your boundless mercy that
You would save me from sin and death. Tie me into
You through the Intermediate, Jesus Christ, and give
me the living water so that I can produce much fruit. I
commit myself to You through your Son, Jesus Christ.
In His name, and in no other, I pray. Amen.*

Pray in this way, and be baptized, and you will live for eternity.

Ephesians 1:9 [NLV]
*God told us the secret of what He wanted to do. It is this: In loving thought He
planned long ago to send Christ into the world.*

3. Thinking Outside the Box

In order to understand the meaning of life, one must think outside the box of
this world. Christ has said,

> *My kingdom is not of this world. [John 18:36 NKJV]*

The Christian life would not make any sense in the absence of the
trustworthy promise that Jesus will return to put an end to sin and to bring us
to a better place.

> *If our hope in Christ is good only for this life, we are
> worse off than anyone else. But Christ has been raised
> to life! And he makes us certain that others will also
> be raised to life. [1 Corinthians 15:19–20 CEV]*

The Nine-Dot Problem offers a good illustration.

Figure 1. The Nine-Dot Problem

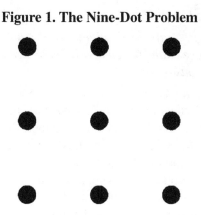

Using only four straight lines, try to hit all nine dots without lifting your pencil from the page. Hint: heed the title of this section.

See Appendix I for the solution to the Nine-Dot Problem.

John 10:1–4 [NIV]
I tell you the truth, the man who does not enter the sheep pen by the gate, but climbs in by some other way, is a thief and a robber. The man who enters by the gate is the shepherd of his sheep. The watchman opens the gate for him, and the sheep listen to his voice. He calls his own sheep by name and leads them out. When he has brought out all his own, he goes on ahead of them, and his sheep follow him because they know his voice.

4. The Gathering of Souls

Some people maintain that there is no real evidence that God exists, let alone that He acts out of love and that He became a human being.

Of all the accusations that one could level against God, this is the one that belongs to the unabashed fool. The following two verses are from the only chapters in the Bible that are entirely the same.

The fool says in his heart,	*The fool says in his heart,*
"There is no God."	*"There is no God."*
[Psalm 14:1 NIV]	*[Psalm 53:1 NIV]*

God repeated Psalm 14 and Psalm 53 into His Holy Word for effect—because it is so bloody stupid to think that He does not exist.

Aristotle noted,

> *As bats' eyes are to daylight, so is our intellectual*
> *eye to those truths which are, in their own nature, the*
> *most obvious of all.*[3]

The evidence for God's existence is everywhere in time, space, and consciousness. But obvious things are always easy to overlook. Since this is *the most obvious thing*, it is the easiest to overlook. Nevertheless, the human being's responsibility for acknowledging God's existence is found in the ability to formulate the question in the first place.

Think of when you are enjoying a well-made movie. We all know the sensation of losing ourselves in the story. Only when you have to use the toilet, or when someone near you is speaking disruptively, or when the movie ends, are you snapped out of the semi–hypnotic state. But while you are involved, you do not pay attention to the most obvious things.[4] Let's take an account of some of these facts for a moment:

- you are engaged in a financial transaction—money in exchange for film-going entertainment;
- there is someone working behind you at the film projector; he is quite possibly looking at the back of your head as you eat popcorn;
- the walls, screen, seats, air conditioning system, etc., all were installed by tradesmen that are now employed elsewhere;
- thousands upon thousands of man-hours went into the production of the film. The actor's portrayals onscreen represent not one percent of that effort;
- the various businesses (e.g., vending, construction, film studio, popcorn farmer) have people in distant offices planning how to keep them profitable;
- if the businesses are publicly-traded companies, someone on the other side of the globe is purchasing their stock based partially upon your patronage.

All of this is undeniably true, though you don't particularly care at the moment. You are trying to enjoy yourself. And you should enjoy yourself. But what a fool you would be to get caught up in the fantasy world of film to such an extent that you believe that it is all that there is. What a fool if you believed that what was going on before your eyes was not all deliberately created for a specific purpose: the gathering of dollars. You are responsible to acknowledge that fact, and to pay an admission fee, by virtue of your ability to enjoy the film. That is why a seeing-eye dog does not have to pay admission, but you do.

He that enjoys a movie production at the ticket price, and without creating a mess or disturbance, is quite different from he that sneaks into the theater or bootlegs the film. The first is welcomed, and the other is ejected.

Now, Christ is the only One that has entered the theater of life via the admittance door, and at the agreed-upon price. In fact, He paid for all of us. He, then, has the right both to enter and to call us out of the charade that is on the screen. He may do so without any fear of consequence.

> *When you arise, O Lord, you will laugh at their silly*
> *ideas as a person laughs at dreams in the morning.*
> *[Psalm 73:20 NLT]*

Have you ever been to a matinee on a hot summer day, and gotten so involved with the plot, that when you emerge you are astounded to find that it is not cool nighttime, but that it is a brilliant afternoon? You get engrossed in the movie to the point that you forget that there is an entire world out-of-doors of that little theater.

The Franciscan monk, Father Benedict Groeschel, put it well:

> *Do you want to know what is going on in human his-*
> *tory? God is going about the business of gathering*
> *souls to Himself. And when He is finished, it will be*
> *over. All the distractions of politics and pop culture,*
> *are just that—the window-dressing of life.*[5]

Imagine the passing away of everything that is vain. No more awards programs; no more endless parade of pop-tart princesses; no more weekly political punditry; no more vogue fashion crazes launched by Hollywood moguls.

Imagine that the whole thing has been a production by God, and a contrivance of that production by the devil.[6] The ultimate purpose behind the images that are being presented to you in this life is anything but vain: it is designed to gather souls unto God. And when He is finished, the world will be over.

Colossians 2:17 [TNIV]
These are a shadow of the things that were to come; the reality, however, is found in Christ.

5. Reality is Found in Christ

One night a gullible man was led to a buried treasure by the devil. The man dug where the devil pointed and found bars of pure gold, but they were too heavy to move.

The devil made a suggestion, "Why don't you cover it up and come back in the morning with your truck? Just make sure that you don't lose the spot because I can't be bothered to help you find it twice."

"But I have no marker with which to stake the ground," said the man.

"Idiot!" said the devil. "If you mark it with an obvious sign, someone else will dig it up before you return. Why don't you pull down your pants and defecate here? Then you will be able to find it, but everyone else will stay away because of the presence of your feces."

"That's a good idea," said the man.

"Of course it's a good idea," said the devil.

The man was excited by the thought of being rich and proceeded to produce an enormous stool.

Then he awoke from the dream to discover that he had ruined his brand-new thousand dollar mattress.

~~~~~~~~~~~~~~~~~~~~~~~

Most people can be brought out of the mesmerization of an engrossing movie simply by the person next to them coughing. But there are outliers in every population, including the movie-going population. There are invariably people that think the stories are real, and that think that their favorite actors really are the characters portrayed on film.

Sometimes they are stalkers; sometimes they are murderers.

A case in point are the two deviants (I will not sully my book with their names) that killed thirteen persons at Columbine High School in AD 1999. The motion picture, *The Matrix*, was released a month before the massacre, and is thought to have pushed them over the edge.

The Matrix is an engrossing movie, to be sure. The premise is that humanity lives in a computer-generated false reality that is controlled by intelligent, but evil, machines. The protagonist, Neo, is pulled from that false reality by Morpheus, and his small band of renegade humans. Morpheus knows the truth, and he teaches Neo how to go back and forth from reality to the Martix. He also shows him how to break the rules of physics while inside the Matrix through the power of his mind. Neo is then given a license to kill people inside the Matrix in order to overcome the machines and destroy their power over mankind.

After the Columbine rampage, several other fans became obsessed with the plot of this movie to the point of violence. Actor Laurence Fishburne had to step out of his memorable role as Morpheus in order to bring his fans back from the brink. He made a public statement,

There is no Matrix; there is only what is real.[7]

In this book I'm not saying that our lives are a movie or a dream. What we experience is real, *but it is not the only reality.* Something else is coming along that is much more real than this proving-ground that we call earth. The thing that is coming will make our experiences in this life seem unreal by comparison. The Apostle Peter assured us,

> *We also have the prophetic message as something completely reliable, and you will do well to pay attention to it, as to a light shining in a dark place, until the day dawns and the morning star rises in your hearts.*
> *[2 Peter 1:19 TNIV]*

Indeed, you will do well to pay attention to Scripture's prophetic message that the reality of life is not to be found in what plays out before our eyes. These things are a shadow; the reality is found in Christ.

~~~~~~~~~~~~~~~~~~~~~~~~

If you're like me, you dissect movie and book plots. I'm the type that is always stopping and rewinding the video to catch every nuance as the plot unfolds, especially if it is a mystery. And all the while I'm saying, "Wait a minute! That doesn't make sense!" I even do that in my dreams; while my dreams are taking place, in the back of my mind, I'm thinking, "Why is it unfolding this way? There's a gaping hole in the plot of this dream."

What I'm recommending to you, dear reader, is that you do that with this life—with your state in the world. Don't just go along with what you've been told. Think about the holes in the plot that the devil is trying to sell you on. There are plenty of them. Try to see through them, to what the point of life really is.

C.S. Lewis (AD 1898–AD 1963) provided this example:

A friend of mine wrote a play in which the main idea was that the hero had a pathological horror of trees and a mania for cutting them down. But naturally other things came in as well; there was some sort of love story mixed up with it. And the trees killed the man in the end. When my friend had written it, he sent it [to] an older man to criticize. It came back with the comment, 'Not bad. But I'd cut out those bits of padding about the trees.' To be sure, God might be expected to make a better story than my friend. But it is a very long story, with a complicated plot; and we are not, perhaps, very attentive readers.[8]

Do you view the Bible and Jesus' ministry as padding in the ten billion year story of the universe? Do you view the devil's distractions as the real story? Can you not see through the satanic deception?

~~~~~~~~~~~~~~~~~~~~~~~

A real-life illustration may be found in North Korea. It is run by the pot-bellied despot, Kim Jong Il. He controls every aspect of life in that country. He requires strict allegiance to the state religion, wherein his father, Kim Il Sung (AD 1912–AD 1994), is the deity (*and what does that make him?*).

The official state ideology, *Juche*, is surprisingly close to the fanatical Shinto Emperor worship of the Imperial Japanese. The Empire of Japan occupied the Korean peninsula immediately before Kim Il Sung seized power in the north. He chose his name, which means 'Kim becomes the sun.'[9] His philosophy was that, "man is the master of everything and decides everything."[10] Thus, the anniversary of Kim Il Sung's birth and death are national holidays, and his birth year is the first year in the North Korean calendar. All people, including foreign tourists, are required to bow down before statues of the elder Kim and pray, "Thank you Father Kim Il Sung."

That is not to say that Kim Jong Il actually loved his father: the older Kim was seriously ill with heart disease at the end of his life. He suffered a fatal heart attack while engaged in a routine, vicious, argument with his son.

You fool! Tonight your soul will be taken from you. Then who will have all the things you have put away?
[Luke 12:20 NLV]

The per capita gross domestic product of the North Koreans is nine percent that of their South Korean brethren.[11] And the small amount of money that is generated in its economy is confiscated by the state to fund Kim Jong Il's weapons programs, his expansive concentration camps for the descendants of political dissidents, and his personal excesses. He keeps a harem of young Eastern European women, has a ten thousand bottle wine cellar,[12] and has the world's largest collection of Daffy Duck cartoons. In the late AD 1990's, his disastrous agricultural policies resulted in the starvation of three million of his subjects.

Nevertheless, most of the remaining twenty-three million North Koreans worship their 5' 2" leader-in-shoe-lifts. Why? Because they are completely cut off from the outside world; all they know is what the government-controlled media tells them. They believe that his IQ really is off the high end of the scale, and that he is an instant expert at everything that he tries (e.g., tennis, skeet shooting, opera composition, etc.).

Do you see the irony here? Kim Jong Il is murdering them, but they still love him; the United States fought a war in the hopes of liberating them, but they revile us.

If only the people in North Korea could see that there is another reality—a life of unimaginable prosperity—just over the demilitarized zone. If only they knew of the newborn North Korean babies that are stomped to death in front of their imprisoned mothers, and the outlawed Christian pastors that have been run over by steamrollers in the name of Kim Il Sung.

The North Korean dynasty is especially threatened by Christianity, and it reserves the steamroller torture for Christian leaders. There have been at least two documented cases, thirty years apart. Witnesses report that the victims' craniums make a horrible popping sound as their brains squirt out.[13]

What the common people of North Korea do not realize is that their Great Leader is holding all of them hostage. The United States could annihilate North Korea at any time simply by dropping a dozen thermonuclear weapons. But we are waiting for an opportune moment to overthrow the leadership, so as to not kill the innocent people with the guilty. In the meantime we are hoping for the best, and trying to get their government to accept our food aid.

If the North Korean citizens used their reason for a moment, it would be clear who is at fault for their desperate condition; it would be clear the lengths to which Kim Jong Il has gone to preserve his control. Some of them do use their reason, but millions of them believe in their despot unto death. To do otherwise would do them no immediate material good, and would force them to come to terms with their complicity in supporting his regime through their good citizenship.

~~~~~~~~~~~~~~~~~~~~~~~

Jesus Christ taught us that the devil is the prince of this world, and that he is ultimately responsible for all injustice, pain, disease, and death. The devil's subjects believe his unceasing propaganda. They remain steadfastly loyal to him, and accuse God of doing the very things that the devil is doing. But those of us that have employed Providential reason have dissected this poorly-made plot, and the news reports that support it. Our hearts have been turned against the despotic prince. We are sorry for ever having anything to do with him, and have become underground agents for that Overseas Power that once came for us, and that will surely come again.

> *I am going away and I am coming back to you. [John 14:28 TNIV]*

If you were behind enemy lines during a war, and you received coded radio transmissions from your comrades-in-arms saying that they were coming for you, would it encourage you? If the messages adjured you to hang on and to be tough, if they assured you that the final victory was close at hand, would you allow yourself hope? If you subsequently heard the bombers and the artillery of your allies on the other side of the front (Section 100), would you marshal your spirit? Would your heart swell with patriotic pride?

With Christ you are on a winning team. Read the communiqués from your Providential headquarters. Listen to the sounds of battle from your Lord High Commander and His legions of seraphim. Can you hear them? They are coming like a wave. There is no power in Heaven, or on earth, or under the earth, that can halt the advance of Christ.

> *Of the increase of His government and peace there will be no end ... with judgment and with justice from henceforth even for ever. [Isaiah 9:7 KJV]*

One last battle, and the victory is ours. An end to war is at hand, and afterward a never-ending springtime for you and me.

> *Now is the time for judgment on this world; now the prince of this world will be driven out. [John 12:31 TNIV]*

God is only waiting for the right moment, when we are no longer in mortal jeopardy. He doesn't want to lose anybody.

> *The Lord is not slack concerning His promise, as some count slackness, but is longsuffering toward us,*

> *not willing that any should perish but that all should*
> *come to repentance. [2 Peter 3:9 NKJV]*

Not one member of Christ's family will be left behind from His redeeming work.

> *... and so all Israel shall be saved ... [Romans 11:26*
> *ASV]*

God has a plan to save souls, and it involves the overspreading of His Word.

Genesis 16:13 [TNIV]
She gave this name to the Lord who spoke to her: "You are the God who sees me ..."

6. You are Being Monitored—You are Being Sustained

People do not acquit themselves well on the telephone. There's something about having a black box to speak into that brings out the heart of man.

> *... out of the abundance of the heart the mouth spea-*
> *keth. [Matthew 12:34 KJV]*

E-mail is even worse. You think you are whispering into your best friend's ear, when really you are a mouse-click away from having your most mortifying secret broadcast to a million computer screens. It's as plain as the nose on our face that these are non-secure means of communication, but we don't take notice.

I once heard my neighbor's Polish accent coming through my television speaker. I looked out the window and saw her jabbering into a wireless telephone on the sidewalk. The neighbor did not care when she was alerted to the problem. "I'm a busy person. If people want to listen, let them!" She rented apartments in the neighborhood and was busy making money.

We are all busy making money. Do we ever stop to consider that God can see everything we do in secret? Consider these pieces of Scripture:

> *Nothing in all creation is hidden from God's sight.*
> *Everything is uncovered and laid bare before the eyes*
> *of him to whom we must give account. [Hebrews 4:13*
> *NIV]*

> *... the eyes of the Lord ... see everything on this earth.*
> *[Zechariah 4:10 CEV]*
>
> *Where can I go from your Spirit? Where can I flee*
> *from your presence? If I go up to the heavens, you are*
> *there; if I make my bed in the depths, you are there.*
> *[Psalm 139:7–8 NIV]*

One has a sense of being watched—as though the entire world were a bird nest beside a bird blind, or perhaps a hospital bed beside a mirrored examination room. One gets used to the mirror. One comes to the point where one takes no notice of it. But the Bible teaches that we are not only being monitored by the Person on the other side of the mirror—we are being sustained by Him.

> *From heaven the Lord looks down and sees all man-*
> *kind; from his dwelling place he watches all who live*
> *on earth—he who forms the hearts of all, who con-*
> *siders everything they do ... the eyes of the Lord are*
> *on those who fear him, on those whose hope is in his*
> *unfailing love, to deliver them from death and keep*
> *them alive in famine. [Psalm 33:13–15,18–19 NIV]*

If you pay close attention, or I should say if you adopt the right mindset, you'll notice that the Observer behind the mirror has a singular purpose in what appears to be the meaninglessness of life. There is cause-and-effect in an ostensibly random world. His cause is for us to acknowledge Him in faith; the effect is our salvation.

> *... if I settle on the far side of the sea, even there your*
> *hand will guide me, your right hand will hold me fast.*
> *[Psalm 139:9–10 TNIV]*

To an unbeliever this is abhorrent;[14] to a believer it is most comforting.

~~~~~~~~~~~~~~~~~~~~~~

When I was a child, my family went along on one of my father's month-long business trips. His work took him to western Kansas toward the end of the year—a bleak place. The grass was short and brown, the sky was overcast, and the wind never stopped blowing. Coming from the east coast, I was struck by the lack of landscape formations and trees. One felt alone, even amongst one's family.

I loved maps and spent a good amount of time daydreaming about the fascinating places just west of us. I mentioned at dinner one evening how cool it would be to see the Rocky Mountains, since we were within driving distance.

At the end of the four weeks, Dad was given a week off. He loaded us into a station wagon and drove us to a dude ranch in northern Colorado. When he announced where we were going, I boasted to my siblings, "See?! You guys always make fun of me for looking at maps, but now we will be able to vacation in Colorado because I had the idea of going there!" This was greeted with derision by the other children, of course.

I must have repeated it one too many times in the car because I remember my father turning his head from the wheel and wryly saying, "Yes, it's a good thing you said something about it last week, Chris, otherwise I never would have had the foresight to make reservations six months ago."

Colorado was a magical place to my young eyes. The mountains really were purple. And at nighttime the mule deer herded in the field abutting my cabin. We went horseback riding, and fly-fished for trout. It was a paradise. But I had to accept that my mind, my words, the work of my hands, had nothing to do with my being there. Father and mother had chosen to bring us there out of the goodness of their hearts.

*Do not fear, little flock, for it is your Father's good
pleasure to give you the kingdom. [Luke 12:32 NKJV]*

It was a gift that was planned for me while I was in ignorance, and utterly incapable of getting there on my own.

John 14:6 [NKJV]
Jesus said to him, "I am the way, the truth, and the life. No one comes to the Father except through Me."

7. The Way Life Really Is

When you enter the State of Maine, there are highway signs that read, "Maine: The way life should be." This fits with Maine's state moniker of 'Vacationland.'

I once drove there with a friend from New Jersey, and when we passed the sign he scoffed, "If Maine is the way life should be, then New Jersey is the way life really is!"

Christianity is the way life really is. Christianity explains life. But some people view life as Vacationland, and think that the purpose of life is anything but communion with the Sovereign. They think that we should pretend that the earth has been around forever and that it will be around forever. They believe in the ability of people, working together, to conquer the problems of war, poverty, crime, disease, and even death.

To think that any human endeavor can correct our miserable fallen state is to live in a Vacationland fantasy. In truth, there is only one way to that paradise: accepting Jesus Christ into your heart (see the prayer at bottom of Section 2).

~~~~~~~~~~~~~~~~~~~~~~~~

I once saw a preacher on television who was wearing a blue suit jacket. He said during his sermon, "This jacket that I am wearing right now is green." He repeated it and paused. Then he explained that he, as a human being in the fallen state, was prone to telling lies. But he said that if God had said that a blue jacket was green, then it really would be green even though it looked blue to us.

This is a useful and true illustration. It shows that our senses are fallible, and that the Word of God is immutable. So it is never the case that God is lying to us—it is always that our senses and conceptual limitations are lying to us. And this is where faith is required.[15]

Think of a person that is completely colorblind from birth. Such a person has no conception of blue versus green versus red. Everything is a shade of grey to him. One cannot adequately describe the wonders of color to this individual. All you can say is, "It is beautiful beyond what you can imagine, and someday if there is a cure for color-blindness, you shall see the majesty that has been right before you all along—trust me, there is such a thing as color, and it is magnificent."

God's sovereignty and power are such that He is able to make things become our reality—things to which we are presently blind. He can do this simply by speaking—simply by His Word.

We find the Word of God in the Holy Bible. It is the full extent of what He has chosen to reveal to us before His final judgment.

Things that are written in the Bible have a way of coming true. For example, Jesus Christ predicted,

> *What you have said in the dark will be heard in the*
> *daylight, and what you have whispered in the ear in*

> *the inner rooms will be proclaimed from the roofs.*
> *[Luke 12:3 NIV]*

That might have seemed quaint to someone living two thousand years ago, or even twenty years ago, but now we have digital audio recorders that fit in our pockets, and satellite dishes on our roofs. It is no problem at all to record what someone whispers to you at night, download it onto your personal computer, and then broadcast it to the world through a satellite link to your Internet server.

One of my proof-readers asked for a real-life example of this: a teenage girl was angry with her mother and her mother's boyfriend because they had grounded her for misbehaving. The teenager found their homemade erotic video in her mother's bedroom, downloaded the file onto her personal computer, and broadcast it to the world. The couple was oblivious to this treachery until one of their neighbors informed them that they were infamous. Their daughter was arrested, but there was no way to undo the damage—it had been downloaded onto untold numbers of computers in every corner of the world. What a nightmare! But Christ warned us that a time was coming when it would be possible for such things to occur.

What the Bible predicted came true. It came true because what God says is, by definition, truth.

In this way, whatever God decides will be is a forgone conclusion no matter how extraordinary or fantastic it seems. It matters not with what power of the will, nor with what persuasion of the arts, God's Word is ignored—sooner or later it will be the undeniable reality of existence.

~~~~~~~~~~~~~~~~~~~~~~~

The Bible says that a host of angels appeared to shepherds in Bethlehem and sang (Luke 2:13–14), and this means that those peasants really did see and hear angelic beings. The Bible says that Jesus walked on water (Mark 6:48), and this means that a human being really did walk on liquid water. The Bible says that Jesus multiplied a few fish and pieces of bread into enough to feed thousands of people (Matthew 15:36), and this means that He really did make delicious food out of thin air. And it says that at a historically verifiable time (Thursday, May 26, AD 29, according to one biblical scholar),[16] and in a place on the face of the earth (Bethany, Judea), Jesus really did ascend to Heaven by floating up into the sky (Acts 1:9).

It does not matter how unlikely any of this may seem to you. These things are historical facts just as surely as your ability to listen in on what someone says in secret on the other side of the world through your personal computer speakers.

The Word of God is just as true when it says that Jesus will come back from the sky at a future calendar date in a manner that everyone on earth shall recognize. It is just as true when it says that the bones of billions of long-dead people will be reanimated on that day. Jesus Christ said,

Don't be surprised! The time will come when all of the dead will hear the voice of the Son of Man, and they will come out of their graves. [John 5:28–29 CEV]

As surely as God was born to the blessed virgin Mary, He will come again in power and in glory. On that calendar day He will raise the dead from every cemetery with incorruptible physical bodies.

The sea gave up its dead, and death and the grave gave up their dead. [Revelation 20:13 NLT]

It will happen on a somewhat normal day, when people are going about their everyday business.

People were eating and drinking, buying and selling, planting and building. But the day Lot left Sodom, fire and sulfur rained down from heaven and destroyed them all. It will be just like this on the day the Son of Man is revealed. [Luke 17:28–30 NIV]

To a person without faith this day of finality seems incredibly improbable—until the moment that it occurs. Then, it shall suddenly become his or her reality, and it will be scientifically impossible for it to not have occurred exactly as it occurred.

Romans 10:14–15 [NKJV]
How then shall they call on Him in whom they have not believed? And how shall they believe in Him of whom they have not heard? And how shall they hear without a preacher? And how shall they preach unless they are sent?

8. "Why Didn't I Never Hear this Before?"

At the end of *Uncle Tom's Cabin*, as Uncle Tom lay dying from a vicious beating, his two Negro tormentors had a change of heart. They were, at long last, moved by his dignity and goodness, and they approached him for forgiveness.

One asked, in Harriet Beecher Stowe's (AD 1811–AD 1896) Louisiana-black dialect,

> *O, Tom! We's been aweful wicked to ye! ... do tell us*
> *who is Jesus, anyhow? Jesus, that's been a standin' by*
> *you so, all this night! Who is he?*[17]

Uncle Tom managed "a few energetic sentences of that wondrous One,—his life, his death, his everlasting presence, and power to save."[18]

Upon hearing this Christian witness, the two brutes wept, and one said,

> *Why didn't I never hear this before? but I do believe!—*
> *I can't help it! Lord Jesus, have mercy on us!*[19]

Such is the power of the message of Christ wherever it is preached.

~~~~~~~~~~~~~~~~~~~~~~

While Jesus Christ was ministering in what is modern-day Lebanon, a Canaanite woman implored Him to heal her daughter. He told her,

> *I was sent only to the lost sheep of Israel. [Matthew*
> *15:24 TNIV]*

By saying this He did not mean that she *as a Canaanite* was not a Child of Israel. Rather, He meant that she *as an unbeliever* was not a Child of Israel. He was telling her that faith mattered, not Jewish roots. She then answered Him in faith, and He accepted her (still as an ethnic Canaanite!) into the Israel of God.

Some confused Evangelicals who are reading this will be indignant. They are saying to themselves, "But Jesus did not use any such caveat when ministering to Jews! He was clearly making a distinction between this unbelieving Canaanite and unbelieving Jews, regardless of their faith in Him."

Well, let's see if Jesus addressed self-righteous Jewish men with more deference than He did this self-righteous Gentile woman. He called the unbelieving Jews:

- a brood of vipers (Matthew 12:34);
- whitewashed tombs (Matthew 23:27);
- unmarked graves (Luke 11:44);
- blind guides (Matthew 23:24);
- fools (Luke 11:40);
- descendants of murderers (Matthew 23:31);
- sons of hell (Matthew 23:15);

- and the progeny of the devil (John 8:44).

Why did He call them by such harsh names if they were the 'lost sheep of Israel' and the Canaanite woman was not the 'lost sheep of Israel'? Why did He end up accepting the Canaanite woman's profession of faith, but He never accepted the Jewish Pharisees that did not profess faith in Him? The reason is that any person that will someday have faith in Jesus comprises the lost sheep of Israel; and any person that now professes faith in Jesus has become the very Israel of God. **Membership in the Jewish nation counts for absolutely nothing in God's calculus.**

Again, the lost sheep of Israel are those that will accept Jesus into their hearts before they die. God knew their names from before they were born. He is waiting for them to believe before He comes again. The Bible assures us that none of the Children of Israel (i.e., those that are destined to believe in Christ) will be shut out of God's Kingdom, for,

> ... all who were appointed for eternal life believed.
> [Acts 13:48 TNIV]

Jesus came for the lost sheep of Israel that were among the Jews; He came for the lost sheep of Israel that were among the Samaritans; He came for the lost sheep of Israel that were among the Canaanites. He came for everyone on earth that would believe that God became a man in Him!

There are yet little brown lost sheep of Israel in the jungles of the Amazon. There are tall, skinny, black ones in the deserts of the Horn of Africa. There are squat yellow ones in the forests of Siberia. There are overfed white ones in the modern cities of Western Europe. And there are yet some olive-skinned ones in the place that Scripture calls,

> ... the Holy Land ... [Zechariah 2:12 NKJV]

It is called the Holy Land because God lived there among men in the Person of Jesus Christ. Arabs and Jews now live in this Holy Land. All have the potential to become the Children of Israel, **with or without descent** from Abraham, Isaac, and Jacob—**but only with the faith** of Abraham, Isaac, and Jacob.

~~~~~~~~~~~~~~~~~~~~~~~

A few years ago *National Geographic* magazine had an article about the final few untouched tribes of the western Amazon jungle. There may be just a few thousand souls left in remote locations that are oblivious to the outside world. The researchers wanted for them to remain untouched so that the world would not lose their diversity. Past experience has shown that from the moment when untouched people gain contact, they start wearing cotton pants and carrying steel machetes. The researchers therefore watched the tribes from a distance, and kept their location a secret from Christian missionaries in the area.[20]

It is not going to stay a secret. God is going to see to it that these people receive the Good News of Jesus Christ. They need an intervention against their oppressive and ignorant culture as much as the North Koreans do—as much as all of us do. God is all about touching previously untouched peoples with the Good News about His Love.

> *For the earth shall be full of the knowledge of the Lord*
> *as the waters cover the sea. [Isaiah 11:9 NKJV]*

In fact, one consequence of the AD 2004 Tsunami was that the Indian government initiated contact with the Sentinelesea, a previously untouched people of the Nicobar Island chain.[21] The Word of God is unstoppable, and God has promised to reach the people of every nation with it.

> *... by your blood you ransomed people for God from*
> *every tribe and language and people and nation ...*
> *[Revelation 5:9 ESV]*

The Bible teaches that there is one crucial historical requirement before Christ's return:

> *... this gospel of the kingdom will be preached in all*
> *the world as a witness to all the nations, and then the*
> *end will come. [Matthew 24:14 NKJV]*

The moment when the technology becomes available for sermons in native tongues to be beamed by satellite into remote villages (perhaps through holograms), it will be done. And when the lost sheep of Israel around the globe, half of whom cannot read, hear the Gospel for the first time they will weep and say, "Why didn't I never hear this before?"

Then the end will come.

Exodus 20:12 [TNIV]
Honor your father and your mother, so that you may live long in the land the
Lord your God is giving you.

9. Honoring Your Father

If some stranger approaches you with an intricate story about your father being a fraud—if he knows details about your father's life (e.g., where he went to school, his address before he was married, his regiment in the army, etc.)—are you going to believe him? Are you going to put validity in his word and never look at your father the same way again?

Any sensible person would say, "Just a moment! Who in hell are you anyway? And what is your motivation in disturbing my peace? Do you think you can so easily estrange me from my Daddy? Where is the proof for what you say? All you have proven to me so far is that you have done rudimentary research into publicly available records, and that you are malicious. Explain yourself, or be gone!"

You'd be a fool to believe the man's report without ample supporting evidence … unless, of course, you wanted to believe it.

Some people have a gnawing desire to accuse their Heavenly Father, or any other authority figure, of wrongdoing regardless of the issue at hand. In fact, the more their Heavenly Father looks out for their interest, the more fault they find.

I am reminded of a discussion that I had with a friend (a citizen of the United States) in AD 1991 during the Persian Gulf War. I was in full support of the decision of President G.H.W. Bush to go to war against Iraq. To me the issue was simple: a ruthless dictator with a history of expansionist ambitions had invaded our ally and trading partner, Kuwait. They supplied a significant fraction of the world's fossil fuel. It would endanger our national security to allow the dictator to monopolize that resource, and to gain the revenue thereof. The dictator, Saddam Hussein (AD 1937–AD 2006), was fond of starting wars, and feeding his political enemies into meat grinders feet-first. It would be prudent to either isolate or depose such a man. Fortunately, another key ally and trading partner, Saudi Arabia, felt threatened by the invasion, and offered their territory as a staging ground to return Kuwait to its previous monarch. The President had every right and responsibility to mobilize the United States for war under these circumstances.

My friend saw things quite differently. He was appalled. He felt that Iraq had a rightful claim to Kuwait, and he saw the Persian Gulf War as another example of American imperialism.

I told him, "I think you are just saying that because you like to be on whichever side is against what is good for the United States of America."

He said that that was not the case, but I told him that I could prove it. He glared at me, as if to say, "How can you prove what is in my heart?" His father, for whom he has little regard, was sitting next to us during this exchange.

I proceeded, "Let's say that, for whatever reason, President Bush had chosen to take up sides with Saddam Hussein when this dispute arose. What if he had said that Kuwait had been unlawfully broken off from Iraq by the British imperialists after the First World War, and that it was, in fact, the nineteenth province of Iraq? What if he had promised American military support to deter Saudi Arabian aggression in stealing Kuwait back away from Saddam? Then would you not be outraged by our actions against the sovereignty of Kuwait, and would you not denounce our hardheartedness toward the poor Kuwaitis who overwhelmingly support independence? I think everyone here knows that you'd be bemoaning the tyranny of our interventionism under that scenario, too."

He was caught off-guard and said something about how we shouldn't be involved one way or the other. But that was precisely my point: he did not have any convictions beyond being opposed to whatever the United States supported. I suspect he'd soon find fault with a foreign policy of indifferent isolationism, as well.

If my friend really had a crumb for a father, or if he really lived in an evil country, he could have found a remedy: adopt a worthy substitute, and honor that as a foster father.

Such a remedy has never been an option for him. In the past, I have challenged him to move to Cuba and allow his life savings to be confiscated by his hero, Fidel Castro. He has yet to do it. He keeps his money in conservative investments in the hated United States. At the same time he chooses rebellion toward God, the United States, his father, and every God-appointed authority, above and before anything.

Why is that?

Because to act in a different manner would cost him something. It would cost him something small—something that he would be far better off without—but something nonetheless. The thing that I am referring to is pride, of course.

Sin boils down to selfish pride. God offers us everything in exchange for our humble trust of Him as our Father. He has forgiven us of all our sins and, if we only accept that gift, He will give us eternal life in Heaven and a more abundant life here on earth. He promises to rework all the sins that we have ever committed such that good will be derived from them. That is how great His providence and love is! The King has chosen us to be His children!

Yet people resist this; people resent it. The main reason is that they think that they will be required to give up some small, precious, sins in the bargain.

This is a misconception.

When a person accepts Christ into his or her heart, God changes that person over time so that they *no longer want to sin*. Through a process called sanctification, what was once precious becomes abhorrent.

> *Find your delight in the Lord. Then he will give you everything your heart really wants. [Psalm 37:4 NIrV]*

It is actually quite astounding. All practicing Christians can tell of changes in themselves—sometimes sudden and sometimes gradual. They look back at their old selves and shake their heads. "Was I ever really like that? What a fool I was! I want no more of it. God is my portion now." They say this with joy, not begrudgingly. If you let go of your pride and embrace Christ, you will see for yourself what it is like to be tied into the Life-Giving Source (Section 2).

Still, it is of no appeal to those that are irredeemably attached to their particular set of sins. Take Kim Jong Il again. He had a serial killer for a father— one of the worst men ever to live. He could have disowned him, defected to the west, and found a worthy father figure (such as President Eisenhower). Or Kim Jong Il could have freed his people after his father was gone. He would remain fabulously wealthy under that scenario. But it would mean giving up his own private country, whose every policy is directed for his pleasure and aggrandizement. It must be an awfully powerful aphrodisiac to starve millions of people to death while you are told that you are a demigod.

It's interesting that Kim Jong Il likes the Daffy Duck cartoons. A memorable episode has Daffy stumble across a treasure chest full of gold. His eyes melt with greed, and he bathes in the coins, sputtering, "It's mine! All mine!"

~~~~~~~~~~~~~~~~~~~~~~~~

There is a scene in the movie *Cold Mountain* where, in the midst of the American Civil War, two women come upon the results of a massacre at their friend's home. The friend, the matron of a family, was left to die by slow strangulation after watching her husband and her boys butchered. The two women freed her from the rope, and one of them prophesied into the air,

> *This world won't stand long! God won't let it stand*
> *this way long!*

Her words are true. God is just and He simply will not permit this world to go on indefinitely. It would be cruel of Him to allow evil to persist for one moment longer than is necessary—and God is not cruel. He has only permitted human history to reach this late stage for the greater purpose of saving souls.

Two thousand years ago Christ was eager for there to be a definitive end to evil; He wished that the fire were already kindled to burn away this sin-laden existence.

> *I have come to bring fire on the earth, and how I wish*
> *it were already kindled! [Luke 12:49 TNIV]*

Therefore I am certain that on a calendar date that is within grasp of our imagination, God will put an end to this world forever. In His mercy, He will do this.

> *For he has set a day when he will judge the world with*
> *justice by the man he has appointed. He has given*
> *proof of this to all men by raising him from the dead.*
> *[Acts 17:31 NIV]*

He will do something else, too—something greater. He will make the pain that we have endured of no consequence. His Holy Word promises,

> *God will wipe away every tear from their eyes; there*
> *shall be no more death, nor sorrow, nor crying. There*
> *shall be no more pain, for the former things have*
> *passed away. [Revelation 21:4 NKJV]*

Many people that carry pain cannot believe this. They are overwhelmed by what they have gone through. They tell God, "Never! It is impossible to cover this hole in my soul. Not even You could make it right. Do not dare to tell me otherwise."

Bitterness against God for allowing this world of sin to continue is common. But the pain of this life—no matter how bad—is both temporary and reversible. Some day faithful Christians shall remember their pain no more than a happy toddler remembers his morning cry for his mother.

This reminds me of a friend's seven year old daughter. I was visiting them for a week because my friend's wife had undergone a caesarian section, and needed to be off her feet. I took over the kitchen duties. One evening the little girl had a fight with her five year old brother. Their parents told them to knock it off, and the girl back-talked to them. She was full of vinegar that day, and couldn't help being prissy over everything.

Her father told her, "Go to the basement until you don't think that this is a big deal anymore."

She screamed, "That's going to be never!" and stormed off in little girl fashion.

I was doing the dishes while all this occurred. Twenty minutes later, I was just finished with the drying of them when she peered around the corner.

"Mr. Jacobsen?" she said timidly.

"Yes, my dear," I answered.

"How long has it been?"

I pursed my lips to hold back my laugh. "I think it has been long enough, dear. Why don't you join them in the den now?"

She sat with her family around the fireplace, and forgot why she had been angry. She fell asleep there, and her father carried her to her room. The poor thing was tired.

I am tired, too. Are you? I suspect so.

It is unavoidable that we view the pains of this life as being beyond God's ability to console. But an eternity of good is quite a lot of good. Twenty minutes into forever will be longer than this old world has existed.

> *For I consider that the sufferings of this present time*
> *are not worthy to be compared with the glory which*
> *shall be revealed in us. [Romans 8:18 NKJV]*

Soon enough we shall nestle into our Heavenly Father's arms and wonder what all the fuss was about.

Mark 8:36 [KJV]
For what shall it profit a man, if he shall gain the whole world, and lose his own soul?

10. Ownership Rights

During the writing of this book I was approached by a friend of a friend about assisting him in launching a business. The business was to be a joint venture between his firm and another company. He was at an impasse in the formulation of a suitable operating and licensing agreement with the other company. He told me that this business opportunity had enormous profit-potential in the first year, but that if they didn't get the joint venture off the ground and secure a market position soon, all would be lost. He said that if I became involved he would make it worth my time.

I became involved. The problem was that the owner of the other company had staked out for himself an absurdly one-sided position in the joint venture legal documents. I read all the documents and rooted out all the potential pitfalls. Then, through painstaking negotiation with the lawyers of the other company, I made the necessary corrections. I then rewrote the research and development schedule of work, the business plan, and the proposed budget. When all were in presentable shape, I printed a prospectus for venture capitalists. While doing this work, I incurred expenses for which I did not immediately request reimbursement, and I was never paid for my time.

Throughout this process the person that had recruited me kept saying that he and the other two principals of his firm were going to cut me in on the deal, and that I was going to end up a rich man. After he said it the third time, and I had already saved the joint venture from collapse, I raised the possibility of making me a full fourth partner in his firm (which was to own half of the joint venture). I told him that I saw great potential in the project and would be willing to invest the same funds that he and his two partners had originally invested. He told me that this was an entirely reasonable proposal, and that he would discuss it with his partners. Later, he said that a final decision on partnership should be put off until we got closer to securing investment funds for the joint venture.

He was delighted with my efforts and complimented me unceasingly; we worked together on a daily basis like brothers, with never a cross word between us. He regaled me with stories of his past business exploits, and how generous he had been with previous partners and employees. He often mentioned the idea of me becoming the president of the joint venture once it was funded, and for a handsome salary. I always told him that I would consider becoming president if I were assured some ownership rights in addition to salary.

One time he smiled, winked, and brushed his hand at me, "What are you worried about? We're going to make a profit of one hundred million on this deal—so how does ten million dollars for yourself sound?"

I said, "A ten percent stake in your firm? That's less than a full partnership of twenty-five percent, but still okay, I guess."

I'm sure you can see where this story is going ... After three months of unpaid work, my prospectus was successful in attracting **ten times** the original funding request from a venture capital firm. In subsequent meetings everyone was exuberant, and my name was used interchangeably with the title of president of the soon-to-be-launched joint venture. I cautioned everyone that I did not yet know if I wanted the job.

Shortly after that, this fellow said that he had decided to revise the budget, and asked if half of the original salary figure (less than I could make elsewhere) would be alright with me. I told him that I believed in the business plan, and that the salary was of no consequence to me. I said that I would still consider such an offer as long as I was assured ownership rights. He said that they were definitely going to cut me in on the deal, and that I would soon be a rich man. He said that the final papers would be signed in a couple weeks, and asked me to start looking for commercial real estate so I would have an office from which to work.

A few days later he called about some other employee-related duty. I finally spoke pointedly to him. I told him that I had never promised to work for him permanently, and I was no longer willing to do legwork without a written agreement on a compensation package.

He snapped at me, "Did you not agree to take the position of president for [one-half the original salary]?!"

I said, "No. You're hearing what you want to hear. I told you that I would consider the job at that salary as long as ownership rights went along with it. My further involvement is contingent upon owning a piece of the action."

He became irritated, "How many times do I have to tell you that we are going to cut you in on the deal?!"

"When? And exactly to what degree?" I demanded.

"I don't know! I don't even know how much of the joint venture I am going to end up with at this time! These things will not be known until all the papers are signed with the venture capitalists and everything is settled concerning the other company!"

I reminded him, "But you said yourself that the window for profitability is short-lived—probably this year. So these things must be laid out in a written compensation package before I would ever commence permanent work. And the details should—"

"It will all be laid out!" he pleaded. "It will all be laid out some day soon!!"

I continued, "And the details should be discussed right now so that you can make plans to recruit another candidate in case I don't like the arrangements that you make for the president in those papers. This conversation is long overdue. We need to come to an agreement right now on how much of your firm I am going to own outright."

"What do you want from me?!"

"How about half as many shares as you have? In other words, I'm asking for a junior partnership in your firm, rather than the full partnership that you told me was within the realm of possibility a few months ago when you desperately needed my help."

He turned on me viciously, "Who the [expletive] do you think you are to make such a demand of me?! All you did was print a pamphlet for us, and you think that you are suddenly worth half as much as I am?! This company is my baby—the joint venture was my brainchild. I have already given away two-thirds of my portion by being in business with my two good-for-nothing partners. I don't want another partner! I'm offering you a job—a good job! You are going to gain great experience in the corporate world! But you've got to realize your place, and rethink things, and not make outrageous demands!"

I reminded him that I owed him nothing, and that it was he who was deeply indebted to me for salvaging the joint venture on several occasions. I told him that I had been helping him out of friendship, and in the hope that he would bring me into partnership after he saw my worth and fidelity. I told him that if he wanted to hire someone else as president and cut me loose, I would have no hard feelings whatsoever (but he would have to stop calling on me for help).

I concluded with, "It's simply a matter of what is best for your firm. If you need me in order to see the project through to profitability, I will require direct and irrevocable ownership rights over half as many shares as you have guaranteed for yourself."

He hung up on me.

Now, the joint venture could not succeed without my expertise—everyone knew this—and his firm was a worthless shell-company without the joint venture's success. So five days later he sheepishly called me and asked where we stood with each other. I said, "My position has not changed. No one in this country tells anyone else what he or she is worth. Everyone asks his price, and if you don't meet it you have to find someone else. I lay no claims against you for my work to date, except for my expenses. But I have hit a wall with you. I am unwilling to spend one more minute or one more dollar on the joint venture until we have an agreement in writing."

He was immediately bolstered because I was still speaking with him. "Not a problem!" he said cheerfully. "We don't need you to spend anything more on it until we are ready for you to commence work as president in a few weeks—at the salary that we agreed upon, mind you. And, as I promised, you will accumulate some amount of options to buy stock in the joint venture based upon your performance as president over time. It's a good opportunity for you. So stick with me, and let's leave this conversation on a good note. Okay?"

I told him that performance-based stock options were not acceptable, and that I would only entertain an offer for direct and irrevocable ownership rights over one half as many shares as he had guaranteed for himself.

He quickly replied, "Yeah, yeah, yeah! Something along those lines will be arranged for you in the final documents. It's all very much up in the air at this point. But we're definitely going to cut you in, and you are going to be a rich man soon. Excellent. You and I are back on track. Now, about that office space, I'm thinking that we need something in the city. I want you to call some commercial real estate agents and check out properties with factory platforms …"

~~~~~~~~~~~~~~~~~~~~~~~

Should I have ever become involved, even one step of the way, with this fellow? I knew that I had nothing in writing. And I knew from the tenor of his voice every time I would ask what he meant by 'cutting me in on the deal' that he was going to try to fool me into accepting performance-based, time-dependent, options to buy stock. His flattery was quite transparent: he wanted a gullible workhorse, not a capable partner.

But I also knew that his underlying business idea had great merit. I wanted to see what he was really made of. So I set a limit in my mind of a few months' work, and a certain number of dollars of personal expenses. I was willing, under the worst case scenario, to write off that amount and walk away.

I took a calculated risk that he would be shrewd enough to ultimately realize that it was in his own best interest to be honest and bring me into partnership.

I also had faith that God would never allow him to continue on to riches based on my previous labors if I did walk away. The Word of God says of people like me,

> *I will bless those who bless you, and I will curse him*
> *who curses you; [Genesis 12:3 NKJV]*

And it says of those that demonstrate contempt toward people like me,

> *Let them all be confounded and turned back that hate*
> *Zion. [Psalm 129:5 KJV]*

That is exactly what happened. He refused to make me a partner, and called me naïve for ever expecting him to keep his word. I refused to help him any longer. The venture capitalists were shocked by the unprofessional quality of the work that was subsequently done by him, and withdrew their funding offer. The window of opportunity for the joint venture closed. I went on my merry way, and he fell flat on his face.

~~~~~~~~~~~~~~~~~~~~~~~

God wants ownership rights over your soul. He is going along with you—working on your behalf—based upon your assurance that you will cut Him in on your life. He is incurring non-reimbursed expenses in keeping your dumb ass alive all these years. But He is not a fool. He has rewritten the business papers of your life many times to get you out of jams; He knows your affairs better than you do. You cannot play Him along; under no circumstances will He sign a contract to give you eternal life without a commitment in which you and He become one entity.

> *The earth is the Lord's and the fullness thereof, the*
> *world and those who dwell therein ... [Psalm 24:1*
> *ESV]*

It is laughable for you to try to buy Him off with a fluctuating salary of legalistic observances—whether high or low. Your good works are of no consequence to Him. He desires your soul. That is the only thing of value in this transaction.

You stand to gain much more than God, should you agree to enter into the blessed partnership. He doesn't need you in order to go on, but you definitely need Him. If you continue to act as a confidence trickster, He will just walk away and leave you to your own destructive and pathetic machinations.

You will not be able to succeed onto heavenly riches without God's expertise.

> *... for if righteousness comes through the law, then*
> *Christ died in vain. [Galatians 2:21 NKJV]*

Christ did not die in vain. He is the only way to eternal life.

A deadline is fast approaching beyond which ownership rights over your soul will be worthless. Signs of your mortality are growing like cancers. Trust Christ, and you shall gain everything. Deny Christ, and you will be the consummate loser.

Amos 5:18–20 [NLT]

What sorrow awaits you who say, "If only the day of the Lord were here!" You have no idea what you are wishing for. That day will bring darkness, not light. In that day you will be like a man who runs from a lion—only to meet a bear. Escaping from the bear, he leans his hand against a wall in his house—and he's bitten by a snake. Yes, the day of the Lord will be dark and hopeless, without a ray of joy or hope.

11. An End to Taunts

Many people taunt God, saying, "How could a God of love allow all the suffering that exists in the world?"

I have been commissioned to tell you that one day soon God is not going to allow that question to just hang in the air rhetorically. The Almighty Sovereign has promised,

> *I will put an end to the arrogance of the haughty ...*
> *[Isaiah 13:11 TNIV]*

One day soon it will be time for Him to put an end to all the wickedness in the world and destroy this sin-laden existence. On that day He will vanquish sin and death, and gather His people unto Himself, and reward them.

> *So he who was seated on the cloud swung his*
> *sickle over the earth, and the earth was harvested.*
> *[Revelation 14:16 TNIV]*

You know very well that the people that fault God for the continuance of suffering will not rejoice on suffering's final day. They will, rather, say, "No, no, no, no! Not yet! It's not so bad, really, God! We take it all back. We are managing—You leave those that suffer to our care. We will gladly euthanize them for You. It's no trouble at all. Please go away. Don't You know that I've rented a timeshare for next weekend?!"

> *Be careful, or your hearts will be weighed down with*
> *dissipation, drunkenness and the anxieties of life, and*
> *that day will close on you unexpectedly like a trap.*
> *[Luke 21:34 NIV]*

Ah, but the faithful Christians will say, "Alleluia! Thank you, God! We have been waiting for You, and it is so good to see an end to this earth!"

~~~~~~~~~~~~~~~~~~~~~~~~

Have you ever given someone a gift, and they look at it with a jaundiced eye?

My friend married a divorced woman with two problem children. Her ex–husband was in prison. My friend stayed married to her for twenty years, and they produced two well-adjusted children. He is a gentle giant, and an incredible handyman. He was able to save enough money to buy two apartment buildings as investment properties.

It snowed a lot where they lived and he would get up before dawn on a snowy day, and clean and salt their driveway and walkway. He would start all the family's cars, and clean their windows of frost. Then he would come in and make breakfast for everyone. His wife stayed in bed while he worked.

He told me that he knew she was planning to get rid of him when she yelled because he had scraped the edge of their lawn while cleaning the snow.

She filed for divorce and took half his property and savings. He and I talked it over, and came to the conclusion that she never would have left him if he had squandered his money and not accumulated real estate holdings. The very fact that he had saved for their retirement together made her decide to take half and leave. She was evil.

My friend is a natural provider—some would say a sap. He soon found another divorcée with children. He explained to her that his wife had thrown him away; she couldn't believe her luck and married him soon thereafter.

My friend's first wife acted like she did not have a husband in the sense that she did not respect him or appreciate him. When she did acknowledge him, it was only to accuse him of not being a good enough provider.

In the same way, unbelievers use God's goodness as an excuse to discount, disparage, and disrespect Him. They criticize Him as a Provider; they take what they have not earned; they refuse to live under His Lordship; they tell Him to give them their share and leave. Even though He is bigger and stronger than they are, He is a gentle giant and will not contest the divorce (see Section 16 for the divorce papers).

> *If we disown him, he will also disown us; [2 Timothy 2:12 TNIV]*

Great will be the judgment upon those that disown God.

Matthew 25:31–34 [NKJV]
When the Son of Man comes in His glory, and all the holy angels with Him, then He will sit on the throne of His glory. All the nations will be gathered before Him, and He will separate them one from another, as a shepherd divides his sheep from the goats. And He will set the sheep on His right hand, but the goats on the left. Then the King will say to those on His right hand, 'Come, you blessed of My Father, inherit the kingdom prepared for you from the foundation of the world ...'

12. A Place for the Penitent

I've seen a study on educational television where behavioral scientists put a baboon in a room in which one of the walls is a mirror. The baboon immediately sees itself in the mirror and attacks—thinking that it is another animal. Sometimes it injures itself by hitting the mirror. This goes on for as long and as often as the baboon is put in the mirrored room. Time after time it screeches and hits the mirror over and over again; it never learns.

Now if they put a chimpanzee alone into the same room, it initially has the same reaction. It thinks that the image in the mirror is a rival and it screeches and attacks the mirror. But an amazing thing happens with the chimp: after a period of time, it begins to notice that the other chimp is itself. It can understand that the image is moving in the exact same way and at the exact same time that it is moving. At that moment the chimp calms down, approaches the mirror, and moves its limbs deliberately—taking note of the movement of the image. Then the chimp scratches its head, and you can see in its eyes that it is self-aware. This is possible because a chimpanzee has considerably more intelligence than a baboon.[22]

The Bible teaches us that the purpose of God's Law (e.g., the Ten Commandments) is to show us our sin—it is a mirror for us to see what our human nature really is—the way that God sees us. And the picture is not a good one: we are fallen creatures; we are beasts.

> *Those who listen to the word but do not do what it says are like people who look at their faces in a mirror and, after looking at themselves, go away and immediately forget what they look like. But those who look intently into the perfect law that gives freedom and continue in it—not forgetting what they have heard but doing it—they will be blessed in what they do. [James 1:23–25 TNIV]*

Now, the children of this world are the ones that would look at the image of themselves in the Word of God and never come to terms with what they see. They do not understand or accept that they are the filthy animals that are reflected back into their eyes. Rather, like the baboon, they only know how to make noise and war against their neighbor, and to destroy themselves.

But the children of God are fundamentally different in this respect: like the chimp we see and understand and accept that we are the filthy animal in the mirror. We see and understand and accept what the Word of God tells us: that we are sinners from the time that we have been conceived.

> *For I was born a sinner—yes, from the moment my mother conceived me. [Psalm 51:5 NLT]*

Both by our nature when we are babies, and by our personal history as we grow old, we are rife with sin; and we are utterly unworthy of God's love and attention. Our response is not to attack the Word of God. That is foolish and vain. There is only one logical response to this state-of-affairs: it is to get on our knees and repent.

And we are most fortunate, for although we are unworthy, the Bible says,

> *If we confess our sins, He is faithful and just to forgive us our sins and to cleanse us from all unrighteousness. [1 John 1:9 NKJV]*

And again it confirms,

> *... if you confess with your mouth, 'Jesus is Lord,' and believe in your heart that God raised him from the dead, you will be saved. [Romans 10:9 NIV]*

Wake up! Admit that you are a part of the problem, and in this way be transformed from an ignorant beast into a Child of the Living God.

> *I tell you, now is the time of God's favor, now is the day of salvation. [2 Corinthians 6:2 TNIV]*

~~~~~~~~~~~~~~~~~~~~~~~~

A Mainline Protestant denomination has been running television advertisements that show a burly bouncer at the door of a church. The bouncer is turning away homosexuals and other nonconformists. The denomination then declares that their church, in contrast, is a place for everyone to come.[23]

One of their New York City congregations has posted a door sign reading:

> *We welcome people of every age, creed, culture, economic standing, ethnicity, gender and gender expression, language, nationality, physical or mental ability, race, sexual orientation, and trade union status. As an Open and Affirming congregation we seek to be a wellspring of Christian faith for a diverse people in the heart of the city.*

They are open and affirming to every lifestyle, except for the 'hate' and 'exclusion' of the Gospel of Jesus Christ.

I know of an old man that used to come to church every week with a completely perfidious heart. Even while he 'worshipped,' he openly admitted, "I don't believe that Jesus is the Son of God, or that He walked on water. I don't think He's the only way to God, and I don't accept all those fairytales in the Bible. I just come here for cultural and social reasons."

Now, there are two types of pastors in the world: One type smiles magnanimously and tells him, "You can't fool me, friend! I've known you for a long time. I know your heart—that you are a good man. In the end, one way or another, you are going to accept Christ's message of love and go to Heaven with me. So you keep on attending and supporting the church, and someday I'll see you in Glory."

The other type of pastor keeps his arsenal in reserve in most situations; he knows that he is there to announce the Good News about forgiveness of sin—no matter what the sin. But there is one thing that he does not countenance, and that is the old man's words. This pastor would grab him by the proverbial collar, and give him a proverbial shake, and say, "You are a fool, friend, and you're in danger of hellfire! That is where you will end up for a certainty if you don't repent of this madness, and believe in Jesus Christ. You're welcome to come to this church again, but you've got to keep your profane mouth shut, and don't even think about coming to the Communion table until you've had a change of heart."

The latter pastor's approach is the biblical one.

> *The apostles did many miraculous signs and wonders among the people. All the believers used to meet together at Solomon's Porch.* **No outsider dared to join them.** *But the people thought highly of them. More and more men and women believed in the Lord. They joined the other believers. [Acts 5:12–14 NIrV]*

A good pastor says, "This is a place for everybody to come—on their knees, like I do."

Luke 23:43 [NIV]
Jesus answered him, "I tell you the truth, today you will be with me in paradise."

13. A Cause for Joy

In AD 96,[24] the Lord Jesus appeared to His last surviving disciple, and said,

> *Behold, I am coming quikly! Blessed is he who keeps the words of the prophecy of this book. [Revelation 22:7 NKJV]*

God is either going to come for us, or He isn't. God is either our loyal doting Father, or He has abandoned us as spiritual bastards. Jesus' promises of return are either true, or they are stinking platitudes.

A few years ago I asked a missionary friend of mine if he had any inside information about the Second Coming of Jesus Christ. He replied, "Nothing specific, but I wouldn't be surprised if He came any day now."

"Really?" I said. "This soon?"

He said, "The requirements have been met—or nearly so. The Gospel is being preached around the world." He nodded with confidence, "He will come soon."

Again, I expressed surprise at his certainty. He said, "I wouldn't be doing this for a living if I didn't believe in the afterlife and in the Second Coming. They are the same thing. The day that you die is the day Jesus Christ comes again for you. So whether I think that the world will end soon, or whether I just accept my own mortality, its going to be in the next few years. Although I may make some provisions in case I become unable to earn money, my trust is not in building a fortune here."

This fellow is in his mid–fifties, and is not from a long-lived family. "So you're laboring for a good retirement in Heaven?" I said.

"Not exactly. My retirement is already secure. I trust Jesus to take care of me in Heaven. I'm laboring for my Lord because He loves me. The sooner He comes, the better."

It's an interesting perspective, isn't it? It is the perspective of the faithful Christian.

> *We know that while we are at home in the body we are away from the Lord, for we walk by faith, not by sight. [2 Corinthians 5:6–7 ESV]*

Therefore, we are exhorted,

> *This is the reason we do not give up. Our human body is wearing out. But our spirits are getting stronger every day. The little troubles we suffer now for a short time are making us ready for the great things God is going to give us forever. We do not look at the things that can be seen. We look at the things that cannot be seen. The things that can be seen will come to an end. But the things that cannot be seen will last forever. [2 Corinthians 4:16–18 NLV]*

We are expecting something joyful. We're expecting an incorruptible physical body, and we know that the aging process is but a pang that must be endured to receive the prize.

> *Your dead will live. Their dead bodies will rise. You who lie in the dust, wake up and call out for joy. For as the water on the grass in the morning brings new life, the earth will bring back to life those who have been dead. [Isaiah 26:19 NLV]*

~~~~~~~~~~~~~~~~~~~~~~

I know an old woman that had five children. Before her children were all grown, her husband, a Roman Catholic believer, was diagnosed with lung cancer. He was hospitalized for several months, but at that time there was no treatment available. Finally, he was discharged to go home and die.

His sons brought fresh oxygen tanks to the house, and the gas fed into his nostrils through a tube. Still, he was barely able to take enough into his lungs to stay alive. He remained bedridden at home for several weeks. His wife was constantly by his side.

One morning while he slept, she knelt at the foot of his bed and prayed something very difficult. "Lord Jesus, I trust that You are going to heal him. But if You are not going to do it on this earth, please take him to Heaven and heal him completely there. I want it to be the way that You want it."

When she finished praying, the man awoke from his sleep. She raised his head slightly so that he could look out the large window that was opposite his bed. She asked him if he wanted his morning coffee. He was weak and whispered, "Not today. Maybe just some spring water." She got up to get a glass, and as she reached the door, he said something. She turned around to find him looking intently at the window. His face was filled with joy, and with a strong voice he was saying, "Hello! Come in, please! You are welcome here!"

She saw nothing at the window, and perceived that he was seeing into another dimension. She prayed in her mind, "Lord, please! Allow me to see what he is seeing."

Immediately, she saw human beings—people that she and her husband had known—coming through the window. They had all died in the Lord. One of them had died only two months beforehand. They were greeting her husband with great joy. Last among them was the human being, Jesus Christ. He was dressed in a blue, red, and gold robe,[i] and was surrounded by a radiant light.

Jesus separated Himself from the crowd of believers. He stood in the corner of the room and looked into the sick man's eyes. His wife was in the doorway on the other side of the room. She saw her husband get out of bed for the first time in weeks. He walked over to Jesus and got on his knees. Jesus offered him of the cup that makes a man live forever, for it is written,

> *To him who is thirsty I will give to drink without cost*
> *from the spring of the water of life. [Revelation 21:6*
> *NIV]*

As the man was drinking, his wife realized that she had neglected to have a priest come to the house to give him Holy Communion. She had been

---

i She did not tell me if she knew why Jesus chose to dress in that manner when He came to their house that day. It seems probable that it was because those are the colors of the High Priests' ephod (see Exodus 28:6).

overwhelmed with caring for his physical needs and she hadn't thought of it. She suddenly had a tremendous sense of guilt.

Just then she heard a popping sound. She looked at the bed where her husband had been, and there was his body. His soul had left it when he got out of bed to meet Jesus. The oxygen had built up in the nasal cavity of the corpse, and the tube had popped out of its nose.

She looked back to the corner of the room, and then to the window. Everyone was gone.

Her husband was dead, but he was really more alive than herself. Jesus Christ of Nazareth came for him.

> *So he is the God of the living, not the dead, for they are all alive to him. [Luke 20:38 NLT]*

~~~~~~~~~~~~~~~~~~~~~~~

On New Year's Eve AD 1987, my uncle and I sat in his living room talking about what the world might be like someday if the Soviet Union were to cease to exist. It was something that neither of us could imagine without a worldwide nuclear war. I remarked that it might happen peaceably in a hundred years, but I couldn't say what series of circumstances would bring about something that wonderful.

Exactly four years later, on New Year's Eve AD 1991, we were in the same room watching the red hammer and sickle flag come down from the Kremlin, and the flag of the Russian Federation go up.

My uncle said, "Isn't that a good sight?"

"It sure is," I said. "I never thought I'd live to see it."

My uncle is a Soviet scholar and noted, "Nobody ever talks about how the collapse of this evil empire has occurred after seventy years—that is a biblical number."

I did some quick arithmetic in my mind, "Well, actually, it has been seventy-four years and two months since the October Revolution."

"That was when the Bolsheviks took over Saint Petersburg, yes, but the Russian Civil War lasted through the year 1920, and the USSR was not officially declared until December 30, 1922 when Russia and some of the other republics came together under a constitution," he noted. "So yesterday was the end of the sixty-ninth anniversary, and this New Year's Eve that we are celebrating is the beginning of the seventieth year. And now, a day and a half into the seventieth year, the flag is down and it's over. In a few more months they will decommission the Red Army, redirect their nuclear missiles, and we won't have to worry about them anymore."

"Oh yeah—seventy years exactly. What could it mean?" I asked.

"I don't know, but I think that we should not discount it as a coincidence. The Bible teaches that empires rise and fall at God's command. All things are in His hands."

This began in me a thought process that has continued to this day. After twelve years of meditation, I saw God's plan for His Chosen People, the Christians.

Something unimaginably wonderful is about to happen. It will be beyond anything the most ostentatious futurist could imagine.

> *Then I saw a new heaven and a new earth, for the*
> *first heaven and the first earth had passed away ...*
> *[Revelation 21:1 NIV]*

The entirety of human history will end on a definitive day in the not-too-distant future; God is going to reveal Himself, and a new Heaven and new Earth will be introduced.

1 Corinthians 7:31 [TNIV]
... this world in its present form is passing away.

14. The Passing Away

I know a ninety-five year old man that complains because his health is failing. He is still lucid—sharp as a tack, actually. He is able to walk, read, feed himself, and use the toilet. He has never spent a night in a hospital. He lives in his own home with no assistance. But he says that life isn't fair because he has pains.

He is a Christian believer, so I told him, "Listen, I know life is not as good as it used to be, but look on the bright side: you've outlived the ages at which your father and mother and all of your siblings died. So we know that the end will be soon for you, and then you are going to get to see Jesus and your loved ones that died in Him. It's really just a matter of months now—maybe weeks! Isn't that exciting? You're so close to your eternal reward. You will finally get to meet Jesus face-to-face!"

He looked at me curiously. It had never occurred to him before.

We can learn three important things about the human condition from my old friend. First, our appetites for the best things in life are insatiable. Imagine a person that sleeps beautifully-deep, glorious, sleep every night of his life until he is ninety-nine years old. Throughout his life he fell asleep the moment when his head hit the pillow and did not wake up for eight hours. And then, in his very old age, he develops an untreatable sleep disorder, and spends the last year of his life horribly sleep-deprived.

Does he say with a heart full of mirth, "Oh, I don't mind! It's okay. I enjoyed a good run of ninety-nine years that most men would pay a fortune for. So I can't complain if only one percent of my life is spent longing for a decent rest. I came out ahead in life's lottery!"

Nobody thinks like that, no matter how privileged he has been in life. If anything, his past good fortune makes him feel all the worse because of it being gone! Let a splinter afflict the most pampered man on earth for one week, and he will moan like a banshee. Quite naturally, one who suffers is miserable until either he recovers, or his voice is silenced by the grave.

That leads me to my second observation about our inherent mindset: if we, by our nature, take no solace in the triumphs of the past, then we certainly don't take any solace in the promise of eternal triumph. For human beings without faith, only the moment—the here-and-now—is of importance.

The Bible teaches us the opposite thing about the here-and-now. It says that our present comforts are of no more consequence than our past because they will soon be in the past themselves. It says that because our bodies (and this earth) do not last forever, they are of infinitely less importance than the end-state of our souls. It says that God will give us a new, incorruptible, and eternal body in Heaven if we accept the correct things about Him in this life. It says that changing one's beliefs to be in-line with God's beliefs is of paramount importance to the destination of one's soul, and is really the only important thing in life.

Heaven is an unending good state of the here-and-now. And it is worth living for.

> Here on earth we do not have a city that lasts forever, but we are looking for the city that we will have in the future. [Hebrews 13:14 NCV]

Thirdly, we can draw the lesson that human beings tend to be delusional. That is to say that we like to be told lies. For example, the buffoon that currently runs Venezuela has recently reported that his friend Fidel Castro is "fighting for his life." This quote was repeated as the headline on the news wires.[25] But everyone knows with complete certainty that Castro will not be victorious in his fight for his life. Even if his current infection from diverticulitis subsides, and he somehow manages to live another few agonizing years, he shall still lose the fight for his life some day soon—it is a one hundred percent certainty.

So why the pretence of the colloquialism 'fighting for his life'—as though he could actually beat death? Could it be that, like a woman that is in love with a bad man, we humans want to be told lies? Could it be that we will believe anything, as long as it affirms our delusion that we can indefinitely defer accountability to God through the strength of our willpower?

~~~~~~~~~~~~~~~~~~~~~~~

A friend was recently complaining to me about his health. Although he is only thirty-one years old, he suffers from epileptic seizures, vertigo that can last weeks, bad knees, and a throat ailment that makes it difficult for him to speak in a normal voice. He either has to yell or whisper. Additionally, for an unknown reason he lost a lot of weight, and contracted pneumonia, and required hospitalization. He is unhappy with his current employment but it is impossible for him to go on job interviews in his state of health.

I quietly listened to the litany. Everything that he said was the truth, but he is not a believer in Christ and I know his real problem is his enmity toward God. I said, "Maybe God is trying to tell you something."

He stopped in his tracks and demanded, "What?"

I opened my palms toward him as though the answer were obvious. "Your body is falling apart. True?"

"Yes. I don't feel well at all," he confirmed.

I said, "Isn't that a sign from above?"

He smirked, "You mean God is telling me that I'm going to end up on disability compensation?"

"No," I said, "God is telling you that you're going to end up in the ground."

He shook his head in shock and disgust, "I've got to stop hanging around with you."

I bought him an ice cream cone to cheer him up, and said, "You mean you didn't know that you are going to die? It is the only truly certain thing."

He licked his ice cream as though he were licking a wound, "I'm not going to die … It's too far off to ever happen."

His health has since taken a severe turn for the worse. He is starting to consider that God is allowing the devil to afflict him in the hopes of getting him to repent of his many sins, and accept the message of the Bible. Therefore, pity the people that live the charmed lives, have the best of health, and have family histories of longevity. How will they ever become attuned to God's message of inevitability? How will they ever learn to number their days?

> ... *teach us to number our days that we may gain a heart of wisdom. [Psalm 90:12 ESV]*

The Bible teaches that just as an abrupt end of our lives is inevitable, so is an abrupt end to the world inevitable.

> ... *you know very well that the day of the Lord will come like a thief in the night. While people are saying, "Peace and safety," destruction will come on them suddenly, as labor pains on a pregnant woman, and they will not escape. [1 Thessalonians 5:2–3 NIV]*

This day of the Lord will be preceded by a short period of trouble and unusual natural phenomena—the likes of which no one has ever experienced before. The earth will be out of balance immediately before the end, just as people are usually sick immediately before they die.

Christians are told not to be afraid of it, but to be ready for it. And Christ commissioned us to tell others to likewise prepare for the impending doom that will overtake and consume all worldly things.

~~~~~~~~~~~~~~~~~~~~~~

On February 20, AD 2003, a pyrotechnics display during a rock concert at *The Station* nightclub in Rhode Island ignited a fast-moving fire. One hundred people burned to death within a few minutes.[26]

Ironically, a television cameraman happened to be in the building at the time to record a news piece on nightclub safety. One could see the billows of thick, black, smoke roll across the ceiling as the cameraman and scores of nervous people moved through the narrow exit. But others either did not notice the beginnings of the fire, or they were too intoxicated to head for the door.

One person in the middle of the dance floor thought that the smoke was part of the entertainment for the evening. He had no idea that his life was about to end in a holocaust. He looked up and said, "Whoa! This is so-o-o-o cool."

~~~~~~~~~~~~~~~~~~~~~~

Immediately before the AD 2004 Indian Ocean tsunamis, the sea suddenly receded. Many local people did not realize what was about to happen. Tsunamis are unknown occurrences in that part of the world, so they rushed onto the mud flats to pick up stranded fish. Moments later the seawater that was drawn back came crashing ashore in gigantic waves. Those people perished.

There was one precocious English schoolgirl on holiday with her family in Thailand that did recognize the warning signs. When the water frothed and bubbled and then receded, she remembered her geology lesson. She alerted her parents that these were signs of an impending tsunami. They warned the beachgoers to flee, and saved many lives.[27]

In the same way, I am warning you now: the end of all things is coming like a mighty tsunami.

~~~~~~~~~~~~~~~~~~~~~~~~~

It is a large leap to change one's mindset from a virtually unending world to a near-term dissolution of the world. For almost all readers, the notion that Christ will return within this generation will take some mental adjustment.

I, myself, was numb upon the initial realization. It occurred on the coldest day of the year in early AD 2004. I went out from my study and looked at the trees and the sky. I rested my torso against my sedan and felt life-giving warmth drain into the freezing-cold metal. I raised my hands and examined them through the vapor of my respiration, and thought, "My God ... it's all going to pass away ... within my lifetime ... planet Earth is going to disappear ..."

If I succeed in convincing you of the Biblical timelines (Sections 40–49, 71), you may be as shocked as was I. But really, if you think about it, what has changed for you? You were going to die anyway. At that moment—on the inevitable day of your passing—all the comforts and joys of this world would avail you precisely not one thing.

> *For we brought nothing into the world, and we can*
> *take nothing out of it. [1 Timothy 6:7 TNIV]*

So why be disconcerted with the news of the end of the world? Unless, as with my sickly friend, you do not really believe that you are going to die ...

~~~~~~~~~~~~~~~~~~~~~~~

I know a capable businesswoman that enjoyed excellent health her entire life, was professionally accomplished, and dressed impeccably. Then, suddenly, at the age of seventy-two she discovered a small lump in her breast. She had a lumpectomy, and appears to be cancer-free. But she had a nervous breakdown over the health scare. She had never before come to terms with her own mortality. She went from a strong, brash person to a whimpering, insecure person.

We have all seen this many times during our lives. It's common. Those entrenched within the human condition have an uncanny ability to ignore the most obvious of facts.

His hair is sprinkled with gray, but he does not notice.
[Hosea 7:9 TNIV]

Again and again, the Bible teaches us to be very much aware that life is fleeting.

Lord, remind me how brief my time on earth will be.
Remind me that my days are numbered, and that my
life is fleeing away. [Psalm 39:4 NLT]

But even if the worldly man accepts the inevitability of his own passing, he is comforted by the idea of 'leaving the world a better place than he found it.' Legacy, in the form of children, businesses, social causes, publications, etc. is a powerful, though illusionary consolation.

When I began my doctoral degree, I worked with a fellow that had just finished his own doctorate. That summer he succeeded in publishing a paper on his dissertation results in a peer-reviewed journal. I took him out for a beer after work to celebrate. He took a deep drink, gazed out the window, and said, "I feel like it'd be a little less bad if I were to die now, than if I died last year."

"Huh?" I said.

He explained, "I'm not saying it'd be okay if I died, of course. I'm just saying that now that my son has been born, and now that my paper has been published and distributed to libraries around the world, my name will not be forgotten from the face of the earth. I have a legacy."

I put down my beer, and turned toward him with a dumb smile, "You're serious?"

"Yeah!" He was surprised by my incredulity, "I've contributed to the world. I've produced two things. These things will exist, even if I do not. That's important to me."

~~~~~~~~~~~~~~~~~~~~~~~

It's a difficult thing for people to accept that the world that we leave behind shall suffer the same fate as us. It's abhorrent that, all at once—at a time that has been predetermined by a Power outside our petty affairs—everything will end. It's inconceivable that that which is dearest to us has only been tolerated by Him—as a grown-up tolerates a child's fantasy world until it is time for that child to face the real world.[28]

It takes some time to get used to the idea. But it is the truth. God has been up to something larger than any good that we know. He's about to wrap it all up. He won't allow it to continue one moment longer than is necessary to accomplish His good purpose.

That revelation has had a great calming effect upon me. I simply don't care about vain things any longer. One sees the futility of most human strife—the race to get ahead, to show-up one's friends, to accumulate wealth, even to keep certain people out of your family. It just doesn't matter.

Sweet peace for knowing that the end is in sight! Sweet and restful peace! My joy is not circumstance-dependent!

> *Though the fig tree does not bud and there are no grapes on the vines, though the olive crop fails and the fields produce no food, though there are no sheep in the pen and no cattle in the stalls, yet I will rejoice in the Lord, I will be joyful in God my Savior. [Habakkuk 3:17–18 NIV]*

Are you not weary of the angst of life? Do not enjoin the divine sublimity any longer; enter the serenity of the saints.

As I said earlier, the day of the revelation that forms the thesis of this book came to me in early AD 2004. I was in such a daze from realizing that the world would end that I became late for a dinner appointment. I raced down the highway to make up time, blew-out a tire, and had a terrifying single-car automobile accident. My vehicle—the one that I had rested my torso upon a few hours before—was totaled. The people at the junkyard said that they had never seen anything like it.

I walked away from the crash shaken, but completely unscathed. I looked upon the wreck, and then raised my freezing hands toward my face. I examined them through the vapor of my respiration and thought, "Truly this world will pass away. Truly my body will pass away. Truly Christ is coming back to remake all things."

The next day, a friend told me that my narrow escape must mean that God had a purpose in keeping me alive. He said that I should find out what it is and then do it. But I already knew: I had to write this book.

2 Thessalonians 2:3 [NKJV]
... that Day will not come unless ... the man of sin is revealed, the son of perdition ...

15. The Son of Perdition is One of Many Antichrists

There was much speculation during the time of the Apostles' ministries about the passing away of this age and the return of Jesus Christ. Some thought it was imminent. The Apostle Paul addressed this concern in his second epistle to the Thessalonians in AD 53.[29] He began by assuring them that they had not missed the great event:

> *Now, brethren, concerning the coming of our Lord Jesus Christ and our gathering together to Him, we ask you, not to be soon shaken in mind or troubled, either by spirit or by word or by letter, as if from us, as though the day of Christ had come. [2 Thessalonians 2:1–2 NKJV]*

He went on to give them a prophetic precondition for Christ's return:

> *Let no man deceive you by any means: for that day shall not come, except there come a falling away first, and that man of sin be revealed, the son of perdition; who opposeth and exalteth himself above all that is called God, or that is worshipped; so that he as God sitteth in the temple of God, shewing himself that he is God. [2 Thessalonians 2:3–4 KJV]*

The issue of the identity of this 'Son of Perdition' immediately produced more speculation. Within a generation the name 'Antichrist' was coined to describe that person. Writing some forty years later, the Apostle John cautioned his readers about the mythology that was developing around the anticipated Antichrist personality. He told them not to make the mistake of thinking that all the evil that was to come in the world would be conducted by one bombastic and terrible Antichrist:

> *Little children, it is the last hour; and as you have heard that the Antichrist is coming, even now many antichrists have come, by which we know that it is the last hour. [1 John 2:18 NKJV]*

This piece of Scripture tells us two things: Firstly, the period of human history after Jesus' Ascension is the last hour—the End Time. No matter how long it lasts, it is the encore to what God has done on earth (Section 70). The time when the Apostle John was writing (i.e., the end of the first century) was the End Time; and the time when I am writing (i.e., the beginning of the twenty-first century) is the End Time. The Apostle Peter also confirmed,

> *The end of all things is near. [1 Peter 4:7 TNIV]*

The end will not be in four to five billion years when the sun reaches its red giant phase and burns up all life on earth. The end will, rather, be within the biblical timeframe—in the neighborhood of the six thousand years that the Bible teaches us our universe has been in existence.

The second thing that 1 John 2:18 tells us is that there will be many, many, antichrists before Christ comes again. We think of the Antichrist as a single maniacal boogieman that will come near the end of human history, but the Bible teaches that there have been innumerable antichrists.

The Apostle John goes on to define an antichrist:

> *Who is a liar but he who denies that Jesus is the Christ? He is antichrist who denies the Father and the Son. Whoever denies the Son does not have the Father either; he who acknowledges the Son has the Father also. [1 John 2:22–23 NKJV]*

And again, in his second epistle:

> *For many deceivers have gone out into the world who do not confess Jesus Christ as coming in the flesh. This is a deceiver and an antichrist. [2 John 7 NKJV]*

An antichrist, then, is any person or institution that does not acknowledge that God became a man in the person of Jesus of Nazareth. They deny that Jesus is the Messiah or Christ. Such a person, even if he is a monotheist, does not worship the true God; he is in service to the devil, whether he knows it or not.

~~~~~~~~~~~~~~~~~~~~~~~~

The Bible speaks highly of grace, mercy, kindness, and peaceful living, but the word 'nice' does not appear in most English translations. In the passage below, from the New Living Translation (a paraphrased Bible), the word 'nice' does appear, but negatively. It is set up as the antithesis of what is true.

> *... these people are stubborn rebels who refuse to pay any attention to the Lord's instructions. They tell the prophets, "Shut up! We don't want any more of your reports." They say, "Don't tell us the truth. **Tell us nice things. Tell us lies.** Forget all this gloom. We have heard more than enough about your 'Holy One of Israel.'"* [Isaiah 30:9–11 NLT]

The truth is often a hard thing to accept, and the message of the truth-teller is often an unwelcome one. It is a difficult but true thing to say that many of the antichrists that will go to eternal punishment are quite nice people. A nineteenth century theologian put it this way:

> *A person is either a child of the devil or a child of God; either in the kingdom of darkness or in the kingdom of light; either in a state of grace with God or under His wrath. There is no middle ground.*[30]

Antichrists are not all monsters like the father and son rulers of North Korea, or like Stalin (AD 1878–AD 1953), or like Mao (AD 1893–AD 1976). Some are great humanitarians like Thomas Paine (AD 1737–AD 1809), Mahatma Gandhi (AD 1869–AD 1948), or the Dalai Lama. And some are my near-kin and friends that donate to their local food pantries and are kind to animals. But they all have one thing in common: they don't believe in a personal God—a God that became flesh in Christ. This denial keeps them in a state of alienation from God. They are nice antichrists.

John 3:36 [NIV]
Whoever believes in the Son has eternal life, but whoever rejects the Son will not see life, for God's wrath remains on him.

16. How to Become an Antichrist

As I illustrated with the story of Mr. Shepherdson's squash (Section 2), a clipping of a plant only appears to be alive. It is actually in the process of dying from the moment when it becomes detached from the root. Even if it is put in a vase, it's just a matter of time.

We have been detached from our Creator—the only source of life in the universe. He loves us and has been working overtime to get us grafted back into Him. An antichrist is any person that refuses to be spiritually grafted into eternal life.

Do you aspire to be an antichrist? Is it something that appeals to you? This is easily achieved. Puff up your chest and say, "I do not believe that God became a man. I do not believe that Jesus is God Almighty. I do not accept Him as Christ. I do not believe that He was born of a virgin, or that He rose bodily from the dead. I think his bones are somewhere on the face of the earth, like everybody else's. I do not believe that He ascended into Heaven, or that He will come back on a specific calendar date to give me a new body." That's all you have to do.

Of course, I recommend against it. But if you are a nominal 'Christian' that acquiesces to any part of the above, vile, confession, then I say to you: Why the pretense? Why not have the courage of your convictions and admit what you are? You are not fooling God, I can assure you. He knows every human heart.

> *... for the Lord searches every heart and understands the intention of every thought. [1 Chronicles 28:9 HCSB]*

If one insists upon unbelief, I think it is better to be honest with oneself about it.[31] You will soon lose the illusion of being a good person and discover that a devil—nay, seven devils—have taken up residence inside your brain. And then, I pray you will come into a right mind and stop resisting the Spirit of God that is working overtime to save you.

Mark 16:16 [NKJV]
He who believes and is baptized will be saved;

17. How to Become a Christian

To become a Christian you must entrust your soul to the care of Jesus Christ, the God-man, and be baptized with water in the name of the Father, and of the Son, and of the Holy Spirit.

John 4:23 [KJV]
... the hour cometh, and now is, when the true worshippers shall worship the Father in spirit and in truth: for the Father seeketh such to worship him.

18. What Exactly Do Christians Believe?

The following is an excellent synopsis of the Christian faith. I think it is the most beautifully comprehensive piece of prose ever composed.

> *Whoever desires to be saved must, above all, cling to the universal Christian faith.*
>
> *Whoever does not keep it whole and undefiled will, without doubt, perish eternally.*
>
> *Now this is the universal Christian faith: We worship one God in Trinity and the Trinity in Unity, neither confusing the persons nor dividing the substance.*
>
> *For the Father is one person, the Son is another, and the Holy Spirit is still another.*
>
> *But the Godhead of the Father and of the Son and of the Holy Spirit is one: the glory equal and the majesty coeternal.*
>
> *What the Father is, the Son is, and so is the Holy Spirit.*
>
> *The Father is uncreated; the Son is uncreated; the Holy Spirit is uncreated.*
>
> *The Father is infinite; the Son is infinite; the Holy Spirit is infinite.*
>
> *The Father is eternal; the Son is eternal; the Holy Spirit is eternal.*
>
> *And yet there are not three Eternal Beings, but one who is Eternal, just as there are not three Uncreated or Infinite Beings, but one who is Uncreated and Infinite.*
>
> *In the same way, the Father is almighty; the Son is almighty; the Holy Spirit is almighty. And yet there are not three Almighty Beings, but one who is Almighty.*
>
> *Thus the Father is God; the Son is God; the Holy Spirit is God. And yet there are not three Gods, but one God.*

Thus the Father is Lord; the Son is Lord; the Holy Spirit is Lord. And yet there are not three Lords, but one Lord.

Just as Christian truth compels us to acknowledge each distinct person as God and Lord, so also Christian faith forbids us to say that there are three Gods or Lords.

The Father was neither made nor created nor begotten by anyone. The Son was neither made nor created, but was alone begotten of the Father.

The Holy Spirit was neither made nor created nor begotten, but is proceeding from the Father and the Son.

Thus there is one Father, not three Fathers; there is one Son, not three Sons; there is one Holy Spirit, not three Holy Spirits.

And in this Trinity none is before or after another; none is greater or less than another; but all three persons are coeternal and coequal with each other, so that in all things, as has been stated above, the Trinity in Unity and the Unity in Trinity is to be worshiped.

Whoever desires to be saved must think in this way about the Trinity.

It is also necessary for eternal salvation that one faithfully believe in the incarnation of our Lord Jesus Christ.

For this is the true faith that we believe and confess: that our Lord Jesus Christ, the Son of God, is at the same time both God and man.

He is God, begotten before all ages from the substance of the Father; and He is man, born into this age from the substance of His mother—existing fully as God and fully as man, with a rational soul and a human body; He is equal to the Father with respect to His divinity, but subordinate to the Father with respect to His humanity.

Although He is God and man, He is not divided, but is one Christ.

He is united because God has taken humanity into Himself; God does not transform divinity into humanity.
He is completely one in the unity of his person, without confusing his natures.
For as the rational soul and body is one person, so God and man is one Christ.
He suffered death for our salvation.
He descended into hell and rose on the third day from the dead.
He ascended into heaven and is seated at the right hand of God the Father Almighty.
He will come again to judge the living and the dead.
At His coming all people will rise bodily to give an account of their own deeds.
Those who have done good will enter eternal life; those who have done evil will enter eternal fire.[ii]
This is the universal Christian faith; one cannot be saved without believing this firmly and faithfully.[32]

[ii] A note to Protestants and Catholics who will argue with each other over this clause: we know that salvation is through faith alone—apart from good works— for Christ said, *"I tell you the truth, whoever hears my word and believes him who sent me has eternal life and will not be condemned; he has crossed over from death to life." [John 5:24 NIV]* Nevertheless, five verses later Christ said, *"... those who have done good will rise to live, and those who have done evil will rise to be condemned." [John 5:29 NIV]* And also the Apostle John saw that in the Judgment Day, *"... the dead were judged according to their works ..." [Revelation 20:12 HCSB]* And also the Apostle Paul said, *"... we must all appear before the judgment seat of Christ, that each one may receive what is due him for the things done while in the body, whether good or bad." [2 Corinthians 5:10 NIV]* In this way, Christians receive eternal life as a gift from God in response to faith, while at the same time they are judged on the basis of works. *"For by grace you have been saved through faith. And this is not your own doing; it is the gift of God, not a result of works, so that no one may boast. For we are his workmanship, created in Christ Jesus for good works, which God prepared beforehand, that we should walk in them." [Ephesians 2:8–10 ESV]* Needless to say, no person's good works are worthy of eternal life apart from Christ, for, *"There is none who does good, no, not one." [Romans 3:12 NKJV]* We need pardon of our sins through Christ's atonement, and the accreditation of the good works of Jesus Himself, for, *"... by one Man's obedience many will be made righteous." [Romans 5:19 NKJV]*

This statement of Christian faith is called the Athanasian Creed. It was probably composed by Ambrose of Milan (AD 339–AD 397) and his disciples in the late fourth and early fifth centuries. It is named after Athanasius of Alexandria (AD 293–AD 373) who strongly influenced the text. The creed is accepted as dogma by Roman Catholics and Confessional Protestants (i.e., Creedal Christians). The Eastern Orthodox accept its teachings as a guideline, but do not use it liturgically. It is rejected by the Oriental Orthodox (i.e., Monophysites), Nestorians, and liberal Mainline Protestants.[33]

The damnatory clauses of the Athanasian Creed are problematic for some limp-wristed Christians. Some parts of the Anglican Communion, for example, have distanced themselves from this creed as a result of its rigidity.[34] Specifically, they are uncomfortable with:

> *Whoever desires to be saved must, above all, cling to the universal Christian faith. Whoever does not keep it whole and undefiled will, without doubt, perish eternally ... Whoever desires to be saved must think in this way about the Trinity. It is also necessary for eternal salvation that one faithfully believe in the incarnation of our Lord Jesus Christ ... This is the universal Christian faith; one cannot be saved without believing this firmly and faithfully.*[35]

My view is that the damnatory clauses are absolutely necessary. For example, one of my friends spoke with a Pentecostal woman that professed to be a Christian, but rejected the concept of the Trinity. She said, "I just believe in Jesus—only Jesus—not all that three Persons crap of the Roman Catholic Church. Their God is not my God—Jesus is my God."

My friend, a member of the Evangelical Covenant Church, said, "But the Roman Catholics' God is my God. The Pope and I are both baptized and believing Christians, after all."

The Pentecostal woman curled up her nose, "The Pope? That's just sad."

He tried to explain to her how Jesus is of the same substance, or being, or essence as the Father, but that He is not the same Person as the Father.

She mocked him, "Substance! Being! Essence! Person! Those are just words. 'Father' and 'Son' are just words, too. There is only one God: Jesus. He is real. Stop trying to confuse who God is with the words of men."

He said, "I agree that there is only one God, and that Jesus is that one God."

"That's right," she clucked.

He continued, "And the Father is that one God, too; and the Holy Spirit is that one God, too."

"No, no. You're confused," she shook her head. "The Prophet Isaiah refers to Jesus as the Everlasting Father."

"That is scriptural and we accept it," said my friend. "Jesus is the Everlasting Father because He is the same Divine Being as both the Father and Holy Spirit. But at the very same time Jesus is a different Person than the Father and a different Person than the Holy Spirit. These three Persons are the one and only, indivisible, God of the Godhead."

"No! There are not three Persons—only Jesus! And that awful, pagan, word that you just used: 'Godhead!' That word is not found in the Bible. You are trying to trick me into accepting the Trinity. You are trying to trick me into confessing something that does not make any sense."

"It's not a trick," he pointed out. "Jesus said that unless you become like a little child you will not get into the Kingdom of Heaven. The Holy Trinity is incomprehensible and inexplicable; it makes us feel like little children because there in no way to get our heads around it. We must stop trying to rationally explain it, and simply accept and express with our mouths what the Bible teaches: the Holy Trinity is the Christian God."

She was indignant, "Holy?! Your so-called 'Trinity' is just an idea concocted by dead Italian popes that persecuted the true Christians that believed in Jesus. 'Trinity' is another blasted word that is not found in the Bible. My church baptizes in the name of Jesus Christ alone, *not in the name of the Father and of the Son and the of Holy Spirit*. And we believe in Jesus Christ alone, *not in the Father and the Son and the Holy Spirit*."

"But the Bible speaks of Jesus, and the Father, and the Holy Spirit as being distinct, remember? Jesus prayed to the Father—He did not pray to Himself. And the Holy Spirit anointed Jesus at His baptism—He did not anoint Himself," noted my friend.

"No, no," she said. "You're confused again. It's like when the Bible calls Jesus the 'Son of Man,' then it calls Him the 'Son of God.' It does not mean that He was two different persons. These were just titles for the one person, Jesus."

"Right," my friend said. "Jesus was one Person: the Son of God and Son of Man."

"Right," said the Pentecostal woman. "And God is one Person—no matter what words are used for Him. So when the Bible talks about the Father or the Holy Spirit, it means the individual known as Jesus Christ. It's like when you call a person by their first name, and then a minute later you call that same person by their middle name, and then a minute later you call that same person by their last name. And then another time you call the person by a title like 'doctor,' and then another time you call him by a suffix like 'junior.' It's not five distinct persons, but only one person with five different names or titles. So when the Bible talks about the Father, it's talking about the same person as Jesus. If it makes it easier for you, think of Jesus' full name as 'Son-of-Man-Jesus-Father-Holy-Spirit-Christ-Son-of-God.'"

My friend told her that although she might be a good Pentecostal, she was definitely not a Christian. He advised her to stop thinking that she is smarter than the God of the Bible, and to accept Trinitarianism before she died. He said that any human being that dies while rejecting that the One and Only God exists in three Persons will definitely go to Hell.

When he related this story to me, I commended him, "Bravo, faithful Christian! You are a truth-teller!"

If it were not for the clear wording of the Athanasian Creed, my friend might have committed the sin of telling the Pentecostal woman that she was in adequate spiritual shape because of her 'faith' in Jesus. She had, in fact, fallen into a third century antichrist heresy known as Sabellianism.[36] It held that the Heavenly Father, the Resurrected Son, and the Holy Spirit are different manifestations of the one true God, just as steam, liquid water, and ice are different manifestations of the chemical, H_2O. Rather than believing in three distinct Persons in the single Godhead, the Sabellians thought of Jesus morphing into the Father and the Holy Spirit for the sake of our conceptualization of God—just as H_2O changes phase for the sake of atmospheric pressure and temperature. [Except that Trinitarianism is anything but an aid to our understanding.]

Not all Pentecostals are 'Oneness Pentecostals'—most are, in fact, Trinitarian. But all non-creedal churches are inherently susceptible to a return to such ancient heresies.[37]

In truth, the Holy Trinity is the eternal God, and would exist, as such, even if there were no humans to believe in Him. It is a matter of God's own three-in-one essence, not a formulation acquiesced to by God for our puny brains.

> *I keep asking that the God of our Lord Jesus Christ,*
> *the glorious Father, may give you the Spirit of wis-*
> *dom and revelation, so that you may know him better.*
> *[Ephesians 1:17 NIV]*

It was not the Person of God the Father that suffered on the Cross, but the Person of God the Son. Yet there is only one God: Father, Son, and Holy Spirit.

Do you see how indispensable the three Ecumenical Creeds are to the Christian Church? The Athanasian Creed makes things especially plain and inarguable. You cannot subscribe to it and then return to the Pentecostal woman's jejune, Jesus-only, argument. The Trinitarian issue was settled for all time in the fourth century. If you are not Trinitarian, you are not Christian.

The devil hates for truth to be plain and settled for all time. He likes ambiguity and wiggle-room and word games, especially when it comes to the particulars about God. The devil knows that this is a productive way to damn souls.

Again, I warn you: if you ever hear a 'Christian' proclaim ...

- "What does it even mean for there to be one God, but three Persons? This is a nonsensical dogma introduced after the Church was corrupted by politics," or ...

- "What does it even mean for the Christ to be one Person, but with separate divine and human natures? This is just the academic babbling of people with too much time on their hands,"

... then know for a certainty that this 'Christian' is an agent of Satan (Sections 61–67).

There will be no person in the Kingdom of Heaven that does not confess both the doctrine of the Trinity and the doctrine of the Dual Nature, for the Lord Jesus has decreed,

> ... *if you do not believe that I am the one I claim to be, you will indeed die in your sins. [John 8:24 NIV]*

~~~~~~~~~~~~~~~~~~~~~~~~

The second oldest ecumenical creed is called the Nicene Creed. It was a response to the heresy of Arianism (Section 61).

> *I believe in one God, the Father Almighty, maker of heaven and earth and of all things visible and invisible.*
>
> *And in one Lord Jesus Christ, the only-begotten Son of God, begotten of His Father before all worlds, God of God, Light of Light, very God of very God, begotten, not made, being of one substance with the Father, by whom all things were made; who for us men and for our salvation came down from heaven and was*

incarnate by the Holy Spirit of the virgin Mary and was made man; and was crucified also for us under Pontius Pilate.

He suffered and was buried.

And the third day He rose again according to the Scriptures and ascended into heaven and sits at the right hand of the Father. And He will come again with glory to judge both the living and the dead, whose kingdom will have no end.

And I believe in the Holy Spirit, the Lord and giver of life, who proceeds from the Father and the Son, who with the Father and the Son together is worshiped and glorified, who spoke by the prophets.

And I believe in one holy Christian and apostolic Church, I acknowledge one Baptism for the remission of sins, and I look for the resurrection of the dead and the life of the world to come. Amen.[38]

This creed was drafted at the first ecumenical council in Nicaea in AD 325; it was amended with the Holy Spirit paragraph at the second ecumenical council in Constantinople in AD 381; and it was unofficially amended with the addition of the Filioque clause at the Council of Toledo in AD 589. The 'Filioque' refers to the inclusion of the wording "and the Son" (above) about the Holy Spirit's procession. The rest of the western Church adopted this change by the year AD 1014[39] (see Section 69).

Please note that the Nicene Creed affirms "one Baptism for the remission of sins." This is, of course, baptism with water (either by sprinkling, pouring, or immersion) in the name of the Father, and of the Son, and of the Holy Spirit. Again, this Creedal clause is indispensable, and brings to light the waywardness of churches that neglect the recitation of the three Ecumenical Creeds.

Indeed, I know some Reformed Evangelical Protestants that do not believe in original sin, and on that basis reject infant baptism (or consider it optional and unnecessary)—as if these little bundles of wickedness that we call babies would go to Heaven even if God the Son had not become incarnate and been sacrificed upon the cross. Such people mistakenly view sin as only a conscious choice, rather than an inheritance from Adam and Eve. But the Apostle Paul tells us plainly:

I know there is nothing good in my sinful nature.
[Romans 7:18 NIrV]

Nevertheless, the Reformed Evangelicals maintain that a person becomes a Christian by 'getting saved' at an altar-call when they are of the age of accountability and are cognizant of their sinful choices. This is nowhere supported in the Bible. Rather, the Scriptures teach that we are steeped in sin while in our mothers' amniotic fluid.

> Surely I was sinful at birth, **sinful from the time my mother conceived me.** [Psalm 51:5 TNIV]

Some Reformed Evangelicals go even farther and blaspheme God by saying that if there is such a thing as original sin, then God Himself is unjust. They repeat Anne Hutchinson's[iii] bathetic credo,

> I cannot look into the eyes of a child and see sin therein.[40]

Such people say that baptism is just a symbol or testimony of one's faith, like wearing a cross around your neck. They say that since they are already committed to Christ, baptism is unimportant (unless the person is emotionally weak enough to feel that they need to go through the showmanship of a public ceremony to demonstrate their faith).

Many of these people talk about the Bible all the time, but have never been baptized themselves, and feel no compunction about not baptizing their teenaged, professing, children. They say of their unbaptized children, "They can choose to be baptized if they want to do so." They are 'Abaptists'—those for whom infant baptism has been deferred, and who then neglect to get baptized in adulthood because they are already saved by means of praying the sinner's prayer at an altar call.

> But the Pharisees and the lawyers **rejected God's purpose for themselves, not having been baptized** ...
> [Luke 7:30 NASB]

Such people chuckle at old fashioned Christians that view baptism with water in the name of the Father, and of the Son, and of the Holy Spirit, as a means of grace by which a person is forgiven of his or her original sin and gains trust in the Lord Jesus.

We must remember that children cannot trust in God of their own volition. They are born hell-bent against the will of God and they require the intervention of the Holy Spirit—as is the case with everybody else. God is able to instill that faith through the Sacrament of Holy Baptism.

---

iii   A holier-than-thou Puritan heretic that moved to The Bronx, New York before colonial settlement. She and all her clan (including ostensibly sinless children) were scalped by Siwanoy Indians in AD 1643.

You made me trust in you *even when I was at my mother's breast. [Psalm 22:9 NIV]*

By what mechanism is a suckling infant able to trust in Christ's atonement if not through the mystery of Holy Baptism? It could not be through reason—they have only drool.

Abaptists that reject this tenet of faith are, at the same time, perplexed as to why their prayers for their unbaptized children go unanswered. There is nothing to be perplexed about—such people are, in fact, living in direct disobedience to the Lord Jesus' command,

> *Go to the people of all nations and make them my disciples. Baptize them in the name of the Father, the Son, and the Holy Spirit ... [Matthew 28:19 CEV]*

Did Jesus mean to baptize ignorant natives in other nations, but not the dependents in one's own household?!

Every breath that an unbaptized Christian draws is an offense to God Almighty, for He has provided a way for them to become His Chosen People and they are dismissive of the process. They have put themselves very much in the position of Moses, who neglected to circumcise his sons:

> *On the way to Egypt, at a place where Moses and his family had stopped for the night, the Lord confronted him and was about to kill him. But Moses' wife, Zipporah, took a flint knife and circumcised her son ... After that, the Lord left him alone. [Exodus 4:24–26 NLT]*

If God's anger was aroused against His servant Moses for not observing the ceremony to make his children into Jews, do Abaptists think that it will not be aroused against them for not observing the ceremony to make their children into Christians?

The shame—the foolish shame—of Abaptist Reformed Evangelicals that know better than to wash themselves and their children with water and the Word! They are in peril; their children are in peril. Truly, truly, theirs is a pride that cries out to be humbled.

~~~~~~~~~~~~~~~~~~~~~~

The most ancient ecumenical creed is the second century Apostles' Creed. It is not as deliberative as the other two creeds because the heresy of Gnosticism that it addressed was not as intricate as later heresies. This creed was meant to affirm that Jesus was a real physical person, and that He really died and really came back to life.

> *I believe in God, the Father Almighty, maker of heaven and earth.*
> *And in Jesus Christ, His only Son, our Lord, who was conceived by the Holy Spirit, born of the virgin Mary, suffered under Pontius Pilate, was crucified, died, and was buried.*
> *He descended into hell.*
> *The third day He rose again from the dead.*
> *He ascended into heaven and sits at the right hand of God the Father Almighty. From thence He will come to judge both the living and the dead.*
> *I believe in the Holy Spirit, the holy Christian Church, the communion of saints,[iv] the forgiveness of sins, the resurrection of the body, and the life everlasting. Amen.*[41]

These three Ecumenical Creeds contain the truth about God. Accept Him and you will have eternal life.

~~~~~~~~~~~~~~~~~~~~~~~

Before closing this section, I must point out an obvious fact, but one that will not sit well with most Protestants: quoting from the Bible is not an adequate means to establish the truth about God.

My grandfather once demonstrated this to me, saying, "It's not enough to believe in the Bible. The devil believes in the Bible."

"What?!" I said. "How can that be?"

He explained, "The Bible says, '... there is no God,'—the devil likes that very much."

"But Grandpa, the Bible teaches us the truth about God. Where does it say that He does not exist?"

He smiled, "In the Psalms it is written, 'A fool says that there is no God.' The last four words of that verse are a mantra for the devil and his people. You see, they believe in the Bible; they just don't believe in it correctly."

My grandfather was wise: Bible verses can be misinterpreted; they are misused all the time. Mormons and Jehovah's Witnesses profess to adhere to

---

iv   The 'communion of saints' refers to the family of messianic faith throughout human history (see Sections 53–56).

the Bible and profess to worship the Lord Jesus, yet they are anti-Trinitarian and do not accept the Virgin Birth.

Recall that the devil quoted Bible verses as a means to tempt Jesus in the desert.

> *Then the devil took him to the holy city and set him on the pinnacle of the temple and said to him, "If you are the Son of God, throw yourself down, for it is written, 'He will command his angels concerning you,' and 'On their hands they will bear you up, lest you strike your foot against a stone.'" [Matthew 4:5–6 ESV]*

Now, there was an irony! Using the written Word to tempt the Word Incarnate!

Jesus wisely answered the devil with another Bible verse that correctly applied to His situation.

> *Jesus said to him, "Again it is written, 'You shall not put the Lord your God to the test.'" [Matthew 4:7 ESV]*

But Jesus was simply refuting the devil here—He was not trying to teach a human being what He believed, or to establish the true Church at that moment. When the latter was Jesus' purpose, He surely did use original sentences and thoughts!

It is, in fact, impossible to articulate a debate, or to preach a sermon, or to describe a theological position using only a string of conjunction-less Bible verses. Of course Bible verses must be the foundation of any truthful metaphysical argument, and of course they should be liberally quoted (as I have done in this book), but it is incumbent upon the Christian Church to have standard formulations (e.g., creeds, a catechism, position statements, press releases) that inform the lost world, and reminds the saints, what it means to be a Christian and to accept the Bible.

So when I am having a spiritual discussion with a person, I do not ask, "Are you a Christian?" or "Do you accept the Bible?" These are meaningless questions. They are very much the same as, "Are you a good person?" or "Do you accept Shakespeare?" Rather, I ask questions derived from the creeds:

- *Do you worship one God in three Person, and the Trinity in unity?*
- *Do you believe that God the Son was incarnate by the Holy Spirit of the virgin Mary?*

- *Do you believe that Jesus is fully God and fully man—one person with two natures?*
- *Do you believe that Jesus will return to this earth in judgment, and that the dead will rise with new bodies and give account to Him?*

Any true Christian will immediately and emphatically answer, "Yes!" to all these questions. In fact, that affirmative answer will often be followed up with mild irritation, "Why are you even asking me such things? How could I doubt any of them? Don't you know that I am a baptized and believing Christian?"

In short, the Bible is the Christians' language, and the three Ecumenical Creeds are the fundamental grammatical rules for using that language. The Bible, as the Word of God, is the complete and inerrant truth about God; the creeds make clear how to correctly speak that truth about God. They are a confession of allegiance to the King, in the King's English (the King being Jesus, of course, and the King's English being Christian orthodoxy).

That is the beauty of the creeds: They were deliberately designed in response to the devil's early barrage of Pidgin English corruption upon the Christian language. Specifically:

- the Apostles' Creed refuted the *antichrist heresy* of Gnosticism;
- the Nicene Creed refuted the *antichrist heresy* of Arianism;
- the Athanasian Creed refuted the *Christian heresies* of Nestorianism, Monophysitism, and Anti-Filioqueanism[42] (see Sections 62–69).

The three Ecumenical Creeds inculcate Christian minds to the truth. When they were completed, with the AD 589 addition of the Filioque to the Nicene Creed (see Section 69), the proper use of the Christian language was no longer subject to heretical debate. The grammatical rules were written in three concise packages, and recited by Christians in their houses of worship as a reminder of what the Holy Scriptures mean. Those that accepted the grammatical rules of the three Ecumenical Creeds were safely within the Christian Church. Their own mouths testified to the world that they were subjects of the Heavenly Crown.

So at the end of the sixth century the devil changed tactics and started to breed a royal-line of his own in the dry sands of the Arabian Peninsula. It was time for the Antichrist Beast to arise from the salty Red Sea and challenge the Christian Church with a book of lies about God (i.e., the Qur'an), and five new creeds for how to speak those lies (i.e., the regimen of daily Muslim prayers).

And woe to those eastern Christians who specifically rejected any portion of the King's grammatical rules in the three Ecumenical Creeds. Their own Pidgin English mouths testified to the world that they were expatriates of the Heavenly Crown. Many of them were still quasi–Christians, but they were Christians that had placed themselves beyond the protective boundaries of the universal Christian faith. Woe! Woe!

Daniel 7:8 [NLT]
… suddenly another small horn appeared among them. Three of the first horns were torn out by the roots to make room for it. This little horn had … a mouth that was boasting arrogantly.

19. Beware of Little Horns with Big Mouths

Hundreds of years before Christ, the Prophet Daniel had a number of visions that turned him pale and left him bedridden for days. They foretold of the rise and fall of the Babylonian (626 BC–539 BC), Medo–Persian (539 BC–334 BC), and Grecian Empires (334 BC–30 BC). They were seen by him in the form of a lion, a bear, and a leopard, respectively. Then he described the ascendancy of the Roman Empire (27 BC–AD 1453), comparing it to a strong and unnatural animal (Daniel 7:7). He also predicted that the Son of God would be born during the time of Roman supremacy, and that this Rock would break the Romans' feet of clay (Daniel 2:34–35). Finally, he describes a last, fifth, empire arising out of the breakup of the Roman Empire that would uproot three kingdoms, tread upon the saints, and arrogantly defy the God of the Bible (Daniel 7:25).

This has been misinterpreted by modern so-called biblical scholars as a single personality that shall arise out of today's European Union and reign for seven years. But Daniel's vision was of a contiguous series of empires: first, Babylonian; second, Medo–Persian; third, Grecian; fourth, Roman. The little horn is another empire that defeated the [Eastern] Roman Empire in the seventh century—it is not one person called the Antichrist who shall emerge from the twenty-first century European Union. So what is the empire that is represented by the little horn?

If you look at a map of the Roman Empire in AD 600, and a map of the Roman Empire in AD 700, the answer will be right before your eyes.

~~~~~~~~~~~~~~~~~~~~~~

The failing Roman Empire was split into two pieces by Diocletian in AD 286 to make it more manageable.[43] The Western Roman Empire ceased to be when the child emperor Romulus Augustus was deposed in AD 476.[44] *But it is an ignorant, west-centric, opinion to say that the Roman Empire ended in that year!* The Roman Empire lived on as a formidable, though waning, superpower for centuries after that in the form of *the Eastern* Roman Empire.

The Eastern Roman Empire is commonly called the Byzantine Empire, but that name was coined by a German historian in the nineteenth century. It would have been unknown contemporaneously—they thought of themselves as the intact portion of the Roman Empire. To the people of that day, the Eastern Roman Empire was the Roman Empire, and its capital of Constantinople was known as 'New Rome.' In fact, the city of Rome was, for many years, part of the holdings of the Eastern Roman Empire.

Then suddenly, in the first half of the seventh century, the Eastern Roman Empire permanently lost all its eastern and southern provinces. By the time of the eleventh century crusades, it was a paper tiger. The capital itself finally fell in AD 1453, and the Roman Empire ceased to be.[45]

What one empire took over nearly all of the land holdings of the [Eastern] Roman Empire during the latter half of the first millennium? Moreover, what happened to the three empires that had preceded the Roman Empire? What happened to the lion, which represented Babylo–Mesopotamia or modern Iraq? And what happened to the bear, which represented Medo–Persia or modern Iran? And what happened to the leopard, which represented Greece[v], or modern Turkey, Syria, Palestine, and Egypt? What became of these 'three horns'? As the Bible predicted, they were wrenched out by the roots—their customs, languages, and religions were abruptly changed. But by whom?

The Arab and Turkish Muslim empires. Islam is the little horn that consumed these Christian lands and boasted arrogantly against the Living God (Revelation 13:5–8).

~~~~~~~~~~~~~~~~~~~~~~

In AD 1980 I visited a wealthy friend at his estate on Prudence Island in Narragansett Bay. This fellow was always boasting about the moderating oce-

---

v   What we now call Greece is a tiny fraction of what was Greece and the Greek-speaking satellites 1,500 years ago; and, of course, they have lost their capital, Constantinople (now renamed Istanbul by the Turks). The *lingua franca* of much of the Near East used to be Greek—not Arabic, and certainly not Turkish. For example, the New Testament was written by Jews in the Greek language.

anic climate they enjoyed. He said, "Coastal Rhode Island is the Florida of New England! You are living up in the Arctic tundra of Vermont. You should spend a winter here! The snow melts as fast as it falls. Even Brazilian birds can make a home here."

He insisted that we walk down to the pier so he could show me a colony of feral Monk Parakeets that had taken up residence beside an electrical transformer. I could see a dozen gray and green, chubby-cheeked, birds squawking around an enormous, round, nest of sticks. He explained that their ancestors had been imported for the pet trade, but a few had escaped into the wild when a JFK Airport handler dropped a crate. The birds had been able to adapt to the coastal weather, and had established colonies up and down Long Island Sound.

"Impressive," I conceded.

Five years later, I ferried back to Prudence Island. The first thing I asked my friend was, "How are the Brazilians?"

"Those damned birds!" he scowled. "They're everywhere, and they never shut up. The whole colony swooped down on my apple trees and ate the fruit in one day. I tried to scare them away with a broom and they shit on me! They're even stripping off the bark! They're a menace!"

I pointed at the antique shotgun that was mounted above his hearth, "That would solve the problem."

"Are you kidding? We can't shoot them. The animal rights nuts won't even let us put them in cages!"

I made a bad pun, "Rather imprudent to have ever allowed those aliens to invade Prudence, wasn't it?"

He was not in the mood, but this time I insisted on walking him down to the pier. My friend said that the old nest had reached two hundred kilograms and brought down the utility pole during a gale. The indefatigable birds had just relocated to another pole. They were swarming like bees when we saw them, and making a horrendous noise.

He sighed, "It's just a matter of time before we lose power again ..."

~~~~~~~~~~~~~~~~~~~~~~~~~~

The Eastern Roman Empire was the sole superpower in the biblical world in AD 632. They were fresh-off a decisive victory over the Sassanid Persians in Mesopotamia. Then, within ten years, they lost control of all of their eastern and southern provinces. Palestine, Syria, Mesopotamia, Egypt, and Cyrene quickly fell to a previously unknown group from Arabia.[46] The new invaders even swept through the heartland of Persia, where the Romans had never dared to tread.

How could this have happened?

Islamic tradition holds that the Arabs broke out of their desert homeland, fervent to spread the religion of their recently-deceased prophet, Muhammad (AD 570–AD 632). Virtually every subsequent history book promulgates the tale that the Arabs won a fantastic series of battlefield victories, culminating with the slaughter of thousands of Roman troops at the Yarmuk River. This ostensibly forced the Christians into retreat, and the Muslims conquered the Middle East and North Africa.

This is simply not true. The facts are that the Arabs had no identifiable religion when they started marauding outside Arabia.[47] They could have been easily annihilated by the superpower that they invaded. However, the Eastern Roman emperor delayed an engagement while enacting ecclesiastical policies that made his subjects resent him (Section 64). When he finally sent an army against the Arabs, a significant number of his soldiers defected.[48] The remaining faithful soldiers were slaughtered. After that one disastrous battle, the Eastern Roman Empire withdrew to Anatolia, and handed the Arabs all of eastern Christendom. The Arabs then took Persia with ease because of the dynastic and military chaos that prevailed there in the wake of their recent defeat by the Eastern Roman Empire. The rapidity and sustained success of the Arab expansion later gave rise to lore that became religion and history.

The Arab Empire initially made few impositions upon its Christian subjects.[49] They simply took many wives and were industrious in their nighttime activity.[50] They waited three generations for their numbers to increase within the new lands. Then, at the end of the seventh century, they suddenly introduced the Cult of Muhammad[51] and imposed Islam.

Revelation 13:1–2 [YLT]
And I stood upon the sand of the sea, and I saw out of the sea a beast coming up, having seven heads ... and upon its heads a name of evil speaking, and the beast that I saw was like to a leopard, and its feet as of a bear, and its mouth as the mouth of a lion ...

20. The Beast Coming Up Out of the Sea

In AD 96,[52] the Apostle John was exiled by the pagan Romans to the Aegean Island of Patmos. There, near the end of the first century, he wrote the last book of the Bible, Revelation. During his period of writing, he stood upon the aqua-blue seashore and had a vision. He saw, across the Mediterranean Sea, a

Beast arising. He likened it to an animal with the traits of a leopard, bear, and lion.

The Apostle John's vision has parallels to the vision of the Prophet Daniel that I covered in Section 19. Daniel saw three kingdoms arising which he described as a lion, a bear, and a leopard (Daniel 7:2–6). These are universally recognized by biblical scholars as representing the empires of Babylon, Medo–Persia, and Greece.

Daniel goes on to describe the advent of another world power:

> *After that, in my vision at night I looked, and there before me was a fourth beast—terrifying and frightening and very powerful. It had large iron teeth; it crushed and devoured its victims and trampled underfoot whatever was left. It was different from all the former beasts, and it had ten horns. [Daniel 7:7 NIV]*

This is also universally recognized as representing the Roman Empire. Then, in verse 8, Daniel says that a "little horn" would arise from the vacuum of power left at the end of the Roman Empire. He said that it would subdue three kingdoms.

> *After them another king will appear. He will be different from the earlier ones. He'll bring three kings under his control. [Daniel 7:24 NIrV]*

I here proffer that the Apostle John's "beast rising up out of the sea" and the Prophet Daniel's "little horn" are one-and-the-same entity: the two texts are referring to the ascension of the Arab Muslim Empire (or Caliphate) that originated in the Mediterranean/Red Sea region and overwhelmed the territories of the former empires of Babylon, Medo–Persia, and Greece with remarkable speed and ease.

The seventh century Arabs conquered North Africa and the Middle East[53] just as if it had been prophetically predetermined.

The Apostle John says that the Beast that rose from the sea will have,

> *… seven heads and ten horns, and upon his horns ten crowns, and upon his heads the name of blasphemy. [Revelation 13:1 KJV]*

The seven heads are the seven early successors of Muhammad, or caliphs, of the Arab Empire (they are not to be confused with the seven heads of Revelation 12 or 17). These seven heads are:

1. Abu Bakr, caliph from AD 632 to AD 634;[54]
2. Umar, caliph from AD 634 to AD 644;[55]

3. Uthman, caliph from AD 644 to AD 656;[56]
4. **Ali ibn Abi Talib**, caliph from AD 656 to AD 661;[57]
5. Muawiyah, caliph from AD 661 to AD 680;[58]
6. Yazid, caliph from AD 680 to AD 683;[59]
7. Abd al-Malik,[vi] caliph from AD 685 to AD 705.[60]

There would eventually be one hundred caliphs.[61] I have chosen to name only the first seven major caliphs because it was during Abd al-Malik's reign that the Muslim religion was codified and permanently identified with the Arab Empire. The careers of these seven men were preparatory for the establishment of what the Bible calls 'the abomination that causes desolation.' This will be discussed at length in Sections 22 and 46.

The ten crowns are the Christian lands that the Caliphate conquered and held. They include Syrio–Phoenicia, Palestine–Transjordania, Babylo–Mesopotamia, Egypt, Cyrene, Medo–Persia, Armenia, Carthage–Tripolitania, Mauretania–Numidia, and eventually the entirety of Asia Minor. Most of the people in these areas were eventually Islamicized (Revelation 13:7–8). The once great Christian churches that Christ's Apostles founded there have been extremely marginalized or exterminated.

Of the early Patriarchates, only the Apostle Peter's church in Rome was left unmolested by the Muslims. This was predicted by Christ Himself:

> Now I say to you that you are Peter (which means 'rock'), and upon this rock I will build my church, and all the powers of hell will not conquer it. [Matthew 16:18 NLT]

The Islamists are very well aware of their failure to destroy Rome, and it is a sore point with them. The Iraqi arm of al-Qaeda recently threatened,

> We shall break the cross and spill the wine ... God will [help] Muslims to conquer Rome ... [May] God enable us to slit their throats, and make their money and descendants the bounty of the mujahideen.[62]

The name of blasphemy that is upon the seven heads of the Beast is the name of Muhammad. To the seventh century Arabs the word 'Muhammad' was as much a description as it was a relatively uncommon name. Its literal transla-

---

vi   I have left out Muawiya II who ruled for four months, and Marwan I who ruled for one year. They served sequentially during a power struggle for the empire. After Yazid's unexpected death in AD 683 the Caliphate was not reunited and firmly in al-Malik's hands until AD 692.

tion is 'the desired one' or 'the chosen one,'[63] so it was a suitable name/moniker for a man like Muhammad that claimed to be the one that God wanted to be His messenger. But the implication was larger: if the Arab, Muhammad, was a chosen prophet, apostle, and slave of Allah, then the Jew, Jesus, must also be no more than a chosen prophet, apostle, and slave of Allah.

Consider the similarity of these two Qur'anic verses:

> *Muhammad is no more than an apostle; other apostles have already passed away before him;*[64]

> *The Messiah, son of Mary, is no more than an apostle; other apostles before him have indeed passed away;*[65]

That is quite a theological distinction from the "Son of God, begotten of the Father before all worlds." Christians believe Jesus was begotten of God Himself; the Arab conquerors believed that Jesus was like Muhammad and the previous human mouthpieces of God's choosing. They honor Jesus as a good prophet only. They insist that He did not die on the cross, and that He was not the Son of God.

In this manner, Muslims have put the Arab man, Muhammad, into the place of the Jewish man, Jesus. Indeed, you will often hear Muslim clerics of today sermonizing about Muhammad as the 'ideal' or 'perfect' type for men to follow. But Christ is the perfect man; Christ led the sinless life; Christ is our model for behavior.

If you see Jesus and Muhammad as flip-sides of the same coin—if you view Christianity and Islam as a distinction without a difference—then you have not been paying attention. Islam is primary among the many antichrist sects. Islam is the Antichrist Beast.

~~~~~~~~~~~~~~~~~~~~~~~

Islam appeals to the worst in human nature. It teaches its young men to steal, rape, and kill.

> *This horn had eyes like the eyes of a man ... [Daniel 7:8 NIV]*

A Muslim man may get divorced simply by stomping his foot and saying, 'I divorce you,' three times.[66] There is no requirement for female consent to the divorce, or even for female consent before intercourse. No menstruating girl was safe in Afghanistan during the reign of the Taliban. They would be stolen without their fathers' permission and given to a Taliban mujahideen in their early teens.

Islam teaches that if these things are done in conjunction with the Pillars of Islam, one is not sinning, but earning one's way to paradise. And it teaches blind leader-worship through the incessant repetition that Muhammad is the Prophet of God. They insist that he is only a man, yet they venerate him five times per day in the call to prayer—as though he were a deity.

During the siege of Constantinople in AD 1453,

> *Every Moslem believed that the Prophet himself would accord a special place in Paradise to the first soldier who should force an entry into the ancient Christian capital ... Of the Sultan's own enthusiasm there could be no doubt. Many times he was heard to declare his determination to be the prince who should achieve this supreme triumph for Islam.*[67]

It would be the same if we Americans recited a veneration of George Washington (AD 1732–AD 1799) five times per day, and were told to invade Canadian households whenever we saw fit, and steal, rape, and kill there.

Islam is a pyramid scheme—a recipe for expansion as more and more young fighters covet their piece of the pie at the expense of a shrinking pool of infidels.[68]

~~~~~~~~~~~~~~~~~~~~~~~~

On November 2, AD 2004 Dutch filmmaker Theo Van Gogh (AD 1957–AD 2004) was brutally murdered in the streets of Amsterdam. He was followed while riding to work on his bicycle. A Moroccan immigrant to the Netherlands shot him, slit his throat, and then stuck a knife in his heart with a note attached to it. The note threatened his friends with the same fate.

Van Gogh's crime? He had directed a ten minute film that the Muslims consider blasphemous against their holy book, the Qur'an.

The murder was committed in broad daylight, in front of a number of horrified witnesses. The murderer took so long to decorate the crime scene that the police arrived. There was a shootout. He was wounded and arrested. At his sentencing he told the judges,

> *I take complete responsibility for my actions.* **I acted purely in the name of my religion** *... I can assure you that one day, should I be set free, I would do the same, exactly the same.*[69]

He told the mother of the victim,

> *I don't feel your pain. I have to admit that I don't have*
> *any sympathy for you. I can't feel for you because*
> *you're a non-believer.*[70]

There was a conspiracy to kill Theo Van Gogh. A dozen other men from the murderer's Muslim prayer group have been implicated.

~~~~~~~~~~~~~~~~~~~~~~~~

There are many antichrist sects in the world. After the various fits-and-starts of Gnosticism, Rabbinic Judaism, and Arianism in the first few centuries after Christ, the devil played his trump card: Islamism.[71] It has been his most successful bulwark against the Gospel of Jesus Christ.

What is unique about Islam (besides its violence) is its numbers: Islam (~ 1.2 billion) is second only to Christianity (~ 2 billion) in adherents. Islam has over a billion pair of human eyes, and over a billion human mouths that agree to speak boastfully against God five times per day. They are willing to use this network of evil to kill anyone that speaks against their god, their prophet, or their book.

The Beast of Islam is the largest and longest-lasting organized crime network in the world. The members of this organized crime network intend to extort and murder in every corner of the globe.

This is what we should expect from people that have read only one book their entire lives—and that, a very wicked book.

Revelation 13:2b [TNIV]
The dragon gave the beast his power and his throne and great authority.

21. The Dragon

The dragon or serpent is the devil, Allah, who gave power, seat, and authority to the Islamic Caliphate. The Apostle John said,

> *So they worshiped the dragon who gave authority to*
> *the beast; and they worshiped the beast, saying, "Who*
> *is like the beast? Who is able to make war with him?"*
> *[Revelation 13:4 NKJV]*

This passage tells us that the Muslim adherents worshiped the devil, Allah, because the spread of the Arab Empire was so impressive. It seemed that nothing could stop the Beast of Islam:

> *It was granted to him to make war with the saints and to overcome them. And authority was given him over every tribe, tongue, and nation. All who dwell on the earth will worship him, whose names have not been written in the Book of Life ... [Revelation 13:7–8 NKJV]*

Although God is sovereign and nothing happens without His allowing it, the devil is the one that instituted the Beast of Islam. Those that are of the Beast are servants and worshipers of their master, Allah.

The devil, Allah, is simply one. The Living God is worshiped as Trinity in unity, and Unity in trinity.

> *... I do not want you to be participants with demons. You cannot drink the cup of the Lord and the cup of demons too; you cannot have a part in both the Lord's table and the table of demons. Are we trying to arouse the Lord's jealousy? Are we stronger than he? [1 Corinthians 10:20–22 NIV]*

You have to be careful when using the word 'Allah' because it is the name of the Trinitarian God in the Arabic language Bible, but it is the name of the non-Trinitarian god (or Termagant) in the Qur'an. The Allah of the Qur'an is definitely the devil, and I use the word in this sense exclusively in this book.

The same distinction applies to the use of the word 'Jesus' between Christians and Mormons, or the use of the word 'Yahweh' between Christians and Rabbinic Jews. The devil loves to play word games, but every Christian should recognize that only the Trinitarian God of the Holy Bible is the True, Living God. Anyone that does not worship Father, Son, and Holy Spirit is serving the devil whether they call him by 'Allah' or by any other name.

More on the spiritual commonality between Muslims and other antichrists is presented in Sections 74, 86–87.

Revelation 13:3 [NLT]
I saw that one of the heads of the beast seemed wounded beyond recovery—but the fatal wound was healed! The whole world marveled ...

22. The Mortal Head-Wound and its Symbolic Healing

The Apostle Paul predicted that the Son of Perdition is the one who,

> *... opposes and exalts himself above all that is called God or that is worshiped ... [2 Thessalonians 2:4 NKJV]*

This person is the same as the head of the Seven Headed Beast that had a mortal wound in Revelation 13. **The Son of Perdition is the person known in history as Ali ibn Abi Talib (AD 599–AD 661)**—the fourth of the major seventh century Caliphs.

> *For I am going to raise up a shepherd over the land who will not care for the lost ... [Zechariah 11:16 TNIV]*

Ali was the first male convert of Muhammad, as well as his cousin, stepson, and son-in-law.[72] As a youth, he risked his life to protect Muhammad and to carry out his orders.[73] He was a commander of Arab forces from the very beginning of their expansion. He single-handedly killed two dozen enemy at the pivotal Battle of Badr in AD 624.[74] He was commended by Muhammad for bravery,[75] and granted his daughter's hand in marriage.[76]

Ali was the central charismatic figure of the post–Muhammad period. His supporters have always claimed that he should have been the first caliph. They say that he was usurped by the first three Sunni caliphs.

> *After the death of Muhammad, rival claims were put forth for the caliphate which was the office that was the supreme secular authority of Islam. In Shi'a history, Muhammad designated Ali as his successor, so that all the others who served in this capacity were illegitimate. The "Partisans of Ali," [Shi'a Ali] ... gave the name to the religious schism that divided the Islamic world from the very beginning. Eventually the Shi'ites would develop a religious doctrine that differs in fundamental respects from orthodox, or Sunni Islam. Nevertheless, at the cornerstone of Shi'a his-*

*tory is the figure of Ali and his persecution by the ille-
gitimate caliphs.*

*Upon Muhammad's death, a hastily collected group
of prominent Muslim leaders elected Muhammad's
father in law, Abu Bakr, to be the secular head of
Islam. However, Ali, Muhammad's son-in-law and
cousin, was not part of this committee nor were other
members of Muhammad's immediate family, and
many believed that Muhammad had designated Ali as
a successor, for the Traditions had Muhammad nam-
ing him as both his brother and his successor. Ali had
been raised with Muhammad and was the ... first of
Muhammad's tribe, the Quraysh, to declare himself
an apostle. But the Meccan and Medinan leaders
... gave their allegiance to Abu Bakr as Caliph, or
Successor to Muhammad and supreme head of Islam,
and attempted through force of arms to coerce Ali into
acknowledging Abu Bakr as well.*[77]

In AD 654 a Jewish admirer of Ali began to preach that Ali was the only
legitimate successor of Muhammad until (as he believed) Muhammad would
return to life. The Jew was so enamored of Ali that he spread his message
throughout Iraq and Egypt, and gained a following. Soon five hundred rabble
made their way to Medina to protest that the Arab Empire had been taken over
by godless tyrants (i.e., the first three caliphs). In AD 656, they demanded the
resignation of the third caliph, Uthman (AD 580–AD 656). When he refused,
they stormed his palace and killed him.[78]

With Uthman's death came Ali's big chance. Finally, at the age of
fifty-seven,[79] he ascended to the Caliphate. He delayed in punishing Uthman's
assassins and they escaped. This resulted in two insurrections against Ali,[80] and
delayed him from instituting a new religious orthodoxy concerning whatever
Muhammad had taught him in his youth. He moved the capital from Medina
(in modern Saudi Arabia), to Kufa (in modern Iraq), and made some unpopular
changes in political appointments. Concerns about his religiosity grew, as did
Ali's paunchy waistline.[81]

What we know about the historical person named Muhammad comes
from literary sources that begin four to five generations after his death.[82] We
would have known more, and an Arab religion would have been formalized
under Ali, except for a singular quirk of history: the slain Caliph Uthman's
nephew, Muawiyah (AD 602–AD 680), had by that time risen to the power-

ful position of governor of Syria. Muawiyah suspected that Ali had a hand in Uthman's lynching and vowed revenge. He seized control of Egypt, and a civil war ensued in AD 657. After heavy fighting in Syria, Muawiyah began to lose the Battle of Siffin against Ali's forces. Muawiyah pleaded for a truce and Ali acquiesced. During an arbitration in AD 661 Ali was conveniently assassinated by an anti-establishmentarian third party called the Kharijites. The assassin stuck a poison-tipped spear into Ali's brain while he was praying.[83] With no rival, Muawiyah easily seized the caliphate. This set the stage for the development of the two main branches of Islam (i.e., Shi'a and Sunni).

> *From [AD 661] onwards, authority was divided in the Islamic world. The Umayyads continued to pass the Caliphate down through the ages among their family; but there now existed in Iraq a separate Islamic community that did not recognize the authority of the Umayyad Caliphs. Rather they recognized only the successors to Ali as authorities, and they gave these successors the title Imam, or spiritual leader of Islam, both to differentiate their leaders from the more worldly and secular Umayyads and because ... the second Imam, ceded the Caliphate to the Umayyads. This meant, of course, that the Shi'ite leaders could not legitimately assert themselves as Caliphs, so they invented a separate title. In Shi'ite history, Ali is the first Imam (although Sunni and Western historians do not believe that he assumed this title but rather that it was retroactive). A grand total of eleven Imams succeeded Ali ... passing the Imamate down to their sons in hereditary succession.[84]*

It is ironic that Muawiyah ended up the uncontested leader of the Arab Empire—especially by usurping Muhammad's stepson and heir, Ali.[85] Muawiyah was the son of one of Muhammad's staunchest opponents, and had fought against Muhammad during his early campaigns in Arabia. When Muhammad conquered Mecca in AD 630, Muawiyah became a follower of Muhammad's teaching in order to save his life.[86] Muhammad accepted him since he came from the most powerful family in Mecca. Muawiyah was given both civil and military posts, at which he proved politically adept. For example, he had no qualms about employing Christians in prominent positions of his government in Syria—even if they came from families that previously served the Eastern Roman Empire. Their duplicity was something that Muawiyah could understand.

Muawiyah instinctively knew, after only thirty years in control, that the Arabs were in no position to force a new religion onto their almost-entirely Christian subjects. One of the secrets to their success had been to stay out of the doctrinal squabbles that divided Christendom. The new caliph was pragmatic, soulless, and smart enough not to unnecessarily provoke the Eastern Roman Empire with religiosity. The time was not yet right for religious provocation.

Caliph Muawiyah drank wine, lived lavishly, and had little regard for Muhammad's legacy. He poisoned many of Muhammad's remaining old guard once he gained absolute control of the empire.[87] He forced Ali's eldest son, Hasan (AD 624–AD 670), into retirement in Medina. Hasan married many times, and was eventually poisoned by one of his wives at the instigation of Muawiyah.[88] Ali's second son and heir, Husayn (AD 626–AD 680), tried to retake the Caliphate by force after Muawiyah's death. He and his seventy-one true-believers were massacred at the Battle of Karbala by Muawiyah's son, Caliph Yazid. It was a purge of the party ranks of those that followed Ali's ideology.

Muawiyah has always been loathed by Shi'a Muslims as a cruel, irreverent, and calloused opportunist. From his time onward, the Muslims were split between those loyal to Ali (i.e., the Shi'a), and those that reluctantly accepted Muawiyah (i.e., the Sunni).

~~~~~~~~~~~~~~~~~~~~~~~

At this point, it may be helpful to draw a loose parallel between the Arabs and Soviets. The Arabs usurped the Eastern Roman Empire and the Oriental Orthodox Church; the Soviets usurped the Czarist Russian Empire and the Eastern Orthodox Church. But neither Muhammad nor Lenin (AD 1870–AD 1924) bequeathed a successor in the form of written instructions. Subsequent to their deaths, both of their empires experienced early leadership struggles and assassinations, as shown in the table below.

Table 1. Comparison of Early Satanic Empires

Satanic Empire	Fallen Founder	Martyred Ideologue	Oppressive Tyrant	Pure / Calloused Ideology	Subsequent Purge
Arab	Prophet Muhammad	Caliph Ali	Caliph Muawiyah	Shi'aism / Sunnism	Battle of Karbala
Soviet	Vladimir Lenin	Leon Trotsky	Joseph Stalin	Trotskyism / Stalinism	Great Terror

The comparison is self-evident and requires little explanation. Antichrist movements inevitably turn inward upon themselves, and the true ideologues are devoured by opportunists during post–revolutionary purges.

It is notable, however, that Leon Trotsky (AD 1879–AD 1940) was the founder of the Red Army,[89] and Ali was Muhammad's most trusted warrior.[90] Also, Trotsky was killed by an ice pick strike with his head bowed to read, and Caliph Ali was killed by a poisoned spear strike with his head bowed in prayer. Both men did not lose consciousness immediately, and ordered their bodyguards to spare the life of their assassin.

~~~~~~~~~~~~~~~~~~~~~~~~~

The Apostle John goes on to tell us in this section's verse heading that the head that was wounded was healed. But because Ali is the prototypical Antichrist, his healing from a mortal wound must be the opposite of Christ's actual conquest over physical death. [For more on how Shi'a Islam is the inverse of Christianity, see Section 73.]

As the antithesis of Christ, Ali did not rise from the dead. Christ's tomb is empty, but Ali's bones still lie in a mausoleum in Najaf, Iraq. The site is holy to Shi'a Muslims, and nearly all Shi'as in Iraq request that they be buried in its six square kilometer cemetery.[91] Eighty kilometers away is Karbala, where Ali's younger son and second heir, Husayn, was killed and dismembered.[92] The Shi'a gather there every year for a passion play[93] called the Day of Ashura,[94] and wail and beat themselves until they are bloody. This is to show their anguish because they were not able to be present to give their life for the valiant Husayn.

The contrast is striking: Christ endured scourging and a crown of thorns on His head; by His stripes we are healed, and through His shed blood we are redeemed from death. It is for this reason that we refer to the day of Christ's Crucifixion as Good Friday. It is a day of solemn and sober worship for the Good Work that He did in dying for us. But the Shi'a work themselves into a loud self-flagellating frenzy, and inflict razor cuts on their heads in a vain effort to reverse history for their fallen leader, Husayn. And when they die they want to be buried near their fallen leader's father, Ali.

It took Ali three days to die of his wound,[95] whereas it took Jesus three days to emerge from the grave. I find the symbolism beautiful: three days to die in agony versus three days to rise in glory. And unlike Christ's real bodily Resurrection, the healing of Ali's brain was purely figurative—the 'resurrection' of his dream of a world religion to challenge Christianity.

~~~~~~~~~~~~~~~~~~~~~~

The final caliph of the seventh century was Abd al-Malik (AD 646–AD 705). He represented the last of the Beast's seven heads.

Abd al-Malik had become caliph in AD 685 after a year and a half power struggle, but he initially did not have firm control of the entire Arab Empire. He sent his most capable general to Mecca to put down a rebellion by a pretender to the caliphate,[96] and later to put down a rebellion in Iraq.[97] By AD 692, al-Malik was the absolute ruler of the Arab Empire. He decided to construct an ornate building on the Temple Mount in Jerusalem to represent the triumph of the Caliphate over Christianity.[98] Much of the construction material for this project was looted from Christian churches. The Christians of Jerusalem attempted to prevent this abomination, but they were violently suppressed and a portion of the city was destroyed.[99] Al-Malik's building, the Dome of the Rock, still stands on the old Temple Mount. It symbolizes the 'abomination that causes desolation' spoken of in Daniel 12:11.

It is commonly held that the Dome of the Rock was completed in AD 692, but a convincing argument is made by Blair[100] that AD 692 *was the date of the beginning of the construction project* because al-Malik was not in a position to pursue such an ambitious project while fighting a multi-front war. His simultaneous victories in AD 692 over rebels in Mecca and over the Eastern Roman Empire at Sebastopolis[101] left al-Malik with much booty.[102] He considered a new coin from Constantinople with the full-face image of Christ to be idolatrous,[103] and began minting Islamic coins in Damascus.[104] He also commissioned the cultic structure on the Temple Mount in Jerusalem.[105] The completion date could have been anytime over the next nine years, as was the case with the contemporaneous construction of a mosque in Damascus.[106] I suggest a date of AD 699 for the completion of the Dome of the Rock,[107] as this is the year that the Caliphate finished its anti-Trinitarian currency reforms.[108]

Prior to AD 692, there was still no official sanction of the prophethood of Muhammad in the Arab Empire.[109] Over the next seven years, Abd al-Malik changed all that.[110]

The despotic and irreligious fifth caliph, Muawiyah, was al-Malik's grandfather's cousin, so al-Malik did not directly inherit the disdain that Muawiyah had toward Muhammad's teachings. In fact, al-Malik identified more with the third caliph, Uthman, who was a more closely related cousin, and who was an early follower of Muhammad. However, you will recall that Caliph Uthman was killed by over-enthusiastic supporters of Ali, and when Ali became the fourth caliph he neglected to punish Uthman's assassins. So it is easy to understand how al-Malik desired to venerate and preserve the memory of Muhammad, while at the same time ignoring Ali (whose descendants remained potential rivals for power until the AD 870's).

Thus, through the Dome project[111] and the implementation of an Islamic monetary system,[112] al-Malik began a decades-long process that firmly institutionalized the Cult of Muhammad.[113]

And why not? For the new Arab Empire to have an Arab prophet as its founder worked for the Arab political establishment.[114] That the Prophet Muhammad was a greater prophet than the Jew, Jesus (whom they also accept as a prophet), was likewise expedient. And what better place to proclaim the new religion than from the Temple Mount in Jerusalem?

Caliph al-Malik stated of his own motivation in building the Dome of the Rock,

> *Verily he was right, and he was prompted to a worthy work. For he beheld Syria to be a country that had long been occupied by the Christians, and he noted there are beautiful churches still belonging to them, so enchantingly fair, and so renowned for their splendour, as are the Church of the Holy Sepulchre, and the churches of Lydda and Edessa. So he sought to build for the Muslims a mosque that should be unique and a wonder to the world. And in like manner is it not evident that Caliph Abd al-Malik, seeing the greatness of the martyrium of the Holy Sepulchre and its magnificence was moved lest it should dazzle the minds of Muslims and hence erected above the Rock the dome which is now seen there.*[115]

In this way, al-Malik changed the goal of the Arab Empire from just gaining land as an independent monotheistic third party, to forcibly changing the religion of its subjects. From that point forward the Arabs required not just the respect due any civil authority, but the submission of the mind. This is the Islam that we know today.

~~~~~~~~~~~~~~~~~~~~~~~~

At the moment when Caliph Ali was struck in the head by a spear, he is purported to have cried out,

> *By the Lord of the Kaaba, I have succeeded!*[116]

He apparently knew that his martyrdom would have the desired effect in time.

The period between Ali's death (AD 661)[117] and the resurrection of his dream of a new world religion by Abd al-Malik (AD 692)[118] is symbolically significant: it is the same period of time between Christ's incarnation (6 BC)[119] and His anointing by the Holy Spirit in AD 26[120] (see Table 2).

The period between the initiation (AD 692)[121] and completion (AD 699)[122] of Dome construction is also significant: it is the same period of time between the beginning of Christ's ministry in AD 26[123] and the spread of His Gospel to the Gentiles in AD 33[124] (see Table 2).

So, as Christ's work was done while He and His Apostles lived and walked among us, Ali's work was done while he and his followers were being eaten by worms. And just as Christ really did rise from the dead bodily, Ali's healing is simply his dream reaching beyond the grave. The Gospel authors tell us that the resurrected Jesus talked with people, and cooked breakfast, and let the Apostle Thomas touch Him before His Ascension. But Ali was never heard from again.

The political benefits of the thirty-one year respite (i.e., AD 661–AD 692) from Arab religious fervor was enormous. When Ali took control in AD 656, the Arab Empire was only twenty-four years old, and still fragile. It was not at all clear whether they would be able to effectively administer their vast new territories and establish lasting control over their overwhelmingly Christian subjects.[125] Just one organized campaign from the Eastern Roman Empire, combined with a popular uprising among their Christian subjects, could have brought quick ruination. But by the time of the Dome construction project, the empire was sixty years old, and the Arabs had firm control over the eastern Christians.

~~~~~~~~~~~~~~~~~~~~~~~

It was on the future-caliph Ali's advice that the Arabs first besieged Jerusalem in AD 637,[126] instead of the more logical choice of Caesarea Palaestina on the Mediterranean coast.

> *[The Arab officers] consulted the caliph [Umar] whether they should march to Caesarea or Jerusalem; and the advice of Ali determined the immediate siege of the latter. To a profane eye, Jerusalem was the first or second capital of Palestine; but after Mecca and Medina, it was revered and visited by the [Arabs], as the temple of the Holy Land which had been sanctified*

by the revelation of Moses, of Jesus, and of Mahomet himself.[127]

Ali wanted the Arabs to conquer the city that was holy to Christians, but,

> *... the city was defended on every side by deep val-*
> *leys and steep ascents; since the invasion of Syria,*
> *the walls and towers had been anxiously restored; the*
> *bravest of the fugitives of [the Battle of] Yermuk had*
> *[retreated there as] the nearest place of refuge; and in*
> *the defense of the sepulchre of Christ, the natives and*
> *strangers might feel some sparks of the enthusiasm,*
> *which so fiercely glowed in the bosoms of the [Arabs].*
> *The siege of Jerusalem lasted four months; not a day*
> *was lost without some action of sally or assault;*[128]

The Arabs of that time were not Muslim as we know them today, and they did not write of a person named Muhammad, but they were oppressors from the beginning. Their belief was loosely monotheistic, but emphatically non-Trinitarian.[129] Their earliest inscriptions tersely state, "do not say three, for Allah is One," and "God neither begets, nor is he begotten."

Patriarch Sophronius of Jerusalem (AD 560–AD 638), was not so much alarmed by Arab savagery over his Christian flock (there was little at the time)—he just couldn't believe that such pagan oafs could defeat the Eastern Roman Empire and be entrusted to run the affairs of government.[130] Although appalled at the prospect of having godless barbarians in charge of the holy city, the faithful old patriarch finally had no other choice than to appear at the walls of Jerusalem to negotiate surrender. Defeat was inevitable and he wanted to avoid the slaughter that had befallen the city during the Sassanid Persian conquest of AD 614.

The second caliph, Umar (AD 580–AD 644), made his way from Medina to Jerusalem to personally take control of Jerusalem. And the future fourth caliph, Ali, made the historic pilgrimage as well.

> *After signing the capitulation, [the Caliph] entered*
> *the city without fear or precaution; and courteously*
> *discoursed with the patriarch concerning its religious*
> *antiquities.* **Sophronius bowed before his new master,**
> **and secretly muttered, in the words of Daniel, "The**
> **abomination of desolation is in the holy place."** *At*
> *the hour of prayer they stood together in the church of*
> *the resurrection; but the caliph refused to perform his*

devotions, and contented himself with praying on the
steps of the church ... [131]

Sophronius' *mot juste* is amazing. The man had the erudition of the Holy Spirit. He knew that the Arab Empire was the Abomination.

I can only imagine that Ali, the first convert to Muhammad's religious ideology, walked the short distance from the Church of the Holy Sepulchre to the Temple Mount and there said something blasphemous—perhaps "Ali Akbar!" ["Ali is great!"] But he would have to wait nineteen more years before it would be his turn to lead the Arab Empire.

He will oppose and will exalt himself over everything
that is called God or is worshiped, so that he sets
himself up in God's temple, proclaiming himself to be
God. [2 Thessalonians 2:4 NIV]

With Ali's tacit approval, his followers hailed him with the messianic shout, "Ali Akbar!", when he finally assumed the Caliphate in AD 656. His grandson was even named Ali Akbar[132]—a common name among Shi'a Muslims to this day. This put Ali in the place of God in men's hearts.

Every single day the Shi'a muezzin proclaims the call to prayer,

I bear witness that Ali is the vice-regent of God and
his infallible sons are the proofs of God.[133]

And the Shi'a believe that Ali and the other eleven Imams were,

... free from all sin or fault ... therfore, they are the
most perfect of humans ... [and] the one who teaches
human beings the mystical truths of the universe. The
Shi'ites believe that [within the person of the Imam]
... the esoteric, mystical aspects of God are transmit-
ted to human beings.[134]

If Ali had lived on as Caliph in AD 661 and imposed this new non-Trinitarian religion, the Eastern Roman Empire might have awoken to the reality of the situation. They could have organized a crusade, crushed the interloping Arabs, and made them nothing more than a historical blip. Instead, Ali was assassinated, and the Arabs bode their time until the turn of the eighth century.

The Eastern Roman emperor was deposed from Constantinople in AD 695. His nose was chopped off and he was sent into exile in the Crimea. Two subsequent emperors failed to stabilize the situation, and the angry noseless emperor returned to power in AD 705.[135] So it was in AD 699,[136] while the Eastern Roman Empire was in this period of dynastic chaos, that the new

Islamic religion was codified in the gilded Dome and sent forth from Jerusalem. The Arabs were the new superpower, and they had a new religion.

This is the 'healing' that the Apostle John tells us made the world wonder after the Beast. Ali had lost the civil war and been killed in AD 661, but his dream was resurrected by his political enemies once the Arab Empire was self-sufficient in AD 699. The Arabs simply modified their earlier "Ali Akbar!" to a more presentable "Allah Akbar!"[137]

The year AD 699 was *exactly* six hundred and sixty-six years after a Jewish mob stoned the Deacon Stephen to death in AD 33.[138] The stoning marked the first persecution that the Christian Church was to experience.

> *On that day a great persecution broke out against the*
> *church at Jerusalem, and all except the apostles were*
> *scattered throughout Judea and Samaria. [Acts 8:1*
> *NIV]*

The devil was celebrating an anniversary. But as the saints fled the persecution, the Gospel of Christ—the only hope for mankind—went forth from Jerusalem with them.

Revelation 13:18 [ASV]
... it is the number of a man: and his number is Six hundred and sixty and six.

23. The Number of the Beast

The Romans had destroyed the Second Temple in AD 70 after a disastrous Jewish revolt.[139] The vacant Temple Mount eventually became a place of prayer for Christians. There was only a small open-walled enclosure to protect pilgrims from the rain when the Arabs captured the city in AD 637. By the AD 670's, the Arabs were also congregating there for prayer.[140] But beginning in AD 692,[141] Caliph Abd al-Malik constructed yet another temple there called the Dome of the Rock, and initiated the Cult of Muhammad. The Christians in Jerusalem revolted, and part of the city was destroyed by al-Malik's army when they crushed the rebellion.[142]

In the year AD 699,[143] amid cries of "Allahu Akbar," or "[The Non-Triune] God Alone is great!" the Dome of the Rock was gilded with gold[144] and the Temple Mount became a place exclusively for people that submitted to a new religion that denied Trinitarianism, the Incarnation, the Easter-Resurrection, and the Holy Bible.[145]

The Dome of the Rock remains the focal point of Jerusalem to this day. The gold of the gilded dome symbolized the Islamic monetary system, finalized at the very end of the seventh century.[146] This later became manifest in the Dhimmi religious caste system by which millions of people were coerced away from Christianity (Section 24).

In one of the few places in Scripture where the number six hundred and sixty-six is used, it refers to money.

> *The weight of gold that came to Solomon yearly was six hundred and sixty-six talents of gold ... [2 Chronicles 9:13 NKJV]*

And we know that,

> *... the love of money is a root of all kinds of evil, for which some have strayed from the faith in their greediness, and pierced themselves through with many sorrows. [1 Timothy 6:10 NKJV]*

It is, therefore, poetic that the Son of Perdition died by piercing with a spear, and that his religion spread through Antichrist inscriptions on pieces of gold coin and a gilded dome of gold.

~~~~~~~~~~~~~~~~~~~~~~

Most biblical scholars agree that Jesus Christ was born to the blessed virgin Mary in the year 5 BC or the year 6 BC. The 6 BC date is favored by some scholars that interpret the Star of Bethlehem to be a rare double eclipse of Jupiter that occurred that year.[147] Whether Jesus' birth was in 6 BC or 5 BC, it is probable that God became incarnate as a zygote in the womb of the virgin Mary in 6 BC. Therefore, throughout this book I will use 6 BC[148] as the year that God became a male human. It was His plan to save those who would believe.

The devil also had a plan. His answer to the Christian religion was six hundred and sixty-six years in-the-making. By the year AD 661 the Arab Empire had engulfed the whole of eastern Christendom, and was busy dispatching the Buddhists in Afghanistan. In its first decade it had captured three of the most important Christian centers: Jerusalem, Antioch, and Alexandria.

As we discussed in the preceding section, the fourth caliph was a man named Ali ibn Abi Talib—the cousin, stepson, and son-in-law of Muhammad. Ali is the prototypical Antichrist—the man that the Apostle Paul called the 'Son of Perdition' (2 Thessalonians 2:3).

This section's verse heading tells us that the Number of the Beast is a man's number. That man is Caliph Ali, the Son of Perdition. His number is the number of years between the birth of the Son of God and the death of the Son of Perdition.

The Apostle Paul said of himself to the church elders of Ephesus,

I tell you this day that I am clean and free from the blood of all men. I told you all the truth about God. [Acts 20:26–27 NLV]

Therefore, egomaniacs like Ali that tell lies about God are guilty of men's blood as they aid them on toward Hell. Ali was an effective warrior who subjugated enormous areas of land, coveted Jerusalem, and extracted tribute from Christians. Then he began to think of himself as the vice-regent of God, and an infallible incarnation of divine wisdom.

It was not unusual for sycophants to compare their leaders to God in the Middle East. In the Bible we read of the fate of King Herod Agrippa:

Then Herod went from Judea to Caesarea and stayed there a while. He had been quarreling with the people of Tyre and Sidon; they now joined together and sought an audience with him. Having secured the support of Blastus, a trusted personal servant of the king, they asked for peace, because they depended on the king's country for their food supply.
On the appointed day Herod, wearing his royal robes, sat on his throne and delivered a public address to the people. They shouted, "This is the voice of a god, not of a man." Immediately, because Herod did not give praise to God, an angel of the Lord struck him down, and he was eaten by worms and died. [Acts 12:19–23 NIV]

Like Herod, Ali allowed himself to be hailed as God with the words, 'Ali Akbar,' and he was struck down.

Again, there is a marked contrast with Christianity: whereas the Christian religion began with the birth of a poor baby, the Muslim religion began with the assassination of a wealthy dictator. The death of Caliph Ali occurred *exactly* six hundred and sixty-six years after the 6 BC incarnation of Jesus Christ.[vii] As the birth of Christ brought forth a Christian era of benefi-

---

vii One year has to be subtracted since there is no 'year zero' in the Christian calendar. Throughout this book I have subtracted one year from date-intervals that extend from BC through AD, and added a year to timelines that extend from BC to AD.

cence, so the death of Ali only cemented the historical changes that would usher in the new, oppressive religion, Islam.

> *So don't boast about following a particular human leader. For everything belongs to you—[1 Corinthians 3:21 NLT]*

My Christian readers will now begin to see how it is that Ali is the prophesied Son of Perdition—the prototypical Antichrist.

Jesus is …

> ➢ the Son of God …
>> ➢ and the sinless Incarnation of the Word of God …
>>> ➢ His birth began the Christian religion.

Ali claimed to be …

> ➢ the vice-regent of God …
>> ➢ and the infallible incarnation of divine wisdom …
>>> ➢ his assassination began both Shi'a and Sunni Islam.

That Ali and Islam are the devil's anti-type of Christ and Christianity is made clear in the table below. Note that the six hundred and sixty-six year parallel is consistent between the four rows.

Table 2. The Six Hundred and Sixty-Six Year Parallel

Jesus of Nazareth, Son of God	Date	Cumul. Duration	Date	Ali ibn Abi Talib, Son of Perdition
Incarnation of sinless zygote.	6 BC[149]	--	AD 661[150]	Assassination of violent dictator.
Anointing by the Holy Spirit at His baptism. The Heavenly Father confirms, "This is My beloved Son, in whom I am well pleased."	AD 26[151]	31.25 years	AD 692[152]	Inscriptions of the Dome of the Rock composed by al-Malik; construction begun; Christians revolt and are crushed; Islamic monetary system introduced with a coin stating, "Muhammad is the Messenger of God."
Mid–point of final seven year period prophesied in Daniel 9:27. Resurrection from the dead, proof shown, ascension to Heaven.	AD 30[153]	34.75 years	AD 696[154]	Mid–point of Dome of the Rock construction; the first Islamic gold coin is issued. It denies the Trinity, the Incarnation, and it calls for the new religion to prevail over all other religions.
Persecution of the Church and sending forth of Christ's Gospel from Jerusalem.	AD 33[155]	38.25 years	AD 699[156]	Islamic currency reforms completed. Dome is gilded gold—symbolic sending forth of Ali's dream of a new world religion from Jerusalem.

The Apostle John wrote in Revelation,

> *This calls for wisdom: let the one who has under-standing calculate the number of the beast, for it is the number of a man, and his number is 666. [Revelation 13:18 ESV]*

The table that you just reviewed is the fulfillment of this prophecy. Out of the tens of billions of people that have lived, I am the only one that has seen and written that the Antichrist died *exactly* six hundred and sixty-six years after the Christ was born,[157] and that the Antichrist's heinous religion was institutionalized *exactly* six hundred and sixty-six years after Christ's blessed ministry.

> *I will brag only about what I have done in the area God has given me. It is an area that reaches all the way to you. [2 Corinthians 10:13 NIrV]*

The 666-mystery has been hidden since the first century completion of the Bible. Now, in the early twenty-first century, God has brought forth the one with understanding to calculate the Number of the Beast.

There is only one wise conclusion: the end of all things is near.

Revelation 13:16–17 [CEV]
All people were forced to put a mark on their right hand or forehead. Whether they were powerful or weak, rich or poor, free people or slaves, they all had to have this mark, or else they could not buy or sell anything. This mark stood for the name of the beast and for the number of its name.

24. Burns and Calluses: the Mark of the Beast

There are many sincere Christians that expect a one-world currency to be instituted by a coming Antichrist personality that will have power throughout the globe. This notion is especially prevalent among those of Anabaptist sects (i.e., those that believe a person that was baptized as an infant must be re-baptized as an adult—usually by immersion). These Christians tend to hoard gold bullion, and are absolutely paranoid about credit cards, social security numbers, and paper money that has magnetic fibers in it.

When considering the verses that head this section we must remember that the Apostle John lived his entire life in the eastern Christian lands that eventually became part of the Caliphate. That was his world. The Prophet Daniel had used similar language in 550 BC[158] when he wrote that the coming Roman Empire would,

> ... *devour the whole earth* ... *[Daniel 7:23 NKJV]*

So when John wrote that no one would be able to buy or sell unless they had the Mark of the Beast, he meant that the entire Middle East would be engulfed by some type of economic tyranny. Of course, it would always be possible for Christians to buy or sell with each other, or to barter with people under-the-table. This verse is not meant to indicate a suspension of the economic laws of supply-and-demand, but to show that there would be official, religious, laws that would affect commerce, and there would be effective religious boycotts against Christians. This refers to the Islamists' Dhimmi religion cast system that makes business transactions less advantageous for those 'infidels' that remain true to Christ.

~~~~~~~~~~~~~~~~~~~~~~~~~

You don't have to affect people's pocketbooks very far before you move them to action. My childhood chum once ate a bug for five cents. He said he did it to prove the point that bugs are not poisonous. But he loved money, and I can assure you that he would not have taken up the challenge if he had to pay six cents to procure the bug instead of picking it up off the ground! His motivation was profit, and not the virtue of entomological cuisine.

Now, there is no freedom of religion in Islamic countries. Christians, Jews, Mandaeans, Zoroastrians, and Hindus have all been oppressed under the Dhimmi religious caste system. The infidels were taxed unequally—often at twice the rate for Muslims.[159] My grandmother used to tell stories about how the Muslim Kurds were allowed to pillage their Christian neighbors in the Ottoman Empire at certain times of the year. The Qur'an is often touted as commending good treatment of the 'people of the book,' but elsewhere it encourages discrimination and brutality.

The second caliph, for example, threatened that the Christians of Jerusalem must pay a tax in order to continue to confess the Trinity.

> *We require of you to testify that there is but one God,*
> *and that Mahomet is his apostle. If you refuse this,*
> *consent to pay tribute, and be under us forthwith.*
> *Otherwise I shall bring men against you who love*
> *death better than you do the drinking of wine or eating*
> *hogs' flesh. Nor will I ever stir from you, if it please*
> *God, till I have destroyed those that fight for you, and*
> *made slaves of your children.*[160]

Throughout the centuries, murder and coercion have been the ways that Islam has spread. I know a Nigerian Christian pastor that was brought to the hospital for malaria in the Muslim part of that country. The hospital staff asked him to convert to Islam. He refused, and then lost consciousness. They then told his wife that he needed open-heart surgery. They were planning to kill him on the operating table! She wisely called upon a number of male relatives; they congregated at the hospital and took her husband home.

Even in the best of circumstances, religious minorities have been forbidden from engaging in certain businesses, or were forced into only the lowest professions. In the Islamic Republic of Iran, for example, the Ayatollah Khomeini (AD 1900–AD 1989) protected the tiny Christian minority from violence, but wrote that a Muslim would be ritually unclean if he touched urine, feces, sperm, carrion, a dog, a pig, *or an unbeliever*. He declared that when a person is converted to Islam, their body, saliva, nasal secretion, and sweat suddenly become ritually clean.[161] Khomeini is considered the greatest Islamic thinker of modern times. Therefore, Shi'as in Iran will not buy produce from non-Muslim merchants because they are considered unclean. Under the same mentality, members of the Coptic Church were relegated to being the garbage-men of Egypt centuries ago.

There is one way out of these economic hardships: convert.

Indeed, I know three formerly-Christian brothers that live in a Muslim capital and have converted to Islam in order to keep their meager candy store afloat. Their relatives in the United States would gladly have sponsored them for immigration, but that was too much trouble for them. They were more will-ing to pray to the devil, Allah, than to pack up and start over in a free land.

> *If anyone worships the beast and his image and receives his mark on the forehead or on the hand, he, too, will drink of the wine of God's fury, which has been poured full strength into the cup of his wrath. He will be tormented with burning sulfur in the presence of the holy angels and of the Lamb. And the smoke of their torment rises for ever and ever. There is no rest day or night for those who worship the beast and his image, or for anyone who receives the mark of his name. [Revelation 14:9–11 NIV]*

Sometimes the cost of doing business is bugs in your teeth; other times it is an eternally burnt and calloused soul.

~~~~~~~~~~~~~~~~~~~~~~

The Bible tells us that Christians also have a mark, but it is invisible and it is put in place through the indwelling of the Holy Spirit.

> *Having believed, you were marked in him with a seal, the promised Holy Spirit, who is a deposit guaran-teeing our inheritance until the redemption of those who are God's possession—to the praise of his glory. [Ephesians 1:13–14 NIV]*

So our mark is a gift, and we live in thankful response for the gift. The Psalmist says,

> *Seven times a day I praise you for your righteous laws. [Psalm 119:164 TNIV]*

Seven is a number signifying completeness and perfection. This verse shows that a mature Christian praises God in his heart continuously, not at legalistic intervals.

I find it significant that the Muslims settled upon a strict five-per-day prayer regimen, as well as five pillars of Islam, and a fifth-work-day (i.e., Friday) Islamic Sabbath. The symbol of Satanists is an inverted pentagram—making the devil often associated with the number five. And remember that the Son of Perdition, Ali, and the Beast of Islam came into being during the fifth millennium of human history.

We have already established that the Beast is the religion of Islam that was established by the Arab Caliphate (Section 20). The mark of an observant Beast-worshiper is to pray five times per day, every day, toward the Kaaba in Mecca. And when the Muslims pray, they strike a kneeling pose, and lower their hands and foreheads to the ground. The right hand is the hand of business and oaths in Islamic lands. The left hand is for personal hygiene—never try to shake a Muslim's hand with your left hand. But to lower one's right hand has special significance to them; it is a sign of oblation.

To survive economically in Islamic countries people literally genu-flected at the invocation of the name of blasphemy, Muhammad. When it is time for Muslims to lower their foreheads to the rug in prayer, the muezzin in the minaret calls out, "I bear witness that Muhammad is the Messenger of Allah." Pious Muslims develop rug burns on their foreheads and calluses on their hands and fingers from the incessant rug-worship.

Do not doubt this explanation. Repetitive use of any kind results in injuries and marks. I, for example, have developed a discomforting callus on the last digit of my index finger by using my mouse's scroll button during the writing of this book.

The Qur'an itself predicted that a mark would be left in the faces of those that seek to earn favor from Allah through prostration.

> *Muhammad is the Apostle of Allah, and those with him are ruthless against the unbelievers, but compas-sionate among themselves; you will see them bowing down, prostrating themselves, seeking grace from Allah and pleasure;* **their marks are in their faces** *because of the effect of prostration;*[162]

Significantly, this is one of the few places in the Qur'an where Muhammad is specifically named. That is why the Apostle John writes in this section's Scripture heading that the mark, "stood for the name of the beast."

The name of blasphemy is 'Muhammad,' and another word for the Beast of Islam is 'Muhammadanism.'

Dr. Ayman al-Zawahiri, the second-in-command of al-Qaeda, has a pronounced prayer burn on his face. Like the swastika that is tattooed on Charles Manson's face, it does not wash off. For some reason, mass murderers like to carry the sign of their depravity on their foreheads. This is the Mark of the Beast.

Figure 2. The Mark of the Beast in al-Zawahiri
The Mark of the Beast in the forehead of Dr. Ayman al-Zawahiri, second-in-command of al-Qaeda (retouched). It is a rug burn that comes from bowing to the Antichrist Beast of Islam that came into being six-hundred and sixty-six years after the time of Jesus Christ. Note the model cannon pointing at his head on the right—nicely representing the sentence of eternal death that is upon those with this mark (Revelation 14:9–11). U.S. federal government public domain image.

Revelation 13:11 [YLT]
And I saw another beast coming up out of the land, and it had two horns, like
a lamb, and it was speaking as a dragon ...

25. The Beast Coming Up Out of the Land

Immediately after describing the Beast that arose from the sea (i.e., the Arab Muslim Empire), the Apostle John wrote of another Beast. This time it originated from a land mass, rather than the Mediterranean region. The second Beast is the Oghuz Turks that invaded the Middle East from the very center of the Asian continent[163]—as far away as you can get from the ocean on this planet.

Please note that the text does not say that the Land Beast looked like a lamb. There was nothing lamb-like or gentle about the Beast except that it had two horns, as a lamb does. The two horns are the Seljuk Empire (AD 1055–AD 1327) and the Ottoman Empire (AD 1299–AD 1922) that arose from the Oghuz.

The Oghuz Turks[164] originated from the Altai Mountains—the furthest east and north area that the Arabs were able to impose Islam. The Islamic religion suited the bloodlust of Turkic peoples quite well, and in time they turned upon the Arabs and came to brutally subjugate them. The Turks were early practitioners of gunpowder warfare, and used bronze cannons to break through the thick walls of Constantinople.[165]

> *He performs great signs, so that he even makes fire*
> *come down from heaven on the earth in the sight of*
> *men. [Revelation 13:13 NKJV]*

The Turkish sultans assumed the Caliphate from the Arabs,[166] and were known by the blasphemous moniker, 'The Shadow of God on Earth.'[167]

The Apostle John predicted all of this:

> **He exercised all the authority of the first beast on**
> **his behalf**, *and made the earth and its inhabitants*
> *worship the first beast, whose fatal wound had been*
> *healed. [Revelation 13:12 NIV]*

~~~~~~~~~~~~~~~~~~~~~~~~

At the beginning of the Arab Empire towers were built as lighthouses[168]—used for the conveyance of information through light signals.[169] Later, they were used to glorify rulers, and to proclaim a political message.[170] But there are almost no references to prayer towers in early Arabic writings.[171] There was originally no special place for the muezzin to issue the call to prayer.[172] The earliest mosques did not have minarets,[173] but only small staircases that sometimes led to the roof.[174] Ali himself had commanded,

> *Do not raise [the muezzin's place in] the mosque above its wall. And its structure—what is attached to it—is to be equal in height to the roof of the mosque.*[175]

The few early towers, therefore, did not have any religious significance, Shi'a, Sunni, or otherwise.[176] Before the eleventh century, mosques either had no tower or only one tower.[177] Even in the fifteenth century (before Ottoman control of Syria), only ten percent of the mosques in Damascus had minarets.[178]

To prove their Islamic *bona fides*, the Turks would build many minarets from which the incessant calls to prayer were broadcast.

> *... Sunni Islam [was given] a much-needed shot in the arm ... [through] the zeal of the ... Seljuq Turkish leaders. They may not have fully understood theological intricacies, but they made up for this lack with their enthusiasm for proving themselves as good Muslims as anyone else.*[179]

In fact, the word 'minaret' is Turkish in origin,[180] and means,

> *A slender lofty tower attached to a mosque and surrounded by one or more projecting balconies from which the faithful are summoned to prayer by the muezzin.*[181]

The Turks swept into Anatolia from the east, and on their way they adopted the design of the traditional Mesopotamian ziggurat as a symbol of Islam.[182] With the improvement of baked-brick technology, the Turks were able to build taller, thinner, minarets.[183] These towers then became,

> *... one of the most characteristic features of Islamic architecture. By the middle of the eleventh century the tower was widely considered an Islamic sign and could be placed virtually anywhere.*[184]

Only at this point did the towers become firmly associated with the Islamic call to prayer.[185] The Turks built minarets next to mosques, mausoleums, schools, and oftentimes independently of any other structure.[186]

Under the Turks, prayer towers sprouted everywhere in former Christian lands.[187] They surrounded the Church of the Holy Wisdom (i.e., the

Hagia Sophia in Constantinople) with four giant minarets after they stole the magnificent building from the Greek Orthodox in AD 1453.

In this way the Beast of Islam spoke and demanded worship.

> [He told] those who dwell on the earth to make an image to the beast who was wounded by the sword and lived. He was granted power to give breath to the image of the beast, that the image of the beast should both speak and cause as many as would not worship the image of the beast to be killed. [Revelation 13:14–15 NKJV]

Through their military might and brutality, the Turks kept the Islamic religion going, and forced millions more people to submit to the Beast of Islam.

Figure 3. The Image of the Beast that Could Speak
The Seljuk mosque Menucehr Camii (right, foreground, circa AD 1072) and the Armenian Cathedral of the Mother of God (left, background, circa AD 1001) in the ruins of the City of Ani on the current Turkish–Armenian border (retouched). The mosque is the oldest in Anatolia, and prominently displays the Turks' popularization of the minaret by which the Beast of Islam issued threatening calls to prayer (Revelation 13:15). Photograph by author.

Daniel 9:25,27 [NKJV]
... from the going forth of the command to restore and build Jerusalem until Messiah the Prince, there shall be seven weeks and sixty-two weeks ... Then he shall confirm a covenant with many for one week;

26. The Seventy Week Timeline for the First Coming of Christ

In his old age, the Prophet Daniel studied the Book of Jeremiah and had a singular epiphany: from Jeremiah 25:11–12 he realized that the Scriptures predicted that the time period from the destruction of the First Temple to the dedication of the Second Temple would be seventy years (from 586 BC to 516 BC).[188]

> *... I, Daniel, understood from the Scriptures, according to the word of the Lord given to Jeremiah the prophet, that the desolation of Jerusalem would last seventy years. [Daniel 9:2 NIV]*

It was 539 BC,[189] and reconstruction work was about to commence on the Temple Mount in Jerusalem. When Daniel realized the prophecy, he was overcome by God's faithfulness to His covenant of love. He prayed a long prayer of confession for his own sin, and for the sin of the people of Israel:

> *O Lord, the great and awesome God, who keeps covenant and steadfast love with those who love him and keep his commandments, we have sinned and done wrong and acted wickedly and rebelled, turning aside from your commandments and rules. We have not listened to your servants the prophets, who spoke in your name to our kings, our princes, and our fathers, and to all the people of the land. To you, O Lord, belongs righteousness, but to us open shame, as at this day, to the men of Judah, to the inhabitants of Jerusalem, and to all Israel, those who are near and those who are far away, in all the lands to which you have driven them, because of the treachery that they have committed against you. To us, O Lord, belongs open shame, to our kings, to our princes, and to our fathers, because we have sinned against you. To the Lord our God belong mercy and forgiveness, for we*

have rebelled against him and have not obeyed the voice of the Lord our God by walking in his laws, which he set before us by his servants the prophets. All Israel has transgressed your law and turned aside, refusing to obey your voice. And the curse and oath that are written in the Law of Moses the servant of God have been poured out upon us, because we have sinned against him. He has confirmed his words, which he spoke against us and against our rulers who ruled us, by bringing upon us a great calamity. For under the whole heaven there has not been done anything like what has been done against Jerusalem. As it is written in the Law of Moses, all this calamity has come upon us; yet we have not entreated the favor of the Lord our God, turning from our iniquities and gaining insight by your truth. Therefore the Lord has kept ready the calamity and has brought it upon us, for the Lord our God is righteous in all the works that he has done, and we have not obeyed his voice. And now, O Lord our God, who brought your people out of the land of Egypt with a mighty hand, and have made a name for yourself, as at this day, we have sinned, we have done wickedly. O Lord, according to all your righteous acts, let your anger and your wrath turn away from your city Jerusalem, your holy hill, because for our sins, and for the iniquities of our fathers, Jerusalem and your people have become a byword among all who are around us. Now therefore, O our God, listen to the prayer of your servant and to his pleas for mercy, and for your own sake, O Lord, make your face to shine upon your sanctuary, which is desolate. O my God, incline your ear and hear. Open your eyes and see our desolations, and the city that is called by your name. For we do not present our pleas before you because of our righteousness, but because of your great mercy. O Lord, hear; O Lord, forgive. O Lord, pay attention and act. Delay not, for your own sake, O my God, because your city and your people are called by your name. [Daniel 9:4–19 ESV]

During the prayer, the Angel Gabriel was sent by God to tell Daniel something of even greater significance than the end of the period of exile. Gabriel said,

> *O Daniel, I have now come forth to give you skill to understand. At the beginning of your supplications the command went out, and I have come to tell you, for you are greatly beloved; therefore consider the matter, and understand the vision. [Daniel 9:22–23 NKJV]*

Gabriel informed Daniel that after the restoration from Babylonian captivity, the Jewish people had 'seventy weeks' (i.e., 490 years) to change their wicked ways. He said that they must, at that time, venerate the Most Holy One in Jerusalem.

> *Seventy weeks are determined for your people and for your holy city, to finish the transgression, to make an end of sins, to make reconciliation for iniquity, to bring in everlasting righteousness, to seal up vision and prophecy, and to anoint the Most Holy. [Daniel 9:24 NKJV]*

Daniel had been praying out of thankfulness that their house of prayer—a temple made of stone—was going to be rebuilt, but Gabriel told him that the Messiah (Daniel 9:27) was on the way!

The angel told Daniel that the 490 year countdown would begin when permission was given (Daniel 9:25) by the political authorities to rebuild all of Jerusalem (not just the Temple, but the walls, fortifications, streets, etc.). That took place in 458 BC[190] when King Artaxerxes of Medo–Persia issued the decree for which the Jews had waited, prayed, and hoped. The first 'seven weeks' (i.e., 49 years) of the period would be for the difficult task of reconstructing the city in the face of opposition (Ezra 4:7–23).[191]

> *... there shall be seven weeks ... the street shall be built again, and the wall, even in troublesome times. [Daniel 9:25 NKJV]*

The troublesome times occurred in 445 BC when the enemies of the Jews tore down and burned their recent work (Nehemiah 1:3). Nevertheless, the city was successfully rebuilt by 409 BC.[192]

> *So the wall was finished ... when all our enemies heard of it ... they were very disheartened in their own*

eyes; for they perceived that this work was done by our God. [Nehemiah 6:15–16 NKJV]

Then, Gabriel said, there would be another 'sixty-two weeks' (i.e., 434 years) until the Messiah would be anointed as Prince and rejected by His people.

... from the issuing of a decree to restore and rebuild Jerusalem until Messiah the Prince there will be ... sixty-two weeks; ... Then after the sixty-two weeks the Messiah will be cut off and have nothing ... [Daniel 9:25–26 NASB]

This occurred in AD 26 when Jesus was baptized in the River Jordan,[193] and rejected in His hometown of Nazareth.[194] During Jesus' baptism He was anointed by God the Holy Spirit descending upon Him as a dove, and by God the Father saying,

This is My beloved Son, in whom I am well pleased. [Matthew 3:17 NKJV]

Also, at that time John the Baptist declared,

I have seen and have borne witness that this is the Son of God. [John 1:34 ESV]

This event marked the beginning of Jesus' earthly ministry.

The angel said that because of the Jewish nation's rejection of the Messiah, the city of Jerusalem and the Second Temple would one day be destroyed by a future invader.

... the people of the ruler who is to come will destroy the city and the holy place. The end will come like a flood. Even to the end there will be war. For the Lord has said that much will be destroyed. [Daniel 9:26b NLV]

The destruction occurred in AD 70,[195] by the Roman legions of General Titus (AD 39–AD 81). It was predicted by Jesus Himself:

Your enemies will not leave a single stone in place, because you did not accept your opportunity for salvation. [Luke 19:44 NLT]

The fate of the Second Temple would, then, be the same as that of the First Temple: a heap of rubble. This was the very temple whose construction was about to be started in Daniel's old age—the very reconstruction effort that had moved Daniel to pray earnestly.

Finally, the Angel Gabriel told Daniel that during the final 'week' (i.e., seven years) of the 490 year period the Messiah would confirm a new covenant upon many Jewish people. But, he cautioned, three and a half years into the Messiah's ministry, He would put an end to the Jewish sacrificial system of atonement.

> ... in the middle of the week He shall bring an end to sacrifice and offering. [Daniel 9:27 NKJV]

This event was, of course, the institution of Holy Communion and the Crucifixion of Christ, the Lamb of God.

God was not mocking Daniel by sending the angel to burst his bubble. Quite the contrary: Gabriel told Daniel that he was so greatly beloved that God was giving him the entire story. The contemporary political miracle that was happening to allow the exiled Jews to return and rebuild was about more than the Jewish nation; the impending restoration of their center of worship was about more than a stone building; the remaking of Jerusalem into a respectable capital was about more than a single city: these things were about God becoming a man and saving all those that would accept Him. Daniel was being given a preview of God's plan for the salvation of men.

Gabriel told Daniel that in the middle of the final seven years in which the Jewish people had the truth about God in their midst, the Messiah would take upon Himself the abominations of the sinful world, and be made desolate, and die. The angel said that this had been determined to be necessary.

> ... in the midst of the week ... for the overspreading of abominations he shall make it desolate, even until the consummation, and that determined shall be poured upon the desolate. [Daniel 9:27 KJV]

Indeed, the Prophet Isaiah had written much earlier,

> ... the punishment that brought us peace was upon him ... [Isaiah 53:5 TNIV]

Jesus' earthly ministry lasted three and a half years past His baptism.[196] In the year AD 30[197] Jesus allowed Himself to be sacrificed on a cross. During His passion, the sins of the whole world were poured upon Him.

> God made him who had no sin **to be sin for us** ... [2 Corinthians 5:21 TNIV]

He drank the cup that the Father had given Him to drink, was crucified for our sake, and was left desolate. While bereft upon the cross Jesus cried out,

> *My God, My God, why have You forsaken Me? [Mark*
> *15:34 NKJV]*

Then He died as the perfect sacrifice. At that moment there was an earthquake in Jerusalem and the altar on the nearby Temple Mount was disrupted—its time had past.

> *And Jesus cried out again with a loud voice and*
> *yielded up his spirit. And behold, the curtain of the*
> *temple was torn in two, from top to bottom. And*
> *the earth shook, and the rocks were split. [Matthew*
> *27:50–51 ESV]*

The final three and a half years of Gabriel's 490 year period concerns Christ's early Church in Jerusalem. After the Crucifixion, Resurrection, and Ascension of Jesus, the Church was established at Pentecost and flourished. God gave the almost-entirely Jewish believers a three and a half year period of peace there in the Judean capital past the three and a half years of Christ's ministry (for a total of seven years since Christ's baptism in AD 26).[198]

> *He will make a firm covenant with many for one week,*
> *but in the middle of the week ... the decreed destruc-*
> *tion is poured out ... [Daniel 9:27 HCSB]*

This seven year period ended with the stoning of the first Christian martyr, the Deacon Stephen (Acts 7:54–60), and the scattering of the saints from Jerusalem into the rest of the Roman Empire in AD 33.[199]

> *At that time a great persecution arose against the*
> *church which was at Jerusalem; and they were all scat-*
> *tered throughout the regions of Judea and Samaria ...*
> *Therefore those who were scattered went everywhere*
> *preaching the word. [Acts 8:1,4 NKJV]*

The 490 years had come to an end, and it was time for the Good News about the truth of God's love to be spread outside of Jerusalem. It was time for the rest of the Jews, Samaritans, Greeks, and the whole world to hear the Gospel.

Daniel 12:10 [TNIV]
... those who are wise will understand.

27. Dispensationalism: the Seventy Weeks Misconstrued

The Angel Gabriel visited the Prophet Daniel to instruct him about a 'seventy week' timeline. The account, given in Daniel 9:20–27, is among the most poorly translated sections of the Bible. The angel was announcing the coming of the Messiah, but Dispensationalists maintain he was announcing the coming of both Jesus Christ (during the first sixty-nine weeks) and a future Antichrist punk (during the final week). What an insult to the Lord Jesus!

The problem has arisen as a result of the difficult Hebrew grammar and syntax of Daniel.[200] The Prophet wrote at the time of the Babylonian Captivity, and transliterated a number of foreign words into Hebrew. Later scholars have wrestled with the arcane language of the Book of Daniel.

Consider this King James Version translation of the latter part of Daniel 9:27:

> *... for the overspreading of abominations he shall*
> *make it desolate, even until the consummation, and*
> *that determined shall be poured upon the desolate.*
> *[KJV]*

Compare it with the same part of Daniel 9:27 from the New International Reader's Version®:

> *In one part of the temple a hated thing that destroys*
> *will be set up. It will remain until the Lord brings the*
> *end he has ordered. [NIrV]*

And compare it again with the same passage from the Contemporary English Version™:

> *Then the "Horrible Thing" that causes destruction*
> *will be put there. And it will stay there until the time*
> *God has decided to destroy this one who destroys.*
> *[CEV]*

The first translation is completely different from the other two! When one looks at a literal word-for-word translation,[201] the King James Version is much closer to the original Hebrew. But almost all the recent English language versions of the Bible contain the erroneous phrasing that allows for the charge that this is a prophecy about a modern-day Jewish temple being defiled by a modern-day Antichrist figure. See the three tables below for the false eschatological theory that has grown out of the mistranslation.

Because I come from an immigrant people, my ear has been trained to understand the meaning of those that do not speak English as a first language. I am able to read the word-for-word Hebrew–English translation and to see Daniel's meaning. Also, I do not come to the matter with a preconceived doctrinal position, as do so many Evangelicals and Anabaptists.

The prophetic passages that require some interpretation to make sense in English have been mistranslated in order to fit a school of eschatological thought, popular among American Evangelicals, called 'Dispensational Premillennialism' (see Appendix II for detailed definitions of these terms). This ideology was unknown through eighteen hundred years of the Church, but was introduced in the mid–nineteenth century by the Anglo–Irish evangelist, John Nelson Darby (AD 1800–AD 1882). He was one of the founders of a Dispensationalist denomination called the Plymouth Brethren.[202] The AD 1909 publication of the Scofield Reference Bible was a tremendous boon for Dispensationalism within the American Evangelical movement. During the twentieth century the doctrine spread widely throughout Baptist, Pentecostal, and ostensibly non-denominational churches.[203]

The Dispensationalists have an inferiority complex when comparing their spiritual state to that of ethnic or 'natural' Jews. As a consequence, their eschatology is replete with racially-based red herrings. They have seized upon ambiguities in Daniel (and also in Revelation), and amplified them with mistranslations and misinterpretations. They viewed the restoration of the twentieth century Jews to Palestine as divine validation of their message, and have created an intricate, futurist, layout of world events that 'must' take place before Christ may return.

In this particular case, they say that the Angel Gabriel was referring to God's blessing upon mankind for the first 'sixty-nine weeks' or 483 years. Then, they say that the timeline is suspended, and the final 'week' refers to the last seven years during which the Antichrist will be revealed. They say that the subject of the last week's text is not Jesus' holy ministry, but that of the despicable world leader who is to come.

The Dispensationalists assert that the Antichrist will have the power of persuasion, and will be popular at the beginning of his rule. He will supposedly make a deal with worldly people whereby they will allow him to become their absolute dictator and to institute a one-world currency. Dispensationalists insist that he will be a Jew,[204] probably from the tribe of Dan, and that he will take over the European Union and invade Jerusalem. Apparently, this will be at a time when the Israelis have torn down the Dome of the Rock, and replaced it with yet another Jewish temple. They say that after three and a half years of rule, the Antichrist will stop the animal sacrifices that the Jews have re-instituted in their new temple, and set up some sort of abomination there, and declare that he is God. Then, they say, he will rule as a tyrant for the remaining three and a half years before Christ returns.

People that subscribe to this nonsense also say that just before the Antichrist's ascension to power, all the Christians and young children in the world (whom they consider to be not old enough to possess sin, and therefore not old enough for baptism to be required) will disappear in their birthday suits.[205] This is known as the Rapture. The unbelievers that do not disappear will see their friends' and relatives' clothes lying on the spot where they last stood, and many of them will then repent, come to Christ, and oppose the Antichrist. These events, needless to say, appear nowhere in the Bible.

The word, 'rapture,' comes from the Apostle Paul's use of the Greek word, *harpazo*, in his first letter to the Thessalonians. In English language Bibles it is translated as 'caught up.'

> *For the Lord himself will descend from heaven ... And the dead in Christ will rise first. Then we who are alive, who are left, will be* **caught up** *together with them in the clouds to meet the Lord in the air ... [1 Thessalonians 4:16–17 ESV]*

Note that Paul is explicit that **this event will occur immediately after the resurrection of the dead**—thus on the day of the Second Coming of Christ and not seven years beforehand. Jesus will return once, not twice!

I hate to upset everyone's martyr complex, but there is not going to be an advent of a Danite Jewish Antichrist in Europe or anywhere else. And there is not going to be a focused world-wide persecution of Christian believers from this fictional Antichrist's central authority (a general worldwide persecution of Christians is taking place right now if anyone would care to notice it).

The latter part of Daniel 9:27 has nothing to do with the Antichrist defiling a future Jewish building on the Temple Mount. It refers to the sin of the human race that Christ took upon Himself during the Crucifixion. It is a prophecy concerning the time when Jesus—the true Third Temple (Section 28)—was bereft upon the cross, crying out,

> *My God, My God, why have You forsaken Me? [Mark 15:34 NKJV]*

In the three tables that follow, I summarize the correct and incorrect interpretations of the Angel Gabriel's revelation to the Prophet Daniel in 539 BC.[206]

Table 3a. The Correct Interpretation of Daniel's Forty-Nine Weeks

Date	Cumul. Duration	Traditional Christian View	Supporting Biblical References [scriptural prophecy] [scriptural fulfillment]
458 BC[207]	--	King Artaxerxes of Medo–Persia issues a decree allowing post–exilic Jews to rebuild Jerusalem and restore order.	... from the issuing of a decree to restore and rebuild Jerusalem until Messiah the Prince there will be seven weeks and sixty-two weeks; [Daniel 9:25a NASB] **The king's decrees were delivered to his highest officers ... who then cooperated by supporting the people and the Temple of God. [Ezra 8:36 NLT]**
409 BC[208]	49 years	Reconstruction of Jerusalem is completed despite opposition from the surrounding Gentiles.	... the street shall be built again, and the wall, even in troublous times. [Daniel 9:25b KJV] **So the wall was finished ... when all our enemies heard of it... they were very disheartened in their own eyes; for they perceived that this work was done by our God. [Nehemiah 6:15–16 NKJV]**
AD 26[209]	483 years	Jesus is baptized, and anointed by the Holy Spirit. The Heavenly Father testifies that He is the Son of God. Jesus is rejected in His hometown of Nazareth, and begins His three and a half year earthly ministry as an itinerant preacher.	Seventy weeks are decreed... to anoint the most holy. [Daniel 9:24b ASV] **As soon as Jesus was baptized, he went up out of the water. At that moment heaven was opened, and he saw the Spirit of God descending like a dove... And a voice from heaven said, "This is my Son, whom I love; with him I am well pleased." [Matthew 3:16–17 NIV]** ... after the sixty-two weeks the Messiah will be cut off and have nothing... [Daniel 9:26a NASB] **And all the people in the synagogue were filled with rage ... they got up and drove Him out of the city... [Luke 4:28–29 NASB]**

Table 3b. The Correct Interpretation of Daniel's Forty-Nine Weeks

Date	Cumul. Duration	Traditional Christian View	Supporting Biblical References [scriptural prophecy] [scriptural fulfillment]
AD 30[210]	486.5 years	Jesus quickly gains a following. He institutes the New Covenant, takes upon Himself the sins of the world, and puts an end to the Old Testament sacrificial system. He dies desolate, but is resurrected and ascends into Heaven. The early Church is begun at Pentecost and flourishes under Christ's protection in Jerusalem for another three and a half years.	... he shall confirm the covenant with many for one week... [Daniel 9:27a KJV] **Large crowds from Galilee, the Decapolis, Jerusalem, Judea and the region across the Jordan followed him. [Matthew 4:25 NIV]** **This cup is the new covenant in my blood, which is poured out for you. [Luke 22:20 NIV]** **So the word of God spread. The number of disciples in Jerusalem increased rapidly... [Acts 6:7 NIV]** ... for the overspreading of abominations he shall make it desolate, even until the consummation, and that determined shall be poured upon the desolate. [Daniel 9:27c KJV] **... Jesus cried out... "My God, My God, why have You forsaken Me?" [Mark 15:34 NKJV]** ... in the middle of the week He shall bring an end to sacrifice and offering. [Daniel 9:27b NKJV] **Jesus said, "It is finished." With that, he bowed his head and gave up his spirit. [John 19:30 NIV]**
AD 33[211]	490 years	The Church of Pentecost is scattered to Judea and Samaria after the martyrdom of Deacon Stephen. The Gospel begins to be disseminated to all peoples.	Seventy weeks are determined upon thy people and upon thy holy city, to finish the transgression ... and to bring in everlasting righteousness, and to seal up the vision and prophecy... [Daniel 9:24a KJV] **On that day a great persecution broke out against the church at Jerusalem, and all except the apostles were scattered throughout Judea and Samaria... Those who had been scattered preached the word wherever they went. [Acts 8:1,4 NIV]**

Again, the Dispensationalists accept the traditional Christian view for the three rows shown in Table 3a. But they maintain that the prophecy then jumps far ahead in time, and that the two rows of Table 3b are a prediction of the dictatorship of a future Antichrist ruler, rather than a prediction of Christ's blessed ministry.

Table 4. The Incorrect Interpretation of Daniel's Forty-Nine Weeks

Date	Cumul. Duration	Dispensational Premillennialist View
458 BC[212]	—	Same as above.
409 BC[213]	49 years	Same as above.
AD 26[214]	483 years	Same as above, except that they add in all the events of Christ's earthly ministry here (not just His baptism and initial rejection)—thus making their timeline 3.5 years off (see the boldface portion of the H.A. Ironside quote below).
AD 20xx	~2500 years	They claim that there is a chronological break in the text, and the final 'week' refers to the very end of human history when a new Jewish temple will be constructed and consecrated on the Temple Mount in Jerusalem. Some of the modern Israeli Jews will then abandon Rabbinic Judaism and renew ancient Jewish animal sacrifice practices in the temple. The Rapture of Born Again Christians and young [supposedly sinless] children will take place seven years before Christ's Second Coming. The disappearance of all the Christians will somehow result in a new Church, as previously unbelieving people around the world are converted en masse to Christianity. The seven year reign of the Antichrist despot will then begin. They call this the 'beginning of sorrow.'
AD 20xx	~2500 plus 3.5 years	The Antichrist will have the power of persuasion. He will make an insincere peace treaty with the modern State of Israel, and he will introduce a one-world currency. Although popular for the first half of his reign, the Antichrist despot will then turn against the Jews of modern Israel, and defile their new temple in Jerusalem, and there proclaim himself to be God. This will result in a persecution of the post–Rapture Church. Things will get very bad on earth (politically, economically, climatically, etc.) during this three and a half year 'Great Tribulation.'
AD 20xx	~2500 plus 7 years	The Battle of Armageddon will take place in modern Israel at the end of the three and a half year 'Great Tribulation.' The Antichrist and his forces will be defeated by Christ Himself when He returns to save the modern State of Israel and the post–Rapture Church. Then the devil will be thrown into a pit, and Jesus will rule from this earth's Jerusalem (presumably with secretaries, chauffeurs, and butlers) for one thousand years.
AD 30xx	~3500 years	The devil is loosed from the pit and leads a revolt against Christ's government in Jerusalem. Fire comes down from Heaven to destroy the devil and his army. There is the final Judgment Day.

Notice, in the third row of Table 4, that the Dispensationalists prevaricate on the historical timeline: They are three and a half years off in saying that Christ was crucified at the end of sixty-nine 'weeks' (i.e., 483 years after King Artaxerxes' command to rebuild Jerusalem). Christ was, of course, crucified *exactly* in the middle of the seventieth 'week' (i.e., 486.5 years after King Artaxerxes' command to rebuild Jerusalem).

Consider this excerpt from the 'Archbishop of Fundamentalism,'[215] Harry A. Ironside (AD 1876–AD 1951):

> *[The period of Daniel 9 is] divided into three parts,—*
> *7 weeks, or 49 years, in which the streets and the*
> *wall of the city were to be re-built. Then, 62 weeks,*
> *or 434 years, immediately following the completion*
> *of this work, unto the appearing and cutting off of*
> *Messiah the Prince. Then, one final week, or 7 years,*
> *to complete the cycle, at the end of which the King*
> *would be reigning in the holy city and all prophecy*
> *fulfilled by the establishment of the kingdom so long*
> *foretold. The starting-point is clearly defined as,*
> *"The going forth of a commandment to restore and*
> *build Jerusalem," which is the decree of Artaxerxes*
> *as recorded in Nehemiah, chap. 2. During the next 49*
> *years the city was rebuilt.* **Then, 434 years later, our**
> **Lord rode into Jerusalem and was acclaimed by the**
> **multitudes as King, the Son of David, but a few days**
> **later was rejected and crucified. Thus Messiah was**
> **cut off and had nothing.**
> **What then of the last week? Has it been fulfilled? It**
> **has not.** *When His Son was cast out, God cast off the*
> *nation, and that week will not be fulfilled till a future*
> *day, when He takes up Israel again.*
> *… The last week, of 7 years, cannot begin to run till*
> *the Jews are again in the land, and Jerusalem becomes*
> *the Jewish capital, after the church has been caught*
> *up to meet the Lord in the air. Of this last week the*
> *greater part of the book of the Revelation treats. It is*
> *only when this is seen that all becomes plain and the*
> *prophecy becomes intelligible.*
> *… the return of the Lord to the air … is the first stage*
> *of His second coming. The second stage will be when*

He comes to the earth in manifested glory to reign.
The 70th, or last week of Daniel, comes in between
these two momentous [sic] events. The Lord spoke of
this period as the "end of the age" in Matt. 24, and
He divides it into two parts, "the beginning of sor-
row" and "the great tribulation."[216]

You will hear this same ridiculous scenario retold on 'Christian' television today. For all the Dispensationalists' supposed non-creedalism, they are
stuck-like-glue to this false teaching.

To believers in Jesus Christ that have been swayed by Dispensationalism,
I have several things to say: Firstly, always go back to the Holy Bible. Don't
just take at face value teachings by people that claim to be Christians (including me). It is your responsibility to see if the Bible really is saying what someone is telling you that it is saying. If it is an especially difficult or controversial
topic, get yourself a King James Version, a New International Version®, and
one or two more; compare them; and if you're still stumped, get an Interlinear
Bible, with the original Hebrew, Aramaic, and Greek text translated word-
for-word into English. Then look and see how the Bible measures up to what
you're being force-fed. Remember, the devil quoted Holy Scripture to Jesus
during His period of temptation (Matthew 4:1–11). This episode teaches us
that all things—including biblical prophecy—must be interpreted correctly,
and within context, in order to be credible.

Secondly, stop being an ugly American and gain some perspective. Dispensationalist-thought represents a narrow segment of worldwide
Christendom. Despite their loud voices in our culture, they actually emanate
from only a portion of the United States' Baptist community. But these Über-
Baptists have crossed over into many of the Reformed Protestant churches that
consider themselves 'Evangelical' and 'Born Again.' These terms do not represent formal denominations; non-creedal and non-sacramental churches have
no ecclesiastical polity or doctrine that grounds them. Such a state-of-affairs
creates an opening for anyone carrying a Bible and a confident attitude, regardless of the nuts-and-bolts of that person's beliefs. But, again, with as much
success as the Dispensationalists have had in influencing the Second Coming
expectations of naïve Christians, one must remember that they still represent
a tiny fraction of believers: Eastern Orthodox, Roman Catholic, Anglican,
Lutheran, Presbyterian, and most other organized Protestants, all reject the
Dispensational interpretation out-of-hand.

Thirdly, realize that the Dispensationalist movement is predicated
upon a morbid preoccupation with the modern State of Israel and people of

Jewish bloodlines. Some of the Dispensationalists have formed 'Christian' Zionist cults.[217] You'll find them saying that God will bless you if you are kind to a Jewish person or if you travel to Israel and spend money there. I've known some of them to work for Jewish businessmen specifically because they want to be in servitude to Jews. I've even heard of an old-time radio evangelist that sponsored a female Israeli immigrant in his home. He thought he would be favored by God for getting the young lady into the United States, and by meeting her physical needs. It was only natural when she became his mistress. What better way to obtain a blessing from the God of Israel than to give the gift of an orgasm to a Jewess? The Evangelist's aged wife approved of the arrangement: she, too, believed the Jews to be God's Chosen People, and the presence of the Jewish woman gave her respite from her husband's insatiable sexual demands. This hedonism lasted until he was finally imprisoned for embezzlement and tax evasion.[218]

Clarify your minds, and remember what the Apostle Peter, a pious Jew, said:

> *I now realize how true it is that **God does not show favoritism but accepts men from every nation who fear him** and do what is right. [Acts 10:34–35 NIV]*

True Christianity, therefore, precludes both the racism of 'Christian' Aryanism and the racism of 'Christian' Zionism.

Fourthly, learn something about history. The story of human civilization is six thousand years old. We are at the very end of the two thousand year post–Christ period. Hundreds of millions of believers have come-and-gone before you were born; many have been through unimaginable hardships at the hands of antichrists. Many today—this very day!—are suffering death at the hands of antichrists. Your ignorance and ambivalence toward the suffering of your Christian brothers and sisters throughout history is embarrassing and shameful. The Antichrist Beast has already come and forced his mark upon the world and you have not even noticed it!

The Book of Revelation was written,

> *... to show his servants **what must soon take place**.*
> *[Revelation 1:1 NIV]*

That means that its prophecies cover the entire End Times period—from the first century onward.

Do you really think that all of the interesting prophecies concern one seven year period immediately preceding the Second Coming? Has God just ignored all the epic battles for the advance of the Gospel since AD 96? Is it not more likely that you have bought into the allure of End Times fiction because you, as a pampered American consumer, have a need to see everything through a story that can fit into a two hour film?

Finally, accept that God is in no way limited by your willful misunderstanding of His Holy Word. He is going to do what He is going to do in His Second Coming, just as surely as He did in the Incarnation. He has told us what will come to pass; whether or not people will listen and understand is another matter altogether.

There were pious and believing Jews during the early first century that completely misunderstood the prophecies concerning the Messiah. One of them, Nicodemus, actually met with Jesus face-to-face because he couldn't understand how *He* could be the One for which they were waiting (John 3:9). A carpenter from Nazareth didn't fit with the commonly held interpretation of the Scriptures. Nevertheless, Jesus was the One. Those that were truly the Chosen People (i.e., chosen by God to believe that Jesus is the Messiah and to have eternal life through Him), came to realize that they were mistaken about what God had written. For Nicodemus it was a gradual process (John 19:39).

I pray that you will also come to see the sin of your ways, and repent of the heresy of Dispensational Premillennialism.

Revelation 12:1–2 [NKJV]
Now a great sign appeared in heaven: A woman clothed with the sun, with the moon under her feet, and on her head a garland of twelve stars.

28. The Woman Clothed with the Sun

This woman represents the People of God. They include the ones before Christ's time that believed that God would become a man (mostly Jews); they also include the ones after Christ's time that believed that God became a man in Jesus (mostly non-Jews). The 'woman clothed with the sun' is the Church—both of the Old and New Testament periods.

To make this perfectly clear, the text goes on,

> *Then being with child, she cried out in labor and in pain to give birth … She bore a male Child who was to rule all nations with a rod of iron. [Revelation 12:2,5 NKJV]*

The labor pain that the woman experienced represents the long wait of the People of God for their Messiah.

The Apostle John then provided a flashback of how the devil tried to kill the baby Jesus by moving King Herod to massacre the young male children of Bethlehem (Matthew 2:16).

> *... behold, a great, fiery red dragon having seven heads and ten horns, and seven diadems on his heads ... And the dragon stood before the woman who was ready to give birth, to devour her Child as soon as it was born. [Revelation 12:3–4 NKJV]*

But, of course, the dragon failed.

> *And her Child was caught up to God and His throne. [Revelation 12:5 NKJV]*

Jesus completed His task on earth in AD 30,[219] and ascended to Heaven to prepare a place for the Woman Clothed With the Sun (John 14:3).

~~~~~~~~~~~~~~~~~~~~~~~

The colonists that founded the United States were God-fearing people. They were mostly Protestant Christians, looking for religious liberty. They became the first nation in which ordinary people had the Bible, the very Word of God, in their homes. And they read it.

Historian Paul Johnson has commented upon them:

> *... most Americans ... believe[d] that knowledge of God comes direct to them through the study of the Holy Writ. They read the Bible for themselves, assiduously, daily. Virtually every humble cabin in Massachusetts colony had its own Bible ... Adults read [the Bible] alone silently. It was also read aloud among families, as well as in church, during Sunday morning service ... Many families had a regular course of Bible-reading which meant that they covered the entire text of the Old Testament in the course of each year. Every striking episode was familiar to them, and its meaning and significance earnestly discussed; many they knew by heart. The language and lilt of the Bible in its various translations, but particularly in the magnificent new King James version, passed into the common tongue and script. On Sunday the minister took his congregation through key passages, in carefully attended sermons which rarely lasted less than an*

hour. But authority lay in the Bible, not the minister, and in the last resort every man and woman decided 'in the light which Almighty God gave them' what the Bible meant.[220]

These Anglo–American Protestants had an English-language term for the place where they would gather together on Sundays: 'The Meeting House.' They did not call that building a church. They knew from the Holy Scriptures that they—the Chosen People—were collectively the Church.

Now you are the body of Christ, and members individually. [1 Corinthians 12:27 NKJV]

They took to heart the Jeremiad,

This is what the Lord Almighty, the God of Israel, says: Reform your ways and your actions, and I will let you live in this place. Do not trust in deceptive words and say, "This is the temple of the Lord, the temple of the Lord, the temple of the Lord!" If you really change your ways and your actions and deal with each other justly, if you do not oppress the alien, the fatherless or the widow and do not shed innocent blood in this place, and if you do not follow other gods to your own harm, then I will let you live in this place, in the land I gave your forefathers for ever and ever. [Jeremiah 7:3–7 NIV]

Therefore, Christians do not venerate any building, nor worship icons, nor pray in any particular geographic direction.

*The God who made the world and everything in it, being Lord of heaven and earth, **does not live in temples made by man**, nor is he served by human hands, as though he needed anything, since he himself gives to all mankind life and breath and everything. [Acts 17:24–25 ESV]*

Christians know that Jesus is the Third Temple who was raised on the third day (John 2:19). And Christians also know that those that keep God's Word in their hearts are one with Christ, as a wife is one with her husband.

For you are the temple of the living God. [2 Corinthians 6:16 NKJV]

The Church is not a building or an institution. It is the invisible, indivisible, Body of Christian believers that accepts the three Ecumenical Creeds (with the Filioque). We are the Body that is being prepared to be made into one flesh with the groomsman, Jesus Christ. He is betrothed to us. We have become the Temple of the Living God.

> *I tell you, something greater than the temple is here.*
> *[Matthew 12:6 ESV]*

~~~~~~~~~~~~~~~~~~~~~~

God had chosen the spot in Jerusalem on which the First Temple would be built. He showed it to King David during a plague.

> *The Lord's angel told the prophet Gad to tell David*
> *that he must go to Araunah's threshing place and*
> *build an altar in honor of the Lord. David followed*
> *the Lord's instructions ... David said, "The temple of*
> *the Lord God must be built right here at this threshing*
> *place. And the altar for offering sacrifices will also be*
> *here." [1 Chronicles 21:18–19, 22:1 CEV]*

David's son and heir, Solomon, built the First Temple there. Four hundred years later the Babylonians destroyed it, and seventy years after that the Second Temple was built on the same spot. Just prior to Christ's birth, that Second Temple was remodeled and expanded by King Herod the Great.

It was on that same Temple Mount where Abraham had offered his son Isaac eight hundred and fifty years[221] before David's time. And it was on that same Temple Mount where the money changers were driven out by Jesus a thousand years after David's time.[222] The Pharisees asked Jesus for a sign to justify His authority in cleansing the Temple. He replied,

> *Destroy this temple, and in three days I will raise it*
> *up. [John 2:19 NKJV]*

The Apostle John tells us explicitly,

> *He was speaking of the temple of His body. [John*
> *2:21 NKJV]*

The Resurrected Body of Christ is the Third Temple. It is incorruptible and indestructible, and the Christian Church is one with Him. The Apostle John reported that in his vision of Heaven,

*I did not see a temple in the city, because the Lord God
Almighty and the Lamb are its temple. [Revelation
21:22 NIV]*

After Christ's sacrifice there was no more need for animal sacrifices
in a temple made of stone—the first two were simply a foreshadowing of
Christ's body. Therefore, God allowed the Second Temple to be laid waste by
the Romans, just as the Angel Gabriel had predicted (Daniel 9:26b).

Daniel 7:25 [NIV]
*He will speak against the Most High and oppress his saints and try to change
the set times and the laws.*

29. The Changing of Set Times and Laws

Islam is the Beast, and the Beast changes set times and laws. In the year when
they conquered all of Palestine (AD 638), the new Arab rulers introduced the
so-called Hijra calendar, where the first year was changed from the Incarnation
of Christ to the Hijra, or the flight of Muhammad from Mecca to Medina, in
AD 622.[223]

This new dating system was lunar, with the average month lasting
twenty-nine and a half days. The Christian (or Gregorian) calendar that they
tried to replace was solar and averaged 365.24 days per year. For this reason
the Muslims' year is eleven days shorter than the time for the earth to circle
the sun, and their calendar falls a full year behind the Christian calendar every
thirty-three years.[224]

The ninth day of September AD 622 is the first day of the Muslims'
year number one.[225] A rough conversion to the Christian calendar may be made
by multiplying the Muslims' year number by 0.97, and then adding 622.[226]

Much later, in the late eighth century,[227] the Arabs changed the religious laws by writing the Qur'an. They introduced new laws about women
covering their faces, praying five times per day, making a pilgrimage to Mecca,
and so forth.

Many of these rules are extra–Qur'anic. For example, the Qur'an does
not say that a Muslim must pray five times per day—it indicates that three times
per day is sufficient.[228] You may draw your own conclusions on the veracity of
Islamic legalism.

Revelation 12:6 [NASB]
Then the woman fled into the wilderness where she had a place prepared by
God, so that there she would be nourished for one thousand two hundred and
sixty days.

30. Ataturk and the End of the 1,260 Days

Here the Apostle John prophesies about a time after the death of the prototypical Antichrist (i.e., Caliph Ali—the Son of Perdition). As we have discussed,
because he is the antithesis of Christ, his death (AD 661) is a comparable event
to Jesus' incarnation (6 BC). The series of events that led to the codification of
the Islamic religion as we know it were set into motion by Ali's assassination,
just as Jesus' incarnation began Christianity.

The verse that heads this section is referring to the retreat of the People
of God from the eastern Christian lands into the wilderness of the west. The
eastern Christian lands were occupied by the Arab Muslims in the seventh century, and by the Turkish Muslims in the eleventh century.

> *When you are persecuted in one place, flee to another.*
> *[Matthew 10:23 TNIV]*

The Turks were very much aware that in conquering Asia Minor and
the Balkans, they were finishing what the Arabs had started: they were claiming for Islam the last land holdings of the ancient Roman Empire. The Seljuks
even called their empire the Sultanate of Rum—'Rum' being the Turkish
word for Rome. They were proud that all of the cities of the seven ecumenical
councils (i.e., Nicaea, Ephesus, Chalcedon, and Constantinople; see Table 11)
became seats of Islam.

The duration of the Christian retreat into western lands was predicted
to be 1,260 days after the inception of the Antichrist religion of Islam. In prophetic Scripture, days usually symbolize years. This number of years past Ali's
assassination in AD 661 puts us at AD 1921—the time of the formal end of
the First World War,[229] the loss of power of the Caliphate with the Turkish
Constitution of AD 1921,[230] and the colonization of Arab lands by the Republic
of France and the United Kingdom.[231] The following year Sultan Mehmed VI
(AD 1861–AD 1926), the one hundredth caliph (or 'successor of Muhammad')
in line from Abu Bakr, was deposed from Constantinople, and the Ottoman
Empire ceased to be.[232] A new caliph took his place, but he was a pretender
without the title of Sultan or any political power. The Republic of Turkey's
revised AD 1924 constitution formally abolished the Caliphate and exiled all
members of the Ottoman dynasty.[233]

~~~~~~~~~~~~~~~~~~~~~~~~

Mustafa Kemal (AD 1881–AD 1938) was the most effective general in the Ottoman Army during the First World War. A cunning and ruthless man, he adopted the moniker 'Ataturk' (i.e., Father of the Turks) to bolster his reputation. Although outnumbered, he won a decisive victory at the Battle of Dumlupinar to end the Greco–Turkish War in AD 1922.[234] It was his superior artillery and superior battlefield strategy that made the difference. Ataturk's forces then cornered their enemy in Smyrna and set fire to the city, killing one hundred thousand Greeks and Armenians.[235] Ataturk gave orders that his troops not massacre Christian civilians, but these orders were widely ignored without reprisal. His lead general incited a Turkish mob to lynch the Greek Orthodox Metropolitan of Smyrna. They gouged out his eyeballs, cut off his nose, ears, and hands, and hanged him by his beard until he bled to death.[236]

This catastrophe spelled the end of the four thousand year long Greek presence in Asia Minor. Within a year, western Turkey was ethnically-cleansed of Christians, and the Turkish people hailed Ataturk as 'The Victorious One— The Destroyer of Christians.'[237] The Republic of Turkey celebrates these events every August 30th with their national holiday, Victory Day.

[Yes, the Turks are terribly nice people. To any of my readers that believe in celebrating diversity, I suggest that they buy a summer cottage in the Anatolian countryside. Every miscreant in the province will soon know that they are non-Muslims, and that they have handsome children, and that they have some money with which to improve their property. Then their neighbors will visit them with laughs and smiles, like a pack of hungry hyenas, and the liberal newcomers will experience first-hand the thousand-year-old Turkish culture of armed robbery, rape, sodomy, mutilation, and murder. But if my multicultural-minded readers would feel more comfortable settling in with the Alpine Swiss than with the Pontic Turks, I have a question: are not the Greeks and Armenians justified in calling you damned hypocrites?]

Ataturk continued on to become a shrewd and visionary politician. He was adept at playing the western powers against each other for the benefit of Turkey. He gained control of the parliament at its inception in AD 1920, passed a new constitution negating the Caliphate in AD 1921, and was proclaimed President of the new Republic of Turkey in AD 1923. He waged war to reverse the land concessions that the Sultan had made upon capitulation in the Treaty of Sevres.[238] Ataturk's government then managed to forcibly expel one and a half million Asian Greeks in exchange for accepting one third as many European Turks.[239] This stabilized the new boundaries and resulted in a state visit from the Greek Prime Minister in AD 1932.[240]

Ataturk attempted democratization twice, but had to retreat to a policy of 'enlightened authoritarianism' (i.e., dictatorship) because each time the Turkish people moved sharply away from his ideal of laicism. He had his chief political opponent, Kazim Karabekir (AD 1882–AD 1948), placed under house arrest for fifteen years because Karabekir wanted to reinstate the Caliphate and annex Mosul from the British Mandate of Iraq.[241] Ataturk was resolute in his opinion:

> *The Caliphate is nothing but a myth of the past having*
> *no place in modern times.*[242]

Ataturk was a secularist and an extreme Turkish nationalist—he was definitely no Islamist. He drank heavily and dressed in pinstripe suits. He discouraged women's head scarves, outlawed polygamy, and introduced childhood education for both sexes; he outlawed the fez and required that Turkish citizens take on surnames; he replaced the Islamic (or Hijra) calendar with the Christian (or Gregorian) calendar, and moved the Turkish capital from Constantinople to Ankara; he converted the Hagia Sophia from a mosque to a museum, and restricted public expressions of religion; he replaced the Arabic script, which he considered illegible chicken scratches, with a modified Latin alphabet; and he removed many Arabic and Persian words from the Turkish language.

Ataturk adopted the Italian penal code for his overwhelmingly-Muslim country. He would never have considered the imposition of Qur'anic law within the Republic of Turkey—it would have meant his own beheading. He ordered that the ubiquitous call from the minaret of "Allah Akbar!" (Arabic for "God is Great") be changed to "Tanri Uludur!" (Turkish for "God is Great!").[243] He insulted Islam, Muhammad, and the Qur'an,

> *Islam, this theology of an immoral Arab, is a dead*
> *thing.*[244]

Once the highest ranking sheik in Turkey complained to the president about Turkish women dancing in public; Ataturk threw a Qur'an at him and chased him out of his office with a stick.[245]

The reforms that Ataturk instituted were inline with what may be called 'Americanism *sans* Christianity': well-defined borders, a strong defense, a universal language, a secular national identity, and a focus on diplomacy, education, and economic development. But his Turkification program has met with limited success. A significant number—perhaps a third—of the people in today's Republic of Turkey have cultural, religious, and linguistic differences that preclude them from considering themselves full Turks. These include Kurds, Avelis, Zazas, Lazes, Hamshemis, Pomaks, Kabardins,

Nusayris, Crimean Tatars, Arabs, as well as underground Greeks, Armenians, and Assyrians. Eastern Turkey today is full of military checkpoints and garrisons to keep the Kurds from forming a separate state. Ataturk's party is routinely outvoted by a greater than two-to-one margin.

Ataturk's numerous quotes are memorable and revealing:

> *[My ideology is] patriotism blended with a lofty humanist ideal.*[246]

> *The nation's land is sacred. It cannot be left to fate.*[247]

> *The economy is everything. It is the totality of what we need to live, to be happy.*[248]

> *Only teachers and educators are the saviors of a nation.*[249]

> *Science is the only true guide in life.*[250]

> *Culture is the foundation of the Turkish Republic.*[251]

> *We do not accept a religion which ignores fine arts.*[252]

> *Happy is he who says, 'I am a Turk.'*[253]

Poor Ataturk! He was a Renaissance Man governing a nation of Neanderthals. His frustration over their true character may explain his vices: he was a chronic alcoholic and a notorious womanizer. He drank raki by the liter and died at age fifty-seven from cirrhosis of the liver. He also frequented whorehouses and suffered from a recurrent syphilis infection.

The Republic of Turkey is a fool's paradise, and its most poorly kept state secret is that its founder had a fetish for young flesh.[254] One of Ataturk's methods of dismissing the virgin adolescents that he often bedded was to subsequently adopt them as his children. At the time of his death, he had seven adopted daughters, an adopted son, as well as two other boys that were, ahem, 'under his care.'[255] It was a new twist on the sultans' harem.

Indeed, the Hungarian–American actress Zsa Zsa Gabor lost her virginity at the age of fifteen to a fifty-one year old Ataturk. The first time they met, he plied the beautiful ingénue with belly dancers, an opium-laced hookah, and a jewel-encrusted raki goblet. She was, even at that tender age, beguiled by diamonds.[256] She wrote in her autobiography,

> *... every Wednesday afternoon ... he dazzled me with his sexual prowess and seduced me with his perversion. Ataturk was very wicked. He knew exactly how to please a young girl ... he was a professional lover,*

a god, and a king ... I spent most of the time with him
in a semi–awake state, a sleepwalker unable to see
straight or to focus on reality ... He also ruined for
me every other man I would ever love, or try to love ...
For the rest of my life I would search for another god
to eclipse him.[257]

In between child rape sessions he intensely questioned her about the Turkish politicians that—his spies had informed him—were secretly meeting at her home. Despite being in an opium-induced haze, young Zsa Zsa, was careful not to tell Ataturk anything that would get her houseguests killed. The dictator tired of her after six months and sent her away.[258]

Rape and pederasty remain persistent social ills within Ataturk's utopia.

~~~~~~~~~~~~~~~~~~~~~~~~

The Father of the Turks would have been well-advised to heed the words of the Colossus of American Independence, John Adams (AD 1735–AD 1826). Concerning our system of government's success, Adams said,

The general principles upon which the Fathers
achieved independence were the general principles of
Christianity.[259]

We recognize no Sovereign but God, and no King but
Jesus![260]

We have no government armed with power capable of
contending with human passions unbridled by moral-
ity and religion ... Our Constitution was made only
for a moral and religious people. It is wholly inad-
equate to the government of any other.[261]

Also, contrast Adams' dismissive and utilitarian view of scientific endeavor (quoted at bottom of Section 89) with that of Ataturk (above).

After Ataturk's death in AD 1938, his successor fostered a personality cult for him. Today, Kemal Ataturk is very nearly worshiped in the Republic of Turkey. His demon-eyed picture is ubiquitous and obligatory in shops and homes, and it is a criminal offense to say anything unflattering about him or Turkism. To the modern Turk, he is Jesus Christ, Martin Luther, and George Washington in one. The Turkish people, as inclined as they are toward the Beast of Islam, are quite aware that without Ataturk their national borders would extend half as far as they do today.

I think of Kemal Ataturk as Andrew Jackson (AD 1767–AD 1845), but without the Christian baptism. Like Jackson, he:

- saved the nation from European invasion through cannons,
- ethnically-cleansed it from [the remaining] indigenous minorities through treaty,
- expanded its borders to the maximum extent that was practicable,
- purged the central government of an entrenched and ineffective oligarchy,
- adopted the orphaned children of his enemy[262] (albeit for entirely different reasons).

Ataturk's absence of Christian faith made all the difference to God, of course. Though a practical man, he lived and died without repentance in the name of the Lord Jesus.

Ataturk and his people were still under God's wrath after the passing of their AD 1921 constitution, but the time of the Turkish State upholding the banner of Islam had ended.

Revelation 12:7–9 [NKJV]
And war broke out in heaven: Michael and his angels fought with the dragon; and the dragon and his angels fought, but they did not prevail ... So the great dragon was cast out, that serpent of old ... who deceives the whole world; he was cast to the earth, and his angels were cast out with him.

31. The War in Heaven and the Great Eagle

Toward the end of AD 1922, there was a war in Heaven. The devil lost; he always loses.

An angel broke out in song over the victory:

> *Now have come the salvation and the power and the kingdom of our God, and the authority of his Christ. For the accuser of our brothers, who accuses them before our God day and night, has been hurled down. They overcame him by the blood of the Lamb and by the word of their testimony; they did not love their lives so much as to shrink from death. Therefore rejoice, you*

*heavens and you who dwell in them! But woe to the
earth and the sea, because the devil has gone down to
you! He is filled with fury, because he knows that his
time is short. [Revelation 12:10–12 NIV]*

The last part of this song gives a warning to the people on earth:
because the devil had lost the power of the Caliphate, and because he knew
that the time before the Second Coming of Christ was short, he was filled with
fury.

Indeed, one of Osama bin Laden's chief gripes is that the Caliphate
ended with the collapse of the Ottoman Empire.[263] He wants it restored at
any cost. And Ayman al-Zawahiri has said that he wants the restoration of the
Arab Islamic Empire "from Spain to Iraq."[264] The terrorists are angry that the
Caliphate—once the most powerful and expansionist empire on earth—has
ended. The terrorists are angry that they can no longer force the people of the
world to submit to the Beast of Islam.

The devil, having been humiliated through the destruction of
the Caliphate, looked to a new source of violence and perversion: Soviet
communism.

~~~~~~~~~~~~~~~~~~~~~~~

The devil was keen to destroy the Church after the Caliph was deposed on
November 1, AD 1922.[265]

*... when the dragon saw that he had been cast to the
earth, he persecuted the woman who gave birth to the
male Child. [Revelation 12:13 NKJV]*

The first thing that the devil did was to establish the Union of Soviet
Socialist Republics on December 30, AD 1922.[266] This was his new bulwark
against the People of God. It lasted seventy years, until the dissolution of the
Red Army and the redirection of their nuclear missiles in AD 1992.[267]

Fortunately, the previous few decades had seen unprecedented immigration of Christian peoples to the United States of America.

*... the woman was given the two wings of the great
eagle so that she might fly from the serpent into the
wilderness, to the place where she is to be nourished
for a time, and times, and half a time. [Revelation
12:14 ESV]*

This symbolically ended with the Emergency Quota Act of AD 1921
that limited the annual number of immigrants from any country to three per-

cent of the number of persons from that country living in the United States in AD 1910.[268]

As I mentioned at the bottom of Section 13, it did not escape the notice of all Christian believers that the Soviet Union ended seventy years after it began. Christians are attuned to periods of oppression that last seventy years.

The seventy year Soviet period represents the "time, times, and half a time" during which God nourished the Christian Church within the United States. Each 'time' corresponds to the twenty years that Jacob spent in Laban's house, protected from Esau's fury (Genesis 27–32).

To understand this analogy, we must recall that the pre–Christian Church was called Israel, and that Israel was the name that God gave to the Patriarch Jacob when he wrestled with God (see the dedication of this book).

> *Your name shall no longer be called Jacob, but Israel,*
> *for you have striven with God and with men, and have*
> *prevailed. [Genesis 32:28 ESV]*

Also, remember that the malevolent Esau had wanted to kill Jacob.

> *So Esau bore a grudge against Jacob because of the*
> *blessing with which his father had blessed him; and*
> *Esau said to himself, "… I will kill my brother Jacob."*
> *[Genesis 27:41 NASB]*

So Jacob fled to his dishonest Uncle Laban's territory for safety between 1736 BC[269] and 1716 BC.[270] At the end of this period Laban was resentful because Jacob wanted to leave him and return to his homeland. Jacob answered him,

> *These twenty years I have been with you; your ewes*
> *and your female goats have not miscarried their*
> *young, and I have not eaten the rams of your flock.*
> *That which was torn by beasts I did not bring to you;*
> *I bore the loss of it. You required it from my hand …*
> *Thus I have been in your house twenty years … and*
> *you have changed my wages ten times. Unless the*
> *God of my father, the God of Abraham and the Fear of*
> *Isaac, had been with me, surely now you would have*
> *sent me away empty-handed. [Genesis 31:38–39,41–*
> *42 NKJV]*

I suggest that Esau represents the Soviet Union that wanted to kill Christianity. I also suggest that selfish Uncle Laban represents selfish Uncle

Sam that protected the Christian Church for its own financial benefit, and was blessed by God as a result of the Church's presence in the country.

Have you ever wondered why it is that the United States of America has risen from non-existence to the greatest power the world has ever known in a mere 230 years? I have.

The history of the United States is the history of unlikely fortuitous events. For example, General George Washington made a colossal mistake at the beginning of the Revolutionary War: he faced the British Army on an open plain in Long Island in August AD 1776. If that wasn't enough, he had no retreat path because he was boxed into the corner of Brooklyn Heights. But Providence provided thick fog and calm seas, as well as British General Howe (AD 1729–AD 1814) who didn't want to continue the battle past night-fall. This was just what Washington needed to get his troops into small boats and cross the East River into Manhattan. If it were not for the fog, the fledgling Continental Army would have been annihilated and there would never have been a United States.[271]

There are many more examples. We had incredibly unlikely victories in New Orleans (AD 1814), San Jacinto (AD 1836), Gettysburg (AD 1863), and Midway (AD 1942). Without these we would not be a superpower today. Don't you think this is strange? We were competing against more established empires and peoples, but we overtook them all.

If God is sovereign—and He is—what has He been up to here? Is it because we sing "God bless America" and "America, America, God shed His grace on thee"?

Spare me, please. Americans are no better than the Turkish Kemalists without Jesus in our hearts. And a good number of our countrymen give Christ no heed.

> *Will you steal and murder, commit adultery and per-*
> *jury, burn incense to Baal and follow other gods you*
> *have not known, and then come and stand before me*
> *in this house, which bears my Name, and say, "We*
> *are safe"—safe to do all these detestable things?*
> *[Jeremiah 7:9–10 NIV]*

God is not impressed by the United States; God is impressed by His Son. The reason that God allowed the US to hold such influence over human civilization is that He knew that with it would come the protection and prom-ulgation of the Gospel. President John Quincy Adams (AD 1767–AD 1848) was well aware of this:

> *Why is it that, next to the birthday of the savior of the world, [the Americans'] most joyous and venerated festival [is Independence Day]? Is it not that, in the chain of human events, the birthday of the nation is indissolubly linked with the birthday of the savior? **[Is it not that] it forms a leading event in the progress of the gospel dispensation?** Is it not that the Declaration of Independence first organized the social compact on the foundation of the redeemer's mission on earth?*[272]

The United States was providentially designed for a singular purpose: the mass production and distribution of the Word of God. That was not our aim, of course—we were out for commerce. President Calvin Coolidge (AD 1872–AD 1933) was more realistic than his predecessor in office:

> *The chief business of the American people is business.*[273]

Nevertheless, our system of governance has been such that the Gospel was freely spread along with our economic hegemony. And our ascendancy has just happened to coincide with the approach of the Second Coming of Christ.

The United States of America is the Great Eagle—Revelation 12:14 is referring to the US national symbol. The great immigration wave of the early twentieth century was the bulk of the Church being transported from Europe into our wilderness where we would be nurtured, and protected from the devil and his Soviet communism.

Revelation 12:15–17 [NKJV]
So the serpent spewed water out of his mouth like a flood after the woman, that he might cause her to be carried away by the flood. But the earth helped the woman, and the earth opened its mouth and swallowed up the flood which the dragon had spewed out of his mouth. And the dragon was enraged with the woman, and he went to make war with the rest of her offspring, who keep the commandments of God and have the testimony of Jesus Christ.

32. The Flood of Lies

The United States was a refuge for the People of God during the twentieth century. From this place we have spread the Good News of Jesus Christ to the entire world. The devil could not touch us in this place of care and protection.

But that didn't mean that he gave up. The devil never wins, but he never gives up either.

The verse above says that the devil emitted something from his mouth in hopes of washing away the Church. What is it that comes out of the mouth of the devil? Christ said of the devil,

> *When he lies, he speaks his native language, for he is*
> *a liar and the father of lies. [John 8:44 NKJV]*

When I was a freshman engineering student, I was required to take a nineteenth century English literature course. The professor spoke often of secular humanism, and once he said that modern philosophers think that Christianity will soon be swept into the trash bin of history by Rationalism. What this had to do with Austin and Dickens and Stevenson, I knew not. But what it had to do with the natural impulse of the intellectual to be against all that God desires for man was plain to me even then.

The devil threw a lot at the Church between AD 1922 to AD 1992. The Christians around the world suffered through the Great Depression, the Second World War, and the Cold War. But in areas of relative peace and affluence, especially in the United States, the Culture Wars were raging. It was a time of judicial activism, feminism, hedonism, liberal media bias, and the cult of science. This liberal degeneration was predicted:

> *... in the last days perilous times will come: For men*
> *will be lovers of themselves, lovers of money, boasters,*
> *proud, blasphemers, disobedient to parents, unthank-*
> *ful, unholy, unloving, unforgiving, slanderers, without*
> *self-control, brutal, despisers of good, traitors, head-*
> *strong, haughty, lovers of pleasure rather than lovers*
> *of God, having a form of godliness but denying its*
> *power. And from such people turn away! [2 Timothy*
> *3:1–5 NKJV]*

If you are a secular humanist, this book should make you happy. I am yielding that in fewer than thirty years the scales will tilt irreversibly in your favor. If Christ does not come as He promised, the Anglo–American, Bible-Believing, Protestants that you so loathe will be completely dismayed. If human history reaches New Year's Day, AD 2040, then Christianity really will be swept into the trash bin of history, and your Rationalism will fill the void and finally usher in a great utopian existence.

I'm quaking in my boots to see who will ultimately win the Culture Wars.

~~~~~~~~~~~~~~~~~~~~~~~

Good old mother earth. *Terra firma*. The earth in this section's Scripture heading represents solid facts that keep us grounded.

The devil is greatly assisted when lies go unchecked, or when they are repeated; but he cannot stand up to scrutiny. If you pay attention, lies are propagated all the time in our culture. Often times they are recycled—like a bad penny they keep turning up over and over.

For example, when I grew up it was not uncommon for my peers, and the television programs I watched, to warn of the dangers of 'spontaneous human combustion.' That was a phenomenon whereby some people's body temperature would suddenly and inexplicably rise, and they would burst into flames like a pile of oily rags. They were always alone when this would happen, and all that would be found later were the hands and feet—nothing else in the room would burn beside their bodies. It was a commonly held myth that it was completely spontaneous. Spiritualists in Great Britain tried to line up the occurrences of spontaneous combustion on their island with the constellations.

This nonsense continued until an intrepid French detective had an immolation case in his town. Through proper investigative techniques he realized that spontaneous combustion was, in actuality, accidental burning. The victims were always either permanently disabled, or they had suffered an accident and become unconscious. They also had always not been seen by anyone for at least twelve hours. The detective theorized that somehow their clothes had caught fire. A healthy and alert person would stomp or smother the initial flame out, but these victims were unable to do so. The clothes set fire to the skin, and they burned to death.

Now, the alarmists had said that since the human body is mostly water, there must be an immense source of heat within the people that spontaneously combust and turn to ashes. But the Frenchman said that although that is true (about the water), humans also carry a large amount of body fat just under the skin, and in the bone marrow. The fat smolders at high temperatures for long periods of time, like a candlewick. This causes a hot, localized, flame that vaporizes the body fluids and combusts the proteins. For this reason plastic objects near the burning bodies often melt, though the house does not necessarily burn down.

The theory was tested on a pig carcass that was covered with a shawl. A few drops of perfume were added to the shawl as a mild accelerant. Sure enough, a simple ignition source applied to the shawl resulted in a sustained combustion of the entire carcass over a period of many hours. By the next day only the hooves were left because they did not have enough fat to sustain the smoldering-wick fire.[274]

The myth was debunked—or was it? Every now and then I still hear the term 'spontaneous human combustion' bandied about. I'm sure that a feverish boy somewhere tonight is asking his mother if he is really burning up.

~~~~~~~~~~~~~~~~~~~~~~~~

I saw a television program in which special needs educators had insisted that their severely retarded and physically disabled students were able to communicate. The educators were paid by the local school district to sit next to the disabled children in a normal classroom, and facilitate their learning. The special needs educators would hold the hand of the disabled student to steady them, and guide them to the key on a computer keyboard that they wanted to type. The children would type out messages in this manner for the teacher of the class. Some would be quite intelligent questions about the lesson, some would be requests concerning their physical needs. All the while, the disabled students would be drooling and looking out the window as they typed.

The special needs educators really believed that it was the children communicating, and that they themselves were just the facilitators. They were adamant and emotional about their belief that the children that were in their care were intelligible savants. Any suggestion to the contrary was met with a sharp rebuke.

To settle the matter some behavioral scientists did a double-blind study where they gave the special needs educators a lecture through headphones, and gave the special needs students a different lecture through different headphones. They did not inform the educators that the lesson that they were hearing was different from the students'. The facilitators typed messages with the students' hands for the lesson that they themselves were hearing! The behavioral scientists proved beyond a doubt that it was the special needs educators that were, in fact, writing their own messages while holding the students' hands. The students really were as unable to understand or communicate as they appeared to be. The educators had been sincere in their belief, and were devastated by the findings.[275]

Obviously, there is a boredom problem in their profession, and also a deep human need to do something beyond babysitting an incoherent child.

~~~~~~~~~~~~~~~~~~~~~~~~

I offer these two, out of innumerable examples, to show how careful one has to be when accepting something as the truth. Our attitude should be like that of the Apostle Paul:

> *I destroy every claim and every reason that keeps people from knowing God. I keep every thought under control in order to make it obey Christ. [2 Corinthians 10:5 NIrV]*

There are, of course, more obvious examples about affronts to Christian teaching and ethics in our culture than the two I have cited. I have much to say about the ceaselessly propagated myth that there is no fundamental difference between men and women apart from the underwear. Also, I could comment upon the absurdity that dolphins are, on some levels, smarter than human beings. But I chose two innocuous examples to show that the devil is out for any lie that he can sell. It doesn't have to be a vicious or terribly destructive lie. The shear quantity of misinformation is sufficient for his aim: to either keep people diverted from Christ, or to keep them too skeptical to consider Christ.

After all, with so much ambiguity in the world no One Person could ever come along with a claim of absolute truth … Right??

~~~~~~~~~~~~~~~~~~~~~~

This is the state-of-affairs to date—since the time that the Beast first arose in the year of the number of the Beast (AD 661) until now. The threat of Soviet tyranny ended in AD 1992, and the devil is beside himself with anger. He has failed to destroy the Church through early heresies (e.g., Gnosticism, Arianism), Arab Islam, Turkish Islam, worldwide communism, and a myriad of morally relativistic lies. Still these blasted Christians believe in their Savior.

What's a dragon to do? How about a worldwide persecution of Christians??

> *As I looked, this horn made war with the saints and prevailed over them, until the Ancient of Days came, and judgment was given for the saints of the Most High, and the time came when the saints possessed the kingdom. [Daniel 7:21–22 ESV]*

I don't know if you realize what is going on, but Christians are being massacred and oppressed around the world. In East Timor, Egypt, Kosovo, North Korea, Pakistan, the Philippians, the Sudan, and other places. Recently three Christian schoolgirls were beheaded in Indonesia by Muslim savages armed with machetes.[276] In AD 1999 a pastor and his two boys were burned to death by a mob of Hindu fanatics in India.[277] Several Protestants have been shot and killed in Iran for the suspected proselytism of Shi'a Muslims to Christianity.[278] Underground church leaders are being imprisoned in China; and now an above-ground pastor has been imprisoned in Sweden for violating speech codes.[279] That same law was proposed in Canada.[280]

Revelation 11:3 [NKJV]
And I will give power to my two witnesses, and they will prophesy one thousand two hundred and sixty days, clothed in sackcloth.

33. Two Witnesses

We have already discussed that the 1,260 'days' is the time between Ali's assassination in AD 661 and Ataturk's rise to power in AD 1921. This is reinforced in Revelation 11:2, where we are told that the Gentiles (i.e., those that do not believe that God became a man in Jesus) will "tread the holy city underfoot for forty-two months." If a 'month' represents thirty years, then forty-two months represents 1,260 years. That timeline elapsed with the end of the First World War,[281] the occupation of Palestine by the British,[282] and the dissolution of the Ottoman Empire,[283] the Sultanate,[284] and the Caliphate.[285] Since that time Christians have been free to practice their faith in Jerusalem without the menace of the post-Ali Islamic Caliphate.

The two witnesses, referred to above, are the faithful believers within the Roman Catholic and Confessional Protestant churches (i.e., Creedal Christians). Undoubtedly there are Christian believers among the Mainline Protestant, Eastern Orthodox, Oriental Orthodox, and Nestorian churches, as well. But they are excluded from the two witnesses because of their heretical christologies. They 'fell away' from Christian orthodoxy, and are like foolish women that downgrade their husband's manliness and virility. It is a serious sin. [See Section 76 for a detailed explanation.]

So faithful Christians that accept the three Ecumenical Creeds (i.e., Apostles', Athanasian, and Nicene with the inclusion of the Filioque) are the two witnesses. The sackcloth they wear represents the poverty and oppression that they endured under the Caliphate once it began the process of adopting the Son of Perdition's religion in AD 661.

Yet these two witnesses that are clothed in sackcloth have awesome spiritual power. They stand before the living God as chosen vessels of honor.

These are the two olive trees and the two lampstands standing before the God of the earth. And if anyone wants to harm them, fire proceeds from their mouth and devours their enemies. [Revelation 11:4–5 NKJV]

The rest of Chapter 11, from verse 7 on, refers to things that will happen once the two witnesses "… have finished their testimony …" [Revelation 11:7 NIV] That is distinct from the completion of the 1,260 days of prophesy. The finishing of their testimony will be close to the time when the Gospel is preached to all nations. At that time a group of faithful Roman Catholics and Confessional Protestants will proclaim the Good News in Jerusalem (or possibly Rome or Istanbul), and will be massacred. Then, immediately before the Second Coming of Christ, they will be risen from the dead before video cameras.

~~~~~~~~~~~~~~~~~~~~~~~

Christians are truth-tellers. If lies flood forth from the devil's mouth like a torrent (Section 32), then truth emanates from the mouths of believers like a flame thrower. The power that we have is the power of prayer and of prophecy. I have seen this many times in myself and other believers: we will say something, and it will come to pass. It's really quite astounding.

Faithful Christians experience this regularly.

… the afflicted of the flock who were watching me realized that it was the word of the Lord. [Zechariah 11:11 NASB]

My great grandfather, for example, was a skilled textile craftsman who lived in the Ottoman Empire while it was in its death throes before the First World War. He was a Bible-believing Protestant—one of the Christian saints that would prophesy in sackcloth under the subjugation of the Caliphate for 1,260 years past the time of the head-wound of Ali.

Great grandfather would travel to find work. In one city he received a substantial contract: the mayor promised to pay him a handsome sum to make all the drapery in his mansion. He worked like a bee for weeks—dying, sewing, and hanging ornate fabric on the mayor's walls and windows. When he finished everything, the mayor claimed to be dissatisfied with the job and refused to make payment. He said that he had fed my great grandfather his family's leftovers, and had allowed my great grandfather to sleep in his basement during his work, and that was enough compensation for a shoddy job. My great grandfather argued with him, but there was no recourse for a Christian claimant against a Muslim authority in the Ottoman Empire. My great grandfather was an infidel, after all, and he was fortunate that he did not just disappear while he was away on business. So he left the mayor on a cold and rainy morning with these words, "I hand you over to God for stealing my labor and my material. May He be as generous with you as you insist that you have been with me."

Great grandfather went to another region to try to earn some money before returning home. On his way back he went into the city again, thinking that perhaps the passage of time had made the mayor rethink the matter. But he could not find the mansion. It was gone. He thought for a moment that he was on the wrong street, but then the Turkish women of the neighborhood recognized him and started wailing. They knew about the argument, and said that he must be a mighty man of God. They told him that the evening after he left town, a heavily-armed group of chatahs[viii] came to the mayor's mansion for lodging. This was customary since they were fellow Turkish Muslims and they worked for the people that kept the mayor in power. With typical Middle Eastern hospitality the mayor's family made a warm fire, prepared a large dinner, and set out bed linen for the men. Their munitions were damp from the rain, so they lay them a safe distance from the fire to dry overnight. But a spark from the fire jumped onto a sack of gunpowder, smoldered through the canvass, and blew up the sleeping quarters of the house. The drapery that my great grandfather had lain acted like accelerants and fueled the resulting fire into the walls. The mansion was completely destroyed in a holocaust. The mayor, his family, and most of the chatahs perished.

As it is written,

> Surely the great houses will become desolate, the fine
> mansions left without occupants. [Isaiah 5:9 TNIV]

Great grandfather left the city quickly, and safely returned home in the blessed fear of the Lord.

Revelation 17:1–6 [NKJV]
"Come, I will show you the judgment of the great harlot who sits on many waters, with whom the kings of the earth committed fornication, and the inhabitants of the earth were made drunk with the wine of her fornication." So he carried me away in the Spirit into the wilderness. And I saw a woman sitting

---

viii   A Turkish word for the highwaymen of the local warlord.

on a scarlet beast which was full of names of blasphemy, having seven heads and ten horns. The woman was arrayed in purple and scarlet, and adorned with gold and precious stones and pearls, having in her hand a golden cup full of abominations and the filthiness of her fornication. And on her forehead a name was written: MYSTERY, BABYLON THE GREAT, THE MOTHER OF HARLOTS AND OF THE ABOMINATIONS OF THE EARTH. I saw the woman, drunk with the blood of the saints and with the blood of the martyrs of Jesus. And when I saw her, I marveled with great amazement.

34. The Great Harlot

The Great Harlot in the wilderness represents the secular American culture or American liberal values, headquartered in New York City. Please note that the debased culture and value system (i.e., the Great Harlot) is distinct from the liberal and socialist political institutions (i.e., the ten horns).

The kings of the earth becoming drunk with the wine of the Harlot's fornication are symbolic of the export of our music, movies, and moral degradation. The Harlot's gaudy purple and scarlet apparel is representative of western prosperity.

The many waters on which she sits is New York Harbor, the headwaters of American Liberalism. Later in the chapter the angel explains,

> *The waters which you saw, where the harlot sits, are peoples, multitudes, nations, and tongues ... And the woman whom you saw is that great city which reigns over the kings of the earth. [Revelation 17:15,18 NKJV]*

In Scripture, cities are conventionally symbolized as women.[286] New York City is the largest melting pot in the world and the center of worldwide commerce. And New York State is quite appropriately monikered 'the Empire State.' It is the seat of the worldwide, secular, American empire.

The Harlot being drunk with the blood of the martyrs is not an indication that she was actively involved in the killing of Christian saints. It is, rather, an acknowledgment that the previously unheard of prosperity that she enjoys is a result of spiritual blessing that came from the sacrifice of the Christians within her midst. She perverted what others built at the expense of their lives for her shameless debauchery.

For example, my friend and her husband rented a summer house on the Connecticut coastline and invited me there for the weekend. It was a beautiful spot. I told her that she should consider buying property there. She said that it was out of the question because all her neighbors did was drink and party.

"Don't they have jobs?" I asked.

"No," she said. "They all live off trust funds that their parents or grand-parents set up for them. They are so bored that they stay drunk all summer long."

~~~~~~~~~~~~~~~~~~~~~~~

The angel went on to explain that the seven heads of the Scarlet Beast represent seven kingdoms (these are not to be confused with the seven heads of the Sea Beast in Revelation 13).

> *... the angel said to me, "Why did you marvel? I will tell you the mystery of the woman and of the beast that carries her, which has the seven heads and the ten horns." [Revelation 17:7 NKJV]*

Five of the kingdoms had ceased to be, and one was currently reigning, and one was coming and must remain for a little while.

> *This calls for a mind with wisdom. The seven heads are seven hills on which the woman sits. They are also seven kings. Five have fallen, one is, the other has not yet come; but when he does come, he must remain for a little while. [Revelation 17:9–10 NIV]*

These represent the great worldly empires that are spoken of in the Bible. Each threatened to quench God's plan for salvation. The Bible gives examples of each trying to wipe out the Chosen People that trusted that God would become a man. The first five kingdoms that verse 10 says "have fallen" were:

1. Egypt, whose pharaoh tried to destroy Moses and his flock of Israel's children (1462 BC);[287]
2. Assyria, which destroyed the northern kingdom of Israel (721 BC), and tried to destroy Judah (701 BC);[288]
3. Babylonia, which destroyed Jerusalem, and led Judah into captivity (586 BC);[289]
4. Medo–Persia, whose king gave an order to extirpate all the exiled Jews (474 BC);[290]

5. Greece, whose Seleucid ruler desecrated the Second Temple by sacrificing a pig to Zeus upon the altar, and also killed many Jews (168 BC).[291]

The sixth kingdom, the Roman Empire, crucified the Lord and killed the early church Fathers. It was at its peak of power when John wrote the Book of Revelation. Hence verse 10 refers to it when it says that "one is." The seventh kingdom was the Caliphate, which at that time had "not yet come." It remained for the "little while" of 1,260 years beyond the assassination of Ali!

> This calls for patient endurance and faithfulness on
> the part of the saints. [Revelation 13:10 NIV]

The Harlot was riding on this Seven-Headed Scarlet Beast, showing that modern American Liberalism is riding upon the legacy of these wicked kingdoms' historic hostility toward God's salvation plan.

The United States' rationalist neo–paganism is partially evidenced by our classical, columned, architecture and monuments. These designs are heavily drawn from Greek and Roman pagan temples. Even the U.S. Capitol Building is named after Capitoline, the highest of the seven hills of ancient Rome. It was the historic and religious center of Rome, and hosted a temple to the pagan god, Jupiter.[292]

The Scarlet Beast itself is a kingdom distinct from its heads, but is also a derivative of them. It is said to be something that,

> ... was, and is not, and will ascend out of the bottom-
> less pit and go to perdition. [Revelation 17:8 NKJV]

This represents the recurrence of lawlessness and terrorism, which were the roots of the above kingdoms before they became established powers. There will be more and more anarchy as we get closer to the last day.

The ten horns represent the socialist political and cultural forces within American society.

> The ten horns which you saw are ten kings who have
> received no kingdom as yet, but they receive author-
> ity for one hour as kings with the beast. These are of
> one mind, and they will give their power and author-
> ity to the beast. These will make war with the Lamb ...
> [Revelation 17:12–14 NKJV]

These are the hodgepodge of anarchist, anti-establishmentarian, liberal groups (e.g., the mainstream news media, Hollywood, American Civil Liberties Union, academia, the Democratic Party, National Abortion Rights Action League, teachers' unions, Public Broadcasting Service, etc.). They always talk of celebrating diversity because they are set against God's absolute truths. They would make a pact with the devil before agreeing to live in peace with the Word of God. The war that they wage against the Lamb refers to the Culture Wars[293] that have been fought in the United States since ~ AD 1960.

The one hour in which they receive authority signifies the attack of September 11, AD 2001. Remember that the political battle cry during the AD 1992 presidential election was, "Character doesn't matter." It resulted in the very unlikely victory of Bill Clinton over George H.W. Bush, after Bush plummeted from his record ninety percent job approval ratings.

The Secretary of State during the Clinton Administration bemoaned the United States' new status as the sole superpower after the collapse of the Soviet Union. She saw it as a destabilizing geopolitical phenomenon, and thought that we needed to be challenged on the world stage. She actually traveled to North Korea and clinked champagne glasses with its butcher, Kim Jong Il.

While the United States was under the neglectful leadership of the Clinton Administration, the Scarlet Beast of terrorism arose. The Liberals' distain for biblical values is so great that they would rather see the Great Harlot (i.e., their own homebase) destroyed than for the People of God (i.e., the Christians) to be politically victorious. This is self-destructive because the ten horns (i.e., the Liberals) would be the first ones rounded up and executed if the Scarlet Beast (i.e., terrorist forces) ever came to power within the Great Harlot. Still, they advocate tolerance for multicultural values, and oppose an aggressive war on terrorism. They are, in the word of Vladimir Lenin, 'useful idiots' to the cause of the Antichrist Beast of Islam.

The chapter concludes:

> *The beast and the ten horns you saw will hate the prostitute. They will bring her to ruin and leave her naked; they will eat her flesh and burn her with fire. For God has put it into their hearts to accomplish his purpose by agreeing to give the beast their power to rule, until God's words are fulfilled. [Revelation 17:16–17 NIV]*

We have all witnessed this alliance between anti-American terrorism (i.e., the Scarlet Beast) and the American left (i.e., the ten horns) against the liberal cultural mecca of New York City (i.e., the Great Harlot upon many waters). It was a horrific day.

Revelation 18:10 [NIV]
O Babylon, city of power! In one hour your doom has come!

35. The Fall of Babylon the Great

At the heart of the Great Harlot (i.e., New York City) that sits on many waters (i.e., New York Harbor) is Babylon the Great (i.e., the World Trade Center). Its awful fate is foretold in Revelation 18—the entire chapter points to the attacks on the World Trade Center on September 11, AD 2001. The 'one hour' represents the one hundred and two minutes for the collapse of the North Tower, and the fifty-six minutes for the collapse of the South Tower.[294] The space that they occupied may be rebuilt upon, but there will be no restoration of the World Trade Center buildings. They were beyond repair, and every bit of them has been taken to landfills and blast furnaces.

I have reprinted the entire, chilling, account of the fall of the towers, given in stunning apocalyptic prose.

> *After this I saw another angel coming down from heaven. He had great authority, and the earth was illuminated by his splendor. With a mighty voice he shouted:*
>
> > *"Fallen! Fallen is Babylon the Great! She has become a home for demons and a haunt for every evil spirit, a haunt for every unclean and detestable bird. For all the nations have drunk the maddening wine of her adulteries. The kings of the earth committed adultery with her, and the merchants of the earth grew rich from her excessive luxuries."*
>
> *Then I heard another voice from heaven say:*
>
> > *"Come out of her, my people, so that you will not share in her sins, so that you will not receive any of her plagues; for her sins are piled up to heaven, and God has remembered her crimes. Give back to her as she has given; pay her back double for what she has done. Mix her a double portion from her own cup. Give her as much torture and grief as the glory and luxury she gave herself. In her heart she boasts,*

'I sit as queen; I am not a widow, and I will never mourn.'
Therefore in one day her plagues will overtake her: death, mourning and famine. She will be consumed by fire, for mighty is the Lord God who judges her. When the kings of the earth who committed adultery with her and shared her luxury see the smoke of her burning, they will weep and mourn over her. Terrified at her torment, they will stand far off and cry:

'Woe! Woe, O great city,
O Babylon, city of power!
In one hour your doom has come!'

The merchants of the earth will weep and mourn over her because no one buys their cargoes any more—cargoes of gold, silver, precious stones and pearls; fine linen, purple, silk and scarlet cloth; every sort of citron wood, and articles of every kind made of ivory, costly wood, bronze, iron and marble; cargoes of cinnamon and spice, of incense, myrrh and frankincense, of wine and olive oil, of fine flour and wheat; cattle and sheep; horses and carriages; and bodies and souls of men. They will say,

'The fruit you longed for is gone from you.
All your riches and splendor have vanished, never to be recovered.'

The merchants who sold these things and gained their wealth from her will stand far off, terrified at her torment. They will weep and mourn and cry out:

'Woe! Woe, O great city,
dressed in fine linen, purple and scarlet,
and glittering with gold, precious stones and pearls!
In one hour such great wealth has been brought to ruin!'

Every sea captain, and all who travel by ship, the sailors, and all who earn their living from the sea, will stand far off. When they see the smoke of her burning, they will exclaim,

'Was there ever a city like this great city?'
They will throw dust on their heads, and with weeping and mourning cry out:

'Woe! Woe, O great city,
where all who had ships on the sea
became rich through her wealth!
In one hour she has been brought to ruin!
Rejoice over her, O heaven!
Rejoice, saints and apostles and prophets!
God has judged her for the way she treated you.'"

Then a mighty angel picked up a boulder the size of a large millstone and threw it into the sea, and said:

"With such violence the great city of Babylon will be thrown down, never to be found again. The music of harpists and musicians, flute players and trumpeters, will never be heard in you again. No workman of any trade will ever be found in you again. The sound of a millstone will never be heard in you again. The light of a lamp will never shine in you again. The voice of bridegroom and bride will never be heard in you again. Your merchants were the world's great men. By your magic spell all the nations were led astray. In her was found the blood of prophets and of the saints, and of all who have been killed on the earth."
[Revelation 18 NIV]

When I told a couple Christian friends that this referred to the attacks of September 11th, their reaction was surprising. They were not indignant. They did not say that we Americans were [spiritually] innocent and that we did not [spiritually] deserve what happened. Rather, they said that Revelation 18 could not possibly refer to the World Trade Center because it *was not a bad enough disaster*. 'Only' three thousand people died. 'Only' a fraction of Manhattan was razed. The land was not contaminated—it can be rebuilt upon. They were expecting for the entire city to disappear and become uninhabitable.

You must remember that God is longsuffering and gracious. He does not give to us as our sins deserve.

... he is gracious and compassionate, slow to anger and abounding in love, and he relents from sending calamity. [Joel 2:13 TNIV]

In Scripture God is always loath to allow the destruction of an entire city. He would not have destroyed Sodom and Gomorrah if there were ten righteous persons in it.

For the sake of ten, I will not destroy it. [Genesis 18:32 TNIV]

Again, eleven hundred years later, God held back from destroying a pagan and cruel city, Nineveh, because He was concerned about its many inhabitants.

And should I not have concern for the great city Nineveh, in which there are more than a hundred and twenty thousand people who cannot tell their right hand from their left—and also many animals? [Jonah 4:11 TNIV]

And when God did finally tire of centuries of idolatry by the Jews, their destruction was severe, but not complete. He predicted the result of the conquest by King Nebuchadnezzar,

I will make Jerusalem a heap of ruins, a haunt of jackals; and I will lay waste the towns of Judah so no one can live there. [Jeremiah 9:11 TNIV]

But that only meant that the First Temple would be destroyed, the royal line of Judah would cease governance, and the best and brightest Jews would be killed or exiled. It did not mean that the land would be completely devoid of human beings. Jerusalem became a haunt compared with the glory of the time of Solomon, but still some Jewish and non-Jewish peasants carried on daily life among the ruins.

This raises an important point: there is a difference between believing that the Bible is inerrant (as I do), and taking the Bible literally. Where a metaphor is clearly being used, we can still believe in the inerrancy of the Scriptures while appreciating the literary device. For example, when the devil is called a dragon in Revelation 12:9, we know that the devil is not literally a dragon flying in the sky and exhaling fire—we're not stupid.

Now, New York City has eight million inhabitants. Undoubtedly hundreds of thousands of those people truly and sincerely trust in the Lord Jesus, and are thus the Chosen People of God in whom His favor rests. So the Sovereign Lord allowed a great judgment to come upon Babylon the Great (i.e., the World Trade Center), but He spared most of the people. This is in His character; He often defers cataclysms—His interest lies in saving as many human souls as possible.

> *And God sent an angel to destroy Jerusalem. But*
> *as the angel was doing so, the Lord saw it and was*
> *grieved because of the calamity and said to the angel*
> *who was destroying the people, "Enough! Withdraw*
> *your hand." [1 Chronicles 21:15 NIV]*

Nationalist Americans that do not know Jesus Christ will object to the characterization of our culture as the Great Harlot, and of the Twin Towers as Babylon the Great. But *Nationalist American Christians* will know better.

> *If we say that we have no sin, we deceive ourselves,*
> *and the truth is not in us. [1 John 1:8 NKJV]*

Christians are very well aware, for example, that it was the Tribe of Judah that produced both:

- the Messiah, Jesus of Nazareth;
- and the betrayer, Judas Iscariot.[295]

So it is that within our country, there are Christians and Antichrists living in peace, side-by-side, oftentimes as friends.

The United States is, at once, the Great Eagle upon which the Church 'flew' into the wilderness and was nourished, and the Great Harlot that sits on many waters. In order to see the place of the Great Harlot, the Apostle John says that the angel,

> *... carried me away in the Spirit **into the wilderness**.*
> *And I saw a woman sitting on a scarlet beast which*
> *was full of names of blasphemy, having seven heads*
> *and ten horns. [Revelation 17:3 NKJV]*

The Greek word for 'wilderness' is the same word that is used elsewhere in Revelation to describe the place to which the Church was flown for protection.

This is the American dichotomy: it is a land of goodness and wickedness.

> *Then the angel who was talking with me came for-*
> *ward and said, "Look up and see what's coming."*
> *"What is it?" I asked.*

He replied, "It is a basket for measuring grain, and it's filled with the sins of everyone throughout the land."

Then the heavy lead cover was lifted off the basket, and there was a woman sitting inside it. The angel said, "The woman's name is Wickedness," and he pushed her back into the basket and closed the heavy lid again.

Then I looked up and saw two ... wings like a stork, and they picked up the basket and flew into the sky.

"Where are they taking the basket?" I asked the angel.

He replied, "To the land of Babylonia, where they will build a temple for the basket. And when the temple is ready, they will set the basket there on its pedestal." [*Zechariah 5:5–11 NLT*]

The United States of America is a free country. The Chosen People (i.e., Christians) have flocked here for religious liberty, and worldly people (i.e., Antichrists) have flocked here for economic gain and licentiousness. There is no such thing as an exemplary nation upon the earth. Believers and unbelievers alike share each country, as was the case in ancient Israel. And because the United States is a democracy, there is a natural tendency for the population to determine if something is moral and true by virtue of its popularity. This is serious business because every day that passes brings us closer to the Judgment Day.

Though grace is shown to the wicked, they do not learn righteousness; even in a land of uprightness they go on doing evil and regard not the majesty of the Lord. O Lord, your hand is lifted high, but they do not see it. [*Isaiah 26:10–11 NIV*]

The unbelievers have had far more influence on the American popular culture than the believers since the advent of the Culture Wars (Sections 32, 34); they also aggressively seek political power. They are diametrically opposed to the Gospel of Jesus Christ, and they love to be deceived.

If a liar and deceiver comes and says, 'I will prophesy for you plenty of wine and beer,' he would be just the prophet for this people! [*Micah 2:11 NIV*]

Christian citizens of the United States share in the shame and sin of our harlot-like culture, and priests and pastors here have an obligation to speak out against our hedonism and blasphemy.

Fortunately, the remedy is free and uncomplicated: turn to the Word of God, Jesus Christ, and repent, and you will be cleansed.

2 Corinthians 7:10 [CEV]
When God makes you feel sorry enough to turn to him and be saved, you don't have anything to feel bad about.

36. The Way Out

Much of this book is predicated upon prophetic messages delivered by angels to saints in the Bible. Do angels still visit earth to help God's Chosen People, the Christians?

It is certain that they do.

> *Are not all angels ministering spirits sent to serve those who will inherit salvation? [Hebrews 1:14 TNIV]*

I know a Christian woman that was raised to be a fortune teller. She was good at it. She could figure people out by looking at them, and gain their confidence by telling them what she knew they wanted to hear. Then she would prescribe to them an elaborate scheme to rid themselves of their bad luck. Needless to say, the scheme always involved her somehow gaining a large amount of money. She made a good living this way, and her husband did not need to work.

Somehow the Holy Spirit led she and her husband to Christ. But they could not bring themselves to leave their fortune telling business. They had a baby on the way, and there was no other source of income; they had no education, and their family had disowned them because they were now Christians. So she still scammed people for money, but just not as badly as before.

Our Savior said,

> *No one who puts a hand to the plow and looks back is fit for service in the kingdom of God. [Luke 9:62 TNIV]*

After a few months of confessing Christ, but practicing evil, a stranger came into her shop to have his palm read. As I said, she was good at reading people and she sensed right away that the man was bad news. She decided to read his palm quickly and tell him something that would not make him want to come back again. But the man pulled out a large knife, and pushed her to the floor. She was alone and eight months pregnant. The blade passed an inch from her baby's head as he cut off her clothes. Then he put the knife to her throat and ordered her to be silent.

She might have lost the baby. She might have been killed herself. The Bible says,

> *May the Lord answer you when you are in distress;*
> *may the name of the God of Jacob protect you. [Psalm*
> *20:1 TNIV]*

She called out in her mind, "Lord Jesus, have mercy on me! Help me!"

Immediately the rapist looked up, above the top of her head. He got a terrified expression on his face, and ran out of the house.

She said that she did not know what he saw. But I think I know what he saw. It was an angel of the Lord with his sword drawn.

> *The angel of the Lord encamps around those who fear*
> *him, and he delivers them. [Psalms 34:7 TNIV]*

This woman never practiced fortune telling again. God changed her so that she can no longer stand to have anything to do with the black arts.

~~~~~~~~~~~~~~~~~~~~~~~~

The Bible teaches that bad things (e.g., accidents, diseases, natural disasters, wars, suffering, death) happen as a result of the presence of sin in the world. It is ultimately the devil's fault, but all human beings have contributed to the collective amount of sin. Therefore, we should each repent of our hand in the state of this fallen world, and nurture the Word of God in our heart.

It is a different issue whether specific sins directly cause specific bad things. It's certainly possible, but Jesus warned against idle speculation in this regard—especially by outsiders. Concerning an accident that had occurred at the southeast walls of Jerusalem, He said,

> *... those eighteen on whom the tower in Siloam fell*
> *and killed them, do you think that they were worse*
> *sinners than all other men who dwelt in Jerusalem? I*
> *tell you, no; but unless you repent you will all likewise*
> *perish. [Luke 13:4–5 NKJV]*

Jesus thus taught that vigilant repentance was the key to avoiding a coming calamity.

> *When you see Jerusalem being surrounded by armies,*
> *you will know that its desolation is near. Then let those*
> *who are in Judea flee to the mountains, let those in the*
> *city get out, and let those in the country not enter the*
> *city. For this is the time of punishment in fulfillment of*
> *all that has been written. [Luke 21:20–22 NIV]*

These words came true when the entire city of Jerusalem, swollen with Jewish pilgrims that had rejected Jesus Christ, was destroyed forty years later. At that time the Jewish Christians heeded His warning, and fled Judea for the safety of the Transjordanian mountains.[296] They knew from the prophecy in Daniel 11:41 that those particular mountains would be a safe place to escape the invasion.

People should turn to God, rather than point fingers, when they hear of specific bad things happening to others. God wants us to live, and turning to Him is the way of eternal life.

~~~~~~~~~~~~~~~~~~~~~~~

In early AD 1915 the son of a Syriac Orthodox priest in a town in eastern Turkey blasphemed God: the teenager got drunk, went into the town square, and yelled, "If Jesus is the Messiah, then let Him kill me right here! I challenge Him!" When nothing happened, he laughed at Christ. Some of the wiser Assyrian women of the town cried when they heard this because they knew something bad was going to happen.

A few weeks later, the Turkish authorities rounded up a group of criminals and hanged them in the town square without a trial (the Turks are experts at building gallows and hanging people without a trial). Among the condemned suspects was the priest's son. He had not committed a crime, but somehow he was implicated with the criminals. Some of the Assyrian townspeople felt righteous when they saw him hanging on the very spot of his blasphemy; they said that the priest's son had brought a curse upon himself.

Shortly after that, the deportations and massacres of innocent Armenian, Assyrian, and Greek Christians were organized by the Ottoman government in Constantinople. One and a half million Armenians,[297] six hundred thousand Greeks,[298] and three hundred thousand Assyrians[299] were systematically murdered. Untold numbers of women and children were enslaved into Turkish households and forced to convert to Islam, or sold to Turkish whorehouses until they died from abuse. By the end of the First World War there were only a few thousand Christians left in the land mass of Anatolia.

This was the final horrific gasp of the Islamic Caliphate. It died at the end of AD 1922,[300] and with it ended the large-scale massacres.

The mass killings only ceased because there were no other infidel population centers to exterminate. The flames of malice had burned themselves out in the last great Christian stronghold of Smyrna.[301] But hostility toward Christianity and opposition to the norms of civilized behavior continued on in the Republic of Turkey: it remains a police state—without freedom of speech or conscience—and a place of vigilante Sharia justice. To this very day, the few remaining Assyrians, Greeks, and Armenians must adopt Turkish surnames and stay quiet about their ancestry and faith. They could lose their jobs, or even their lives, if they are openly Christian. In AD 2006, for example, a Roman Catholic priest that was celebrating Mass in Trabzon was murdered by a Muslim youth shouting "Allahu Akbar!"

> *Yes, the time is coming when those who kill you will think they are offering service to God. [John 16:2 NCV]*

Another priest was knifed later that year.[302] And in AD 2007 a journalist that was outspoken about his Armenian heritage was gunned down outside his office in Istanbul. His young assailant shouted, "I shot the non-Muslim!" as he fled the murder scene.[303]

The Turks will be judged for this. It is written,

> *... I will judge them for harming my people, my special possession, for scattering my people among the nations, and for dividing up my land. They threw dice to decide which of my people would be their slaves. They traded boys to obtain prostitutes and sold girls for enough wine to get drunk. [Joel 3:2–3 NLT]*

And the angel of the Lord has proclaimed,

> *... the Glorious One has sent me against the nations that have plundered you—for whoever touches you touches the apple of his eye—I will surely raise my hand against them so that their slaves will plunder them. Then you will know that the Lord Almighty has sent me. [Zechariah 2:8–9 TNIV]*

The people of the Republic of Turkey will soon turn upon each other because of their bloodguilt against the Apple of God's Eye (i.e., the Christians).

Accepting Christ is the Turks' only way to avoid the coming calamity, but they will not accept Him.

> *The fifth angel poured out his bowl on the throne of the beast, and his kingdom was plunged into darkness. Men gnawed their tongues in agony and cursed the God of heaven because of their pains and their sores, but they refused to repent of what they had done. [Revelation 16:10–11 NIV]*

On April 18, AD 2007 a Turkish fraternal group assaulted three Protestant missionaries during their morning Bible study in Malatya. The victims were tied to chairs and tortured with knives before their throats were slit.[304]

This is nothing new. The Turks have been doing this to Greeks, Armenians, Assyrians, and Christian Arabs for a thousand years. My grandfather lost every one of his friends and relatives to the Turks' unquenchable barbarism. He had left the Ottoman Empire immediately before the outbreak of the First World War; a year later he found himself in the United States, at the age of thirty-three, with not a loved one left in this world.

You don't have to be a prophet to perceive that divine judgment is on the horizon. I am not a prophet, but a discerner of prophecy. I can see that trouble is imminent for the Turkish people. And when the coming Turkish Civil War erupts, know that the interpretations of Biblical prophecy within this book are true and that the Tribulation has begun.

~~~~~~~~~~~~~~~~~~~~~~~

It is easy to see the sin that [spiritually-speaking] led to the Syriac Orthodox priest's son being killed in AD 1915. He literally asked for it. But then all the other Christian peoples suffered. And not only did the genocide extirpate the Oriental Orthodox (i.e., the priest's people), but also virtually all the Eastern Orthodox, Protestants, Roman Catholics, and Nestorians of Anatolia. What, specifically, had they done to be driven from their homes and killed?

> *Remember how Achan son of Zerah refused to obey the command ... That one man broke God's law, but all the Israelites were punished. Achan died because of his sin, but others also died. [Joshua 22:20 NCV]*

The young man being unjustly hanged was a sign not just to his family, but to the entire community. They all needed to get on their knees and repent—quickly! They all had contributed to the high level of collective sin and [spiritually-speaking] deserved death, too. Their rejection of the Word of God was just not as overt and complete as the young man's.

That same principle applies to us, as well. We are all fallen creatures.

The only One that did not have any sin was Jesus. And He allowed Himself to be killed like a criminal to take our eternal punishment! Therefore, Christ's first and primary message was repentance.

> *From that time on Jesus began to preach, "Repent,*
> *for the kingdom of heaven has come near." [Matthew*
> *4:17 TNIV]*

I am by no means exempt from the accusation of rejecting the Word of God. It is for this reason that I hold steadfastly to the faith of the three Ecumenical Creeds (i.e., Apostles', Athanasian, and Nicene with the inclusion of the Filioque), read the Bible, and begin everyday on my knees with the prayer, "forgive us our trespasses, as we forgive those that trespass against us." I am afraid not to do so! Whether the Good Lord calls me home unexpectedly or not, I want to be armed to deal with this dangerous world.

Practicing Christians should repent and be thankful that we are forgiven when bad things happen. We should likewise repent and be thankful when good things happen, and it outwardly appears that repentance is not necessary. We should trust God in this way in all seasons.

> *... he commands everyone everywhere to repent of*
> *their sins and turn to him. [Acts 17:30 NLT]*

Repentance is like bathing: a clean person does it everyday—then he clothes himself with the Word of God.

Revelation 17:14 [NKJV]
... the Lamb will overcome them, for He is Lord of lords and King of kings; and those who are with Him are called, chosen, and faithful.

37. Good News About the War

To review: the eastern Church has been under assault from the devil since the prophesied coming of the Son of Perdition (2 Thessalonians 2:3). This occurred, as prophesied, six hundred and sixty-six years after the Incarnation of Christ, and it marked the beginning of the formulation of the Islamic religion (Revelation 13:18). Specifically, Islam was:

- initiated in AD 661 through Ali's mortal head wound;[305]
- proclaimed in AD 692 with the inscriptions in the Dome of the Rock and upon Muslim coinage;[306]
- and sent forth in AD 699 by the completion and gilding of the Dome of the Rock.[307]

The Islamic Caliphate lasted for the prophesied 1,260 years past the initiating episode of Ali's martyrdom (Revelation 12:6; 13:5). During that time the eastern branches of Christianity (i.e., Eastern Orthodox, Oriental Orthodox, and Nestorian) went into serious decline (Revelation 13:8). Each fell away into a flawed Christology (i.e., Anti-Chalcedonianism and Anti-Filioqueanism; Sections 62–69) that God did not want propagated (2 Thessalonians 2:3). As prophesied, the Church moved into the wilderness of Western Europe, North and South America, Australia, and New Zealand, for care (Revelation 12:6,14). Even the Eastern Orthodox Russians were dislodged from Alaska when Providence arranged for Czar Alexander II (AD 1818–AD 1881) to sell it to the United States in AD 1867.[308] Indeed, there is no country in North America, South America, or Oceania in which Roman Catholics and Protestants do not outnumber other sects.

Immediately after the fall of the Caliphate, there came a seventy year period of communist persecution (Revelation 12:13–14). But God had brought the Church west, into the wilderness of the United States and the rest of the Free World for nourishment. Towards the end of the Cold War, the devil was more enraged than ever. He began to spew out a torrent of lies in hopes of washing the Church away (Revelation 12:15). Those that accept lies as truth are the 'ten horns' of liberal special interest groups in the United States (Revelation 17:12). They are relentless in their efforts to break down the Church's influence over society. This struggle came to be known as the Culture Wars. The liberal radicals of the Culture Wars were able to gain control of both the legislative and executive branches of government in AD 1992. The Clinton Administration neglected to protect the nation and wage war against the reemerging Scarlet Beast of anarchy and terrorism. This is the alliance of convenience between the Ten Horns (i.e., the Liberals) and the Scarlet Beast (i.e., the Terrorists)—they both had a common enemy in Jesus Christ (Revelation 17:17). The alliance resulted in the September 11th attack on the Great Harlot that sits on many waters (i.e., New York City; Revelation 17:16) and the fall of Babylon the Great (i.e., the World Trade Center; Revelation 18).

The success of the attack was bound to captivate the imagination of the enemies of God.

The inhabitants of the earth whose names have not been written in the book of life from the creation of the world will be astonished when they see the beast because he once was, and now is not, and yet will come. [Revelation 17:8 NIV]

There has always been a perverse fascination with pointless revolution and lawless tribalism among fallen human souls. They see it as a chance to get humanity back into a 'pristine,' non-God-fearing, state of nature. So it is no surprise that the antichrist forces around the world are now conspiring to wage war against Jesus Christ.

... the beast and the kings of the earth with their armies gathered to make war against him who was sitting on the horse and against his army. [Revelation 19:19 ESV]

What shall the end of this struggle be?

Their entire army was killed by the sharp sword that came from the mouth of the one riding the white horse. And the vultures all gorged themselves on the dead bodies. [Revelation 19:21 NLT]

Christ will be victorious. He is Lord and it has been prophesied.

This is great news, but be careful to keep your eyes on the real prize. Remember the example of Daniel and the Angel Gabriel (Daniel 9:20–23; Section 26): the Prophet Daniel was jubilant about the restoration of the Jews to Judea, and the imminent construction of the Second Temple in Jerusalem. But the Angel Gabriel told him that something more important was at hand— the return of the Jews from exile in Babylon actually began a timetable that was to end in Christ's redemption of mankind (Daniel 9:24–27).

So, with us, our inevitable victory in the Culture Wars and in the War on Terrorism is about much more than the United States. These victories will immediately precede the ultimate victory: the Second Coming of Christ and the end of this sinful world.

The kingdom of the world has become the kingdom of our Lord and of His Christ; and He will reign forever and ever. [Revelation 11:15 NASB]

~~~~~~~~~~~~~~~~~~~~~~~

Are you suffering in this life? Do you have an ailment? Are you forlorn because of unrequited love? Do you carry a sorrow that will not go away? Hold on. Jesus is coming.

> *Be strong. Do not fear. Your God will come. [Isaiah 35:4 NIrV]*

If you were assured that it would only last for twenty-five more days and then everything would be well with you forever after, could you bear it? Would the hope be enough for you?

The Bible is telling you that it will end, and it will end soon. This miserable world will not go on forever. Only twenty-five more years, and then sin, suffering, and death will be vanquished forever. At that time Christ will remake all things, and we shall forever be free with Him—we shall never again be put into bondage.

> *He who testifies to these things says, "Yes, I am coming soon." Amen. Come, Lord Jesus. [Revelation 22:20 TNIV]*

You might say that twenty-five years is a lot longer than twenty-five days, but when you divide either number by the infinity of eternity, you come up with a negligible amount of time that you are afflicted. What seems like forever is zero compared with the blessed eternity that God has prepared for us.

Hold on. Jesus is coming. You will be healed.

Habakkuk 2:2 [NIV]
Write down the revelation and make it plain on tablets so that a herald may run with it. For the revelation awaits an appointed time; it speaks of the end and will not prove false. Though it linger, wait for it; it will certainly come and will not delay.

38. The Herald

When I lived in Indiana, I used to go hunting for morel mushrooms. They are only ripe for a couple weeks in the springtime, and they are elusive. Some days you are blessed to find just one. But it is worth the time for this prize of French cuisine.

My favorite hunting grounds were near the banks of the Tippecanoe River. One day I entered a grove of quaking aspen and my eyes immediately fixed upon a perfectly-camouflaged mushroom poking through the leaf debris. I kept my gaze upon it as I walked forward, knowing that if I looked away I would lose it. As I bent down and put my hand upon the fungal cup, I unfocused my eyes and looked around. Suddenly the forest floor came alive with morels! They were everywhere, staring back at me like the gnomes of an enchanted forest.

There were more morels in that grove than I could possibly eat—there were even too many to carry in my basket. I picked every morel and took the shirt off my back to bundle them up. Then I prepared a special dinner for my friends.

It was a magical moment when I discovered the shire of morels—like the moment of epiphany when one looks through three-dimensional poster-art.

I had that same magical feeling when I began to write this book. God had only de-cloaked the Abomination Timeline (Section 46) when I set out upon this odyssey. I had doubts whether I would be able to make a book out of the little that I knew. But I kept my eyes fixed upon His Word, and wrote down the morsel of information that He had shown me. I asked Him to show me more, even as I was first putting my hand upon the cup of knowledge. Then, suddenly, my mind was opened to a panoply of eschatological truths! Pearls of wisdom were everywhere, staring back at me through history, literature, and Scripture.

> *When the Spirit of truth comes, He will guide you into*
> *all the truth ... He will also declare to you what is to*
> *come. [John 16:13 HCSB]*

There were more truths than I could mentally digest—there were even too many to write down. I bought a digital voice recorder and spoke every idea into it. Then I prepared a special gift for my brethren.

> *Remember me for this, O my God, and do not blot out*
> *what I have so faithfully done for the house of my God*
> *and its services. [Nehemiah 13:14 TNIV]*

~~~~~~~~~~~~~~~~~~~~~~~

My revelations about the End Times are not the result of a prophetic gift. I have had no visions or meaningful dreams, as with the old man I described at the bottom of Section 51. I have written nothing in this book that could not have been discerned by reading the Bible, reading history, walking with God, and employing simple logic and arithmetic.

I do have a gift of the Holy Spirit, but it is not the gift of prophecy (otherwise I would tell you exactly what is going to happen in the coming Tribulation)—it is the gift of discernment. Through no merit of my own, the

Holy Spirit has enabled me to tell the truth about spiritual messages, as well as to recognize spiritual associations in world events.

> *He gives one person the power to perform miracles, and another the ability to prophesy. He gives some- one else the ability to discern whether a message is from the Spirit of God or from another spirit. [1 Corinthians 12:10 NLT]*

Beginning in Section 40, you will read of a number of Biblical time- line markers that narrow to within a few years (i.e., AD 2033–AD 2039) the time when Christ will return and put an end to this world of sin. I expect at least three objections:

Firstly, most Christians erroneously believe that it is impossible to know the year of Jesus' return, and they consider speculation on the year to be taboo. They base this on Jesus' words:

> *No one knows about that day or hour, not even the angels in heaven, nor the Son, but only the Father. [Matthew 24:36 NIV]*

But the only thing that He was warning against is guessing the day or the hour; He said nothing about the year or the decade. I do not know the day or the hour of Christ's return. I am offering a few predictions of the likely year based on Biblical timelines.

In fact, the Old Testament prophets did just as I am now doing to deter- mine the time for the First Coming of the Messiah.

> *The prophets searched very hard and with great care to find out about that salvation. They spoke about the grace that was going to come to you. They wanted to find out when that salvation would come. The Spirit of Christ in them was telling them about the suffer- ings of Christ that were going to come. He was also telling them about the glory that would follow. It was made known to the prophets that they were not serv- ing themselves. Instead, they were serving you when they spoke about the things that you have now heard. [1 Peter 1:10–12 NIrV]*

This searching of the Scriptures and searching for signs was actually recommended by Jesus Christ when He said,

> *Look at the fig tree and all the trees. When they sprout leaves, you can see for yourselves and know that sum-*

mer is near. Even so, when you see these things happening, you know that the kingdom of God is near. [Luke 21:29–31 NIV]

And,

... keep on the alert at all times, praying that you may have strength to escape all these things that are about to take place, and to stand before the Son of Man. [Luke 21:36 NASB]

Likewise, the Apostle John instructed us to cipher the Number of the Beast,

Let him that hath understanding count the number of the beast ... [Revelation 13:18 KJV]

It is the unbelievers that will rationalize away all the prophecies and signs of the Second Coming.

... in the last days scoffers will come, mocking the truth and following their own desires. They will say, "What happened to the promise that Jesus is coming again? From before the times of our ancestors, everything has remained the same since the world was first created." [2 Peter 3:3–4 NLT]

This will be their undoing.

While people are saying, "Peace and safety," destruction will come on them suddenly, as labor pains on a pregnant woman, and they will not escape. [1 Thessalonians 5:3 NIV]

But in the very next verse, the Apostle Paul exhorted Christian believers to not be taken by surprise by the Second Coming of Christ.

***But you, brothers, are not in darkness so that this day should surprise you like a thief.** You are all sons of the light and sons of the day. We do not belong to the night or to the darkness. **So then, let us not be like others, who are asleep,** but let us be alert ... [1 Thessalonians 5:4–6 NIV]*

So for the faithful Christians, the return of their Lord will be a most expected occurrence.

For sure the Lord does not do anything without mak-
ing His plan known to His servants who speak for
Him. [Amos 3:7 NLV]

Secondly, some Christians may be skeptical as to why the explanation of these matters has been made known now—after centuries of fruitless
speculation. It is precisely because the end is so near that the prophecies are
now made clear.

Go your way, Daniel, for the words are shut up and
*sealed **until the time of the end.** [Daniel 12:9 ESV]*

God kept it hidden from earlier peoples so that they would not grow
complacent, but be on their toes.

[He has made] that day unknown to men, that they
may shake off all carnal security, and be always
watchful ... [309]

Remember, the day that people die is the Judgment Day for them—
they are instantaneously transported to the Second Coming of Christ (Section
13). God's purpose has always been to gather souls (Section 4), and He is
using all available means—including keeping us unaware of things that only
required faith until now.

In reading this, then, you will be able to understand
my insight into the mystery of Christ, which was not
made known to men in other generations as it has now
been revealed by the Spirit ... [Ephesians 3:4–5 NIV]

Thirdly, if I were you, I would wonder why the mystery has been
revealed to me, of all people. There has previously been some vague speculation and tip-toeing around the truth concerning the Antichrist Beast. For
example,

- Maximus the Confessor identified the Arabs as
  Apocalyptic Beasts when they first invaded the
  Eastern Roman Empire in AD 632;[310]
- Patriarch Sophronius said that the Abomination
  of Desolation was in the holy place when he sur-
  rendered Jerusalem to Caliph Umar and the future
  Caliph Ali in AD 637;[311]
- Pope Innocent III associated Muhammad with the
  Son of Perdition when he summoned the fifth cru-
  sade in AD 1213;[312]

- when the last remnant of the Roman Empire was conquered by the Ottoman Caliphate in AD 1453, the citizens of Constantinople reminded themselves of the prophecies concerning the coming of the Antichrist;[313]
- Peter the Venerable (AD 1092–AD 1156), who ordered the translation of the Qur'an into Latin, regarded Muhammad as the precursor of the Antichrist and the successor of Arius;[314]
- some early Protestants speculated that the Turks were the Antichrist when they threatened Vienna in the sixteenth century;[315]
- a French philosopher has recently noted, "Jesus is a master of love, Muhammad a master of hate."[316]

But apart from this, Christian authors have had the good sense not to speculate about unclear End Times passages in Scripture (except for the glaring example of the Dispensationalists).

Thus, no eschatological construct has developed around the idea that Islam is the antithesis to Christianity. I am the first person to clearly explain how it is that the Arab Caliphate is the Sea Beast (Section 20), the Turkish Caliphate is the Land Beast (Section 25), and Ali is the Son of Perdition (Section 22). I have also unveiled the Mark of the Beast (Section 24), the Number of the Beast (Section 23), the Fall of Babylon the Great (Section 35), and the False Prophet (Section 87). And I have found eleven intersecting timelines in the Holy Scriptures for the Second Coming of Christ (Sections 40–49, 71).

Should I say it? Is it necessary for me to say it? Okay, I will say it …

Whilst the Dispensational Premillennialists have been dreaming of a new Jewish temple, and the rapture of naked Born Agains, and a myriad of other sugarplum fairies, I have been worshiping God in Spirit and in truth, and studying the Bible, and employing reasoned thought. If you have bought into any of the Dispensationalists' End Times twaddle (Section 27), you should be ashamed of yourself, and repent, and consider my work judiciously. In other words, stop being wicked children, and take on wisdom—even the wisdom of this book.

It was foretold that wise people would understand the prophecy near the end of human history.

> *None of the sinful will understand, but those who are wise will understand. [Daniel 12:10 NLV]*

But how did I become wise enough to see this much of the picture?

I will tell you: I repented of my sins in the name of Jesus Christ. I repented, and I repented, and I repented.

> *... because your heart was penitent ... I also have heard you ... [2 Kings 22:19 ESV]*

I ate the Lord's body and drank His blood. I made it my hobby to read the Bible, and then to read reliable books about the Bible. I did not approach God with pride or preconception. Rather, I emptied myself until God was finally able to utilize the natural gifts that He had given me for observation, logic, and writing.

> *This is in writing because His hand was upon me. He helped me to know all the plan. [1 Chronicles 28:19 NLV]*

I became weak physically, emotionally, and financially; I felt the devil's breath against the base of my throat; I became vulnerable for the sake of my God.

> *And He said to me, "My grace is sufficient for you, for My strength is made perfect in weakness." Therefore most gladly I will rather boast in my infirmities, that the power of Christ may rest upon me. [2 Corinthians 12:9 NIV]*

If I had not sought God, my gifts would have been given over to vain pursuits, and I would be nothing more than a negativist. But God has promised to be a,

> *... rewarder of those who diligently seek Him. [Hebrews 11:6 NKJV]*

So it was that I diligently sought God, and He esteemed me to become the Herald of the Second Coming of Christ.

> *Daniel, you who are highly esteemed, consider carefully the words I am about to speak to you ... Do not be afraid, Daniel. Since the first day that you set your mind to gain understanding and to humble yourself before your God, your words were heard, and I have come in response to them. [Daniel 10:11–12 NIV]*

I have made the revelation plain, and have run with it. Now is the appointed time, Faithful Christian. There will be an end to evil; it will certainly come and will not delay.

Matthew 22:2 [TNIV]
The kingdom of heaven is like a king who prepared a wedding banquet for his
son.

39. Christians are Expectant People

A few years ago I was invited to a college roommate's wedding at a resort on the coast of Oregon. The out-of-town guests stayed in bungalows near the ocean. I was in the wedding party, so I was registered in the central building. It had a common area with a large fireplace.

On the afternoon of the wedding, I finished reading the newspaper and decided to make a fire with it. As I struck the match, the bride and her mother came in to prepare for the ceremony. They went into the bride's quarters and the mother began to brush her daughter's golden hair. They left the door open a crack and talked softly. I stayed in the common area just long enough to ensure that the fire was safe and would stay lit. Then I went outside to give them privacy.

As I quietly exited, I overheard the bride say, "You know, Mummy, I never thought that a man would come along who would actually choose to marry ... *me* ..."

They were married that very sunset, in a picture-perfect ceremony on the Pacific seashore.

She made a lovely bride, but she had a poor self-image. She thought that she had a horse face, and doubted that she would be chosen for marriage. Every woman that is reading this knows that anxiety.

Then, a good man came along, and gave her his name ... and then he gave her three beautiful children. She was chosen after all.

Dear Christian reader, allow me to assure you of something: you have been chosen by Jesus Christ—the only truly good man ever to live—to be a part of the Holy Conglomerate that is His Bride, the Church. He desires her hand in marriage. He wants to make an honest woman out of her, horse face and all.

> *I made you. I am now your husband. My name is The*
> *Lord Who Rules Over All. I am the Holy One of Israel.*
> *I have set you free. I am the God of the whole earth.*
> *[Isaiah 54:5 NIrV]*

Each Christian is a minute part of the Bride. As a healthy, normal, Christian man, I cannot identify with that role.

> *Do not lie with a man as one lies with a woman; that*
> *is detestable. [Leviticus 18:22 NIV]*

It may be that I am destined to be a eukaryotic cell in one of the Church's functional organs—her duodenum, or peritoneum, or sacroiliac. A man that donates a kidney to a female transplant recipient does not consider his kidney to have become homosexual.

I am being facetious, of course. Surely the Lord will have a purely platonic bond with the males within the Church. David said of close friend, Jonathan,

> *Your love to me was wonderful, surpassing the love of*
> *women. [2 Samuel 1:26 NKJV]*

Whatever the case, I am honored to be a minute constituent of the Body that the manly man, Jesus, will soon possess and ravish. That Union in Heaven will be more harmonious and full of ecstasy than any wedding night bliss of a good groomsman and his virgin bride.

> *You will be a crown of splendor in the Lord's hand, a*
> *royal diadem in the hand of your God ... As a young*
> *man marries a young woman, so will your Builder*
> *marry you; as a bridegroom rejoices over his bride, so*
> *will your God rejoice over you. [Isaiah 62:3,5 TNIV]*

There is an entire book in the Bible, the Song of Songs, that is dedicated to the heated lovemaking that will take place between Christ and His Bride, the Church. The Apostle Paul commented upon this scriptural allegory:

> *Husbands, love your wives, just as Christ also loved*
> *the church and gave Himself for her, that He might*
> *sanctify and cleanse her with the washing of water*
> *by the word, that He might present her to Himself a*
> *glorious church, not having spot or wrinkle or any*
> *such thing, but that she should be holy and without*
> *blemish. So husbands ought to love their own wives as*
> *their own bodies; he who loves his wife loves himself.*
> *For no one ever hated his own flesh, but nourishes*
> *and cherishes it, just as the Lord does the church. For*
> *we are members of His body, of His flesh and of His*
> *bones. [Ephesians 5:25–30 NKJV]*

We were betrothed to Christ when He ascended to Heaven at the close of the fourth millennium. He went to prepare a place for His beloved in the Father's house.

> *There is more than enough room in my Father's home.*
> *If this were not so, would I have told you that I am*
> *going to prepare a place for you? When everything*

> *is ready,* ***I will come and get you****, so that you will*
> *always be with me where I am. [John 14:2–3 NLT]*

Christ also sent the Holy Spirit to create the Christian Church on Pentecost. Then, at the close of the fifth millennium (i.e., about one thousand years ago), He sanctified us so that we were worshipping properly with three Ecumenical Creeds (i.e., Apostles', Athanasian, and Nicene with the Filioque). Since that time He has cleansed us "with the washing of water by the word." He has waited this long for our benefit—that we might be "holy and without blemish."

> *I saw the Holy City, the new Jerusalem, coming down*
> *out of heaven from God, prepared as a bride beau-*
> *tifully dressed for her husband. [Revelation 21:2*
> *TNIV]*

The sixth millennium is about to close. It will close within our life-times. The time of the two thousand year engagement is over. There will not be another million years—there will not be another thousand years. Jesus Christ is a man of His word.

It is time. It is time for the marriage ceremony. It is time for the con-summation. Christ will wait no longer. He comes for His own—to take what is rightfully His. No one will deny the Groomsman His beloved Bride.

~~~~~~~~~~~~~~~~~~~~~~~

Again, there remains the question of what, specifically, the Church is expect-ing from Christ after He return for us collectively. Let us not evade the issue.

> *As the Scriptures say, "A man leaves his father and*
> *mother and is joined to his wife, and the two are*
> *united into one." This is a great mystery, but it is an*
> *illustration of the way Christ and the church are one.*
> *[Ephesians 5:31–32 NLT]*

A bride expects vaginal intercourse on her wedding night. What of the Church? Will the collection of believers have vaginal intercourse with the Resurrected Jesus when He returns for His Bride?

I think not. One could use one's imagination and think of the mil-lions of members of the Church swarming together to form one Body, as in a movie—the female members taking up position as skin, nerves, and female organs (I assume there will be more women in Heaven than men, given church attendance figures). And one could envision such a Body having carnal rela-tions with its Lord in Heaven. But this is too simplistic and three-dimensional to be true.

The Holy Scriptures suggest that the Union will be an intimacy for which joyous marital sex is only a foreshadowing.

> *I am my lover's,*
> > *and he claims me as his own.*
>
> *Come, my love, let us go out to the fields*
> > *and spend the night among the wildflowers.*
>
> *Let us get up early and go to the vineyards*
> > *to see if the grapevines have budded,*
> > *if the blossoms have opened,*
> > *and if the pomegranates have bloomed.*
>
> *There I will give you my love.*
> *There the mandrakes give off their fragrance,*
> > *and the finest fruits are at our door,*
> > *new delights as well as old,*
> > *which I have saved for you, my lover.*
>
> *[Song of Songs 7:10–13 NLT]*

Imagine such frolicking, except throughout the entire universe—and with the Lover being the very Prince of all things!

> *Then God will rejoice over you as a bridegroom rejoices over his bride. [Isaiah 62:5 NLT]*

It is a mistake to think of the Risen Christ as being constrained by our physics—sexual and otherwise. The Apostle Paul tells us,

> *God has put all things under the authority of Christ and has made him head over all things for the benefit of the church. And the church is his body; it is made full and complete by Christ, **who fills all things everywhere with himself**. [Ephesians 1:22–23 NLT]*

Remember that when the Deacon Stephen was about to be stoned, he,

> *… looked up to heaven and saw the glory of God, and Jesus standing at the right hand of God. "Look," he said, "I see heaven open and the Son of Man standing at the right hand of God." [Acts 7:55–56 NIV]*

Now, if the Risen Christ had the same physical frame as when He walked among us, He would have been no larger than a flea from Stephen's earthly viewpoint. But Stephen was clearly conveying that Christ was discernable at a great distance.

For this reason, one of the early Protestant confessions states,

*[The resurrected body of Christ exists in an] incomprehensible, spiritual mode [of presence], according to which He neither occupies nor vacates space, **but penetrates all creatures wherever He pleases (according to His most free will)**; as, to make an imperfect comparison, my sight penetrates and is in air, light, or water, and does not occupy or vacate space; as a sound or tone penetrates and is in air or water or board and wall, and also does not occupy or vacate space; likewise, as light and heat penetrate and are in air, water, glass, crystal, and the like, and also do not vacate or occupy space ... [Jesus employed this mode of presence] when He rose from the closed (and sealed) sepulcher, and passed through the closed door (to His disciples), and in the bread and wine in the Holy Supper ... **[it follows that in heaven] all creatures must be far more penetrable and present to Him than they are [now].** For if, [at this time,] He can be in and with creatures in such a manner that they do not feel, touch, circumscribe, or comprehend Him, **how much more wonderfully will He be in all creatures according to this sublime ... mode**, so that they do not [merely] circumscribe nor comprehend Him, but rather that He has them present before Himself ...* [317]

Sublime? Sublime, indeed.

~~~~~~~~~~~~~~~~~~~~~~~

Again, I do not know the day or the hour when this consummation will take place—that is impossible. I do not even know the year of the nuptials, for sure. I am, however, on the watch for the invitation.

> ***Therefore keep watch**, because you do not know on what day your Lord will come. [Matthew 24:42 TNIV]*

By being on the watch I have come to know the time period of the Second Coming plus or minus a few years; God has revealed to me that the Resurrected Christ will return bodily to earth between AD 2033 and AD 2039. The scriptural timelines that show this are outlined in the next ten sections, and also in Section 71.

My revelation is not as uncommon as it might, at first, seem. There are Christians all around the globe that know what I know (see Section 51). They might not have all the Biblical timelines that I have—they may have others that have not yet occurred to me. But I'm by no means the only Christian believer that is expecting the end within a generation. In the pages of this book I am simply affirming what others already sense and anticipate.

Christians are expectant people. When we pray, we expect an answer. And when the Bible promises something, we know that it is a sure promise. The Bible says that we are not spiritual bastards, but that we have a Father in Heaven. The Bible says that God would be humbly borne into the world on a specific calendar date, and it says that He would return for us as a King on a specific calendar date. The Bible says that there would be signs—obvious signs—that would accompany both events. Therefore, we tend to have our eyes on the sky, in anticipation of His bodily return. Jesus Christ predicted,

> *There will be signs in the sun, moon and stars. On the earth, nations will be in anguish and perplexity at the roaring and tossing of the sea. Men will faint from terror, apprehensive of what is coming on the world, for the heavenly bodies will be shaken. [Luke 21:25–26 NIV]*

The purpose of these signs is not to scare us, but to prepare us.

The believers at the time of Jesus' birth were also expectant, upward-looking, people. Based upon the Holy Scriptures, and upon personal revelations, some of them knew that the Messiah would appear soon. King David wrote,

> *The Lord confides in those who fear him; he makes his covenant known to them. [Psalm 25:14 TNIV]*

Two old Jewish prophets sat in the Second Temple in Jerusalem at the time of the Incarnation because it had been revealed to them that they would see the Christ Child before they died (Luke 2:25–38). Likewise, non-Jewish Magi traveled from Persia to Judea because it had been revealed to them that God would become a man (Matthew 2:1–12).

The believing people were not disappointed in 6 BC[318] when God became a baby boy, right on schedule.

> *Everyone was expecting the Messiah to come soon, and they were eager … [Luke 3:15 NLT]*

They were not disappointed in AD 30[319] when the man, Jesus, conquered sin, death and every power of the devil, right on schedule.

We who believe in these last days shall not be disappointed between the years AD 2033 and AD 2039, when He returns as a King, right on schedule.

> *At that time they will see the Son of Man coming in a cloud with power and great glory. When these things begin to take place, stand up and lift up your heads, because your redemption is drawing near. [Luke 21:27–28 NIV]*

Christ has died! Christ is risen! Christ will come again!
Alleluia to the Lamb of God!

Daniel 7:23–25 [NKJV]
The fourth beast shall be a fourth kingdom on earth, which shall be different from all other kingdoms, and shall devour the whole earth, trample it and break it in pieces. The ten horns are ten kings who shall arise from this kingdom. And another shall rise after them; He shall be different from the first ones, and shall subdue three kings. He shall speak pompous words against the Most High, shall persecute the saints of the Most High, and shall intend to change times and law. Then the saints shall be given into his hand for a time and times and half a time.

40. The Handover Timeline

The fourth Beast in the passage given above is the Roman Empire—all biblical scholars are agreed upon that interpretation. I have already demonstrated that the horn that arose after the breakup of the Roman Empire is the Arab Empire, or Caliphate (Sections 19–20). The three kings that it subdued were the remnants of the three kingdoms that preceded the Romans: the Babylonian, Medo–Persian, and Grecian lands all became Muslim lands (Daniel 7:8). The Arab Caliphate was the one that was "different from the first ones" and that spoke "pompous words against the Most High". They also persecuted the saints, changed the dating system and the day of the Sabbath, and changed the laws of God (Daniel 7:25; Section 29).

What interests me here is the prediction that the saints shall be handed over to him for "a time and times and half a time." This was an ancient way of saying three and a half times. But how long is the three and a half times? I think it is a different length of time from when the same phrase is used in

Revelation 12:14 (see Section 31). But if that is so, then what is the period of each 'time' in this case?

There is an axiom within the field of systematic theology that "Scripture interprets Scripture." When trying to understand an obscure or difficult passage, one must go back to a pertinent episode or lesson for a point of reference. In this verse, the clue for a point of reference is the phrase, "given into his hand." This is a flashback to the time when the people of Israel lived as strangers in Canaan, and later as slaves in Goshen, Egypt.

That period began when Abraham's second son, Isaac, was persecuted by his first son, Ishmael, in 1862 BC.[320] It ended with the Exodus under Moses in 1462 BC.[321] God had earlier informed Abraham that it would last for these four hundred years:[ix]

> *Your children who live after you will be strangers*
> *in a country that does not belong to them. They will*
> *become slaves. They will be treated badly for 400*
> *years. [Genesis 15:13 NIrV]*

The Apostle Paul makes an analogy between Isaac's childhood situation and that of Christian believers:

> *Brothers and sisters, you are children because of*
> *God's promise just as Isaac was. At that time, the*
> *son born in the usual way tried to hurt the son born*
> *by the power of the Holy Spirit. It is the same now.*
> *[Galatians 4:28–29 NIrV]*

The time of the handover of the Christian saints in Daniel 7, then, is three and a half oppression periods of four hundred years, or fourteen hundred years. The believers within the small horn's realm will be oppressed for fourteen hundred years. During that time, the small horn will speak pompous words against the Most High. But fourteen hundred years from what starting point?

The watershed moment in Arab expansion was their overwhelming victory at the Battle of Yarmuk in AD 636.[322] From that moment on, antichrist peoples have had military and political power over the Christians of the Levant

---

ix   Elsewhere the Bible records, *"... the people of Israel had lived in Egypt [and Canaan] for 430 years." [Exodus 12:40 NLT]* But this refers to the period from when Abraham buried his father in Haran (1892 BC) and entered Canaan until the Exodus. The period of persecution refers to his son, Isaac, and Isaac's descendants through Jacob, and is therefore thirty years shorter. Also, the Apostle Paul says *"All this took about 450 years." [Acts 13:20 NIV]*, but he is including the forty years of wandering in the desert as well as Joshua's subsequent conquest of Canaan.

(except for brief respites during the Crusades, and British and French coloni-zation). Although the Caliphate ended more than eighty-five years ago, non-Christian peoples (both Muslims and Jews) have subsequently ruled, and used their civil authority as it suited their interest.

Daniel 7:25 predicts that this state-of-affairs will come to an end four-teen hundred years after the time when the saints were first handed-over. This points to the Second Coming in the year AD 2036.

Ezekiel 35:10–13 [ESV]
Because you said, 'These two nations and these two countries shall be mine, and we will take possession of them'—although the Lord was there—therefore, as I live, declares the Lord God, I will deal with you according to the anger and envy that you showed because of your hatred against them. And I will make myself known among them, when I judge you. And you shall know that I am the Lord. I have heard all the revilings that you uttered against the moun-tains of Israel, saying, 'They are laid desolate; they are given us to devour.' And you magnified yourselves against me with your mouth, and multiplied your words against me; I heard it.

41. The Conquest Timeline

When Jerusalem was destroyed by the Babylonian Empire in 586 BC,[323] their Edomite neighbors to the south swept in to plunder the city. They were the descendants of the Patriarch Jacob's malevolent twin brother, Esau.

Edom was the longtime enemy of Jacob's descendants, Israel. We are told in Scripture,

> *Jacob I have loved, but Esau I have hated. [Romans*
> *9:13 NKJV]*

Esau was an outdoorsman, a hunter, and a person that looked after his appetites for food and sex and fun. But Esau had no time or regard for God. He did not give God a moment's consideration, even though he was the son of the Patriarch Isaac and the grandson of the Patriarch Abraham. He knew the great ways that God had revealed Himself to them, and he thought it trivial and womanish. God hates that indifference.

Jacob, though a man of many faults, earnestly sought the God of Abraham. God loves that interest.

Therefore, God renamed the man that He loved, 'Israel,' which means, 'He who strives with God' (Genesis 32:28; see the dedication of this book).

In the verses heading this section, God was angry with the descendants of Esau because they rejoiced to see the descendants of Israel come to ruination.

> *O Lord, remember what the Edomites did on the day the armies of Babylon captured Jerusalem. "Destroy it!" they yelled. "Level it to the ground!" [Psalm 137:7 NLT]*

God had allowed devastation to come upon the Jews because of their sin of idolatry, but the Edomites had nothing against idolatry. They were simply happy to be rid of their neighbors—some of whom had faith that the God of Abraham, Isaac, and Jacob would become a man someday. The Edomites took advantage of God's purifying action, and then boasted against the Almighty.

God saw the Edomites' cruelty, and heard their words against Him, and promised to bring judgment upon them.

> *You should not have plundered the land of Israel when they were suffering such calamity. You should not have gloated over their destruction ... You should not have stood at the crossroads, killing those who tried to escape ... The day is near when I, the Lord, will judge all godless nations! As you have done to Israel, so it will be done to you. All your evil deeds will fall back on your own heads ... Just as you swallowed up my people on my holy mountain, so you and the surrounding nations will swallow the punishment I pour out on you. Yes, all you nations will drink and stagger and disappear from history ... There will be no survivors in Edom. I, the Lord, have spoken! [Obadiah 13–16,18 NLT]*

And God did, in fact, judge Edom and completely eliminated them as a people from the face of the earth.

> *... I have turned his mountains into a wasteland and left his inheritance to the desert jackals. [Malachi 1:3 NIV]*

That was a foreshadowing of what will happen to the ungodly on the Judgment Day.

~~~~~~~~~~~~~~~~~~~~~~~

In Scripture, Edom is often associated with all people that hate God and rejoice to see the saints' lands no longer be a suitable place for them to reside. Again, in the writings of the Prophet Isaiah, the judgment against Edom is a foreshadowing of God's ultimate judgment upon the ungodly. Isaiah had a vision of the pre–incarnate Christ emerging victorious from battle in Edom:

> *Who is this man coming from the city of Bozrah in Edom? His clothes are stained bright red. Who is he? He is dressed up in all of his glory. He is marching toward us with great strength. The Lord answers, "It is I. I have won the battle. I am mighty. I have saved my people." Why are your clothes red? They look as if you have been stomping on grapes in a winepress. The Lord answers, "I have been stomping on the nations as if they were grapes. No one was there to help me. I walked all over the nations because I was angry. That is why I stomped on them. Their blood splashed all over my clothes. So my clothes were stained bright red. I decided it was time to pay Israel's enemies back. The year for me to set my people free had come."* [Isaiah 63:1–4 NIrV]

And once again, God spoke through Isaiah about the finality and totality of the judgment upon Edom and all the ungodly:

> *Come near, you nations, to hear; And heed, you people! Let the earth hear, and all that is in it, the world and all things that come forth from it. **For the indignation of the Lord is against all nations, and His fury against all their armies**; He has utterly destroyed them ... All the host of heaven shall be dissolved, and the heavens shall be rolled up like a scroll ... My sword shall be bathed in heaven; Indeed it shall come down on Edom, And on the people of My curse, for judgment ... For it is the day of the Lord's vengeance, the year of recompense for the cause of Zion.* [Isaiah 34:1–2,4–5,8 NKJV]

We have already discussed that in the Prophet Daniel's dream of four beasts (Daniel 7; Sections 19–20), the first one represents the Babylonian Empire and the fourth one represents the Roman Empire. The 'Little Horn' that arose later to conquer [the eastern] part of the Roman Empire represents the Caliphate (Sections 19–20).

The first beast (i.e., Babylon) completed its conquest of Zion (i.e., the people that believed that God would become a man in Christ) in 586 BC[324] when Jerusalem fell. The 'Little Horn,' or Islamic Caliphate, may be thought of as a fifth beast (remember, five is the number of the devil—see Section 24). And this fifth beast completed its most expansive conquest of Zion (i.e., the people that believed that God became a man in Christ) in AD 1453 when Constantinople fell to the Ottomans.[325]

I have, in the past, wondered why Constantinople fell in AD 1453. It had been surrounded and attacked previously many times, but always the city stayed in Christian hands. When it finally fell to the forces of Islam, the western nations could hardly believe that the last vestige of the Roman Empire was finally extinguished.[326]

The Ottoman Turks had a tradition that their Judgment Day (one that would ostensibly vindicate them) would not occur until Islam was imposed upon the great Christian capital of Constantinople.[327] After its victory, the Caliphate (i.e., the Little Horn) spoke boastfully against Almighty God. Daniel tells us about its ultimate end,

> *... I continued to watch because of the boastful words the horn was speaking. I kept looking until the beast was slain and its body destroyed ... and there before me was one like a son of man, coming with the clouds of heaven. [Daniel 7:11–13 NIV]*

~~~~~~~~~~~~~~~~~~~~~~~~

God has promised to make Himself known though a,

> *... year of recompense for the cause of Zion. [Isaiah 34:8 ESV]*

Those that believe that God became man in Jesus Christ constitute Zion. For our sake, God will come and dispatch evil once and for all.

> *I looked, and there before me was a white horse! Its rider held a bow, and he was given a crown, and he rode out as a conqueror bent on conquest. [Revelation 6:2 NIV]*

There will be no survivors among those that reject God's salvation. The Lord has spoken.

I here hypothesize that the duration between Jesus' joyous incarnation and Jesus' glorious return will be the same as that between the fall of Jerusalem to the Babylonians (in 586 BC)[328] and the fall of Constantinople to the Caliphate (in AD 1453).[329] The time period between these two cataclysmic events in the lives of God's people is 2,038 years.

There is another amazing historical reinforcement of this timeline: just as the rebuilding of the Temple in Jerusalem occurred seventy years after Jerusalem's fall, so also Martin Luther (AD 1483–AD 1546) reformed the order of Christian worship seventy years after Constantinople's fall.[330] This is demonstrated in Table 5, where each row represents a span of 2,038 years.

Since Christ became incarnate in 6 BC,[331] this parallel would put His return for judgment upon the ungodly at AD 2033.

Table 5. The Conquest Parallel

Prelude to Christ's First Coming	Date	Cumul. Duration	Date	Prelude to Christ's Second Coming
Fall of Jerusalem to the Babylonians	586 BC[332]	—	AD 1453[333]	Fall of Constantinople to the Ottomans
Rebuilding of the Jerusalem Temple	516 BC[334]	70 years	AD 1523[335]	Reformation of the order of Christian worship
Incarnation as Baby	6 BC[336]	580 years	AD 2033*	Return as King

* Calculated from the columns on the left.

Jonah 3:2 [NKJV]
Arise, go to Nineveh, that great city, and preach to it the message that I tell
you.

42. The Jonahic Timeline

King Tiglath-Pileser was the founder of the Assyrian Empire. He subjugated the Babylonians and the Hittites, and extended his empire throughout Cappadocia, Cilicia, Syria, and Phoenicia. His influence extended from the Persian Gulf to the Black Sea to the Mediterranean Sea. He reached the zenith of his evil power in 1076 BC, the year of his death.[337]

Some people will argue that my date for the beginning of the Assyrian Empire is arbitrary. Of course, there were Assyrian kings before Tiglath-Pileser.[338] But he was the ruler that began their bloodthirsty expansionism, and in 1076 BC he incurred the just penalty for his wicked ways—just as Adam and Eve spiritually died in 3975 BC for their sin.[339]

For the wages of sin is death ... [Romans 6:23 TNIV]

Over the following three centuries the Assyrians ravaged their neighbors and grew wealthy off the plunder. Then, in 767 BC,[340] God instructed the Prophet Jonah to preach against the Assyrian capital, Nineveh. God planned to destroy it, saying,

> *Announce my judgment against it because I have seen*
> *how wicked its people are. [Jonah 1:2 NLT]*

At first, Jonah fled from God toward modern day Spain—as far away as he could get from Nineveh. But his ship was caught in a fierce storm, and he found himself in the sea, and a great fish swallowed him whole. With his skin being burned by the fish's digestive acids, and his mouth pressed against a tear in the fish's air bladder, he prayed to the One and Only God,

> *In my distress I called to the Lord, and he answered*
> *me. From deep in the realm of the dead I called for*
> *help, and you listened to my cry. You hurled me into*
> *the deep, into the very heart of the seas, and the cur-*
> *rents swirled about me; all your waves and breakers*
> *swept over me. I said, 'I have been banished from your*
> *sight; yet I will look again toward your holy temple.'*
> *The engulfing waters threatened me, the deep sur-*
> *rounded me; seaweed was wrapped around my head.*
> *To the roots of the mountains I sank down; the earth*

beneath barred me in forever. But you, Lord my God, brought my life up from the pit. When my life was ebbing away, I remembered you, Lord, and my prayer rose to you, to your holy temple. Those who cling to worthless idols forfeit God's love for them. But I, with shouts of grateful praise, will sacrifice to you. What I have vowed I will make good. I will say, 'Salvation comes from the Lord.' [Jonah 2:2–9 TNIV]

So it was that Jonah's irritation of the fish's internal organs resulted in ichthyological nausea, and God made the leviathan vomit Jonah onto a beach in the eastern Mediterranean. The prophet found his way to Nineveh, and boldly marched throughout the city proclaiming,

Forty days from now, Nineveh will be destroyed! [Jonah 3:4 CEV]

For an unknown reason, rather than lynching the prophet, both the people and the king of Assyria immediately responded to his message.

The people of Nineveh believed God's message, and from the greatest to the least, they declared a fast and put on burlap to show their sorrow. When the king of Nineveh heard what Jonah was saying, he stepped down from his throne and took off his royal robes. He dressed himself in burlap and sat on a heap of ashes. Then the king and his nobles sent this decree throughout the city: "No one, not even the animals from your herds and flocks, may eat or drink anything at all. People and animals alike must wear garments of mourning, and everyone must pray earnestly to God. They must turn from their evil ways and stop all their violence. Who can tell? Perhaps even yet God will change his mind and hold back his fierce anger from destroying us." [Jonah 3:5–9 NLT]

So God relented and did not destroy the city during the time of Jonah.

The Ninevites' repentance did not last long, though, and over the next hundred and fifty years they went back to their ways of robbing, enslaving, and heinously murdering. They conquered the Kingdom of Israel in 721 BC,[341] and carried the ten northern tribes into oblivion.

Finally, in 612 BC,[342] the emergent Babylonian Empire conquered and destroyed Nineveh, and the Assyrian Empire forever ceased to exist.

~~~~~~~~~~~~~~~~~~~~~~~

Jonah was an Old Testament prophet from Galilee, the same region as Jesus Christ. In the year AD 28,[343] Jesus taught that Jonah's time inside the fish would be analogous to His own time inside the tomb.

> *This evil generation keeps asking me to show them a miraculous sign. But the only sign I will give them is the sign of Jonah. What happened to him was a sign to the people of Nineveh that God had sent him. What happens to the Son of Man will be a sign to these people that he was sent by God. [Luke 11:29–30 NLT]*

Jesus also taught that Jonah's warning to the Ninevites was analogous to His own warning to unbelievers.

> *The people of Nineveh will stand up against this generation on judgment day and condemn it, for they repented of their sins at the preaching of Jonah. Now someone greater than Jonah is here—but you refuse to repent. [Matthew 12:41 NLT]*

And after predicting the destruction of Assyria, the Prophet Isaiah added,

> *This is the plan prepared for the whole earth ... [Isaiah 14:26 HCSB]*

I here suggest that the end of the world can be predicted through the simple algebra (1:13 ratio) of the Jonah/Jesus analogy. The table below demonstrates the method.

Table 6. The Jonahic Insular Allegory

Evil Force	Began	1st Interval	Warned	2nd Interval	Ended
Assyrian Empire	1076 BC [344]	309 yrs	767 BC [345]	155 yrs	612 BC [346]
Fallen World	3975 BC [347]	4001 yrs	AD 28 [348]	(X - 28) yrs	X

If Jonah is a type for Christ, then it follows that the occasion of his ministry to the Assyrian Empire would correspond to the occasion of Christ's ministry to the fallen world. The ratio of the first interval to the second interval in the Assyrian Empire row of this table is 309/155 or 1.9935484.

Solving for the End of the Fallen World, **X**, in the second row,

$$4001/(\mathbf{X} - 28) = 1.9935484$$

$$\mathbf{X} - 28 = 2006.9741$$

$$\mathbf{X} = 2034.9741$$

I round the year up to AD 2035.

According to this timeline and Christ's own words, the repentant Ninevites of 767 BC will rise from the grave in the year AD 2035 and condemn the people that reject the Gospel message.

I very much look forward to that spectacle. It will occur across the Tigris River from the modern day city of Mosul, Iraq.[349] The dust of tens of thousands of ancient Assyrians will be reanimated into incorruptible human flesh on that day, and those resurrected people will stand in judgment against their terrified, twenty-first century, Muslim descendants.

> *The Lord took hold of me, and I was carried away*
> *by the Spirit of the Lord to a valley filled with bones*
> *... Suddenly as I spoke, there was a rattling noise*
> *all across the valley. The bones of each body came*
> *together and attached themselves as complete skel-*
> *etons. Then as I watched, muscles and flesh formed*
> *over the bones. Then skin formed to cover their bod-*
> *ies ... and breath came into their bodies. [Ezekiel*
> *37:1,7–8,10 NLT]*

Language differences will not be an issue on the Judgment Day, and there will be no answers to their questions, "How could you not heed the Son of God's message of repentance? How could you despise His exculpatory sacrifice for your sins? By what recompense will your Allah save you from the wrath of the Triune God? See, here is Christ in the flesh with His legions of angels following! Prepare for justice to be administered!"

Mark 12:26–27 [NLT]
... as to whether the dead will be raised—haven't you ever read about this in
the writings of Moses, in the story of the burning bush? Long after Abraham,
Isaac, and Jacob had died, God said to Moses, 'I am the God of Abraham,
the God of Isaac, and the God of Jacob.' So he is the God of the living, not the
dead.

43. The Mosaic Timeline

An algebraic methodology may also be applied to the events in the life of
Moses. I had always found it curious that Moses' life story was set into three
periods of roughly forty years. Now, I see that the Lord intended Moses' tra-
vails as a mid–story synopsis of the entire salvation plan.

> *For the law was given by Moses, but grace and truth*
> *came by Jesus Christ. [John 1:17 KJV]*

Moses was born in 1543 BC[350] to Levite parents during the Children of
Israel's sojourn in Egypt. By that time Pharaoh had become wary of the growing minority in his midst. He ordered the people of Israel into enslavement,
and decreed that their male offspring be killed (Exodus 1:22).

Moses' mother hid him for three months after his birth. When she
could no longer hide him, she made a waterproof basket and set the baby
afloat in the shallows of the Nile River. God arranged for Pharaoh's daughter
to come to that portion of the river to bathe, to discover the baby Moses, and
to bond with him. Moses' precocious sister, Miriam, was watching this serendipitous encounter and stepped forward to volunteer a Hebrew wet nurse for
the Egyptian princess' new baby. The princess agreed, and offered a salary if a
suitable candidate could be found. In this way, Moses' mother was allowed to
safely take her son home until he was weaned (Exodus 2:2–9).

In biblical times children were nursed for two to three years.[351] But the
princess must have been eager to get her adopted boy back, so for the purposes
of this timeline I will assume that Moses was nursed for just under sixteen
months, and entered the royal palace in the year 1541.7 BC[352] (Exodus 2:10).

This is significant because the Bible tells us that it was forty years after
he was given to the princess that Moses took an interest in his humble roots.

> *... the daughter of Pharaoh took him up, and did rear*
> *him to herself for a son; Moses was taught in all wis-*
> *dom of the Egyptians, and he was powerful in words*
> *and in works. And when forty years were fulfilled to*

him, it came upon his heart to look after his brethren,
the sons of Israel ... [Acts 7:21–23 YLT]

While inspecting the Hebrew labor camp, in 1501.7 BC,[353] Moses saw an Egyptian slave master abusing one of his blood-brethren. Thinking there were no witnesses, Moses killed the Egyptian and buried his body (Exodus 2:11–12).

The next day it became apparent that the deed was known, and that Moses was a wanted man. To save his life, Moses fled eastward—to a land outside of Egyptian control. There, at the age of forty-one, he married the daughter of a local priest and sheepherder (Exodus 2:21).

Thirty-nine years later God decided to deliver the people of Israel from their bondage. He called Moses to lead His Chosen People out of bondage in Egypt:

I have surely seen the affliction of my people who are
in Egypt and have heard their cry because of their
taskmasters. I know their sufferings, and I have come
down to deliver them out of the hand of the Egyptians
and to bring them up out of that land to a good and
broad land, a land flowing with milk and honey ...
[Exodus 3:7–8 ESV]

We know that the year that God called Moses out of exile to be His representative to Pharaoh was 1463 BC,[354] for,

At the time, Moses was eighty years old ... [Exodus
7:6 CEV]

By God's powerful hand, Moses was successful in leading the people of Israel across the Red Sea, and to Mount Sinai where he,

... received life-giving words to pass on to us. [Acts
7:38 NLT]

Unfortunately, the people of Israel balked at God's guidance and provision, and they were cursed to wander in the desert for forty years. God said that the adults that were led out of Egypt would not enter the Promised Land.

... not one of the men who saw my glory and the mirac-
ulous signs I performed in Egypt and in the desert but
who disobeyed me and tested me ten times—not one of
them will ever see the land I promised on oath to their
forefathers. [Numbers 14:22–23 NIV]

Then, when Moses was one hundred and twenty years old, he led the next generation of Israel's children to the edge of the Promised Land and blessed them.

> *Blessed are you, O Israel! Who is like you, a people*
> *saved by the Lord? He is your shield and helper and*
> *your glorious sword. Your enemies will cower before*
> *you, and you will trample down their high places.*
> *[Deuteronomy 33:29 NIV]*

In 1423 BC[355] Moses climbed a mountain, and God showed him all of Canaan and said,

> *This is the land which I sware unto Abraham, unto*
> *Isaac, and unto Jacob, saying, I will give it unto thy*
> *seed: I have caused thee to see it with thine eyes, but*
> *thou shalt not go over thither. [Deuteronomy 34:4*
> *ASV]*

At that time, God decided that Moses would pass away and be with Him in Heaven. The people of Israel observed a thirty day period of mourning for their fallen leader.

> *So Moses the servant of the Lord died there in the*
> *land of Moab, according to the word of the Lord ...*
> *Moses was one hundred and twenty years old when*
> *he died. His eyes were not dim nor his natural vigor*
> *diminished. And the children of Israel wept for Moses*
> *in the plains of Moab thirty days. So the days of weep-*
> *ing and mourning for Moses ended. [Deuteronomy*
> *34:5,7–8 NKJV]*

A few days later,[356] Moses' successor, Joshua, instructed the people of Israel,

> *Sanctify yourselves, for tomorrow the Lord will do*
> *wonders among you. [Joshua 3:5 NKJV]*

Finally, under Joshua's leadership, the people of Israel crossed the Jordan River and entered the Promised Land (Joshua 3:17).

"Jesus" is the Greek pronunciation for the Hebrew name "Y'shua" or "Joshua" (meaning "God saves"). That is more than a coincidence: Joshua's destruction of the Canaanites after crossing the Jordan is an anticipation of Jesus' destruction of the ungodly upon His return.[357]

~~~~~~~~~~~~~~~~~~~~~~~~~

As I suggested at the beginning of this section, this story is an insular allegory for the length of man's time on earth and the deliverance of God's Chosen People, the Christians, to the Promised Land of Heaven. Specifically:

- the birth of Moses represents the creation of Adam (Genesis 1:27);
- the flight of Moses from Egypt to Midian represents the move of the Patriarch Abraham from Ur of Chaldea to Canaan (Genesis 12:1);
- the deliverance of God's Chosen People from bondage in Egypt by Moses represents the deliverance of God's Chosen People from bondage to sin by Jesus (Luke 9:31; John 19:30);
- Moses looking upon the Promised Land from the mountaintop represents the anticipation of the Christians immediately preceding the Second Coming of Christ (Luke 21:28);
- the crossing of the Children of Israel over the Jordan River into the Promised Land by Joshua represents the crossing of the Christians from this world to the next by Jesus at his Second Coming (1 Thessalonians 4:16–17).

The precision of this analogy is uncanny, as demonstrated in the central column of the table below.

According to the Mosaic Timeline, God's Chosen People, who were delivered from bondage to sin in AD 30,[366] will enter the Promised Land of Heaven in the year AD 2036.

Table 7. The Mosaic Insular Allegory

Mosaic Event	Date	Interval	Interval Ratio	Interval	Date	World Event
Moses' birth	1543 BC [358]	—	—	—	3976 BC [359]	Adam's creation
Moses' separation from home in Egypt	1501.7 BC [360]	41.3 years	50.07	2068 years	1908 BC [361]	Abraham's separation from home in Chaldea
Moses frees the Chosen People from bondage to Egypt	1463 BC [362]	38.7 years	50.05	1937 years	AD 30 [363]	Christ frees the Chosen People from bondage to sin
Moses looks upon the Promised Land of Canaan	1423 BC [364]	40 years	50.05	2002.07 years	AD 2032.07*	Chosen People anticipate the Promised Land of Heaven
Joshua brings Chosen People to the Promised Land	1422.90 BC [365]	0.096 years	50.06	4.8 years	AD 2036.87*	Jesus brings Chosen People to the Promised Land

* These future dates have been calculated from the columns on the left.

Esther 8:17 [NKJV]
... the Jews had joy and gladness, a feast and a holiday. Then many of the people of the land became Jews, because fear of the Jews fell upon them.

44. The Purim Timeline

Jerusalem was destroyed in 586 BC,[367] and the Jews of Judah were taken into exile by the Babylonian Empire. But the Babylonians were defeated by the Medo–Persians in 539 BC:[368]

> *That very night Belshazzar the king of Babylon was killed. So Darius the Mede became the king ... [Daniel 5:30–31 NLV]*

The new Medo–Persian rulers immediately allowed the Jews to begin to return to Jerusalem for temple construction (in 539 BC).[369]

In the first year of King Cyrus of Persia, the Lord ful-
filled the prophecy he had given through Jeremiah. He
stirred the heart of Cyrus to put this proclamation in
writing and to send it throughout his kingdom: This is
what King Cyrus of Persia says: "The Lord, the God of
heaven, has given me all the kingdoms of the earth. He
has appointed me to build him a Temple at Jerusalem,
which is in Judah. Any of you who are the Lord's peo-
ple may go there for this task. And may the Lord your
God be with you!" [2 Chronicles 36:22–23 NLT]

The Second Temple in Jerusalem was completed and dedicated in 516 BC,[370] *exactly* seventy years after the First Temple was destroyed. But the Jews were still not out of their precarious position:

- there were many hostile non-Jews living in what had been the Kingdoms of Israel and Judah;[371]
- the city of Jerusalem itself was still in ruins;[372]
- and many of the Jewish people were still scattered across an empire that stretched from Ethiopia to India.[373]

After seventy years of foreign domination and exile, the Jews still had no political power or security (Ezra 4:1–5; 5:3–4). Because of this unfavorable situation, an angel made a petition to God in 521 BC.[374]

… the angel of the Lord prayed this prayer: "O Lord
of Heaven's Armies, for seventy years now you have
been angry with Jerusalem and the towns of Judah.
How long until you again show mercy to them?" And
the Lord spoke kind and comforting words to the angel
who talked with me. [Zechariah 1:12–13 NLT]

God was planning something great for His Chosen People. [See Sections 53–56 for a detailed explanation of how the believing Jews of that day were the pre–Christ Church, and are one Body with we who have entrusted our souls to Jesus.]

~~~~~~~~~~~~~~~~~~~~~~

A new king, Xerxes, came to the throne of Medo–Persia in 485 BC,[375] and he made a poor political appointment: he put a proud and evil man named Haman in charge of the kingdom. Haman wanted to be worshiped, but a faithful and pious Jew named Mordecai would not bow to him.

After these events, King Xerxes honored Haman son of Hammedatha, the Agagite, elevating him and giving him a seat of honor higher than that of all the other nobles. All the royal officials at the king's gate knelt down and paid honor to Haman, for the king had commanded this concerning him. But Mordecai would not kneel down or pay him honor. Then the royal officials at the king's gate asked Mordecai, "Why do you disobey the king's command?" Day after day they spoke to him but he refused to comply. Therefore they told Haman about it to see whether Mordecai's behavior would be tolerated, for he had told them he was a Jew. When Haman saw that Mordecai would not kneel down or pay him honor, he was enraged. Yet having learned who Mordecai's people were, he scorned the idea of killing only Mordecai. Instead Haman looked for a way to destroy all Mordecai's people, the Jews, throughout the whole kingdom of Xerxes. [Esther 3:1–6 NIV]

Haman set his heart on the extermination of God's People because of Mordecai's impudence. But like all people that hate God, Haman was a superstitious fool: he decided to cast lots to determine a suitable date for the massacre.

In the twelfth year of King Xerxes, in the first month, the month of Nisan, they cast the pur (that is, the lot) in the presence of Haman to select a day and month. And the lot fell on the twelfth month, the month of Adar. [Esther 3:7 NIV]

Haman did not appreciate that the Lord God of Israel was in charge of such matters. It is written,

The lot is cast into the lap; but the whole disposing thereof is of the Lord. [Proverbs 16:33 KJV]

So, Haman proceeded toward his own destruction.

Then Haman said to King Xerxes, "There is a certain people dispersed and scattered among the peoples in all the provinces of your kingdom whose customs are different from those of all other people and who do not obey the king's laws; it is not in the king's best interest to tolerate them. If it pleases the king, let a decree be issued to destroy them, and I will put ten thousand talents of silver into the royal treasury for the men who carry out this business." So the king took his signet ring from his finger and gave it to Haman son of Hammedatha, the Agagite, the enemy of the Jews. "Keep the money," the king said to Haman, "and do with the people as you please." Then on the thirteenth day of the first month the royal secretaries were summoned. They wrote out in the script of each province and in the language of each people all Haman's orders to the king's satraps, the governors of the various provinces and the nobles of the various peoples. These were written in the name of King Xerxes himself and sealed with his own ring. Dispatches were sent by couriers to all the king's provinces with the order to destroy, kill and annihilate all the Jews—young and old, women and little children—on a single day, the thirteenth day of the twelfth month, the month of Adar, and to plunder their goods. A copy of the text of the edict was to be issued as law in every province and made known to the people of every nationality so they would be ready for that day. [Esther 3:8–14 NIV]

Despite these preparations, Providential serendipity was on the side of the Jews: five years before this, Mordecai's cousin and stepdaughter, Esther, had become Xerxes' queen.

Mordecai had a cousin ... known as Esther, [who] was lovely in form and features, and Mordecai had taken her as his own daughter when her father and mother died ... [She was] taken to the king's palace and entrusted to Hegai, who had charge of the harem. The girl pleased him and won his favor. Immediately he provided her with her beauty treatments and special food. He assigned to her seven maids selected from the king's palace and moved her and her maids into the best place in the harem. Esther had not revealed her nationality and family background, because Mordecai had forbidden her to do so. Every day he walked back and forth near the courtyard of the harem to find out how Esther was and what was happening to her ... Now the king was attracted to Esther more than to

any of the other women, and she won his favor and
approval more than any of the other virgins. So he
set a royal crown on her head and made her queen ...
[Esther 2:7–11,17 NIV]

When Mordecai learned of Haman's scheme, he appealed to Queen Esther to do something.

... who knows but that you have come to royal posi-
tion for such a time as this? [Esther 4:14 TNIV]

It was, however, against the law for anyone to approach the king without being summoned. The penalty was death—even for the queen—unless the king subsequently granted an indulgence. So Esther asked Mordecai and the Jews to fast for three days, and then she approached her husband.

On the third day Esther put on her royal robes and
stood in the inner court of the palace, in front of the
king's hall. The king was sitting on his royal throne
in the hall, facing the entrance. When he saw Queen
Esther standing in the court, he was pleased with her
and ... asked, "What is it, Queen Esther? What is your
request? Even up to half the kingdom, it will be given
you." [Esther 5:1–3 NIV]

Esther wisely did not ask the king immediately for her wish, but waited a day to build up the king's testosterone and suspense, and to give Haman a false sense of security.

So it was that in 474 BC[376]—one hundred and twelve years after the exile began—God arranged for Mordecai to be honored by the king, for the Jews to be delivered from destruction, and for Haman and all the other enemies of the pre–Christ Church to fall into their own trap.

On the thirteenth day of the twelfth month, the month
of Adar, the edict commanded by the king was to be
carried out. On this day the enemies of the Jews had
hoped to overpower them, but now the tables were
turned and the Jews got the upper hand over those who
hated them. The Jews assembled in their cities in all
the provinces of King Xerxes to attack those seeking
their destruction. No one could stand against them,
because the people of all the other nationalities were
afraid of them. And all the nobles of the provinces, the
satraps, the governors and the king's administrators

helped the Jews, because fear of Mordecai had seized
them. Mordecai was prominent in the palace; his repu-
tation spread throughout the provinces, and he became
more and more powerful. [Esther 9:1–4 NIV]

The Jews remembered their deliverance through a perpetual holiday, named 'Purim,' after the serendipitous casting of the lots.

Mordecai recorded these events and sent letters to
the Jews near and far, throughout all the provinces
of King Xerxes, calling on them to celebrate an
annual festival ... [to] commemorate a time when
the Jews gained relief from their enemies, when their
sorrow was turned into gladness and their mourn-
ing into joy. So the Jews accepted Mordecai's pro-
posal and adopted this annual custom. Haman son
of Hammedatha the Agagite, the enemy of the Jews,
had plotted to crush and destroy them on the date
determined by casting lots ... But when Esther came
before the king, he issued a decree causing Haman's
evil plot to backfire ... That is why this celebration is
called Purim, because it is the ancient word for cast-
ing lots. So because of Mordecai's letter and because
of what they had experienced, the ... Festival of Purim
would never cease to be celebrated among the Jews,
nor would the memory of what happened ever die out
among their descendants. [Esther 9:20–28 NLT]

The following year, Mordecai was promoted to the highest office in the land.

... the full account of the greatness of Mordecai,
whom the king had promoted, are recorded in The
Book of the History of the Kings of Media and Persia.
Mordecai the Jew became the prime minister, with
authority next to that of King Xerxes himself. [Esther
10:2–3 NLT]

~~~~~~~~~~~~~~~~~~~~~~

The Book of Esther is the only book in the entire Bible in which there is a,

*... complete absence of any explicit reference to God, worship, prayer, or sacrifice. This "secularity" has produced many detractors who have judged the book to be of little religious value. However, it appears that the author has deliberately refrained from mentioning God or any religious activity as a literary device to heighten the fact that **it is God who controls and directs all the seemingly insignificant coincidences** that make up the plot and issue in deliverance for the Jews. God's sovereign rule is assumed at every point, an assumption made all the more effective by the total absence of reference to him.*[377]

Esther is, of course, an indispensable part of the Christian Canon; God has been at work, behind the scenes, to protect His faithful people from the very beginning. This is the unavoidable conclusion if you dissect the plot of life, as I recommended in Section 5.

In fact, my eschatological study has revealed this superb story to be the culmination of a Providential plan that began with Abraham, the Father of Faith. Throughout 1434 years of history, God preserved the line of Abraham from which the Messiah would be born until the Jews' great triumph of Purim and Mordecai's exaltation.

This was again a foreshadowing—an exact parallel—for the coming of the end of the age. But in this instance there is a twist: the 1434 year parallel is for the devil's "anti-plan," or his answer to the Messiah's earthly ministry. Of course, everything that the devil attempts is destined to failure, so the end of the matter will again be the Christians' great triumph and exaltation at the Second Coming.

... they will go to war against the Lamb, but the Lamb will defeat them because he is Lord of all lords and King of all kings. And his called and chosen and faithful ones will be with him. [Revelation 17:14 NLT]

The table below shows the Abraham-to-Purim saga juxtaposed against historical events since the Incarnation.

As the Jews of Mordecai's day were living in the post–exile period, so the Christians of today are living in the post–Soviet period. Like them, the Church today remains in a precarious position. Evil forces all around the world would be pleased to see the Christians annihilated.

But, according to this Purim Timeline, Christ will return to deliver God's Chosen People (i.e., the Church) and destroy the wicked in AD 2034.

Table 8. The Parallel of the Plan and the Anti-Plan

God's Plan to Bless His People Before the Incarnation	Date	Cumul. Duration	Date	Satan's Plan to Thwart God's People After the Incarnation
God promises that the Christ will be born through Abraham.	1908 BC [378]	—	AD 599 [379]	The Son of Perdition and first Muslim apostle, Ali, born to Muhammad's uncle.
Abrahamic covenant leads to the Israelites' conquest of Canaan.	1883 BC [380]	25 years	AD 624 [381]	Muhammad's victory in the key Battle of Badr leads to his conquest of Mecca.
Abraham's offering of Isaac initiates the 'Age of Faith.'	1846 BC [382]	62 years	AD 661 [383]	The assassination of Ali initiates the two main branches of Islam.
Jacob, the future Israel, is born to Isaac and Rebekah.	1808 BC [384]	100 years	AD 699 [385]	The Abomination is born through the completion of the Dome of the Rock.
Presence of the Lord departs from the First Temple; sacrifices to God cease.	592 BC [386]	1316 years	AD 1915 [387]	Armenian and Assyrian genocides begin. Christians systematically exterminated by the Caliphate.
Jerusalem is conquered by the Babylonians; the First Temple is destroyed, High Priest slain, and the Jews are exiled *en masse*.	586 BC [388]	1322 years	AD 1921 [389]	Caliphate loses all political power. The next year Smyrna is burned, Greeks are expelled from Anatolia, and the USSR is formally established.
The Second Temple is dedicated; the enemies of the Jews conspire to impede their complete restoration.	516 BC [390]	1392 years	AD 1991 [391]	Churches are planted as the USSR crumbles; Islamic terrorism is inspired by the presence of US troops in Arabia for Persian Gulf War.
Jews are delivered from the threats of the evil Haman.	474 BC [392]	1434 years	AD 2033*	Christians will be delivered from the threats of the Antichrist Beast of Islam.
Mordecai is exalted by Xerxes' order.	473 BC [393]	1435 years	AD 2034*	Christians will be exalted by Christ's Second Coming.

* These future dates have been calculated from the columns on the left.

Daniel 12:7 [KJV]
... and when he shall have accomplished to scatter the power of the holy peo-
ple, all these things shall be finished.

45. The Scatter Timeline

At the very end of the Prophet Daniel's life-long work of history and prophecy, he recorded a vision of three heavenly beings.

> *Then I looked up and saw two other angels. One was*
> *on this side of the Tigris River. And one was on the*
> *other side. The man who was dressed in linen was*
> *above the waters of the river. [Daniel 12:5–6 NIrV]*

The man hovering above the river was probably the pre–incarnate Son of God. One of the angels asked this Man about the end of the world,

> *How long will it be before these amazing things come*
> *true? [Daniel 12:6 NIrV]*

The Man hovering above the river lifted up his hands and said,

> *In the name of the God who lives forever, I solemnly*
> *promise that it will be a time, two times, and half a*
> *time. [Daniel 12:7 CEV]*

Then the Man specified,

> *... and when he shall have accomplished to scatter*
> *the power of the holy people, all these things shall be*
> *finished. [Daniel 12:7 KJV]*

The period that is represented by the "time, two times, and half a time" is different from both that of Revelation 12:14 (see Section 31) and Daniel 7:25 (see Section 40). In this case the key is understanding the meaning of "scatter the power of the holy people."

There is no doubt in my mind that the Word of God, the Holy Bible, is what is being referred to in the above verse as "the power of the holy people."

> *For the word of God is living and powerful, and*
> *sharper than any two-edged sword, piercing even to*
> *the division of soul and spirit, and of joints and mar-*
> *row, and is a discerner of the thoughts and intents of*
> *the heart. [Hebrews 4:12 NKJV]*

The 'scatter' issue is also easily understood. Other translations say 'shatter' or 'broken,' but the meaning is clear: think of a piece of fine crystal that is dropped on a hardwood floor. It shatters into innumerable tiny fragments, and spreads into every corner of the room.

So it is with the Gospel of Jesus Christ. Immediately after his account of the stoning of the Deacon Stephen in AD 33,[394] Luke tells us,

> *On that day a great persecution broke out against the*
> *church at Jerusalem, and all except the apostles **were***
> ***scattered throughout Judea and Samaria ... Those***
> ***who had been scattered preached the word** wherever*
> *they went. [Acts 8:1,4 NIV]*

It has been God's plan from the beginning to send the Savior (i.e., the Word of God in man's flesh) into the world. He promised this when condemning the devil and chastising Eve in 3975 BC[395] (Genesis 3:15). The process of writing the Word of God was begun much later, when the Ten Commandments were given to Moses in 1462 BC[396] (Exodus 20:1–2). The Bible was written over the next 1557 years, ending with the book of Revelation in AD 96.[397] Then it was compiled, canonized, and meticulously hand-copied. About five hundred years ago it was translated into the vernacular, and made available to believers through the printing press. In the past ten years it has been put on the Internet, and beamed by satellites into every corner of the globe. Half the world is illiterate, so the last frontier in spreading Jesus' message of love is to make audio broadcasts of the Bible in every language. We are nearing the completion of Christ's Great Commission.

> *... My Word which goes from My mouth will not return*
> *to Me empty. It will do what I want it to do, and will*
> *carry out My plan well. [Isaiah 55:11 NLV]*

The moment when the finger of God carved out the words on the Ten Commandment tablets rang in a new era in human history: the glories of the Word of God had begun to be revealed. Such an era is spoken of in Scripture as a millennium, or a thousand year period.

> *This was to keep Satan from fooling the nations any-*
> *more until the 1,000 years were ended. [Revelation*
> *20:3 NIrV]*

In Daniel 12:7 we are told that there will be three and a half such periods before the Word will be completely scattered over the face of the earth. Three and a half thousand years past the beginning of the writing of the Bible puts us at AD 2039.

By that time all the amazing things that the Prophet Daniel witnessed will have been fulfilled, and Christ will have returned.

Daniel 12:11–12 [NKJV]
And from the time that the daily sacrifice is taken away, and the abomination
of desolation is set up, there shall be one thousand two hundred and ninety
days. Blessed is he who waits, and comes to the one thousand three hundred
and thirty-five days.

46. The Abomination Timeline

After the timeline given in Daniel 12:7, the prophet wrote,

> *Although I heard, I did not understand. Then I said,*
> *'My lord, what shall be the end of these things?'*
> *[Daniel 12:8 NKJV]*

We can hardly blame Daniel for not understanding. He was a prophet, not a mind-reader (except in the case of King Nebuchadnezzar's dream—Daniel 2:45). He did not have the benefit of the whole picture of God's plan for salvation, as we do at this late date, but he dutifully recorded it for us. In the very next verse the book ends with God telling him that he should not trouble himself, and that on the last day he would be resurrected.

> *Daniel, go on your way until the end. Your body will*
> *rest in the grave. Then at the end of the days you will*
> *rise from the dead. And you will receive what God has*
> *appointed for you. [Daniel 12:13 NIrV]*

What is the clue that helps us now decipher this mysterious 'Abomination Timeline'? It is in the starting point, "from the time that the daily sacrifice is taken away." Realize that young Daniel was among the first Jews deported to Babylon in 605 BC.[398] Nineteen years later the First Temple was destroyed and Jerusalem was flattened by the same Babylonians.[399] The only temple that Daniel knew was this First Temple built by Solomon. The "taking away" refers to the cessation of daily sacrifice in this First Temple.

The Prophet Ezekiel tells us that he witnessed the presence of the Lord abruptly departing from that Temple.

> *Then the glory of the Lord departed from the thresh-*
> *old of the temple ... [Ezekiel 10:18 NKJV]*

This event has been dated to 592 BC[400]—six years before the razing of the city, and the capture and execution of the High Priest, Seraiah (Jeremiah 52:27). So although the Temple stood until 586 BC,[401] and rituals were presumably performed there until that time, the perpetual sacrifices stopped in 592 BC[402] when God was no longer present to receive it.

Again, using years for days, 1,290 years past that event brings us to AD 699. That is the year that the seventh head of the Seven-Headed Beast, Caliph al-Malik, completed and gilded an abominable 'Third Temple' on the Temple Mount (Sections 22–23).[403] We know it as the golden-topped Dome of the Rock.[404]

Christianity was the majority religion in Jerusalem at that time, and Christians used to congregate to pray on the Temple Mount. But by the power of the sword, the martyred Caliph Ali's vision of a new religion was resurrected thirty-eight years after his death (Table 2). Christian icons were replaced with Antichrist inscriptions on the coinage of the Middle East; and the Abomination that Causes Desolation was set up in the form of the Dome of the Rock.

Since that time the highest point in Jerusalem—where God once received pleasing sacrifices that foreshadowed the sacrifice of His Son—has been wholly reserved for the denial of Jesus as Christ.

Figure 4. The Abomination that Causes Desolation of Daniel 12:11

The interior of the Dome of the Rock in Jerusalem. The inscription denies the divinity of Jesus Christ over the very spot where ancient Israelite sacrifices were made in anticipation of His Incarnation. This represents the sending forth of Islamic orthodoxy in AD 699, and the 'abomination that causes desolation' of the Antichrist Beast (Daniel 12:11). Reprinted by permission of Art Explosion, Nova Development.

For the record, the abominable inscription on the inner face of the octagonal arcade of the Dome says:

> *People of the Book! Do not exceed the limits of your faith and do not say anything about Allah except the truth.*
>
> ***The Messiah, Jesus, the son of Mary, is but a messenger of Allah** and His word which He gave to Mary, and a revelation proceeding from Him.*
>
> *So trust Allah and His messengers and **do not say 'three.' Desist! It is to your advantage to admit that Allah is a singular God only.** Blessed is He—**How could it be that He has a son?!***
>
> *To Him belongs what is in the heavens and what is on earth. Allah is able to take care of it unassisted.*
>
> ***The Messiah does not consider it beneath his dignity to be a slave to Allah** nor do the angels who are nigh unto Him.*
>
> *He who considers it beneath him to worship Allah, and whoever is arrogant, He shall summon both together for judgment.*
>
> *O Allah! **Incline unto Your messenger and slave Jesus**, son of Mary and greet him with peace on the day he was born, and the day he died, **and the day when he shall be raised alive.***
>
> ***The following is the truth about Jesus, son of Mary, about whom you dispute: It is unseemly that Allah should acquire a son.***
>
> *Blessed is Allah! Should He decide a thing, He only says to it 'Become!' and it becomes, just like that.*
>
> *Indeed Allah is my Lord and yours. Therefore worship Him, for this is a straight path.*
>
> *Allah Himself is the witness that there is no God but He. The angels and those endowed with knowledge establish it with justice.*
>
> *There is no God but He—the Mighty, the Ruler.*
>
> *Faith in Allah means unity, but **those who were given the Book split into factions after receiving knowledge and endlessly disputed among themselves.***

Whoever denies the evidence of Allah, let him be aware that Allah is swift in reckoning.[405]

And on the exterior of the octagonal arcade of the Dome is inscribed:

*There is no God but Allah alone, **without any other person**. Say that He is God—One God—the Everlasting, **who has not begotten and has not been begotten**. He is without equal. Muhammad is Allah's messenger, may Allah bless him.*

*There is no God but Allah alone, **without any other person**. Muhammad is Allah's messenger. Allah and His angels send blessings on the Prophet. O you who believe, ask blessings upon him and salute him with all respect.*

*There is no God but Allah alone. **Praise be to Allah who has not taken a son, and who doesn't have any other person in sovereignty, nor is he humbly depen-dent upon any other person as a protector**. Magnify Him with repeated magnificats.*

Muhammad is Allah's messenger, may Allah, His angels and His messengers bless him and Allah grant him peace and mercy.

*There is no God but Allah alone, **without any other person**. To Him belongs sovereignty and to Him belongs praise. He gives life and He makes to die; He is powerful over all things.*

Muhammad is Allah's messenger, may Allah bless him and accept his intercession on the day of resurrection for his community.

*There is no God but Allah alone, **without any other person**. Muhammad is Allah's messenger, may Allah bless him.*

God's servant, Abd al-Malik, commander of believ-ers, built this dome in the year seventy-two. May Allah accept it from him and be pleased with him. Amen, Lord of worlds. Praise be to Allah.[406]

After reading these two Antichrist screeds, do you have any doubt about this being the 'abomination that causes desolation' referred to by the Prophet Daniel? What could be more abominable than encircling this message over the spot where the Israelites once offered sacrifices in anticipation of the

Son of God? What could cause more desolation than requiring people to submit to the denial that God is Triune and that He became a man? Jesus Christ said,

> *Where I go, you cannot come ... You are from below;*
> *I am from above. You are of this world; I am not of*
> *this world. I told you that you would die in your sins;*
> ***if you do not believe that I am the one I claim to be,***
> ***you will indeed die in your sins*** *... I have much to say*
> *in judgment of you. [John 8:21,23–24,26 NIV]*

Islam is the abomination. Islam causes desolation. Islam has made every land that it has overtaken desolate.

Believers in Jesus Christ are encouraged in Daniel 12:12 to look forward to a time 1,335 years after the abomination was set up in AD 699.[x] That brings us to AD 2034. At that time the abomination will come to an end, and Christ will deliver His Chosen People (i.e., the Christians) from this sinful world.

The Dispensationalists have never been able to account for the 1,290 days and the 1,335 days. There is no way for it to fit into their misguided eschatology. The noted Dispensationalist, J. Vernon McGee, admitted of the Daniel 12:11–12 passage,

> *No one has the interpretation of this—it is sealed until*
> *the time of the end. I think sometimes we try to know*
> *more than is actually given to us.*[407]

In the table below the mystery is revealed for the first time. Once again, there is only one wise conclusion: the end of all things is near.

---

x   The 1335 days are misinterpreted by Dispensationalists to mean 45 days in addition to the 1290 days that were first mentioned. This is incorrect. There is a total of 2625 prophetic days (i.e., 2625 years) between the cessation of the perpetual sacrifice in 592 BC and the long-awaited blessing in AD 2034. This period is punctuated by the setting up of the abomination that causes desolation in AD 699.

Table 9. The Mystery of Daniel 12:11–12 Revealed

Historical Event	Date	Interval	Scriptural Prophecy
Departure of the presence of the Lord from Solomon's Temple	592 BC [408]	—	And from the time that the daily sacrifice shall be taken away... [Daniel 12:11a KJV]
Completion of the Islamic currency reforms, and the gilding of the Dome of the Rock	AD 699 [409]	1290 years	...and the abomination that causes desolation is set up, there will be 1,290 days. [Daniel 12:11b NIV]
Second Coming of Christ	AD 2034	1335 years	Blessed is the one who waits for and reaches the end of the 1,335 days. [Daniel 12:12 NIV]

Pay special attention to what you have just read: the Abomination Timeline is the most definitive of the eleven timelines that I have discovered in Scripture, and it was the inspiration for this book (see bottom of Section 14).

Genesis 6:13 [TNIV]
So God said to Noah, "I am going to put an end to all people, for the earth is filled with violence because of them."

47. The Noahic Timeline

One of my roommates once took notice of my faith and asked if he could borrow a Bible. His enthusiasm lasted for only that evening. He got ten pages into Genesis, came to my room, and said, "I think I've had enough of this."

"So soon? What's the problem?" I asked.

"You believe this to be the inerrant Word of God?"

"Yes."

He frowned with skepticism, "Isn't it convenient how so many of these early men in chapter five had children on round-numbered years of age, and had lifespans that extended until round-numbered years?"

"Yeah, I've noticed the same thing," I conceded.

"I just read about Noah," he continued. "Noah was five hundred years old when he had three sons and God spoke to him about the ark. That's quite a feat to live childless for five hundred years—I've been having sex with my new girlfriend for five weeks and I've been worrying the whole time about whether she's going to miss her next period! They must have had some great family planning back in Noah's day in order for his wife to be childless for hundreds of years, and then suddenly get pregnant three times just when Noah needed help building a giant ship!"

I did not have an intricate explanation for him. I just said, "We take such things on faith. God can do anything."

He returned the book to its place on my shelf, "I need something more than faith, Christian. It seems like a made-up story. When they find that ark, let me know and I'll read some more."

~~~~~~~~~~~~~~~~~~~~~~~~

I believe that the story of Noah and his ark is true. But what I did not yet appreciate when I spoke to my roommate is that God had prearranged history such that it is another insular allegory (1:10 ratio) for what will happen at the end of the age.

Jesus Christ said,

> *In those days before the flood, the people were enjoying banquets and parties and weddings right up to the time Noah entered his boat. People didn't realize what was going to happen until the flood came and swept them all away. That is the way it will be when the Son of Man comes. [Matthew 24:38–39 NLT]*

We are told that it was the Patriarch Noah's walk with God that set him apart.

> *Noah was a righteous man, blameless among the people of his time, and he walked faithfully with God. [Genesis 6:9 TNIV]*

And his floating ark carried the People of God.

> *God was patient while Noah was building the ark. He waited, but only a few people went into the ark. A total of eight were saved by means of water. The water of the flood is a picture of the baptism that now saves you also. [1 Peter 3:20–21 NIrV]*

So the Christian Church, likewise, is a singularly holy thing on this wicked earth. It now contains the People of God.

> *Christ also loved the church and gave Himself for her, that He might sanctify and cleanse her with the wash-*

ing of water by the word, that He might present her to
Himself a glorious church, not having spot or wrinkle
or any such thing, but that she should be holy and
without blemish. [Ephesians 5:25–27 NKJV]

Noah was born in 2919 BC;[410] he was *exactly* 500 years old in 2419
BC[411] when God told him to start building the ark. Noah faithfully obeyed.

Noah did everything just as God commanded him.
[Genesis 6:22 NKJV]

Similarly, Adam's descendants were 5,000 years into human history
when the invisible, indivisible, Church accepted the three Ecumenical Creeds
(i.e., the Apostles', Athanasian, and Nicene with the inclusion of the Filioque),
in faithful obedience to God.

The one hundred years in which Noah prepared the ark is equivalent to
the thousand years in which the Holy Spirit has built the Church by spreading
the true faith of the Creeds, and adding believing people. Both were done in
preparation for the end of the world.

Noah was *exactly* 600 years old in 2319 BC[412] when the flood washed
away the Antediluvian world; the world will be 6,000 years old in AD 2025
when a great tribulation begins to burn away this world of sin. The last ten
years of human history will bring a firestorm of troubles.

... the world that then existed was deluged with water
and perished. But by the same word the heavens
and earth that now exist are stored up for fire, being
kept until the day of judgment and destruction of the
ungodly. [2 Peter 3:6–7 ESV]

Noah was *exactly* 601 years old in 2318 BC[413] when God commanded
him to leave the ark which had gone aground in ancient Armenia. When Noah
set foot on the new world, he built an altar and worshipped the Lord; the world
will be 6,010 years old when Christ returns and we who make up the Church
worship at His altar in a new Heaven and new Earth.

Then I saw a new heaven and a new earth ... And I
heard a loud voice from the throne saying, "Now the
dwelling of God is with men, and he will live with
them ..." He who was seated on the throne said, "I
am making everything new!" [Revelation 21:1,3,5
NIV]

The Six Day Creation occurred in 3976 BC.[414] According to this time-line, Christ will make everything new 6,010 years after the Creation, in AD 2035.

Table 10. The Noahic Insular Allegory

Noahic Event	Date	Interval	Interval Ratio	Interval	Date	World Event
Noah's birth	2919 BC[415]	—	—	—	3976 BC[416]	Adam's creation
One hundred year building of the ark commences	2419 BC[417]	500 years	9.98	4989 years	AD 1014[418]	One thousand year building of the Church commences
Eight souls are preserved during the Flood	2319 BC[419]	600 years	10	6000 years	AD 2025*	Christian Church is preserved during the Tribulation
Noah worships God on Mount Ararat	2318 BC[420]	601 years	10	6010 years	AD 2035*	Christians worship God in Heaven

* These future dates have been calculated from the columns on the left.

Exodus 21:2,5–6 [NIV]
If you buy a Hebrew servant, he is to serve you for six years. But in the seventh year, he shall go free ... But if the servant declares, 'I love my master ... and do not want to go free,' then ... he will be his servant for life.

48. The Sabbath Timeline

From the preceding section you will see that the six days—both the six days of Creation and of the work-week—are themselves a repeating insular allegory. They are a foreshadowing of the length of man's toil on earth. For from the time of Adam's fall in 3975 BC,[421] man has had to work to live.

> *Since you listened to your wife and ate from the tree*
> *whose fruit I commanded you not to eat, the ground is*
> *cursed because of you. All your life you will struggle*
> *to scratch a living from it. [Genesis 3:17 NLT]*

But when the time of man's toil is ended, the entire Creation that supports it will be replaced by something new.

Since everything around us is going to melt away, what holy, godly lives you should be living! You should look forward to that day and hurry it along—the day when God will set the heavens on fire and the elements will melt away in the flames. But we are looking forward to the new heavens and new earth he has promised, a world where everyone is right with God. [2 Peter 3:11–13 NLT]

There will be an end to what we know of as Heaven and Earth, and Christians will live anew in God's presence.

In the beginning you laid the foundations of the earth, and the heavens are the work of your hands. They will perish, but you remain; they will all wear out like a garment. Like clothing you will change them and they will be discarded. But you remain the same, and your years will never end. The children of your servants will live in your presence; [Psalm 102:25–28 NIV]

Every time Christians look at the weeks on a calendar—every time Christians look forward to meeting together on Sunday—we are remembering God's covenant to rescue us from this miserable world through the reign of His Son after six millennia of human history (see Table 13).

*Remember that you were a slave in the land of Egypt, and the Lord your God brought you out of there with a strong hand and an outstretched arm. **That is why the Lord your God has commanded you to keep the Sabbath day**. [Deuteronomy 5:15 HCSB]*

The word 'Sabbath' means 'Rest.' So when Jesus said …

The Son of Man is Lord of the Sabbath. [Matthew 12:8 NIV]

… He meant that He was the One that would provide rest for His people that have been slavishly subject to the sinful world. For it is written,

… in condemning [Jesus] they fulfilled the words of the prophets that are read every Sabbath. [Acts 13:27 TNIV]

This is why the Sabbath, which *was previously celebrated* on the seventh day of the week (before the time of Christ), *is now celebrated* on the first day of the week: the Sabbath Day represents both the end of the old period of slavery, and the beginning of the new period of freedom. Sunday is both the seventh day from the beginning of the work week on Monday, and the first day of an entirely new week!

For Christians, Sabbath worship is an anticipation of the end of the six thousand years of the human saga, and the beginning of the blessed and eternal rest in Christ.

> *So there is a special rest still waiting for the people of God. For all who enter into God's rest will find rest from their labors, **just as God rested after creating the world**. [Hebrews 4:9–10 NLT]*

Again, God established the Sabbath as a promise to His people,

> *[The Sabbath] will be the sign of the covenant I have made between me and the people of Israel forever. **I made the heavens and the earth in six days**. But on the seventh day I did not work. I rested. [Exodus 31:17 NIrV]*

And we know that God's measurement of time is not the same as ours.

> *... a thousand years mean nothing to you! They are merely a day gone by or a few hours in the night. [Psalm 90:4 CEV]*

This brings into focus an unlikely, but intuitive, truth: to God, the six thousand years of human history have been merely six days gone by. Recall that the Transfiguration occurred *exactly* six days after Jesus predicted that it would occur.

> ***After six days** Jesus ... led them up a high mountain by themselves. There he was transfigured before them. His face shone like the sun, and his clothes became as white as the light. [Matthew 17:1–2 NIV]*

God not only created the world in six days, He has also done the complete redeeming work in six days!

> *... Jesus answered them, "My Father has been working until now, and I have been working." [John 5:17 NKJV]*

We will surely rest with Him at the advent of the seventh day, for,

> *By the seventh day God had finished the work he had been doing; so on the seventh day he rested from all*

*his work. **And God blessed the seventh day and made it holy** ... [Genesis 2:2–3 NIV]*

The end of six thousand years after the fall of man will be in AD 2026. We are that close to the glorious morning foretold throughout Scripture.

I wait for the Lord, my soul waits, and in his word I put my hope. My soul waits for the Lord more than watchmen wait for the morning, more than watchmen wait for the morning. [Psalm 130:5–6 NIV]

After the six thousand years there will be a dawning, and with it will come a surprise, as of the surprise on Easter morning.

*Very early on Sunday morning, **just as the sun was coming up**, they went to the tomb. On their way, they were asking one another, "Who will roll the stone away from the entrance for us?" But when they looked, they saw that the stone had already been rolled away. And it was a huge stone! [Mark 16:2–4 CEV]*

The stone that kept the God-man entombed was huge, but it rolled away like a child's ball one Sunday morning.

Some Christians think that we celebrate Christ's Resurrection only on Easter Sunday, and the other fifty-one Sabbath worships are for topical issues of the faith. Not true! We celebrate the bodily Resurrection *especially* on Easter Sunday, but this Good News should be the focus of every single Sabbath service—it is our blessed hope!

For as often as you eat this bread and drink this cup, you proclaim the Lord's death till He comes. [1 Corinthians 11:26 NKJV]

I must confess that the Sabbath Timeline is my favorite of all the Biblical timelines that foretell the Second Coming of Christ. I was always happy on Sunday morning, but I did not know why I was happy. It is so obvious—how could I not have seen it before? This timeline has been plain to us since the day that Jesus rose from the dead; it is the reason why we awake early, and gather with our Christian friends, and say,

This is the day the Lord has made; let us rejoice and be glad in it. [Psalm 118:24 NIV]

Surely we will rejoice and be glad on the Glorious Sunday when Jesus returns! Until then we sing of Him in worship:

The King shall come when morning dawns

And light triumphant breaks,
When beauty gilds the eastern hills
And life to joy awakes—
Not as of old a little child
To bear and fight and die,
But crowned with glory like the sun
That lights the morning sky.
Oh, brighter than the rising morn
When Christ, victorious, rose,
And left the lonesome place of death
Despite the rage of foes.
Oh, brighter than that glorious morn
Shall dawn upon our race,
The day when Christ in splendor comes
And we shall see his face.[422]

Be prepared for an end to this world as dawn breaks on the seventh millennium. If we think of "just as the sun was coming up" as the first fifteen minutes of Easter morning, then this is the equivalent of ten years into the seventh millennium of human toil, or the year AD 2036.

The new day will offer a new paradigm for human continuance, for in it we shall see the face of the Resurrected Christ.

Revelation 9:1–3 [NKJV]
Then the fifth angel sounded: And I saw a star fallen from heaven to the earth. To him was given the key to the bottomless pit. And he opened the bottomless pit, and smoke arose out of the pit like the smoke of a great furnace. So the sun and the air were darkened because of the smoke of the pit. Then out of the smoke locusts came upon the earth. And to them was given power, as the scorpions of the earth have power.

49. The Locust Timeline

The Book of Revelation describes a series of plagues upon the earth. Each is heralded by angels blowing trumpets. Upon the fifth trumpet's sounding, a star fell to earth. The star is given a key to the 'bottomless pit.' The pit is opened, and smoke arises "like the smoke of the great furnace." The sun and the sky are darkened because of the smoke, and "out of the smoke locusts came upon the earth."

Revelation says that these locusts were not the type that feed upon vegetation. Their form is described as,

> ... *horses prepared for battle. On their heads were crowns of something like gold, and their faces were like the faces of men. They had hair like women's hair, and their teeth were like lions' teeth. [Revelation 9:7–8 NKJV]*

Some of the locusts could fly.

> ... *they had breastplates like breastplates of iron, and the sound of their wings was like the sound of chariots with many horses running into battle. [Revelation 9:9 NKJV]*

Their purpose was not to kill people, but to torment those that are not of the Kingdom of God. Their tails were like stinging scorpions, and their energy source was named 'Destruction' (Revelation 9:11).

~~~~~~~~~~~~~~~~~~~~~~~~

Karl Benz (AD 1844–AD 1929) designed the first gasoline-powered motorcar in AD 1885.[423] At the heart of Benz' machine was a modified Otto Engine, powered by smoke-producing material from a bottomless pit in the earth. The smoke emanated from a searing-hot exhaust pipe at the back of the vehicle—if you touch it, it hurts like a scorpion sting. The headlights and grill of the motorcar resembled eyes and teeth.

Benz launched the age of automated transport that year by testing his machine on the streets of Mannheim, Germany. In AD 1886, he was granted a patent, and in AD 1888 his wife Bertha borrowed the car without her husband's permission for the first long-distance trip.[424]

The locusts represent automobiles, along with their noisy descendants motorcycles, airplanes, and helicopters. We are told that,

> ... *their power was to hurt men five months. [Revelation 9:10 NKJV]*

If a prophetic month is a period of thirty years, as has been my interpretation throughout this book, then five months past Benz' patent would put us at AD 2036. That is the year when the power of petroleum-fueled automotives to harm mankind will end. This can only signify the end of the age, and Christ's return.

1 Corinthians 6:12 [CEV]
Some of you say, "We can do anything we want to." But I tell you that not everything is good for us. So I refuse to let anything have power over me.

50. The Sting of the Scorpion

One of my friends read this entire manuscript, and only found fault with the previous section. He said, "Do you *really* think that cars and planes are the demon locusts?"

I said, "The Bible doesn't say demon locusts—just locusts. 'Demon locusts' is from a stupid movie."

He came back, "True, but the locusts in Revelation torment men, and automobiles do not torment men. In fact, they make people's lives easier. Do only unbelieving drivers suffer in car crashes, or do only unbelieving mechanics burn their hands on hot tailpipes?"

I told my friend that no one can explain why some people end up as highway statistics and others do not. But I told him that the Scripture is not necessarily referring to bodily injuries in Revelation 9. It is also a mistake to think that the torment is through environmental degradation. The point is actually more subtle and fundamental: every invention of mankind can be an agent of good or of evil. That is to say, every innovation can be a vehicle (pardon the pun), through which people can be driven (again, pardon) to their personal betterment or to personal destruction.

Take the Internet, for example. It is the greatest thing that has come along during my lifetime. You'll see from my citations that I could not have written this book without the Internet. All I have to do to find the answer to any question that pops into my mind is type it into a good search engine. It is a vehicle for news, and knowledge, and even the spread of the Gospel of Christ. And now it is becoming wireless and handheld. Amazing! If you had told me twenty years ago that this was coming, I simply would not have believed you. It is a dream-come-true for me.

But what about other people? For some it is a nightmare. What if a person has a weakness for pornography? When I was a child, people had to go to the seedy part of town to view X–rated films. It was inconvenient. And when I was in college, people had to go into the backroom of the video store to rent X–rated videos. Still, inconvenient and embarrassing. But now one can be online twenty-four hours per day in the privacy of one's bedroom. And there is an unending supply of pornography, as long as you have the money (or credit) to pay for it. Is that good for them? Is it good for those around them?

What about the people that have a weakness for gambling? They don't have to travel to Las Vegas anymore. There is twenty-four hour online gambling now. What has it done to them and their families? The same point could be made for innovations in pain killers (that can lead to drug addiction), food processing (that can lead to obesity), or personal music systems (that can lead to deafness).

So, likewise, people can use automobiles to get groceries, and to take their children to the park. Or they can use it to get themselves to places where they ought not to be—such as to a mosque for Friday prayers, or to a madrasah to be taught that Allah wants them to kill infidels. Before automobiles, it might have been impossible for them to travel so far as to get into certain kinds of trouble. But now it is a much smaller world.

Moreover, the automobile itself can become an object of obsession or vanity through which one neglects the important things of life. If men can become obsessed with a morally-neutral thing like a lawn, and women can become obsessed with a morally-neutral thing like shoes, then how much more enticing are things like automated transport or motion pictures (see example in Section 5)?

In a paradoxical way, the conveniences of life make unbelieving people's lives worse. The American author and transcendentalist, Ralph Waldo Emerson (AD 1803–AD 1882), noted,

> *Things are in the saddle and [they] ride mankind.*[425]

For those that die without Christ, everything that has happened has ensured that they do not entrust their souls to Jesus and enter the Kingdom of Heaven. Everything, including automobiles, work for their personal destruction (Section 106). The very things that they desired in order to have a better life take hold of them, and run the life out of them, because they will not accept that God became a man in Jesus Christ.

> *For this reason God sends them something pow-erful that leads them away from the truth ... [2 Thessalonians 2:11 NCV]*

They thus become fodder for demons, and suffer torments as from scorpions.

The opposite is true for Christians. The Bible promises that all things work together for good for those that love God and are called according to His purpose (Romans 8:28). That is because everything that happens in the life of someone that dies in Christ has, in some way, been used to bring them to Jesus and to fulfill Jesus' good purposes in the world (Section 105).

> ... *His name shall be on their foreheads. [Revelation 22:4 NKJV]*

Such a person enjoys every innovation, but is careful not to allow any to have the power to draw him into sin. He sees things from the heavenly perspective, and is happy because his Lord reigns and not one of the Lord's people will be lost.

Therefore, when the prophecy about the locust-like automobiles states ...

> *The locusts were told not to harm the grass on the earth or any plant or any tree. They were to punish only those people **who did not have God's mark on their foreheads**. [Revelation 9:4 CEV]*

... I propose that this is an oblique reference to the Muslims. Remember that Muslims, as rejecters of the Lord Jesus, do not have the Holy Spirit's invisible mark on their foreheads. In fact, a good many of them pray toward Mecca so religiously that they have a visible rug-burn on their foreheads (i.e., the Mark of the Beast; see Section 24).

I have often wondered if Providence had a special purpose in placing a large portion of the world's petroleum reserves in Saudi Arabia, Iraq, Kuwait, the United Arab Emirates, Iran, and many other Muslim nations. Although Muslims make up only 21% of the global population, they supply 70% of the world's oil and gas requirements.[426] Normally, such an abundant natural resource would be a great blessing. But in the Muslims' case there is a spiritually-deleterious effect: the oil wealth causes them to be even more entrenched in their Antichrist religion.

God ordained that the energy source for the locust-like automobiles would not come from a pit beneath Christian soil, but primarily from a pit beneath Muslim sand.

> *The locusts were allowed to make them suffer for five months, but not to kill them. The suffering they caused was like the sting of a scorpion. [Revelation 9:5 CEV]*

Are the Muslims better off for their oil wealth? Should we envy them?

Do not be overawed when a man grows rich, when the splendor of his house increases; for he will take nothing with him when he dies ... A man who has riches without understanding is like the beasts that perish. [Psalm 49:16–17,20 NIV]

Other tribal peoples in Africa and Asia have been proselytized to Christianity since the advent of the automobile—but not the tribes of Arabia, and not the Iranians. The Muslims' locust-revenue has afforded them the ability to print Qur'ans, to build mosques, to fund madrasahs, and to wage war for the Beast of Islam. Osama bin Laden came from a family worth five billion dollars,[427] yet he chose to declare war on the United States of America. And nearly all the terrorists fighting in Iraq are recruited from the oil-rich Persian Gulf states.[428]

*In those days people will want to die, but they will not be able to. **They will hope for death, but it will escape from them**. [Revelation 9:6 CEV]*

It is well-known that the greatest aspiration of a true Islamist is to die while in battle against infidels (Section 82).

*... al-Qaeda offers them a chance to make history—all they have to do is die ... if you [interview] jihadi veterans of the Afghan War, they'll tell you [that] the reason they went to Afghanistan was not to defeat the Soviets, it was to become a martyr—they went there to die. And those who survived it feel that in some way they failed. That's the soil in which al-Qaeda was planted. **There is a longing for death—a glorification of it**—and rooting that out is going to be very difficult.[429]*

Some Muslims do carry out suicide attacks, and thus 'secure their place' in the Islamic paradise. But the vast majority only spit curses upon the Chosen People (i.e., the Christians) and long for a glorious death.

Judges 6:17 [TNIV]
If now I have found favor in your eyes, give me a sign that it is really you talk-
ing to me.

51. A Sign that it is Really God Talking

I remarked at the bottom of Section 39 that there are Christians all around the globe that know what I know about the timing of the Second Coming. I will now give you an example …

Immediately after finishing the rough draft of this book, I flew to a remote capital, rented a Jeep, and drove nine hours into the mountains of the oldest civilization on the face of the earth. I was in search of a rare ornamental plant. A female friend from Sweden joined me for the journey.

While driving, I expressed some self-doubts about my work. My friend is a Christian, and I had previously given her an early version of the manuscript to proofread. She listened to my litany, "Has God really chosen me to carry the message of His bodily return to the earth? I am a nobody, and a lot of people don't like me. Maybe I am self-deceived. Could I have worked myself up into a froth over a falsity, and then written hundreds of pages to justify my idea?"

My traveling companion said, "I have only read half the book so far. It is slow-going because your writing is dense, and I am fact-checking every-thing. But I have been baptized with the Holy Spirit, and the Holy Spirit is giv-ing me peace about the contents of your book. I know that I will have to answer on Judgment Day if I give you the green light, and the premise of your book is incorrect. But so far I am giving you the green light. God knows your heart. He knows that you are writing this out of a passion for Him, and not as an ego trip. He has guided you throughout this project. You know all this."

I was in a whiny mood. "Maybe you're seeing things favorably because you are my loyal friend."

"Is there anything unbiblical in the book?" She asked. "Are you misus-ing Holy Scripture?"

"Definitely not," I replied resolutely. "I use Bible verses to validate my points. I use them in their proper context. I know that my interpretation of Scripture is orthodox and correct."

She continued, "And you're having other Christian friends verify this?"

"Yes. Several. All from different denominations."

"And what about the history? Is it true history?"

"Yes, as far as I know," I said. "Everything is coming out of encyclopedias and reference books."

"Then what are you worried about? Why do you doubt?"

"I just wish I had an external sign from God that I am not a loon. Predicting the end of the world is something about which one should be certain. I want a sign that it is really God talking through my book. And I want to know that a Christian that I have never met before will agree with it and be eager to read it."

"You'll get your sign," she said. "God will do something unmistakable."

The next morning we went to the bazaar for some light tourist shopping. I was surprised to stumble upon the exact horticultural specimen that I desired growing in a pot in the window of a leathergoods store. We went inside and perused some jackets as I thought of a good way to broach the subject of the plant.

The shopkeeper approached me with a mischievous grin and said something in an obscure dialect. My female friend, who is a linguist, laughed, "He's saying that you want a piece of the plant in his window."

I turned to him, "Well, yes! How did you know?"

"I saw you admiring it while you were outside. You must be a botanist," he said.

"I'm just an amateur. I'd be happy to pay you for it. I really don't need any leather jackets. I just want a cutting from the root." I took out my wallet.

"No! I won't hear of it. The plant is my gift to you."

I thanked him. He was a humorous man—full of idioms and jokes. After further conversation he offered us a guided tour of his town. He got in the passenger's side of the Jeep and directed me to a bucolic meadow. "You'd better get ready to stop because there is a two hundred meter cliff ahead," he warned.

I stopped abruptly and applied the emergency brake. We exited the Jeep and surveyed the landscape. Sheep were grazing in the meadow, which was dotted with pine trees. It ended with a steep granite canyon. At the bottom of the canyon was a raging river. On the other side was a mountain covered with a thick deciduous forest. In between, eagles were soaring. It was the most beautiful place I have ever seen, and the weather was perfect.

The setting was conducive to discussing deep subjects. We began to speak about life and religion. The shopkeeper told me that he was drinking-buddies with all the priests in his province, and that he didn't have much respect for any of them as men of God. I asked some follow-up questions and eventually realized that he was telling me that the priests frequent houses of prostitution.

I asked him directly, "Do you believe that true God became true man in Jesus of Nazareth?"

"Yes. Most certainly. I read the Bible and have entrusted my soul to the Lord. And I've been faithful to my wife throughout thirty years of marriage, by the way. But I don't go to church anymore since I moved back here. There are no good churches in these remote parts."

I told him that I wanted to buy him lunch, and asked if he knew of a good restaurant. We descended into the forest and found a place to order roast lamb and wine. By the time the bottle was empty I had told him my theories about the judgment of God upon nation-groups with incorrect Christologies. He was pensive in considering what I said.

I liked him and wanted to tell him more, so I asked him a leading question—what has become my favorite question—"Do you believe that Jesus will descend from the sky one day and put an end to human history?"

He opened his arms wide, "How can I not believe that? It is the very thing for which every righteous person is waiting."

I leaned in close to him and tapped my finger on the side of the wine bottle, "When?"

He then said something that astounded me, "Definitely not before the completion of the year two thousand and thirty-two."

A shiver went down my spine. I whipped my head toward my friend, who was acting as translator, "What?! What did he say?!"

She smiled, "Do you remember our talk in the Jeep, Chris?"

I was overcome with emotion for my God. My eyes welled and I barked at her, "You must ask him why he gave us that year! Be careful to tell me every word that comes out of his mouth!"

He told us that while working at a factory in the capital in AD 1988 he saw a strange old man standing on a street corner looking at him; he saw the old man for many consecutive days, standing and staring at him as he rode the bus to work. One day the shopkeeper rang for the bus to stop at that corner, although it was not his destination. He approached the old man, "Do we know each other?"

"No," said the old man, "But I have received a prophecy from God, and I have been guided by God to relate the prophecy specifically to you."

The old man was a Christian believer, and he told the shopkeeper that the Soviet Union would collapse in the next few years, and that Russia and the United States would become loose allies. The old man said that both nations would end up fighting fanatical Islamic forces around the world. He said that the war would intensify after AD 2011, and would result in chaos and lack of cohesion in many Muslim countries. The civil strife would last at least through AD 2032. During that time great natural disasters would occur on land and at sea. And immediately before Jesus Christ's return some strange things would happen in the sky.

"So what is the year of the Second Coming, then?" I asked.

"The old man was pretty sure it would be in the year two thousand and thirty-four—or maybe the year after that," he confirmed.

"Who was he? What was his name?"

"I don't know. I stupidly didn't get his name because I was late for work. And I never saw him again after that, although I looked for him and asked many people. I think he was an angel, but I'm not sure. I just always remember what he told me because the Soviet Union collapsed three and a half years after we spoke. And then in 1993 the World Trade Center in the US was truck-bombed by Muslims, and then the war started in Russia against the Chechen Muslims, and also in Bosnia and Kosovo. And now, of course, we have the wars resulting from September 11th and the mess in Iraq."

I told the shopkeeper that I already knew most of what he had related from the old man because I had just finished writing a book about the Second Coming with a similar timeline.

His eyes twinkled, "I'd like to read that book, my friend!"

"I'm afraid it won't be available in your language for some time."

"Never mind! Now I know why I made my kids learn English. Just promise that you will send me a copy!"

Acts 1:11 [NASB]
Men of Galilee, why do you stand looking into the sky? This Jesus, who has been taken up from you into heaven, will come in just the same way as you have watched Him go into heaven.

52. How Will Jesus Return?

At the beginning of AD 2006 I visited an elderly friend in the hospital. He was a veteran from the Battle of the Bulge, and immediately after the Second World War he was an aid-de-camp to General Eisenhower (AD 1890–AD 1969).

He was dying of old age and calmly stated, "I sure hope I don't have to spend another Christmas apart from Jesus. I keep asking Him to let me come up there."

"Aren't you afraid of dying?" I asked, already knowing the answer.

"No!" he scowled. Then his countenance softened with the thought of the Savior, "I know my God is waiting for me on the other side."

I said, "The Good Lord, in His time, is going to answer your prayer. You'll see Him soon enough. And then, not too long afterward, I'll see you again because Jesus will come back for the rest of us and put an end to this old world once and for all."

His perspicacity undiminished, he raised his head from the hospital bed and gave me a hopeful look, "I've always wondered about that. How, exactly, is it going to happen?"

I shrugged my shoulders and looked out the window, "One fine day, when the message of Jesus has been spread around the world, the sky will open up and He will descend in glory. Christ will give a shout and the dead will be raised with incorruptible bodies. The cemeteries will be busy places on that day—and everyone that has been lost at sea, or burnt to nothing, will somehow be physically reconstituted. The non-Christians will be sent to Hell, and the Christians will be brought to Heaven. Then the same thing will happen with the rest of humanity that is still alive at that time, and all God's people will live eternally with Jesus." I turned to look him in the eye, "It won't be much longer now."

He nodded in approval and rested back on the pillow.

Before I left he asked me to permanently disable the television in his room. I did so, and he raised his arms in triumph, "Hurrah!" Then we prayed about the things we had talked about.

He died a few weeks later, surrounded by four Christian women from his congregation, singing hymns.

God is so good: my old friend not only got to spend Christmas with Jesus, he also got to spend Easter with Him.

~~~~~~~~~~~~~~~~~~~~~~~~

My explanation above is what the Bible tells us about the mechanism of Jesus' return. The last time the disciples saw Jesus, He ascended upward, and two angels appeared.

> *... [Jesus] was taken up into a cloud while they were watching, and they could no longer see him. As they*

strained to see him rising into heaven, two white-robed men suddenly stood among them. "Men of Galilee," they said, "why are you standing here staring into heaven? Jesus has been taken from you into heaven, but someday he will return from heaven in the same way you saw him go!" [Acts 1:9–11 NLT]

Immediately preceding Jesus' Second Coming there will be fantastic signs in the sky. The Christians will know what this means, but the people whose treasure is on this earth will not be glad to see it. The Prophet Joel predicted,

I will pour out my Spirit on all people. Your sons and daughters will prophesy, your old men will dream dreams, your young men will see visions. Even on my servants, both men and women, I will pour out my Spirit in those days. I will show wonders in the heavens and on the earth, blood and fire and billows of smoke. The sun will be turned to darkness and the moon to blood before the coming of the great and dreadful day of the Lord. [Joel 2:28–31 NIV]

Jesus Christ said,

*Immediately after the tribulation of those days the sun will be darkened, and the moon will not give its light, and the stars will fall from heaven, and the powers of the heavens will be shaken. **Then will appear in heaven the sign of the Son of Man**, and then all the tribes of the earth will mourn, and they will see the Son of Man coming on the clouds of heaven with power and great glory. And he will send out his angels with a loud trumpet call, and they will gather his elect from the four winds, from one end of heaven to the other. [Matthew 24:29–31 ESV]*

This world will come to a close like the sudden end of a movie, or like being jolted awake from a bad dream. It will occur quickly, and be unmistakable.

For as the lightning that flashes out of one part under heaven shines to the other part under heaven, so also the Son of Man will be in His day. [Luke 17:24 NKJV]

Jesus Christ will descend from the sky in such a way that the living and the dead will see Him.

> *Look! He is coming with the clouds! Every eye will*
> *see him. Even those who pierced him will see him. All*
> *the nations of the earth will be sad because of him.*
> *This will really happen! [Revelation 1:7 NIrV]*

At that moment, those that have died in Christ will arise with new bodies, and we who are left on earth will also receive new bodies.

> *For the Lord Himself will descend from heaven with*
> *a shout, with the voice of an archangel, and with the*
> *trumpet of God. And the dead in Christ will rise first.*
> *Then we who are alive and remain shall be caught up*
> *together with them in the clouds to meet the Lord in*
> *the air. And thus we shall always be with the Lord. [1*
> *Thessalonians 4:16–17 NKJV]*

This is not the so-called 'rapture' that the Dispensational Premillennialists assert will occur seven years before the Second Coming—it will occur at the very moment of the Second Coming. This is the Judgment Day.

> *And just as it is appointed for man to die once, and*
> *after that comes judgment, so Christ, having been*
> *offered once to bear the sins of many, will appear a*
> *second time, not to deal with sin but to save those who*
> *are eagerly waiting for him. [Hebrews 9:27–28 ESV]*

Therefore, Christ will return to take away His people once, not twice. Saint Peter indicated that this event will be accompanied by a holocaust from the sky—possibly an asteroid, comet, or meteor impact.

> *… the day of the Lord will come as a thief in the night,*
> *in which the heavens will pass away with a great noise,*
> *and the elements will melt with fervent heat; both the*
> *earth and the works that are in it will be burned up. [2*
> *Peter 3:10 NKJV]*

And the Prophet Zephaniah predicted,

> *Neither their silver nor their gold shall be able to*
> *deliver them on the day of the wrath of the Lord. In*
> *the fire of his jealousy, all the earth shall be con-*
> *sumed; for a full and sudden end he will make of all*
> *the inhabitants of the earth. [Zephaniah 1:18 ESV]*

Such an event took place on the planet Jupiter in AD 1994 with the impacts of the Shoemaker-Levy Comet. That was God's forty year warning to planet Earth.

> ... there will be fearful sights and great signs from heaven. [Luke 21:11 NKJV]

Indeed, the asteroid Apophis is scheduled to pass close to Earth in AD 2029, **and could impact our planet during its second pass on Easter Sunday, April 13, AD 2036.**[430]

Despite the impending cataclysm, people that trust in Christ's bodily return should not be afraid. Christ promised to protect His faithful Church from the Tribulation that precedes His return.

> Since you have kept my command to endure patiently, I will also keep you from the hour of trial that is going to come on the whole world to test those who live on the earth. [Revelation 3:10 TNIV]

Jesus will send His angels to deliver us.

> At that time Michael, the great prince who protects your people, will arise. There will be a time of distress such as has not happened from the beginning of nations until then. But at that time your people— everyone whose name is found written in the book— will be delivered. Multitudes who sleep in the dust of the earth will awake: some to everlasting life, others to shame and everlasting contempt. Those who are wise will shine like the brightness of the heavens, and those who lead many to righteousness, like the stars for ever and ever. [Daniel 12:1–3 NIV]

On the other hand, those whose trust is not in Christ's bodily return should be very afraid.

> When I come to bring justice, you will trample those who are evil, as though they were ashes under your feet. [Malachi 4:3 CEV]

If you are waiting for supernatural occurrences in the heavens before you will accept that Jesus is the Messiah and give your heart to Him, there will not be enough time for you to repent—only to weep.

Deuteronomy 32:5 [KJV]
They have corrupted themselves, their spot is not the spot of his children: they
are a perverse and crooked generation.

53. What About the Jews?

In AD 1934 some Australian gold prospectors flew into a remote valley in New Guinea. They were greeted by the chief of a previously untouched tribe. The chief thought they were gods that had ridden to them from heaven on a giant eagle. He wanted to know the sex of the airplane.[431]

The Australians did not discourage these misconceptions. They soon had the Aborigines busy building an airstrip, and acting as jungle guides. Aboriginal virgin girls were given to them for nighttime pleasures.

Eventually, two enterprising natives secretly followed one of the White 'gods' while he went into the woods to defecate. They hid and watched until he finished, and then they investigated the gift from heaven. In short order one observed, "His skin is white, but his shit smells like ours." After a moment's reflection on the personal conduct of the white Australians, the other native gesticulated with indignation and exclaimed, "They're the same as us!"

Those aboriginal New Guineans had more sense than some churches in the United States that fly Israeli flags and hold Yiddish folk dancing classes. They are putzes, all of them.

There is an idolatrous movement afoot in evangelical Christian circles. It teaches that Jews and the modern State of Israel are especially loved by God—in a way that other human beings and other nations are not loved. These ideas are propagated by the non-creedal 'Christian' Zionists[432] that I mentioned in Section 27. They are a cult within the Dispensational Premillennialists. I call them Über-Baptists.

That very same element was present when the first Christian churches were planted. Judaizers infiltrated the Apostle Paul's churches in order to secure loyalty for Jewish national and cultural causes at the expense of the Gospel.

> *Those people are zealous to win you over, but for no*
> *good. What they want is to alienate you from us, so*
> *that you may have zeal for them. [Galatians 4:17*
> *TNIV]*

And, again, forty years later the same element afflicted the Smyrnan church that the Apostle John oversaw.

*I know the blasphemy of those opposing you. They say
they are Jews, but they are not, because their synagogue belongs to Satan. [Revelation 2:9 NLT]*

The devil is nothing if not persistent in his pathetic schemes. The
'Christian' Zionists of today have infiltrated not just Baptist churches, but
many supposedly nondenominational churches with their wicked dogma. They
receive attention disproportionate to their numbers because they have monopo-
lized End Times teaching, and people have been baffled by that part of the
Holy Scriptures (until the publication of this book). Also, they are outlandish
in dress and goofy in mannerism. Certainly the devil is keen to show off his
handiwork: demonic spirits entice foolish American women to respond to the
Über-Baptists' television appeals with enormous sums of money.

I make no apologies for this assertion. The Bible says that the rejection of Jesus as God in man's flesh is the spirit of the antichrist (1 John 4:3).
Anyone that declares that people with such a spirit (in this case, unbelieving
Jews) are favored by God and destined for Heaven is himself a false prophet
and an antichrist. And if unbelieving Jews are not destined for Heaven, then in
what sense are they a blessed people? Are they not a most piteous people?

How could it be that a particular group of antichrists gathering in a
particular eastern Mediterranean country are the Apple of God's Eye? Is God
a dog that He should shove His snout into our crotch and judge based upon
molecules, rather than upon belief?! Are you that muddleheaded and ignorant
of the Holy Scriptures?! Do they not universally testify that God is interested
in spiritual and not carnal traits?

*... there will be more joy in heaven over one sinner
who repents than over ninety-nine righteous persons
who need no repentance. [Luke 15:7 ESV]*

Will you not at least listen to Moses? The verse that heads this section
was spoken by him concerning those unbelieving Jews among his flock—the
very people that were about to claim the land of Canaan as the land of Israel.
**Moses said that the place of unbelieving Jews is not the place of God's
Children.** In other words, he is saying that they, as unbelievers, are destined
for Hell.

*Your accuser is Moses, on whom you have set your
hope. [John 5:45 HCSB]*

If Jews that deny Jesus Christ are the Chosen People, and the Chosen
People are destined for Hell, then by all means let me be unchosen for this
short life and saved for eternal life!

> *He who has the Son has life; he who does not have the*
> *Son of God does not have life. [1 John 5:12 NKJV]*

By what logic, then, can anyone say that unbelieving Jews are God's Chosen People? It can only be by the devil's logic. And if it is the devil's logic, then we should not be surprised to see concomitant with it the devil's gaudy polyester suits, the devil's slick hairstyling, and the devil's inappropriate emotionalism on 'Christian' television.

~~~~~~~~~~~~~~~~~~~~~~~

I know and like many Jewish people. They have been my neighbors, colleagues, and friends. They are generally friendly and insightful, and make quite good citizens. I could say similar things of Muslim people. That is why I am writing this book: I want for those that reject Christ's redemptive gift to know the truth about God's love; I want them to accept Him into their hearts, and to thus become the Chosen People. The most loving thing that you can do is to make someone aware of Jesus Christ.

However, in contrast to Dispensational Premillennialists, I am not obsessed with Jews. I do not believe—not for a moment—that 'natural Jews' are the Apple of God's Eye by virtue of their parentage or national identity.

The Jews are the Chosen People only in so far as God chose to bring His Word into the world through the bloodline and stories of Jacob, Judah, David, and the rest.

> *[King David] knew that God had promised him on*
> *oath that he would place one of his descendants on*
> *his throne. [Acts 2:30 TNIV]*

This is what Jesus meant when He told the Samaritan woman,

> *... salvation is of the Jews. [John 4:22 NKJV]*

He meant that it had been prophesied in the Old Testament Scriptures that He, the Messiah, was going to be a Jew (see Isaiah 59:20, for one of many examples). That's it. Nothing more. It is a boasting right that means precisely nothing to a person of Jewish ethnicity that has not personally accepted Jesus into his or her heart. Therefore, Jesus told the Jews in the Capernaum synagogue,

> *The Spirit gives life; the flesh counts for nothing.*
> *[John 6:63 TNIV]*

Sadly, many early Jewish followers of Jesus could not accept that being a Jew counted for nothing in God's eyes.

From this time many of his disciples turned back and
no longer followed him. [John 6:66 TNIV]

Jesus then asked His twelve Jewish disciples if they, too, would leave.
The Apostle Peter replied for them with faith.

Lord, to whom shall we go? thou hast the words of
eternal life. And we believe and are sure that thou art
that Christ, the Son of the living God. [John 6:68–69
KJV]

In this way, Peter showed that it was what he believed, and not his
Jewish lineage, that made him truly an Israelite.

And Christ Himself, when He first saw the Apostle Nathaniel, said,

Here is a true descendant of our ancestor Israel.
[John 1:47 CEV]

Does that not imply that there were false descendants of Israel within
Judea? Indeed there were then, and there are today. The false descendants of
Israel are those that do not acknowledge the Messiah, Jesus of Nazareth.

Christ explicitly told those Jews that did not love Him that although
they had descent from Abraham (John 8:37), they were not truly Abraham's
children (John 8:39).

It is an utter corruption of the Gospel to call those that reject the Son
of God 'the Chosen People on whom God's favor rests.' But many that claim
to be Christians do just that! I know a man that is a Jewish Christian and is
an evangelist to the Jews. He told me that when his organization contacts certain Bible societies in order to pool their outreach efforts, they receive a reply
like this: "Oh, no, we would never partner with your group. You Jews are the
Chosen People; you have your own covenant with God, as do the Arab descendants of Ishmael. The Bible teaches that you folks don't need Jesus like we
unclean Gentiles do."

That is a racist statement. But more importantly, it blasphemes the
name of Christ. God our Father is just, for,

*[He] shows no partiality. But in every nation **whoever***
fears Him and works righteousness is accepted by
***Him**. [Acts 10:34–35 NKJV]*

God did not show favoritism between the races either in the Old
Testament or in the New Testament. Nor did He ever make a covenant based
upon race. A Messianic Jew recently said on 'Christian' television,

You Gentile Christians have the New Covenant, and
its promise is in the afterlife. But we Jewish Christians

*have two covenants, New and Old: One promise is
for the afterlife, and the other is here on earth. The
promise of the Old Covenant involves real estate in
the Middle East! The land of Israel belongs to us Jews
because God has given it to us through Abraham.*

How racist, and ignorant, and twisted, and satanic! What has always
mattered to God is what one believes, not what blood-type runs through one's
veins!

*For the Father Himself loves you, **because you have
loved Me and have believed** that I came from God.
[John 16:27 HCSB]*

Genealogy reveals that there is no such thing as a pure race, in any
case. Such a thing is impossible without multi-generational endogamy. And
even a small amount of incest leads to genetic deformities and sterility.[433] If the
Jews had completely pure genetic lines, they would not exist today. Of course
they have not inbred, but interbred—like every other physically-viable group
on the face of the earth.

We know from the Holy Scriptures that Judah, the father of the Jews,
married a Canaanite woman.

*About that time Judah left his brothers in the hill
country and went to live near his friend Hirah in the
town of Adullam. While there he met the daughter of
Shua, a Canaanite man. Judah married her, and they
had three sons. [Genesis 38:1–3 CEV]*

And because of meticulous record-keeping, we know that one of his
sons by her had descendants. Those descendants mixed with the ancestors of
today's Jordanians.

*Shelah was one of Judah's sons. The descendants of
Shelah were Er (the father of Lecah); Laadah (the
father of Mareshah); the families of linen workers at
Beth-ashbea; Jokim; the men of Cozeba; and Joash
and Saraph, who ruled over Moab and Jashubi-
lehem. These names all come from ancient records.
They were the pottery makers who lived in Netaim and
Gederah. They lived there and worked for the king. [1
Chronicles 4:21–23 NLT]*

This happened throughout the Old Testament. For example, Moses'
wife was the daughter of a Midianite priest.

Now a priest of Midian had seven daughters ... Moses agreed to stay with the man, who gave his daughter Zipporah to Moses in marriage. [Exodus 2:16,21 NIV]

And King David's great grandmother was Ruth the Moabitess.

[Ruth's son, Obed] became the father of Jesse and the grandfather of David. [Ruth 4:17 NLT]

And Israel's greatest king, Solomon, produced children with hundreds of non-Jewish women.

Solomon loved his wife, the daughter of the king of Egypt. But he also loved some women from Moab, Ammon, and Edom, and others from Sidon and the land of the Hittites. Seven hundred of his wives were daughters of kings, but he also married three hundred other women. [1 Kings 11:1–3 CEV]

Even after the Babylonian captivity, in 432 BC,[434] Nehemiah documented intermarriage with the enemies of Israel.

I discovered that some Jewish men had married women from Ashdod, Ammon, and Moab. About half of their children could not speak Hebrew—they spoke only the language of Ashdod or some other foreign language. [Nehemiah 13:23–24 CEV]

And the penultimate pre–Christ prophet lamented,

You men have married women who worship other gods. [Malachi 2:11 NIrV]

This being the case, in what sense is a modern Jew a genetic Jew? By descent from Abraham, Isaac, and Jacob?? Lots of people in Europe, Africa, and Asia carry DNA from Abraham, Isaac, and Jacob (including the author of this book). The assimilation of Jewish bloodlines—from the foreign marriage of Judah in 1715 BC[435] onward—necessarily means that most of today's people that carry some small amount of DNA from Abraham, Isaac, and Jacob do not self-identify as modern-day Jews. Their ancestors may have been subject to ethnic cleansing and forcible conversion and a host of other atrocities, but the descendants themselves—by their freewill this very day—are members of other nation-groups and are likely ignorant of their genetic heritage. This includes millions of people in Jordan, Egypt, Iran, Iraq, Morocco, Russia, Ethiopia, and even South Africa and India.

So the position of 'Christian' Zionists is completely untenable and contradictory. Consider the disconnect between (a) and (b) below:

a. 'Christian' Zionists insist that modern Jews are the Chosen People. They insist that this is the case without regard to the percentage of DNA that the modern Jew carries from Abraham, Isaac, and Jacob. They insist upon it simply because the modern Jew self-identifies as a Jew. In other words, 'Christian' Zionists venerate the Jews based upon their belief and profession that they are Jews.

b. AT THE VERY SAME TIME, 'Christian' Zionists insist that the belief and profession of Creedal Christians (with or without DNA from Abraham, Isaac, and Jacob) is not enough to overcome God's prejudice for the Jewish race as the 'Apple of His Eye' and the rightful occupants of the land west of the Jordan River.

Now, there are only two ways to become a Jew: be born of a Jewish mother (even if she, herself, is only a Jew from her maternal grandmother), or convert in a ceremony that usually involves the renunciation of Jesus as Christ. Indeed, if there is but one thing that ninety-nine percent of self-identified Jews agree upon, it is that Jesus of Nazareth is not the Messiah. As it is written,

He came unto his own, and his own received him not.
[John 1:11 KJV]

Therefore, 'Christian' Zionists are saying that God favors faith in the Jewish national identity over faith in His Only Begotten Son, Jesus Christ—at least when it comes to ancestral inheritance to real estate and other special offspring-allowances.

I can understand this coming from a Jewish nationalist: zealots of every ethnic stripe preen their feathers, and make a spectacle of themselves, and maintain that they are God's gift to the world. But for it to come from someone that claims to be a Christian—such a notion is the product of a sick mind!

I maintain that the measure of belonging in (a), above, is sufficient for the purpose of establishing a national claim for the modern Jewish state within Palestine, but it is in no way sufficient for executorial purposes concerning God's promise to Abraham. Legally-speaking, ancestral inheritance must be quantifiable—through direct descent. And modern DNA fingerprinting affords us the ability to do just that.

Now, if such tests were run against the bones of the Patriarch Jacob, and if a certain Palestinian Arab fruit farmer were found to have a more substantive Israelite lineage than a certain Ashkenazi Jewish software engineer, then intellectual consistency would require that 'Christian' Zionists switch allegiance for that pair. Their preoccupation would have to go from the Ashkenazi Jew taking control of an orchard in the West Bank (at the expense of the Arab) to the Palestinian Arab taking control of a condominium within the State of Israel (at the expense of the Jew).

Of course, such a change in allegiance would never be forthcoming because the position of the 'Christian' Zionist is not based upon godliness—it is based upon worldliness.

The hypocrisy is nauseating. But what does the Bible have to say about this issue of land title and direct descent from Abraham, Isaac, and Jacob?

In God's eyes, the title to the real estate in the Levant, the whole earth, and the entire universe, belongs to any and all Christians, *but never to people (with or without descent from Abraham, Isaac, and Jacob) that reject the Son of God, Jesus Christ*. This is the case precisely because God made a spiritual (rather than genetic) covenant with Abraham.

> *Lift up now thine eyes, and look from the place where thou art northward, and southward, and eastward, and westward:* **For all the land which thou seest, to thee will I give it, and to thy seed for ever.** *And I will make thy seed as the dust of the earth: so that if a man can number the dust of the earth, then shall thy seed also be numbered. Arise, walk through the land in the length of it and in the breadth of it; for I will give it unto thee. [Genesis 13:14–17 KJV]*

When Abraham lifted up his eyes, he was looking into the horizon; he was looking, as it were, over the whole earth and all the stars of heaven. The land thereof was promised by God to Abraham and his seed forever.

> *Wherever you set foot, you will be on land I have given you … [Joshua 1:3 NLT]*

And who is this seed to whom God referred?

> *The promises were spoken to Abraham and **to his seed … who is Christ**. [Galatians 3:16 TNIV]*

Now, we know that Jesus Christ, the One and Only Seed of Abraham, did not sire any children by a woman.

> *Unjustly condemned, he was led away. No one cared that **he died without descendants**, that his life was cut short in midstream. [Isaiah 53:8 NLT]*

So who on the face of the earth today is the heir of the promise made to Abraham, the Father of Faith, and to His Seed, Jesus?

> *Understand, then, that **those who believe are children of Abraham**. [Galatians 3:7 NIV]*

> ***For Abraham is the father of all who believe.** [Romans 4:16b NLT]*

Those who believe what, exactly?

> *Both Gentiles and Jews **who believe the Good News** share equally in the riches inherited by God's children. Both are part of the same body, and both enjoy the promise of blessings because they belong to Christ Jesus. [Ephesians 3:6 NLT]*

Believe the Good News for what purpose, exactly?

> *This people I have formed for Myself; **They shall declare My praise**. [Isaiah 43:21 NKJV]*

It is we that entrust our souls to Jesus and declare Christ's praise that are one with Him and Abraham as heirs of every good thing in Creation!

> ***If you belong to Christ, then you are Abraham's seed, and heirs according to the promise**. [Galatians 3:29 TNIV]*

Never make the mistake of calling unbelieving people 'the Israel of God' or 'the Chosen People.' The Chosen People were always those that believed that God would become a man in accordance with the divine prophecies given in the Old Testament, no matter from what nation they emanated. In the two thousand years before Christ, most of the people that believed the promise were chosen from among the Jews. Some, however, were Gentiles, such as Job, Rahab, Ruth, the widow of Zarephath, Naaman, Ebed-Melech, and the Magi.

> *I have other sheep which are not from this sheep-pen. [John 10:16 NLV]*

In the two thousand years after Christ, most of the people that believed the fulfillment have been chosen from among the Gentiles. But some were

Jews, such as Barnabas, Silas, Eunice, Philip, Priscilla, Aquila, and Apollos. There never was a distinction between God's acceptance of Jewish believers and Gentile believers, nor God's blessing upon Jewish believers and Gentile believers.

> *Everything depends on having faith in God ...*
> *[Romans 4:16a CEV]*

The Apostle Paul and his companion Barnabas boldly said to the unbelieving Jews,

> *We had to speak the word of God to you first. Since you reject it and do not consider yourselves worthy of eternal life, we now turn to the Gentiles. [Acts 13:46 NIV]*

Jesus underscored this point when His family sent word through the thronging followers that they wished to speak with Him. He responded,

> *"Who is my mother, and who are my brothers?" Pointing to his disciples, he said, "Here are my mother and my brothers. For **whoever does the will of my Father in heaven is my brother and sister and mother**." [Matthew 12:48–50 NIV]*

Jesus Christ was prepared to disown His own immediate family if they did not become His disciples—even the blessed Virgin Mother!

Remember, Jesus' family was of direct lineage to King David. Do you not now see the true position of today's Jews that deny Jesus' divinity (whether descended from David, or Samuel, or Aaron)? They are utterly lost and destitute without Christ in their hearts!

But anyone that entrusts his or her soul to Jesus Christ is an heir with Him to all the fullness of God. For it is written,

> *The Father loves the Son, and has given all things into His hand. [John 3:35 NKJV]*

So stake a claim for Christ, and stop showing deference to antichrists!

> *The righteous shall inherit the land and dwell upon it forever. [Psalm 37:29 ESV]*

If you do so, Jesus promises that unbelieving people—of all possible combinations of human genomic sequence—will acknowledge your holiness.

> *I will make them come and fall down at your feet and acknowledge that I have loved you. [Revelation 3:9 NIV]*

The True Israel is, and always has been, whosoever will believe that the God of love became a man in Jesus Christ. Heaven and earth are for them alone, and the last verse in the entire Bible confirms a blessing upon them alone:

> *May the grace of the Lord Jesus be with God's holy people. [Revelation 22:21 NLT]*

~~~~~~~~~~~~~~~~~~~~~~~~

Before closing this section, I should point out that I am not obsessed with Jews in a condemnatory sense either. Some Christians overemphasize the shout of a hundred-or-so paid political hacks during Jesus' 6:00 AM trial[436] before Pilate,

> *Let his blood be on us and on our children! [Matthew 27:25 NIV]*

It is suggested that if a Jew does not expunge every aspect of his ethnic Jewish identity and take-on the identity of some *non-Jewish ethnicity*, then he is a Christ-killer.

This has been a rally cry of Jew-baiters for centuries. We should not be surprised. The devil always misuses the Word of God for his own destructive ends.

Those that espouse Jewish cultural nihilism are invariably hypocrites: they are the least likely people to admit that they must divest themselves of the unchristian influences in their own culture. Rather, they insist that their own [non-Jewish] culture, idioms, cuisine, and manner of picking their teeth, are so completely infused with the Bible's teachings that it would be efficacious for those that wish to become true Christians to take-on their ethnic identity as a spiritual primer!

It is the theological addendum to Rudyard Kipling's (AD 1865–AD 1936) White Man's Burden: inasmuch as the Jews must eschew their Jewishness in order to make it into heaven, they themselves must embrace their heritage and revel in their favored cultural destiny. How convenient for these modern-day Pharisees!

Don't laugh. Tribalism is a powerful delusion. I have heard certain [non-ethnically-Jewish] Christians make these assertions with my own ears. They don't see the irony that God brought forth His Word from within the Jewish paradigm—the very people that they correctly consider to be unworthy without throwing-off the handicaps of the Jewish culture in favor of a relation-ship with Jesus Christ. How, then, can some non-Jewish culture, which isn't even mentioned in the Bible (or if it is mentioned, it is only in the most loathsome terms), be a vehicle of divine virtue? Most certainly it cannot be.

> *Do not be arrogant, but be afraid. For if God did not spare the natural branches, he will not spare you either. [Romans 11:20–21 NIV]*

Like a thick bank account, every comfort of this life is only and always an impediment to the Lordship of Jesus Christ over one's heart.

> *For where your treasure is, there your heart will be also. [Matthew 6:21 NKJV]*

And the more resonant and far-reaching one's cultural history is (as is arguably the case with the Jews), the more difficult it is to see one's way through it.

Jesus said about a fellow Jew that closely observed the Mosaic Law,

> *It's terribly hard for rich people to get into the kingdom of heaven! [Matthew 19:23 CEV]*

Jesus was referring to money here, but not solely to money. This pitiful rich man had everything that life could offer—everything except the Son of God in his life. He walked away dejected after Christ instructed him to forsake it all in favor of the Blessed Relationship. Christ then noted,

> *... it's easier for a camel to go through the eye of a needle than for a rich person to get into God's kingdom. [Matthew 19:24 CEV]*

It is no stretch to also say that it is easier for a camel to go through the eye of a needle than for ...

- an Abaptist Evangelical to baptize his young children, and confess that they gain faith in Christ and have their original sin forgiven at that moment by the Holy Spirit's mysterious power (see Section 18);
- an Über-Baptist to confess, "The Jews never were the Apple of God's Eye—it was only those Jews (and Gentiles) that believed that God would become a human being that were the Apple of God's Eye. It has always been those that believe in the promise of salvation through the God-man, Jesus Christ, that are the Apple of God's Eye and

God's Chosen People" (continue reading through Section 56);

- an Oriental Orthodox to confess, "Jesus of Nazareth had the separate nature of God and the separate nature of man in one undivided Person" (see Sections 62–67, 80);
- an Eastern Orthodox to confess, "The Holy Spirit proceeds from both the Father and the Son" (see Section 69);
- a Mainline Protestant to confess, "Spreading the Gospel of Jesus Christ is good, and spreading liberalism is evil" (see Sections 76–80);
- a Roman Catholic to confess, "A Christian is justified by faith apart from the works of the law" (see bottom of Section 81).

There are hundreds of millions of stiff-necked Christians that cannot shake off their unbiblical cultural/religious heritage and confess these simple truths about God.

Many of these same Christians will hate this book and will hate its author. And if you think that the weaning of human souls away from imprinted fealty is a trivial matter, **take some practice by getting in between the teats of a lioness and her cubs, and explaining to them the virtues of a non-dairy diet.**

Things would look bleak for the salvation of human souls, except that,

> *There are some things that people cannot do, but God can do anything. [Matthew 19:26 CEV]*

Because God loves you, He will work throughout your life, in the most extreme ways possible, to get you to confess the truth about Him and thus to be one with Him.

> *As many as I love, I rebuke and chasten. Therefore be zealous and repent. Behold, I stand at the door and knock. If anyone hears My voice and opens the door, I will come in to him and dine with him, and he with Me. [Revelation 3:19–20 NKJV]*

Do not harden your heart toward the God of Love. Make it easier on yourself and stop resisting the Holy Spirit, for,

*It is hard for you to kick against the goads. [Acts
26:14 NKJV]*

And whether you are rich in finance, or rich in heritage, or rich in any
other worldly good, take no solace in it. Rather, follow the example of the
Apostle Paul:

*Indeed, I count everything as loss because of the sur-
passing worth of knowing Christ Jesus my Lord. For
his sake I have suffered the loss of all things and count
them as rubbish ... [Philippians 3:8 ESV]*

In this light, my answer to the 'Let-his-blood-be-on-us-and-on-our
children' charge is simple: today's Jew is only [spiritually-speaking] responsible for Jesus' Crucifixion if, in his heart or with his mouth, he approves of
the death sentence pronounced upon Him. Any Jew (or Gentile, for that matter)
that thinks that Jesus was a blasphemer that got what He deserved, is as guilty
in God's eyes as the High Priests Annas and Caiaphas, the Sanhedrin, and the
Temple guards. Such a person would not be renouncing his ancestral sin, but
would be laying claim to the murder of God as part of his or her rich cultural
heritage. On the other hand, any Jew that thinks that the AD 30 Jewish leadership were dangerous religious fanatics with no regard for freedom of speech, is
by no means a child of the mob in Pilate's court. In that case, he or she is only
responsible for personal sin—not the sin of the Sanhedrin.

Can we not all agree that that is a fair judgment?

Luke 21:24 [NKJV]
*Jerusalem will be trampled by Gentiles until the times of the Gentiles are
fulfilled.*

54. Modern Israel has Virtually No Eschatological Significance

Jesus predicted that Jerusalem would be trampled by the Gentiles until near
the time of His Second Coming. The word 'Gentile' is a pejorative that means
'heathen' or 'pagan.'

Some Christians maintain that Jesus' prophecy was fulfilled in AD
1967 when Roman, Arab, Crusader, Turkish, British, and Jordanian rule

finally ended. Since that time, Jewish Israelis have been the civil authorities in Jerusalem.

This view is incorrect because, according to the Bible, the unbelieving Jews (i.e., those that practice Rabbinic Judaism) are themselves Spiritual Gentiles or antichrists. Christians must take care to distinguish between the religion of the Old Testament (sometimes referred to as 'Yahwism') and the Rabbinic Judaism that developed after the destruction of the Second Temple in AD 70.[437]

Today's Jews do have a genetic similarity with the faithful Jews, or Israelites, or Hebrews of biblical times (as do many other people in Europe, Africa, and Asia), but the degree of their spiritual similarity is entirely based upon how they think about the God that revealed Himself to Abraham, Isaac, and Jacob. If they reject the Messiah, Jesus, their spiritual similarity is with both the ancient Gentile sinners and the ancient Israelites that rejected Yahwism.

> *Son of man, the people of Israel are the worthless slag*
> *that remains after silver is smelted. They are the dross*
> *that is left over—a useless mixture of copper, tin, iron,*
> *and lead. [Ezekiel 22:18 NLT]*

The Word of God is, therefore, not at all schizophrenic when it both blesses and curses Israel: Wherever the word 'Israel' is used favorably in the Old and New Testaments, it is always a reference to the Spiritual Israel or True Israel (i.e., those that would accept and practice Creedal Christianity if they were alive in the last Millennium).

> *I will grant salvation to Zion, and my splendor to*
> *Israel. [Romans 11:26 NIV]*

And wherever the word 'Israel' is used negatively in the Old and New Testaments, it is always a reference to those that are not of the Spiritual or True Israel (i.e., those that would not accept and practice Creedal Christianity if they were alive in the last Millennium).

> *I will give Jacob to the curse, and Israel to reproaches.*
> *[Isaiah 43:28 NKJV]*

This is a completely-consistent explanation—one that transcends race.

> *There is no difference between the Jews and the peo*
> *ple who are not Jews. They are all the same to the*
> *Lord. [Romans 10:12 NLV]*

The promises of the Old Testament and fulfillment of the New Testament are a continuum—the Law of Yahwism showing us our sin, and the

Gospel of Christianity showing us our Savior. In this way the believing Jews of the Old Testament period and the believing Christians of the New Testament period (i.e., the End Times) are one Body. And every single person that has been chosen by God to be part of the true, spiritual, Israel (i.e., to become a Christian before they die) will be saved.

> For the promise is for you and your children and for
> all who are far off, as many as the Lord our God will
> call to Himself. [Acts 2:39 NASB]

So when Muslim Jordanian authority in Jerusalem was replaced by the Jewish Israeli authority, there was no spiritual changeover. Both governments are made up of individuals that disbelieve that God became a man in Jesus. Thus they are both antichrists, and rule of the city went from Spiritual Gentile to Spiritual Gentile.

~~~~~~~~~~~~~~~~~~~~~~

The modern State of Israel is a parliamentary democracy, aligned with the political and economic values of the United States. It is a secular nation, populated by peoples that are [religiously] seventy-seven percent Judaic, eighteen percent Islamic, and only two percent [mostly Arab] Christian.[438] They very well could have called themselves the modern 'State of Judea,' or the modern 'State of Ashkenazi, Mizrahi, and Sephardi,' or the modern 'State of Southwest Coastal Levant.' The word 'Israel' is a tribute to their forefathers of three thousand years ago—very nice indeed, but that does not make them the True Israel because,

> ... not all who are descended from Israel are Israel.
> [Romans 9:6 TNIV]

How much more clearly does God have to state it in His inerrant Word?! **You have to accept Jesus Christ into your heart in order to be descended from Israel.** God has promised,

> In the Lord all the offspring of Israel shall be justi-
> fied ... [Isaiah 45:25 ESV]

And the Apostle Paul taught us,

> ... a man is justified by faith apart from observing the
> law. [Romans 3:28 NIV]

Therefore, faith in Christ makes one an Israelite, rather than circumcision, or Judaic descent, or any other machination of the law. And just as secularist Kemal Ataturk and his Islamic nation are still under God's wrath

(Section 30), so secularist David Ben-Gurion[xi] and his Judaic nation are still under God's wrath.

It is a useful comparison. As non-Christian, secular, states that aspire to the western political and economic model, Turkey and Israel are quite naturally strategic allies. If you want to see what modernism and democracy are like apart from the mitigation of God's Word, visit Turkey, or Israel, or India, or even Japan. If you walk away enamored of their cultural diversity, there is something wrong with you.

> *But Jesus didn't trust them, because he knew human*
> *nature. No one needed to tell him what mankind is*
> *really like. [John 2:24–25 NLT]*

The same principle applies to loyal, patriotic, Americans that vote the correct way, but refuse to entrust their souls to the care of the God-man, Jesus. We must not make the mistake of assuming that our personal allies, however much we like them, are spiritually alive. Whoever, regardless of nationality or bloodline, rejects Jesus as coming in the flesh is himself or herself rejected; whoever accepts Him is accepted as one of the very Chosen People of God and the very Apple of His Eye.

Despite the proofs offered above, Dispensational Premillennialists stubbornly maintain that the successful establishment of the modern State of Israel, eighteen hundred years after the short-lived bar Kokhba Jewish state (AD 132–AD 135), is too major an event to be coincidental. They say that it must be a sign of the end of the world. The 'Christian' Zionists go farther, maintaining that the sign of the end of the world will be when all the land west of the Jordan River is occupied by Jews and only by Jews. They anxiously await the demolition of the Dome of the Rock and the construction of another temple by Jews on the Temple Mount.[439]

In point of fact, such speculation does portend the end, but not for the reason that these people assert.

Spiritually-speaking, nothing is a coincidence. Spiritually-speaking, the entire period after Christ's Ascension to Heaven is the End Time. Every wicked and tragic thing that is reported in the news is a sign of the end of this age. So is the appearance of every false teacher. The Bible says,

> *These men are blemishes at your love feasts, eating*
> *with you without the slightest qualm—shepherds who*
> *feed only themselves … they follow their own evil*

---

xi   The first Prime Minister of the modern State of Israel. He was not Christian. He was not a practicing Jew, either. He dabbled in Buddhism.

desires ... and flatter others for their own advantage.
But, dear friends, remember what the apostles of our
Lord Jesus Christ foretold. They said to you, "In the
last times there will be scoffers who will follow their
*own ungodly desires." **These are the men who divide***
you, who follow mere natural instincts and do not
have the Spirit. *[Jude 12,16–19 NIV]*

This speaks of those that send out glass vials filled with dirt (an idol of stone) from the Holy Land in exchange for donations. It speaks of those that teach that God needs for Christians to make certain that modern-day Jews inhabit all the land west of the Jordan River. It is the emergence of these snake oil salesmen within Christ's Church (rather than Jewish control over Palestine) that is the real sign of the end of the world. But the Apostle Paul assures us that God will judge the Judaizing agitators.

The one who has gotten you all mixed up will pay the
price. It doesn't matter who that may be. [Galatians
5:10 NIrV]

And the Apostle Peter says of false prophets,

Many people will follow their evil ways and cause
others to tell lies about the true way. They will be
greedy and cheat you with smooth talk. But long ago
God decided to punish them, and God doesn't sleep.
[2 Peter 2:2–3 CEV]

I testify to you as a dyed-in-the-wool Protestant: I would sooner attend a Latin Mass and kiss the ring of the Bishop of Rome than listen to the Über-Baptists speak of their fictional rapture and the desecration of a future Jewish temple.

Be forewarned: Dispensationalism is not merely idiocy—it is wickedness!

~~~~~~~~~~~~~~~~~~~~~~~~

Christ's Gospel is, in reality, utterly indifferent toward the issue of modern-day Jews residing between the Mediterranean Sea and the River Jordan. The founding of the modern State of Israel is simply not mentioned in Biblical End Times prophecy. Those that insist that the return of the Jews to their ancestral homeland is the central event heralding Christ's imminent return are false prophets.

God allowed the twentieth century Jews to retake their ancestral homeland for the same reason that He allowed Ataturk to form the Republic of Turkey: His Holy Word prophesied that the [post-Ali] Caliphate's power would last for only 1,260 years (Revelation 12:6). Indeed, the Ottoman Empire did end—right on schedule—with the ratification of the Turkish Constitution in AD 1921 (Section 30).[440]

God's Holy Word did not, however, prophesy that the entire region that had been desolated by the Caliphate would be Christianized—only that the Gospel would be spread there before the end would come.

> *The Lord has made His saving power known. He has shown to the nations how right and good He is ... All the ends of the earth have seen the saving power of our God. [Psalm 98:2–3 NLV]*

We are approaching that calendar date, so Providence is making provision for the final overspreading of the Gospel message.

Although it is true that fewer than one percent of identifiably ethnic Jews are Christians,[xii] modern-day Jewish people are undeniably western in their sensibilities. Consider the comments of Harvard University Professor Samuel P. Huntington concerning the culture of the United States:

> *... our culture has been a Protestant culture ... I [am] talking about a set of values and customs and beliefs which are the product of the [English] settlers, but ... are also ... absorbed ... by other people. It's not limited to Protestants. When I've talked about my ideas with Jewish friends and talked about Anglo-Protestant culture, they very frequently say, "Oh, yes. Of course. And I'm an Anglo-Protestant Jew." And that's ... the overwhelming case.*[441]

He is referring to the self-identification of American Jews,[442] but the principle translates to Israeli Jews, as well. They are an anchor for modernity in the heart of the Muslim world. And with modernity comes the dissemination of information and freedom of conscience. Just ask any Muslim fanatic.

---

xii   Many people with Jewish blood are Christians, but they are not ethnic Jews because they have been assimilated into other cultures. It is probable that today's Palestinian Christians, for example, are largely mixed-blood Jews that converted to Christianity before the Arab invasion necessitated that they adopt the Arabic language and culture. There was a flourishing Christian civilization in Palestine between the fourth and seventh centuries.

To them the eleventh century Crusader and the twenty-first century Zionist are one-and-the-same being: an oppressive occupier of a land where people are not supposed to be allowed to choose their own religion.

Mr. Ben-Gurion, a person of Jewish ethnicity, chose Buddhism for himself in a former part of the Caliphate. Needless to say, the suicide-bomb manufacturers of Gaza City would not countenance their vest-carriers' converting to Buddhism. They would not tolerate religious pluralism of any sort if they gained control of Palestine.

Indeed, a female friend of mine once had her gold cross ripped off her neck by the religious police while she was working in Kuwait. Infidel symbols are not tolerated on the Prophet's sand. Now, Christianity may not be popular in Israel, but the western value system is popular. Thus, the Israeli civil authorities do not countenance religious radicalism against Christians or secular Jews.

There have been riots in Orthodox Jewish neighborhoods when secular Jews drive on the Sabbath, and there have been instances of Christian clergy being spat upon by Jewish fanatics in Jerusalem. Also, an Anglican theologian friend of mine is routinely strip-searched and harassed by Israeli customs when he travels through Tel Aviv for biblical research. They are discriminating against him on the basis of his religion. But, relatively-speaking, it is a more tolerable situation than exists in Islamic countries. I don't know of any murders of secularists or Christians in Israel, as is commonplace in Muslim lands.

In this way an adult child that becomes a Creedal Christian would have his throat slit by his Muslim family in a country that observed Sharia law. But in the modern State of Israel he or she would just stop being invited over for matzo ball and gefilte fish—not exactly a punitive reward!

God is sovereign. The Israeli attitude, although non-Christian, is more useful for God's current plan-of-action. Hence, it exists and is made to be viable through US government subsidization.

If the Palestinian Arabs really wish to regain control over their lives, there is one, and only one, course to take: *en masse* they should get on their knees and confess the Lordship of Jesus Christ over their hearts, their minds, their children, and their property. They should repudiate the devil, Allah, and the name of blasphemy, Muhammad. They should flood into whatever Christian churches there still are in their cities and get baptized with water in the name of the Father and of the Son and of the Holy Spirit. They should eat the body and drink the blood[xiii] of the Risen Christ. They should throw out their

---

xiii   Yes, that means drinking a sip of wine! The devil, Allah, has commanded Muslims to not consume any alcohol in order to keep them away from the

Qur'ans and start reading the Holy Bible in Arabic. They should confess the three Ecumenical Creeds (with the Filioque! See Sections 18, 69), and say the Lord's Prayer, and attend Sunday worship. Then the Arabs would become the Chosen People on whom God's favor rests, and God Himself would contend with the mighty Israeli army and their American sponsors.

If the Israeli Jews simultaneously did the same thing, then the Arabs and the Jews would together be the Chosen People on whom God's favor rests. God would make them love each other and defer to each other. Our God is omnipotent—He is not impotent like the Islamic god or the Judaic god. Jesus Christ can do anything.

It is a common misconception that the Triune God of the Bible is the same as the god of the other Monotheistic faiths—especially Judaism. This is absolutely false. The Bible tells us clearly,

> *Whoever transgresses and does not abide in the doc-*
> *trine of Christ does not have God. [2 John 9 NKJV]*

And also,

> *Who is the liar? It is the man who denies that Jesus is*
> *the Christ. Such a man is the antichrist—he denies the*
> *Father and the Son. [1 John 2:22 NIV]*

The god of Judaism and Islam is most definitely the devil. Jesus did not tell the unbelieving Jews, "Both you and I have Yahweh as our Father." Certainly not! Jesus was not a liar. Instead, He told the unbelieving Jews,

> *You belong to your father, the devil. [John 8:44*
> *NIrV]*

Only people that accept and trust that the co-eternal Person of the Holy Trinity, God the Son, became a man in the Jewish carpenter, Jesus of Nazareth, worship the Living God.

The solution to the problems of the Arabs and the Jews is right under their identical Semitic[xiv] noses: accept Christ. But Jesus prophesied about the hardness-of-heart of the people that inhabit this region of the world:

---

live-giving blood of Jesus Christ. Appallingly, some Reformed Protestants do the same: I once heard a non-denominational preacher tell his radio audience to get some orange juice and a muffin from their refrigerators and partake in Communion from home. God help us! That is a snack, not the very body and blood of Christ!

xiv Both the Arabs and Jews are Semitic peoples. That is to say that they are both descended from Noah's son, Shem. He was the father of the Assyro–Chaldeans, from whence Abraham originated.

O Jerusalem, Jerusalem, the one who kills the proph-
ets and stones those who are sent to her! How often
I wanted to gather your children together, as a hen
gathers her chicks under her wings, but you were not
willing! See! Your house is left to you desolate; for
I say to you, you shall see Me no more till you say,
'Blessed is He who comes in the name of the Lord!'
[Matthew 23:37–39 NKJV]

By this He meant that there would be no peace there until they accept Him as Christ. The area could be one hundred percent Jewish or one hundred percent Arab, and still there would be no peace there. God has spoken; they must accept Him, or live in want of peace.

In any case, there is less than one generation left until the end of the world.

Look! I am creating new heavens and a new earth,
and no one will even think about the old ones any-
more. [Isaiah 65:17 NLT]

The God of glory has promised that a new Heaven and a new Earth will be given, thus making the entire point of land-control in Palestine moot.

Luke 11:27–28 [NIV]
... a woman in the crowd called out, "Blessed is the mother who gave you birth
and nursed you."
[Jesus] replied, "Blessed rather are those who hear the word of God and obey
it."

55. God Does Not Want You to Celebrate Jesus' Diversity

The American public school curriculum has lately become infused with diversity madness. Liberals assert that it is not enough to simply teach geography and social studies, but that the children have to experience and celebrate other ways of living. They say that this is necessary so that the children do not 'freak out' later in life when they meet people of another culture, race, or sexual orientation. Invariably, the traditional Anglo–American Protestant heritage is disparaged during these neo–religious sessions. That is the hidden agenda, really.

Likewise, some Christians say that since Jesus was a first-century Jew, and the Scriptures teach us to emulate Him, we should adapt ourselves to every cultural particular that He experienced. They want to follow Jesus' diet, get their boys circumcised, get baptized in the Jordan River as adults, celebrate a Seder dinner on Maundy Thursday, and other such Hebraic nonsense. This is thought to deepen the Christian experience.

It is, in reality, a backdoor way to venerate the Jewish culture at the expense of the Savior that came out of the Jewish culture. Indeed, the Apostle Paul advised,

> ... *pay no attention to Jewish myths or to the commands of those who reject the truth. [Titus 1:14 NIV]*

Nevertheless, if you insist upon playing this game, then at least let me have some fun:

- Have you given up English for Aramaic as your primary tongue?
- When was the last time you filled a basin and rubbed your fingers between the toes of twelve houseguests (one of whom was planning to murder you)?
- Is your robe superior to the trousers that you used to wear?
- How is your carpentry apprenticeship going?
- Do you squat (rather than sit) and defecate into a festering hole in the ground? How are the biting flies treating your backside?

According to you, doing these things will better prepare you to have a rapport with the Jewish man, Jesus, on Judgment Day.

~~~~~~~~~~~~~~~~~~~~~~~~

The story of Old Testament Israel is the story of God's continual faithfulness, and the Jewish peoples' continual unfaithfulness. It was never, even once, the other way around.

The Lord says of them,

> ... *I called but you did not answer, I spoke but you did not listen. [Isaiah 65:12 TNIV]*

And,

> *... the more I called Israel, the further they went from*
> *me. [Hosea 11:2 NIV]*

God simply worked around the Jews' unfaithfulness in order to bring Himself into the world. Therefore, it cannot be that the diversity of Jewish people has any intrinsic merit for the purpose of getting closer to God.

Christians worship *a Jew*, Jesus of Nazareth.

> *As a human being, the Son of God belonged to King*
> *David's family line. [Romans 1:3 NIrV]*

And He is known in the heavenly realm by the unmistakably Jewish monikers:

> *... the Lion of the tribe of Judah, the Root of David ...*
> *[Revelation 5:5 NKJV]*

God was made into a man as *a Jew of the tribe of Judah and the lineage of David.*

Indeed, when Pilate asked Jesus if He was King of the Jews, Jesus affirmed,

> *It is as you say. [Matthew 27:11 NASB]*

Christians are people chosen by God to worship *that Jew*, Jesus Christ, in spirit and in truth. But Christians do not worship, venerate, or even honor *the Jews*—neither those of the Exodus, nor those of the modern State of Israel.

> *Now I want to remind you, although you once fully*
> *knew it, that Jesus, who saved a people out of the*
> *land of Egypt, afterward destroyed those who did not*
> *believe. [Jude 5 ESV]*

In this way it is plain that we Christians do not have to make ourselves, nationally-speaking, into something that we are not. And we do not have to make Jesus, nationally-speaking, into something that He is not. He was a Jew that became a pariah to people of His ethnicity; we are mostly non-Jews that have become pariahs to people of our own ethnicity.

> *All men will hate you because of me ... [Matthew*
> *10:22 NIV]*

> *Yes, and everyone who wants to live a godly life in*
> *Christ Jesus will suffer persecution. [2 Timothy 3:12*
> *NLT]*

We are to connect with Jesus on a spiritual level, not a national one. It will not avail you anything to become blood-brothers with the Jews, to grovel before them, or to adapt yourself to any Jewish custom. John the Baptist told those who found comfort in Jewishness,

> *Produce fruit in keeping with repentance. And **do not*** *
> **begin to say to yourselves, 'We have Abraham as our*** *
> **father.'** For I tell you that out of these stones God can* *
> *raise up children for Abraham. [John 3:8 NIV]*

It is important to repent. It is important to think about God as did Jesus Himself. It is not important to refrain from eating pork products (Deuteronomy 14:8), or to wear only unblended textiles (Deuteronomy 22:11), or to not cut your sideburns (Leviticus 19:27). As long as you follow the Bible's teaching about Jesus (as opposed to the Bible's teaching about Jewish customs), it does not matter from whence you came.

God, therefore, does not want you to celebrate Jesus' diversity. He wants you to accept in your heart that Jesus is the only begotten Son of God. He wants you to be transformed into the Chosen People of the Christian nation (i.e., the Church, or the invisible, indivisible, body of Christian believers)—under one King, Jesus Christ Himself.

> *Do not conform any longer to the pattern of this* *
> *world, but be transformed by the renewing of your* *
> *mind. [Romans 12:2 NIV]*

I, as a twenty-first century American, will have no qualms when I meet Jesus face-to-face on Judgment Day.

> *So we will not be afraid on the day of judgment, but* *
> *we can face him with confidence because we are like* *
> *Christ here in this world. [1 John 4:17 NLT]*

I already know Jesus personally as my Lord, and I am already known by Him as a precious adopted child. It does not matter how foreign the Jewish culture is to me. God will never reject me now that I am in Christ.

Galatians 3:1 [NKJV]
O foolish Galatians! Who has bewitched you that you should not obey the truth?

56. Do Christians Become Jews by Adoption?

No! Good garden party, what a revolting suggestion! I can barely tolerate the people of my own ethnicity. You're proposing to give me yet another group of horses' asses with which to deal?

Notice that I said 'the people of my own ethnicity' and not 'my own people.' That was purposeful: Christians are my own people. My ethnicity, on the other hand, is an artifact of the fallen world. **I utilize that part of it that glorifies God; I am ice cold toward that part of it that is unprofitable for Christ**.

Also, in Section 53 I said that I like Jewish people; now I am calling them (and every other ethnic group) horses' asses. So am I a universal humanitarian, or am I a universal curmudgeon? Think of all your unbelieving aunts, uncles, and cousins: you love them and want the best for them, but the last thing that you need is to live on a commune, surrounded by twice the number of them telling you what to do. What you need is to be left alone by them so that you can worship God in spirit and in truth.

> *... where the Spirit of the Lord is, there is liberty. [2 Corinthians 3:17 NKJV]*

I am appalled enough by the sins of the ethnicity into which I was born. I don't need to supplement my transgressions by becoming a Jew, thank you very much! The favor of God is not evidenced by being a part of any nation's culture. To the contrary, we should throw off our worldly culture (Jewish, Greek, or otherwise), and take on Christ. Taking on Christ means taking on the spiritual culture of love that is taught in the Bible—it does not mean taking on Jewish ethnicity in any fashion.

> *If we belong to Jesus Christ, it means nothing to have or not to have gone through the religious act of becoming a Jew. But faith working through love is important. [Galatians 5:6 NLV]*

This is true! Faith expressing itself through love is the only culture that Jesus Christ cares about!

The very reason that the Jewish leadership in Jerusalem objected to Jesus is that He, acting in faithful love, *was not Jewish enough* for their tastes. They complained to Him,

> *Why don't your disciples live according to the tradi-*
> *tion of the elders ...? [Mark 7:5 TNIV]*

They feared losing their phony-baloney jobs to Jesus' way of love; they sought His murder as a means to salvage their personal interest in the Jewish culture.

> *"What shall we do? For this Man works many signs.*
> *If we let Him alone like this, everyone will believe in*
> *Him, and the Romans will come and take away both*
> *our place and nation." And one of them, Caiaphas,*
> *being high priest that year, said to them, "You know*
> *nothing at all, nor do you consider that it is expedient*
> *for us that one man should die for the people, and not*
> *that the whole nation should perish." [John 11:47–50*
> *NKJV]*

I ask you, dear Christian reader: are you going to cast your lot with their myopic concern for their ethnic identity and land? Do you agree that the preservation of their cultural diversity is paramount over the continuance and propagation of God's Holy Word? [I am wincing as I write this.]

Beware what Christ said of the Jews when they claimed to have Abraham as their father:

> *... you are not able to listen to My word. You are of*
> *your father the devil, and the desires of your father*
> *you want to do. [John 8:43–44 NKJV]*

This does not only apply to unbelieving Jews. It is His verdict on any person that puts any culture in place of the Word of God.

Our Heavenly Father is not impressed with Jewishness, or with any other artifact of this fallen world. He is impressed with His Son who came into this world from Heaven. The inerrant Holy Scriptures say,

> *Now to Abraham and his Seed were the promises*
> *made. He does not say, "And to seeds," as of many,*
> *but as of one, "And to your Seed," who is Christ.*
> *[Galatians 3:16 NKJV]*

In Christ, God took into the Holy Trinity all those that would believe— He did not deconstruct the Holy Trinity into millions of Jewish seedlings. If it were not so, the doorstep of each Jewish household would be a shrine for us. Then the Jews and their children would be divine beings and we would gladly lick up their footsteps as a means to grace.

God forbid! God's Chosen People are the Christians! We have been chosen to worship at the foot of the Cross and nowhere else! We have been chosen to eat the body and drink the blood of the Risen Christ, and not to salivate after false gods!

Don't you know that Jesus Christ is the only begotten Son of God? Don't you know that He came to make you a Christian by adoption, as opposed to a Jew by adoption? If the latter were God's cause, Jesus would not have had to be crucified in order to save us. God could have simply directed that every Jewish mother circumcise and raise ten Gentile boys, and within a few generations we would all be Jews by adoption. What a world it would have been! Plates and plates of kosher food, but no victory over death!

Praise be to our God, whose mind is set on saving our souls and not on widening our waistlines.

> *... He chose us in Him before the foundation of the world, that we should be holy and without blame before Him in love, having predestined us to adoption as sons by Jesus Christ to Himself ... [Ephesians 1:4–5 NKJV]*

We have been adopted as sons of God, not as sons of the Jewish nation! The Apostle Paul, a Jew, called the Gentile believers his brothers by adoption in Christ, and in the same sentence he called his Jewish kinsmen that do not know Christ slaves!

> *Therefore, brothers, we are not children of the slave woman, but of the free woman. [Galatians 4:31 NIV]*

And again,

> *... you are all sons of God through faith in Christ Jesus. [Galatians 3:26 NKJV]*

God greatly desires that Jews and all other peoples should become sons and daughters of God (i.e., Christians), and not the other way around. Therefore, Isaiah prophesied in 712 BC[443] that an unfathomably generous gift would be given,

> *... you will be called by a new name that the mouth of the Lord will bestow. [Isaiah 62:2 TNIV]*

That promise was fulfilled in AD 43,[444] while two Jewish saints, Paul and Barnabas, were preaching to Greeks in Syria.

> *And the disciples were called Christians first in Antioch. [Acts 11:26 KJV]*

He has not given us the name of people that are dying (e.g., Jews, Greeks, Syrians, Americans, or any other name of the world), but the name of One that lives forever.

> *Holy Father, protect them by the power of your name—*
> *the name you gave me ... [John 17:11 NIV]*

Alleluia! We are called Christians—after our Brother, the very Son of God, Jesus Christ.

> *For this reason I kneel before the Father, from whom*
> *his whole family in heaven and on earth derives its*
> *name. [Ephesians 3:14–15 NKJV]*

Our family name is CHRISTIAN because God's surname is CHRIST!

> *... praise God that you bear that name. [1 Peter 4:16*
> *TNIV]*

The Lord was undeniably Jewish, but His name is not 'Jesus Jew'—it is 'Jesus Christ.' He is the Anointed One—our High Priest. Realize and accept that Creedal Christians (i.e., people of the new name) are the true, spiritual, Israel of God.

> *Then all the nations may look for the Lord, **even all***
> ***the people who are not Jews who are called by My***
> ***name**. [Acts 15:17 NLV]*

Realize and accept that the ethnic Jews that continue to reject Jesus (i.e., people of the old name) are not the true, spiritual, Israel of God. They themselves are rejected, and are utterly despondent—making music in the form of wails and dirges.

> *I say to you, many people will come from the east*
> *and from the west. They will sit down with Abraham*
> *and with Isaac and with Jacob in the holy nation of*
> *heaven. But those who should have belonged to the*
> *holy nation of heaven will be thrown out into outer*
> *darkness, where there will be crying and grinding of*
> *teeth. [Matthew 8:11–12 NLV]*

God has counted them as Spiritual Gentiles because of their preoccupation with the soil of Palestine and because they do not renounce the **old religious name** of 'Jew' in favor of the **new religious name** of 'Christian.'

> *Therefore, I will make you a desolate place and the city's residents an object of contempt; you will bear the scorn of My people. [Micah 6:16 HCSB]*

And again,

> *You will cry in sorrow and despair, while my servants sing for joy. Your name will be a curse word among my people, for the Sovereign Lord will destroy you and call his true servants by another name. [Isaiah 65:14–15 NLT]*

By logic, that same curse extends to other people that do not renounce their unbiblical ethnicity, unbiblical religiosity, and unbiblical heritage in favor of citizenship in Christ. If God expects today's Jews to jeopardize their status as Jews in order to be a part of Him, then it follows that He expects the same from people of other cultural traditions, including Christian churches. Even in the most doctrinally-pure branches of Christianity it is all-too-easy for sin to swagger in and eclipse the Gospel of Jesus Christ.

Renounce the sin of your heritage, and then you will be free to glory in the true purpose of your heritage!

> *In those days ten men from the nations of every tongue shall take hold of the robe of a Jew, saying, 'Let us go with you, for we have heard that God is with you.' [Zechariah 8:23 ESV]*

~~~~~~~~~~~~~~~~~~~~~~~

Because I value my privacy, I am not going to tell you the exact details of my own unbiblical ethnicity, unbiblical religiosity, and unbiblical personal history. It will have to suffice to say that I am a second-generation American, whose four grandparents were Mainline Protestant, Nestorian, Oriental Orthodox, and Roman Catholic. And one of my great-grandparents was Eastern Orthodox.

How did such enmity ever get together for procreative love-making?! I am the unlikely product of a motley crew!

Whatever the case, if I were not willing to renounce the cursed names of my own heritage, then you would know that this exegesis is nothing more than Jew-bashing and self-serving demagoguery. But I think you will find me rather plain-spoken toward the sins into which I was born, as well as the sins of my chosen profession (see Sections 35, 60, 67, 77, and 104).

Indeed, God had a plan of exultation even for a sinner like me.

~~~~~~~~~~~~~~~~~~~~~~~

The Apostle Paul was an ethnic Jew with a long pedigree from the tribe of Benjamin.

> *If anyone else thinks he has reasons to put confidence*
> *in the flesh, I have more: circumcised on the eighth*
> *day, of the people of Israel, of the tribe of Benjamin,*
> *a Hebrew of Hebrews ... a Pharisee; [Philippians*
> *3:4–5 NIV]*

He wrote to the Gentile people of Galatia, in what is now central Turkey. He offered them a blessing if they would cease from the sin of adopting the Jewish culture, and only believe in Christ.

> *Peace and mercy to all who follow this rule—to the*
> *Israel of God. [Galatians 6:16 TNIV]*

He called them the Israel of God based solely on their acceptance of Christ. This necessarily means that there is no synergism whatsoever between being the Israel of God and being a Jew. The true Israel of God has always been a spiritual nation, every member of which trusted that the God of Abraham, Isaac, and Jacob would become a man. When you accept Christ, you become a member of the True Israel without in any way becoming Jewish.

The Apostle Paul specifically discounted any reveling in his own ethnic identity.

> *God forbid that I should glory except in the cross of*
> *our Lord Jesus Christ, by whom the world has been*
> *crucified to me, and I to the world. [Galatians 6:14*
> *NKJV]*

The Apostle Paul did later say that being an ethnic Jew was advantageous for those that accepted Christ because it helped them appreciate His sacrificial role (Romans 3:2). But one must remember that in Paul's day the Old Testament was mostly available in only in the Hebrew language. And although the Septuagint was also available in Greek, a classical Jewish education was necessary in order to fully understand Christ's mission. The Apostle Paul surely used his [Jewish] knowledge of the inspired text to its fullest extent in writing half of the New Testament!

However, when Jerusalem was destroyed in AD 70,[445] a new Rabbinic Judaism began to be developed that explicitly rejected Jesus as Christ. The literary leg-up that the Apostle Paul referred to was largely lost by the end of the first century. It is completely gone today because English-speaking Christians have numerous Study Bibles in our own language. We can understand the prophecies concerning Christ much better than even first century Jewish believers.

We Christians—the True Israel of God—can see for ourselves His complete plan for salvation. How blessed we are! And how foolish to throw it all away for the practice of neo–Judaism!

> *Stand fast therefore in the liberty by which Christ has made us free, and do not be entangled again with a yoke of bondage. [Galatians 5:1 NKJV]*

If the Apostle Paul was willing to place no glory in being Jewish, then what twisted logic makes us think that we are unworthy without adoption into the Jewish race? We are adopted into Christ, rather than into any worldly thing.

This has always been God's rule. Even in the Old Testament any notion of reciprocity between Jewish ethnicity (or blood, or culture) and saving spirituality was specifically forbidden.

> *Foreigners who worship me must not say, "The Lord won't let us be part of his people." [Isaiah 56:3 CEV]*

And also,

> *I will record Egypt and Babylon among those who know me—also Philistia and Tyre, and even distant Ethiopia. They have all become citizens of Jerusalem! And it will be said of Jerusalem, "Everyone has become a citizen here." [Psalm 87:4–5 NLT]*

And again,

> *Blessed be Egypt my people, Assyria my handiwork, and Israel my inheritance. [Isaiah 19:25 TNIV]*

God repeats over and over that the Abrahamic blessing is not restricted to the Jewish race.

> *… the Israelites will be like the sand on the seashore, which cannot be measured or counted. In the place where it was said to them, 'You are not my people,' they will be called 'sons of the living God.' [Hosea 1:10 NIV]*

Remember that in the Prophet Elijah's day God said,

... I have reserved seven thousand in Israel, all whose knees have not bowed to Baal, and every mouth that has not kissed him. [1 Kings 19:18 NKJV]

Only seven thousand out of the millions of Jews were His People!

From these verses it is clear that both Jews and non-Jews that worship the God of the Bible constitute His people, Israel. But Jews and non-Jews that do not worship the God of the Bible are by no means His people.

Indeed, Christ prophesied to the Jewish nation,

... the Kingdom of God will be taken away from you and given to a nation that will produce the proper fruit. [Matthew 21:43 NLT]

And the Apostle Paul explains how this is true:

Because of the price Christ Jesus paid, the good things that came to Abraham might come to the people who are not Jews. [Galatians 3:14 NLV]

I am not preaching the so-called 'replacement theology' (or Supersessionism) whereby God's covenant has shifted from Jews to Christians. Hardly! **I am preaching that there never was a covenant with Jews** *per se*; there was a covenant with individuals (mostly Jews) that believed that God would become a man. These people were known as the Israel of God. And now that God has become a man, that very same covenant resides with individuals (mostly non-Jews) that believe that God did become a man. These people are also known as the Israel of God. It is in this most logical and plain way that God's promises remain unbroken.

For the gifts and the calling of God are irrevocable. [Romans 11:29 ESV]

Both in the Old Testament and in the New Testament people were saved by God through their faith.

I am the Lord, and I do not change. [Malachi 3:6 NLT]

Nothing has changed in the mechanism by which a human being becomes one of the Chosen People! The definition and designation of the Chosen People are the same except for the name. Do not complain to me about the change in name, for that change was foretold and instituted by God Himself.

I will give them an everlasting name ... the foreign-ers who join themselves to the Lord, to minister to him, to love the name of the Lord ... these I will bring

to my holy mountain, and make them joyful ... for my
house shall be called a house of prayer for all peo-
ples. [Isaiah 56:5–7 ESV]

The advent of Christ is not a cause for racial resentment, but for joy!

City of Zion, sing and celebrate! The Lord has prom-
*ised to come and live with you. When he does, **many***
nations will turn to him and become his people.
[Zechariah 2:10–11 CEV]

Now more than ever, Jews are free to leave the sin in their culture and worship the God of Abraham, Isaac, and Jacob; non-Jews are free to leave the sin in their culture and worship the God of Abraham, Isaac, and Jacob.

The Apostle Peter wrote to both the Jewish Believers and Gentile Believers of Asia Minor,

... you were redeemed from the empty way of life
handed down to you from your forefathers ... [1 Peter
1:18 NIV]

Both groups inherited emptiness and death from their forefathers, but fullness and life from the God of Abraham, Isaac, and Jacob.

Without any doubt there was, in Old Testament times, more sin in non-Jewish cultures. But this is irrelevant because God looks through nationality and into the heart of the individual. There never was any genetic or linguistic distinction in His eyes! He has always cared about what we believe (i.e., culture based upon belief), and not from whom we are descended (i.e., culture based upon race).

He did not discriminate between us and them, for he
purified their hearts by faith. [Acts 15:9 TNIV]

In fact, a Christian that is not an ethnic Jew, but that insists upon adopting Jewish customs, has pronounced a curse upon himself. The Apostle Paul sternly admonished the Gentile believers in Galatia,

Mark my words! I, Paul, tell you that if you let your-
selves be circumcised, Christ will be of no value to
you at all ... You who are trying to be justified by law
have been alienated from Christ; you have fallen
away from grace. [Galatians 5:2,4 NIV]

Therefore, I say to Dispensationalists with all my heart: redirect your infatuation with the Jews to an infatuation with Jesus Christ.

And do not grieve the Holy Spirit of God, by whom
you were sealed for the day of redemption. [Ephesians
4:30 NKJV]

You, as a Christian and not a Jew, are right now the Israel of God. If you then proceed to become a Jew, you will no longer be the Israel of God.

You who seek the Lord: Look to the rock from which
you were hewn ... [Isaiah 51:1 ESV]

That Rock is the Son of God! Look to Jesus Christ, and to Him alone!

~~~~~~~~~~~~~~~~~~~~~~

In review, it is correct and salutary to say that:

- Christians are the True Israel;
- Christians are the Spiritual Israel;
- Christians are the Children of Israel;
- Christians are the Israel of God;
- Christians are the Remnant;
- Christians are the Chosen People;
- Christians are the Children of Promise;
- Christians are the Apple of God's Eye;
- Christians are the Head and Not the Tail;
- Christians are an Acceptable People;
- Christians are a Blessed People;
- Christians are God's Children;
- Christians are People of the New Name;
- Christians are the People of God;
- Christians are the Elect;
- Christians are the Church.

But it is incorrect and an utter corruption of the Gospel of Jesus Christ to say that:

- ethnic Jews that reject Christ are any of the above;
- Christians are ethnic Jews by adoption or by any other means (unless, of course, they happen to already be ethnic Jews that turn to Jesus as Lord and Savior—a small number indeed);
- Christians have any affinity to Zionism or to the modern State of Israel (unless, of course, they

happen to live in that particular country and gain
suffrage and the other rights of citizenship).

Isaiah 1:13 [NIV]
Stop bringing meaningless offerings! Your incense is detestable to me. New
Moons, Sabbaths and convocations—I cannot bear your evil assemblies.

57. Against Meaningless Offerings and Evil Assemblies

The Apostle Paul's treatise against so-called 'Jewish adoption' naturally
extends to other unbiblical influences. If, as he taught the Galatians, a person's
claim of Christianity is invalidated by co-mingling it with the Jewish culture,
then it follows that it is also invalidated by co-mingling it with the [fill-in-the-
blank] culture.

Why is that?

Because God loves us. He knows that life is found in Him and in
no human institution. He desires for us to have the life that is found in Him.
Therefore, God is jealous for our fidelity, and says,

> *Do not worship any other god, for the Lord, whose*
> *name is Jealous, is a jealous God. [Exodus 34:14*
> *TNIV]*

Why jealous? We usually associate jealousy as a negative emotion.
But God is jealous for us in a good way—in the way that a father is protective
of his teenage daughter's virtue. If he discovers that she has been having sex
with various members of the high school football team, he grieves for the loss
of the life that she could have had if she had maintained her purity. God feels
this way when we take our purity in Christ and put it under subjugation to
worldly influences.

Primary among the influences that putrefy our worship is the culture-
at-large. Are not priests that subjugate Christians to the sins of the culture-
at-large just another manifestation of the Judaizers with whom the Apostle
Paul contended? Unfortunately, many churches are interwoven with the cul-
ture-at-large to such an extent that separating them would be like separating
conjoined twins that share a single central nervous system—it cannot be done.
Reformation is impossible in these institutions; a new church must be planted.

> *... pour new wine into new wineskins ... [Matthew 9:17 TNIV]*

Take, for example, the Ethiopian Orthodox Tewahedo[xv] Christians. If you ask them what nationality they are, they will say 'Ethiopian'; if you ask them what religion they are, they will say 'Ethiopian.' There is no way out of this: if you are Ethiopian and Christian, then you are, by-default, Orthodox Tewahedo. Even if you have left the old church and are of a biblical denomination, there is no mechanism whereby you can resign. In this way, when the membership of the Ethiopian Orthodox Tewahedo Church is counted, a national census is taken rather than a count of weekly communicants.

The people of this nation-group demand at least tacit acquiescence to this formulation. If an Ethiopian Christian does not at least tip his hat to the ancient 'Mother Church,' he is thought to have cast aside his ethnicity and to be a traitor to the nation—just as Jews that become Born Again Christians are also considered traitors to their nation. In fact, one of the Monophysites' main epithets for Protestants is translated "the Outsiders."

Is this not as pernicious as saying that a Christian must adopt the ethnicity of the Jews? We will later discuss at length how the Ethiopian Orthodox' [Monophysite] christology is heterodox to the point of being quasi–Christian (Sections 62, 67). Also, their liturgy is incomprehensibly turgid. Yet their ecclesiastical structure is such that Ethiopian Christians are coerced into embracing the shame of their nation, rather than repenting of it and arming themselves with the Word of God.

This principle is not limited to ethnic churches, by the way. The exact same point could be made with whitebread American Protestant churches that have no identifiable ethnicity, but that have subjugated Biblical Christianity to American Liberalism. I was once in an American Baptist Church (a heretical Mainline Protestant denomination) where the preacher said that when a Christian advocates for a woman's right to choose an abortion, he may expect the same unjustified persecution that Jesus predicted for His faithful disciples in Matthew 5:11.

True Christians in the United States feel a profound sense of shame for the innumerable ways in which Americans have misused our Christian liberty. We gladly say, "If being an American means subjugating my faith to this heathen culture, then I am not an American."

---

xv   A Ge'ez word meaning 'being made one'—reflecting their [heretical] Monophysitic belief that in Jesus of Nazareth there was a complete union of the divine and human natures. See Sections 62, 66–67.

Come out from her, my people. Do not be a part of her sins so you will not share her troubles. [Revelation 18:4 NLV]

The Chosen People (i.e., Christians) are a people of penance, not national pride. And the best way to celebrate and revel in your nation, denomination, or any other part of this world, is to turn away from it for the sake of your Lord.

If anyone would come after me, he must deny himself … For whoever wants to save his life will lose it, but whoever loses his life for me will find it. [Matthew 16:24–25 NIV]

~~~~~~~~~~~~~~~~~~~~~~

The Lord told Joshua,

See, I have delivered Jericho into your hands, along with its king and its fighting men … march around the city seven times … [Joshua 6:2,4 TNIV]

A few years ago I visited one of the oldest churches in the world that is still in operation. It happened to be a Sunday morning. Our tour guide led us inside, into a surreal scene of incense and emptiness: there were a number of priests upon the altar saying Mass, and a choir singing a Gregorian chant in an alcove. But in the middle of the church there were no pews and no worshipers—there was just open space with milling tourists. People were speaking quietly with each other and admiring the architecture, music, and ceiling paintings. The church was a combination of performing artistry (upon the altar and in the alcove), and a museum of antiquities.

An old priest came out from behind a curtain and stood next to the choir. Foreign tourists in tank-tops and hot pants knelt in a semicircle around him. They bowed their heads and folded their hands as he shook an ornate silver cross over them. The priest frowned with boredom as his arm repeated the same motion for ten minutes. He looked at me. I could discern nothing in his eyes but a desire to sit down and be rid of the simpletons beneath him.

I felt uncomfortable—even queasy—and left the building. As people exited, they turned around and walked out backwards, so as to not turn their backsides upon the altar. I exited the normal way, and may have passed some flatulence when I reached the vestibule.

I found a Christian friend in the courtyard and asked her to walk around the building with me. I was silent at first, collecting my thoughts. Without any prompting she said, "Can you feel it? These poor people are under a curse."

I took her by the hand, raised it to Heaven, and said, "I bind this church in the name of Jesus Christ of Nazareth!"

We circled seven times, and left.

~~~~~~~~~~~~~~~~~~~~~~~~

I have a friend that is a Pentecostal Christian and speaks in tongues. This is a gift of the Holy Spirit whereby some Christian believers can pray to God, or receive words of knowledge from God, in an angelic language. It sounds like babbling. In some cases, the tongue is a human language that the speaker does not know, but someone else in the gathering does know. There are many documented cases of this.

> *Paul placed his hands on them. Then the Holy Spirit*
> *came on them. They spoke in languages they had not*
> *known before. [Acts 19:6 NIrV]*

This friend once asked my opinion of the practice. I told her that speaking in tongues is biblical but that it should never be done in the hearing of another person, and certainly not during a worship service, unless there is someone there to interpret word-for-word what is being said. The Apostle Paul expressly proscribes public worship in unknown languages without a translator.

> *... if no one is present who can interpret, they must be*
> *silent in your church meeting and speak in tongues to*
> *God privately. [1 Corinthians 14:28 NLT]*

Paul points out that without a translator it can rightfully be challenged as fakery or lunacy or bedlam (1 Corinthians 14:23). God does not want the Church to open itself up to such criticism.

> *... everything should be done in a proper and orderly*
> *way. [1 Corinthians 14:40 NIrV]*

To me, the idea that a Christian clergyman would allow an unknown, untranslated, language to be used during any part of a worship service is abhorrent. Jesus Christ commanded,

> *... when you pray, do not keep on babbling like pagans,*
> *for they think they will be heard because of their many*
> *words. [Matthew 6:7 TNIV]*

It takes a twisted sense of piety to cause parishioners to sit through a service that they cannot understand. Yet apologists for the eastern churches that use dead and dying dialects say that we would view their services as beautifully ornate and symbolic if we only took the time to understand the ancient language.

> *They take pride in things they should be ashamed of. All they think about are the things of this world. [Philippians 3:19 NLV]*

God wants to be worshiped by all His human creatures, not by priests alone! He is already righteous. He does not need for us to return to Medieval religious customs and languages to increase the appearance of piety. Should a person seeking to worship the Living God have to go to a college of linguistics first?! Who dares to impose such a rule over and above God's desire to be known by His Chosen People, the Christians?!

> *You skillfully sidestep God's law in order to hold on to your own tradition. [Mark 7:9 NLT]*

Let us look to Christ for the answer: He did not tell the believing Jews, "If you would only go back and understand the classical, pre–exilic, Hebrew of the Prophets Isaiah and Daniel, then you would truly know Me to be the Anointed One." To the contrary, He taught the people in the vernacular of Aramaic, rather than Hebrew. Later, Jesus commanded the Apostle Peter,

> *Feed My lambs. [John 21:15 NKJV]*

And the Apostle Peter dutifully fed them in the *lingua franca* of Greek (although it was not his own first language)—Peter did not baptize them and then starve them of hearing the Word of God!

Those that preach and read and recite liturgies in obscure tongues in order to appear more venerable have their portion. Their portion is not Christ—it is their culture. And they have choked upon it.

~~~~~~~~~~~~~~~~~~~~~~~

I know a Canadian woman that was raised a Congregationalist, lost faith in Christ in adulthood, became Born Again and joined an Anabaptist church, lost faith again, and eventually became a New Age spiritualist. She wrote me a letter that mentioned her own death in a way that alarmed me. I called her and pointedly asked if she had plans to take her own life.

"No, no. Not remotely," she laughed. "I'm quite at peace. Sure, I went through some tough times before, but I've found complete freedom now. I've found the true way."

I asked if she was worshipping anywhere. She said, "Yes. I attend Greek Orthodox services—"

I was so excited that I cut her off, "Oh, thank God! I thought you might have been in an unchristian environment. The Eastern Orthodox recite the Nicene Creed. They have the Holy Bible, and Holy Baptism, and Holy Communion. They're certainly no cult—"

She cut me off, "Hold on. I didn't tell you *why* I go to a Greek Orthodox church. It's precisely because you can't tell that you're in a Christian environment. They may have the Bible, but they don't affect me with it. I am a Zen Practitioner now. I go for the incense, and the candles, and the stained glass, and the chanting choir. It's a spiritually-enriching place. I just enter into the haze and meditate upon the true god that does not care what you believe, or how you worship, or who you worship. God accepts everyone in his or her own way. God is in everyone, and he or she is in everything. The smoke from the incense are tiny particles of God; the wooden carvings of the Orthodox saints are pieces of God; I am a piece of God. You have no idea the fullness that you are denying yourself by being part of organized Christian religion the way that you continue to be."

I warned her, "Do you realize that if you were to tell your ideas to the Greek priest at your parish, he would not serve you Communion and he would tell you that you are headed to Hell?"

She said, "I don't care. It doesn't matter. I don't believe in Hell anymore. I am beyond all that now. Their words are just background noise. If the services were comprehensible, it would ruin the effect. I just use it for meditative purposes—to reach a higher level of consciousness and achieve a state of peace with the world that you hate so much."

Hebrews 11:13–16 [NIV]
[The Old Testament people of faith] admitted that they were aliens and strangers on earth. People who say such things show that they are looking for a country of their own. If they had been thinking of the country they had left, they would have had opportunity to return. Instead, they were longing for a better country—a heavenly one. Therefore God is not ashamed to be called their God, for he has prepared a city for them.

58. A Better Country

I lived in the Bible Belt of the United States for a time, and my company contracted some work from a British immigrant that was an atheist. One day while I was driving him to a job site I asked him why he had moved to the United States.

He said, "I wanted to start my own business and it's too difficult in the United Kingdom. The laws are against entrepreneurship, and the taxes are outrageous. I really like the United States. It's so much freer, and the people are more friendly and honest."

"*We Americans are honest?*" I was incredulous. "You can't mean that."

"I do! In many ways you people are warmer, and less bloody devious than the British." He thought for a moment and came up with an example, "The fast food restaurants here leave the ketchup and sugar packets out in the open, and they trust people to take only what they need. But if you did that in England, little old ladies would come in, empty all the condiments into oversized handbags, and leave. When you go to a restaurant over there, you have to ask a waitress to bring you only what you need for your meal."

I laughed, "Well, this is a prosperous country and those teaspoon packets of sugar don't really have any value here. God has blessed us with plenty of low-priced food. But tell me, is there anything that you don't like about the US?"

"There is one thing, and you just said it without even realizing what you were doing." He paused and looked at me, wondering if he should have started along this path.

"—it's the Christians. There are so many Christians here. They're on television, and they go to those mega-churches, and they speak about God blessing them. Even the politicians speak about God all the time, and say, 'God bless America.' You can't get away from it."

"That's a problem for you?" I asked innocently.

"Well, yes. I hate it. There's too much religion in the people here. In England, nobody talks openly about God. We have separation of church and state there."

"Actually, that's the opposite of the truth," I said without showing any irritation. "In your homeland, the head of state, Queen Elizabeth II, is also the head of the Church of England."

"Oh, yeah. But she doesn't really do anything—I mean she is not an especially religious person. It's only a formality."

"True enough, but in the US it is unconstitutional for taxpayer dollars to be used to support a church. It's all supported by volunteerism and donations over here, whereas in the UK the clergy are essentially civil servants. And that's the case all over Europe. Wherever the faith is in decline, you'll find a dead national church at work. It has been the bane of European Christianity."

He thought for a moment. "You're right about that; the government does pay our vicars over there. But somehow it doesn't offend me. They're impotent and sheepish. They just motion toward the ceiling and speak vaguely of some god that wants us to be nice."

"Ah-hah!" I pointed at him. "Exactly my point! You're not at all offended by the lack of the separation of church and state. You're offended by the presence of sincerely believing people within the public realm."

"Yes. Yes, that's it precisely," he admitted. "Why do people have to be so bloody religious here? It's such a good country apart from that element."

"First of all, why should it bother you? Just ignore them if you don't agree," I recommended. "But secondly, you're a man of science: did you ever think that there might be a correlation between our adherence to the Bible as the Word of God, and our relative honesty, warmth, low taxes, and prosperity? Isn't it possible that the things that you ran away from in England are caused by a lack of freely-expressed Christianity among your countrymen?"

He found that difficult to believe, but he told me that he'd have to think about it. He was surprised to find himself admitting that Europe did not have separation of church and state, and that the United States did have it.

The United States is a better country than the United Kingdom—there's little doubt about that. But it is not better for any other reason than that there is a greater concentration of Christian people here.

As an American Christian, I know that I am not really a citizen of the United States, or even a permanent resident. My United States passport is just a piece of paper, and some day I shall permanently immigrate somewhere else. The Apostle Peter said that God's Elect were,

> *... strangers in the world, scattered throughout [various countries] ... [1 Peter 1:1 NIV]*

In a very few decades all Christians shall immigrate to a truly better country—a heavenly one.

1 Peter 2:9–10 [NIV]
But you are a chosen people, a royal priesthood, a holy nation, a people belonging to God, that you may declare the praises of him who called you out of darkness into his wonderful light. Once you were not a people, but now you are the people of God;

59. A Holy Nation

At the beginning of His earthly ministry Jesus stood up in His hometown synagogue on the Sabbath day and, in the process of stating His credentials, insulted the Jews. He said,

> *I assure you that there were many widows in Israel in Elijah's time, when the sky was shut for three and a half years and there was a severe famine throughout the land. Yet Elijah was not sent to any of them, but to a widow in Zarephath in the region of Sidon. And there were many in Israel with leprosy in the time of Elisha the prophet, yet not one of them was cleansed—only Naaman the Syrian. [Luke 4:25–27 NIV]*

Jesus told the people of Nazareth that God purposely sent the Prophets Elijah and Elisha to help a Lebanese and a Syrian, rather than to help Jews. His Jewish neighbors were infuriated and tried to throw Him off a cliff. The Scriptures tell us that Jesus walked through the mob without them being able to harm Him, and then He went on to another city with His message of repentance.

~~~~~~~~~~~~~~~~~~~~~~~

Christians are a peculiar people: as the People of God, we follow Christ above and beyond every other loyalty—even that of nation and family. Jesus said,

> *If anyone comes to me and does not hate father and mother, wife and children, brothers and sisters—yes,*

even life itself—such a person cannot be my disciple.
[Luke 14:26 TNIV]

The Apostle John admonished us not to be enamored of culture, language, nationhood, or any other temporal influence.

Do not love the world or the things in the world. [1
John 2:15 NKJV]

The Apostle Paul reminded us of our true citizenship, and the rewards of it.

... our citizenship is in heaven. And we eagerly await
a Savior from there, the Lord Jesus Christ, who, by the
power that enables him to bring everything under his
control, will transform our lowly bodies so that they will
be like his glorious body. [Philippians 3:20–21 NIV]

Thus, we have always been looked upon with suspicion and contempt by those whose interests lie in national unity at the expense of our ability to live lives in anticipation of Christ's return. I am not referring to the so-called Christian pacifists that refuse to be conscripted into military service or to pay taxes. I am referring to principled Christian citizens that take exception to the government or the national church dictating their ecclesiastical policies, including:

- what they can preach from the pulpit and teach in their schools;
- to whom they can serve Communion;
- who they may ordain into pastorship;
- when and where they can build churches and gather in them;
- whether they can proselytize their neighbors through free speech and free assembly;
- taking a sober position on the sins of the nation.

To a spoiled American, none of these things is an issue because of our excellent Bill of Rights, and our tradition of 'mind your own business.' But in Muslim countries, communist countries, Canada, the State of Israel, and the socialist democracies of Europe and the former Soviet Union, there are various restrictions on religious freedom in the name of statehood.

... you will be hated by all nations for My name's
sake. [Matthew 24:9 NKJV]

Many governments have wanted to throw Christians off the edge of the earth, but God chose for the bulk of His Church to come out of that part of the world that was to be enveloped by the Beast of Islam and other tyrannies.

> *Your own people hate you and throw you out for being*
> *loyal to my name. [Isaiah 66:5 NLT]*

In accordance with biblical prophecy, God made a new people in the wilderness of the New World out of a melting pot of many nations.

~~~~~~~~~~~~~~~~~~~~~~~~

In AD 1817, King Friedrich Wilhelm III (AD 1770–AD 1840) decreed that the Lutheran and Reformed congregations of Potsdam, Germany must be merged under the single banner of the 'Evangelical Christian Church.' This was known as the Prussian Union.[446]

After his disastrous experience with Napoleon (AD 1769–AD 1821) during the previous decade, the king decided that the northern Germans needed to be religiously united in order to be a viable nation within the European community. He chose the three hundredth anniversary of the Reformation to push forward a common liturgy and a compromised Communion consecration. Churches that believed in the Real Presence of Christ in the Communion elements were 'encouraged' to serve the Lord's Supper to people that denied the Real Presence of Christ in the Communion elements. Seminarians were required to swear allegiance to the new formulations. Sectarian groups were outlawed, and dissenting pastors were defrocked and imprisoned. The effect was to punish those that took Christ's professions about His body and blood seriously enough to have a 'members-only' Communion table.

The German–Jewish poet, Heinrich Heine (AD 1797–AD 1856), converted to Protestantism during this period. Writing from Paris in AD 1834, he issued a chilling prophecy about the effects that de-Christianization would have on German society. His words came true one hundred and seven years later during the Nazi campaigns in North Africa and Russia.

> *'Nature philosophers' ... will reestablish contact with*
> *the telluric forces ... conjuring up the satanic powers*
> *of old-Germanic pantheism. Within their breast there*
> *will come to life a war-lust ... which makes fighting an*
> *end in itself ... If the time should ever come when the*
> *Christian Cross will break down, then the savagery of*
> *the ancient warriors will reappear ... the ancient gods*
> *of stone will rise from their graves ... Thor with his*

*hammer will rise and destroy the Gothic cathedrals.
We must expect the same revolution in the world of
phenomena that we have witnessed in the realm of the
spirit. Thought precedes action as lightning precedes
thunder ... And when you hear it crash as it has never
crashed before in the history of the world, then you
will know that the German thunder has reached its
mark. There will be such a commotion that the eagles
will drop dead to the ground, and the lions in the
distant deserts of Africa will put their tails between
their legs and withdraw to their royal dens. Germany
will then offer a spectacle which will make the great
French Revolution appear as a harmless idyl ...* [447]

By AD 1838 the dissenters to the Prussian Union had had enough of
King Wilhelm's heavy-handed political expediency. Calling themselves 'Old
Lutheran,' they sold their property in Saxony and made for the United States
and Australia where they would be left alone to practice the Christian faith
according to conscience.

No sooner had the Old Lutherans settled in St. Louis, Missouri than
they discovered that their bishop had begun to lead a double life on the other
side of the Mississippi River. He was embezzling funds, and was an adul-
terer and drunkard. He would not repent and resign from pastoral office. They
excommunicated him and elected a capable young holy man. [448]

They were willing to separate themselves—twice!—in order to declare
the praises of God who called them out of the darkness and into His wonderful
light.

The story of King Friedrich Wilhelm's Prussian Union is remarkably
similar to that of Emperor Heraclius' (AD 575–AD 641) Monothelite initiative
in the Eastern Roman Empire twelve hundred years before. The Prussian Union
gave rise to Prussian militarism and Nazi fascism; similarly, Monothelitism
gave rise to Islam and al-Qaeda terrorism. In this way, the current world war
has the same roots as the first two world wars.

Beginning in Section 64 I provide a detailed discussion of
Monothelitism's disastrous effects on eastern Christendom and its pertinence
to eschatology.

~~~~~~~~~~~~~~~~~~~~~~

It is for this principle of religious liberty that the Church of Pentecost was first driven from Jerusalem in AD 33.[449] It is for this same principle that the Pilgrim Fathers were driven from England in AD 1620. God was allowing them to claim the wilderness of North America for Christ.[450] That pattern has continued to this day, as God has gathered those that were once not a people to become a holy nation (i.e., the Church, or the invisible, indivisible, Body of Christ).

> ... with your blood you purchased men for God from every tribe and language and people and nation. You have made them to be a kingdom ... [Revelation 5:9–10 NIV]

The next movement of His people shall not be along the face of the earth; it will be upward.

> Open the gates that the righteous nation may enter, the nation that keeps faith. [Isaiah 26:2 TNIV]

The Christian nation will enter Heaven on the day of the Second Coming.

Judges 2:17 [KJV]
... they went a whoring after other gods, and bowed themselves unto them: they turned quickly out of the way which their fathers walked in ...

60. Cultural Christianity Leads to Demonic Submission

Is it possible for the people of a region to change from being overwhelmingly Christian in their sensibilities to being overwhelmingly unchristian in their sensibilities? Certainly; it happens all the time. Read the account of the Benjamites' warfare in defense of sodomy only one hundred years after Joshua led them into Canaan (Judges 19–20).[451]

Likewise, this is the story of nearly all the Congregationalist churches in the United States that the Pilgrims and Puritans founded. Most are now members of an amalgamated denomination called the United Church of Christ, and are essentially Unitarian-Universalist in their philosophy. That process only took about three hundred years.

~~~~~~~~~~~~~~~~~~~~~~~~~

I once went on a tour of an extinct Christian civilization in an overwhelmingly Muslim country. The architectural ruins were magnificent. But at the same time it was depressing to think that the people had been annihilated genera- tions ago by their Muslim neighbors.

One of the Yale University Episcopals with whom I was traveling approached me while I was photographing a roofless Monophysite church. The building had been turned into a mosque, and then into a shithouse after the roof caved in. He whispered in my ear like the devil, "Does this experience weaken your faith?"

"Pardon?" I said, lowering my camera.

"Think about it. You are a Christian. There were Christians here. They are gone—wiped off the map. Logically, what are our options? Is God a Muslim? After all, he gave this country to them. Or is God cruel and indiffer- ent? What kind of a God allows good people to come to this fate?"

"Hold on a minute," I said. "Who says that the Christians that were living here were good people? Only God is good. The premise of your question is faulty."

He was not expecting me to say that, since part of my bloodline traced me to the Christians of that city. I continued, "Maybe they had the truth about God, but insisted upon worshipping Him in an incorrect manner, and living in a sinful lifestyle. Maybe this went on for centuries, though He warned them repeatedly, and gave them many opportunities to change their wicked ways. There comes a point when God would rather put up with an ignorant people that are His enemy, than an enlightened people that are His in name only. So perhaps He finally had enough of their stiff-necked-ness and let them be devoured by a less righteous foe. I'm not giving the Muslims a pass—they have blood on their hands for what they did to these innocent people. But God, in His righteousness, allowed it; and I assure you that He did not allow it because they were penitent Biblicists."

"Are you telling me that if I don't worship God correctly, He will allow me to be killed?"

"I'm telling you that if you don't worship God correctly, you are already dead. The devil has succeeded in murdering your eternal soul, whether you acknowledge it or not. Being in this place does not weaken my faith. It strengthens it! God has a purpose in our being here and seeing this. God is speaking to me through this place."

"Speaking to you?! What is He saying exactly?!"

"He's saying, 'You're in danger! Grave danger! Repent and take up the Word of God as your shield, or the same thing will happen to your so-called Christian civilization in the United States!' God doesn't bless the way of death;

He blesses the way of life because He is loving and He wants people to follow that way and be saved."

"But these Muslims have been blessed—"

"Have they??" I shot back.

"They possess the land," was his rejoinder. "You can't deny the reality on the ground."

"They do possess the land, and it is a beautiful and fertile land. But they don't look too blessed to me. They look stupid, and unemployed, and desperate. And I can only assume that their women are desperate because I haven't seen one of them in days. Every local that has spoken to us honestly has asked how they can get the hell out of this unhappy place and into the United States."

"Are you happy?!" he snapped.

I threw my head back and laughed, "You can see that I am! I am happy that I don't live here among these Muslim dogs, for one thing. I am happy that I am an American with money in my pocket and a gun under my arm. And most of all I am happy that I am free to worship the true God—the God that is not a Muslim."

"What is God?" he said disdainfully.

"Mmm! Good question! God is love. And the God of love became a Jewish man—He was born to a virgin girl in Judea and circumcised on the eighth day. But He, acting in love, renounced the Jews a long time ago—just as I happily renounce these ancestors of mine, and I also happily renounce the liberal Protestant church of my childhood in New York. If you'd really like to know, Jesus Christ would be most at home today among conservative American Protestants—excuse me, *Biblical* American Protestants.[xvi] You know … people like me! People who trust that true God became true man in Him; people that read and think about His Book all the time; people that confess their sins every chance they get, and eat and drink His body and blood every chance they get, and sing praises to His name every chance they get. It makes me happy. Very, very, happy! What a joy that God Almighty became a man with a nature like my own, and that this man is my personal friend!"

The Yale Episcopal walked away from me, and did not answer his hotel door that evening when I knocked to invite him to dinner.

Was it something I said? Tee-hee-hee.

---

xvi   I said 'American' only because that is the major wilderness destination into which God sent His Church to be nurtured and protected from the devil, Allah (see Section 31). Of course, Jesus would be at home among people of any nationality that truly believe that He is the God-man.

~~~~~~~~~~~~~~~~~~~~~~~~

God does sometimes allow individual Christian saints to be martyred by Muslims and other Satanists, as was the case with all of the Apostles except John. But nowhere in the Bible does God allow every man, woman, and child to be extirpated from the land as a sign that He is well-pleased with them. To the contrary, God always protects His Chosen People (i.e., the true Christian Church), and watches over them like a doting father.

> *As the mountains surround Jerusalem, so the Lord surrounds his people both now and forevermore. [Psalm 125:2 TNIV]*

Our Heavenly Father is not a louse; He is the Great Provider.

> *... I have never seen the righteous forsaken or their children begging bread. They are always generous and lend freely; their children will be blessed. Turn from evil and do good; then you will dwell in the land forever. [Psalm 37:25–27 NIV]*

God cannot be faulted for what happens when His people are unfaithful and leave His care.

De-Christianization occurs by taking what the Bible teaches and transmuting it according to a myriad of unbiblical cultural influences. As we will soon discuss, the Nestorian and Monophysite Christians of the Middle East did this, and their descendants slowly came into submission to the devil: they are now overwhelmingly Muslim, or dominated by Muslims.

Islam is short for 'al-Islam' which literally means 'Submission to Allah.' We know that the Termagant Allah is a non-Triune god, and we know that,

> *No one who denies the Son has the Father. [1 John 2:23 NIV]*

Therefore, Islam is submission to the devil.

John 14:8–9 [NKJV]
Philip said to Him, "Lord, show us the Father, and it is sufficient for us." Jesus
said to him, "Have I been with you so long, and yet you have not known Me,
Philip? He who has seen Me has seen the Father; so how can you say, 'Show
us the Father'?"

61. The Doctrine of the Trinity

The Edict of Milan, issued by Emperor Constantine in AD 313, removed penalties for professing-Christians within the Roman Empire. Christians came out of hiding from the Diocletian persecution, and were appointed to government posts. But no sooner had Constantine consolidated his control over the eastern and western parts of the empire than doctrinal disputes erupted regarding the definition of Christianity. The issue was partially settled when Constantine called the first ecumenical council, the Council of Nicaea, in AD 325. At this gathering hundreds of bishops[452] from around the Christian world denounced an Anti-Trinitarian, rationalist, heresy called Arianism (not to be confused with Aryanism, the racist theory that was prevalent in early twentieth century Europe).

The Arians were followers of Arius of Alexandria (AD 256–AD 336) who taught that God the Father is the one Supreme Deity. He did not have many followers, but those that did support his position were primarily in Egypt and Syria. Sixty years before Arius, a similar heresy had been taught in Syria by Paul of Samosata (AD 200–AD 275). He said that Jesus was born a mere man, and became divine at His baptism. The Christians of that time voted him out as Bishop of Antioch.[453]

The Arians separated Jesus from the essence, nature, and substance of God the Father, declaring that He was a created being, and not truly divine. In this way, Arians thought of Jesus as a second, inferior, god—someone that God the Father created out of nothing, and then used to create the world; they accepted Jesus as the Son of God only as a figure of speech. They said that He had the reasoning powers of God, but not the eternal nature or omnipotence of God. They also maintained that God the Father had subsequently created the Holy Spirit as a helper for Jesus. Thus they made a hierarchy between the Father, the Son, and the Holy Spirit.[454]

The teachings of Arius will immediately be recognizable to all Christians as blasphemy. Arius taught that …

> … *God was not always the Father, but that there was*
> *a period when he was not the Father; that the Word of*
> *God was not from eternity, but was made out of noth-*

ing; for that the ever-existing God ('the I AM'—the eternal One) made him who did not previously exist, out of nothing; wherefore there was a time when he did not exist, inasmuch as the Son is a creature and a work. That he is neither like the Father as it regards his essence, nor is by nature either the Father's true Word, or true Wisdom, but indeed one of his works and creatures, being erroneously called Word and Wisdom, since he was himself made of God's own Word and the Wisdom which is in God, whereby God both made all things and him also. Wherefore he is as to his nature mutable and susceptible of change, as all other rational creatures are: hence the Word is alien to and other than the essence of God; and the Father is inexplicable by the Son, and invisible to him, for neither does the Word perfectly and accurately know the Father, neither can he distinctly see him. The Son knows not the nature of his own essence: for he was made on our account, in order that God might create us by him, as by an instrument; nor would he ever have existed, unless God had wished to create us.[455]

Rubbish! Christians, in contrast, believe in the mysterious doctrine of the Holy Trinity whereby there is one God with three co-eternal, co-equal, and uncreated Persons. The Apostle John plainly said of Jesus Christ,

He is the True God. [1 John 5:20 NIrV]

Athanasius of Alexandria was a contemporary of Arius, and was a champion of the Biblical, Nicene, view of Christ. He passionately opposed a Christian compromise with Arianism. He argued that establishing a proper Christian creed would prevent future generations from believing in a non-saving type of 'christianity.' He astutely noted,

What is at stake is not just a theological theory but people's salvation.[456]

The Council of Nicaea overwhelmingly upheld Athanasius' view by a vote of roughly 300 to 2.[457] They created the first draft of the Nicene Creed to reflect that the Christian Church is Trinitarian.

Emperor Constantine accepted Nicene Trinitarianism as Christian orthodoxy, but he had an interest in pacifying his subjects and averting civil war. He knew that at least three of the bishops had voted for the Nicene formulation under duress—they secretly held sympathies for Arianism. One of Arius' friends eventually wormed his way back into the Emperor's good graces. He convinced Constantine to banish Athanasius and two other bishops because they refused to stop striving against the evils of Arianism.

The Emperor then ordered the ninety-five year old Patriarch of Constantinople to admit the eighty year old Arius back into Communion. The old Patriarch knew that he would be banished to his death if he did not comply. He asked the faithful Christians of Constantinople to pray that God would show His will by having either he or Arius die before the fateful Sunday in AD 336.[458]

The day before the service faithless Arius was again questioned by Emperor Constantine. Arius covered over the most outrageous parts of his theology. His equivocation satisfied Constantine, who again found him worthy of eating Christ's body and blood. The account of what followed is worthy of a full quotation …

> *It was then Saturday, and Arius was expecting to assemble with the church on the day following: but divine retribution overtook his daring criminalities. For going out of the imperial palace, attended by a crowd of [Arian] partisans like guards, he paraded proudly through the midst of the city, attracting the notice of all the people. As he approached the place called Constantine's Forum, where the column of porphyry is erected, a terror arising from the remorse of conscience seized Arius, and with the terror a violent relaxation of the bowels: he therefore enquired whether there was a convenient place near, and being directed to the back of Constantine's Forum, he hastened thither. Soon after a faintness came over him, and together with the evacuations his bowels protruded, followed by a copious hemorrhage, and the descent of the smaller intestines: moreover portions of his spleen and liver were brought off in the effusion of blood, so that he almost immediately died. The scene of this catastrophe still is shown at Constantinople, as I have said, behind the shambles in the colonnade: and by persons going by pointing the finger at the place, there is a perpetual remembrance preserved of this extraordinary kind of death … and the report of it quickly spread itself over the city and through the whole world.[459]*

Many years later, writing from Egypt, Athanasius was pensive about his old adversary's horrific fate:

> *With all men the common end of life is death. We must not blame a man, even if he be an enemy, merely because he died, for it is uncertain whether we shall live to the evening. But the end of Arius was so singular that it seems worthy of some remark ...* [460]
>
> *Constantine was amazed when he heard of [Arius' death], and regarded it as the proof of perjury ... for a long period subsequently no one would make use of the [toilet] on which he died. Those who were compelled by necessities of nature, as is wont to be the case in a crowd, to visit the public place, when they entered, spoke to one another to avoid the seat, and the place was shunned afterwards, because Arius had there received the punishment of his impiety. At a later time a certain rich and powerful man, who had embraced the Arian tenets, bought the place of the public, and built a house on the spot, in order that the occurrence might fall into oblivion, and that there might be no perpetual memorial of the death of Arius.* [461]

A year after Arius' death, Emperor Constantine also died. Soon after Athanasius was restored as Patriarch of the See of Alexandria.

Nevertheless, the imperial vacillation begun by Constantine was continued by his heirs over the next fifty years. Also, because the first draft of the Nicene Creed did not mention the Holy Spirit, a new form of Arianism developed: a bloodthirsty acolyte of Arius' named Macedonius eventually became the bishop of Constantinople and introduced the false teaching that although God the Father and God the Son were of the same substance, the Holy Spirit was not divine at all.[462] Again, it was an assault upon Trinitarianism.

The blasphemous Creed of Ulfilas reflects this type of thinking.

> *... I believe in one Holy Spirit, an enlightening and sanctifying power ... neither God nor Lord, but the faithful minister of Christ; not equal, but subject and obedient in all things to the Son.* [463]

Toward the end of this period, one of the Trinitarian bishops received the following, disconcerting, correspondence from his brother in Constantinople:

This city is full of mechanics and slaves who are all of them profound theologians, and preach in the shops and the streets. If you desire a man to change a piece of silver he informs you wherein the Son differs from the Father; if you ask the price of a loaf ... you are told that the Son is inferior to the Father; and if you inquire whether the bath is ready, the answer is, the Son was made out of nothing. [464]

This was a Greek trait going back to biblical times.

All the Athenians and the foreigners who lived there spent their time doing nothing but talking about and listening to the latest ideas. [Acts 17:21 TNIV]

The Arian versus Nicene controversies swirled until AD 381 when Emperor Theodosius I convened the second ecumenical council, the Council of Constantinople. It unequivocally accepted the Nicene Creed, and added to it a supplemental phrase concerning the divinity of the Holy Spirit. The Emperor put his stamp on the council's findings, and proclaimed Trinitarianism to be the official state religion of the Roman Empire. [465]

~~~~~~~~~~~~~~~~~~~~~~~~

Nicene Trinitarianism is the religion in which the gracious Founder, Jesus of Nazareth, died on a cross for our sins, and issued blood and water from a spear hole under His ribs. Anti-Nicene Arianism is the religion in which the supercilious founder, Arius of Alexandria, died on a toilet for his sins, and issued blood and abdominal organs from his anus.

As it is written of Christ's betrayer,

... he burst open in the middle and all his bowels gushed out. And it became known to all the inhabitants of Jerusalem, so that the field was called in their own language Akeldama, that is, Field of Blood. [Acts 1:18–19 ESV]

Arianism lost the ecclesiastical battles of the fourth century, but the devil is relentless in his opposition to the notion that the Triune, preexistent, God literally became a man with a nature like our own. That core issue was to be questioned again and again, under other guises.

Galatians 4:4–5 [NKJV]
... when the fullness of the time had come, God sent forth His Son, born of a
woman, born under the law, to redeem those who were under the law, that we
might receive the adoption as sons.

62. The Doctrine of Two Natures in One Undivided Person

The first two ecumenical councils had firmly established the doctrine of the Trinity by the close of the fourth century. However, christological differences were still unaddressed. If Jesus is one of the Persons of the Holy Trinity, and hence true God, then how could He also truly be a man?

A heresy known as Nestorianism emerged in AD 428 which maintained that Jesus existed as two distinct Persons—one human and one divine—sharing the same body. This essentially relegated Jesus to a dual personality, and threw into question the whole concept of the Incarnation. The Nestorians rejected the idea that God literally became a helpless baby inside the womb of the virgin Mary,[xvii] or that God was scourged, or that God suffered and died on the cross. They said that those things were only experienced by the man-part of Jesus, and not by the God-part of Jesus.[466] This belief is in direct contrast to the teachings of the Holy Scriptures.

> *See to it that no one takes you captive through hollow*
> *and deceptive philosophy, which depends on human*
> *tradition and the basic principles of this world rather*
> *than on Christ. For **in Christ all the fullness of the***
> ***Deity lives in bodily form** ... [Colossians 2:8–10 NIV]*
>
> *The Son is the radiance of God's glory and **the exact***
> ***representation of his being** ... [Hebrews 1:3 TNIV]*

To settle the matter, Emperor Theodosius II convened the third ecumenical council, the Council of Ephesus, in AD 431. The Council denounced Nestorianism, and held that Christ was incarnate of the virgin Mary as a single person with both divine and human properties.[467]

---

xvii   This was later revived in the West by certain Reformed Protestant sects that teach that the blessed virgin Mary, as a human being, is merely the mother of "Christ's humanity" and not the mother of God the Son. The correct doctrine, of course, is that the historical figure known as the virgin Mary is the mother of God. Eternal God became a man inside her womb.

AD 2036 Is The End

The immediate result was that the Assyrian Church of the East separated from the rest of Christianity. The Sassanid Persian kings, who were constantly at war with the Eastern Roman Empire, were pleased to see their Nestorian Christians ecclesiastically-separated from the west. Although the Persian kings were of the Zoroastrian religion, they took an interest in the church within their midst and even nominated candidates as bishops.[468] Missionaries of the Assyrian Church of the East spread their heretical brand of Christianity over the next two centuries throughout Persia, Central Asia, and even China. There is one Assyrian parish remaining in China, established in AD 635.[469]

Technically, the eastern Assyrians followed the modified Nestorianism of Babai the Great (AD 551–AD 628) which taught that Jesus had two essences or souls inside one Person.[470] They have recently distanced themselves from Babai and reconciled with the Roman Catholic Church.[471] Only the break-away Ancient Church of the East still follows Babai's false teachings.

Both Nestorianism (i.e., belief in two persons in Christ) and Babaiism (i.e., belief in one person, but two souls in Christ) are extremely heretical. If there were two persons in Christ, which one died for our sins? If there were two souls in Christ, which one went to Hell for three days to preach against the condemned? And did the God-person and God-soul of Jesus rise from the dead on Easter morning, or was it the man-person and man-soul of Jesus?

Clearly Christ had to be a single, divino-human, Person, with a single, divino-human, Soul, in order to conquer death for us. This is the very Christ that ascended to Heaven in AD 30[472] and will return for His Chosen People within [plus or minus] three and a half years of AD 2036.

~~~~~~~~~~~~~~~~~~~~~~~

Some theologians within the Eastern Roman Empire overreacted to Nestorianism. They maintained that Jesus was not only one Person with one Soul, but that He also had only one nature. This teaching came to be known as Monophysitism. In its most radical form the Monophysites held that the human nature of the incarnate Christ was overwhelmed, subsumed, and obliterated by the divine nature, as a drop of honey disappears in an ocean of water.[473] That made His human body essentially different from other human bodies. Taken to its extreme, this is a sort of reverse-Arianism, where the humanity of Jesus is denied rather than His divinity being denied.

Officially, the Monophysites adopted a more nuanced position, saying that in Christ the two natures were simply united into one nature that retains all the characteristics of both. They are careful to say that His perfect humanity was not transmuted or absorbed by His perfect divinity. In this way the Monophysites acquiesce to the term 'perfectly man,' but strictly avoid the term 'fully man.'

The Monophysites taught that Christ's one divino-human nature consists of two sub-units that are united without any mixture or mingling or transformation.[474] Nevertheless, they insisted that the two natures were somehow combined into one—making the manner in which Jesus would have experienced His surroundings something quite inhuman.

The semantics of the 'nature' issue aside, the Monophysites show their true colors by recoiling at the following statements of plain Christian truth:

- Jesus of Nazareth was fully man;
- Jesus of Nazareth was tempted to sin just as men are tempted to sin;
- Jesus of Nazareth was subject to the effects of sin in this fallen world just as men are subject to the effects of sin in this fallen world.

The Monophysitic doctrine that Jesus had a single, unmingled, divino-human nature is quite simply unbiblical. The Apostle Paul records in Scripture an early Christian hymn that testifies of the two natures:

> *Your attitude should be the same as that of Christ Jesus:* ***Who, being in very nature God,*** *did not consider equality with God something to be grasped, but made himself nothing,* ***taking the very nature of a servant,*** *being made in human likeness. [Philippians 2:5–7 NIV]*

And Christ Himself taught about His two natures:

I and my Father are one.	*My Father is greater than I.*
[John 10:30 NKJV]	*[John 14:28 NKJV]*

Emperor Marcian (AD 396–AD 457) called a fourth ecumenical council, the Council of Chalcedon, which, in AD 451, repudiated Monophysitism in all its forms. It established the doctrine that a fully human and a fully divine nature are inseparably present within the single Person of Christ. Pope Leo the Great (AD 400–AD 461) cited the two verses above, and said that the human nature of the Christ is inferior to the Father, but the divine nature of that very same Christ is equal to the Father. This also fits with Jesus' two principal monikers: Son of Man and Son of God.

The Armenian bishops were unable to attend the Council of Chalcedon because of their nation's epic battle against the Sassanid Persians on the Plains of Avarayr. The Eastern Roman Emperor Marcian favored the Armenian Christians in their struggle for religious liberty against the Zoroastrian Persians, but could not send military aid because he was preoccupied with Attila the Hun (AD 406–AD 453) on the western frontier.[475] Hence, the Armenians were predisposed to oppose anything they perceived as a reconciliatory gesture toward the Nestorian church that was within the borders of their enemy, Persia.

Many other eastern bishops also considered the Council of Chalcedon a step back toward the Nestorian heresy that resided within Persia. They did not recognize the difference between Christ being said to exist as one Person with two natures (i.e., Chalcedonianism), and Christ being said to exist as two persons (i.e., Nestorianism). As a consequence, the Armenian Apostolics, the Egyptian Copts, the Ethiopian Tewahedos,[xviii] Eritrean Tewahdos,[xix] Syriac Orthodox,[xx] and the Malankara Orthodox[xxi] all split off from the rest of Christianity. They eventually formed the Oriental Orthodox Communion[476] which to this day holds that in Jesus Christ the divine and human natures are united into a single, unmingled, divino-human nature (see Sections 66–68 for a full exposition on this wicked dogma). **This massive schism of half of that period's Church represents the 'falling away' from Christian orthodoxy that the Apostle Paul predicted would occur before the advent of the Son of Perdition (2 Thessalonians 2:3).**

Just as the Assyrian Church of the East did not like to be called Nestorian, the Oriental Orthodox chafe at being labeled Monophysite. They consider it a misrepresentative epithet, since they reject radical Monophysitism. They prefer the terms 'non-Chalcedonian' or 'Miaphysite' to distinguish themselves from the Roman Catholics, Eastern Orthodox, and Protestants.[477]

Although Monophysites consider themselves to be the theological opposites of Nestorians, they have a commonality: both try to rationally explain the unknowable mystery of how God could become a man. Any explanation, of course, is insufficient—just as any explanation of the Holy Trinity also falls short. God's identity is bigger than our ability to fully grasp, and we must simply accept what the Bible reveals about Him.

---

xviii The Ethiopians were part of the Coptic Church until AD 1959, when the Patriarch of Alexandria, Egypt granted them their own patriarchy.

xix The Eritreans were part of the Ethiopian Church until AD 1993, when the Ethiopian Patriarch granted them autocephaly. Five years later the Eritrean archbishop became a patriarch.

xx Also known as the Jacobite Church (a moniker they reject), after their influential sixth century theologian and bishop, Yaqub Baradaeus. This church is inclusive of the western Assyrian people, but many of their communicants consider themselves to be Christian Arabs and other ethnicities.

xxi The Malankara Christians of India are under the oversight of the Syriac Patriarch.

Psalm 127:1 [TNIV]
Unless the Lord builds the house, the builders labor in vain. Unless the Lord
watches over the city, the guards stand watch in vain.

63. The Rise of Heraclius

A fifth ecumenical council was held in Constantinople in AD 553 to confirm the findings of the first four councils—especially Chalcedonianism, whose authority was constantly contested. But by the beginning of the seventh century, ecclesiastical controversies took a back seat to more immediate concerns: the entire Eastern Roman Empire was on the verge of collapse.

In AD 602 unpaid troops were ordered to over-winter on the hostile Danube frontier. They mutinied, marched on Constantinople, and killed Emperor Maurice and all his sons.[478] A non-commissioned officer named Phocas seized the throne. Phocas was seen as a usurper, and implemented savage purges to keep control of the throne.[479] The frontiers of the empire began to collapse at this time, with Avars and Slavs penetrating as far as Athens in the west, and the Persians advancing to the Euphrates River in the east. A civil war ensued within the Eastern Roman Empire, and the Persian Sassanid Empire took advantage of the chaos to move into Syria.

In AD 610 the son of an ethnically-Armenian military viceroy named Heraclius entered Constantinople without resistance and was made Eastern Roman Emperor by acclamation. He personally executed Phocas and had his body cut into pieces and burned.[480]

The first (and last) ten years of Heraclius' thirty-one year reign were a disaster. The Persians captured the entire Middle East, sacked Jerusalem in AD 614, and surrounded Constantinople. The Persian King sent the Emperor a taunt:

> *Khosru, greatest of gods and master of the whole*
> *earth, to Heraclius, his vile and insensate slave: You*
> *say that you trust in your god. Why, then, had he not*
> *delivered Jerusalem out of my hands?*[481]

This is reminiscent of the taunt sent in 704 BC[482] from the Assyrian King Sennacherib to King Hezekiah of Judah.

> *Do not let the god you depend on deceive you when*
> *he says, 'Jerusalem will not be handed over to the*
> *king of Assyria.' Surely you have heard what the kings*
> *of Assyria have done to all the countries, destroying*

them completely. And will you be delivered? [Isaiah 37:10–11 NIV]

God tends to take notice when kings challenge Him.

Rise up, O God, and defend your cause; remember how fools mock you all day long. Do not ignore the clamor of your adversaries, the uproar of your enemies, which rises continually. [Psalm 74:22–23 NIV]

So the fate of the Assyrian King Sennacherib was a foreshadowing of the fate of the Sassanid Persian King Khosru thirteen hundred years later.

That night the angel of the Lord went out and put to death a hundred and eighty-five thousand men in the Assyrian camp. When the people got up the next morning—there were all the dead bodies! So Sennacherib king of Assyria broke camp and withdrew. He returned to Nineveh and stayed there. One day, while he was worshiping in the temple of his god Nisroch, his sons Adrammelech and Sharezer cut him down with the sword, and they escaped to the land of Ararat. And Esarhaddon his son succeeded him as king. [2 Kings 19:35–37 NIV]

God eventually used Emperor Heraclius to punish King Khosru. While the Persians advanced and overstretched themselves, Heraclius bode his time and prepared for an offensive campaign. He rooted out corruption in Constantinople, reorganized the army, and instituted a popular policy of land grants for military service. Finally, in AD 621, he audaciously led the army deep behind enemy lines and invaded Persia from the north.[483] He destroyed the Clorumia fire-temple that was sacred to the Zoroastrians, and extinguished its eternal flame.[484] He enlisted Ethiopian allies to pressure the Persians from the south in Egypt. He defeated the Persians time-and-again in the Armenian Highlands, slowly working his way into Mesopotamia. He sowed dissention among enemy officers, and took the Sassanid Persian capital near what is now Baghdad.

King Khosru was usurped and killed by his son. The plague spread within Persia and the empire fell into anarchy.[485] By the end of the decade the Persians had withdrawn from all Christian lands.[486] The Persians had previously desecrated the Church of the Holy Sepulchre (in AD 614) and made off with the relic of the True Cross. Heraclius made them return what he believed to be Christ's True Cross.[487]

Emperor Heraclius was a hero. He revitalized the Eastern Roman Empire, and in AD 628 rescued Christianity from the Zoroastrian menace. God had given him the whole world. After seven years of successful warfare he triumphantly rode into Constantinople with a parade of Persian elephants.[488]

There was no indication then that Heraclius was about to preside over the most enduring catastrophe that the Christian Church would ever suffer.

Proverbs 14:12 [NKJV]
There is a way that seems right to a man, but its end is the way of death.

64. The Hubris of Heraclius

Up until that time, the Eastern Roman Empire was synonymous with the Roman Empire, and Constantinople's pseudonym was New Rome.[489] Heraclius, though, spoke only Greek and Armenian—his Latin was quite poor. He decided to abruptly Hellenize the Empire that he had just saved, and changed the official language from Latin to Greek.[490]

Heraclius had developed a messiah complex as a result of his spectacular success over the Sassanid Persian 'King of Kings' Khosru. He stopped using the Roman imperial title, Augustus, in favor of the Greek equivalent of 'King of Kings.' He also assumed the blasphemous titles 'self-ruler' and 'savior of the universe.'[491] He even impersonated Christ by having the common people lay their cloaks before his horse as he approached the walls of Jerusalem in triumph. Then he dismounted, donned a plain robe, and actually carried the relic of the True Cross into the city on his back. This was the third (after Hadrian in AD 131, and Julian in AD 363) and the last time a reigning Roman Emperor would visit Jerusalem.[492]

Despite his wild success and massive ego, Heraclius was terribly insecure. He had risen from the son of an obscure bureaucrat stationed in North African to the undisputed leader of the world's sole superpower. It was as if the earth had been shaken just so that he would be tossed to the top. With such instability, he wondered: could it pass out of his hands just as easily? He looked to the occult for answers, and received an omen of impending evil. It concerned a threat from a circumcised people. Heraclius assumed that this threat was from Jews, but he failed to appreciate that Arabs also circumcise their boys.[493]

You can't believe idols and fortunetellers, or depend on the hope you receive from witchcraft and interpreters of dreams. But you have tried all of these, and now you are like sheep without a shepherd. [Zechariah 10:2 CEV]

So it was that Heraclius set out upon the opposite course-of-action than he should have. He felt that he needed national unity to counter whatever was looming. The Eastern Roman Empire had been beset with christological squabbles for two hundred years. The fourth and fifth ecumenical councils (that upheld the dual-nature doctrine known as Chalcedonianism) had only enflamed internal dissent to the point where the entire empire had nearly collapsed. Heraclius saw himself as just the man to revisit the Chalcedonian controversy. He determined that his crowning glory would be to dictate, once and for all, Jesus Christ's true character.

He knew that he couldn't simply reverse the ecumenical orthodoxy that was emphatically affirmed at the AD 451 council, and again at the AD 553 council. On the other hand, most of the inhabitants of the lands that he had just recovered (especially in Syria and Egypt) were Monophysite. His cousins in Armenia, whose support was instrumental in his Persian campaign, were Monophysite. The Ethiopians, by whose cooperation he had pressured the Persians from the south, were Monophysite. Moreover, his loathsome predecessor, Phocas, had supported Chalcedonianism, and had given the Roman Christians the Pantheon as a church. In gratitude the Pope erected a column in Emperor Phocas' honor. It was the last monument erected in the Roman Forum, and it still stands today.[494] Over twenty years later, Heraclius still resented this fraternization. Why should he be the standard-bearer for the narrowly-defined doctrines of long-dead popes? Italy was on the western fringe of his empire, and he was the King of Kings.

Heraclius pressed forward a compromise doctrine called Monothelitism that held that Christ had two natures, but only one [divinohuman] will. He thought of this as the ideal political solution: By specifying 'two natures,' he gave lip-service to the Chalcedonians. By adding 'one will' he essentially yielded the theological point to the Monophysites.[495]

As a diplomatic intermediation, it was brilliant; as a christological doctrine, it was preposterous. It could never have stood the test of time,[xxii] but no one with a job wanted to inform the Emperor. The obsequious Patriarch in Constantinople resolutely supported Monothelitism—just as he had resolutely supported Heraclius' incestuous second marriage to his brother's daughter. There was also an intellectually-dim pope in Rome at the time, and he indicated amenability to Monothelitism in a letter.[496]

There were other hopeful signs: on his way back to Constantinople, Heraclius met with the Nestorian Catholicos concerning the new frontier between the Eastern Roman and Persian Empires. The latest Persian monarch had sent him to negotiate terms of surrender. Heraclius offered to revert to the AD 602 border in exchange for a Monothelitic statement of faith from the Catholicos. The Persians were defenseless after recent battles and could hardly believe that such a generous treaty was being offered. The Nestorian Catholicos promptly produced an ecclesiastical document that explained away over two centuries of bitter antagonism.[497] Then he served the Eastern Roman Emperor the sacrament of Holy Communion—something that would have been unthinkable a few years before. Heraclius was ridiculously encouraged by this ass-kissing, and harbored delusions that the Persian Zoroastrians would convert *en masse* to his Monothelitic form of Christianity.[498]

The Emperor subsequently demanded an oath from Sophronius, the newly-elected Patriarch of Jerusalem, to never speak against Monothelitism before allowing him to be installed.[499] He continued on to Syria to add another layer to his house of cards. He met for two weeks with the Monophysite Patriarch of Antioch, and twelve of his Monophysite bishops.[500] They reluctantly acquiesced to the Emperor's Monothelitic formulation. Heraclius felt tremendous satisfaction in having forced the eastern Assyrian Nestorians (i.e., the Assyrian Church of the East) and the western Assyrian Monophysites (i.e., the Syriac Orthodox Church) to both commune with he, the Greek Orthodox Emperor from Constantinople.

Heraclius next bought the good graces of the Cypriot Archbishop with a generous public works project on the island.[501] He made his way back to Armenia and offered its Apostolic Catholicos a lucrative salt mine in exchange for embracing Monothelitism. When he hesitated, Heraclius threatened to

---

xxii   The only church that was Monothelite for more than one generation was the Maronites of Lebanon. They were steadfastly supportive of Heraclius' formulation for more than five hundred years, refusing communion with Chalcedonians and Monophysites alike. Finally, during the Crusades of the twelfth century, they came under the Chalcedonian orthodoxy of the Roman Catholic Church.

establish a rival church hierarchy in his country. The Catholicos called together a synod of Armenian bishops in modern Erzurum, Turkey,[502] which yielded to the Emperor's demand. They had little choice in the matter: Heraclius actually sat through the entire proceedings, and again at the end demanded Holy Communion from the Armenian Apostolic Catholicos.[503] Once the Armenians saw things his way, the Emperor rewarded them by ordering that all the recalcitrant fire-worshipers in their region be exterminated.

He was traveling northwest and did not have time for personal diplomacy in Egypt.[504] Also, he was afraid of water and could not bring himself to sail there.[505] Egypt was the most staunchly Monophysitic province in the Empire. Heraclius appointed one of his flunkies as both Prefect of Egypt and Patriarch of Alexandria. With that unprecedented level of power, the Prefect/Patriarch implemented a reign of terror to force the Coptic clergy to accept Monothelitism. Many fled into the desert rather than be tortured into submission.[506]

As a crowning achievement, on May 31, AD 632, Heraclius ordered that the Jews of the Eastern Roman Empire be forcibly baptized.[507]

Heraclius had done what Jesus Christ Himself had failed to do: he had brought the entire world—from Gibraltar to the Indian Ocean—into religious unanimity. Everyone was now a Monothelite Christian. There was no longer anything to fear.

~~~~~~~~~~~~~~~~~~~~~~~

Later in AD 632, a simple Christian monk saw ominous signs in the land and in the air of an approaching apocalypse: there was an earthquake in Palestine, and a comet appeared in the southern sky. It was sword-shaped, and moved progressively northward, from the Arabian peninsula into the Levant, over the period of a month. At the same time, godless barbarians were ravaging the Empire's southeastern frontier. He wrote,

> *What more unfortunate circumstances could be here than these that hold the inhabited world in their grip? ... What could be more lamentable and more terrible to those upon whom they fell? To see how a people, coming from the desert and barbaric, run through land that is not theirs, as if it were their own ...* [508]
> *... to see our civilzation laid waste by wild and untamed beasts who have merely the shape of a human form.*[509]

The monk was Maximus the Confessor (AD 580–AD 662). He was writing about Arab raiders on camelback. It was the beginning of an eight hundred year long invasion that culminated with the fall of Constantinople on May 29, AD 1453.[510]

Maximus was a passionate believer in Jesus Christ, and a brilliant theologian. Much of his writing has survived to this day. He was of a noble Constantinopolitan family and rose to become first secretary to Emperor Heraclius.[511] The Emperor valued him highly, but was disappointed when Maximus decided to take on religious orders and enter a monastery. Maximus moved to the Asian side of the Bosporus and quickly rose to the level of abbot. In AD 620 he was forced to flee to Carthage because of the Zoroastrian Persian encroachment.

Maximus had no way of knowing it, but Providence had an important purpose in his evacuation to Carthage: there he would meet and earn the respect of General Peter of Numidia. That same general sought Maximus' advice on whether to defend Egypt from the Arab invasion twenty years later.[512] Maximus knew that the Arabs were God's judgment upon the false christologies of Monophysitism and Monothelitism.[513] He advised Peter that Providence was against Heraclius' success; Alexandria, Egypt was then taken by the Arab Caliphate without a fight.

From the moment when Maximus heard of the Monothelite initiative, he knew that it was an unorthodoxy. He wrote, gently at first, to inquire if it was simply a semantic misunderstanding. It quickly became clear that this was a political initiative from the Emperor himself. Heraclius actually meant to dictate that Jesus Christ had two natures, but only one will. Maximus rose to His Lord Jesus' defense, and began a campaign to stop the pernicious new doctrine.

> *Again and again I sent my servants the prophets, who said, 'Do not do this detestable thing that I hate!' But they did not listen or pay attention; they did not turn from their wickedness or stop burning incense to other gods. [Jeremiah 44:4–5 NIV]*

By AD 634 Maximus had raised enough theological objections that the Archbishop of Cyprus convoked a synod to discuss Monothelitism. Maximus sensed a trap and declined an invitation to attend. The bishops could not come to an agreement, so they sent a report on their deliberations about Maximus' doctrinal position to the Emperor.[514]

> *We ought to obey God rather than men. [Acts 5:29 KJV]*

Heraclius was apoplectic about his former secretary's impudence and had an Imperial Edict put forth that any clergyman that rejected Monothelitism should be tried for heresy.[515] That meant more than just losing your title in those days—it meant certain death.

Jeremiah 6:19 [NIV]
Hear, O earth: I am bringing disaster on this people, the fruit of their schemes, because they have not listened to my words and have rejected my law.

65. The Fall of Heraclius

On the very day when Emperor Heraclius restored the relic of the True Cross to the Church of the Holy Sepulchre in Jerusalem, a previously unknown band of Arabs attacked one of his garrisons on the Jordan River.[516]

Heraclius was fifty-seven years old when he finally took notice of the Arabs' move northward. That was an advanced age in those days, and he was not in a good state of health.[517] He suffered from chronic depression and debilitating dropsy. Nonetheless, he clung to power until the end.

Heraclius was never as good a field commander as his propaganda machine made him appear. His victories during the Persian campaign had not been huge battlefield epics, but something more like a series of duplicitous communications and buyoffs, punctuated by routs. Heraclius excelled at subverting his enemy through espionage, spreading false information, exploiting internal divisions, and encouraging enemy officers to commit treason. He could not adjust to fighting an enemy that was not a stale imperial dynasty with a large bureaucracy. His new enemies were Bedouin raiders—immune to Byzantine intrigue.[518]

The Emperor never again took the field after crushing the Persians at their capital in Mesopotamia. After a long victory tour, he made the Syrian coast his home.[519] He avoided Constantinople because his second marriage to his niece was a scandal there.[520]

Syria should have been an advantageous outpost for dealing with the new Arab threat, but Heraclius foolishly delayed taking the fight to the enemy before they had gained a serious toe-hold.[521] That was a calculation more than an oversight: he knew that the people of Palestine and Transjordania did not buy into his Monothelitism.[522] He could not come to terms with his failure to purchase their religious fidelity. He questioned the loyalty of Maximus the Confessor, and of Patriarch Sophronius of Jerusalem, and wanted to give them a taste of life outside his lordship. For four crucial years he allowed the Arabs to run wild while he looked for tribal divisions that he could exploit within them.[523]

Patriarch Sophronius was strongly Chalcedonian. He saw the Arab raids as divine retribution for the eastern peoples' christological heresies (i.e., Nestorianism, Monophysitism, and Monothelitism).

> *[The Arabs] would not have achieved or gained such*
> *strength to be able to do and utter such things, **if we***
> ***had not first insulted the gift** and if we had not first*
> *defiled the purification, and by this we injured the*
> *gift-giving Christ and impelled this wrath against us*
> *... [the Arabs have] risen up unexpectedly against*
> *us because of our sins and ravaged everything with*
> *violent and beastly impulse and with impious and*
> *ungodly boldness.*[524]

At long last, Emperor Heraclius had no choice but to act: territory around Damascus had been taken by the Arabs, and his residence in the north of Syria was threatened. He mustered soldiers. But in a horrendous act of negligence, he allowed half of his army to be composed of Monophysite Christian Arabs from southern Syria. Their ancestors had migrated from Yemen during the late Roman Empire, and they could converse freely in Arabic with the invaders. Heraclius' ecclesiastical strong-arming only succeeded in alienating these soldiers. Worse, he had not paid them for years.[525]

The armies faced each other in August, AD 636. It was terribly hot, giving an advantage to the desert enemy.[526] Heraclius' generals delayed a decisive engagement for a month, while searching for vulnerabilities in the Arab ranks.[527] But the Arabs were not interested in bribes when the whole of the land was theirs for the taking.[528] In fact, they turned the tables and used the time to secretly negotiate with their Syrian kin. The Eastern Roman army was finally drawn into a vulnerable position near the Yarmuk River, a tributary of the Jordan. Their only line of retreat was a bridge that the enemy controlled. The Caliph's army attacked and, at a critical point in the battle, a significant number of Heraclius' Syrian Arab soldiers (i.e., Monophysite Christians) defected on the promise of back wages. Tens of thousands of Roman soldiers were trapped, and most were slaughtered.[529]

Heraclius gambled the whole of this army on one battle, and he lost that battle. He made scapegoats of his generals, and had his own brother imprisoned for poor battlefield performance.[530] From that time on, he avoided open combat with the Arabs. The Eastern Roman Empire did not battle the

Arabs again in Syria until AD 995 under Emperor Basil the Bulgar-Slayer (AD 958–AD 1025).

Heraclius negotiated a truce with the Arabs that allowed for a year-long evacuation of the Romans from Syria. A year was necessary because he assumed that everyone would want to leave their land and follow him in retreat. Also, he wanted time to carry out a scorched-earth policy in northern Syria. On his orders, Roman troops pillaged everything they could find and created a wasteland up to their new front lines in Cilicia.[531] At the same time, Heraclius expected fortified cities that he left deep within enemy lines to fight to the bitter end.[532] When one of them negotiated its own surrender to the Arabs, he advanced his troops and burned the city to the ground.[533]

Heraclius thought that he could concede the whole of the Levant, and still hold Mesopotamia and Egypt. He assumed that the Arabs would consider themselves fortunate to have won at Yarmuk and would not try their luck. He could not conceive that the enemy would advance again and again. Even he had not forayed deeply into Persia-proper in his campaign against the Sassanid Dynasty. If the *status quo ante* was good enough for him, then the Arabs conquest of all of the Levant should surely satiate them for generations.[534]

The Arabs, for their part, knew that the more territory they could occupy, the less tax revenue and the fewer military recruits there would be for the defense of Eastern Roman lands. They also knew that there was little resistance to them among the populace.[535] The Arabs were well aware of the christological controversies that were exacerbated by Heraclius. They countered with an evenhanded, even pluralistic, approach.[536] They could not care less whether someone believed in one nature or two natures within Christ, and thus appeared to be refreshingly non-partisan.[537] At that time there was no hint that the Arabs meant to impose a new religion—they were still godless barbarians.

The idea of calling for a crusade with help from Christians outside the Empire would have been laughed at in those days.[538] The Syriac Monophysites were pleased to be rid of Heraclius,

> ... *it was by bargaining with [the Arabs] that we secured our deliverance. This was no small gain, to be rescued from Roman imperial oppression.*[539]

The citizens of Jerusalem also did not see any point in fighting to the death for a tyrant that imposed nonsensical religious doctrines. They had offered stiff resistance to the Persians in AD 614, and there was a mass-slaughter when the city fell.[540] They did not want to provoke a repeat of that just twenty years later.[541] Heraclius knew that Jerusalem would fall, and ordered the relic of the True Cross evacuated to Constantinople. Again, this avoided pitting the Arab invasion in religious terms.[542]

There was a cascading fiscal crisis in the Empire after the loss at Yarmuk. Heraclius' re-conquest of the east in AD 628 had necessarily caused economic hardships. These continued unabated for eight years between the last battle with the Persians and the delayed first battle against the Arabs. Nonetheless, Heraclius spent lavishly on reconstruction and beautification projects in reclaimed areas. That spending weakened the Empire's military readiness just when Arab storm clouds were gathering.[543]

Tax revenue was down even before the humiliating retreat from Syria. Now huge numbers of displaced Chalcedonians and Monophysites moved into the remaining, western, provinces of the Empire. The economy suffered terribly. Heraclius desperately needed money so more troops would not rebel against him. He instituted a debilitating tax on maritime commerce, the lifeblood of the Empire's economy.[544] He became furious when the Prefect of Mesopotamia negotiated to pay tribute to the Arabs to forestall an invasion. He insisted that all tax money go into his coffers.[545] That resulted in the Arab invasion of Mesopotamia, and set the stage for the Arab conquest of all of Persia. With that, Heraclius lost any possibility of forming a military alliance with the Persians against the Arabs.[546]

Meanwhile, a new pope had been chosen that refused to sign the Imperial Edict on Monothelitism. In retaliation, Heraclius refused to officially confirm him to the Papal See for two years, and plundered church property in Italy, Sicily, and Carthage for revenue.[547] He did the same to the churches in Egypt on the eve of their loss to the Arabs. Heraclius made no effort to arm the Egyptian people to resist invasion. The Copts were known to be culturally averse to warfare, and they had no incentive to fight for the tyrannical Prefect/ Patriarch that Heraclius had appointed.[548]

Things started to unravel. Heraclius ordered General Peter of Numidia (modern day Algeria) to defend Egypt from the imminent Arab invasion.[549] Maximus the Confessor, who had ties to the region, advised the general to ignore the order.[550] He sensed that the Arabs were God's judgment upon both the Monophysite and Monothelite heresies,[551] and he knew that the Egyptian Copts would not support an Eastern Roman army at that time. The general heeded Maximus and stayed in Algeria.

There was an attempted *coup d'état* in Constantinople that involved Heraclius' illegitimate son and his nephew. Unfortunately, the plan was discovered beforehand. A youthful leadership in the Eastern Roman Empire probably would have been able to crush the incipient Arab Empire. Heraclius had the young men's noses and hands cut off, and sent them into exile.[552] This was a custom that he learned from the Sassanid Persians: a rival to the throne would be considered ineligible if he was physically mutilated.

Capable and powerful generals were also implicated in the conspiracy. They were relieved of command and recalled to Constantinople for punishment. One escaped into the mountains of Armenia and succeeded in weakening Heraclius' influence in that rich recruiting ground for new soldiers.[553] All of this worked to make Heraclius more depressed, paranoid, and distracted from responding to the Arab threat.

Heraclius knew that he was dying from dropsy. His organs became distended, and he suffered from a severe hernia which caused his urine to be discharged toward his face.[554] He retreated to Constantinople. His phobia of crossing open water was so acute that he ordered ships to be tied together sideways to form a pontoon bridge across the Bosporus. Branches of trees were affixed to the bow and stern of each ship to give the illusion that he was on a road.[555] He raced his horse across the bridge and inside the walls of the capital forever.

His entire focus after the coup attempt was to entrench his heirs into a lasting dynasty. This was of paramount importance, far outweighing the disintegrating situation in the east. His vigilance was on prospective usurpers within his court. He removed any soldiers whose loyalty was the least bit suspect, and kept his best troops close to himself.[556] Whereas in the past he avoided Constantinople, now he secluded himself there.[557]

In the end, all Heraclius managed to do was to put upon the throne a hundred year dynasty of incompetence that was tailor-made for the incubation of what became Islam. By the time his last descendant was killed in AD 711, Islam was permanently established in what had been Christian lands.

~~~~~~~~~~~~~~~~~~~~~~~~

Emperor Heraclius finally died in AD 641. By then, Egypt was in the hands of the Arabs. The Egyptian Monophysites publicly rejoiced at news of the emperor's death.[558] As it is written,

> *... you ruined your country and murdered your people. You evil monster! We hope that your family will be forgotten forever. [Isaiah 14:20 CEV]*

His first wife had died young from epilepsy; he remarried, but his second wife was also his brother's daughter. Both consorts produced sickly heirs to the throne. Heraclius' son by his first marriage became Emperor, but died of tuberculosis four months later.[559] The people of Constantinople suspected

Heraclius' second wife (never a popular figure) of poisoning the new emperor for the sake of her own son. They cut out her tongue, and cut off her son's nose, and sent them both into exile.[560] They then made Heraclius' grandson through his first wife emperor. The grandson proceeded to kill his brother so that his position would remain unchallenged.

Heraclius' grandson held the Monothelite doctrine in high esteem, and made a renewed push for it to be accepted as orthodoxy. But by that time Maximus the Confessor had found a stalwart ally in Pope Martin I. The Pope held a Lateran council in AD 649 and unequivocally denounced Monothelitism.[561] The Emperor sent an assassin to kill the Pope during Mass in Rome. The assassin was struck with blindness and could not carry out his evil assignment.[562] Finally, in AD 653, the Emperor arranged for Pope Martin to be kidnapped from Rome and brought to trial in Constantinople. For his probity, Martin was tortured and then exiled until his death in AD 655.[563]

Maximus the Confessor was also brought to trial in AD 662. When he refused to submit to Monothelitism his right hand was cut off, and his tongue was cut out, so that he could no longer write or speak against the Imperial Edict.[564] He was stripped of his clothes, exiled, and died from exposure. His disciple, who was also mutilated and exiled, reported that an angelic light would appear around Maximus' grave at night.[565] Martin and Maximus were later made saints in the Roman Catholic and Greek Orthodox churches.

Heraclius' despicable grandson then had the brilliant idea of moving the capital of the Eastern Roman Empire to Sicily in order to spread Monothelitism to the west. The people of Constantinople balked, and he was assassinated in his bathtub by his chamberlain.[566]

Heraclius' great grandson became Emperor. By this time the Arabs had an army in Anatolia, and had assembled a navy to attack Constantinople. He called the sixth ecumenical council (termed the Third Council of Constantinople) in AD 680 to denounce his fathers' Monothelitism and once again affirm Chalcedonianism. This was politically convenient to do since all the churches that had acquiesced to Heraclius' original formula were now irrevocably in the hands of the Arab Caliphate. Constantinople was the only Patriarchal See left within the Empire; it needed to be united in doctrine with the Roman Papacy in order to withstand the relentless Arab attacks.

With the return to Chalcedonian orthodoxy, God gave Heraclius' great grandson simultaneous land and sea victories over the Arabs. He celebrated in family tradition by having his two brothers mutilated. Then he promptly died of dysentery.[567]

Heraclius' great-great grandson, Justinian II (AD 669–AD 711), became emperor in AD 685. During his reign Caliph Abd al-Malik consolidated his rule over the Arab Empire, and began to formalize the Muslim religion. While the Dome of the Rock was under construction by the Arabs in Jerusalem, there was a *coup d'état* in Constantinople. Emperor Justinian's nose was cut off, and he was deposed for ten years. In AD 699—the middle of this especially unstable period within the Eastern Roman Empire—the Arabs completed the Dome, thus codifying Islam.[568]

Justinian II managed to regain the throne in AD 705, and instituted savage purges against his enemies. There was another *coup d'état*. He and his sole heir were killed, and the Heraclian Dynasty finally ended in AD 711.[569] Islam was entrenched, and the dynasty's providential purpose was over—one hundred and one years after Heraclius seized the throne.

Luke 22:41–42 [NKJV]
He knelt down and prayed, saying, "Father, if it is Your will, take this cup away from Me; nevertheless not My will, but Yours, be done."

66. The Doctrine of the Temptation of Christ

Heraclius' Monothelite compromise was a colossal flop. It only served to highlight the underlying problem with Monophysitism: one nature implies one will, and one will implies no enticement to sin. That is, if Jesus is said to have only a single [divino-human] nature (as is the main tenet of Monophysitism), then He would necessarily have only a single will.[570] **If He had only a single [divino-human] will, as opposed to a distinct divine will and a distinct human will, then how could He have been tempted to sin?** He could not have been. Sin is abhorrent to God, but quite attractive to us.

> *God is never tempted to do wrong ... [James 1:13 NLT]*

And,

> *... it is impossible for God to lie. [Hebrews 6:18 NLT]*

Since all Christians are agreed that Jesus had only one type of action (i.e., sinless), His single [divino-human] will under Monophysitism would have to be one for which sin had no appeal. And if He never experienced human temptation as we know it, then how could His ability to live sinlessly be a suitable recompense for our inability to do so? It could not be—it would have been an effortless trick.

Prior to the Incarnation of our Lord Jesus Christ, God never had the choice to sin or not to sin. For the Holy Scriptures tell us that,

> *God is love. [1 John 4:16 TNIV]*

And,

> *Love never fails. [1 Corinthians 13:8 NKJV]*

God is inherently virtuous: He did not choose to be love—love is His fundamental and inalterable characteristic—it is His state of being. It was therefore necessary for God to take on a fully human nature and a fully human will in order to be tempted about loving conduct.

Only when God the Son found Himself as the Son of Man was He able to face down the choice to sin—and under the most extreme circumstances, no less. It was only in this way that He was able to reverse our [eternal] death sentence. The Apostle Paul wrote,

> *For I do not do the good I want, but the evil I do not want is what I keep on doing ... it is no longer I who do it, but sin that dwells within me ... Wretched man that I am! Who will deliver me from this body of death? Thanks be to God through Jesus Christ our Lord! [Romans 7:19–20, 24–25 ESV]*

How heinously sinful is Monophysitism's attempt to negate Christ's monumental intercessory work on Calvary!

~~~~~~~~~~~~~~~~~~~~~~~~

You will never get a straight answer from Monophysite priests or deacons concerning the difference between their church and the Roman Catholic or Eastern Orthodox or Protestant churches. They're maddeningly coy about it. They will dismissively shake their heads if you try to explain their theology as I have done here, but they won't plainly tell you what it is. They guard their Christology, I suspect, because of an inability to defend it against Maximus the Confessor's cogent arguments.[571]

> *For I will give you words and wisdom that none of your adversaries will be able to resist or contradict. [Luke 21:15 TNIV]*

The Monophysites' homilies are usually not delivered in English, and their liturgy is not even performed in the vernacular of the third-world countries in which the churches are based. You have to be a Medieval linguistic specialist to understand their Masses.

Nevertheless, if you spend enough time within these churches, and if you can get around the language barrier, you'll eventually hear one of their priests say that Jesus Christ was not tempted in the same way that we are tempted. That's the house secret of Monophysitism: they circumscribe Jesus' real and true humanity by saying that the two natures are united into a single *inhuman* nature. In so doing, they compromise the purpose for which God became a human being in the first place.

Can you imagine how infuriating the Monophysites' position is to the Lord Jesus? Let's look at it from His perspective for a moment:

- He left His rightful place as King of the universe and beyond;
- He entered time and space on planet Earth and took on human form;
- He was born into a livestock trough;
- He was tempted in every conceivable way, and yet He [divinely] willed to resist His [human] nature and thus stayed true to His Heavenly Father;
- He lived without worldly goods, and yet was reviled by the authorities as a glutton;
- He was humiliated and beaten;
- He bled to death while nailed to a piece of wood.

All of this is surely true, and yet the Monophysites cannot accept that it was a work worthy of the redemptive purpose! They do not want to think that God could ever lower Himself to experience the same lustful, gross, and perverse enticements that we all know from our own human experience.

May I be blunt? Jesus was a man, so I am speaking to men that remember their adolescence: do you know that tight feeling inside the crotch of your pants that you had every time an intriguing vixen flashed through your mind— or even when your chair was jostled? The Monophysites want to say that the adolescent Jesus of Nazareth did not suffer with it. They are unyielding in their implication that Christ had a limp noodle.

This is a supreme insult to a man that suffered all things in order to die and save us.

~~~~~~~~~~~~~~~~~~~~~~~~~~~~

In point of fact, the single Person of the Trinity, Jesus Christ, did have two distinct natures (divine and human) and two distinct wills (divine and human). His human nature was tempted as we are tempted; He felt the will to sin as a man does because He had the nature of a human.

> *Temptation comes from our own desires, which entice*
> *us and drag us away. These desires give birth to sinful*
> *actions. [James 1:14–15 NLT]*

Jesus endured it all with grace and without ever giving in to the will to sin because He also had the nature of God. He, as true man, could have given in to the will to sin. He did not. It appealed to His human nature, but it was repugnant to His divine nature. Both existed in perfect harmony within His single personality. He always gave way to the desires of the divine nature. It was a conscious decision, made out of love for the Father and for us.

I am not making this up because I am a Confessional Protestant (i.e., a Chalcedonian, or Anti-Monophysite).

> *I want you to know, brothers, that the gospel I preached is*
> *not something that man made up. [Galatians 1:11 NIV]*

Rather, the Holy Scriptures specifically testify of Jesus Christ,

> *… we do not have a high priest who is unable to sym-*
> *pathize with our weaknesses, but **we have one who has***
> ***been tempted in every way, just as we are—yet was***
> ***without sin.** Let us then approach the throne of grace*
> *with confidence, so that we may receive mercy and find*
> *grace in our time of need. [Hebrews 4:15–16 NIV]*

And also,

> *Because **he himself suffered when he was tempted**, he*
> *is able to help those who are being tempted. [Hebrews*
> *2:18 TNIV]*

His suffering as a result of temptation is absolute proof that He had a separate human nature. A single divino-human nature would not suffer as a result of temptation in any way that can be comparable to the suffering of a man because a nature that is partially divine is not tempted by sin.

> *After **the devil had tempted Jesus in every way**, he left*
> *him to wait until a better time. [Luke 4:13 NCV]*

Therefore, Christ's Holy Week passion was not pointless masochism or showmanship. He endured it for us, with pain, in advance of His death. It was necessary for our salvation. May we never discount it for the sake of ecclesiastical politics or prudish propriety.

Matthew 16:21–23 [NKJV]
From that time Jesus began to show to His disciples that He must go to Jerusalem, and suffer many things from the elders and chief priests and scribes, and be killed, and be raised the third day.
Then Peter took Him aside and began to rebuke Him, saying, "Far be it from You, Lord; this shall not happen to You!"
But He turned and said to Peter, "Get behind Me, Satan! You are an offense to Me, for you are not mindful of the things of God, but the things of men."

67. Satan's Christology

The Monophysite 'protection' of Jesus from His divine purpose of overcoming temptation reminds me of the preceding discourse between the Apostle Peter and the Lord Jesus. Peter's visceral reaction to the news that Jesus would suffer unimaginable indignities was, "Far be it from You, Lord; this shall not happen to You!"

Jesus' sharp reply shows the seriousness with which He regarded His passion: taking upon Himself the sins of the world was the very reason that He had come—it was the very cup that His Father had given Him to drink. He was not going to deny His purpose because the Apostle Peter found it unseemly.

We call Peter a saint because he repented of his false notions of what the Messiah was to experience; Peter ended up accepting that Jesus suffered (against His human will!) for the sins of mankind. The Apostle Peter emptied himself of pride, and later confessed his allegiance to the risen Christ three times.

Unfortunately, the Monophysites have not followed Peter's example—they have not repented of their Anti-Chalcedonian Christology. The heresy remains dogma within their [ever-shrinking] churches to this day.

~~~~~~~~~~~~~~~~~~~~~~~~

On December 13, AD 1996 Pope John Paul II (AD 1920–AD 2005) and the Armenian Apostolic Catholicos Karekin I (AD 1932–AD 1999) issued a common declaration aimed at reconciliation. It carefully avoided the dual nature issue, but expressed,

> *... hope for and commitment to recovery of full com-*
> *munion between [the two churches]*[572]

The two old men had become friends, and the Pope harbored hope that the Armenians might be the easiest of the Oriental Orthodox churches to return to Christian orthodoxy. But Karekin I was warned by his bishops that he would be removed from office if he proceeded toward a formal reconciliation with Rome.

Karekin I later died of throat cancer and was replaced by Karekin II. The new Catholicos is younger, healthier, and is a staunch defender of Monophysitism. Pope John Paul II visited Armenia under Karekin II, but of course was not served Holy Communion because Roman Catholics are Chalcedonian and Armenian Apostolics are Anti-Chalcedonian.

~~~~~~~~~~~~~~~~~~~~~~~~

Leo the Great—the pope that dissuaded Attila the Hun from sacking Rome—wrote the foundational document of Chalcedonianism in AD 449. Known as the Tome of Leo, it is a brilliant treatise on how the single, undivided, Person of the Trinity—God the Son—became incarnate with a separate divine nature and a separate human nature. It reads beautifully:

> *... **the proper character of both natures was main-**
> ***tained and came together in a single person**.*
> *Lowliness was taken up by majesty, weakness by*
> *strength, mortality by eternity. To pay off the debt of*
> *our state, invulnerable nature was united to a nature*
> *that could suffer; so that in a way that corresponded*
> *to the remedies we needed, one and the same media-*
> *tor between God and humanity, the man Christ Jesus,*
> *could both on the one hand die and on the other be*
> *incapable of death. Thus was **true God born in the***
> ***undiminished and perfect nature of a true man,***
> ***complete in what is his and complete in what is ours.***
> *By 'ours' we mean what the Creator established in us*
> *from the beginning and what he took upon himself to*
> *restore. There was in the Savior no trace of the things*
> *which the Deceiver brought upon us, and to which*
> *deceived humanity gave admittance. **His subjection***
> ***to human weaknesses in common with us** did not*
> *mean that he shared our sins. He took on the form*

*of a servant without the defilement of sin, thereby enhancing the human and not diminishing the divine. For that self-emptying whereby the Invisible rendered himself visible, and the Creator and Lord of all things chose to join the ranks of mortals, spelled no failure of power: it was an act of merciful favor. So the one who retained the form of God when he made humanity, was made man in the form of a servant. **Each nature kept its proper character without loss;** and just as the form of God does not take away the form of a servant, so the form of a servant does not detract from the form of God.*

It was the devil's boast that humanity had been deceived by his trickery and so had lost the gifts God had given it; and that it had been stripped of the endowment of immortality and so was subject to the harsh sentence of death. He also boasted that, sunk as he was in evil, he himself derived some consolation from having a partner in crime; and that God had been forced by the principle of justice to alter his verdict on humanity, which he had created in such an honorable state. All this called for the realization of a secret plan whereby the unalterable God, whose will is indistinguishable from his goodness, might bring the original realization of his kindness towards us to completion by means of a more hidden mystery, and whereby humanity, which had been led into a state of sin by the craftiness of the devil, might be prevented from perishing contrary to the purpose of God.

*So without leaving his Father's glory behind, the Son of God comes down from his heavenly throne and enters the depths of our world, born in an unprecedented order by an unprecedented kind of birth. In an unprecedented order, because one who is invisible at his own level was made visible at ours. The ungraspable willed to be grasped. Whilst remaining pre–existent, he begins to exist in time. The Lord of the universe veiled his measureless majesty and took on a servant's form. **The God who knew no suffer-***

ing did not despise becoming a suffering man, and, deathless as he is, to be subject to the laws of death. By an unprecedented kind of birth, because it was inviolable virginity which supplied the material flesh without experiencing sexual desire. What was taken from the mother of the Lord was the nature without the guilt. **And the fact that the birth was miraculous does not imply that in the Lord Jesus Christ, born from the virgin's womb, the nature is different from ours. The same one is true God and true man.**

There is nothing unreal about this oneness, since both the lowliness of the man and the grandeur of the divinity are in mutual relation. As God is not changed by showing mercy, neither is humanity devoured by the dignity received. **The activity of each form is what is proper to it in communion with the other: that is, the Word performs what belongs to the Word, and the flesh accomplishes what belongs to the flesh.** One of these performs brilliant miracles the other sustains acts of violence. **As the Word does not lose its glory which is equal to that of the Father, so neither does the flesh leave the nature of its kind behind.** We must say this again and again: one and the same is truly Son of God and truly son of man. God, by the fact that in the beginning was the Word, and the Word was with God, and the Word was God; man, by the fact that the Word was made flesh and dwelt among us. God, by the fact that all things were made through him, and nothing was made without him; man, by the fact that he was made of a woman, made under the law. **The birth of flesh reveals human nature; birth from a virgin is a proof of divine power.** A lowly cradle manifests the infancy of the child; angels' voices announce the greatness of the most High. Herod evilly strives to kill one who was like a human being at the earliest stage; the Magi rejoice to adore on bended knee one who is the Lord of all. And when he came to be baptized by his precursor John, the Father's voice spoke thunder from heaven, to ensure that he *did not go unnoticed because the divinity was concealed by the veil of flesh: 'This is my beloved Son, in whom I am well pleased.'* **Accordingly, the same one whom the devil craftily tempts as a man, the angels dutifully wait on as God.** *Hunger, thirst, weariness, sleep are patently human. But to satisfy five thousand people with five loaves; to dispense living water to the Samaritan woman, a drink of which will stop her being thirsty ever again; to walk on the surface of the sea with feet that do not sink; to rebuke the storm and level the mounting waves; there can be no doubt these are divine.*

So, if I may pass over many instances, **it does not belong to the same nature to weep out of deep-felt pity for a dead friend, and to call him back to life again** *at the word of command, once the mound had been removed from the four-day old grave; or to hang on the cross and, with day changed into night, to make the elements tremble; or to be pierced by nails and to open the gates of paradise for the believing thief. Likewise,* **it does not belong to the same nature to say 'I and the Father are one,' and to say 'The Father is greater than I.' For although there is in the Lord Jesus Christ a single person who is of God and of man, the insults shared by both have their source in one thing, and the glory that is shared in another.** *For it is from us that he gets a humanity which is less than the Father; it is from the Father that he gets a divinity which is equal to the Father.*

So it is on account of this oneness of the person, which must be understood in both natures, that we both read that the son of man came down from heaven, when the Son of God took flesh from the virgin from whom he was born, and again that the Son of God is said to have been crucified and buried, since **he suffered these things not in the divinity itself whereby the Only-begotten is co-eternal and consubstantial with the Father, but in the weakness of the human nature.** *That is why in the creed, too, we all confess* *that the only-begotten Son of God was crucified and was buried, following what the apostle said, 'If they had known, they would never have crucified the Lord of majesty.' And when our Lord and Savior himself was questioning his disciples and instructing their faith, he says, 'Who do people say I, the son of man, am?' And when they had displayed a variety of other people's opinions, he says, 'Who do you say I am?'— in other words, I who am the son of man and whom you behold in the form of a servant and in real flesh: Who do you say I am? Whereupon the blessed Peter, inspired by God and making a confession that would benefit all future peoples, says, 'You are the Christ, the Son of the living God.' He thoroughly deserved to be declared "blessed" by the Lord. He derived the stability of both his goodness and his name from the original Rock, for when the Father revealed it to him, he confessed that the same one is both the Son of God and also the Christ. Accepting one of these truths without the other was no help to salvation; and to have believed that the Lord Jesus Christ was either only God and not man, or solely man and not God, was equally dangerous.*

*After the Lord's resurrection—which was certainly the resurrection of a real body, since the one brought back to life is none other than the one who had been crucified and had died—the whole point of the forty-day delay was to make our faith completely sound and to cleanse it of all darkness. Hence he talked to his disciples and lived and ate with them, and let himself be touched attentively and carefully by those who were in the grip of doubt; he would go in among his disciples when the doors were locked, **and impart the Holy Spirit by breathing on them**, and open up the secrets of the holy scriptures after enlightening their understanding; again, he would point out the wound in his side, the holes made by the nails, and all the signs of the suffering he had just recently undergone, saying, 'Look at my hands and feet—it is I. Feel and* *see, because a spirit does not have flesh and bones as you see that I have.' All this was so that it would be recognized that the proper character of the divine and of the human nature went on existing inseparable in him;* **and so that we would realize that the Word is not the same thing as the flesh, but in such a way that we would confess belief in the one Son of God as being both Word and flesh.**

This Eutyches must be judged to be extremely destitute of this mystery of the faith. **Neither the humility of the mortal life nor the glory of the resurrection has made him recognize our nature in the only-begotten of God.** *Nor has even the statement of the blessed apostle and evangelist John put fear into him: 'Every spirit which confesses that Jesus Christ came in the flesh is from God, and every spirit which puts Jesus asunder is not from God, and this is Antichrist.'* **But what does putting Jesus asunder consist in if not in separating his human nature from him, and in voiding, through the most barefaced fictions, the one mystery by which we have been saved?** *Once in the dark about the nature of Christ's body, it follows that the same blindness leads him into raving folly about his suffering too. If he does not think that the Lord's cross was unreal and if he has no doubt that the suffering undergone for the world's salvation was real, then let him acknowledge the flesh of the one whose death he believes in.* **And let him not deny that a man whom he knows to have been subject to suffering had our kind of body, for to deny the reality of the flesh is also to deny the bodily suffering.** *So if he accepts the Christian faith and does not turn a deaf ear to the preaching of the gospel,* **let him consider what nature it was that hung, pierced with nails, on the wood of the cross.** *With the side of the crucified one laid open by the soldier's spear, let him identify the source from which blood and water flowed, to bathe the church of God with both font and cup ...*

... it is by this faith that the catholic church lives and grows, by believing that neither the humanity is without true divinity nor the divinity without true humanity ...

*... **It is just as wicked to say that the only-begotten Son of God was of two natures before the incarnation as it is abominable to claim that there was a single nature in him after the Word was made flesh ...** [573]*

Notice Pope Leo's use of the word 'abominable' in the final sentence of this excerpt. He knew something about the 'abomination that causes desolation' (Sections 46, 68). He knew—two hundred and fifty years before it was set up on the Temple Mount in Jerusalem—that the abomination derived its power from the denial that God the Son took on a dual nature at the Incarnation (i.e., the denial that He became fully man). This is the domino that, once tipped, leads inexorably to every other gross depravity—including Islam.

~~~~~~~~~~~~~~~~~~~~~~~~~

I find Leo's encyclical indisputable, but to Monophysites it is anathema—especially the parts that I have set in boldface.

In AD 728, the Armenian Apostolic Church and the Syriac Orthodox Church held the Synod of Manzikert in which they denounced Pope Leo and Chalcedonianism, and formally embraced the Monophysite heresy. They adopted ten canons whereby they 'venerated' the body of Jesus Christ as being:

... neither subject to sin nor destined to decay.[574]

What does this really mean? A great deal, actually. It means that while Jesus was growing and ministering and dying, He was [according to these Armenian and Assyrian reprobates] the prototypical superman. They maintained that for Him, the discomforts of life were not naturally-derived because He was a human being with a nature like our own, but that they were either divinely abrogated or divinely authorized because of His [supposedly] unique, divino-human, nature.

In practical terms, they were really asserting that while He was living in this fallen world, Jesus Christ:

- never blinked *because* He was startled;
- never had to hurry to the latrine *because* His bladder was full;
- never wept *because* He was sad;

- never felt more achy climbing out of His bivouac *because* He was getting older;
- never caught the common cold *because* His ear, nose, and throat membranes were infected by a rhinovirus;
- never found Himself unable to keep His eyes open *because* of exhaustion;
- never found Himself unable to fall asleep *because* of irritation;
- never had sour breath *because* He ate garlic the night before;
- never grunted *because* of the pain of the lashes upon His back;
- never asked the Father if there was some other way to complete His task *because* He did not relish the passion that He was beginning to endure in the Garden of Gethsemane.

The Synod of Manzikert held that to the extent that these sufferings and corruptions of the flesh did happen to the Son of God, they were only voluntarily permitted by His [supposedly] unique, divino-human, will. In other words, they held that the above examples were conscious acts of self-flagellation. They would not accept that these things were naturally-necessitated by the vicissitudes, frailties, and afflictions of human existence in a fallen world. They would not accept that [human] nature ever 'took its course' within the Person of Jesus, or that He ever responded reflexively to the onslaught of the devil.

Now, as far as we know, all human beings grow up to die some day. The only exceptions in Scripture are Enoch (Genesis 5:24) and Elijah (2 Kings 2:11). By the will of God, these two saints were taken directly to Heaven without dying. They are not ghosts there, but have trans–corporeal bodies like that of the Resurrected Christ.

> *Why are you troubled, and why do doubts arise in your hearts? See my hands and my feet, that it is I myself. Touch me, and see. For a spirit does not have flesh and bones as you see that I have. [Luke 24:38–39 ESV]*

The translation of Enoch's (Hebrews 11:5) and Elijah's (2 Kings 2:16–17) bodies into incorruptible flesh was an act of God that foreshadowed the events that will take place among those who are alive on the day of the Second Coming. Indeed, the bodies of many of today's people will never even experience *rigor mortis* because they will be taken to Heaven directly on the last day (1 Thessalonians 4:17)—and needless to say none of these people is the Only Begotten Son of God!

So there is nothing inherently venerable about not undergoing decomposition and reduction to the elements. And even in the case of favored-Enoch and favored-Elijah, their bodies grew both strong and weak during the natural cycles of organic life. The effects of time in a fallen world were not suspended for them; they experienced the aging process that is common to humanity.

It was the same with the Christ Child who,

> *... grew up healthy and strong. [Luke 2:40 NLT]*

And yet He faced the inevitable death of every man.

> *You were made out of the ground. And you will return to it. You are dust. So you will return to it. [Genesis 3:19 NIrV]*

Clearly, as a descendant of Eve, Jesus' body was destined to decay both during His lifetime and during His entombment.

> *Because God's children are human beings—made of flesh and blood—the Son also became flesh and blood. For only as a human being could he die, and only by dying could he break the power of the devil, who had the power of death. [Hebrews 2:14 NLT]*

At the same time, Jesus knew the Scripture that pertained to the Messiah's ultimate fate:

> *No wonder my heart is glad, and I rejoice. My body rests in safety. For you will not leave my soul among the dead or allow your holy one to rot in the grave. [Psalm 16:9–10 NLT]*

The Scripture had to be fulfilled as surely as the prediction that Jesus would be born of a virgin, for He said,

> *... all things must be fulfilled which were written in the Law of Moses and the Prophets and the Psalms concerning Me. [Luke 24:44 NKJV]*

Jesus knew that He would die and enter into decay; and yet He thoroughly trusted that the Heavenly Father would not abandon His body to muck and mire, nor His soul to Hell, once He paid for sin. He boldly predicted both these eventualities:

> *As they were gathering in Galilee, Jesus said to them,*
> *"The Son of Man is about to be delivered into the*
> *hands of men, and they will kill him, and he will be*
> *raised on the third day." [Matthew 17:22–23 ESV]*

Likewise, we trust the Heavenly Father when we face sin, death, and decay everyday because we know the promises of Holy Scripture that pertain to our ultimate fate.

> *It will happen in a moment, in the blink of an eye,*
> *when the last trumpet is blown. For when the trumpet*
> *sounds, those who have died will be raised to live for-*
> *ever. And we who are living will also be transformed.*
> *For our dying bodies must be transformed into bodies*
> *that will never die; our mortal bodies must be trans-*
> *formed into immortal bodies. Then, when our dying*
> *bodies have been transformed into bodies that will*
> *never die, this Scripture will be fulfilled: "Death is*
> *swallowed up in victory. O death, where is your vic-*
> *tory? O death, where is your sting?" [1 Corinthians*
> *15:52–55 NLT]*

Our Faithful Brother, Jesus, was giving us this hope when, on Easter morning, He instructed Mary Magdalene,

> *... go to My brothers. Tell them that I will go up to*
> *My Father and your Father, and to My God and your*
> *God! [John 20:17 NLV]*

The same Father and God that delivered Jesus' body from its [temporary] subjection and its [temporary] destiny will deliver our bodies at the Second Coming!

The point of the Resurrection was not that Jesus' body was too holy to be subjected to natural post–mortem processes—His body was indeed subject to those processes for tens of hours during His entombment! Rather, the point of the Resurrection was that God had predetermined that the decay of the corpse of Christ would abruptly end after three days—a sufficient period of time to confirm the surety of His death by crucifixion, but an insufficient period of time for advanced decomposition.

> *It was my plan to crush him and cause him to suffer.*
> *I made his life a guilt offering to pay for sin. But he*
> *will see all of his children after him. In fact, he will*
> *continue to live. [Isaiah 53:10 NIrV]*

The Apostle Paul used this prophetic point as proof during his first missionary journey in AD 46:[575]

> ... *the One whom God raised from the dead did not rot*
> *away. [Acts 13:37 NIrV]*

Christ crucified, buried, decaying for three days—and yet not rotting, but abruptly coming back to life—this is the blessed hope of every Christian!

> *I decided that while I was with you I would forget*
> *about everything except Jesus Christ and his death on*
> *the cross. [1 Corinthians 2:2 NCV]*

Notwithstanding this truth, the Monophysite priests persist in error. Their dogma puts them in the awkward position of consoling their suffering parishioners with, "Christ can not quite identify with what you are going through—His nature was different from your own. He could pick and choose what happened to His body, and prepare Himself for it. He intervened for Himself on a moment-to-moment basis in a way that He is obviously unwilling to do for you, since you remain ill. Some day you will undergo decay and be eaten by worms, but His venerable body was never destined to the grotesquery of decay."

Saying this about Jesus is like saying about a Medal of Honor winner, "Sure, he ran into enemy machine-gun fire and saved his comrades, but he was cloaked with an invisible forcefield that deflected the bullets until the job was done. He had control over the effectiveness of the enemy's arsenal. He could choreograph the exact details in which he was to die a hero's death, and then miraculously come back to life after receiving a mortal wound. He was not taking a chance in acting as he did—the whole thing was contrived to make him look like the savior of the regiment."[576]

This conception of Jesus of Nazareth is wholly unlike the reality of His experience on earth. The Old Testament Scriptures foretold that the Christ would be,

> *A man of **pains**, and acquainted with **sickness** ...*
> *[Isaiah 53:3 YLT]*

Just because Jesus healed others, it does not mean that His own health and wellness were never travailed.

> *Surely you will quote this proverb to me: 'Physician,*
> *heal yourself!' [Luke 4:23 TNIV]*

The Holy Scriptures clearly teach that,

> *God had the power **to save Jesus from death**. And while Jesus was on earth, **he begged God with loud crying and tears to save him**. He truly worshiped God, and God listened to his prayers. **Jesus is God's own Son, but still he had to suffer** before he could learn what it really means to obey God. **Suffering made Jesus perfect**, and now he can save forever all who obey him. [Hebrews 5:7–9 CEV]*

A person that is not genuinely tormented by ungodliness and the inevitability of bodily infirmity cannot truly suffer. Jesus, as a human being, was genuinely tormented. The natural order was not suspended or mitigated for Him—it is the same natural order that afflicts us. Christ Himself said,

> *[The wicked] have done to [John the Baptist] everything they wanted to do. **In the same way**, they are going to make the Son of Man suffer. [Matthew 17:12 NIrV]*

And what is the ultimate source of the afflictions of the human race?

> *Our fight is ... against the leaders and the powers and **the spirits of darkness in this world**. It is against **the demon world** ... [Ephesians 6:12 NLV]*

Now, some men can live for decades without an emotional outburst against the spirits of darkness that are oppressing them. They are ignorant men, but nevertheless they have the intestinal fortitude to plod on without appealing to God. So, if Jesus had a directorial leg-up over us, then why the loud crying on His part? Why the tears, if His struggle was not every bit as real as our own? Why the begging, if His flesh was not bound over to the exact same natural death to which we are bound? Was it all just thespianism to elicit our sympathies?

No! A thousand times, no! Jesus groaned for the same reason that Christian believers groan during this miserable life.

> *While we live in these earthly bodies, we groan and sigh, but it's not that we want to die and get rid of these bodies that clothe us. Rather, **we want to put on our new bodies so that these dying bodies will be swallowed up by life**. God himself has prepared us for this, and as a guarantee he has given us his Holy Spirit. [2 Corinthians 5:4–5 NLT]*

Jesus wanted to do His Heavenly Father's will, and attain the resurrection, and be done with the devil's oppression. That is precisely what all Christians want.

> ***I want to know Christ and the power of his resurrection and the fellowship of sharing in his sufferings***, *becoming like him in his death, and so, somehow, to attain to the resurrection from the dead. [Philippians 3:10–11 NIV]*

Jesus is our kith and kin, you see. He was not partially God and partially man within one nature, but fully God and fully man with two separate natures in one undivided Person.

Although it is most certainly true that ...

- everything that has ever happened to anyone (including Jesus) has happened with God's tacit permission,
- and Jesus was and is the Almighty Sovereign that gives that tacit permission,
- and there were instances when Jesus took miraculous action in order to prevent burgeoning consequence and to fulfill His earthly mission,

... it in no way follows that Jesus' mind and body were immune from cause-and-effect treatments administered by demonic forces.

If He was immune to the effects of a forty day fast, for example, then He would not have been vulnerable to the devil's temptation in the desert.

> *After Jesus had gone without eating for forty days and nights, **he was very hungry**. Then the devil came to him and said, "If you are God's Son, tell these stones to turn into bread." [Matthew 4:2–3 CEV]*

The devil knew that Jesus could not just shrug off His experience like a prize fighter that receives a glancing blow in the first round, and then hike back to civilization like a fresh marathoner. Jesus was physically weak and probably near death from starvation, such that it was necessary that,

> *... angels came and took care of Jesus. [Matthew 4:11 NLT]*

I suspect that the reason that Jesus did not turn the stones into bread is that He knew that He needed an intravenous, and He trusted that the Father would provide angelic nursing care for Him the moment that the fast was over and the temptation ceased. His trust was well placed, for that is precisely what happened.

... he has not despised or scorned the suffering of the
afflicted one; [Psalm 22:24 TNIV]

If you call yourself a Christian, you must realize and appreciate that
when God the Son took humanity into the Godhead at the Incarnation, **He vol-**
untarily suspended His rightful Godly powers for a period of thirty-four and
a half years (including His time inside the Virgin's womb).

[Jesus] did not consider equality with God something
to be used to his own advantage; rather, he made him-
self nothing ... [Philippians 2:6–7 TNIV]

During that period of human history (6 BC to AD 30),[577] **the Person of**
God the Son was involuntarily subject to sin.

My Father! If it is possible, let this cup of suffering be
taken away from me. Yet I want your will to be done,
not mine. [Matthew 26:39 NLT]

This is why Christ's mode of activity during His earthly ministry was
not one of omnipotence and omniscience, but faith and trust in God the Father.
Jesus readily admitted to His disciples that He did not know everything.

No one knows the day or the time. The angels in
heaven don't know, and the Son himself doesn't know.
Only the Father knows. [Mark 13:32 CEV]

And when a woman was healed by touching Him from behind,

... Jesus kept looking around. He wanted to see who
had touched him. [Mark 5:32 NIrV]

Just as we are in the dark about what challenges tomorrow might bring,
so Jesus of Nazareth was in the dark. He had to deal with that same feeling of
insecurity that we know so well. In fact, with Him it was worse: imagine that
the Chief of Operations for a maximum security prison voluntarily became
one of the prisoners. Would he not feel vulnerable? The only security that he
would have during his time as a prisoner is believing that the Warden would be
continuously monitoring him through a video feed, and that he could call upon
the guards for aid. But he would still be bound to suffer abuse throughout such
a period.

I assure you: The Son is not able to do anything on
His own, but only what He sees the Father doing.
[John 5:19 HCSB]

Just as bad things happen to us as a result of the presence of sin in the
world, so bad things happened to Jesus of Nazareth as a result of the presence

of sin in the world (but never as a result of His own sin, for He had none). As with us, the bad things that Jesus endured were often unexpected, objectionable, and seemingly senseless. They required trust on His part, and He always trusted. Although the devil succeeded in making Jesus flinch, he did not succeed in making Jesus doubt the Father.

> *Jesus wept ... Then Jesus raised His eyes, and said,*
> *"Father, I thank You that You have heard Me. I knew*
> *that You always hear Me; but because of the people*
> *standing around I said it, so that they may believe that*
> *You sent Me." [John 11:35,41–42 NASB]*

I'm sure that the Baby Jesus sometimes involuntarily vomited onto His blessed mother's breast, for example, and then cried like any other infant. But the child was comforted, and His human nature learned what obedience really meant. And Jesus the carpenter surely experienced splinters, cuts, and jammed fingers for which He did not immediately beforehand pronounce, or even think, "AND NOW THE SON OF GOD WILL INCUR AN INJURY!" but for which He immediately afterward exclaimed, "OW! THAT HURT! HELP ME, HEAVENLY FATHER!" And again He was comforted, and His human nature learned what obedience really meant.

His flesh was trained in this manner throughout His earthly walk, as is the case with all people that have the Holy Spirit.

> *... He humbled Himself and became obedient to the*
> *point of death, even the death of the cross. [Philippians*
> *2:8 NKJV]*

For this reason, on the evening before His Crucifixion—when He could have used some rest—He was on guard to train His flesh to be subject to the onslaught of sin. Jesus cautioned the Apostle Peter to follow His example.

> *Watch and pray, lest you enter into temptation. The*
> *spirit indeed is willing, but the flesh is weak. [Mark*
> *14:38 NKJV]*

Jesus' flesh was weak in the same way that Peter's flesh was weak. He did not have any superhero physical powers that Peter lacked. Jesus needed to be alert and to pray so that the will of His human nature would accept the will of His divine nature.

It was, in fact, because His humanity was so unremarkably common that the Jews rejected His Christhood and first attempted to stone Him.

> *You are just a man, and here you are claiming to be*
> *God! [John 10:33 CEV]*

They would never have attempted to stone Him if His flesh was overtly extraordinary, because then they would have been afraid that the stones would bounce off Him and hit them back. People would have known (without the necessity of saving faith) that He was the Son of God if He never perspired, or if He was never stung by a mosquito, or if He never burped in the middle of a sentence. But His body was like ours—limited, and very much in the process of decay from the moment that it was born into the world.

The Jewish masses were perfectly prepared to accept a Messiah that was the same as them in regard to avarice.

> ... *they were about to come and take Him by force to make Him king ... [John 6:15 NKJV]*

But they were not prepared to accept a Messiah that was the same as them in regard to physicality.

> ... *we know where this man comes from. When the Messiah comes, he will simply appear; no one will know where he comes from. [John 7:27 NLT]*

They were continually vexed because, apart from His miracles and gracious teachings, He was so ordinary.

> *There was nothing beautiful or majestic about his appearance, nothing to attract us to him. [Isaiah 53:2 NLT]*

Therefore, Jesus instructed the dense people of Jerusalem,

> *Stop judging by mere appearances, and make a right judgment. [John 7:24 NIV]*

God chose to become a human being—to take on a humanity that was subject to the pattern (but not the rut) of our pitiful track. If Christ's abdominal cavity had been opened with a scalpel, it would not have been found to be full of chocolate bonbons and budding lilacs, as the Gnostic heretics implied; it would have been found to be full of guts, just like any other person. It was for this reason that life-giving blood and water showered forth when His torso was speared by the Roman executioner. **The separation of blood cells from blood plasma was forensic proof that His body followed the natural decay processes of newly-dead corpses**.

Thus, Jesus Christ *had* to eat *because* His body was hungry (Mark 11:12). Likewise, He *had* to sit down *because* He was tired (John 4:6). And, most significantly for us, He *had* to die *because* His humble frame was scourged and nailed onto wood (Acts 5:30).

The Pharisees would have none of Jesus' loving words because they had long-before decided not to trust God to preserve them.

> *Jesus said to them, "If God were your father, you would love Me. I came from God. I did not come on My own, but God sent Me." [John 8:42 NLV]*

Jesus claimed to be the Heir of the Sovereign that had seen fit to give the Jewish nation into the hands of the hated Roman Empire. For that, they despised Him.

> *This is the heir; come, let us kill him, and the inheritance shall be ours. [Mark 12:7 ASV]*

The Pharisees knew instinctively that Jesus' body was as human as anyone else's, and that it would be possible to kill Him if they could only get their hands on Him (Luke 7:44–46). They were right about that, and the temptation to actually be able to kill the Son of God was enthusiastically embraced when the opportunity finally presented itself.

> *... it was out of envy that the chief priests had handed Jesus over ... [Mark 15:10 TNIV]*

So it was, that three and a half years[578] of infuriation was savagely unleashed upon Him on one mournful day. But God had a plan, as He always does.

> *... He has appeared one time, at the end of the ages, for the removal of sin by the sacrifice of Himself. [Hebrews 9:26 HCSB]*

We call that day Good Friday because God used the worst thing that has ever happened for the best of purposes.

> *See ... I will remove the sin of this land in a single day. [Zechariah 3:9 NIV]*

Will He not similarly work a good purpose from your cancer, or diabetes, or ileitis, or paralysis, o suffering brother or sister of Jesus Christ? Most certainly He will! For through faith and trust we have gained a Corporate Identity with Him. In a mystical Union, what we suffer, Christ also suffered; and what demonic opposition Christ encountered in securing our salvation, we also encounter in spreading His Gospel.

> **In my own body I am doing my share of what has to be done to make Christ's sufferings complete.** *This is for His body which is the Church. [Colossians 1:24 NLV]*

Jesus is the Artisan that suffered for His craft; the Church is the society of Art-lovers that suffer for His Masterpiece (i.e., the Gospel) to be known around the world. How else could Christians be joyful in all circumstances? Indeed, I have heard a faithful woman, suffering in the hospital, say, "If this is somehow all for my dear Lord Jesus' sake, then it is worth it, and I have no regret."

It is, in fact, precisely through the experiential similitude between the pain of Jesus and the pain of the Christian believer that we have the hope of eternal life.

> We will also share in the glory of Christ, **because we
> have suffered with him**. [Romans 8:17 CEV]

And that same experiential similitude accounts for Christ's judicial credentials.

> God has given Him the right and the power to say
> if people are guilty, **because He is the Son of Man**.
> [John 5:27 NLV]

So, in the most fundamental way possible, the Armenians and Assyrians of the Synod of Manzikert were sacrilegious when they pronounced that Jesus of Nazareth had one divino-human nature that was neither subject to sin nor destined to decay. That was the entire purpose of the incarnation of God as man: to make Christ subject to the circumstances and destiny of sinners (i.e., bodily death and entry into Hell) in order that we may be made subject to the circumstances and destiny of the Sinless One (i.e., resurrection from the dead and entry into Heaven).

> For God made Christ, who never sinned, to be the
> offering for our sin, so that we could be made right
> with God through Christ. [2 Corinthians 5:21 NLT]

The devil tremendously enjoyed subjecting Christ to the effects of sin for thirty-four and a half years (including His time inside the Virgin's womb). He had no qualms about losing the souls of millions that were in his clutches because he knew that the Baby Jesus was destined for suffering, death, burial, decay, and Hell.

> For just as Jonah was three days and three nights in
> the belly of the great fish, so will the Son of Man be
> three days and three nights in the heart of the earth.
> [Matthew 12:40 ESV]

But what the devil did not appreciate when God set out upon His cosmic rescue mission is that God would use the devil's greatest weapon (i.e., death) against him.[579]

> *... he has reconciled you by Christ's physical body through death to present you holy in his sight, without blemish and free from accusation ... [Colossians 1:22–23 NIV]*

Indeed, Christ's entry into Hell was for but three days of triumphalism.

> *For Christ also suffered once for sins, the righteous for the unrighteous, to bring you to God. He was put to death in the body but made alive in the Spirit. **In that state he went and made proclamation to the imprisoned spirits** ... [1 Peter 3:18–19 TNIV]*

Remember that it was only when Jesus physically died that His Soul was manifested to be victorious over sin and death and every power of the devil. And it was only on Easter morning, after three days in the grave, that His Body was manifest to be something extra–human—something trans–corporeal[580]—something completely free from the effects of sin.

> ***After He had suffered much and then died**, He showed Himself alive in many sure ways for forty days. [Acts 1:3 NLV]*

Hence, in between Jesus' Resurrection and Ascension in AD 30,[581] He demonstrated to His disciples that His reanimated flesh could:

- both eat, and not eat;
- both breath, and not breath;
- both be touched, and not be touched;
- both show His face, and obscure His face;
- both travel by walking, and travel by teleportation;
- both enter through open doors, and enter through solid walls;
- both stand firmly upon the ground, and float upward into the sky.

These were not traits that Jesus demonstrated before His death (except on the day of the Transfiguration when His Body both absorbed light and radiated light). But once the devil's oppression of the Son of God was over, **it was over for good**.

Even though we have known Christ according to the flesh, yet now we know Him thus no longer. [2 Corinthians 5:16 NKJV]

So the Apostle Peter was right when he later preached,

... it was impossible for death to keep its hold on him. [Acts 2:24 TNIV]

It *was* impossible! The Resurrected Jesus remains scarred with a gaping mortal wound.

Then I saw a Lamb, looking as if it had been slain ... [Revelation 5:6 TNIV]

Yet that wounded Body is both glorious and immortal, and He,

... rules over all forces, authorities, powers, and rulers. [Ephesians 1:21 CEV]

The same glory and immortality awaits those that have died in Christ and whose bodies have already returned to the elements. Christ's destiny was for only three days of decay and after that eternal rejuvenation; the average Christian's destiny is for only a few centuries of decay and after that eternal rejuvenation.

... in Christ all will be made alive. But each in his own turn: Christ, the firstfruits; then, when he comes, those who belong to him. [1 Corinthians 15:23 NIV]

The time difference is, at once, both trivially inconsequential and entirely appropriate.

... he is the beginning and the firstborn from among the dead, so that in everything he might have the supremacy. [Colossians 1:18 TNIV]

But most assuredly we Believers shall be supermen at the Second Coming, for,

*When Christ, who is your life, appears, then **you also will appear with him in glory**. [Colossians 3:4 TNIV]*

Until then our weak human nature is wholly like that of our Brother, Jesus of Nazareth, whilst He sojourned among us.

As for the miracles that Christ preformed while clothed in carnal flesh, we ourselves are capable of them if only we have enough faith.

Truly, truly, I say to you, whoever believes in me will also do the works that I do; and greater works than these will he do, because I am going to the Father. Whatever you ask in my name, this I will do, that the Father may be glorified in the Son. [John 14:12–13 ESV]

All this being the case, how can I not now break forth in praise?

O merciful Sovereign, how grateful I am that You became a man with a separate nature exactly like my own! You have shown Your love by lowering Yourself, and making the sinless and eternal Son of God both subject to sin and destined to decay. Then, at a time that was in accord with the Old Testament prophecies, You destroyed the power of the devil through means of the devil's destruction of Jesus Christ, and You raised Him from the dead. You did this for my sake—to save me from an eternity in hell. Now I shall be like You in the resurrection! Truly, truly, You love me!

~~~~~~~~~~~~~~~~~~~~~~~~

The political consequence of the Synod of Manzikert was that the Armenians, Syriacs, and Egyptian Copts entered into the [Monophysitic] Oriental Orthodox Communion, as they remain to this day. This delighted the Antichrist Beast (i.e., the Muslim Arab Empire), which by that time (AD 728) exercised firm control over all three regions.[582] But the Georgian Orthodox Church split from Armenian ecclesiastical authority during this period, and aligned with the Chalcedonian Communion of the Greeks.[583] Although the Georgians are known to be a crass and impious people, they were largely spared the massacres that followed the Monophysite heresy in later centuries.

It is significant that Christian sovereignty over Anatolia was permanently lost to the Antichrist Beast (i.e., the Muslim Seljuk Empire) in the province of Manzikert in AD 1071.[584] This occurred *exactly* six hundred and sixty-six years after the Armenian saint, Mesrop Mashdots (AD 360–AD 440) invented the Armenian alphabet for the purposes of spreading Christianity in AD 405.[585] Mashdots was from Hatsekats—a village within the province of Manzikert.

Tragically, that same province of Manzikert (the modern province of Mush, Turkey) was a complete disaster for the indigenous Armenian and Assyrian population during the genocides of the First World War. They were unarmed, and surrounded by the Antichrist Beast (i.e., the Muslim Ottoman

Empire). Almost no one survived. Men were impaled, children were hurled into bedrock crevasses, and pregnant women were eviscerated.[586]

As it is written,

> *The people of Samaria must bear their guilt, because they have rebelled against their God. They will fall by the sword; their little ones will be dashed to the ground, their pregnant women ripped open. [Hosea 13:16 NIV]*

There are no more Monophysitic Christians living in Manzikert, Turkey. None. I have been there and looked for them.

> *'When I called, they did not listen; so when they called, I would not listen,' says the Lord Almighty. 'I scattered them with a whirlwind among all the nations, where they were strangers. The land was left so desolate behind them that no one could come or go. This is how they made the pleasant land desolate.' [Zechariah 7:13–14 NIV]*

Satan's demons squeal with delight when the Chosen People confess untruths about the Living God. They know that it means for them a divinely-authorized license to commit atrocities against the Elect.

> *Who gave Jacob to the robber, and Israel to the plunderers? Was it not the Lord? Have we not sinned against Him? They were not willing to walk in His ways, and they would not listen to His instruction. So He poured out on Jacob His furious anger and the power of war. [Isaiah 42:24–25 HCSB]*

~~~~~~~~~~~~~~~~~~~~~~

Again, please note the similarities between:

1a. The Apostle Peter's "protection" of Jesus with the statement, "Far be it from You, Lord; this shall not happen to You!"

1b. And Jesus Christ's response to Peter, "Get behind Me, Satan! You are an offense to Me, for you are not mindful of the things of God, but the things of men."

2a. The Dome of the Rock inscription "magnifying" God with, "Praise to Allah who has not taken a son, and … [is not] humbly dependent upon any other person. Magnify Him with repeated magnificats"[587] (see Section 46 for full text).

2b. And Daniel 12:11 prophesying this structure as the "Abomination that Causes Desolation."

3a. The Monophysites' "veneration" of Jesus with the canon, "[His body] was neither subject to sin nor destined to decay."[588]

3b. And the horrific fate of that branch of the Christian Church.

My point? **A curse follows any suggestion that Jesus of Nazareth was not subject to the devil's harassment in the exact same manner that you and I are subject to the devil's harassment** (Section 78).

> *This is the curse that is going out over the whole land; for according to what it says ... everyone who swears falsely will be banished ... it will enter the house of ... him who swears falsely by my name. It will remain in his house and destroy it, both its timbers and its stones. [Zechariah 5:3–4 NIV]*

Dear Christian reader, do yourself, your family, and your nation a great favor: no matter how tempting it is to say otherwise, or to be ambivalent, never compromise on the truth that God the Son became incarnate inside the womb of the blessed virgin Mary in the form of ...

- a single divino-human Person,
- and a single divino-human Soul,
- with a separate divine nature and a separate human nature,
- and a separate divine will and a separate human will.

And yet He was undivided, unconfused, sinless, and completely at home within His own skin.

I recommend reciting the following out loud, as a cathartic liturgy:

- ❖ *Jesus was subject to sin exactly as men are subject to sin;*
- ❖ *Jesus was tempted exactly as men are tempted;*
- ❖ *Jesus died and entered into decay exactly as men die and enter into decay;*
- ❖ *Yet Jesus lived the sinless life to save us, and rose from the dead on the third day.*

This is the Christian faith.

For God so loved the world, that he gave his only begotten Son, that whosoever believeth in him should not perish, but have everlasting life. [John 3:16 KJV]

~~~~~~~~~~~~~~~~~~~~~~~

Some years ago, I developed the following axiom:

Small-minded persons flock to opposite extremes of the same issue, for in extremism is emotional safety and a lack of intellectual vigor.

It applies here: as we have discussed, the illogical inverse of Monophysitism is Nestorianism (Section 62); so whereas the Monophysites erred in insisting that Christ had one nature, the Nestorians erred in insisting that Christ was two different persons, each with a different nature. The truth lies in between these extremes (i.e., one Person with two natures). And whereas the Monophysites were brutalized by [Sunni] Turks and Kurds, the Nestorians were brutalized over the centuries by [Shi'a] Persians and Kurds (Section 68).[xxiii]

The number of Nestorians declined earlier and more precipitously than that of the Monophysites. Tamerlane (AD 1336–AD 1405), who claimed descent from Ali, beheaded one hundred and sixty thousand Nestorians in Iraq.[589] Their number has become even smaller since two branches have come back into communion with Rome: the Chaldean Catholic Church came under Vatican oversight in AD 1552;[590] the Assyrian Church of the East (now based in Chicago) returned to orthodoxy by signing a Common Christological Declaration with the Roman Catholic Church in AD 1994.[591] Only a tiny remnant of the Nestorian heresy remains today in the form of the breakaway Ancient Church of the East.

Fortunately, Nestorianism is well on its way to extinction.

~~~~~~~~~~~~~~~~~~~~~~~

The next two tables review the seven ecumenical councils, and the spectrum of christological formulations.

---

xxiii This is a general rule, but several thousand Nestorian civilians were murdered by [Sunni] Ottoman troops that invaded western Iran specifically for that purpose during the winter of AD 1915.

Table 11. The Seven Ecumenical Councils and Their Major Decisions

Council	Held in	Year	Major Decision of the Christian Church
1st	Nicaea	AD 325	Denounced Arianism. Affirmed Trinitarianism.
2nd	Constantinople	AD 381	Denounced Arianism again. Reaffirmed Trinitarianism.
3rd	Ephesus	AD 431	Denounced Nestorianism. Affirmed one undivided Person in the Incarnation of Christ.
4th	Chalcedon	AD 451	Denounced Monophysitism. Affirmed two separate natures in the one undivided Person of Christ (i.e., affirmed Chalcedonianism).
5th	Constantinople	AD 553	Denounced Monophysitism again. Reaffirmed two separate natures in the one undivided Person of Christ (i.e., reaffirmed Chalcedonianism).
6th	Constantinople	AD 680	Denounced Monothelitism. Affirmed two separate wills in the one undivided Person of Christ (i.e., reaffirmed Chalcedonianism again).
7th	Nicaea	AD 787	Denounced Iconoclasm. Affirmed that images of Jesus remind Christian worshipers of His dual nature in the miraculous Incarnation.

Table 12. Chalcedonianism vs. the Christological Heresies

Christology	Meaning
Arianism	Christ is not a divine person, but only appeared to be divine (an antichrist heresy that denies the Trinity).
Nestorianism	Christ is two persons with two souls,[i] two wills, and two natures.
Babaiism	Christ is one person, but with two souls, two wills, and two natures.
Chalcedonianism	Christ is one person with one soul, but with two wills and two natures (the orthodox Christology of the Christian Church).
Monothelitism	Christ is one person with one soul and one will, but two natures.
Monophysitism	Christ is one person with one soul, one will, and one nature.
Gnosticism	Christ is not a human person, but only appeared to be human (an antichrist heresy that denies the Incarnation).

[i] Two 'souls' or 'essences.' In Greek the word is *ousia*.

The Apostle Paul noted to the Corinthians,

... there must be also heresies among you, that they which are approved may be made manifest among you. [1 Corinthians 11:19 KJV]

I hope that I have sufficiently demonstrated to you "they which are approved," and you agree with me that Chalcedonianism is the only true form of Christianity. The others are quasi–Christian, at best. The two extremes in Table 12 are antichrist, by definition.

But if you are so stiff-necked as to still be unconvinced, we will investigate God's historic verdict on the matter in the following sections.

Micah 5:13,15 [TNIV]
... you will no longer bow down to the work of your hands ... I will take vengeance in anger and wrath upon the nations that have not obeyed me.

68. Anti-Chalcedonianism was the Precursor of Anti-Christianism

There is precious little Christian joy in Anti-Chalcedonian churches, whether Nestorian or Monophysite. You won't catch the janitor whistling a hymn in the sanctuary while it is empty. I made that mistake once and a scowling deacon came out of the woodwork and told me to shut my trap. These are somber places. The Anti-Chalcedonians speak a lot about their tragic histories and their rich languages. Curiously, they don't speak a lot about the Bible. They don't translate the Bible into the vernacular, or encourage individuals to read it. They don't hold Bible studies or prayer groups. They are national churches and don't proselytize persons of other ethnicities—thus disobeying the Great Commission of Jesus Christ (Matthew 28:19–20). They don't teach that Christians should have private devotional lives at home. They don't emphasize a loving, personal, relationship with Jesus Christ. These things are foreign to them.

Woe to you, teachers of the law and Pharisees, you hypocrites! You are like whitewashed tombs, which look beautiful on the outside but on the inside are full of dead men's bones and everything unclean. In the same way, on the outside you appear to people as

righteous but on the inside you are full of hypocrisy
and wickedness. [Matthew 23:27–28 NIV]

Once a Protestant evangelist asked an Egyptian Copt layman if he knew Jesus Christ personally. The Copt replied, "I've heard the name before. The priests sometimes speak of him. He must have been a great saint in order for them to remember the man in prayer after all these years." This anecdote is close to the state-of-affairs among the entire Anti-Chalcedonian laity.

The church officials do, however, snap into action when they find one of their own receiving Christian nourishment from Protestants. They don't care a whit whether their parishioners attend worship services, but they are tremendously bothered if their parishioners attend worship services *someplace else.* They say that their people are theirs; they say that their people can never really leave them.

Woe to you, teachers of the law and Pharisees, you
hypocrites! You travel over land and sea to win a
single convert, and when he becomes one, you make
him twice as much a son of hell as you are. [Matthew
23:15 NIV]

It's a lot like the mafia—a place for the dead, and for the dying. I am aware of a Monophysite parish in California that has a baptized membership of two thousand, but a weekly attendance of three dozen old ladies.

My grandfather was raised in a devout Monophysite home. His mother would reserve the first-fruits from her kitchen for the local priest to bless. The priest would take a liberal portion of the food for his troubles.

One day she made a big batch of yogurt, put it in the root cellar to cool, and told my grandfather not to touch it until the priest arrived. The boy was overcome with hunger and mischief, so he helped himself to the yogurt and then dipped their cat head-first into the pot to cover-up his crime. The cat then ran through the house, leaving a white trail.

He used to tell this story and laugh uproariously. He felt badly for fooling his old mother, and sorry for the poor cat that took his punishment. But he did not feel guilty for eating the priest's portion. He had no use for Monophysite priests. He used to call them 'black devils' because of their black-hooded vestments.[xxiv]

This attire is suggestive: black is the preferred color of the Antichrist Beast's imams, sheikhs, ayatollahs, and muftis.

---

xxiv Some Protestant pastors also dress in black upon the altar of God. They should not. I think white or off-white is appropriate to reflect their role as Christ's priests.

~~~~~~~~~~~~~~~~~~~~~~~~~

One of my friends is a pastor within the Christian Reformed Church. He has observed that different demonic forces appear to have dominion over different parts of our country. He used to work for a senator in the United States Capitol Building. He noted that Washington, D.C. is most definitely dominated by a demonic spirit of love-of-power. New York, he said, is likewise dominated by a spirit of money; Los Angeles is dominated by a spirit of fame; Boston is dominated by a spirit of intellectualism; and New Orleans is dominated by a spirit of decadent corruption.

If you have lived and worked in any of these cities, you can sense it. The air is thick with the people's sin-laden individuality. The Bible warns believers not to be reintegrated by these cultural influences.

> ... you once walked according to the course of this world, according to the prince of the power of the air, the spirit who now works in the sons of disobedience ... [Ephesians 2:2 NKJV]

And the Bible affirms the notion that certain demons have spiritual authority over certain pieces of territory. One of God's angels told the Prophet Daniel,

> ... for twenty-one days the spirit prince of the kingdom of Persia blocked my way. Then Michael, one of the archangels, came to help me, and I left him there **with the spirit prince of the kingdom of Persia** ... Soon I must return to fight against the spirit prince of the kingdom of Persia, and after that **the spirit prince of the kingdom of Greece will come**. [Daniel 10:13,20 NLT]

This shows that the principle of demonic oversight of particular regions applies to the lands of the Anti-Chalcedonian heresy, as well. It is not simply a coincidence that the lands of the Nestorian falling away (i.e., the lands of the Assyrian Church of the East) were overtaken by Shi'as. And it is also not a fluke of history that the lands of the Monophysite falling away (i.e., the lands of the Oriental Orthodox Church) were overtaken by Sunnis.

Pope Leo I put it well:

> ... what does putting Jesus asunder consist in if not in [denying his separate human nature, and thus] voiding ... the one mystery by which we have been saved?[592]

It is my contention that the most important thing in this life is what one believes about Jesus Christ. **It is my conviction** that the correct belief is that the single, undivided, Person of the Holy Trinity, Jesus Christ, is both fully God and fully man, with the separate nature of God and the separate nature of man. **It is my thesis** that wrong christological beliefs have the most substantive of consequences upon nation-groups. This includes genocide, for God has said,

> *My people are destroyed for lack of knowledge.*
> *[Hosea 4:6 NKJV]*

I here and now propose that the demonic spirits of the Nestorian heresy overtook Iran,[xxv] Iraq,[xxvi] and the surrounding regions with Shi'a Islam; **I here and now propose** that the demonic spirits of the Monophysite heresy overtook Ethiopia,[xxvii] Eritrea,[xxviii] Egypt,[xxix] Syria,[xxx] Armenia,[xxxi] and the surrounding regions with Sunni Islam. In accordance with this rule, the barbarous Azeri Turks (of the northeastern Middle East) became Shi'a Muslims, and the barbarous Anatolian Turks (of the northwestern Middle East) became Sunni Muslims.

In contrast, the western (i.e., Chalcedonian and Filioquean) Church was not conquered by Muslims. Although Roman Catholics suffered occupation in Sicily, Iberia, and Hungary, they eventually emerged victorious over the Antichrist Beast of Islam.

~~~~~~~~~~~~~~~~~~~~~~

President Harry Truman (AD 1884–AD 1972) apocryphally said,

---

xxv   Christians are a one percent minority in Iran.

xxvi   Christians are a three percent minority in Iraq.

xxvii   Ethiopia has, by far, the largest population of Monophysite Christians, but they are still slightly in the minority within their own country.

xxviii Christians make up almost half the population of Eritrea.

xxix   Christians are a six percent minority in Egypt.

xxx   Christians are a ten percent minority in Syria.

xxxi   The only country in the entire world with a Monophysite Christian majority (ninety-three percent) is the tiny Republic of Armenia. It's the size of Maryland, with a population of less than three million. Even so, the current Republic of Armenia is one tenth the size of Historic Armenia; the vast majority of the people residing within Historic Armenia are now Muslim.

*Give people a choice between a Republican and a
Republican, and they will pick the Republican every
time.*[593]

Truman's axiom may be transposed to this situation: if demons are
offered two choices, and one is an Anti-Christian heresy (i.e., Nestorianism or
Monophysitism), and the other is an Anti-Christian world religion (i.e., Shi'a
Islam or Sunni Islam), they will obviously choose the latter.

Thinking-out Anti-Chalcedonian Nestorianism to the extreme leads
one to conclude that the Virgin's zygote could possess a divine soul without
actually being the sovereign God. In this way, the Nestorians did not fully
accept Christ's kingly sovereignty over mankind, and have fallen away (2
Thessalonians 2:3) into mysticism. That [spiritually-speaking] gave rise to the
mystical, Shi'a, branch of Islam which venerates Ali as a type of Christ-King,
without him actually being Allah-in-the-flesh.

Thinking-out Anti-Chalcedonian Monophysitism to the extreme leads
one to conclude that God is a distant, even cold, being—detached from man's
debased level of existence. They find abhorrent the notion that He could ever
lower himself to take on the full human experience. Thus, the Monophysites
have not fully accepted Christ's priestly intermediation for humanity, and have
fallen away (2 Thessalonians 2:3) into legalism. That [spiritually-speaking]
gave rise to the cold-hearted, Sunni, branch of Islam which disregards everyone and everything except the Qur'an.

Sunnis have even less regard for books than they do for Ali. They
consider the Qur'an to contain all the information that is truly worth knowing. Sunni Arabs are thought to have burned the great and ancient library of
Alexandria, Egypt.[594]

The Shi'a are emotional, and consider the Sunni's antipathy toward
Ali's claim to the Caliphate to be venal. They say that Ali, as the patriarch
of the post–Muhammad family line, was the best source of knowledge about
God. They charge that the Sunnis turned their backs on Ali after Muhammad's
death for the sake of worldly concerns.

The Alawite offshoot of Shi'a Islam is even more bent in this direction.
They consider Ali and his descendants to be vehicles of divine incarnation, and
the very purpose of life. A portion of the Alawites' secretive catechism states,

*I turn to the door of knowledge, in order for the father
to provide me with a key; thus receiving the reward
which is the knowledge of Ali.*[595]

The Alawite cult had formed before Ali's death and he supposedly dis-
approved of their worship of him. On the pretense of being offended, he ban-

ished them from his headquarters in Iraq to Syria. Conveniently, Syria was the stronghold of his enemy and rival for the Caliphate, Muawiyah.[596] After Ali's assassination, Muawiyah became Caliph and the Alawite minority remained within his home base as perpetual second-class citizens. That only changed in AD 1970 when the 'Corrective Revolution' brought the secular Alawite dictator, Hafez al-Assad (AD 1930–AD 2000), into power. Today, Assad's son and his Alawite clique control the Syrian government.

Most Shi'a utterly reject the Alawites' ultra-devotion to Ali as being outside the bounds of Islam (somewhat as Mormonism is outside the bounds of Christianity). It is true that the Alawites worship Ali, whereas the Shi'a merely venerate him. Nevertheless, the Alawites are a derivative of the Shi'a branch of Islam, and definitely not a derivative of the Sunni branch of Islam. It is instructive in this eschatological study to place the Alawite ideology at the tail end of a Nestorian–Shi'a–Alawite continuum.

The Sunnis are austere, and consider the Shi'as' obsession with Ali and his family to be carnal. The Kharijite offshoot of Sunni Islam is even more dispassionate in this regard. They were not simply ambivalent toward the Caliphate of Ali—they declared his Caliphate invalid on the grounds that he was too compromising. They rebelled from his army and assassinated him during the first Islamic civil war because he had accepted a truce with Muawiyah. A dormant branch of the Kharijites forms the majority in Oman[597] and rules that country under Sultan Qaboos.

The Kharijites taught uncompromising observance of the Qur'an, radical anti-authoritarianism, and the killing of infidels with impunity. They thought that the Caliph should be the purest and most heartless Muslim, without regard to political connections or aristocratic pedigree. Each new Kharijite recruit was required to cut the throat of an enemy captive as a sign of dedication.[598] The leaders of al-Qaeda, who hail from the relatively-recent Salafi or Wahhabi sect, would be quite at home among the ancient Kharijites.

The Sunnis would say that the Kharijites are not an offshoot of them. They would point out that the Kharijites also sought to assassinate Muawiyah— the person that they accepted as the rightful Caliph after Ali. But most of the Kharijites fury was directed at Ali-veneration. It is instructive in this eschatological study to place the Kharijite ideology at the tail end of a Monophysite–Sunni–Kharijite continuum.

The two sides (i.e., Shi'a and Sunni) are currently blowing each other up by the hundreds in Iraq. In the reverberations of the explosions is the distant echo of enmity between the two extremes of the fifth through seventh century christological controversies (i.e., Nestorian and Monophysite). At one time the demonic spirits at work on each side had to satisfy themselves with the Syriac Orthodox' Patriarch (i.e., Monophysite or western Assyrian) and the Assyrian Church of the East's Catholicos (i.e., Nestorian or eastern Assyrian) anathematizing each other.

To anathematize is the theological equivalent of saying, "I wish you'd die and go to Hell." This is the one thing that a Christian must never say to another human being. God has been gracious and has led us to repentance, though we did not deserve it. We must always wish that others would repent and come to that same saving knowledge—even condemned criminals and war enemies.

Eventually the demons found a protagonist in Caliph Ali, the Son of Perdition (2 Thessalonians 2:3). From the year AD 661 onward, anathematization was considered passé—the evil spirits wanted gushing blood and flying body parts. On Ali's account they gleefully induce the heirs of perdition (i.e., the Shi'a and Sunni) to murder their neighbors in Baghdad today. Thirty-five thousand Iraqis were killed in sectarian violence in AD 2006.[599]

Have you seen the pictures of the dead? Who but demons could inspire such carnage?

This is the ongoing drama of the Antichrist Beast that is Islam.

Luke 7:23 [NKJV]
... blessed is he who is not offended because of Me.

69. The Final Falling Away of the East

We have discussed at length the failure of the eastern Assyrian (i.e., Nestorian) and Oriental Orthodox (i.e., Monophysite) churches to adhere to orthodox Christian doctrine. I have detailed my theory that their heretical christological beliefs led [spiritually-speaking] to their forced conversion to Shi'a Islam and Sunni Islam, respectively.

The Anti-Chalcedonian schisms, and the subsequent mass-conversion of their adherents to Islam, represents the 'falling away' that the Apostle Paul said would precede the Second Coming.

> *Let no man deceive you by any means: for that day shall not come, **except there come a falling away first** ... [2 Thessalonians 2:3 KJV]*

As a result, the three major branches of the Christian Church are all Chalcedonian: the Roman Catholic, Protestant, and Eastern Orthodox churches (listed in order of numerical strength) all hold-fast to the doctrine that Jesus Christ was one undivided Person with separate divine and human natures, and separate divine and human wills. **There is, however, one last schismatic 'falling away' that allowed for the Islamic Beast to overtake the entirety of eastern Christendom ...**

Emperor Heraclius—that wicked man—had opened the door for Islam through his incompetence and ill-conceived Monothelitic formulation. He also initiated the cultural withdrawal of the Eastern Roman Empire from Rome and the rest of Christian Europe with his Hellenization program. From his time onward, the [Eastern] Roman Empire could fairly be called the 'Byzantine' Empire, with all the human-limb-chopping negativity that the phrase conjures. Although a future Patriarch of Constantinople eventually renounced the Monothelite heresy and re-established communion with the Roman Pope, there continued to be a simmering animosity between the two offices. At the very least the Greek/Latin language barrier that Heraclius instituted was a source of friction.

The breaking point came centuries later, though, and centered around the so-called Filioque controversy. The word 'Filioque' is Latin for 'and the Son.' When the Nicene Creed was amended and finalized by the second ecumenical council in AD 381, it stated,

> *I believe in the Holy Spirit, the Lord and Giver of Life;*
> *who proceeds from the Father; who with the Father*
> *and the Son together is worshipped and glorified;*
> *who spoke by the prophets.*

The bishops that crafted the Nicene Creed just copied "who proceeds from the Father" verbatim from the Gospel According to John:

> *... the Spirit of truth who proceeds from the Father, He*
> *will testify of Me. [John 15:26 NKJV]*

But we know that the Holy Spirit proceeds from God the Son as well.

> *And with that [Jesus] breathed on them and said,*
> *"Receive the Holy Spirit." [John 20:22 TNIV]*

Also, Jesus told his disciples,

> *... it is for your good that I am going away. Unless I*
> *go away, the Advocate will not come to you; but if I*
> *go, **I will send him to you.** [John 16:7 TNIV]*

In recognition of this, many early Church Fathers wrote of the Spirit proceeding from both the Father and the Son. In fact, that very phrasing was included in the Athanasian Creed of the same period, which the Eastern Orthodox accept as a guideline (though they do not use it liturgically). It explicitly states (see Section 18 for full text),

> ... *the Spirit was neither made nor created nor begotten, but is proceeding from the Father and the Son.*

This inconsistency shows that the Eastern Orthodox' indignation over the West's inclusion of the Filioque in the Nicene Creed was nothing more than an excuse to be offended.

In truth, there was no contemporaneous theological controversy that caused the Nicene Creed's writers to specifically not include the Filioque. In stating that the Holy Spirit proceeds from the Father, the second ecumenical council did not mean to imply that He does not also proceed from the Son. In the same way, when the Apostles' Creed states ...

> *I believe in God the Father Almighty, Maker of heaven and earth ...*

... it does not mean to imply that God the Son, and God the Holy Spirit, are not the makers of Heaven and earth. In short, everyone understood that the absence of the Filioque from the Nicene Creed *was never intended as a statement of processional exclusionism.*

~~~~~~~~~~~~~~~~~~~~~~~

In AD 589, the Visigoth King, Reccared (AD 554–AD 601), was converted from Arianism to Trinitarianism by Bishop Leander of Seville (AD 534–AD 601). A local council was held in Toledo, Spain in which seventy-three metropolitans and bishops signed onto Christian orthodoxy. Twenty-three doctrinal canons were issued so that none of the people could later claim ignorance. One of the canons was that the Filioque was to be inserted into the Nicene Creed, and recited at Holy Communion. Bishop Leander insisted upon this,[600] so that there would be no cause to view God the Father as a primary god, and God the Son as a secondary god (as the Arians falsely asserted).

Christian people saw this as a sensible and inarguable point. The three simple words of the Filioque put to rest all the confusion that the Arians had raised about whether Jesus was God Almighty, or something less as God's "first creation." In truth, Jesus is God the Son: begotten, not made; and of one substance with the Father and the Holy Spirit.

Over time believers in Western Europe routinely started reciting the Nicene Creed so that it stated the Holy Spirit, "... proceeds from the Father *and the Son* ..."

In the latter half of the first millennium after Christ, the Eastern Roman Empire was continually buffeted in Anatolia by the Muslims. But in Western Europe, France's Charles 'The Hammer' Martel (AD 686–AD 741) decisively defeated a superior number of Muslims at the Battle of Tours in AD 732.[601] Martel's peasant infantry brought down the Muslims' armored cavalry and forever halted their advance toward Rome. His grandson, Charlemagne (AD 742–AD 814), then re-established a semblance of the Western Roman Empire in AD 800 and pressed the Muslims further back in Spain. The Normans and the Italian city-states later beat back the Muslims throughout the western Mediterranean—reconquering all of Sicily by AD 1091. The Eastern Roman Empire felt threatened by this resurgence of the West, and pointed to the liberal use of the Filioque in the Nicene Creed as a sign that their Pope was going astray from Christian orthodoxy.

Significantly, it was not the Pope that was championing the cause of the Filioque, but the believers in Christian Europe. Finally, in AD 1014, the Saxon Holy Roman Emperor, Henry II, requested that the Filioque be used during his coronation Mass. This was the first time that the Pope used the Filioque in Rome.[602] From that point on it was accepted as a legitimate part of the Catholic service.[603] The Greek Orthodox cited the official Roman use of the Filioque in order to justify their Great Schism forty years later.

Once again an eastern Church had embraced a false christological argument in order to justify political separation. It was a mistake that would eventually cost them their capital, Constantinople.

~~~~~~~~~~~~~~~~~~~~~~~~~

One could, of course, make the case that the Nicene Creed should be recited precisely as it was finalized at the second ecumenical council in AD 381 (i.e., without the Filioque). But any church that recites the Nicene Creed in that manner should make it perfectly clear in its statements of doctrine that it believes that the Holy Spirit proceeds from both the Father and the Son. It is in no way justifiable to read the Nicene Creed without the Filioque, and then to continue on to make a doctrinal construct out of that omission.

In their eagerness to separate themselves from the Pope, this is precisely what the Eastern Orthodox did. There were plenty of justifiable reasons to separate from Rome (as Luther discovered five hundred years later), but the

Filioque was not one of them. Nevertheless, the Eastern Orthodox staked their claim there, and started digging their own grave.

As is the case with Anti-Chalcedonianism, the problem with Anti-Filioqueanism[xxxii] was in what it implied about the Personhood of Jesus. The former heresy led to the idea that God the Son was not tempted in the same way that we are tempted (thus nullifying His sacrifice); the latter heresy led to the idea that God the Son is not operational in the same way that God the Father is operational (thus nullifying the Oneness of the Trinity).

If you catch a Greek priest in an honest moment he will tell you that the Eastern Orthodox think that someone in the Trinity has to be the boss and that the other two have to be subordinates. They think of God the Father as the fountainhead of the Trinity. They see Him as the great dispatcher—begetting the Son—sending forth the Spirit. But, again, this is a rationalist heresy. No one Person is in charge of the other Persons in the Holy Trinity because there only is one God. He is One: Father, Son, and Holy Spirit.

This is incomprehensible to us, but one must always remind oneself that we are pea-brains. The Personhood of God is not supposed to be rationally explainable. I, personally, find it comforting rather than maddening that God is bigger than my ability to comprehend.

The irony is that Anti-Filioqueanism was a step backward to the Anti-Trinitarian Arianism of the fourth century, which held that Jesus was only a derivative god. The reason that the Church Fathers created the Nicene Creed in the first place was to combat this idea! What a shame upon the Eastern Orthodox to embrace Anti-Filioqueanism, of all things, as their cause for separation from the Roman church! I would say that the Eastern Orthodox are even worse sinners than the Oriental Orthodox, except that the latter also divide the Father and the Son by rejecting the Filioque.

~~~~~~~~~~~~~~~~~~~~~~~

Even though the Eastern Orthodox and Oriental Orthodox are both Anti-Filioquean Christians, the former are still Chalcedonian whereas the latter are Anti-Chalcedonian. This spiritual difference-of-opinion accounts for the animosity that exists between Greek (Eastern Orthodox) and Armenian (Oriental Orthodox) peoples to this day. The hostility is palpable, even upon a first meet-

---

xxxii I have made up this word. It means 'one that attempts to divide the Holy Trinity by disbelieving that the Holy Spirit proceeds from both the Father and the Son.' I am not an Anti-Filioquean. I am a Filioquean Christian because Filioqueanism is an entirely Biblical doctrine.

ing of perfect strangers. The lack of brotherhood is no ethnological accident—it is a Providential curse.

> *... I broke the stick named "Unity" and canceled*
> *the ties between Judah and Israel. [Zechariah 11:14*
> *CEV]*

The opportunistic Turks exploited this state-of-affairs between their two archenemies and brutally expelled them both from Anatolia. The Turks have an astute idiom about the Christian peoples on their western and eastern frontiers:

> *You cannot make a dog's hide into pillow fabric,*
> *and you cannot make a Greek and an Armenian into*
> *friends.*

What is wrong with these Eastern Christians?! Why can't they see the association between their wrongheaded ideas about Jesus Christ and their lack of political freedom and economic and military strength?!

But it is written,

> *When I please, I will punish them; nations will be*
> *gathered against them to put them in bonds for their*
> *double sin. [Hosea 10:10 TNIV]*

Ah, the double sin that is present within the eastern churches: to be against Chalcedonianism and to be against Filioqueanism. It is a recipe for massacre and mendicancy!

Anti-Filioqueanism was a transparent effort to preserve the Greeks' Hellenistic culture from the growing influence of the Roman church. Preserving their culture would have been a morally-neutral thing to do, except that it was done at the expense of Christ (as with the Armenians, Copts, and Assyrians before them).

Like the previous schism, it necessarily had consequences in the minds of the believers: theologically, the Eastern Orthodox evolved to view Christ's sacrifice as simply having set humanity back on the right track after our detour into sin. That acknowledges our indebtedness to Jesus, but in a significantly less overflowing fashion than the correct view. They call getting back on the right track the 'deification process'[604]—an entirely unchristian concept and phrase.

The Eastern Orthodox' deification concept confuses sanctification (the process of growing in your Christian walk during your earthly life) with justification (which is instantaneous upon trusting in Christ as Lord and Savior).

In truth, Christ freely gives us full justification after our having been completely separated from God. We had fallen hopelessly into sin. We were face-down, dead-in-the-water, to sin—we didn't simply detour into sin. And we have gained full acceptance from Him upon first believing—it is not a process of deification.

> For he has rescued us from the dominion of darkness
> and brought us into the kingdom of the Son he loves,
> in whom we have redemption, the forgiveness of sins.
> [Colossians 1:13–14 NIV]

Historically, the consequence of the Eastern Orthodox' diminished emphasis on Christ was the permanent loss of Anatolian Greece to the Turks, and the temporary loss of Eastern Europe and Russia to the Communists.

The only justification for the continuance of a nation-state is the propagation of the Gospel of Jesus Christ. But if a state that was once useful for that purpose becomes no longer useful, it has no value.

> ... if even the salt have lost its savor, wherewith shall
> it be seasoned? It is fit neither for the land nor for the
> dunghill: men cast it out. [Luke 14:34–35 ASV]

The Eastern Orthodox of the Eastern Roman Empire perverted Christian doctrine by insisting that the eternal Person of the Holy Trinity, God the Son, had a boss. God then gave them over to bosses like the Sultan in Constantinople, and Stalin in Moscow, and Tito in Belgrade. And, once again, the center of gravity of the Church moved into the wilderness of the west.

Isaiah 10:15 [NIV]
Does the ax raise itself above him who swings it, or the saw boast against him who uses it? As if a rod were to wield him who lifts it up, or a club brandish him who is not wood!

70. The Divine Idiom

It was not at all clear in the mid–seventh century that Dual-Nature, Filioquean, Christology would emerge triumphant within the Church of God. Rome was the only Patriarchal See that was holding firmly to Chalcedonianism. It was a weak satellite holding of the Eastern Roman Empire. It could not even prevent Pope Martin from being forcibly brought to Constantinople and killed.

The world would have had a radically different 'christianity' if Emperor Heraclius had competently waged war against a puny band of camel-riding raiders. The Arabs were in the process of being Christianized at the beginning of the seventh century, as the Avars and Slavs later were in Europe. The entire Near East, North Africa, Russia, and East Africa[xxxiii] would likely have become Monophysite. Iran, Iraq, Central Asia, and China would probably have become largely Nestorian. The Subcontinent of India may have been split between Monophysites and Nestorians, as they both had a toehold there. In this way, the two Anti-Chalcedonian branches of Christianity were poised to become larger, more powerful, and more influential than the western, Chalcedonian, churches eventually did become.

All of this potential was abruptly extinguished by the arrival of the Caliphate. The Sea Beast (i.e., Arab Islam) arrived immediately after the Monothelite controversy of AD 630. And the Land Beast (i.e., Turkish Islam) arrived immediately after the Anti-Filioque controversy of AD 1054. Both forces devastated eastern Christendom. As a consequence, we ended up with an overwhelmingly Chalcedonian and Filioquean Christianity in the form of Roman Catholicism and Protestantism. Since God is sovereign, my conclusion is that God simply did not desire the increase of Anti-Chalcedonian or Anti-Filioquean doctrines. He allowed them to become very nearly annihilated, and the Beast of Islam was His dreadful winnowing tool.

> *Cover their faces with shame so that men will seek your name, O Lord ... Let them know that you, whose name is the Lord—that you alone are the Most High over all the earth. [Psalm 83:16,18 NIV]*

The Christianity that most Christians profess is the Christianity that God desires that we profess. Jesus Christ is Sovereign and has seen to it that His Church believes in Him the way that He wants us to believe in Him.

> *The Lord was on our side! Let everyone in Israel say: "The Lord was on our side! Otherwise, the enemy attack would have killed us all, because it was furious ... " Let's praise the Lord! He protected us from enemies who were like wild animals ... The Lord made heaven and earth, and he is the one who sends us help. [Psalm 124:1–3,6,8 CEV]*

---

xxxiii The Ethiopian Orthodox (Monophysite) Church is the only pre–colonial Christian church in black Africa.

~~~~~~~~~~~~~~~~~~~~~~~

If you tie-in the establishment of the Caliphate to the End Times prophecies in the books of Daniel and Revelation as I have done, a startling fact comes to your attention: it had to happen as it happened because it had been prophesied to happen as it happened.

During the United States Constitutional Convention in AD 1787, the American patriot Benjamin Franklin (AD 1706–AD 1790) addressed the chairman:

> *I've lived, Sir, a long time, and the longer I live, the more convincing proofs I see of this truth—that God governs in the affairs of men. And if a sparrow cannot fall to the ground without his notice, is it probable that an empire can rise without his aid? We have been assured, Sir, in the Sacred Writings, that except the Lord build the house they labor in vain who build it. I firmly believe this,—and I also believe that without his concurring aid, we shall succeed in this political building no better than the builders of Babel: we shall be divided by our little partial local interests; our projects will be confounded, and we ourselves shall become a reproach and bye-word down to future ages.*[605]

I am suggesting a form of 'Prophetic Providentialism' whereby God actively directs the vicissitudes of both historic and everyday events. I say 'prophetic' because most of the time we can not make heads-or-tails out of His divine purpose. But there are occasions in human history when God, in His foreknowledge, has predicted in Scripture what will come to pass through the actions of people that He then 'provides' for such purposes. It is written,

> *The horse is made ready for the day of battle, but victory rests with the Lord. [Proverbs 21:31 TNIV]*

And,

> *When disaster comes to a city, has not the Lord caused it? [Amos 3:6 TNIV]*

And Jesus told the Roman governor,

> *You would have no power over me if it were not given to you from above. [John 19:11 TNIV]*

In this manner, God predicted that the messianic believers of the Prophet Daniel's day would be exiled in order to purify them from the idol worship that had plagued Israel for centuries (Jeremiah 9:11). That exile turned out to be to the east—to Babylon and Medo–Persia.

Similarly, God predicted that the messianic believers after the ministry of Christ would twice move into the wilderness (Revelation 12:6,14). According to prophecy there was going to be a purification from the predominant and false Christologies in the Middle East (2 Thessalonians 2:3), and a refuge from the Antichrist Beast's savagery. That wilderness turned out to be the west—first Central and Western Europe, and then the Americas and Australia.

That miserable Beast of Islam—the abomination that causes desolation—had to be set up 1,290 years after the end of sacrifices in the First Temple (Daniel 12:11), just as surely as the Anointed One, Jesus Christ, had to be crucified 486.5 years after the post–exilic call for the Jews to rebuild Jerusalem (Daniel 9:26).

Likewise, the Soviet Union had to be established at the end of AD 1922,[606] and had to fall seventy years later (Revelation 12:12–14). Then the duplicitous Bill Clinton had to win an unlikely presidential victory over George H.W. Bush in order to allow al-Qaeda terrorism to emerge (Revelation 17:12–14). All of this was foretold (see Sections 34, 37).

When I came to this realization, it became clear that all my hand-wringing about Heraclius' woefully poor leadership of the Eastern Roman Empire was for naught. If I could travel back in time and convince obstinate Heraclius—at the very height of his power—to march into western Arabia, then no one ever would have heard of Islam. Hundreds of millions of Christians, Zoroastrians, Jews, Hindus, and Buddhists would have been spared massacre and forced-conversion to Islam if Ali and one hundred of Muhammad's fighters had been slain at the pivotal Battle of Badr in AD 624.[607] But that is impossible. God is sovereign, and in His foreknowledge He recorded what must take place—what did, in fact, take place.

God is indeed sovereign. Even devout Christians do not appreciate the breadth of His sovereign power. He is in direct control of every atom in the universe. God has granted we humans free will, and yet nothing happens without His permitting it. The history of wicked Emperor Heraclius is God's history; the history of the entire world is God's history. The new Pope has said,

> *God writes straight even on the crooked lines of our*
> *human history.*[608]

Therefore, God's Word promises something so great that it is worth having His people endure 1,335 years of the abomination that causes desolation (i.e., the Beast of Islam; see Section 46).

> *This calls for patient endurance on the part of the saints who obey God's commandments and remain faithful to Jesus. [Revelation 14:12 NIV]*

Be of good cheer. The time of the abomination is almost over. The time of Christ's return is near.

> *Trust in the Lord with all your heart, and lean not on your own understanding; In all your ways acknowledge Him, and He shall direct your paths. [Proverbs 3:5–6 NKJV]*

~~~~~~~~~~~~~~~~~~~~~~

There is a technique in woodland management called coppicing whereby a forester cuts unwieldy trees down to their stumps. The roots are left in place and one shoot is allowed to come forth from the stump. It is then trained to grow straight.

Throughout history, God has continually coppiced the civilizations in which His people have lived. He has cut off unwieldy growths, and then allowed a renewal. There are numerous instances of this among the Israelites of the Old Testament. It has happened at least once in the United States when the culture of the Antebellum South was cut off by God's instruments of wrath for the sin of slavery: Lincoln, Grant, and Sherman.

In my eschatological study, I have identified six major coppicing, or purification events, in human history. They have come at ~ 1,000 year intervals. These have each been preceded by ~ 500 years with a promise of Christ's cosmic rescue mission.

The sequence of God's historical plan for salvation may be further categorized into three main acts.[609] The period from the Fall of Man until the choosing of Abraham may be called God's Prelude. The period from Abraham to Jesus' earthly ministry may be called God's Main Presentation. The period from the Ascension to the present time may be called God's Encore. We are living at the very end of the Encore period—God's Finale, if you will.

The entire human drama is set to last 6,010 years, as foreshadowed by the 601-year epic of Noah and the Flood (Section 47).

The theatrical program for God's production is detailed in the table below.

Table 13. The Divine Idiom of the Human Drama

Date	Promissory Event	Purification Event	Interval	Bibl. Ref.
P R E L U D E				
3975 BC[610]	Promise of Christ's Reign through Eve		235 years	Gen. 3:15
3740 BC[611]		Purified through Calling Upon Name	752 years	Gen. 4:26
2988 BC[612]	Promise of Christ's Reign through Enoch		569 years	Heb. 11:5
2419 BC[613]		Purified through Ark Project	511 years	Gen. 6:14
P R E S E N T A T I O N				
1908 BC[614]	Promise of Christ's Reign through Abraham		446 years	Gen. 12:3
1462 BC[615]		Purified through Exodus	448 years	Ex. 14:21
1014 BC[616]	Promise of Christ's Reign through David		498 years	2 Sam. 7:13
516 BC[617]		Purified through Exilic Restoration	545 years	Ezra 6:21
E N C O R E				
AD 30[618]	Promise of Christ's Reign through Ascension		523 years	Acts 1:11
AD 553[619]		Purified through Chalcedonianism	461 years	Rev. 12:6
AD 1014[620]	Promise of Christ's Reign through Three Proper Creeds		516 years	Rev. 20:4
AD 1530[621]		Purified through Reformation	506 years	Rev. 12:14
F I N A L E				
AD 2036	Promise of Christ's Reign Fulfilled!		–END–	Rev. 19:11

Total Duration of the Human Drama   **6,010 years**

Please note that the Word of God became incarnate at the close of the second act of the human drama (6 BC). That was *exactly* 1,456 years after Moses[xxxiv] began recording the Word of God in Sinai, and *exactly* 1,456 years before Gutenberg[xxxv] began printing the Word of God in Mainz. There is a symmetry here in-keeping with the divine idiom.[622]

I have tried to avoid numerology in this book, yet I cannot help noticing that the square root of 1,456 is 38.16—the particular number of years between the Word of God's Incarnation as a zygote inside the blessed virgin Mary, and the promulgation of His Gospel from Jerusalem three and a half years after the Crucifixion (as predicted in Daniel 9:27—see bottom of Section 26). To be specific:

- Christ spent the normal gestation of nine months, or three-quarters of a year, inside the Virgin's womb (Luke 2:6);
- and Christ was in His thirtieth year (Luke 3:23)— so I assume thirty and a half years old—when His public ministry began;
- and Christ was crucified three and a half years after that (Daniel 9:27b),[623]
- and Christ's Church was protected in Jerusalem for another three and a half years after that (Daniel 9:27a), before it spread the Good News to the world (Acts 8:4).[624]

$$0.75 + 30.5 + 3.5 + 3.5 = 38.25 \text{ years}$$

The Divine Producer-Director is great, and greatly to be praised.

Revelation 20:1–4 [NKJV]
Then I saw an angel coming down from heaven, having the key to the bottomless pit and a great chain in his hand. He laid hold of the dragon, that serpent

---

xxxiv God wrote the first words of the Bible in the form of the Ten Commandment tablets in 1462 BC, and gave them to Moses who recorded them on parchment.

xxxv After many years of experimenting with cutting and casting movable metal type, Johannes Gutenberg (AD 1398–AD 1468) began printing pages of the Latin Vulgate Bible in AD 1451. He sold the first copy of what came to be known as the Gutenberg Bible in AD 1455.

of old, who is the Devil and Satan, and bound him for a thousand years; and he cast him into the bottomless pit, and shut him up, and set a seal on him, so that he should deceive the nations no more till the thousand years were finished. But after these things he must be released for a little while ... Then I saw the souls of those who had been beheaded for their witness to Jesus and for the word of God, who had not worshiped the beast or his image, and had not received his mark on their foreheads or on their hands. And they lived and reigned with Christ for a thousand years.

71. The Millennial Timeline

Concurrent with the Filioque Controversy was an awakening in the West concerning Islam. People began to see that this was not simply a land-grab by another non-Christian people. Europe had encountered that before with the Vandals, Huns, Avars, Goths, Lombards, Vikings, etc. Those people came, plundered, assimilated, and eventually disappeared. But the Muslims actually meant to conquer the entire world, and to force everyone to worship the devil, Allah, five times per day in the Arabic language. Also, Western Europe finally realized that the Eastern Roman Empire was utterly incapable of dealing with its side of the problem, as the West had dealt with the Muslims in France, Spain, and Sicily.

In AD 966, the doors and roof of the Church of the Holy Sepulchre in Jerusalem were burned by a Muslim mob.[625] That was *exactly* six hundred and sixty-six years after Roman Emperor Diocletian (AD 245–AD 312) received a bad omen and embraced a zealous policy of Christian persecution in AD 300. The Diocletian Persecution was the final and most severe suppression of the Church by the Roman Empire.[626]

The year AD 300 was also the last year in which the devil could, with impunity, kill Christians by the power of the civil authority everywhere in the world. In AD 301 Christianity was proclaimed the state religion in Armenia and San Marino.[xxxvi] Twelve years after that penalties against Christians were abolished within the entire Roman Empire.[627]

---

xxxvi The title of 'First Christian Nation' is claimed by the Armenians, but on September 3, AD 301 a stonemason named Marinus the Dalmatian founded the tiny state of San Marino as a Christian refuge from the persecutions of Roman Emperor Diocletian. In the mid–nineteenth century the Roman Catholic Sammarinese citizens wisely made an alliance with Giuseppe Garibaldi (AD 1807–AD 1882) to avoid being swallowed up during his Italian unification campaign. San Marino has remained an independent republic to this day, and is a member of the United Nations. So Armenia and San Marino are tied for first place among Christian nations.

In AD 1009 Caliph al-Hakim (AD 985–AD 1021) went farther than the Muslim mob of AD 966 and completely destroyed the Church of the Holy Sepulchre.[628] He hacked out the church's foundations until he hit bedrock. The empty tomb of Christ inside the church was desecrated; and two of the walls of the tomb were torn down. This outrageous act of vandalism occurred approximately six hundred and sixty-six years after the church had been constructed in AD 336.[xxxvii] The devil is fixated upon that number.

In AD 1048 another Caliph permitted some small chapels to be built on the site of Christ's tomb, but a new church was not permitted. Severe restrictions were placed upon Christian pilgrims to Jerusalem.[629]

Of course, the desecration of the Church of the Holy Sepulchre had no effect upon Christ's life-giving work in the hearts of millions of Christian believers. But Medieval European public opinion was fueled by news of the Muslim atrocities. The people of the Church realized that the Muslims were not going to stop killing, any more than Christians were going to stop proselytizing. The difference in value systems was irreconcilable.

Meanwhile, in AD 1071, the Eastern Roman Empire's army lost the Battle of Manzikert to a smaller Seljuk force.[630] The loss occurred just seventeen years after the Great Schism of AD 1054 in which the Greek Eastern Orthodox split from Christian orthodoxy over the inclusion of the Filioque in the Nicene Creed.[631] As it is written,

> *Though the army of the Syrians had come with few men, the Lord delivered into their hand a very great army, because Judah had forsaken the Lord, the God of their fathers. [2 Chronicles 24:24 ESV]*

The Seljuks had first appeared in the Middle East in AD 1055 when they conquered Baghdad.[632] This marked the beginning of the 'Land Beast' of Oghuz Turkic peoples that the Apostle John wrote of in Revelation 13:11. The Eastern Roman Empire subsequently grew so weak that by the end of the century the Seljuks were threatening Constantinople. Emperor Alexius I (AD 1048–AD 1118) sent ambassadors to beg mercenaries from the Pope.[633]

In November AD 1095 Pope Urban II (AD 1042–AD 1099) called for the First Crusade.[634] Within four years the Crusaders, under the leadership of Godfrey of Bouillon (AD 1060–AD 1100), had routed the Turks from large parts of Asia Minor and retaken Jerusalem. Instead of assuming the name 'King

---

xxxvii This year differential is 673, not 666, but often the date given for the construction of an ancient building is the *terminus a quo* (i.e., the year that the foundation stone was lain). The completion and consecration of the Church of the Holy Sepulchre could have been up to ten years later.

of Jerusalem,' Godfrey declared himself 'Defender of the Holy Sepulchre'—showing that the repeated desecration of Christ's tomb was the issue that motivated him to invade.[635]

The relative ease with which the Crusaders conquered the Muslims embarrassed Emperor Alexius. He was less than enthusiastic about the Latin hegemony that was taking form in the Levant. It was at this time that the Maronite Christians of Lebanon finally abandoned Emperor Heraclius' Monothelitism and reestablished communion with Rome. In subsequent years the Crusaders of the Holy Roman Empire and the soldiers of the Eastern Roman Empire often did not work in concert.

~~~~~~~~~~~~~~~~~~~~~~~

The desecration of the Lord's tomb in AD 1009 was the high-water mark for Islam—especially for Arab Islam. Shortly after that (AD 1016) there was an earthquake in Jerusalem, and the Dome of the Rock was partly destroyed.[636] It was an omen of the commencement of the millennial reign of the saints with Christ.

In the coming centuries God allowed the Arabs to get a taste of their own medicine: they were overrun and massacred by the Turkish Muslim hordes, and kept in subjugation until the twentieth century. The age of Arab expansion was over.

More significantly, the eleventh and twelfth centuries saw a series of victories by western Christianity over the Muslims. Although the Crusaders were forced to surrender Jerusalem to the Kurdish Muslim, Saladin (AD 1138–AD 1193), in AD 1187,[637] the message was clear: 'Stop messing with us.' Christians were allowed to visit the city under a subsequent treaty, and there were no more desecrations of holy sites.

Meanwhile, the Moors were pushed back in the Iberian Peninsula. The final Christian victory over the Muslim stronghold of Granada occurred on January 2, AD 1492.[638] The remaining Muslim and Jewish population was completely expelled to North Africa. On August 3rd of that same year, Christopher Columbus (AD 1451–AD 1506) set sail for the Americas on behalf of the Spanish monarchs.[639] That is more than a coincidence: God had made an edict that the wilderness of the New World was reserved for His Chosen People, the Christians, and not for the Beast of Islam, or any other antichrist sect (Revelation 12:14). Indeed, North America, South America, Australia, and New Zealand are overwhelmingly populated by Roman Catholics and Protestants (inclusive of the current aboriginal population).

As the Moors were being pushed back in the Roman Catholic Iberian Peninsula, the Turks were advancing in the Eastern Orthodox Balkan Peninsula. The Ottoman Turks did succeed in overtaking the moribund Eastern Roman Empire, and they even threatened Venice and Vienna at various times. But again, we see the hand of Providence in history: the fanatically Catholic Holy Roman Emperor, Charles V (AD 1500–AD 1558), was unable to pursue war against the Protestant princes of German Saxony as a result of the Turkish distraction. When the Ottoman Sultan prepared his second march on Vienna in AD 1532, the Emperor reluctantly entered into a temporary peace with the Schmalkald League of Lutherans.[640] Once again, God used the Beast of Islam (i.e., the Ottoman Turks) to rebuff those that were not steadfastly true to His Word (i.e., the Roman Catholics), and to allow His faithful people (i.e., the Lutherans) a western refuge (i.e., northern Germany, in this case).

In AD 1571 the Ottoman fleet was obliterated by the Holy League at the Battle of Lepanto. It was the most decisive naval battle in world history—and the last battle involving rowing vessels.[641] It forever ended Turkish control over the Mediterranean high seas. The Ottomans suffered another devastating naval defeat at the Battle of Navarino in AD 1827. That happened to be the last major battle involving sailing vessels, and it paved the way for Greek independence.[642]

Even the fledgling United States Navy bombarded and blockaded the Barbary States in AD 1803 to put an end to Mediterranean piracy by the Muslims. It was the United States' first act of war since becoming a sovereign nation, and the ship that was used is now the oldest commissioned ship afloat in the world.[643] And on November 1, AD 1911, the first-ever aerial bomb was dropped upon Turkish troops in Libya during the Italo–Turkish War.[644] This marked the beginning of eleven years of warfare that resulted in the end of the Ottoman Empire. Finally, after the First World War, the Middle East was colonized by western powers.[645] Since that time the Muslim states have essentially been vassals of the [Protestant] United Kingdom and the [Protestant] United States.

This state-of-affairs will change somewhat during the Tribulation as various Muslim states revert wholesale to their heritage of savagery.

~~~~~~~~~~~~~~~~~~~~~~

The adoption of the Filioque into the Nicene Creed by the Roman Catholic Church in AD 1014[646] marked the beginning of the so-called Millennium—the thousand year reign of the saints with Christ that is referred to in this section's Scripture heading. The current period is actually the sixth millennium since the creation of the world. But it is the final one before the end of the world, and the one specifically mentioned in Revelation 20:4 as a thousand year reign of the saints with Christ.

With three proper Christian Creeds (i.e., Apostles', Athanasian, and Nicene with the inclusion of the Filioque), the Church had the true message of faith that God wanted spread around the world. It is the confession of the true faith that empowered the Church to be on the offensive against its sempiternal enemy, the Beast of Islam. During this period Providence orchestrated the pre-eminence of the Christian Church over the face of the earth.

> *During the reigns of those kings, the God of heaven will set up a kingdom that will never be destroyed or conquered. It will crush all these kingdoms into nothingness, and it will stand forever. [Daniel 2:44 NLT]*

If you have an anti-Catholic prejudice, you will have difficulty accepting that the Medieval Roman Church was God's primary Millennial agent. But for all their inquisitions and wickedness, the Romanists were carrying the Word of God, just as the ancient Israelites were carrying the Ark of the Covenant. And if King Ahab and Queen Jezebel led part of the Israel of God before the time of Christ, we should not be shocked that the much more fair-minded King Ferdinand (AD 1452–AD 1516) and Queen Isabella (AD 1451–AD 1504) led part of the Israel of God after the time of Christ.

Nevertheless, some Christians may ask, "Has the devil really been bound for a thousand years since AD 1014? It hardly seems like it."

Allow me to answer with some questions of my own: Have you been murdered by Muslims or any other Satanists? What do you think that the devil would like to do to you if left to his own devices? Has he not been constrained and continually frustrated in his plans for world domination and extermination of the Christian Church? Has not the Word of God survived and spread despite every plan against it? Has not the Antichrist Beast of Islam already failed? Aren't the Muslims' suicide bombings a desperation tactic? Does the world observe an Islamic Calendar or a Christian Calendar? Is the universal language of science and business Arabic (the language in which Allah supposedly revealed the Qur'an to Muhammad), or English (the primary language of the Protestants and of the plurality of printed Bibles)? Are you reading the Bible and other Christian books (i.e., the truth about God), or are you reading only the Qur'an (i.e., lies about God)?

The issue is one of ascendancy versus subordination. During the one thousand year reign of the saints with Christ, the Beast of Islam has been restrained from attacking the Creedal Christian Church in the wilderness of the west. This one thousand year period is scheduled to come to an end in AD 2014 (Section 71). Afterward, the devil will be unleashed to cause mayhem for a short season (approximately twenty years according to the timelines in Sections 40–49).

Something is going to happen upon the expiration of the Millennium. Do you want to know what it is?

Revelation 20:7–10 [NIV]
When the thousand years are over, Satan will be released from his prison and will go out to deceive the nations in the four corners of the earth—Gog and Magog—to gather them for battle. In number they are like the sand on the seashore. They marched across the breadth of the earth and surrounded the camp of God's people, the city he loves. But fire came down from heaven and devoured them.

72. The Tribulation: Satan's Short Season

There's going to be a war—a localized nuclear war.

Throughout this book, I have avoided prognostications about eschatological prophecies that have not yet occurred (except for the timing of the Tribulation and Second Coming, of course). I don't want to stumble into the errors of others. I honestly do not know what most of them mean. But I am willing to say that the part of the Tribulation that is mentioned in the twentieth chapter of Revelation points to a war. The war may not take place in AD 2014, as indicated by the Millennial Timeline (Section 71); according to the Noahic Timeline (Section 47) it would commence in the last ten years—beginning in AD 2025. It will be shorter than most other wars, but it will definitely be a more substantial conflagration than we have seen before.

The words 'Gog' and 'Magog' symbolize all the nations of the earth that join together to attack God's people, the Christians. But before the battle can even begin, the Bible says that fire will come out of the sky and instantly destroy the evil army.

By what mechanism will this occur?

Earlier in Revelation we are told that the martyred saints are continually before God, asking Him to exact punishment on their enemies.

> *I saw under the altar the souls of all who had been*
> *martyred for the word of God and for being faithful*

in their testimony. They shouted to the Lord and said,
"O Sovereign Lord, holy and true, how long before
you judge the people who belong to this world and
avenge our blood for what they have done to us?"
[Revelation 6:9–10 NLT]

Some of my ancestors are among those martyred saints that are today ruling the earth with Christ from Heaven during the Millennium. They keep asking Him to bring the fullness of His righteous judgment against the world. God tells them to wait a little longer. He has a timetable, and He is working according to it.

At a specific hour, day, month, and year, four especially destructive demons are scheduled to be unbound from the vicinity where Ali headquartered to run the caliphate.

'Loose the four messengers who are bound at the
great river Euphrates;' and loosed were the four mes-
sengers, who have been made ready for the hour, and
day, and month, and year, that they may kill the third
of men; [Revelation 9:14–15 YLT]

Their short season of havoc after the Millennium is commonly referred to as the Tribulation. During this period the demons marshal an enormous infantry, as well as an inferno to stop that infantry (see Section 86 for an explanation of this apparent contradiction in purpose). It is described in this way:

And thus I saw the horses in the vision, and those
sitting upon them, having breastplates of fire, and
jacinth, and brimstone; and the heads of the horses
[are] as heads of lions, and out of their mouths pro-
ceedeth fire, and smoke, and brimstone; by these three
were the third of men killed, from the fire, and from
the smoke, and from the brimstone, that is proceeding
out of their mouth, for their authorities are in their
mouth, and in their tails, for their tails [are] like ser-
pents, having heads, and with them they do injure;
[Revelation 9:17–19 YLT]

If the locusts of Revelation 9:3 are automobiles, then the horses of Revelation 9:19 must be substantially larger. I see these horses as intercontinental ballistic missiles tipped with thermonuclear warheads. The Apostle John specifically states,

*The number of the mounted troops was two hundred
million. I heard their number. [Revelation 9:16 TNIV]*

Perhaps that means that they will have the destructive capability of
two hundred million horsemen roaming the countryside, just as we measure
the maximum power of the internal combustion engine in horsepower. If we
take it to mean two hundred million horsepower-hours of discharged energy,
then it would be equivalent to 128 kilotons of trinitrotoluene [TNT]—about
ten times as powerful as the atomic bomb dropped on Hiroshima, Japan in AD
1945.[647]

The largest army in the world can be destroyed in an instant with the
right-sized bomb.

Luke 21:8–9 [NKJV]
Take heed that you not be deceived. For many will come in My name, saying,
'I am He,' and, 'The time has drawn near.' Therefore do not go after them. But
when you hear of wars and commotions, do not be terrified; for these things
must come to pass first, but the end will not come immediately.

73. In Anticipation of the Mahdi

It is now time to discuss the unfulfilled ambitions of the Islamists (i.e., the
Antichrist Beast).

I shared an office with a Turkish student in graduate school. Her
English writing skills were atrocious. I rewrote her entire master's thesis as a
favor. I've noticed that there is something about Ataturk's modern Turkish that
precludes its speakers from writing a simple declarative English sentence. One
of her sentences ran-on for an entire page. She was greatly indebted to me for
my help, as she was terrified of failing at her studies and being sent back to
Turkey. Those Turks that believe in Islam worried her.

One of her university girlfriends had given her a crucifix, and she wore
it around campus for decoration. But she said that she could never have worn
it in her country.

I asked her if the Turks ever speak of Jesus. "Yes!" she said to my surprise, "My grandmother says that He will come back at the end of the age in
order to force everyone to become a Muslim."

I found out later that that is, in fact, Islamic dogma.

~~~~~~~~~~~~~~~~~~~~~~~~

The Mahdi is the prophesied redeemer of Islam. The word 'Mahdi' means 'the [Rightly] Guided One.' It does not appear in the Qur'an, but is mentioned in some of the Hadith (i.e., the extra–Qur'anic reports of the sayings of Muhammad). He is supposed to appear before the Judgment Day to change the world into a perfect Islamic society.

Muhammad is reported to have predicted,

> *During the last times, my people will be afflicted with terrible and unprecedented calamities and misfortunes from their rulers, so much so that this vast earth will appear small to them. Persecution and injustice will engulf the earth. The believers will find no shelter to seek refuge from these tortures and injustices. At such a time, God will raise from my progeny a man who will establish peace and justice on this earth in the same way as it had been filled with injustice and distress.*[648]

Islamic tradition holds that the Mahdi will be a descendant of Muhammad, and that he will be from Mecca. His father's name will be the same as Muhammad's father's name. He will be tall and have the features and character of Muhammad.[649] The Mahdi is to reign over a worldwide Islamic kingdom of peace, justice, and truth. Soon after his arrival, Jesus will return and fight in cooperation with the Mahdi against the Islamic version of the false messiah. The Mahdi and Jesus live out their lives as allies, with Jesus praying behind the Mahdi. Finally, there will be a relapse into sin and the end of the world will come.

This is similar to the [faulty] Dispensational Premillennialism of some Christians in which Jesus comes to reign for a thousand years on earth before a final showdown with the devil (see Table 4).

~~~~~~~~~~~~~~~~~~~~~~

The Sunnis and Shi'a differ on the particulars of the Mahdi. There have been individuals in the past from both major branches of Islam that have claimed to be the Mahdi.

The best example of a Sunni Mahdi is the rebel leader Muhammad Ahmad (AD 1845–AD 1885). He declared himself to be the Mahdi in AD 1881 because he had a v–shaped gap in his teeth. He began a jihad, and in AD 1885 conquered Khartoum, Sudan, and killed the British viceroy Charles Gordon

(AD 1833–AD 1885). He re-instituted slavery and set up an Islamic utopia in Sudan called the Mahdiyya. By the time the British retook the country fourteen years later, **half the population had perished** because of his government's mismanagement and brutal oppression.[650] The Arabs have had an obsession with Islamicizing the remaining black Sudanese Christians ever since then.

The best example of a Shi'a Mahdi is the Safavid ruler, Shah Ismail (AD 1487–AD 1524). He came to power in AD 1494 at the age of seven, and claimed to be the Mahdi (or 'Hidden Imam' as the Shi'a say). He gained a fanatical following while expanding his control over Iran, Iraq, Azerbaijan, and Armenia.[651] He imposed Shi'aism over his largely Sunni subjects, and forced them to curse the first three Caliphs that had circumvented Ali's reign.[652] By this action, Shah Ismail became the father of Shi'a Iran, just as his contemporary King Henry VIII (AD 1491–AD 1547) became the father of Anglican England.

The Shah enjoyed remarkable success until the Ottomans challenged his control of eastern Anatolia. At the Battle of Chaldiran in AD 1514, his Iranian archers and swordsmen rushed into Turkish cannons and muskets. The Iranians thought that their faith in the Mahdi would make them bulletproof. [There is no limit to stupidity, you see.] **Tens of thousands of them were slaughtered**, and the present boundary of Iran and Turkey was roughly established.[653] The Shah's favorite wife was taken prisoner and put into the Turkish harem. He could not win her release and died at a relatively young age of a broken heart.[654] After this experience, the Iranians integrated gunpowder into their military arsenal, but to this day they remain prone to following a quixotic and dangerous leader.

Indeed, predestination and fatalism are prominent elements within Islamic theology. Ali related the following story about Muhammad:

> We were sitting with the Prophet, and he wrote with a stick in the ground, saying: 'There is not one among you whose sitting place is not written by God whether in fire or in paradise.'[655]

One historian has noted that this can be used to,

> ... encourage bravery in battle, since no danger could hasten, nor any caution defer, the predestined hour of each man's death.[656]

The Shi'a are more mystical than the Sunni and, as minority underdogs, they have always had more invested in the Mahdi's unveiling. **Shi'aism may reasonably be considered to be the inverse of Christianity**, as they venerate the Son of Perdition, Caliph Ali, to the point of near-deification.[657] Their annual remembrance of the martyrdom of Ali's son, Husayn, at the Battle of

Karbala (i.e., the Day of Ashura) is somewhat similar to Christian's remembrance of the sacrifice of Christ on Good Friday. The Shi'a often repeat,

> *Husayn is from me, and I am from Husayn.*[658]

This is rather similar to Christ's passion prayer in the Garden of Gethsemane,

> *Father ... just as you are in me and I am in you. I want*
> *them also to be in us. [John 17:21 NIrV]*

The Shi'a have saints and feast day, as do Christians, and they believe in a coming apocalyptic battle of good against evil. They maintain that their redeemer, the Mahdi, entered a cave and then disappeared, as did Christ. They say that a tribulation will immediately precede the return of the 'Light of the World' (i.e., the Mahdi). And just as any writing of the twelve Apostles was canonized into the New Testament, the Shi'a consider the twelve generations of Imams that were directly descended from the Prophet Muhammad (through the bloodline of Ali, and then Husayn) to have been infallible incarnations of divine wisdom.[659] Hence, the Shi'a are also known by the moniker, Twelvers. And just as Christ gave the Great Commission to His Apostles, the job of the twelve Imams is to implement the Shi'a faith on the face of the earth. The bulk of this task was left to the twelfth Imam, since the first eleven were murdered.

The Shi'a legend concerning the twelfth Imam is, again, the mirror-image of the Christian religion: there was a short-lived rumor within the early Christian Church that the Apostle John, would not die, but remain until the Second Coming of Christ. The rumor stems from a seaside conversation between the resurrected Jesus Christ and the Apostle Peter.

> *Jesus answered, "If I want [John] to remain alive until*
> *I return, what is that to you? You must follow me."*
> *Because of this, the rumor spread among the brothers*
> *that this disciple would not die. [John 21:22–23a NIV]*

But the Apostle John clarified,

> *But Jesus did not say that he would not die; he only*
> *said, "If I want him to remain alive until I return,*
> *what is that to you?" [John 21:23b TNIV]*

No serious Christian believes that the Apostle John is still alive on the face of the earth. The early Christian writer Tertullian (AD 155–AD 230) tells us that Emperor Domitian (AD 51–AD 96) had the Apostle John brought to Rome and thrown into a cauldron of boiling oil. He emerged unharmed, so the Emperor banished John to the Aegean island of Patmos where he wrote Revelation. Later, during the reign of Emperor Trajan (AD 53–AD 117), the

Apostle John was allowed to return to his home in Ephesus.[660] The early Christian Bishop Irenaeus (AD 130–AD 202) was the disciple of one of the Apostle John's disciples. He tells us that the Apostle John died there around the year AD 100.[661] He was the youngest of the twelve Apostles, the last of the twelve to die, and the only one not to be martyred.

The Shi'a say that the male child born in the twelfth generation of the Imams was the Mahdi. He was born in the year AD 868, and his name was Muhammad al-Mahdi. His father, the eleventh and penultimate Shi'a Imam, was killed by the Sunnis through poisoning at the age of twenty-seven.[662]

The five year old Mahdi officiated at his father's funeral *and then immediately went into occultation* (i.e., he became concealed from the physical world by Allah) in AD 873 so that he would not be murdered as the other eleven Imams had been. It is said that he will emerge later to fulfill his mission as the ultimate savior of mankind.[663]

Shi'as say that Allah is trying the hearts of true believers by allowing the Mahdi's occultation to last so long. They say that he will reappear, along with Jesus, at a time when all other ideologies, governments, and religions have proven to be failures, and the people are ready to accept his acting as Allah's administrator. Therefore, the time will only be right for him to return if they truly believe in his reality.

> *Twelver Shi'ism is, then, a deeply eschatological religion ... The world, for the Shi'ite, is a deeply immoral, degenerate, and corrupt place; these are the necessary preludes to the appearance of Imam Mahdi. Like Christianity, Shi'ism is also a deeply prophetic religion. Like Christian belief, the end of time and the appearance of the Mahdi will be preceded by a number of events foretold in prophecy. The Shi'ite, then, like many Christians, lives in a world full of signs of the impending concluding chapters of history. This is vitally important in understanding Shi'a culture and political theory. **Most of Iranian history can only be understood in relationship to the Doctrine of Return and the prophecies associated with it** ... In many ways, the [Iranian] Revolutionaries believed that they were engineering or inaugurating the beginning of the reign of justice in the world, just as the radical Protestant English who settled America believed that*

they were inaugurating the one thousand year rule of
saints that would precede the end of the world.[664]

The sixth Shi'a Imam (half way from Muhammad to the generation of the Mahdi) is reputed to have said,

Before the appearance of the one who will rise, peace
be upon him, the people will be reprimanded for their
acts of disobedience by a fire that will appear in the
sky and a redness that will cover the sky. It will swal-
low up Baghdad, and will swallow up Kufa. Their
blood will be shed and houses destroyed. Death will
occur amid their people and a fear will come over the
people of Iraq from which they shall have no rest.[665]

Shi'a eschatologists believe that a diabolical insurgency will occur in Iraq just before the Mahdi's reappearance. The insurgent leader of the forces of evil is supposed to originate from Palestine or Jordan. They say that he will be a direct descendant of Muawiyah, the notorious fifth [Sunni] caliph who fought against Ali during the first Muslim civil war.[666]

Muawiyah has always been reviled by the Shi'a, who blame him for Ali's assassination in AD 661. The tyrannical End Times descendant of Muawiyah is supposed to bring terror throughout the Middle East, from Egypt to Iraq.

A loud noise in the sky is supposed to signal the reappearance of the Shi'a Mahdi from his current state of occultation.[667] He is to rally the faithful, and his followers will then be given great strength to descend upon Mecca. There will be a mass conversion of Sunnis to the Shi'a faith, and the insurgency of Muawiyah's descendant will be crushed.

Something like these events is playing out in Iraq at this very time. Abu Musab al-Zarqawi (AD 1966–AD 2006), the Jordanian-born leader of al-Qaeda in Iraq, was trying to instigate a civil war until an American bomb killed him on June 7, AD 2006. He was a fanatical Sunni, and was deliberately provoking the Shi'a majority by indiscriminately bombing their gathering places. He had said,

There is no difference between Shiites of Iran and the
Shiites in the rest of the Arab world, either in Iraq or
Lebanon. Their beliefs are the same; their hatred of
Sunnis is the same. The roots of Jews and the Shiites
are the same.[668]

He therefore arranged for a suicide bomb blast on February 22, AD 2006 which destroyed much of the al-Askari Mosque in Samarra, Iraq.[669] That is the place from which the Shi'a say that the Mahdi disappeared. It is also the site of his father and grandfather's mausoleum (the tenth and eleventh Imams). It is one of the most holy sites to Shi'as.

Watching all this is the largest and most powerful Shi'a state, Iran. Its president is the radical Shi'a, Dr. Mahmood Ahmadinejad. Although Shi'a Iran has no history of expansionism, they do have a tradition of self-flagellation and senseless martyrdom. They also have a chip on their shoulder for being the minority sect within Islam. They would like to demonstrate to the Sunni Muslims that they are the truly pious branch of the faith.

Dr. Ahmadinejad is a passionate believer in the imminent return of the Shi'a Mahdi, and he just may be willing to instigate a war to hasten the Mahdi's return. He has been breathing out threats since he has been in office, and is vigorously pursuing nuclear arms. During his first speech before the United Nations General Assembly on September 17, AD 2005, he talked at length about Iran's nuclear program, and concluded with these words:

> ... *from the beginning of time, humanity has longed for the day when justice, peace, equality and compassion will envelop the world. All of us can contribute to the establishment of such a world. When that day comes, the ultimate promise of all Divine religions will be fulfilled with* **the emergence of a perfect human being who is heir to all prophets and pious men.** *He will lead the world to justice and absolute peace.*
> *O mighty Lord, I pray to you to hasten the emergence of your last repository, the promised one, that perfect and pure human being, the one that will fill this world with justice and peace.*[670]

The ambassadors in the chamber were aghast.

President Ahmadinejad was a student radical during the AD 1979 Iranian Revolution, and joined the Islamic Revolutionary Guard Corps during the Iran–Iraq War. At that time, the Iranian government was issuing cheaply-made keys to young Shi'a men to wear around their necks. These soldiers would jump out of trenches into Iraqi machine-gun fire under the belief that the key would get them through the door of paradise. The Ayatollah Khomeini had given his infantry orders to take Baghdad and continue on until conquering Jerusalem.

> *There is another aspect to [the Shi'ite observance of] Ashura: the veneration of martyrdom. The events at Karbala have inscribed permanently in the Shi'ite*

*historical consciousness the idea that to be a Shi'ite is
to be a martyr to the correct faith.*[671]

This type of fanaticism is in charge of one of the world's largest oil reserves at a time of record high fuel prices. Iran is using that revenue to join the nuclear club.

*For [President Ahmadinejad], Mutual Assured
Destruction is not a deterrent, it is an inducement ...
We know already that [Iran's ruling ayatollahs] do
not give a damn about killing their own people in
great numbers. We have seen it again and again. If
they kill large numbers of their own people, they are
doing them a favor. They are giving them a quick, free
pass to heaven.*[672]

The Iranian clerical leaders have predicated their entire lives upon the Shi'a religion. Ahmadinejad has said,

*Our revolution's main mission is to pave the way for
the reappearance of the 12ᵗʰ Imam, the Mahdi.*[673]

The Iranians are infiltrating Iraq to promote reprisal killings against Sunnis, as well as killing the American soldiers that are trying to maintain civil order. There is even a large Shi'a Arab militia in Iraq called The Mahdi Army that is fighting against the al-Qaeda Sunnis.

In fact, one of the unintended consequences of the United States' invasion of Iraq has been to put in place a Shi'a president. Since there are twice as many Shi'a Arabs as Sunni Arabs in Iraq, this is likely to continue indefinitely. So now we have a situation where the leadership of Iran, Iraq, and Syria[xxxviii] all belong to religions that teach that a Shi'a-style Mahdi is about to arrive on the scene.

If I have been able to make the connection between al-Qaeda's mayhem in Iraq, and the insurgency that was predicted before the Mahdi's return, don't you think the Iranian leader has done the same? President Ahmadinejad thinks about the return of the Mahdi as often as I think about the return of Christ.

Of course, I trust God to do everything in His time, and would never set off a nuclear weapon to hasten the end of the world. President Ahmadinejad, on the other hand, keeps warning people to expect a loud noise in the sky.

Indeed, the war that Revelation foretells is something like Ayatollah Khomeini's dream—an Anti-Christian infantry marching westward.

---

xxxviii Again, Syria has an overwhelmingly Sunni population, but it is controlled by secular Alawites. And the Alawites are an offshoot of Shi'aism.

> *Then they gathered the kings together to the place that in Hebrew is called Armageddon. [Revelation 16:16 TNIV]*
>
> *They marched across the breadth of the earth and surrounded the camp of God's people, the city he loves. But fire came down from heaven and devoured them. [Revelation 20:9 NIV]*
>
> *Then there came flashes of lightning, rumblings, peals of thunder ... [Revelation 16:18 TNIV]*

Gog and Magog will ignore reality, head into a nuclear holocaust, and a third of their huge army will be incinerated.

Luke 1:34–35 [NKJV]
Then Mary said to the angel, "How can this be, since I do not know a man?" And the angel answered and said to her, "The Holy Spirit will come upon you, and the power of the Highest will overshadow you; therefore, also, that Holy One who is to be born will be called the Son of God."

74. Homegrown Muslims

Some Christians in my reading audience may view the christological controversies of Sections 61–69 as quaint, at best. Others may find them arcane, and maddeningly inconsequential. This is an especially likely response from Reformed Evangelical Protestants (both Abaptists and Anabaptists) who consider themselves as too enlightened to recite the three Ecumenical Creeds (i.e., Apostles', Athanasian, and Nicene with the inclusion of the Filioque).

Of course, the self-avowed 'non-creedal' churches have all kinds of beliefs systems in practice. They tend to be legalistic in their interpretation of the Scriptures. Sometimes these beliefs are written down and recited; other times they are just popularly assumed. But without the anchor of the true statements about God that are found in the creeds, error builds upon error until the comical becomes orthodoxy.

For example, I know of a conservative Christian woman that attended a non-creedal church until she came to a Sunday service wearing a new hat. It had a feather in it. The pastor waved her along when she approached the communion table. When she later inquired about the reason, he said, "Your hat showed pride, and pride was the first sin of the devil. You cannot partake of Communion while wearing a prideful feathered hat—at least not in this church."

She soon found a new church without such a creed.

The word 'creed' comes from the Latin 'credo,' which simply means 'I believe.' So it is a fallacy for a church to say that it rejects formalized creeds. Everybody believes in something. Any church that truly is non-creedal is just a gathering of invertebrates. And any Christian that truly refuses to accept creeds would have to also swear off all Christian books, movies, hymns, sermons, and enriching conversations with other believers. All of them are extra–biblical means of expressing the faith.

So you see that to be non-creedal is to be nonsensical.

Nevertheless, I expect a response from non-creedal Christians along these lines: "Look, it's all very interesting history, but I just don't think that God cares one way or the other. If anything, He's angry at both sides for making such a fuss about an indecipherable point. It's the same type of argument as 'how many angels can stand on the head of a pin?'"

If this is your position, I adjure you to reconsider. Christians ought not to be ambivalent about what the Bible reveals concerning the Incarnation of God as man. This is the most important thing that has happened in the history of the universe. God most definitely wants you to care about the one nature versus two nature issue, and to choose correctly between them; the devil most definitely does not want you to care about it. Read the abominable inscriptions on the Dome of the Rock (the full text is provided in Section 46) and you will see the Antichrist Beast faulting Christians for thinking critically[674] about Christology:

> *Faith in Allah means unity, but those who were given*
> *the Book split into factions after receiving knowledge*
> *and endlessly disputed among themselves.*[675]

The 'endless disputes' are the Christological arguments of the fifth through seventh centuries. Islam's foundational verse proclaims that Christians lost their way by concentrating upon Jesus Christ's nature as God and man. Do you agree with the Antichrist Beast?! Do you concur with the veiled threat (below) that it makes against those that insist that true God became true man?

> *Whoever denies the evidence of Allah, let him be*
> *aware that Allah is swift in reckoning.*[676]

In marked contrast, the Holy Bible commends the early Christians of Berea because,

> *They searched the Scriptures day after day to check*
> *up on Paul and Silas, to see if they were really teach-*
> *ing the truth. [Acts 17:11 NLT]*

Again, I will put words of protest in your mouth, "But how could it be that a God so big would allow the eastern portion of His Church to be annihilated over the semantic difference between two separate natures versus a single nature containing both elements? You make the Christian path too narrow! He can't expect such specificity!"

Amazing behavior on your part. If you are a Protestant or Roman Catholic believer making the above argument, then you are being a complete ingrate and hypocrite. It is, in fact, vitally important. The purifying work that the Holy Spirit did during the Nestorian Schism (AD 428–AD 431), Monophysite Schism (AD 451–AD 728), and the Anti-Filioquean Schism (AD 589–AD 1054) are integral parts of your Christian heritage (see Table 13). Saints were tortured, mutilated, and killed in order to preserve and promote the truth about Christ's Personhood. They were banished into the desert with no food or water or clothing for the sake of Jesus and the Christian Creeds. And you have the nerve to dismiss these issues as puerile and inconsequential? You dare to reargue them at this late date? Have you no shame?

Unfortunately, Protestants tend to take these issues for granted because they were resolved over a thousand years ago. But there are no Protestant denominations deriving from any of the eastern churches, because the eastern churches are fundamentally wrong about the particulars of how God became a man in Christ. Again, there is no such thing as a Protestant church that is Anti-Chalcedonian or Anti-Filioquean.

As Christians, we know that the one and only determinant for the eternal destination of one's soul is confessing and trusting in the truth about God. Jesus Christ—tempted, but sinless—sending forth His Spirit—is the source of our salvation.

Still, it makes you feel like a good person to allow for a wider path than the three Ecumenical Creeds, eh? What would you say about a church that accepts everything in the Creeds except the Virgin Birth? What would you say about a church that accepts everything in the Creeds except that God was always eternal God? Are persons that believe in those things saved? How much of what God has done for you are you willing to discount because of your intellectual laziness and imbecility?!

~~~~~~~~~~~~~~~~~~~~~~~

For those that still don't believe that slightly incorrect dogma concerning the Personhood of Jesus Christ can lead to an Antichrist world religion, consider the example of Mormonism.

I once had a Mormon roommate that posed the following question: "How many times do you think that God had to try before He got someone to live a sinless life? Jesus turned out to be the rarest of persons."

I didn't know how to respond. The premise of the question was queer to me. I know from the Bible and the Nicene Creed that Jesus is the only begotten Son of God, being of one substance with the Father. But my roommate was trying to get me to think that he or I could have been the Savior if we had been born fifty years before Jesus and had avoided sin all our lives. Jesus, he suggested, was just the first to accomplish this remarkable feat.

I later learned that Mormons do not believe that Jesus has always been the one and only Sovereign of the universe and beyond. Their Jesus is an eternal being that *became a God*. They also think that God the Father was once a mere man named Elohim, and that He, too, became a God.[677] They think that He had a father—God the Grandfather, and so on. They think that they will also become Gods someday.[678] They think that when a person becomes a God he gets his own set of planets to govern. Earth is one of God the Father's planets.

They also think that God the Father took physical form in order to sire Jesus. That means that Mary was not a virgin when she married Joseph. They say she was impregnated by carnal relations with the Heavenly Father,[679] rather than being overshadowed by the Holy Spirit (as the Scriptures teach in Luke 1:35). They say that God the Father had other wives, as well. At least one of these women is the 'Heavenly Mother,' or Goddess, of planet Earth.

Are these differences minor, my dear non-creedal Christian skeptic? Does God not care that His own mother, the blessed virgin Mary, is being called a whore? Does He not care that He is being accused of committing incest with her?! If you say that He does care about the doctrine of the Virgin Birth, and at the same time you say that the Christology of the Creeds is unimportant, then where is your consistency?

How can you not denounce Monophysitism as a Christian heresy, and yet condemn Mormonism as an Antichrist cult? On the basis of the Bible?—The Mormons accept the Bible. On the basis of baptism in the name of the Father and of the Son and of the Holy Spirit?—The Mormons baptize in the name of the Father, and of the Son, and of the Holy Spirit.[680] The condemnation can only be *in what they believe* about the Holy Bible and about Holy Baptism.

The three Ecumenical Creeds state, clearly, simply, and irrevocably, what we believe about these things. **Without the belief, speaking of the thing itself is meaningless.** If the three Ecumenical Creeds were unimportant, then the Mormons would be just another variant of Christianity. For that matter, so would the Muslims!

In reality, the Oriental Orthodox and Eastern Orthodox beliefs are Anti-Chalcedonian and Anti-Filioquean heresies (respectively) within the Christian Church; and both Mormonism and Islam are Antichrist sects outside the Christian Church.

There are many similarities between Mormons and Muslims. They both:

- have a 'Damien'-like aversion to crosses;
- elevate post–Christ prophets that supposedly revealed that the truth about God had been distorted by the Christian Church;
- split into two main factions after the death of their prophet—the minor one adhering to blood lineage and the major one adhering to pragmatism;
- extol extra–biblical holy books and maintain that there is an exact copy of it in heaven;
- have a mania for marriage, believing that they will enjoy nose-hair-curling sex with multiple women in the afterlife.[681]

Moreover, like the Muslims, when Mormons live in one isolated society they form murderous bands. A Mormon militia massacred one hundred and twenty unarmed Christian settlers that dared to pass through Utah Territory in AD 1857.[682]

The Mormons, however, have not become a danger to world civilization as the Muslims have thanks to the grace of God and the overwhelming strength of the United States Army. It is only by moderating their religion, and agreeing to live in subjugation to a Protestant Christian people, and in accordance with Protestant Christian laws, that the Mormons survived and prospered (Section 28).

The Muslims have yet to do this. I think it will take the threat of nuclear vaporization to make them reasonable.

Luke 1:68 [NKJV]
Blessed is the Lord God of Israel, for He has visited and redeemed His people ...

75. Jesus' Bride is Attracted Through His Spirit

In Evangelical circles, it is common to hear people declare, "I found the Lord at an altar-call when I was twenty-five years old," or "I made the decision for Christ seven years ago," or "I feel I am ready to become baptized now because I really understand the Bible and my faith has grown strong."

These statements represent terribly incorrect theology. They are fingernails-on-a-chalkboard to any person that understands what God has done for them.

The Scriptures teach that we cannot come to salvation by means of our own willpower or intellect.

> *... no one can say that Jesus is Lord except by the*
> *Holy Spirit. [1 Corinthians 12:3 NKJV]*

As sinners, our will is always hell-bent against the saving knowledge; it is only the Holy Spirit's faithful striving that saves us. The most we can say is that we who are saved have simply stopped resisting long enough for Him to be able to baptize us with water and the Word.

~~~~~~~~~~~~~~~~~~~~~~~

The Holy Spirit is the third Person of the Trinity. He is a distinct Person from the Father and the Son, even while He is one substance with them.

The Holy Spirit has a job and that job may be thought of as, among other things, being Jesus' personal magnetism. The Spirit's primary work is to draw the Church—the Bride of Christ—to be pledged to Jesus.

> *When the Spirit of truth comes, he will guide you into*
> *all truth. [John 16:13 NLT]*

The Holy Spirit proceeds from Christ to secure the Church's heart in betrothal and hand in marriage. This cleansing is done in preparation for the heavenly consummation, for,

> *Who may ascend into the hill of the Lord? Or who*
> *may stand in His holy place? He who has clean hands*
> *and a pure heart ... He shall receive blessing from the*
> *Lord, and righteousness from the God of his salva-*
> *tion. [Psalm 24:3–5 NKJV]*

The Apostle John had a vision of the heavenly host praising Jesus on the wedding day, saying,

> *Alleluia! For the Lord God Omnipotent reigns! Let us be glad and rejoice and give Him glory, for the marriage of the Lamb has come, and His wife has made herself ready. [Revelation 19:6–7 NKJV]*

The Lord's bride is the collection of all who believe, and her adornment is the good works that the Holy Spirit empowers her to do.

> *And to her it was granted to be arrayed in fine linen, clean and bright, for the fine linen is the righteous acts of the saints. [Revelation 19:8 NKJV]*

The marriage in heaven is not to be a plural marriage. Christ is wed with only one: the Christian Church. But the Church is made up of many constituent parts.

> *The human body has many parts, but the many parts make up one whole body. So it is with the body of Christ ... All of you together are Christ's body, and each of you is a part of it. [2 Corinthians 12:12,27 NLT]*

The marriage between Christ and the Church is a blessed institution of which individual Christians are both spectators and participants.

> *And the angel said to me, "Write this: Blessed are those who are invited to the wedding feast of the Lamb." [Revelation 19:9 NLT]*

~~~~~~~~~~~~~~~~~~~~~~~~

The practical implication of the disconnect that the Anti-Filioqueans have established between Christ's atoning work, and the Spirit's guiding work, is that Jesus does not have the ability to get a wife for Himself. They are saying that He needs His Father to make the arrangement for Him.

Again, saying, as the Eastern Orthodox do, that the Spirit proceeds from the Father *but not from the Son* is like saying, "That boy [i.e., God the Son] just doesn't have what it takes to attract a woman [i.e., the Church]! His daddy [i.e., God the Father] had better fetch for the matchmaker [i.e., God the Holy Spirit] to set him up!"

Luke 2:21 [ESV]
*And at the end of eight days, when he was circumcised, he was called Jesus,
the name given by the angel before he was conceived in the womb.*

76. Jesus has a Penis

Heretofore I have detailed two eastern christological heresies[xxxix] and their
implications concerning the sexual identity of God (Sections 62, 69). To
review ...

The Monophysitism of the Oriental Orthodox holds:

> ➤ that Jesus did not have the [separate] nature of a
> man;
>> ➤ which means that He did not have the [separate] will of a man;
>>> ➤ which means that He was not tempted as a
>>> man is tempted;
>>>> ➤ which means that He was unable to
>>>> feel want for a woman as does a man.

The Anti-Filioqueanism of the Eastern Orthodox holds:

> ➤ that the Holy Spirit did not proceed from Jesus;
>> ➤ which means that He does not draw His Bride,
>> the Church, to Himself;
>>> ➤ which means that He is not desirable to
>>> her as a man is desirable to a woman;
>>>> ➤ which means that He was never capable of attracting the affections of His
>>>> Bride, the Christian Church.

As pernicious and destructive as these two false doctrines are, they are
nothing compared with the western christological heresy that has arisen within
Mainline American Protestant churches: they refuse to accept that God is a
man and not a woman, and in so doing, they refuse to accept that Jesus has a
penis. To be perfectly clear ...

The Egalitarianism of the Mainline American Protestants holds:

> ➤ that God the Father is neither masculine nor
> feminine;

---

xxxix Actually, I have detailed three eastern Christological heresies, but Nestorianism
(i.e., the belief that Jesus had a dual personality) is so ridiculous that I shall not
go into its sexual implications.

> ➢ which means that God the Son is neither mas-
> culine nor feminine;
>> ➢ which means that Jesus is not a man, and
>> never had a penis;
>>> ➢ which means that He will be unable
>>> to fulfill his husbandly duties to His
>>> Bride, the Christian Church.

The Athanasian Creed of the Christian religion correctly states that in order to go to Heaven you must believe that God became a man in Jesus Christ. You must believe that He literally became a male human being. If you believe that He became a female human being, or a hermaphrodite, you will undoubtedly die in your sins and go to Hell for all eternity.

~~~~~~~~~~~~~~~~~~~~~~

A feminist theologian of a large Mainline Protestant denomination has written that we should move beyond the notion of God as a male. She writes,

> *The use of male titles, references, names, and pro-*
> *nouns eventually lead many to conclude that God*
> *does have a gender and that God is a male.*[683]

She says that 'father' and 'king' are simply among a myriad of figurative symbols of God. But these two are particularly 'dangerous' because,

> *While we easily realize that God is not literally a rock*
> *or an eagle ... Our own human relationships tend*
> *to literalize those symbols, turning God into those*
> *words.*[684]

She asserts that, "the Church, by using masculine words to describe God, has given God a gender," and "As the One who is, God has no gender." She says that because the Bible uses feminine imagery to portray God's attributes, it is legitimate to refer to God as 'She,' and not just 'He.'[685]

The stumbling block for this clergyperson is the sacrifice of the perfect male Lamb of God, Jesus Christ.

> *... we preach Christ crucified, a stumbling block to*
> *Jews and folly to Gentiles ... [1 Corinthians 1:23*
> *ESV]*

In Judaism, God never took human form, but remains disunited with mankind solely as a spirit. They therefore have developed a female presence of God called 'Shekhina' to counterbalance the patriarchal Yahweh. Indeed,

Hollywood actor Leonard Nimoy has published a photographic book under this title with semi–nude Jewish women representing the Judaic god.[686]

But Jesus of Nazareth is a historical reality. The Christian Scriptures testify that God "became flesh" (John 1:14), and that He had normal male genitalia (Luke 2:21), and that He was without hormonal defect (Leviticus 22:24–25). Remember that it is the male of the human species that possesses the heterogametic sex chromosomes, Y and X. Therefore, it is appropriate that He was sacrificed for all mankind, both male (Y/X) and female (X/X).

> ... *God created man* **in His own image,** *in the image of God He created him;* **male and female He created them.** *[Genesis 1:27 NKJV]*

If Christians believe that Jesus is true God, and if Christians believe that Jesus is true [anatomical] man, then Christians believe that God is masculine to the exclusion of God being womanly or epicene. When the Apostle Peter entered the tomb, he found a burial cloth and strips of linen (John 20:6–7); he did not find a burial cloth, strips of linen, a penis, scrotum, and testicles. Christ rose from the dead intact—with a glorious male body. We do not 'turn God into' a man by imagining Him with male symbolism. He was begotten of the Father, not created of our imaginations. We do not 'give God a gender' by using masculine words. He was incarnate in the blessed virgin Mary as a male human being.

> *For unto us a Child is born, unto us* **a Son is given.** *[Isaiah 9:6 NKJV]*

~~~~~~~~~~~~~~~~~~~~~~

While writing one of my graduate theses, I quipped to a friend that the process was, "as excruciating as giving birth." By using this metaphor, I was in no way giving my friend permission to move beyond the notion that I am a male, and to start referring to me broadly as 'Christine.' My friend would have been taking quite a leap if he were to have assumed that I was conveying to him that a disfiguring accident had befallen me in the laboratory, and that I was now smooth all over. My birth certificate says, 'Christian Jacobsen' and 'Male.' That is who I am.

Likewise, God uses ingenious literary devices—including feminine imagery—to tell us of His love for all people. For example, Jesus compared God to a diligent housewife that sweeps the house to find a lost silver coin— the cultural equivalent of a wedding ring (Luke 15:8–10).[687] It is edifying to use this metaphor to represent God's efforts to redeem the Elect. But this does not mean that God is a woman, and it does not give us license to call God 'She' in addition to 'He.'[xl] Female pronouns are *never* used in Holy Scripture for direct references to God because God was made man in Christ for our sake. That is who He is.

Female pronouns for direct references to God are, however, used in American popular culture all the time. I have read lyrics of two American rock tunes (*Muhammad My Friend* by Tori Amos, and *Suite-Pee* by the heavy metal rock group, System of a Down) that refer to Jesus as a woman. And Jesus has often been portrayed in film and theater as effeminate, or even homosexual.

The devil loves to redefine the Incarnation by casting Jesus as less than a man—he thinks that it is funny. The 'System of a Down' song actually lyricizes about mounting the feminine Jesus. I will not repeat the lyrics here.

~~~~~~~~~~~~~~~~~~~~~~

For further evidence of the Muslim religion being the Antichrist Beast, one may point to their Medieval practice of cutting away all of the genitalia of certain unlucky male African slaves. The mortality rate was as horrific as the procedure itself.[688]

Indeed, even today millions of Muslim parents continue to practice clitoridectomy on female infants and girls. Sometimes even the labia are removed.

The Apostle Paul warned,

> *Watch out for those dogs, those men who do evil, those*
> *mutilators of the flesh. [Philippians 3:2 NIV]*

God does not condone sexual mutilation, but the Antichrist does, and the devil would like for us to think that Jesus was a freak between His legs. Recall that the foundational inscription of Islam states,

> *The Messiah does not consider it beneath his dignity*
> *to be a slave ... O Allah! Incline unto Your messenger*
> *and slave Jesus, son of Mary ...* [689]

The Son of Mary was from Galilee and not Africa, but you see what the Islamists would have liked to do to Him! Are they any more offensive than

---

xl   The early liturgy of the Syriac Orthodox (Monophysite) Church used the pronoun 'She' when referring to the Holy Spirit because the word 'Spirit' in the Syriac translation of the Bible is feminine. This suggested that Jesus was one third effeminate, since He is of one substance with the other Persons of the Holy Trinity. The Syriacs long ago corrected this error—their accepted liturgy only uses 'He' to refer to the three Persons of the Holy Trinity.

the leadership of the Mainline Protestant churches when they refer to Christ as a 'She'?

If you worship in a Mainline Protestant church (Section 77), you are acquiescing to the notion that Jesus Christ of Nazareth did not have a penis. These churches have thousands of ordained clergy that propose that God is a 'She' every bit as much as God is a 'He.' Any four year old child can tell you that the difference between a 'she' and a 'he' is to be found between the legs.

Do not assume that this false teaching has no effect on the American culture! A recent survey[690] found that only thirty-six percent of Americans think that God is male; at the same time forty-eight percent think that God is:

    a.   neither male nor female,
    b.   or both male and female,
    c.   or female.

Christ Himself predicted animus toward the Son of God as a sign of the end.

> *And many will turn away from me ... And many false*
> *prophets will appear and will deceive many people.*
> *Sin will be rampant everywhere, and the love of many*
> *will grow cold. [Matthew 24:10–12 NLT]*

The Mainline Protestants would counter that they are in favor of freedom of conscience among their clergymen and clergywomen. I am also in favor of freedom of conscience—passionately so! Therefore, I think that a Christian denomination should maintain, or not maintain, the credentials of their clergy based on what they freely express. And the primary and immutable requisite for being a Christian is to trust that GOD became a MAN in the Person of JESUS.

It's a matter of qualification, not oppression.

It would be a strange thing for me to join a swim club, and show up at the pool with ice skates. It would be stranger still, and quite obnoxious, for me to then open all the windows in the dead of winter and let the water freeze over in the name of freedom of conscience.

The rule of the swim club is that the pool is for swimming. The rule of the Christian Church is that the Church is for Christians.

In the table below I review the three false teachings concerning the masculine sexual identity of God within heretical churches. Their attitude toward Christ is like that of an unsupportive and demeaning wife toward her husband.

Table 14. Three Insults Concerning the Sexual Identity of God

The Insulter	They Stand...	The Implication of the Insult is that...
Eastern Orthodox	Against the processional ability of the Son	Jesus doesn't have the male magnetism to attract His Bride, the Church
Oriental Orthodox	Against the separate human nature of the Son	Jesus doesn't have the male libido to gratify His Bride, the Church
Mainline Protestant	Against the specific gender of the Son	Jesus doesn't have the male physical equipment to penetrate His Bride, the Church

Again, I find the last one most loathsome. There, the first two insults are incorporated into one supreme insult because a person that does not have male genitalia has neither male magnetism nor male desire.

Think of your young son, or young nephew, or little brother. Imagine if some bully pushed him in the chest, and fell him into the dirt, and said, "Sit down dickless! You are not a man!"

Would you not be in a fighting frame-of-mind for your boy?

Well, now you know how our Heavenly Father feels when we mock His Son by worshipping in the Mainline Protestant churches that are found in every town and hamlet of the United States of America.

1 Timothy 4:1 [NKJV]
Now the Spirit expressly says that in latter times some will depart from the faith, giving heed to deceiving spirits and doctrines of demons ...

77. The Church of the Emasculated Christ

Are you scandalized that I have entitled this section, *The Church of the Emasculated Christ*? Which is worse: to worship in such a congregation, or to tell the truth about it?

The truth is that the Mainline American Protestants have huge numbers of ordained ministers and laymen that openly question the manhood and/or the divinity of Jesus Christ. In some cases the unbelievers actually make up the majority. For example, in AD 2005, eighty percent of the United Church of Christ's synod delegates voted to approve of homosexual marriage ceremonies. That same synod rejected a resolution that would have required its clergy to profess the divinity of Jesus Christ in order to maintain their ordination.[691] The Episcopal Church also refused to affirm that Jesus is the only route to salvation at its AD 2006 convention.[692]

> *... there will be false teachers among you. They will secretly introduce destructive heresies, **even denying the sovereign Lord who bought them**—bringing swift destruction on themselves. Many will follow their shameful ways and will bring the way of truth into disrepute. [2 Peter 2:1–2 NIV]*

Many Mainline Protestant churches no longer baptize in the name of the Father, Son, and Holy Spirit as Jesus commanded because they want to use gender-neutral language. Many do not believe that Jesus was born of a virgin, or that He was necessarily sinless in His earthly ministry. Many do not believe that He rose from the dead, or that He is coming again in bodily form. These churches are all tied to each other through various ecumenical arrangements, and altar-and-pulpit fellowships. The Episcopal Church is now headed by a female bishop who has said,

> *[There are two strands of Christian faith. One is] most concerned with atonement, that Jesus died for our sins and our most important task is to repent. [But the other is] the more gracious strand ... to talk about life, to claim the joy and the blessings for good that it offers, to look forward ... [our task is] ... that we may become divine.*[693]

We know that God is diametrically opposed to this latter 'strand.' God says of those that pervert the Scriptures, and commingle Him with cultural gods.

> *I will cut off ... those who bow down and swear by the Lord and who also swear by Molech, those who turn back from following the Lord and neither seek the Lord nor inquire of him. [Zephaniah 1:4–6 NIV]*

The Mainline Protestants deviated from the Christian faith many years ago. The largest seven of these denominations have been termed the 'Seven Sisters.'[694] Specifically, they are (listed by strength of membership):

United Methodist Church–8.4 million[695]
Evangelical Lutheran Church in America–4.9 million[696]
Presbyterian Church [USA]–2.4 million[697]
Episcopal Church in the USA–2.2 million[698]

American Baptist Churches in the USA–1.5 million[699]
United Church of Christ–1.4 million[700]
Disciples of Christ–0.8 million[701]

Don't fool yourselves: if you are a Christian and you go to one of these churches, or to any that is communion with them (such as the Reformed Church in America), you are acquiescing to the notion that God did not become a male human being. These churches are,

> ... *the Unchurch ... hell-bound ... an enemy of Evangelical Faith, Catholic Truth, Apostolic Order, and Godly Life.*[702]

Even if your congregation is a relatively conservative and spiritual congregation within a Mainline Protestant denomination, it is a sin to ever worship there. Even if your congregation holds 'Alpha Courses' and '40 Days of Purpose' programs, this is not exculpatory. I have nothing against these programs *per se*, except that they are a bit gimmicky for my taste; my point is that good Biblical events do not make up for antichrist teachings within a denomination.

The most important thing to God is that you believe and confess the truth about Him. If your church is a member of the Seven Sisters denominations (or any like them), you belong to a church that does not believe and confess the truth about God. You must leave your congregation in order to worship God in spirit and in truth.

> *Do not be joined together with those who do not belong to Christ. How can that which is good get along with that which is bad? How can light be in the same place with darkness? How can Christ get along with the devil? How can one who has put his trust in Christ get along with one who has not put his trust in Christ? [2 Corinthians 6:14–15 NLV]*

What could possibly be your excuse for not separating from them when there is a plethora of good churches (Section 81) from which to chose—churches from denominations that do not countenance their ordained clergy calling God a 'She'? Is the reason because:

1. You don't want to leave your social, cultural, or business contacts there? Are you not embarrassed to say that?! Do you not realize that the Lord Jesus died for you?!

2. You want your child to marry someone from your home church? I am going to vomit!

3. You want to save the lost souls within your congregation? The purpose of Sabbath-gathering is to worship God in spirit and in truth, not to evangelize your fellow parishioners that never should have been admitted to membership in the first place. The Apostle Paul clearly tells us that a person could die as a result of taking Holy Communion without belief (1 Corinthians 11:28–30). Nevertheless, your sense of right and wrong tells you that it is benevolent to share the Communion table with individuals that openly deny that God became a man?!

In point of fact, you have no excuse because the Holy Scriptures plainly state of Jesus,

> *... he had to be made like his brothers in every way ...*
> *[Hebrews 2:17 NIV]*

The church that you attend refuses to take a stand for that foundational belief of the Christian religion. This omission is not a simple heresy; it is the very spirit of the Antichrist.

> *Many deceivers have gone out into the world. They do not believe that Jesus Christ came to earth in a real body. Such a person is a deceiver and an antichrist. [2 John 7 NLT]*

You have now read a clear explanation of how these churches are members of antichrist denominations. It is all the more incumbent upon you to divorce yourself from them, lest you suffer the consequence of associating with demons. Thanks to me, you can no longer claim innocence by means of ignorance.

You are welcome.

~~~~~~~~~~~~~~~~~~~~~~~~

The Apostle Paul warned the Corinthians that they should remain the virgin Bride of Christ (i.e., the Christian Church). He was concerned because they were easily amenable to the worship of a non-Christian Jesus.

· 373 ·

> *I am jealous over you with a godly jealousy, because*
> *I have promised you in marriage to one husband—to*
> *present a pure virgin to Christ. But I fear that, as the*
> *serpent deceived Eve by his cunning, your minds may*
> *be corrupted from a complete and pure devotion to*
> *Christ. For if a person comes and preaches another*
> *Jesus, whom we did not preach, or you receive a dif-*
> *ferent spirit, which you had not received, or a differ-*
> *ent gospel, which you had not accepted, you put up*
> *with it splendidly! [2 Corinthians 11:2–4 HCSB]*

Although I was raised in a denomination that puts up with false doc-trine splendidly, I have decided in my heart that I will not enter one of their sanctuaries on the Sabbath morning ever again for the rest of my life. God help me, I never will. Such places are not for worshiping the true God. They are places for family, and tradition, and community, and idiocy. In fact, I will not enter one of their sanctuaries at all unless I am to attend a wedding, or a funeral, or a similar event. That is my rule for entering Jewish synagogues and Muslim mosques, so why not for churches that disparage my precious Lord Jesus with antichrist doctrines?

Follow my example. Leave the Church of the Emasculated Christ. Leave them, or live under a curse.

1 Corinthians 10:1–12 [NIV]
For I do not want you to be ignorant of the fact, brothers, that our forefathers were all under the cloud and that they all passed through the sea. They were all baptized into Moses in the cloud and in the sea. They all ate the same spiritual food and drank the same spiritual drink; for they drank from the spiritual rock that accompanied them, and that rock was Christ. Nevertheless, God was not pleased with most of them; their bodies were scattered over the desert.
Now these things occurred as examples to keep us from setting our hearts on evil things as they did. Do not be idolaters, as some of them were; as it is writ-ten: "The people sat down to eat and drink and got up to indulge in pagan revelry." We should not commit sexual immorality, as some of them did—and in one day twenty-three thousand of them died. We should not test the Lord, as some of them did—and were killed by snakes. And do not grumble, as some of them did—and were killed by the destroying angel.

These things happened to them as examples and were written down as warnings for us, on whom the fulfillment of the ages has come. So, if you think you are standing firm, be careful that you don't fall!

78. Can a Saved Person Also Live Under a Curse?

Definitely. The fate of one's eternal soul can be secure, but one can still suffer while on this earth as a direct result of personal sin. God does not save us from the earthly consequences of every single one of our sins. If forgiveness meant that, then God would never allow a Christian to find himself with a speeding ticket, or in a bad marriage, or with a gambling loss.

God is love and He does everything out of love. Oftentimes He does protect us from the physical consequences of our own stupidity—but not always. He is the wise and loving Father, who sometimes bails his children out of binds, and sometimes allows them to stew in their own problems—but always with an eye to their ultimate welfare so that they will grow into Christ-likeness.

This is why God continually calls us to repentance—this is why He continually calls us into His Word. He desires that we be sanctified, and live blessed, full, lives. He desires to spare us from the trouble into which we would get ourselves.

Have you not read of David, and nearly every other Old Testament figure that knew God? We are told of their victories of faith, and of their personal failures. God forgave them of their failures and used it for His good purposes, but sometimes the consequences were bitter. King David, for example, committed adultery and murder. God said to him,

> *I anointed you king over Israel, and I delivered you from the hand of Saul ... Why did you despise the word of the Lord by doing what is evil in his eyes? ... therefore, the sword will never depart from your house ... [2 Samuel 12:7,9,10 NIV]*

As a result of this specific sin, there was incest, murder, rebellion, and infant death among David's children. Yet because he repented, his place in Heaven was secure, and the Messiah was later called the 'Son of David.'

In this section's Scripture heading, we are told by the Apostle Paul that the lives of Old Testament characters are recorded as examples to encourage us to good conduct. Indeed, I have meditated upon the story of David when I have been tempted to take another man's wife, and have come to my senses about the matter. Though my soul was secure, I did not want to live under the curse of adultery.

Now, we know from the loss of eastern Christendom to the Muslims that a false Christology has severe consequences. Therefore, might your tacit acceptance of false doctrines be the root spiritual cause of the lack of peace within your household?

> For our struggle is not against flesh and blood, but ...
> against the spiritual forces of evil ... [Ephesians 6:12
> TNIV]

I am suggesting, dear confused Protestant reader, that you give good heed to my warning against attending worship services in any of the 'Churches of the Emasculated Christ' (i.e., any congregation of the Seven Sisters denominations).

Of course, in Heaven the curses will be removed, and the enmity between God and the factions of [Christian] men will be healed.

> Then the angel showed me a river with the water of
> life, clear as crystal, flowing from the throne of God
> and of the Lamb. It flowed down the center of the main
> street. On each side of the river grew a tree of life,
> bearing twelve crops of fruit, with a fresh crop each
> month. The leaves were used for medicine to heal the
> nations. No longer will there be a curse upon any-
> thing. For the throne of God and of the Lamb will be
> there, and his servants will worship him. [Revelation
> 22:1–3 NLT]

But I don't want to wait until Heaven to begin the healing. I want as many curses gone from this life as possible. Don't you?

Matthew 7:21 [NKJV]
Not everyone who says to Me, 'Lord, Lord,' shall enter the kingdom of heaven, but he who does the will of My Father in heaven.

79. Against Apostasy

Now that I am older, I look back with great appreciation on how much my siblings and I mean to our father. Whenever any one of us calls him unexpectedly on the telephone, his normally steadied voice breaks forth with an ebullient lilt. We are the apple of his eye.

It has always been that way. Even when we were children and he would discipline us, it was done out of love. He did not use corporal punishment unless there was no other way to get through to us; before he would do that, he'd try other means.

One of his most effective tools when we were getting too big for our breeches would be a stern reminder of our status within the family. One time, when I was acting especially uppity, he said, "You need to appreciate just one thing: until you grow up and get a job, you're nothing but a parasite."

Wow! It had an impact.

It had an impact because it was true. We were alive because of Dad and Mom. They provided everything for us. They deserved our respect. We were vital appendages—like the arms and legs—of the main organism of the family. But when we used our privileged status as though we were a foreign agent, we were disciplined.

> *Endure hardship as discipline; God is treating you as sons. For what son is not disciplined by his father? If you are not disciplined (and everyone undergoes discipline), then you are illegitimate children and not true sons. Moreover, we have all had human fathers who disciplined us and we respected them for it. How much more should we submit to the Father of our spirits and live! [Hebrews 12:7–9 NIV]*

The same principle is at work among God's human creatures. He is the only source of life in the universe. He created us to be a cherished and adored part of His family. If we accept that role, we are princes and princesses of the Most High King. But if we leech off His sustenance, and work against our Heavenly Father, He disciplines us in the hope of getting us back as obedient children. Those that never come into harmony with the family of God are using the life that He provided for parasitism.

Children are nurtured; parasites are removed.

~~~~~~~~~~~~~~~~~~~~~~

There are individuals within Mainline Protestant (and other) churches that are more than just confused; there are plenty of people that claim to be Christians, but deny the divinity or manhood of Jesus. These people are foreign agents in the Church. They are cursed not only in this short life, but for all eternity as well.

... for unless you believe that I AM who I claim to be,
you will die in your sins. [John 8:24 NLT]

In AD 1998 I attended a lecture by Dr. Peter J. Gomes, the acclaimed Harvard Divinity School Professor of Christian Morals. He is an ordained American Baptist minister, an African–American, and a homosexual. He referred to himself as a Christian during his talk, so during the question-and-answer period someone asked him how he defined 'being a Christian.' Dr. Gomes said that a Christian is fundamentally one who hears Jesus Christ saying 'Follow me,' and follows Him.

This is anything but true. Jesus had a close companion that followed Him for three years, and went on to betray Him and dwell in Hell (Acts 1:25). Also, crowds followed after Jesus for a free meal, and He chastised them. They asked him,

What must we do to do the works God requires? [John
6:28 TNIV]

He answered,

The work of God is this: to believe in the one he has
sent. [John 6:29 TNIV]

Apostasy, then, is to follow Jesus without true and repentant belief.

Many that follow Jesus today are similarly unbelieving. This includes some that make their living preaching under the sign of the cross. C.S. Lewis, in his inimitable style, described the damned soul of one such Episcopal bishop. The bishop's self-imposed torment was to present papers at Hell's theological society. His ghost eagerly boasted of a new project:

I'm going to point out how people always forget that
Jesus was a comparatively young man when he died.
He would have outgrown some of his earlier views,
you know, if he'd lived. As he might have done, with
a little more tact and patience. I am going to ask my
audience to consider what his mature views would
have been. A profoundly interesting question. What a
different Christianity we might have had if only the
Founder had reached his full stature! I shall end up by
pointing out how this deepens the significance of the
Crucifixion. One feels for the first time what a disas-
ter it was: what a tragic waste ... so much promise cut
short.[703]

I have heard this very line-of-thought preached in Protestant churches for decades. It's not at all unusual. But Christ warned us,

> ... *everyone who rejects me and my teachings will be judged on the last day ... [John 12:48 CEV]*

And also,

> ... *he who rejects Me rejects Him who sent Me. [Luke 10:16 NKJV]*

Therefore, we must repent of the apostasy within our midst, or be eternally damned along with a gaggle of Protestant clergy.

~~~~~~~~~~~~~~~~~~~~~~~~

I met a female friend one evening at a restaurant, and she began the conversation by relating an incident at her church. She knew that I was interested in that sort of thing.

The church is of the Disciples of Christ denomination. The building has beautiful architecture; some of the most established and respectable families in that city are members.

My friend told me that the previous Sunday, her church had a guest preacher that she did not like. She said that the man was presumptuous and spoke matter-of-factly about Jesus Christ as though Jesus Christ was God Himself. She said that his homily was peppered with references to Jesus being raised from the dead, and being the only Savior of the world. This offended her sensibilities, as well as those of her fellow parishioners.

I said, "It is a Christian church, right? That is standard Christian dogma around the globe, regardless of the denominational affiliation, right? So where is the problem?"

She became indignant and said that not everyone believed that the man, Jesus, who lived two thousand years ago was the Son of God. She thought that the guest preacher had some nerve coming into their congregation and speaking in a way that would leave some of the members feeling excluded. According to her, it was wrong to convey the idea that one belief system was valid and another belief system was invalid. She said that everyone could agree that Jesus was a great teacher and that He had something to offer humanity, but not everyone could agree that He was God Almighty.

"I do not go to church to be preached to about the divinity of Jesus Christ," she concluded.

"Uh-huh," I said. "And why do you go to church?"

She said that she was disturbed by all the suffering in the world and that she went to church to hear a word of comfort. She was terribly burdened by wars, man's inhumanity to man, natural disasters, and all the untold human suffering from crime, strife, and disease.

She became a skein of emotionalism as she recited her burdens. She was a schoolteacher, and worried about her students that came from dysfunctional homes. She could sense which ones were in trouble; it bothered her terribly that she could not take them all into her home. She was quick to add that her burden extended beyond human beings, to include animals and all living things. "I am not a speciesist," she emphasized.

"Not a what?"

"A speciesist. That is someone that discriminates between the rights of human beings and animals on the basis of their differing species—just as a racist discriminates between the rights of individuals on the basis of their differing race."

"Interesting," I noted as I dipped my beef tenderloin in *au jus* sauce.

She said that she was a vegetarian because she was sensitive to the suffering of farm animals. She never killed insects in her home, but gently moved them onto a flat piece of paper and transferred them outside. She worried as she walked outside that she might inadvertently squash something, and when she gardened it bothered her to have to pull a weed. She said that she felt the resistance of the weed's roots, and its struggle for life against her hand made her soul ache. She began to cry, saying that even the vegetables that she ate had to die in order for her to remain alive.

It was at that moment that I realized why she was thin. "So you don't enjoy your food, then?" I asked.

She poked at her bean burrito with her fork, "Not really."

She was drinking a wine cooler as we spoke. I couldn't resist eulogizing the countless million fermentative yeast cells that had to give up the ghost in order to make her beverage.

She laughed through her tears, "Thanks a lot! Now I can't even enjoy alcohol!"

After she calmed down we spoke more about churches. I told her that it was wrong of her congregation to invite a preacher to speak and then get upset that he gave a Christian message. "If you and your congregants don't believe in the tenets of Christianity, you have no business having a cross up either outside or inside the church. It's false advertising," I pointed out.

She protested that she had never heard such a message before, and she did not see why it was necessary to say things that would not be universally inclusionary. Also, she said that crosses are nice symbols and they make her feel good.

I told her that her permanent pastor was at fault if a message about the true meaning of the cross was so inconceivable as to make the people feel awkward. If the people in that church really did not believe in Jesus Christ, they should switch the sign outside to make it a Unitarian church and not a Christian church.

I nearly convinced her, but there was something else that the guest preacher had said that morning that gnawed at her. The man had used his message about Christ being mankind's Savior as a launching point to speak of the value that God places upon every human life. He made the point that abortion is evil in God's eyes. My friend said that some of the blue-haired old ladies in the pews found this comment incendiary and started to murmur. Some made motions as though they would walk out if the guest preacher did not refrain from speaking against abortion. The preacher discerned that he was in trouble with the congregation, and changed the focus of his sermon away from the controversy before things got out of hand.

I said to my friend, "You just told me how you are having trouble dealing with reality because of every manner of animal, vegetable, and prokaryotic pain and suffering, and that you go to church because it all bothers you so much."

"Yes," she said, welling up again.

I proceeded, "You vote with the same hand with which you gently carry insects to safety. Does not more than one million abortions per year in the United States weigh upon your conscience at all?"

At this, her tears dried up; her face, which had been flush, lost its color. She coldly replied, "Of course that bothers me too, but I would never presume to second-guess a woman's right to choose what to do with her own body. And the church is no place to speak of personal choices."

I wrote something on a napkin and passed it over to her.

"What's this?" she asked.

"It's the name of an excellent psychiatrist. Don't lose it."

Mark 6:6 [KJV]
... he marvelled because of their unbelief.

80. "But I Still Don't Believe It"

Psychiatrists tell us that every person has his or her own set of truths that he or she will accept. These truths often do not have an absolute standard—they are unique to the individual.

I came to appreciate what this means during the highly-publicized trials of the Menendez brothers in California. The two miscreants had been accused of murdering their parents with shotguns while they dozed on a couch. The boys were poor shots, and had to leave the room of the ambush in order to get more ammunition and finish off their wounded mother. She was blasted ten times with birdshot.

They admitted doing this, but maintained that they were driven to madness by a lifetime of sexual abuse at the hands of their father. They said that they had to kill their mother in addition to their father in order to eliminate her as a witness. The juries in the first trial were deadlocked, and jury members refused to speak with each other by the time the judge declared a mistrial.

In a television interview afterward, a female juror for one of the brothers was questioned about why she had voted for a verdict of not guilty. She was fortyish, blonde, chunky, and had painted her fingernails glossy black. She said, "I just don't think he committed murder."

The interviewer pointed out that he admitted to blowing his mother's face off while she tried to crawl away from him. The female juror said, "Yeah, I know, but I still don't believe it. He has kind eyes. He looked straight at me during his testimony, and we made a bond. I feel so badly for him. He doesn't have a mother anymore, you know."[704]

There's no getting-across to a person like that. She did not want to hear objective truth. She just believed what she wanted to believe.

~~~~~~~~~~~~~~~~~~~~~~~

I have spent many pages explaining in excruciating detail the how-and-why of the heresies within the Nestorian, Oriental Orthodox, Eastern Orthodox, Über-Baptist, and Mainline Protestant churches. They have been laid out before you historically and theologically, as in a court case with overwhelming evidence. And yet, I know that many of my readers simply will not renounce their heretical church in favor of a Christ-centered and Bible-based church.

I know this because I have been explaining these facts to people for years, and they don't listen. For example, the deacon of an Armenian Apostolic (i.e., Oriental Orthodox, or Monophysite) church once asked me to tell him my ideas. After a brilliant five-minute dialectic, I concluded with, "This is the ultimate truth of the universe: God the Son became a human being—a man with the same nature as you and I. Jesus Christ resisted the temptation that a man has to sin, took our destiny upon Himself, and in this way saved believers from eternal separation from God."

He came back with, "But I don't care about these minute doctrines."

I replied, "Your indifference does not make it unimportant. We know from the Bible that God does care very much that you and your church accept that Jesus is the Son of God."

"We do," he said smugly.

"No, sorry," I said. "Accepting that Jesus is the Son of God means accepting that Jesus is fully God and fully man. I've already told you how your church does not accept that Jesus Christ had the separate nature of a man, or that He had the separate will of a man. Therefore your church is saying that He was not subject to sin as we are and He was not tempted as we are. A man that is not tempted to sin is not really a man. Therefore your church does not believe that Jesus was fully man."

He cringed and opened his palms in attempted reconciliation, "The difference between your position and mine is indecipherable ... why do you make so much of it? These are just semantic differences, after all. I mean, what does it even mean to say that Jesus had the nature of a man, or that Jesus was fully man?"

I gestured my head forward in simian challenge, "Are you fully man??"

He got angry and closed his hands.

I continued, "A man that does not have the nature of a man is either a homosexual or a hermaphrodite. Or I suppose he could be just a plain old pussy!"

He became flustered and was about to say something, but I cut him off, "Oh, what's the matter, am I offending you? If you are angry with me for questioning your manhood, then why are you not angry with your church for questioning the manhood of Jesus Christ? Why do you feign confusion over what it means for Christ to have the separate nature of a man? You know very well what it means when the challenge is put in personal terms. You are ready to defend yourself, yet you obfuscate when it comes to your Lord. Don't you think that God notices your loyalty to your religious traditions, and your disloyalty to Him? If you're not fooling me, then I assure you that you're not fooling God."

He shook his head in disgust. "Look, you are an impudent fool, alright? My church was worshiping Christ long before your church was ever dreamt up."

"All right," I said, "and the ancient Jews were worshipping in anticipation of Christ long before your church came into being. So what? Today's Jews stubbornly refuse to accept that Jesus had the separate nature of God; and, like them, today's Armenians stubbornly refuses to accept that Jesus had the separate nature of man. Both groups are handicapped by their culture to such an extent that they stumble over Jesus Christ, the Cornerstone. So what's the difference between Rabbinic Judaism and Monophysitic Christianity, really? Both your manner of worship and theirs have been rejected by God Almighty as mockeries of the truth—rejected through genocide, no less! Is it anything to boast about that they are headed to Hell because of unbelief, and you *might* get into Heaven because of belief in the Savior whose dual nature you do not accept?"

"I can't believe that you just compared us to Jews!" he exclaimed.

Providence had previously arranged for this fellow's only daughter to be dating a Jewish man, and he was at his wit's end about it. His face became contorted with hate, *"You think we are the same as stinking Jews?"*

I shook my head and chuckled.

"What is funny?!" he demanded.

"Christ said that the Jews had made the Word of God of no effect because of their traditions."

"Yes, that is exactly what they did," he confirmed.

"They used their privileged status before God as a means to cultural aggrandizement over their neighbors," I emphasized.

He again nodded.

"It is important that Christians not fall into the same pattern, lest we be open to the charge of hypocrisy," I continued.

He lost patience with me and shouted, "What is your point, sir?!"

"My point is: how can a people that are so stereotypically Jewish in their behaviors, and attitudes, and aspirations, be so wickedly Anti-Semitic?"

He gesticulated wildly, "Fool!" Then he brought the tips of his fingers and thumb together like the point of a scimitar, and wagged it in my face, "You cannot separate the Armenian people from their Christian heritage. Did you hear me, you fool?"

"It is not my intention to separate them from Christianity. To the contrary, I want them to realize the preciousness of their Holy Baptism."

"They already do realize it: they are proud to be Armenians."

"But having Christ in your heart has absolutely nothing to do with being Armenian," I protested.

"You are wrong! It has everything to do with it. The two are utterly inseparable."

"If they are inseparable, then why are some of your people communists, or mafiosos, or prostitutes? Why is church attendance abysmal among the middle class? Why does almost no one that does attend your Masses actually crack open a Bible and read it at home?"

He squinted his eyes at me, "Who are you? What is it you are really after?"

I raised my voice, "I am a sinner! I want all sinners to repent and to be Born Again!"

"Born Again?!" he spat. "What you really mean is that you want all people to become Protestants. Isn't it so? Admit it!"

"Well, sure, ideally," I smirked. "I would be overjoyed if Armenia went from being a ninety-five percent Apostolic country to a ninety-five percent Protestant country overnight. I would love it if the people renounced every ethnic caricature of God that their priests have ever taught them. But that is certainly not necessary for salvation—as long as they hear the Gospel message and accept the dual-natured Christ into their hearts, they will be saved. And surely some of those that are saved will choose to become Protestant, and some will choose to become Roman Catholic, and some will choose to remain Armenian Apostolic. So what's wrong with that?"

"Hah! There it is: you want to proselytize innocent Armenians—you want to brainwash them into renouncing the nation's religious heritage."

"No one is brainwashing anyone here. Sharing your faith through free speech, and assembling freely within a Christ-centered and Bible-based church, is not brainwashing—it's worshipful."

"If you insist on doing that, you'll probably get away with it," he conceded resentfully. "But one cannot swear-off the authority of the Mother Church without becoming a deserter to the race. Every Armenian must acknowledge his or her indebtedness to the Holy Apostolic Church for maintaining the national identity throughout centuries of Turkish oppression."

"I acknowledge no indebtedness except to the Triune God," I professed.

"Remember this, you ungrateful child: if it were not for the faithfulness of the Holy See to that Triune God, you and your ancestors would have been forcibly converted to Islam a long time ago."

"Armenian is such a rich, expressive, and mellifluous language," I said dryly. "You must teach me how to say, 'Kiss my ass,' in your native dialect."

"That is just the type of comment that I would expect from a half-breed like yourself!" he shot back. "Whether you like it or not, His Holiness, the Catholicos, is the Supreme Patriarch of *all Armenians*."

I was filled with passion and jealousy for the memory of my Armenian grandfather, who was a powerful Evangelist in the Middle East. I had learned the Christian faith as a boy on his knee, and when he lay dying he had placed his hands on my head and prayed for me to receive the Holy Spirit. I gritted my teeth, "Well, the Catholicos sure as hell isn't the Supreme Patriarch of me! In fact, I would walk ten kilometers out of my way in order to avoid crossing paths with that filthy whoremonger! My religious leader is whomever I choose to honor in that role—it is wholly dependent upon the man's convictions and his personal conduct, not upon what nation's blood happens to run through my veins."

"Then you sure as hell are not a true Armenian. You're a religious fanatic."

"Listen to yourself!" I urged him. "You know that I love the people, the flag, the independence, the language, the food, and the arts. You know that I want every square meter of land that the murderous Turks stole to be returned to the nation. And yet you say that I am not a member of the nation because my conscience does not allow me to ever attend a Monophysitic Mass, nor to observe Armenian Christmas on the sixth day of January, nor to show the least deference to the so-called Mother Church. Who is the fanatic here?"

He gasped at my rejection of the legitimacy of Armenian Christmas as though I had rejected the legitimacy of the Baby Jesus Himself. "You are the fanatic," he reiterated. "There's nothing Armenian about you except for your face."

"Again, this is exactly the position of the Jews," I was quick to point out. "I once heard Elie Wiesel—who has been called the most important Jew in the world—say that one cannot join a Christian church and still remain a loyal Jew. He said that belief in Jesus as the God-man precludes membership in the Jewish race."

"You idiot!" he shouted. "I told you that we are already a Christian people by virtue of our Christian culture!"

"Oh, really?! Most Armenians that I know don't give two shits about accepting Jesus as their Savior, and cultivating a deep interpersonal relationship with Him as Lord. And I could say the same thing for every other 'Christian' ethnic group in the world, like the Assyrians, or the Greeks, or the French, or the English. So what's the spiritual benefit of a national church, anyway?—especially one that is fundamentally flawed about who Jesus is? Are you telling me that God is going to take His hat off when your people approach the Judgment Seat based upon the piety of their nationality? If God isn't going to do that for Jesus' very own Jewish relatives, I don't think that He can be expected to do it for the Armenians."

He retreated to clichés, "Two of Christ's twelve Apostles were sent to our country! We have been chosen by God to be the first Christian nation! God Himself rested Noah's Ark upon our holy mountain! You are arguing about something that does not matter! Your message will never succeed!"

"My message is not my message—it is the very Gospel of Jesus Christ—and it has already succeeded: Roman Catholics and Protestants outnumber any other religion on the face of the earth. And although none of us are very, very, good Christians, we at least accept that within the undivided Person of Jesus of Nazareth existed the separate nature of God and the separate nature of man. We profess that He was tempted *exactly as a man is tempted*, and yet was without sin *exactly as God is without sin*. We accept this without any of the damned caveats and traditions of your *unorthodox* church. This Gospel is being spread even as I speak, and every person that has been chosen to believe in it will believe in it before the God-man returns from the sky in glory and reanimates the dusty remains of millions of saints with incorruptible skin, and incorruptible muscle, and incorruptible sinew."

I glanced at my watch, and then looked upward, shading my eyes, "I don't see Him yet, but we're expecting Him any moment now."

His fury was assuaged by my last line. "Oh my God, what a fruitcake!" he exclaimed with a laugh. "You really believe that? You really believe that dead people are going to sprout out of the ground one fine day like seedlings?!"

"I don't see why that should surprise you," I said. "We know from Scripture that God formed Adam from the dust of the earth—we know from Scripture that this took place fewer than six thousand years ago on our calendar."

He wagged his head.

"Don't you believe that all human beings are descended from Adam and Eve who were created all-at-once in the eternal springtime of the Garden of Eden?" I asked with mock innocence.

"No," he said with annoyance for even being asked.

"Then I guess you really don't believe that some day soon corpses are going to awake and float upward like Christ did, or that Heaven is going to be populated by resurrected Negroes and Norwegians."

"You can't be serious."

"I am! We shall all gain imperishable physical bodies like Jesus did on Easter morning! The Scriptures say that a multitude of all nations, tribes, peoples, and tongues will praise the throne of Christ. They won't be ghosts—they will be incorruptible flesh and blood that can taste, and smell, and shake hands, and hug tightly. All the Jewish Christians will be there, too, of course. I can hardly wait to meet the Apostle Paul. I've always wanted to sit down with him and talk about the things that he wrote in the Bible."

"You're hopeless. A person's culture is a gift from God. It is something real—right here and right now. It's the fundamental building block of human civilization. It's more important than money, and more personally-enriching than family. I'm expending my life to preserve the Mother Church's ancient and glorious manner of worship from being forgotten from the face of the earth, and you're willing to renounce everything for some fantasy-world tea party with the Apostle Paul—who is dead."

"Brother Paul is not dead! He is alive with Christ at this moment. He is more alive than you and I are right now. And that tea party with the saints is more-or-less what Christ promised. He promised that a time is coming when dead, buried, bodies will hear His voice and rise up from the earth—just like Lazarus did. Lazarus came forth from his burial plot at the command of Jesus and enjoyed high tea with his sisters."

He frowned, "Yeah, a long time ago."

"So?"

"It may have happened with Lazarus, but no one has risen from the dead for two thousand years since then—"

"Except for Christ Himself," I interjected. "He rose from the dead a few months after the raising of Lazarus."

"Yes, yes, yes!" said the Monophysite deacon, "Of course Christ was raised too, but no one else has risen from the dead for two thousand years since then. Yet you're carrying on as though it could happen on a worldwide scale tomorrow."

"But it could happen on a worldwide scale tomorrow! Jesus said, 'Behold, I am coming soon!' That means His return is imminent. Don't you believe the words of Jesus Christ?"

"It's you that I don't believe. Christ never promised to come back to earth at any particular time, and He doesn't want us to look forward to the end of the world as though it were something good. He wants us to be faithful to our forefathers and to honor their traditions—just like He did. He wants us to work hard, and have some damned ambition, and build something for mankind while we are in this world—just like He did."

"Well, I believe in working hard, and being a good citizen, and providing a good home for my family, but as far as honoring religious traditions and building something for mankind—is it okay with you if I live as though Christ really is going to return within my lifetime?"

"Go ahead!" he said. "But don't blame me when you end up a bitter old man with nothing but the Bible in your hands and dreams of a flying Jesus in your head!"

I knew at that moment that his daughter would end up marrying the Jewish man.

She did, in fact, marry him, and the deacon's grandchildren were raised as Reformed Jews. He disowned them all, and quickly grew very old and very bitter; and the stress caused him to develop an early case of dementia.

It was like watching a Shakespearean tragedy unfold on stage—there was nothing that could be done for him.

~~~~~~~~~~~~~~~~~~~~~~~

I have endured essentially the same vitriol from Nestorians, Eastern Orthodox, Über-Baptists, and Mainline Protestants of the Seven Sisters denominations. I will spare you a recitation of every conversation. But allow me to tell you about the United Methodist minister that once cornered me and asked why I did not respond to his repeated invitations to attend his church.

"I've been trying to be polite," I said, "but if you must know it is because the United Methodists do not believe that Jesus Christ has a penis."

"What?! That's preposterous!" exclaimed the Methodist.

"But I read it in the newspaper a few months ago."

"What did you read?"

"An ordained United Methodist minister wrote an editorial in which he referred to God as 'He/She.' Since Methodists *sometimes* maintain that Jesus is God, and since Methodists *sometimes* maintain that God may be a 'She,' then you are obviously leaving it open to debate whether Jesus was a man with a penis or a woman with a vagina."

"You're not as funny or as clever as you think you are," he replied stone-faced.

"Interesting," I responded. "You are put-off by my drawing the logical inference, but you haven't asked for the name of the clergyman/editorialist so that you can demand that your bishop convene an ecclesiastical court and have him defrocked."

"I already know who it is. I read his column all the time."

"Doesn't it bother you?"

"What is there to be bothered about?"

"He is mocking God Almighty! *He is calling Him a woman!*" I said.

"I don't think being a woman is a great insult or anything shameful. God loves both men and women. He is big enough to have a place in His heart for everyone."

"Of course God is all-loving. And of course it's nothing to be ashamed of to be a woman—*provided that you are a woman to begin with*. But if you are a man, then it is quite insulting to be called a woman, and vice-versa."

"But the Scriptures state that God is Spirit. So why can't that Spirit be referred to as 'She' in addition to a 'He'?" he postulated.

"Because the same Scriptures state that that Spirit became a human being—a male human being—for our sake. That is the whole point of the Bible: the Gospel message is that God, acting in love, became a man with a nature like yours and mine. Don't you agree?"

"To be perfectly honest, I've never given it a moment's thought," he said cavalierly. "It's not important."

"God's mechanism for salvation is not important?! The soul of your colleague and brother is not important?!"

"Oh, he's a good chap, and in good standing with God, I'd wager. What you read in the newspaper was just Charlie being Charlie. He likes to tweak people like you."

"Tweak?"

"Yes, and obviously his irreverence has worked. You let him get to you to such an extent that you made the absurd assertion that the United Methodists do not believe that Jesus has a penis."

"Is my assertion absurd?"

"Yes! I'm telling you that I and everyone in my United Methodist congregation believe that Jesus of Nazareth was a man and not a woman."

"But you and everyone in your congregation do not believe that it is important to disassociate yourself from the person that openly questions the Incarnation of God as a man. You don't care that you have a devil as your spiritual kinsmen—speaking lies about God in your name—under your denominational banner."

"I'd hardly call him a devil. There are lots of colorful ministers among the United Methodists—it's our diversity that is our strength, after all."

"I thought Christ's victory over death on Mount Calvary is the strength of Christians."

"Oh, yes, that too. Of course that's a part of it," he muttered. "But it can only be good to have a variety of voices emanating from within our churches so that no one faction gains hegemony."

"Yes, it would be a terrible pity if the Christian Church was to actually be run by confessing Christians. Tell me the truth: Don't you have any indignation about the editorial? What is your real opinion of it?"

"I probably would have written it in a less provocative manner," he conceded. "But whether I like it or I don't like it, there is no sense in getting exercised. We can't police what everybody thinks."

"You can't police what everybody thinks, and I'm not suggesting that you do. But you can police what your ministers write and preach and teach. Your denomination is the licensing board for clergy, after all."

"But it's not part of our tradition to look into such trivial matters after ordination."

"Hey!" I raised my index finger in mock inspiration. "I've got a brilliant idea! Why don't you and your congregation vote to leave your denomination in favor of one that *does have a tradition* that only professing Christians can remain as communicant members and clergymen?"

"And where would we go, pray tell?"

"How about to the Free Methodists?"

"Those kooks?!" he scowled. "Forget it. They're conservatives."

"Conservatives are bad? I thought you just said that you liked diversity."

"I do, but I don't like hate. Those people only see things their own way. They're completely against abortion except when the mother's life is in danger."

"Oh, I see! Now we're getting to the marrow of the bone! Accepting pro-abortion elements is diverse, but faithfully advocating for the life of the unborn is hateful. And tolerating people that say that God is a 'He/She' is diverse, but insisting that God became a man to save us is hateful."

For the first time in this exchange, he gave up his chipper demeanor and became irritated. "Look, Christ taught against hypocrisy, and you and I both know that there are Free Methodists whose lives are full of things that you'd find repugnant—regardless of whatever is their official policy."

"Well, I can't speak for the Free Methodists, but let me tell you, my whole life is full of things that I find repugnant!" I admitted with a laugh.

"How, then, can you dare to find fault with poor Charlie?"

"Because I am penitent and confessing before the cross of Christ, and he is impenitent and blaspheming before the cross of Christ. The Bible says that if we confess our sins, God is faithful and just and will cleanse us from all unrighteousness. Coming to terms with your personal sin is not hypocritical, its cleansing."

"Fascinating!" he said sarcastically. "But how can you be sure that your fellow parishioners and priests are also truly penitent and confessing?"

"I can't," I admitted. "We open every worship service with confession and absolution, but only God knows their hearts."

"Now this is a fine thing! Here you are condemning millions of United Methodists for having Charlie within our fold, and yet you admit that the person worshipping right next to you in your own church might be a fan of his blasphemous editorials!"

"It's possible that some of them also think that God should be referred to with the pronoun, 'She.' Remember, there was an unbeliever even among Christ's twelve. But I'll tell you that if there is anyone among us that questions the Incarnation of God the Son through the virgin Mary they'd better keep their mouth shut about it. We would never tolerate open heretics at our Communion table. They would have to repent first, and accept the inerrancy of the Bible."

"And what would you have us do to old Charlie to bring him to his knees before the cross of Christ? Should we burn him at the stake for blasphemy, or simply lock him into a dungeon for impenitence?"

"No. Unbelief is not a civil crime—nor is mocking God—nor should they be."

"What then?"

"How about showing some loyalty toward God and toward your friend by bringing him into pastoral counseling and guiding him to repentance? How about something more than just shrugging your shoulders and turning the page of the newspaper?"

"Charlie is an old man with a small, progressively-minded, congregation," he explained. "There's no sense in upsetting the applecart and possibly causing a schism. Our bishop is a good man, and is not the type to impose upon his pastors' ministries."

"Offering to teach someone the truth about God is not an imposition," I pointed out.

"And if Charlie refuses such an overture?" he asked.

"Then revoke his ordination and membership, and make it publicly known that he is no longer a United Methodist."

"Ah, splendid—cast him out like trash. And then?"

"Then nothing. Pray for him and leave him alone."

He clasped his hands together and said again in sarcasm, "Sounds ideal! I assume your church has no problems then?"

"We have plenty of problems—we have problems up to our gills—but that is irrelevant. It is the presence of the Word of God in our hearts, and not an absence of sin in our lives, that sanctifies us unto God."

"What does *that* mean?"

"It means that whatever my church's problems are, they are not the result of an antichrist heresy within us, as is plainly the case within the United Methodist Church."

"Antichrist?! Now that's just too much!" He caught himself, regained his composure, and cloyingly returned to his purpose in speaking with me, "I don't think you meant that, friend. Why don't you come and join us for Sunday morning worship? Then you'll see that we are a place full of God's love for all points of view. You're a passionate person. I'd like to see you involved at some level in our house of God. Pray about it, and I'm sure that God will give you a sign to make you reconsider the matter."

I never did pray about it, but the sign came anyway. The Bible says,

> *Because you have rejected knowledge, I also will reject you from being a priest for Me. [Hosea 4:6 NKJV]*

Toward the end of that year this fellow sought out and was offered a prestigious position at the liberal World Council of Churches. He was eager to be rid of his troublesome congregation. But before he relocated and commenced his new job, he had a debilitating heart attack and lost the ability to move freely and to speak above a whisper.

After release from the hospital, he attempted to regain his pastorship despite being permanently disabled. But he was forced into retirement shy of his fiftieth birthday by his bishop—the same bishop that had taken no action against Reverend Charlie.

I shuddered with fear when I heard the news. "This God of ours ..." I said to myself, "... truly He is great, and terrible, and loving beyond measure."

~~~~~~~~~~~~~~~~~~~~~~

The United Methodist minister was correct about one thing: I am a passionate person. Is it wrong for me to have such passion about christological doctrine? I will not fault myself for speaking the truth as long as my motivation is love of God and love of neighbor.

Be mindful of what the Apostle Paul advised his protégés, Titus and Timothy:

> *My son Timothy, I give you these teachings ... Some have not accepted these teachings. By doing that, they have destroyed their faith ... I have handed them over to Satan. That will teach them not to speak evil things against God. [1 Timothy 1:18–20 NIrV]*

> *You must teach what is in accord with sound doctrine. [Titus 2:1 NIV]*

> *Watch your life and doctrine closely. Persevere in them, because if you do, you will save both yourself and your hearers. [1 Timothy 4:16 TNIV]*

> *Warn troublemakers once or twice. Then don't have anything else to do with them. You know that their minds are twisted, and their own sins show how guilty they are. [Titus 3:10–11 CEV]*

People like the Armenian Apostolic deacon and the United Methodist minister that I have described above do not have close personal relationships with the Lord Jesus because they do not accept who He is, in one regard or another. They complain bitterly about the politics within their churches and the disunity among their people. They are continually in inner turmoil and twisted into knots about their churches' God-ordained status as the losers within Christendom. But they will not flee their heretical christological doctrines and cling to the God-man, Jesus Christ.

They will not. They will not. Come what may, they will not.

> *As a dog returneth to his vomit, so a fool returneth to his folly. [Proverbs 26:11 KJV]*

If you are like them, why don't you just admit that you don't give a rat's ass about how God wants you to believe in Him, or where God wants you to worship Him? There is nothing virtuous about your position. It does not stem from scriptural conviction, logic, or intellectual consistency, but from pride and obstinacy and economic convenience. God has allowed you to be put to the test to see how generous you are toward Him when you thought that He was not looking, and you have been miserly and pharisaical in your response.

*For everyone looks out for his own interests, not those
of Jesus Christ. [Philippians 2:21 NIV]*

You want to stay in your heretical church because you want to stay in your heretical church. The truth about Christ is a peripheral consideration in your religious jurisprudence.

You are like an imbecilic blonde with black fingernail polish. You have your own set of truths, and there is no getting-across to a person like you.

Psalm 141:2 [NKJV]
Let my prayer be set before You as incense, the lifting up of my hands as the evening sacrifice.

81. Good Churches

To those of you who think I am being absurdly partisan, and that I am slowly directing you to my own particular church, I say, "Nonsense." There are plenty of Christ-centered and Bible-based churches from which to choose. I will now give recommendations of denominations that a true Christian could attend all across the United States (listed in alphabetical order):

> American Association of Lutheran Churches
> American Baptist Association
> Anglican Catholic Church
> Anglican Church in America
> Anglican Mission in America
> Anglican Province of America
> Anglican Province of Christ the King
> Baptist General Conference
> Christian Reformed Church in North America
> Church of God in Christ
> Church of the Nazarene
> Churches of Christ
> Christian and Missionary Alliance
> Conservative Baptist Association of America
> Conservative Congregational Christian Conference
> Evangelical Covenant Church
> Evangelical Free Church of America
> Evangelical Lutheran Synod

Evangelical Presbyterian Church
Free Methodist Church
General Association of Regular Baptist Churches[xli]
Lutheran Church–Missouri Synod
Orthodox Presbyterian Church
Presbyterian Church in America
Reformed Episcopal Church
Southern Baptist Convention
Southern Episcopal Church
Southern Methodist Church
United Reformed Churches in North America
Wesleyan Church
Wisconsin Evangelical Lutheran Synod
World Assemblies of God Fellowship

There are also thousands of non-denominational churches that have sound, biblical, doctrine and preaching. Of course, the term 'non-denominational' is a crock, for the same reason that the term 'non-creedal' is a crock—they each have very distinct teachings and practices (Section 74). Most often, non-denominational churches are essentially undercover Baptists. But just as often they are soundly biblical on the essentials.

~~~~~~~~~~~~~~~~~~~~~~~~

I cannot in good conscience recommend any Roman Catholic parish because of the many errors that they codified into their faith during the Council of Trent. It was the Roman Catholic answer to the Protestant Reformation (the so-called Counter Reformation), and it is the root cause of the desperate poverty in so many Catholic nations.

> *There should be no poor among you … if you are care-*
> *ful to obey all the commands of the Lord your God that*
> *I am giving you today. [Deuteronomy 15:4–5 NLT]*

The deliberations of the Council of Trent lasted from AD 1545 to AD 1563 due to outbreaks of the plague and war.[705] They did not understand these to be signs of God's displeasure with them. Rather, during the council's sixth and final session, they passed the passed the following, vile, decree:

---

xli   One must be careful among the various Anabaptist churches on this list. Some of their pastors are quite good preachers, but some teach the heresy that the unbelieving Jews are the Chosen People in whom God's favor rests.

If anyone says that men are made righteous solely through the imputation of the righteousness of Christ or solely through the forgiveness of sin, to the exclusion of the grace and love which by the Holy Spirit is poured out in their hearts and is inherent in them; or that the grace by which we are made righteous is nothing else than the favor of God,—let him be accused. **If anyone says that the faith which makes men righteous is nothing else than trust in the divine mercy, which remits sin for Christ's sake, or that it is only this trust that makes us righteous,—let him be accursed** ... *If anyone says that a justified person does not, by reason of the good works which are done by him through the grace of God and the merit of Jesus Christ, whose living member he is, truly merit an increase of grace, eternal life, and the actual obtainment of eternal life, provided he dies in grace,—let him be accursed.*[706]

The Council of Trent also added the apocryphal deuterocanonical books into the Roman Catholic Old Testament canon. To their additional shame, the Vatican continued to grant a specific number of days' indulgence to relieve suffering in Purgatory until the AD 1960's.[707] You can still find these indulgences posted on the walls of devout Catholic households. And, to this day, many of their priests sell masses for the dead and do not encourage their flock to read the Bible at home.

Clearly, it is possible for a church to accept the three Ecumenical Creeds and still be against the teachings of Holy Scripture.

I will, nevertheless, say that the Roman Catholic Church is at least Chalcedonian, Filioquean, and now holds its masses in the language of the worshippers. They have become less works-oriented in recent decades (e.g., giving up the ridiculous rule about not eating meat on Friday), and they are biblical on most of the moral social causes. I have a lot more in common with Roman Catholicism than I do with Mainline Protestantism, which I utterly detest and renounce for not holding resolutely to the doctrines of the Trinity, the Incarnation, and the Easter Resurrection.

Romans 7:5 [NKJV]
For when we were in the flesh, the sinful passions which were aroused by the law were at work in our members to bear fruit to death.

82. The Source of Slaughter

The most striking scene for me in *War and Peace* was when Napoleon first decided to invade Russia. Every place he rode, starry-eyed soldiers broke rank to catch a glimpse of the little corporal, and shouted, "Vive l'Empereur!" His already large army swelled with Polish volunteers, ecstatic over the commencement of the long-expected campaign.

Napoleon reached the banks of the Viliya River in modern-day Belarus, dismounted, and examined a map. He gave an order that a suitable place be found for his army to ford the river.

> *The colonel of the Polish Uhlans,*[xlii] *a handsome old man, flushed and, fumbling in his speech from excitement, asked the aide-de-camp whether he would be permitted to swim the river with his Uhlans instead of seeking a ford. In evident fear of refusal, like a boy asking for permission to get on a horse, he begged to be allowed to swim across the river before the Emperor's eyes. The aide-de-camp replied that probably the Emperor would not be displeased at this excess of zeal.*
>
> *As soon as the aide-de-camp had said this, the old mustached officer, with happy face and sparkling eyes, raised his saber, shouted "Vivat!" and, commanding the Uhlans to follow him, spurred his horse and galloped into the river. He gave an angry thrust to his horse, which had grown restive under him, and plunged into the water, heading for the deepest part where the current was swift. Hundreds of Uhlans galloped in after him. It was cold and uncanny in the rapid current in the middle of the stream, and the Uhlans caught hold of one another as they fell off their horses. Some of the horses were drowned and some of the men; the others tried to swim on, some in the saddle and some clinging to their horses' manes.*

---

xlii   Polish light cavalry. The word literally means, 'brave warrior.'

They tried to make their way forward to the opposite bank and, though there was a ford one third of a mile away, were proud that they were swimming and drowning in this river under the eyes of the man who sat on the log and was not even looking at what they were doing. When the aide-de-camp, having returned and choosing an opportune moment, ventured to draw the Emperor's attention to the devotion of the Poles to his person, the little man in the gray overcoat got up and, having summoned Berthier, began pacing up and down the bank with him, giving him instructions and occasionally glancing disapprovingly at the drowning Uhlans who distracted his attention.

For him it was no new conviction that his presence in any part of the world, from Africa to the steppes of Muscovy alike, was enough to dumfound people and impel them to insane self-oblivion. He called for his horse and rode to his quarters.

Some forty Uhlans were drowned in the river, though boats were sent to their assistance. The majority struggled back to the bank from which they had started. The colonel and some of his men got across and with difficulty clambered out on the further bank. And as soon as they had got out, in their soaked and streaming clothes, they shouted "Vivat!" and looked ecstatically at the spot where Napoleon had been but where he no longer was and at that moment considered themselves happy.[708]

That evening, as an afterthought, Napoleon ordered that the colonel that had needlessly plunged his men into the river be enrolled in the Legion of Honor.

I repeat this piece of the novel to make the point that most people look to God the way that the Uhlans looked to Napoleon: they try to please Him in breathless hope of an approving glance. The Shi'as' enraptured devotion toward Ali is analogous to this. And just today, as I am writing this, three hundred and fifty Sunnis have been trampled to death in a stampede at the Jamarat Bridge in Mecca.[709] This happens every few years during the Hajj, or annual pilgrimage of Muslims to Mecca. During one of the obligatory rituals the pilgrims gather to throw a set number of pebbles at a symbol of the devil.

Everyone wants to make sure that their pebbles hit the symbol, and they tend to trip and get trampled. If something as horrendous as that happened during a Christian rite, the event would be cancelled indefinitely. We would consider the waste of human life to be sacrilegious. Yet Muslims continue to save money their entire lives to make a pilgrimage to the dustbowl of death. They think that pleasing God by visiting Mecca (along with observing the other five pillars of Islam) will get them into paradise. It will not.

God is not at all comparable to the dictator, Napoleon. He is not a warmonger. He is not cold, calculating, and ruthless. He does not lead enormous masses of people into senseless death just to inflate His ego. He is not unconcerned when they throw away their lives. And one more thing: He does not enroll people into the Heavenly Legion of Honor when they 'please' Him with futile efforts at piety and earnestness. He gives us eternal life for trusting Him, not pleasing Him.

It is, in fact, impossible for us to please God by our own works. Think about it for a moment: Does He need our money? Our time? Does He need for us to beat our heads until we faint because we were not alive to defend Ali's son during the Battle of Karbala? Does He need us to march around a symbol of the devil in Mecca and throw pebbles at it? These are silly questions. He is God. He is not in need. He only desires for us to accept the free gift of communion with Him through Christ.

Consider this verse:

> ... *all our righteous acts are like filthy rags; [Isaiah 64:6 TNIV]*

The Hebrew word for 'filthy rags' here means 'used menstrual cloth.' God regards our best efforts the way that we regard soiled feminine napkins—disgusting.

Stop trying to please Him, and just trust Him. Entrust your soul to Christ today.

~~~~~~~~~~~~~~~~~~~~~~~

One of the reasons that Muslim fundamentalists are so mean is that they never get a good night's sleep. Their last prayer of the day is called the Isha'a prayer. It is to be said as close as possible to the middle of the night. Their first prayer of the day is called the Fajr prayer. It is to be said at sunrise,[710] and the muezzin's morning call from the minaret includes the line,

> *Prayer is better than sleep.*[711]

These two prayers can be scheduled fewer than six hours apart. Anyone that has spent a night in a Muslim country can testify to being jolted awake by a whining noise over loudspeakers reminding you to stop sleeping and pray while it is still dark outside.

I, personally, need nine hours of uninterrupted sleep per night, or I become irritable and unpredictable. When I was younger, I required ten hours. If I went for any length of time on six hours of sleep, I'd become a maniac.

Can you imagine reciting the same set of ritualized Arabic prayers five time per day, every single day, with no respite for your entire life (especially if you don't even speak Arabic)?

It's enough to drive a man to kill.

~~~~~~~~~~~~~~~~~~~~~~~

Islam was the devil's six-hundred-and-sixty-six-year-planned answer to Christianity. The Qur'an was written and completed about six hundred and sixty-six years after the Bible was completed in AD 96. There are no fragments of the Qur'an that date from before AD 750 because none ever existed.[712] The final copy was canonized over one hundred and fifty years after the year of Muhammad's death.

To a Muslim, the suggestion that the text of the Qur'an is anything but the exact words that were revealed by God is blasphemy. It is the equivalent of suggesting to a Christian that Jesus did not rise from the dead on Easter morning. Therefore, Islamic apologists maintain,

> *The Qur'an is a record of the exact words revealed by God through the Angel Gabriel to the Prophet Muhammad (peace be upon him). It was memorized by Muhammad (peace be upon him) and then dictated to his companions, and written down by scribes, who cross-checked it during his lifetime. Not one word of its 114 chapters, Suras, has been changed over the centuries, so that the Qur'an is in every detail the unique and miraculous text which was revealed to Muhammad (peace be upon him) fourteen centuries ago.*[713]

Bunk! The Qur'an is, in fact, a pathetic piece of literature. It was hastily written and re-written, with ample plagiarism from the Bible and the apocrypha. It is not ordered in any logical manner, but by the length of the chapter (longer chapters first). It repeats the stories of Adam, Noah, Abraham, and Moses, over and over again, and contradicts itself in doing so.[714] There are anachronisms in the stories, such as the assertion that the ancient Egyptians practiced crucifixion.[715] The word 'Muhammad' is used only four times in the text. Where it is mentioned, it is not associated with the word 'Prophet,' nor with a family or city of origin, so that it is not clear if 'Muhammad' is a title or a proper name.[716] What's more, the Qur'an does not enumerate the five pillars of Islam, which are the tenets of the Islamic faith. It contains two dozen grammatical errors, including a few instances of using the wrong case for a letter.[717] Often times God is referred to in the first person plural, and the third person singular, in the same sentence.[718]

> *The Koran claims for itself that it is 'mubeen,' or 'clear.' But if you look at it, you will notice that every fifth sentence or so simply doesn't make sense. Many Muslims—and Orientialists—will tell you otherwise, of course, but the fact is that a fifth of the Koranic text is just incomprehensible. This is what has caused the traditional anxiety regarding translation. If the Koran ... can't even be understood in Arabic—then it's not translatable. People fear that.[719]*

Muhammad himself was illiterate, and most of his companions were killed in early warfare or assassinated during Muawiyah's reign. The writing of the Qur'an was not even begun until one hundred and twenty years after the death of Muhammad.[720] It would be as if nothing was written down about Vladimir Lenin until the year AD 2044. How much of it would reflect his true views and history? What we are left with in the Qur'an is simply the legacy of Muhammad, which is monotheistic,[721] but emphatically Anti-Trinitarian, Anti-Incarnation, and Anti-Easter-Resurrection.

The earliest extant manuscripts of the Qur'an are rough drafts that have small but significant variances with the canonized version.[722] In order to propagate the myth that the final version of the Qur'an is an exact representation of the copy that resides in heaven, the Caliph ordered all rough drafts destroyed. But they missed a few: in AD 1972 some rough drafts of the Qur'an were found in the loft of the ancient Sana'a Mosque in Yemen.[723] The dating of these parchments puts a lie to the belief that the Qur'an was written all at once by those that personally knew Muhammad. It proves that it was an edited work—demolishing Islam's foundational claim.

The Bible, in contrast, was 1,500 years in-the-making. Most of its books were written contemporaneously with the historical events they record. It is ordered either chronologically or by literary genre. Each book compliments the others, and points to Christ and His gift of eternal life. The Bible is the first book ever published, and the best-selling book of all time.

~~~~~~~~~~~~~~~~~~~~~~~

The message of Christianity is that people are hopelessly lost in sin and can not help themselves out of that situation. God is sinless and good. He is willing to go out of His way to rescue us from certain death. He therefore became a man—it was the only way to save us. He did this out of love; He didn't owe it to us. Eternal life is obtained simply by trusting in His saving work. Nothing more is required than to believe that God became a man in Jesus Christ. This is the foundation for a deeply intimate relationship with Him.

> *Jesus replied, "If anyone loves me, he will obey my teaching. My Father will love him, and we will come to him and make our home with him ..." [John 14:23 NIV]*

The Islamic Termagant is nothing like the personal God of the Bible.

> *Allah, by contrast, is cold, haughty, unpredictable, unknowable, capricious, distant, and so purely transcendent that no "relationship" is possible. He reveals only his will, not himself. Allah is "everywhere," and therefore nowhere relevant to us. He remains uninterested in making our acquaintance, let alone in being near to us because of love. We still are utterly unable to grasp his purposes, and all we can do is what we have to do—to obey his commands.*[724]

Islam is a legalistic faith, requiring perfunctory service and obligation. Islamists agree that people are lost in sin, but they think that a person can rectify that situation for himself by the faithful exertion of effort (like getting up before the sun rises every morning to bow on a rug). This is in marked contrast to true Christians, whose good works are done without compunction, out of thankfulness for Christ's atoning work.

The retired American boxer, Muhammad Ali, converted to Islam in AD 1965 and rejected his birth name of Cassius Marcellus Clay, Jr. Consider his response when he was asked what his Islamic faith meant to him:

> *[It] means [a] ticket to heaven. One day we're all going to die, and God's going to judge us, [our] good and bad deeds. [If the] bad outweighs the good, you go to hell; if the good outweighs the bad, you go to*

heaven. [I'm] thinking about the judgment day and how you treat people wherever you go. Help somebody through charity, because when you do, it's been recorded.

I go to parties, [see] good-looking girls. [I] take a box of matches with me. [I] see a girl I want to flirt with, which is a sin, so I [light] my matches, [touch it to my fingers], oooh, hell hurts worse than this. Buy a box of matches and carry them with you. Put [one] on your finger and see how long you can hold it. Just imagine that's going to be hell. Hell's hotter, and [will last] for eternity.[725]

Muhammad Ali provided a fair summary of Muslim doctrine here: it is a human-works-oriented salvation achieved by closely observing the five pillars of Islam. But salvation through good works is by no means a thought that originated with Islam. All non-Christian religions are based upon a merit system. In ancient Egyptians tomb scenes, for example, the god of the netherworld would weigh human hearts on a scale. If the heart was pure, it would be lighter than a single feather and go onto heaven. If not, it would be devoured by a lion in an act of divine retribution.

The one thing that Muhammad Ali got wrong is that close adherence to Islamic legalism does not earn one a guaranteed "ticket to heaven." Even the best Muslim never knows where he stands in his good works until the Judgment Day. In fact, fundamentalist Muslims believe that the only way that you can be sure to get to paradise is by dying in the struggle to forcibly convert others to Islam. This is called 'jihad.' Murderous martyrdom has been their only sure ticket into their supposed heaven for fourteen hundred years, and it is the impetus for the suicide attacks that we witness today.

Revelation 15:2 [CEV]
Then I saw something that looked like a glass sea mixed with fire, and people were standing on it. They were the ones who had defeated the beast and the idol and the number that tells the name of the beast.

83. The Devil's Obsession

I have made several references in this text to an interval of six hundred and sixty-six years. I've found that this interval keeps coming up when Church history is juxtaposed against world history.

Why?

Because the devil is unoriginal and obsessive.

God made the world and everything in it in one week in the year 3976 BC.[726] Man was created on the sixth day of that week (Genesis 1:26–31). Thus, six is the number associated in Scripture with mankind. The devil found God's invention of the human species most objectionable. In 3975 BC[727] the devil took the form of a snake and seduced Eve to enter into sin (Genesis 3:1–7). Eve, in turn, enticed her husband to join her in sin.

> *... it was not Adam who was deceived by Satan.*
> *The woman was deceived, and sin was the result. [1*
> *Timothy 2:14 NLT]*

Regardless of the sequence of their fall into sin, God promised that He would redeem the human race and destroy the devil. He promised that He would do this through a God-man that would be born to a descendant of Eve.

> *Her son will crush your head. [Genesis 3:15 NIrV]*

That God-man, Jesus Christ, was anointed as the Messiah when He was baptized in the River Jordan in the year AD 26.[728]

> *Then Jesus came from Galilee to the Jordan to be*
> *baptized by John. As soon as Jesus was baptized, he*
> *went up out of the water. At that moment heaven was*
> *opened, and he saw the Spirit of God descending like*
> *a dove and lighting on him. And a voice from heaven*
> *said, "This is my Son, whom I love; with him I am*
> *well pleased." [Matthew 3:13,16–17 NIV]*

This occurred *exactly* four thousand years after the fall of man in 3975 BC.[729]

He gave his life to purchase freedom for everyone.
*This is the message God gave to the world **at just the***
***right time**. [1 Timothy 2:6 NLT]*

That same Christ has promised His people rest after a period that is symbolized by the Six Day Creation (Section 48).

So there is a special rest still waiting for the people of
God. For all who enter into God's rest will find rest
from their labors, just as God rested after creating the
world. [Hebrews 4:9–10 NLT]

The six thousand year period of man's toil will end with the close of the sixth millennium in AD 2026.

Christ's anointing, then, took place four thousand years into the six thousand year period of man's toil on earth. Four thousand divided by six thousand is 66.6%. And don't forget that there are sixty-six books in the Word of God, the Holy Bible.

It was bound to raise the ire of the devil that God sent His answer to sin 66.6% of the way through human history, and that His answer was contained within sixty-six books. We know from Scripture that the devil's product is most often a cheap knock-off of God's. It is written of Lucifer,

You said in your heart, "I will ascend to heaven ... I
*will make myself **like the Most High**." [Isaiah 14:13–*
14 TNIV]

I maintain that the devil sent his answer to Christ 66.6% of the way through the first millennium after Christ. Just as Jesus undid the devil's work by the commencement of His ministry (AD 26), so the devil came back and tried to undo Christ's work by the formulation of the Muslim religion (i.e., al-Malik's inscription in AD 692; see Sections 20–23). Thus, the inscription in the Dome of the Rock that denies Jesus' Sonship was proclaimed in Palestine *exactly* six hundred and sixty six years after,

... a voice came from heaven, saying, "This is My
beloved Son, in whom I am well pleased." [Matthew
3:17 NKJV]

It could not be more simple: the devil likes to pretend that he is God.

~~~~~~~~~~~~~~~~~~~~~~

When the Apostle John put forth six hundred and sixty-six as the Number of the Beast, he advised us to be wise and calculate it (Revelation 13:18). But he wrote in the first century and had never heard of Caliph Ali or Islam. The Apostle John must have come up with the number of the Beast either by:

- direct revelation from God. Christ said to him, "Come up here, and I will show you what must take place after this." [Revelation 4:1 NIV]
- or, perhaps he calculated something that had occurred earlier in Jewish history: Jerusalem was conquered in 597 BC[730] by the Babylonians and the First Temple was plundered at that time.[xliii] Then, during the Apostle John's old age in AD 70, Jerusalem was conquered by the Romans and the Second Temple was plundered and destroyed.[731] These two events occurred six hundred and sixty-six years apart.

In the table below I list chronologically the recurrences of the Number of the Beast in history. They are all interesting, but the second through fifth 666-timelines are the key ones for my argument. Note that all occurrences of the 666-timeline after the Apostle John's death involved the Christian/Muslim struggle for dominion over the souls of men.

---

xliii The First Temple was plundered by the Babylonians in 597 BC; it was finally destroyed by them in 586 BC.

Table 15. The Devil's Obsession Throughout History

No.	First Event	Second Event
1	Sacking of Jerusalem by the Babylonian Empire in 597 BC.[732]	Sacking of Jerusalem by the Roman Empire in AD 70.[733]
2	Christ's Incarnation in 6 BC.[734]	Caliph Ali's assassination in AD 661.[735]
3	Baptism and annointing of Jesus Christ in AD 26.[736]	Inscriptions on the Dome of the Rock are composed in AD 692.[737]
4	Crucifixion, resurrection, ascension of Jesus Christ in AD 30.[738] Sin and death are conquered.	First gold coin minted in AD 696. It denies the Trinity, the Incarnation, and it calls for the new Antichrist religion to prevail over all other religions.[739]
5	Spreading forth of Jesus Christ's Gospel after the stoning of St. Stephen and the persecution of the early Church in AD 33.[740]	Spreading forth of Islamic orthodoxy after the completion of Islamic currency reforms, and the gold-gilding of the Dome of the Rock in AD 699.[741]
6	Completion of the writing of the Bible in AD 96.[742]	Completion of the writing of the Qur'an in mid–eighth century.[743]
7	Final and most severe Roman persecution of the Church initiated by Emperor Diocletian in AD 300.[744]	The doors and roof of the Church of the Holy Sepulchre are burned by a Muslim mob in AD 966.[745]
8	Construction of the Church of the Holy Sepulchre in ~ AD 336.[746]	Destruction of the Church of the Holy Sepulchre by Caliph al Hakim in AD 1009.[747]
9	Mesrop Mashdots of Hatsekats, Province of Manzikert, invents the Armenian script for the purposes of spreading Christianity in AD 405.[748]	Christian sovereignty over Anatolia is lost to the Antichrist Beast of Islam (i.e., Seljuk Empire) at the Battle of Manzikert in AD 1071.[749]
10	Seventh ecumenical council condemns Iconoclasm in AD 787—celebrated by the Eastern Orthodox as the 'Triumph of Orthodoxy.'[750]	Constantinople falls to the Ottoman Turks in AD 1453. Eastern Orthodox mourn the extinguishment of the Eastern Roman Empire and the loss of the Hagia Sophia.[751]

Psalm 119:29 [TNIV]
Keep me from deceitful ways; be gracious to me and teach me your law.

84. The Avoidance of Deceit

When I was five years old, my family moved to a newly developed neighborhood. Our street had previously been part of a sweet corn farm. The farmer was past retirement age, and had decided to subdivide his land. He sold half of it to a real estate developer and kept half for continued farming. Our house lot bordered his barn and his remaining field. My father and I used to meet him at the boundary line between the two properties to buy fresh corn in the late summer.

A couple years later, the farmer died. He was childless, so his field lay fallow for several years. I and the other boys in the neighborhood decided that the land was ours to do with as we pleased. We flew kites, built tree houses, and caught frogs. We filled water balloons with paint and threw them against the side of the farmer's old barn. We set off fireworks and built bonfires. In the winter, we cleared a shallow area and created a skating rink.

The real estate developer eventually tracked down the farmer's heirs and made an offer on the remaining land. The next spring the developer filled in the frog pond and leveled the field with earth movers. Our wild playground became a raw mud lot overnight.

I was furious. What right did they have to do this to my place of refuge? It was a crime against the natural order.

I voiced my outrage to my father. He was unsympathetic. "Get off your high horse," he said. "Our house lot used to be part of that farm, too. Why is it okay for you to park your rich white ass on a former piece of pristine nature, but not okay for some other family to build a house and move in behind us?"

I didn't know it at the time, but I was an early environmentalist—well ahead of the wetland regulations that later came to New York State. I informed my father that the situation in the remaining field was different because there had been a frog pond there. Dad told me that what I called a pond was just an irrigation ditch that the farmer had dug years before, and that it was only filled with stagnant rainwater. He said that the real estate developer had bought the property fairly and he had every right to build upon it.

I remained indignant. I tied a red bandana around my forehead, and set out upon a systematic effort to thwart the development. My comrades and I filled the storm sewers of the new street with refuse, and spray-painted the newly-poured concrete, and vandalized the construction supplies.

The real estate developer knew that it was the children on our street that were responsible. A week later, he barreled into our driveway in his station wagon and confronted my father while I cowered in the attic. They spoke for only one minute before the angry man went off to another house. My father came upstairs directly, took off his belt, and waved it in front of my nose. He promised that if I dared to even step across the boundary line again, he would beat me senseless.

That was the end of my life as a radical.

The root of my sin was that I believed a series of lies:

- I thought that the land was mine. It was not mine.
- I considered it wrong—even criminal—to scrape off the topsoil with diesel-powered bulldozers. It is not wrong.
- I believed that I had the right to defend the surface of Mother Earth by destroying other people's property. I had no such right. Moreover, there is no such thing as Mother Earth—there are only inanimate objects and lower life forms.

These are odd things for a person, even a child, to accept as truths. But, then again, is there anything more definitional of humanity than that we are rational beings that are naturally susceptible to fanciful lies?

We can easily imagine what would have happened to me if my sabotage of the real estate development had gone unchecked. I would have been emboldened in my sin of coveting other people's property. I would have come to believe that I could stake claims on other parcels of land to which I had no legal title. Eventually, I may have run for political office as an Enviro-Nazi and tried to control the lives of millions of my fellow citizens through creative zoning and regulation.

Fidel Castro is a good example of the end-state of such a person. For fifty years he treated the entire island of Cuba as his personal playground. He did this at the expense of tens of millions of ruined lives. He counted himself righteous for the many murders that he committed in order to establish his communist utopia.

What was the mechanism by which I, as a ten year old boy, was brought back from the brink of such a fool's life? It was a strong, godly, father exercising his authority as the head of the household. My father was appalled that I would destroy someone else's property. He let me know it in no uncertain terms. God has instituted the traditional two-parent family for this very purpose.

> *Didn't the Lord make you one with your wife? In body*
> *and spirit you are his. And what does he want? Godly*
> *children from your union. So guard yourself; remain*
> *loyal to the wife of your youth. [Malachi 2:15 NLT]*

This familial sanction is illustrative of a larger point: it is only through correctly interpreting the Bible that we can avoid being drawn in to lies.

> *If you abide in My word, you are My disciples indeed.*
> *And you shall know the truth, and the truth shall make*
> *you free. [John 8:31–32 NKJV]*

Without the mitigation of God's Holy Word, there is no limit to the distortion and depravity to which human beings can accede.

> *The human heart is the most deceitful of all things,*
> *and desperately wicked. Who really knows how bad it*
> *is? [Jeremiah 17:9 NLT]*

You'll find the most bizarre lies propagated in arenas that are devoid of the Word of God. The practitioners of these lies are ridiculously encouraged by their limited successes.

In case you haven't guessed, I am thinking about the Islamic radicals again—the vanguard of the unchecked liars. As I write these words, they are literally up in arms about a series of cartoons of Muhammad by Danish artists. Cartoons! Embassies have been firebombed; death threats have been issued against the cartoonists; Danish flags (which contain the Christian cross) have been defaced; Muslim governments have forced European businesses to close, and recalled diplomats, and imposed trade sanctions. All of this over cartoons that they consider blasphemous.

Who the hell do these people think they are? Where do they get the nerve to make their problem (i.e., Islam) into our problem? How can they not be embarrassed by this behavior?

They believe a series of lies:

- That God did not beget a Son. He did.
- That Muhammad is the Prophet of God. He is not.
- That they have the right and obligation to kill other human beings that do not take their religion seriously. They do not have that right.

They need to be shown, through the use of force as necessity demands, that their sickness cannot be imposed upon their neighbors.

I have seen the cartoons. They are benign. But even if they were obscene, so what? The most that Muslims should do is not purchase the publication that printed them. They also have a right to organize boycotts and to peaceably assemble for protest marches, but I would be embarrassed to do even that—it is excessive and childish, and shows an unhealthy preoccupation with the actions of others.

Christians just avert our eyes and don't patronize art museums that display a crucifix in a jar of urine, or theaters that portray Jesus Christ as a homosexual. We don't fly into a rage when flags with crosses on them are burned by Muslims. We understand that we have no right to threaten violence or to disrupt commerce over an offense to our sensibilities. And we understand that it is unethical and self-defeating for governments to take any sectarian position on issues of conscience.

If we can restrain our passions when the true and living Christ is blasphemed, then are Muslims not putting Muhammad above God by carrying on so?

One can sympathize with the Israelis, Serbians, Armenians, Cypriots, and Russians when things like the cartoon riots occur. Fundamentalist Muslims are sick people acculturated into sick lies.

Romans 7:6 [ESV]
... now we are released from the law, having died to that which held us captive, so that we serve not under the old written code but in the new life of the Spirit.

85. Against Legalism and Sectarianism

I was born and raised in an area where the street signs were white shingles of wood stenciled with black lettering. That is the way that street signs should be—like newsprint.

When I grew up and purchased a home, I made sure that it was in a community that had this feature of cultural normalcy. But much to my abhorrence, the town west of my current residence has plastic street signs with a forest green background and white lettering. How grotesque! Even worse, the town east of my current residence has metal street signs with a Prussian blue background and silver lettering. I avoid driving through that town because the signs burn my retina. The green-signed town and the blue-signed town are high school football rivals and hate each other, by the way.

A few years ago I traveled to South America for business and discovered that some countries do not even name their side streets, let alone sign them. I couldn't stop obsessing about how the mail was able to be delivered correctly there. I was barely able to sleep, and kissed the ground upon returning to the United States.

Of course, I am being absurd to make a point: it does not really matter how the signs are painted (although a wooden sign with white background and black lettering is undeniably the best).

~~~~~~~~~~~~~~~~~~~~~~~~

In Islam, things like street signs do matter. Everything matters in Islam—every particular of life may be cause to kill your neighbor. Under the tyranny of Islam, cartoonists have to go into hiding for drawing Muhammad. Under the tyranny of Islam, people that have the temerity to drink carbonated water in the daylight hours during Ramadan are publicly beaten. Under the tyranny of Islam, young women are hacked to death with axes by their families for being caught alone with a male friend.[752] Their brutality is astounding.

Osama bin Laden, for example, interprets the Qur'an as forbidding music. When he used to go to the horse races he would plug his ears at the sounding of the bugle.[753] He thought that those that did not plug their ears were not as good Muslims as he was. In his perfect world, music would be outlawed in order to keep others from sinning, and there would be summary execution for people that attend rock concerts.

After my pages and pages in condemnation of Anti-Chalcedonianism and Anti-Filioqueanism, you might accuse me of the very legalistic sectarianism that I am denouncing. But there are two important points of distinction here: Firstly, the issues that I raised have to do with the attributes of God. I am arguing religious philosophy, not religious law. But secondly, and more importantly, I would never dream of co-opting my neighbor's freewill and forcing him to adopt my religious philosophy. The fate of his soul is his business; it is in no way my business.

I surely have a citizen's right to work within the democratic system to affect the civil code of laws according to my belief system; and I surely have a Christian duty to share the truth about God's love with others as the opportunity arises; and surely this written forum gives me a free-hand to expound upon eschatological and metaphysical particulars. But I would never force anyone into compliance with my views on either the mechanics of salvation or rock 'n' roll concerts.

Although I cannot help noticing when other people live in ways that I find abhorrent, I make a conscious effort *not to do anything about it*. My God directs me not to desire that one human adult should live in subjection to the whimsical fancies of another.

> *If it is possible, as much as depends on you, live*
> *peaceably with all men. [Romans 12:18 NKJV]*

Now, if you were to speak openly about wiping your ass with the pages of the Qur'an in a Muslim country, you would be murdered for it. But if you were to speak openly about wiping your ass with the pages of the Bible around people like me, you would be cautioned about possibly inflicting upon yourself a paper-cut in an inconvenient spot.

That is not a small difference; I want to be left alone while I am on the toilet, and in every other personal matter. It would be hypocritical of me not to observe the Golden Rule and leave my neighbors alone.

> *So whatever you wish that others would do to you,*
> *do also to them, for this is the Law and the Prophets.*
> *[Matthew 7:12 ESV]*

Love springs from faith that Christ's Resurrection has achieved a perfect hope.

> *The three most important things to have are faith,*
> *hope and love. But the greatest of them is love. [1*
> *Corinthians 13:13 NIrV]*

But Muslims do not have hope, love, or faith, and they do not follow the Golden Rule. There is no Muslim 'holy spirit' that they can trust to draw people to Islam—their religion must be enforced by people with swords. Worse than that, they call we who believe in the Trinity and have the Holy Spirit evil. But Jesus warned,

> *"I tell you the truth, all the sins and blasphemies of men*
> *will be forgiven them. But whoever blasphemes against*
> *the Holy Spirit will never be forgiven; he is guilty of*
> *an eternal sin." He said this because they were saying,*
> *"He has an evil spirit." [Mark 3:28–30 NIV]*

As the Antichrist Beast, Islam naturally has a completely different attitude about personal liberty than does Christianity. And when you ask a Muslim, "What is your religion?" you are not asking him about the work of God in saving his soul. You are really asking him, "What is your law?"

Islam's laws are numerous, invasive, and unyielding. Islam prescribes murder as the answer to deviation from outward observance of religious law.[754]

It teaches that green-sign people should strap bombs to their bodies and blow up blue-sign people if they do not submit to their signage system. But Christ's way of love is so beautifully simple.

> *The entire law is summed up in a single command:*
> *"Love your neighbor as yourself." [Galatians 5:14*
> *NIV]*

The true Christian always follows this. He tries to cajole converts into knowing the peace and joy of his Savior. He works in conjunction with the Holy Spirit to proselytize through reason, and rhetoric, and charity, and many other selfless avenues.

> *Since, then, we know what it is to fear the Lord, we try*
> *to persuade men. [2 Corinthians 5:11 NIV]*

But the true Christian never coerces professions of faith through the application of civil or religious laws.

> *[The Lord] says to his people, "Treat everyone fairly.*
> *Show faithful love and tender concern to one another*
> *... Do not crush strangers or poor people. Do not*
> *make evil plans against one another." [Zechariah*
> *7:9–10 NIrV]*

Accept the freedom that God gives every person. Trust Christ; meditate upon Christ; spread the message of Christ's love for all people. Then you will stop being vexed by your neighbor because his town has different signage than your town.

> *I pray that you will be active in sharing what you*
> *believe. Then you will completely understand every*
> *good thing we have in Christ. [Philemon 6 NIrV]*

~~~~~~~~~~~~~~~~~~~~~~~~~

It is to be expected that the Beast (i.e., Islam) would employ apocryphal stories about biblical characters. Remember, Islam is the devil's contrivance of God's story. It is a derivative of the Anti-Chalcedonian falling away from Christian faith (2 Thessalonians 2:3). So it is likewise to be expected that the Beast would pervert God's plan for salvation with legalistic observance. The devil is interested in death, and,

> *... sin is the sting that results in death, and **the law***
> ***gives sin its power**. [1 Corinthians 15:56 NLT]*

It is greatly to the devil's advantage to keep people in bondage to a set of laws. He prefers nonsensical laws, like those of Islam—but even a legalistic observance of the Ten Commandments would do in a pinch. It keeps one too busy resenting one's neighbor's lack of piety to ever really consider God's grace. C.S. Lewis has noted,

> *The sins of the flesh are bad, but they are the least bad of all sins. All the worst pleasures are purely spiritual: the pleasure of putting other people in the wrong, of bossing and patronizing and spoiling sport, and back-biting; the pleasures of power, of hatred. For there are two things inside me, competing with the human self which I must try to become. They are the Animal self, and the Diabolical self. The Diabolical self is the worse of the two. That is why a cold, self-righteous prig who goes regularly to church may be far nearer to hell than a prostitute. But, of course, it is better to be neither.*[755]

Muslim lunatics, then, are not the only ones that are preoccupied with other people's actions (although they are the only ones currently making war over it). Any form of righteousness that is not based solely upon what God has done for you in Christ, is legalism. Every culture, religion, and cause has a set of rules that one has to measure up to in order to reach a nirvana-like state. These include such differing value systems as:

- holier-than-thou Christian piety;
- the rigorous code of conduct required by radical feminists;
- the radical egalitarianism of the early twentieth century's earnest Bolshevik.

Indeed, it is as ridiculous to admire the Muslims for their observation of moral law as it is to admire the Soviets for their protection of the proletariats' working rights. Both these things are canards!

American Liberals, too, are easily offended, and feel that they have a right to run other people's lives. It is an all too common phenomenon, and it is unprofitable on every level. It makes for an unhappy populous; it makes for an unproductive economy; and it makes for an infuriating level of hypocrisy. The result is always sour, resentful, people looking at the requirement for righteousness that their neighbor hasn't met, and comparing that to the requirement they think they have met.

Christ spoke more forcefully against legalism than any other abomination of the mind of man.

> *Woe to you, teachers of the law and Pharisees, you*
> *hypocrites! You shut the kingdom of heaven in men's*
> *faces. You yourselves do not enter, nor will you let*
> *those enter who are trying to. [Matthew 23:13 NIV]*

He did not mean that the law of God was unimportant, but that all things must be done in love.

> *Woe to you, teachers of the law and Pharisees, you*
> *hypocrites! You give a tenth of your spices—mint, dill*
> *and cummin. But you have neglected the more impor-*
> *tant matters of the law—justice, mercy and faithful-*
> *ness. You should have practiced the latter, without*
> *neglecting the former. You blind guides! You strain*
> *out a gnat but swallow a camel. [Matthew 23:23–24*
> *NIV]*

He accused those that find their righteousness in the practice of observing laws (rather than dependence upon God's grace) of having the ultimate blood-guilt.

> *… upon you will come all the righteous blood that has*
> *been shed on earth, from the blood of righteous Abel*
> *to the blood of Zechariah son of Jeremiah, whom you*
> *murdered between the temple and the altar. [Matthew*
> *23:35 NIV]*

He said that it is a trap.

> *Woe to you, because you are like unmarked graves,*
> *which men walk over without knowing it. [Luke 11:44*
> *NIV]*

Legalism really is the ultimate trap for people's souls. It offers its practitioners the fantasy that they are good people by virtue of what they do or don't do.

> *I tell you that unless your righteousness surpasses that*
> *of the Pharisees and the teachers of the law, you will*
> *certainly not enter the kingdom of heaven. [Matthew*
> *5:20 NIV]*

In truth, nobody is a good person except Jesus Christ who kept the Law of Love perfectly. It is the presence of Jesus Christ in our hearts, and not an absence of sin in our lives, that sanctifies us unto God.

Luke 11:17–18 [NKJV]
Every kingdom divided against itself is brought to desolation, and a house divided against a house falls. If Satan also is divided against himself, how will his kingdom stand?

86. The Unholy Alliance

It seems oxymoronic to lump the American Liberals (or Rationalists) in with Fundamentalist Muslims. After all, the former would be the first to be massacred under a Taliban-style regime. And in the verse for this section heading, Christ says that a house divided against itself will not stand. So if the two are natural enemies, then how can they both be the devil's agents? What kind of operation is Satan running?

One must realize that the devil is a clever and focused fellow. The devil's goal is to damn as many human souls as possible—by any means possible. It is not at all necessary for his agents to work in physical harmony with each other, as long as they work in spiritual concert toward the goal of damning human souls. Above and beyond all divergences of purpose, this unites the unholy alliance of Antichrist Beast (i.e., Islamism) and False Prophet (i.e., Rationalism).

> *O God, do not keep silent; be not quiet, O God, be not still. See how your enemies are astir, how your foes rear their heads. With cunning they conspire against your people; they plot against those you cherish ... With one mind they plot together; **they form an alliance against you** ... Cover their faces with shame so that men will seek your name, O Lord. May they ever be ashamed and dismayed; may they perish in disgrace. Let them know that you, whose name is the Lord—that you alone are the Most High over all the earth. [Psalm 83:1–3,5,16–18 NIV]*

The children of the devil are like the treacherous brothers of a crime family: they sometimes work together to kill others, and they sometimes seek to kill each other. But at all times their minds are turned toward lawlessness. In this way, if a Sunni blows himself up at a Shi'a market, the devil has gained many damned souls. Sunni and Shi'a bodies lie dismembered on the pavement—all without having entrusted their souls to Jesus Christ. It's a win-win for the devil.

Likewise, when liberal Americans vote for a welfare state that results in drug dependency, an increase in crime, and a breakdown of the traditional family, the devil has gained many damned souls. The wealthy Liberals feel good about themselves without entrusting their souls to Jesus Christ, and the *hoi polloi* are quieted without entrusting their souls to Jesus Christ. Again, it's a win-win for the devil.

In this way we can see the commonality-of-purpose between poppy cultivation by the godless Taliban in Afghanistan, and heroin addiction by the godless Libertines in America. The devil is interested in the acquisition of souls; he is not interested in the manner in which they are acquired.

~~~~~~~~~~~~~~~~~~~~~~~

The intellectual father of modern Islamic fundamentalism, Sayyid Qutb (AD 1906–AD 1966), kept a journal as an Egyptian exchange student at Colorado State College. He had an epiphany while visiting a Mainline Protestant church in AD 1949.

> *Churches figured prominently in Qutb's writings. He marveled that, "No people can compete with the Americans in building churches," adding that he counted more than 20 churches in the small town of Greeley.*
>
> *But for all the churches, Qutb was quick to point out that most Americans seemed distant from religion and spirituality, "Most do not go to church on Sunday but rather on general holidays and on the feast days of local saints ..."*
>
> *It was at one of those churches that the most infamous event of Qutb's American journey took place. In a story that remains well-known in the Islamic world today, Qutb attended a dance held at a local church.*
>
> *The dance began after an evening service, and was led by the church's pastor, who, according to Qutb's breathless account, lowered the lights and put a*

recording of "Baby, It's Cold Outside" on the turn-
table in an effort to get the few remaining wallflowers
out on the dance floor.
"The dance hall convulsed to the tunes on the gram-
ophone and was full of bounding feet and seductive
legs," Qutb later wrote. "Arms circled waists, lips met
lips, chests met chests, and the atmosphere was full of
passion."
… Such events were common, often drawing hundreds
of students.[756]

One of Qutb's Arab friends expressed his shock to the pastor about such an event being held in a house of God, moments after the conclusion of prayer. The pastor blithely responded,

Would you rather they were alone out under some tree
where we can't see them?[757]

This experience pushed Qutb over the edge, and motivated him to produce volumes advocating for violent jihad until he was finally hanged by Gamal Abdel Nasser's (AD 1918–AD 1970) government in AD 1966.[758]

The anecdote is illustrative of what I have termed the Unholy Alliance:

- a Mainline Protestant clergyman was hastened to Hell by rationalizing his voyeurism and faithlessness;
- some horny college students were enticed by their chaplain into making poor life choices that lead to sexually transmitted diseases, unwanted pregnancy, unhappy marriages, prescription drug dependency, alcoholism, and divorce;
- and Qutb's brainchild (i.e., modern Islamic Fundamentalism) was born.

All-in-all a fruitful evening for the devil!

In opposition to this legion of malevolence stands the Word of God, and the Word of God alone. Jesus Christ, the only begotten Son of God, came into the world to save sinners from the Unholy Alliance between the False Prophet (i.e., Rationalism) and the Antichrist Beast (i.e., Islamism).

For sin shall no longer be your master, because you
are not under the law, but under grace. [Romans 6:14
TNIV]

In this verse the Apostle Paul calls upon the Christian to walk a line of grace. And unless the Holy Spirit empowers a man to walk the razor's edge between passion and reason, between abandon and prudence, that man lives only amongst the herd—the dogs of licentiousness to the left; the swine of legalism to the right.

> *Don't claim to be better than you are ... [And also]*
> *don't be too sinful ... A man who has respect for*
> *God will avoid going too far in either direction.*
> *[Ecclesiastes 7:16–18 NIrV]*

The saints walk the line of Christ's grace that leads to Heaven.

~~~~~~~~~~~~~~~~~~~~~~~

In base terms, the commonality between the seventh century Caliph Ali and the twenty-first century Liberal scientist is that they both disbelieve that God took human form. This makes them both Antichrists. And they both put forth illusionary and beguiling signs and wonders that have deceived many.

> *For false christs and false prophets will rise and show*
> *signs and wonders to deceive, if possible, even the*
> *elect. [Mark 13:22 NKJV]*

One might ask, "How can you say that the Muslims—Arab Muslims in particular—performed signs and wonders? They are a backward people."

I have two answers to this: First, the speed and near effortlessness with which they conquered and retained eastern Christendom remains an unparalleled marvel in world history. The seventh century Arab expansion is comparable to a street gang taking over the United States government, defeating the United States military, and subjugating the entire American population. Unsaved people tend to get caught up, fascinated, and mesmerized by the reality that such a thing did happen to both the Eastern Roman Empire and the Persian Empire. The Middle East used to be as multicultural as Europe, but all-at-once it became Arab in language, script, religion, and custom. There is an allure to that historical fact.

The Arabs' unprecedented success in killing and oppressing their neighbors leads unsaved people to make false inferences. The unsaved never consider that the God of love might have had a greater purpose in mind than favoring murderers (Section 106); rather they think, "Who else has ever been able to get away with such a coup? Even the Soviets only lasted seventy years—but the Muslims have run roughshod over every standard of decency and fairness for fourteen centuries. Impressive! Amazing! Come, let us try to understand them. What a fascinating custom it is that they do not allow their neighbor sovereignty over his or her own mind and property! We have much to learn through celebrating the diversity of their great culture."

Second, the signs and wonders of every person, society, and field of endeavor that stand foursquare against the Lordship of Jesus Christ counts in the Muslims' column. Remember, Ali is the Son of Perdition; he is the proto-type for all false christs and false prophets that came after him. In this sense, Voltaire, Darwin, Marx, and Freud are all spiritual-kinsmen of Ali. They all blasphemously said, 'I am great!' just as Ali blasphemously said 'Ali Akbar!'

> *These are of one mind, and they will give their power*
> *and authority to the beast. [Revelation 17:13 NKJV]*

Whosoever finds the weight of evidence against Jesus as God in man's flesh—whosoever believes in the preponderance of signs and wonders that speak against a personal, intimately-involved, God—these are the very sons and daughters of Satan.

It does not ultimately matter which signs and wonders the antichrists use in their attempt to disbelieve that God became a man. It is the effect that is important. It could just as easily be a geologist's preoccupation with meta-morphic rock, as a Muslim's preoccupation with the glory days of the Arab expansion.

"After all," the damned geologist muses, "how could Christianity be the Way if the world is billions of years old? The entirety of biblical history only encompasses a tiny fraction of one percent of what we know has occurred on planet Earth. Clearly there is more going on than was ever imagined by that unscientific Jewish Carpenter." He then turns his attention to the wondrous pictures from the Hubble Space Telescope and dismisses the Word of God entirely, saying, "Surely there are innumerable civilizations out there that have never heard of humans, let alone of Jesus Christ. How ignorant and arrogant those Christians are to proclaim their incarnation fable to be ultimate truth!"

Such a person, in his rationalist zeal to debunk his loving Creator, has overlooked the most obvious of facts: the same God that visited us in 6 BC made those galaxies; not a one of them is accidentally placed.

> *Lift your eyes and look to the heavens: Who created*
> *all these? He who brings out the starry host one by*
> *one, and calls them each by name. Because of his*
> *great power and mighty strength, not one of them is*
> *missing. [Isaiah 40:26 NIV]*

The Rationalist is viewing them because God has given them for his viewing-pleasure. But if the Rationalist cannot accept that his eyesight is a gift and not an accident, then how can he accept that the celestial glory upon which his eyes are feasting is a gift and not an accident? He cannot. Thus, he is deceived by signs and wonders, and damned to eternal separation from God.

Revelation 16:13 [NKJV]
And I saw ... unclean spirits like frogs coming ... out of the mouth of the false prophet.

87. The False Prophet

In the AD 1970's there was a television game show called *Name That Tune*. The contestants would be told what type of song was about to be played, and they would bid against each other as to who could guess the name of the tune with the fewest number of notes played.

One person would say, "I can name that tune in seven notes." There would be a moment of dramatic tension, and the person playing against them would say, "I can name that tune in six notes."

The appeal of evolution to Rationalists is that Charles Darwin (AD 1809–AD 1882) won their contest for who could debunk the Christian God with the fewest number of ideas. Darwin's prize-winning idea was that mutative natural selection could account for the mysteries of biological Creation. And the acclaimed atheist philosopher, Dr. Daniel Dennett, is enthralled:

> Let me lay my cards on the table. If I were to give an
> award for the single best idea anyone has ever had,
> I'd give it to Darwin ... In a single stroke, the idea
> of evolution by natural selection unifies the realm of
> life, meaning, and purpose with the realm of space
> and time, cause and effect, mechanism and physical
> law ... My admiration for Darwin's magnificent idea
> is unbounded ... [759]

What irks me is not simply that it is a lie that mammals evolved upward from bacteria as a result of progressive mutations. What irks me is that it is the most outrageous lie ever told in the name of science, and that it is the most vociferously defended.

~~~~~~~~~~~~~~~~~~~~~~

Every endeavor of science has a practical application. Chemistry gives us household products. Geology gives us petroleum and coal. Astronomy gives us satellite communication, and the wonders of space travel. And biology gives us advances in medicine. All of these disciplines are legitimate avenues of scientific inquiry, and ultimately result in the manufacture of products for the betterment of mankind.

There is, however, one glaring exception: evolution. It produces nothing, except unbelief toward the sovereignty of God.

To say that evolution produces *scientific knowledge* of how life came to be is as farcical as saying that the study of the Book of Genesis produces *scientific knowledge* of how life came to be. They are both belief systems that cannot be proven; they are both inherently religious.

It's no use denying that the professors of Evolutionism are actually the high priests and high priestesses of our college campuses. Again, consider this quote from the atheistic religious practitioner, Dr. Dennett:

> When we replace the traditional idea of God the creator with the idea of the process of natural selection doing the creating, the creation is as wonderful as it ever was. All that great design work had to be done. It just wasn't done by an individual, it was done by this huge process, distributed over billions of years.[760]

What is this idea of replacing 'God the creator' with a 'huge process'? God is already a 'huge process'—He is omnipotent and He is unconstrained by time. What Dr. Dennett is really saying is that the theory of natural selection results in our being able to dismiss the personal, Christian, God from consideration.

Herein lies the utility of evolution to the Rationalist: when he sees an insect whose body-shape is nearly identical to a leaf on which it makes its home, he cocks his head and says, "God did not make this all at once in a way in which my limited brain could never come to terms. No, not at all. The insect obviously evolved along with the tree so it could be camouflaged from its predators. These two things look similar—they must have been brought to their current state through a trial-and-error continuum. That's the way that we humans would have built it. That's an explanation that we can fit our heads around."

Such an explanation is of more value to the Rationalist than petroleum or household products or satellite communication. Evolutionism has turned out to be the most effective means that the devil and the False Prophet of Rationalism have developed for blinding people to the immediacy of the end of the world. It sears the conscience so that it ignores accountability to God.

> *Why does the wicked man revile God? Why does he say to himself, "He won't call me to account"? [Psalm 10:13 NIV]*

Now, if you ask Rationalists whether the theory of evolution proves that there is no God, you get a patronizing answer like this:

> *No. Many people, from evolutionary biologists to important religious figures like Pope John Paul II, contend that the time-tested theory of evolution does not refute the presence of God. They acknowledge that evolution is the description of a process that governs the development of life on earth. Like other scientific theories, including Copernican theory, atomic theory, and the germ theory of disease, evolution deals only with objects, events, and processes in the material world. Science has nothing to say one way or the other about the existence of God or about people's spiritual beliefs.*[761]

That's awfully high-minded of them, don't you think, to allow for the possibility that God exists under their theory?

Notice what is being said here: evolution takes no stance on the existence of God, but it takes a most definite stance about "a process that governs the development of life on earth." This is not a religiously-neutral position. It precludes a personal, awesome, and creative God—a God that intervenes in nature through miracles—the Christian God.[762]

The theory of evolution is fundamentally different from the Copernican theory, or the atomic theory, or the germ theory of disease, in that it promises to explain the meaning of life *with or without the existence of a personal God.*

It is for this reason that evolution is a *cause célèbre* among people that disbelieve in the Christian God. We often see car bumper stickers with a Darwin Amphibian mocking or devouring the Christians' ichthys or 'Jesus-fish' bumper stickers. These are often placed alongside other liberal bumper stickers.

Why? Why do you never see a bumper sticker touting the Copernican theory? Why is there not a bumper sticker showing the germ theory of disease eating a Jesus fish?

The answer is simple: those scientific theories are of no use in showing-up God. They do not portend trouble for those meddling Christians and their 'dumb' Bible. The appeal of evolution is that it makes God a take-it-or-leave-it proposition. Those that embrace evolution are invariably the very same people that reject an omnipotent God.

The late evolutionary biologist, Dr. Stephen J. Gould (AD 1941–AD 2002), said,

> *The Darwinian revolution is about who we are; it's what we're made of; it's what life means insofar as science can answer that question ... So it, in many ways, was the singularly deepest and most discombobulating of all discoveries that science has ever made.*[763]

It's distressing how widely-held is this view. In fact, the mania to metaphysically justify one's discipline has jumped across from biological evolution into other fields. The renowned British physicist Stephen Hawking has become something of a High Priest and Prophet of American popular culture. He recently spoke of the scientific advances concerning the expansion of the universe. He concluded with,

> *New observational results and theoretical advances are coming in rapidly; cosmology is a very exciting subject. We are getting close to answering these old questions: Why are we here? Where did we come from?*[764]

Does scientific discovery ever tell us *who we are*, or *why we're here*, or *what life means*?

What a steaming pile of horse excrement!

> *I am the Lord, who made all things. I alone stretched out the heavens. Who was with me when I made the earth? **I expose the false prophets as liars** and make fools of fortune-tellers. **I cause the wise to give bad advice**, thus proving them to be fools. [Isaiah 44:24–25 NLT]*

~~~~~~~~~~~~~~~~~~~~~~~~

Archaeologists have a rule of thumb that if they find a watch on a dig, they don't assume that it is there by the forces of nature. Somebody must have put it there. This rule is so strongly held that if an animal bone is found with even a spiral fracture in it, the assumption is always that a rational mind was once creatively at work there. That kind of fracture is only caused by striking the bone with a stone in order to access the marrow—and only humans use tools in this way.

If a specific bone fracture is enough to prove the existence of a human, then is not the entire universe enough to prove the existence of God? It is if you are an objective observer. The evidence for God is all around us.

> *... since the creation of the world God's invisible qualities—his eternal power and divine nature—have been clearly seen, being understood from what has been made, so that men are without excuse. [Romans 1:20 NIV]*

The problem is that most scientists at universities are not objective. They cannot afford to be because Rationalism is a rigid orthodoxy that endures through intellectual intimidation. There are very real financial and career risks associated with professing belief in the teachings of the Bible.

> *You know that in this world kings are tyrants, and officials lord it over the people beneath them. But among you it should be quite different. [Mark 10:42–43 NLV]*

Rationalism is as intolerant as its cousin, Islamism. The same mentality is at work: using economic power to subsidize certain ideas and coerce allegiance. People at universities that do not believe in biological evolution and do not take on the modernist equivalent of the Mark of the Beast (e.g., liberal modernist icons like rainbow flag stickers, Darwin amphibian symbols, ape-to-man progression posters, etc.) pay a price for their insolence.

It is Rationalism, or Modernism, or Liberalism, or Naturalism that is referred to in the Book of Revelation as the False Prophet.

Are you a Rationalist? If so, you are nothing more than a Neo–Islamist—a comrade-in-cause with those religious fanatics that first emerged six hundred and sixty-six years after Jesus Christ was born into the world.[765] They represent the Beast. You represent the False Prophet. Both of you say, "No!" to an intimately-involved God.

> *Then the beast was captured, and with him the false prophet who worked signs in his presence, by which he deceived those who received the mark of the beast and those who worshiped his image. These two were cast alive into the lake of fire burning with brimstone. [Revelation 19:20 NKJV]*

In the light of truth, there is no real difference between the False Prophet and the Beast because there is no real difference between not believing in God, and believing that Satan (i.e., the Muslims' Allah) is God.

Again, what is the fate of all these evil forces?

> The devil, who deceived them, was cast into the lake
> of fire and brimstone where the beast and the false
> prophet are. And they will be tormented day and night
> forever and ever. [Revelation 20:10 NIV]

Here we have the Unholy Trinity in their eternal destination: Satan (represented by the Termagant Allah) is in Hell forever and ever. The Beast of Anti-Christian religiosity (represented by Islam) is in Hell forever and ever. And the False Prophet of Anti-Christian secularism (represented by Rationalism) is in Hell forever and ever.

1 Corinthians 3:18–19 [ESV]
Let no one deceive himself. If anyone among you thinks that he is wise in this age, let him become a fool that he may become wise. For the wisdom of this world is folly with God.

88. The Cult of Science

A prophet is not so much someone that tells the future, as it is someone that tells the truth about God, and about God's history—past, present, and future. He or she tells the truth in such a way that it convinces people to give their hearts to Christ.

And a false prophet is a liar about God, and about God's history—past, present, and future. He or she tells lies in such a way that it convinces people to keep from giving their hearts to Christ.

God told the Prophet Daniel,

> But you, Daniel, shut up the words, and seal the book
> until the time of the end; many shall run to and fro,
> and knowledge shall increase. [Daniel 12:4 NKJV]

That was a prediction of the advent of intercontinental air travel, and biotechnological advances, and the Information Revolution. It is not simply a coincidence that the Internet was introduced in AD 1993[766]—toward the end of the sixth millennium of human existence. The days in which science has advanced to the point where it can be made into the False Prophet's cult are surely the last days.

~~~~~~~~~~~~~~~~~~~~~~~~

One of my friends is a renown leader in the field of volcanology. He has published scores of peer-reviewed papers in the most prestigious journals. He is an assistant professor at a highly reputed university. He has risked his life, has sacrificed relationships, and has literally shed tears in pursuit of his research. Of all my college friends, he has been the most focused on what he chose to study.

The last time I saw him, he told me that he was thinking of leaving it all to become a public school teacher. I was shocked, and asked why. He explained that he could make as much money in the public schools, and he would only have to work nine months per year. He said that he wouldn't have to do any dangerous field work, neither would he have to raise money by writing grant proposals.

I asked, "But what about your name in the scientific community? You've worked so hard. Everybody knows you. What are people going to say if you quit your field to teach at a high school?"

He rolled his eyes and said that they'd say that he had his moment in the sun, but he got burned out, and had become a has-been. He said that new people would come in to fill the void, and he'd be forgotten within five years of his last publication.

"Wouldn't that bother you?" I asked.

He told me that since he got a mortgage and since his wife became pregnant, he just didn't care any longer about being tops in his field. He wanted a secure job that would allow him to spend time with his family.

I looked at him in amazement, and exclaimed, "Reginald! I'm proud of you!"

~~~~~~~~~~~~~~~~~~~~~~~~

All the labor of this world is ultimately for naught. The False Prophet would not have you believe it, but we are all going to die and the world is going to come to an end. Be careful that the life is not sucked out of you for no good reason. Cults will come and go, and the ostensibly important institutions of this world will grant you accolades while you are useful to their cause; the moment when you are no longer useful, you will be discarded in the name of progress.

We shall not all be fools like the strong and loyal workhorse, Boxer, in George Orwell's (AD 1903–AD 1950) book, *Animal Farm*. He toiled endlessly for the collective farm that was established after the despotic Farmer Jones was deposed. Boxer had blind trust in the new dictator, a pig named Napoleon. He could not see the corruption that was right under his nose. His motto was "Napoleon is always right."[767] That was his undoing: Boxer was ultimately injured on the job and sold for glue by the collective.

Ignorant illiteracy may be symbolized by Mr. Jones, but the cult of science is a pig named Napoleon.

I am much more comfortable devoting my efforts to the One that showed His love by giving up His life for me. He has published my name in the Book of Life, and is preparing an eternal habitation for me.

> Then those who feared the Lord spoke with each other, and the Lord listened to what they said. In his presence, a scroll of remembrance was written to record the names of those who feared him and always thought about the honor of his name. "They will be my people," says the Lord of Heaven's Armies. "On the day when I act in judgment, they will be my own special treasure. I will spare them as a father spares an obedient child. Then you will again see the difference between the righteous and the wicked, between those who serve God and those who do not." [Malachi 3:16–18 NLT]

Jesus is the good Master, and will one day congratulate me with, "Well done, good and faithful servant."

Psalm 131:1–2 [NIV]
My heart is not proud, O Lord, my eyes are not haughty; I do not concern myself with great matters or things too wonderful for me. But I have stilled and quieted my soul.

89. Common Sense that Lesser Minds Deem Madness

Nasr-ed-Din Khoja was a fourteenth century wise man, court jester, and jack-of-all-trades from what is now the Republic of Turkey. The stories about him are endless.

~~~~~~~~~~~~~~~~~~~~~~~~

A foreign professor came to the city of Aksehir and requested permission to hold a public enquiry regarding natural science. Bowing to Emperor Tamerlane, he said through an interpreter, "Dear King, if you have specialists on the deepest and most perplexing issues of our times, please allow us to have a colloquy."

Tamerlane called his notables together and said, "This man is a great intellect from the West. If you cannot bring a gifted professor to meet him, he will spread it abroad that the learned classes in Anatolia are of no account."

The notables held a consultation, and after long reflection came to the conclusion that there really was no such person in the country; but they said, "This will never do. It will bring us into disgrace with Tamerlane, and injure our good name among the nations. We must think of something. We must avoid such a calamity!"

"Come now," said one, "let us hear the opinion of our beloved Nasr-ed-Din Khoja on the subject. He always has an answer. Maybe we shall manage to confound this foreign clown by some odd trick of his."

Finding this an excellent idea, they went to the Khoja and explained the matter. At once he said, "You leave it to me! Mind you if I can shut him up by an apt reply, I will look for a good present from each of you! But if I cannot, all you have to say is, 'Oh! That fellow?! He is half-cracked—a dim-witted Khoja who came to the meeting unbidden. Don't take any notice of him.'"

"O Khoja," they said, "God grant you whatever you ask as long as you can save our faces!"

So they pitched tents in the public square and the ceremony was made august and awe-inspiring by the presence of Tamerlane and his retinue, all covered with gold and jewels and armed with the full panoply of war.

Next came the foreign professor, an egg-headed, queer-looking fellow, who was given a seat near his Majesty.

Then the Khoja entered, wearing an enormous turban and an oversized gown with open sleeves.

After drinking some tea, and taking a moment's repose, the professor stepped forward and announced, "I'm sure interpreters shall not be necessary since the truths of science know no language." He then drew a circle on the ground, and looked into the Khoja's eyes for an answer.

The Khoja at once rose and with his stick drew a line through the center of the circle, dividing it into two equal parts. He looked back at the professor, and seeing that he approved, the Khoja proceeded to draw another line across, dividing the circle into four equal parts. The Khoja then made gestures as if he would draw three of the parts towards himself, and push the other part towards the professor. The professor expressed his approval, and bowed.

After this the professor held his hands together in a ball; then he formed a flower bud with his fingers up; then he opened his fingers, wiggled them, and raised his arms. The Khoja jumped to his feet and made a gesture exactly in the reverse so that his fingers pointed to the ground. The foreign professor again signaled his approval.

Then the professor pointed to himself, clenched his fist, and made a gesture as if he were pulling something out. Then, with his fingers, he imitated a creature walking on the ground.

The Khoja responded by taking an egg from his pocket; he displayed it, put it back, and then raised the back of his hand to his head. He then flapped his arms, and made like he was flying away. The professor approved of this also, and made a profound obeisance to the Khoja, kissing his hands. He then told the interpreter to congratulate Tamerlane on possessing such a national treasure as Nasr-ed-Din Khoja.

Tamerlane and the notables were delighted. Each one thanked the Khoja for having saved the honor of the country and showered him with generous gifts.

After everyone had left, Tamerlane, took the professor aside and said to him through an interpreter, "I could not understand anything from your mime-show. What was it you said? And what answers did the Khoja give which made you retire from the contest?"

The professor explained his object, "Your Majesty, western experts are not agreed on the subject of how the world came to be, and the origin of the species; as I did not know the opinion of the learned Doctors of the East, I requested this forum."

"Consequently, I first showed that the earth is round. The Khoja not only accepted this fact, but he drew a line marking the Equator and dividing the globe into the northern and southern hemispheres. He then drew the meridian line across the center, denoting east and west. And by making waving motions over three of the divisions, he meant to say that three parts of the globe are water and one part dry land."

"Then, in order to show the various species of flora and fauna, and to probe the secrets of their origin, I put my hands into the shape of a ball, and then waved my fingers up in the air, imitating thereby the production from the earth of minerals, vegetation, and animal life. The Khoja replied by pointing his fingers downwards, showing clearly, and in agreement with the most recent investigators, that life would be impossible without the sun's rays and the rain's waters."

"Then I pointed to myself and indicated by a gesture that all beasts that roam the face of the earth originate one from another, through the progressive bearing of their young."

"The Khoja, in reply, brought forth an egg, and touched his head as though he were in deep thought. Then he made a motion as though he were flying. This signified that I had only explained mammalian procreation, but not that of bird life. He thereby brought to our attention the ancient enigma of the chicken or the egg: which came first? By flying off the stage, he showed that this is the primary question, still perplexing the greatest minds of our time. I was thereby satisfied that we are pursuing the mysteries of nature along parallel paths."

"The venerable Khoja is a most gifted sage, with insights both celestial and terrestrial. Tell me, your Majesty, from where did he obtain his degrees?"

Tamerlane stammered, "Our Khoja spent many years studying in the far eastern reaches of my kingdom—time does not allow us to list all his credentials. Thank you, professor."

After seeing the professor safely away, Tamerlane asked the unschooled Khoja his perspective on the encounter.

"My dear King! They call him a professor? Indeed! Your notables need not have fretted about that dog-hungry fellow. When I came he drew a circle, as you saw."

"'Ooo!' says he to himself, 'if only it were a tray full of baklava!'"

"I first divided the circle into two parts, meaning that I am willing to share pastry evenly with my neighbor. But as he made no objection, I divided it into four parts, taking three for myself and leaving him one."

"Imagine what a starveling he is! The poor fellow was satisfied with a quarter tray of baklava!"

"Then he waved his fingers in the air as if to say, 'Oh, I would be alright if a pot of plain rice were boiled for my tray.' So I, in turn, made a sprinkling gesture as if to say, 'I would gladly fill the empty quarter of my tray with pilaf provided that it was flavored with spices, pistachios, and raisins.'"

"Then the professor pointed to his stomach, as though it were wrenched, and made a walking motion, by which he meant to say, 'Ah! If you only knew what a long distance I have come, and how I have longed for a good meal!'"

"I, in mime, answered, 'But I am more hungry than you, my friend! I got up this morning and my wife gave me only one hard boiled egg for breakfast. Then our appointment beckoned and I had not even time to eat it. I put it into my pocket in case I became faint on the way here. I tell you, I am so light on an empty stomach that I could fly like a bird!'"[768]

~~~~~~~~~~~~~~~~~~~~~

The Apostle Paul assures us that if we know God,

> *Then we will no longer be infants, tossed back and forth by the waves, and blown here and there by every wind of teaching and by the cunning and craftiness of men in their deceitful scheming. [Ephesians 14:4 NIV]*

So let us imagine that the western professor and the Khoja could come back to life in the early twenty-first century? What would each say?

The professor would discover that he was incorrect about almost all that he had previously accepted as fact. For example:

- the earth is not circular, it is the shape of an irregular ellipse;
- the surface of the earth is not 75% water, it is only 70.8% water;
- there are entire chemotrophic ecosystems at undersea hydrothermal vents that do not rely on solar radiation or precipitation for the continuance of life;
- many lower organisms (e.g., bacteria, nematodes, etc.) are asexual, and reproduce not by parental intercourse, but by the individual splitting into two independent organisms;
- many higher organisms (e.g., fish, reptiles, etc.) are able to reproduce by asexual parthenogenesis.

I suspect the professor would not be in the least embarrassed by his scientific naiveté throughout his career. Rather, he would take hold of the results of the most recent investigators as if they were his own.[769] Since he believed in science long ago, he would again presently say, "I am gratified that our work laid the foundation that allowed you to continue to probe until you have discovered the very secrets of life itself. We are now unquestionably at the threshold of a fuller, more confident, truth."

This is so because Rationalists are relativists—people to whom there is no absolute truth. For them, the truth changes based upon the circumstance because the very thing in which Rationalists have put their faith—namely science—keeps changing! Hence the psychopathic mantra, "What's true for you may not necessarily be true for me," and the reticence to condemn anything absolutely (except for the absolutism of Creedal Christianity).

But what of Nasr-ed-Din Khoja? What would he say if he were here? He would undoubtedly be looking not toward today's great universities, but toward today's great food warehouses, and saying, "Did you know that they now have places called 'wholesale clubs' where you can buy a twenty-five kilogram sack of rice for only ten dollars?! Just imagine! If you make ten dollars per hour, and you work forty hours in a week, you can buy an entire ton of rice! Oh, what a party we are going to have at my house! The pilaf will flow like water!"

If you asked, "But Khoja, what about the foreign professor's conundrum? What do you say of it in light of modern times?" he would say, "You're right! Where ever am I going to get enough pots to cook that much rice?"

Now, you could test the Khoja's patience, and say, "No Khoja! Listen! What about the mysteries of natural science? What is your answer to how the world came to be, and the origin of the species?"

Then he would say, "Is that all you wanted to know these many years? Is it not obvious? God said may it be so, and it was so. Why are you so vexed, you son of a donkey?"

There are two ways to address the incorrigible Khoja at this point:

One is to bow, and say "Quite right, venerable Khoja! Since the existence of God is certain, men of science are tasked to seek specific methods that demonstrate the wonders of His Creation. In other words, true science is nothing more than an occupation dedicated to bringing to light the glories of God in nature. The ultimate goal is to illustrate the infinite mystery of God's design, in acknowledgment of His miraculous transcendence."

The other is to scoff, and say "Khoja, you are wholly uncredentialed! Since the existence of God is not universally held, men of science are tasked to seek specific methods that are not predicated upon the myth of Creation. In other words, true science is the most altruistic of pursuits, dedicated to explaining all of nature without regard to the question of God. The ultimate goal is to expose and demystify every physical phenomena, in refutation of superstitions about transcendent miracles."

The first statement acknowledges that for every scientific question that we answer, many more questions are raised. It acknowledges that *scientific advancement can never yield ultimate truth or explain the meaning of life.*

The second statement pronounces that for every scientific question that we answer, we get tantalizingly closer to answering all things. It dictates that *scientific advancement can and will answer philosophical questions.*

Which view is correct—the one that yields to the Khoja or the one that yields to the western scientist?

The answer could not be more obvious. Consider the satire of President John Adams toward scientific advancement:

> *[Scientists!] Pursue your experiments with indefatigable ardor and perseverance. Give us the best possible bread, butter, and cheese; wine, beer, and cider; houses, ships, and steamboats; gardens, orchards, and fields—not to mention [hearths] and [stoves]. If your investigations lead accidentally to any deep discovery, rejoice and cry 'Eureka!' But never institute any experiment with a view or a hope of discovering the first and smallest particles of matter.*
>
> *I believe, with Father Abraham and Sir Isaac Newton, in the existence of the Spirit distinct from matter, and resign to the Universal Spirit the government of his heavens and earth.*
>
> *[P.S. -] I pray you to consider this letter as confidential. If it should get abroad, I should be thought a candidate for the new Hospital, before it will be ready to receive your obliged Servant.*[770]

Adams shared something with the Khoja: common sense that lesser minds deem madness.

Luke 12:54–56 [NIV]
When you see a cloud rising in the west, immediately you say, "It's going to
rain," and it does. And when the south wind blows, you say, "It's going to be
hot," and it is. Hypocrites! You know how to interpret the appearance of the
earth and the sky. How is it that you don't know how to interpret this present
time?

90. I Think, Therefore I am Accountable unto God

My soil science professor was a legend at the university. I took the last course
that he taught before retirement. He liked to pontificate as he marched us onto
the Great Plains of the North American continent for field studies.

He listened to our inane chatter one afternoon while searching for a
certain geologic feature. After a period of time, he could no longer restrain his
talent for lecture, "Listen up! You young pups need to learn some perspective,
and it's better for you to learn it now. My little sister is closing in on sixty years
of age, and she calls me on the phone all upset about this or that inconsequential detail of life. She says that she's depressed about getting old. I tell her the
same thing I am going to tell you today: take a studied look at the soil. It was
here long before us, and it'll be here long after us. The human lifespan is just
a blip on the radar screen; it's a nothing. In fact, our entire American civilization is a blip. We've farmed this land for fewer than one hundred and thirty
summers. But the Native Americans were here for thousands and thousands of
years before that. And these plains have been here for millions and millions of
years before that. Now, we think we're something special because we paved
the roads and built shopping malls? We're all going to die, and our way of life
is going to die. And the old rattlesnakes that are sunning themselves on the
south side of yonder butte are still going to be sunning themselves a million
years from now. The earth is going to go on for so long that it will forget men
ever walked on it. So don't fret about it; learn to accept the insignificance of
your place in the sequence of events, and be at peace."

He was an exceptionally good teaching professor. I really liked him.
But a little knowledge is a dangerous thing, and he was a lousy metaphysician.
According to my professor's Planet-of-the-Apes-futurism, when we humans
die out, the offspring of the rattlesnake could evolve into a reptilian super-spe-
cies that would take up our niche. And they may damn-well do a better job in
managing the environment than we have.

This is nonsense, of course. Descartes said,

I think, therefore I am.[771]

That is true, but incomplete. Descartes should have said,

I think, therefore I am accountable unto God.

The very fact that my professor had the intellectual capability to pose the question about our place in the world should have given him the answer to his sister's fretting.

Abstract reason is a curious and unique phenomenon. The rattlesnakes don't have it; we do. If we can think, it means that there must be a God. Otherwise human thought would have no basis.[772] And if God has given us the ability to know that He exists by our very ability to think, then we must be accountable to Him in our thought processes. Otherwise human existence would have no utility. Hence, accepting truthful thoughts about God, and not fatalistic nonsense, is the one and only thing that is really important. And the truth about God is that He loves us enough to redeem us. Otherwise human future would have no hope.

My professor made the mistake of taking what he knew to be true about land formations (i.e., that they are millions of years old) and extrapolating from it something about the meaning of life and the future of mankind. That is going about it backwards. He would have been better advised to use his ability to reason as a basis for formulating the meaning of life, and from that extrapolating something about why the land formations are so old. **The soil is old because it was made in such a way as to be old when we examine it.** The soil was obviously put into place by an Omnipotent Power in order to edify those that have faith in that Power, and, by the same token, in order to vex those that do not have faith in that Power.

How, then, could the earth be anything other than ours as a gift? God was providing my professor with a salary and intellectual stimulation when He made the geology of the Great Plains multidimensional; He was not providing him with an excuse to disbelieve in Him!

The Apostle Paul warned,

> *... keep that which is committed to thy trust, **avoiding profane and vain babblings, and oppositions of science falsely so called**: which some professing have erred concerning the faith. [1 Timothy 6:20–21 KJV]*

To think of human beings as a blip—an anomaly in the natural world—is a fantastic rejection of God's purposes. In truth, all things have been done for our benefit. The earth—the entire universe—was made by God for us. We are the crowning glory of nature, not an accidental byproduct. And, by God's reckoning, we are worth saving.

My professor was right about one thing: given our frenzied pace relative to the Native Americans that preceded us, how can the age of humans last much longer? Our collective efforts are being poured inextricably toward independence from our Creator. In the pursuit of technological comforts, we have very nearly used up what it is to be human. Our purpose is almost over, and with it the purpose for everything else. It will soon no longer be efficacious for there to be a human race (Section 103).

There are not going to be any buttes with rattlesnakes on them in a million years. Within a generation's time, God will intervene because He had a purpose in creating us as rational beings in the first place.

~~~~~~~~~~~~~~~~~~~~~~~~

The preceding discourse raises an important question for people like myself that believe in the biblical account of Creation: is it scientifically-correct for us to say that the buttes are millions of years old? Yes and no. Yes according to the science of geology; but no according to the science of quantum physics. Einstein taught us that time is relative, after all. It is a scientific fact that time duration is not constant; it changes with speed.

> *... do not forget this one thing, that with the Lord one*
> *day is as a thousand years, and a thousand years as*
> *one day. [2 Peter 3:8 NKJV]*

If an astronaut were to get into a spaceship that could accelerate to the point where it approached the speed of light, something curious would happen. When he returned from a several month cruise around the near reaches of the Milky Way, he would find that nobody that he knew would still be alive. He would not have aged appreciably, but the earth would have. Time would have moved slowly for him, but quickly for us.

Don't get angry with me, those of you that believe in science. What I have just stated is an indisputable scientific fact. The only thing that makes it unrealistic is that we don't yet have the technology to travel that fast in outer space.

So why all the scorn for a Six Day Creation? All the dinosaurs could have lived and died in a single twenty-four hour day relative to a fast moving body.

That is a fact of physics, you evolutionary ninnies!

~~~~~~~~~~~~~~~~~~~~~~~

My father and I used to visit my grandmother every other Saturday. She was nearly a hundred years old and had raised her children at a time before electric refrigeration. Perishable food had to be kept in cramped ice chests in her day. So anything that didn't absolutely need to be kept cold was left out.

She made good apple pie—lots of shortening and sugar. She gave me some with milk one July day after I cut her lawn. Two weeks later she gave me some more. The milk had been preserved in the refrigerator, but the pie was in the same spot in the musty cupboard. Fortunately, my good sense was not overcome by hunger, and I lifted the crust for a look. A fungal network had overtaken the filling. What to me had been a fortnight, was eons in pie fungus history. Dad's old Ford Fairlane had traveled along the interstate highway at something near the speed of light relative to fungal travel speeds. Our range from Albany to Syracuse was an intergalactic distance compared with their fourteen inch diameter pie world.

In between the two weeks, epic battles had taken place between the fungi and their sworn enemy, the bacteria. The former had emerged victorious, and were lysing the last few bacterial cells the way that a Medieval conqueror would impale barbarian captives. They may have been surfing on the fungal equivalent of the Internet at the time that my giant fork smashed through their atmosphere of pie crust.

Whatever the case, a sudden end came for which their history of the universe had not accounted: a new heaven and a new earth were introduced when I snuck into the bathroom and flushed the pie down the toilet.

Romans 1:21–22 [NIV]
For although they knew God, they neither glorified him as God nor gave thanks to him, but their thinking became futile and their foolish hearts were darkened. Although they claimed to be wise, they became fools ...

91. Accusing God of Duplicity

There are two ways to make a dish of fluffy white rice. One is to decode the DNA of the rice plant. Then have a computer DNA assembler piece the entire rice genome back together, base-pair by base-pair. Then implant that genome into the nucleus of a vegetable carrier cell, and place the cell in a Petri dish under a grow lamp. Allow it to mature into a rice plant and harvest the kernels. Then plant all of them in a paddy field. Save the kernels from the second generation, and plant them again. After two outdoor seasons, you should have enough for food. Then, in a medium saucepan, place one cup of dried, husked, rice and two cups of water. Bring to a boil, cover, and lower to a simmer for twenty minutes. The entire process should take no more than five years and twenty million dollars with today's technology.

The other way is to buy instant rice in a porous plastic pouch and drop it in boiling water for one minute.

I'm sure that you can see that I am offering a metaphor for the recently-created universe. But whereas a mouthful of instant rice is easily distinguishable from homemade rice, instant earth is so flawless that it is indistinguishable to our senses and scientific measurements. God made the world so excellently—by an instantaneous means that we would never have thought to employ—that many people cannot accept that He made it at all.

> *The Lord made heaven and earth, and he is the one*
> *who sends us help. [Psalm 124:8 CEV]*

Now I ask you: what kind of ingrates use the very evidence of God's omnipotence against Him?

> *The man without the Spirit does not accept the things*
> *that come from the Spirit of God, for they are foolish-*
> *ness to him, and he cannot understand them, because*
> *they are spiritually discerned. [1 Corinthians 2:14*
> *NIV]*

We call such people 'unbelievers' because the truth about the universe's recent creation, and its near-term-end, can only be comprehended through the supernatural logic and metaphysics of the Christian faith (see Section 3).

~~~~~~~~~~~~~~~~~~~~~~~~~

I once had an emotional attachment to a female colleague that was going through her fourth divorce. The nature of my work required me to spend eight hours per day in close proximity to her. In short order, she confided to me about her sad and deprived personal history. She also told me that her soon-to-be ex-husband was a pathological liar, an unemployable leech, and was emotionally abusive. Her incessant crying in the workplace moved me to show her the meaning of true and selfless love. I extended myself to the extreme in the hope that through the power of my personality she might be saved from self-destructive behaviors and addictions.

She had no compunction about utilizing my services as a butler-like attendant, but I soon noticed something that intrigued me on a scientific level: the more that I did for her, the more of an irritant I became to her. Especially when I would treat her like a lady, she would recoil and accuse me of impure motivations. If I held the door open for her, for example, she would say, "Why do you always act that way? What is it that you are after? Are you trying to fool me into giving my heart to you after all the pain that I've been through?"

This was absurd because during that same period she was happily sleeping with a couple of bums that had approached her crudely. She knew very well that I was not interested in her sexually—she was disgusting. My interest was in her personal improvement. And that expectation was precisely what put her on edge.

> Like a gold ring in a pig's snout is a beautiful woman
> who shows no discretion. [Proverbs 11:22 TNIV]

My curiosity about what made her tick was finally satisfied one evening when she invited me to her house for a dinner party. I got there early and informed her that there was fresh dog vomit at the foot of her inner stairs. She said wryly, "You notice everything," and handed me some rags, carpet cleaner, and a bucket.

I set to work on the stain while she watched. Then her phone rang and she went upstairs to answer it. The caller was her estranged husband, about whom she had complained so bitterly, and who had run-up enormous debts on her credit cards. I could clearly hear her speaking in a tender tone, "I can't tonight, baby, I've invited people from work over. Please, don't be upset. You know that I would if I could. Yeah … Tomorrow night, for sure … Okay, I'll meet you there."

She was not embarrassed that I had heard her arranging a liaison. She came downstairs and, as she stepped over me, muttered, "I wish that asshole would just pay back the money he owes me, and accept that it's over between us."

There is a world full of evidence that might indicate that God is not love; there is a world full of evidence that might indicate that He did not create the earth recently for our sake, or that He is not going to cause the world to end soon for our sake. There are plenty of scientific and emotional reasons not to believe that there is one generation left until the God-man, Jesus Christ, returns to remake all things. I admit all this.

We, as human beings, are predisposed to believe the evidence against a God that lovingly intervenes in the natural world—a God that cleans up our dog vomit stains, and works for our personal improvement.

Should we accept the suspicions that are, at first glance, validated by our prejudiced and calloused senses? Should we believe Dr. Sigmund Freud, who advised us all to grow up and accept that we are alone in a negative, meaningless, and accidental existence? Should we trust our whorish, self-interested, nature, and get what pleasure we can while we are alive?

Or should we turn from our evil ways and seek the truth?

~~~~~~~~~~~~~~~~~~~~~~

One of the evidences in favor of an old universe is starlight. We are able to measure how far away the stars are from earth through trigonometry, and we know the speed of light, so we can calculate how long it would have taken for any given star's light to reach planet Earth. Moreover, if we look to the outer edges of the universe, we see new galaxies appearing where a few years ago there was a lightless space in the sky. That means that the star's light has just now traversed the distance to us. These and other measurements consistently show that the edge of the universe is 13.7 billion years old.[773]

Young Earth Creationists have posited that God created the stars with spherical circumferences of light extending from them, so that people could see and enjoy the host of heaven that are actually billions of light years away. This is called the 'in-transit'[774] or 'aged-earth' theory; it is derived from the Omphalos hypothesis of P.H. Gosse (AD 1810–AD 1888).[775] This theory suggests that although the universe is actually only thousands of years old, it appears to be billions of years old.

An ethical issue arises with the aged-earth theory in that there is a lot of complex stellar activity taking place in outer space. If, for example, astronomers observe a supernova explosion in a star that is a million light years away from us, and if they measure the associated invisible radiation that results from such an event, are they witnessing an actual event or just divine fakery? What does it say about God's character if the supernova never actually occurred *but only appears to have occurred?*

I once heard a scientist on a public television program ask, in an extremely patronizing tone, "Why would God want to fool us by setting up all these ruses in outer space just six thousand years ago? What could He possibly be after by going to such lengths? Is He that set on trying our faith in the Bible?"

People that speak in this manner do not understand the meanings of infinity and omnipotence; they do not recognize their own limitations; in short, they have no sense of shame.

The Bible says that God formed the earth in such a way that it would be inhabitable by us.

> The Lord created the heavens. He is God. He formed the earth and made it. He set it firmly in place. **He didn't create it to be empty. Instead, he formed it for people to live on**. [Isaiah 45:18 NIrV]

God did not create the heavens as a *papier-mâché* backdrop, as we do for scenes in stage theater. He made it in a way that bespeaks His greatness. It was not His intention to fool us—it was His intention to provide for us. He gave us the starlight as a gift, so we would not have a pitch black sky to gaze upon.

> He also made the stars. God set them in the expanse of the sky ... [Genesis 1:16–17 NIV]

Our loving Creator gave every good and beautiful part of nature as a gift. And yet with each increase in knowledge concerning His Creation, unbelieving people find more room for resentment. They have the nerve to reply in sarcasm, "Yeah, thanks for making the stars for us! God expects us to be thankful that He put them there when all they do is confound us when we contrast it with His dumb Bible?! Everyone knows that what is old cannot also be young. And then, to add insult to injury, God expects us to believe that He became a Jewish Carpenter and rose from the dead for our sake?! Yeah, right, thanks! Everyone knows that what is dead cannot come back to life! Why does He insist on trying to fool us into thinking that He loves us after all the pain that we've been through?!"

How warped it is to look at nature apart from deference to God, and then postulate backwards about His motivation. How warped it is to do this and simultaneously prostitute ourselves to the things of this world. It requires a galling sense of entitlement. It is the ultimate in ingratitude.

> ... unless you turn from your sins and become like little children, you will never get into the Kingdom of Heaven. [Matthew 18:3 NLT]

God is a gentleman. He does not force His goodness upon those that insist that He has not made the entire universe for mankind to enjoy. He will not force us to accept His redemption from our fallen state. He eventually will lose patience, and leave the impenitent to their pathetic lies and head-games (Sections 10–11).

~~~~~~~~~~~~~~~~~~~~~~

Some Christians think that the six days of Creation in Genesis are only a meta-phor for six epochs of indeterminate length. But the Ten Commandments text plainly tells us,

> ... **in six days** *the Lord made the heavens and the earth, the sea, and all that is in them ... [Exodus 20:11 NKJV]*

And the same Bible teaches that the human race cannot be more than a few thousand years old:

> *From these three sons of Noah came all the people who now populate the earth. [Genesis 9:19 NLT]*

If the Word of God is inerrant, then the universe is six thousand years old. And if the universe is billions of years old, then the Word of God is not inerrant.

My position is that the universe appears *on some grounds* to be thir-teen billion years old, but in reality it is only six thousand years old. I take this not only on faith, but also based on the blatant incongruities in the available scientific evidence (Sections 96–97, 101).

> *For we walk by faith, not by sight. [2 Corinthians 5:7 NKJV]*

In giving God the benefit-of-the-doubt, I subscribe to a modification of the aged-earth theory: I would say that the earth appears to be old only in the same manner that it appears to be flat, or that the sun appears to rotate around the earth, or that the earth appears to be still. It only takes a little faith to accept that the earth is not flat, and that the sun does not circle a still earth. Nevertheless, there was a time—not that long ago really—when the brightest minds among us held the flat-earth and sun-rotation fallacies to be scientific dogma. They believed this based upon what they could observe and measure at that time. They did not recognize or appreciate the obvious powers of gravity that God had set up. We now know better.

Still, when one stands in the Black Rock Desert of northwestern Nevada the land appears to be quite flat. It is, in fact, one of the flattest places on the face of the earth. In AD 1997, Andy Green, a British RAF officer, broke the land speed record there, and became the first person on wheels to travel faster than the speed of sound.[776] Would it have been wrong for Mr. Green to emerge from his jet-powered car and say that his triumph was made pos-sible by the perfectly-level salt flats of Nevada? If he had said such a thing, should someone correct him, "No, no, you ignoramus! It is not a salt flat, it is a *salt round*. Ptolemy proved that the surface of your driving range is actually slightly curved."

Or is it wrong when the local weatherman says that the sun will rise in the east at 5:53 AM and set in the west at 6:12 PM? Should someone correct him, "No, no, you ignoramus! Galileo proved that the sun does not rise and set, but that the spinning of the earth *makes it appear* that the sun is moving in the sky."

Or is it wrong when a war correspondent reports that there was a lull in fighting along the frontlines, and that all was still on a windless day? Should someone correct him, "No, no, you ignoramus! Modern astronomy has shown that the surface of the earth is never still. The earth is constantly revolving upon its axis at 1,000 miles per hour; and the earth is constantly rotating around the sun at 67,000 miles per hour; and our solar system is constantly drifting within the Milky Way galaxy; and our galaxy is constantly on the move within the universe!!"

Do you see how all of this is tedious and unnecessary?

The fact is that the earth is both flat as a pancake and round as a baseball at the same time. And the fact is that the sun both moves in the sky and is stationary relative to earth at the same time. And the fact is that the surface of the earth may be totally still, and moving at supersonic speed at the same time. One is a lesser truth; the other is a greater truth. Sometimes it is efficacious to speak of the lesser truth for the sake of brevity and simplicity. It is a question of scale and perspective and purpose.

Now, I ask you, is it foolish or is it wise to believe that the universe is both thirteen billion years old and six thousand years old at the same time? After all, the theory of relativity incontrovertibly shows that time bends with more liquidity than does the surface of this planet. **Could there be other laws of nature, of which we are yet unaware, that would make the implausible quite axiomatic? Or do we know everything already?**

The great American inventor, Thomas Edison, gladly admitted,

> *We do not know one millionth part of one percent about anything. We do not know what water is. We don't know what light is. We do not know what electricity is. We do not know what gravity is. We do not know what magnetism is.*

If anything is certain—if science teaches us anything—it is that our knowledge is incomplete and always will be incomplete. How stupid, how infantile, how utterly unimaginative and intellectually vacant to believe that all of nature is limited to our experience. That is a behavior characteristic of Pavlov's dog, not of Pavlov himself (AD 1849–AD 1936).[777]

I feel safe in reasoning that the universe was created by super-scientific methods and supernatural laws of which we will never be able to conceive.

> *By faith we understand that the entire universe was formed at God's command, that what we now see did not come from anything that can be seen. [Hebrews 11:3 NLT]*

Spiritual methods and laws are, by definition, beyond our three-dimensional sensual limitations. The hubris, then, lies in believing that we can trust our incomplete and entrenched science with metaphysical certitude.

Therefore, I have no issue with an astronomer releasing a press statement that he has discovered a new galaxy that is fourteen billion light years away. The greater truth of the young-agedness of the universe can yield to his pronouncement, for the sake of brevity, without being deconstructed. But I take great exception to the astronomer concluding his press release with, "Therefore, the God of the Bible is bunk, and Jesus Christ is not coming again to rescue us within this generation, or ever."

How can one possibly draw from the other?

Proverbs 14:15 [CEV]
Don't be stupid and believe all you hear; be smart and know where you are headed.

92. May I Suggest that They are All Deceived Liars?

If you have the opportunity, I suggest that you get to know the custodial staff at your workplace. They are invariably the most interesting people in the building. At my job in Arizona the cleaning crew consisted of a husband, wife, their eight foster children, and their one natural-born daughter. I often worked into the time of their shift, and used to join them behind the building for nighttime smoking breaks. I got to know all of them.

One evening I was alone with the beer-bellied patriarch of this clan, Bruno. He pointed up at the sky and said, "Our friends are saying hello. They want to know your name."

"How's that?" I said.

"Chris, I like you. I trust you," he started. "I'm going to tell you my story because I think you can handle it. You see that star up there—the one that's brighter than all the rest?"

"I think that's Venus."

"No, no. It's a star on the other side of the Milky Way," he said confidently. "It's twinkling at me in code. And if you look at it long enough, you will notice that it is buzzing around in the sky like a mosquito."

"Okay. So how do you know this?"

"Well," he said. "I am a blood-brother with the people from that star."

"Are you?!" I said enthusiastically. "I'd like to hear about this!"

"I knew you would, because you are interested in everything." He took a deep drag off his cigarette and began to tell me about his days as a long-haul trucker. His story ended with he and his partner's losing track of several hours, and their rig being totaled through electrical short-circuitry. "I found myself wandering through the scrubland of northern Nevada at three in the morning without a stitch of clothing on. When I came to my senses, I realized that I had burns all over my body. My eyebrows and moustache were seared off. My partner was lying on the pavement next to the truck, unconscious. The dashboard was melted. We had both been abducted by aliens and probed."

I listened and nodded at appropriate times.

He continued, "Once you get probed, you have a kinship with them—they never really leave you. Like one time, after I got a new rig and got back on the road, I stopped at a bar and a gorgeous brunette came on to me. *Me! A* toothless, bald, old fart. She had tits out to here!" He cupped his hands out at elbow length. "I took her to the cabin of the rig and put it to her, and afterward she was gone—just disappeared right out from underneath me! She was from my star people—they sent one of theirs to mate with me. Then, nine months later, my wife and I finally had a baby after twenty years of trying. You see how it works?"

"No ... you lost me there," I said with uncertainty.

"The spacewoman took my seed, mixed it with one of her own eggs, and put it in my wife's belly. Get it?"

"Oh, yes, of course. But how did the embryo get implanted into your wife's womb?"

"You're not paying attention, Chris! *They probed her.* They can do anything with those probes, I'm telling you."

"Sorry. I see now. Then what happened?"

"Well, like I said, a baby girl comes out of my wife's hole nine months later, and a nurse—a gorgeous brunette nurse with tits out to here—walks into the delivery room and pronounces, 'This child will be called, Shawneesay.' Then she left the room and we didn't see her no more. Nobody at the hospital knew who she was, neither."

"The nurse was the same woman that conceived the child?" I asked knowingly.

"The very same," he confirmed with a wink. "You can tell who the aliens are because their appearance is different from most people around here. They have big dark eyes, and a soulful look. They must have had contact in ancient times with the Native Americans that made the giant geoglyphs in these deserts—they look like today's Navajo, and Shawneesay is the name of a Quechan Indian goddess. And you can see that my little girl is pretty dark-skinned, while my wife and I are both Scotch–Irish. So my little Shawneesay is on her way to becoming a medicine woman priestess. Since the time she was a toddler, she goes into trances and speaks to the space people with hand gestures. They're monitoring her progress because she is the Chosen One: some day in the future she will direct their conquest of planet Earth."

Over the next couple weeks, Bruno added other tales of close encounters, signs in the sky, and how all of this had affected his family and business enterprises. He answered every question that I posed without hesitation.

He said that they were interested in me because I was so smart, and that I should keep an eye out for their spaceship—it was shaped like the Michelin Man.

I was fascinated. He asked me to keep his secret to myself, and I did.

~~~~~~~~~~~~~~~~~~~~~~

I later discovered that the mendacious Bruno had told my officemate a slightly different version of his life and times among the aliens. We compared notes and I asked my officemate what he made of it.

"A story like that's got to be true—at least part of it," he said.

"But what about the things that we know to be damned lies?" I asked.

"Like what?"

"He started his story by telling me that the star was buzzing around in the sky. I looked at it the whole time he was speaking. It was not buzzing at all. And it was not a star; I know enough about astronomy to tell that it was one of the planets of our solar system. He just picked it at random because it was bright, and he wanted a jumping off point for his story."

My officemate said, "But he tells it with so much emotion and conviction and detail. The man was brought to tears while we were speaking—real tears! Besides, there's got to be alien life forms out there somewhere. We can't be the only intelligent species in the universe. And he's not the only one with this type of experience, you know. What other explanation could there be to all the reports of alien abduction?"

"May I suggest that they are all deceived liars?"

"Lying? All of them? All those people around the world that claim to have had close encounters?"

"Every single one of them," I said resolutely.

"But why would someone make up something like that?"

"To be important. To be believed. To gain a following. As a sign that one is something and not nothing. To explain away a shortcoming."

"You think so? You think Bruno is willing to take a chance on such an outrageous story just so we will think he's not a loser?"

"You have to look at it from his perspective: he is very much aware that we see his family cleaning our office every night. He feels a need to explain why his only biological child looks like a Native American. So he concocts a story of himself mating with a space alien, rather than the more obvious explanation of his wife humping one of their teenage foster boys from the Fort Yuma Indian Reservation. And don't forget that he also had to come up with some reason why his rig was totaled. I think it's a lot more likely that he was freebasing cocaine behind the driver's wheel than that he was abducted by the Michelin Man. But if the people around him will swallow that lie, he knows the rest of his underwhelming persona is safe with them too."

"You might be right," my officemate admitted. "I've caught him lying before about unimportant everyday things."

"Yeah, me too. The space aliens are just a natural extension of his habitual lying. Who is going to contradict him? His wife? His daughter? He's probably told the story so many times that on some level he actually believes it himself. The thought of being the father of an alien messiah is a powerful delusion, and the best deceivers are the ones who are themselves deceived."

"Wow," said my officemate. "He's nuts."

"I don't know if he's clinically insane, but he has a habit of making up stories and confidently passing them off to those around him."

My officemate suddenly looked as though he had an epiphany. Then he grimaced and banged his desk with his hand.

"What is it?" I asked.

"I wish I hadn't taken his advice on the stock market! I'm already down two thousand dollars with his picks!"

~~~~~~~~~~~~~~~~~~~~~~

Dear reader, may I suggest that every single one of the Rationalists is a deceived liar? Think about it: is it more likely that they are utilizing invalid scientific methodologies and self-serving propaganda, or that human beings actually evolved upward from pollywogs?

The Rationalists want to be important. They want to be believed. They want to gain a following on the face of the earth. They need to explain away their inability to understand the world around them; they need to explain away their personal shortcomings. They figure that if we swallow their damned foundational lie of evolution, we are sufficiently gullible not to laugh at the rest of their faux-science-construct.

They've told the evolutionary myth so many times that on some level they actually believe it. The thought of being the father of reason is a powerful delusion, and the best deceivers are the ones who are themselves deceived.

Bruno, for all his faults, was a jovial, entertaining, old fellow that never stole from me. I would find the Rationalists as fascinating as I found him if it were not for them using my taxes to propagate the Cult of Science in the public schools and on public television. And they have the temerity to accuse Christians of trying to impose religion into government. It's galling.

Leviticus 15:18 [NIV]
When a man lies with a woman and there is an emission of semen, both must bathe with water ...

93. The Justification of the Ejaculate

Bruno's tall tale leads me to the following two allegories: imagine a man that awakens from an indeterminate sleep to find himself naked, homeless, and wandering. He has no knowledge of any previous existence, or how he got to be naked, homeless, and wandering. He stumbles upon an empty town with fully-furnished houses and thriving gardens. He occupies a choice one, and other people like him occupy others. They form a community, and intermarry.

Because the owner of these properties has left them vacant, and is not present to force rental payment, the new occupants assume control of their new possessions as though they were entitlements. They dress in other people's clothes that they find in the closets of other people's houses. They eat other people's food that they find in other people's gardens.

Moreover, the guilt of this thievery drives them to go one step farther and absurdly propose that the houses, gardens, and town came into being through freak and uncontrolled occurrences. The houses, they maintain, are made up of trees that sequentially grew up and fell in fortuitous directions. The paint is the result of bird dung that was bleached by the sun. The furniture is abandoned termite heaps. The clothing is a result of spiders, silk worms, and nesting birds. No matter what they observe, they find a natural-world-explanation for it. In fact, they say that the existence of so much desolation around the town shows how accidental it is that the town fell together in this way. Of course, if another town is ever found, they will then somehow use that to also validate their freak-occurrence theory.

The citizens are, in fact, ungrateful interlopers that see what they want to see in their surroundings. But they justify themselves by declaring that they are simply victims of circumstance. This becomes their orthodoxy and they tax themselves in order to propagate the myth in their public schools.

~~~~~~~~~~~~~~~~~~~~~~~~

The fundamental problem with evolutionary theory is simply that it is obnoxious. The motivation for being obnoxious is guilt over pleasure, if I may be Freudian for a moment. But what vulgar pleasure could account for something so fancifully imaginative as evolutionary theory?

The evolutionary theorist may be likened to the proverbial child whose father has bought him a bicycle for his birthday. The father comes home early from work one afternoon to teach him to ride. As we have seen in film, there's a magical moment after the initial instruction when the father lets go of the seat of the bicycle and the child realizes that he is pedaling on his own. He has control of where, and how fast, he is going.

Now, let's say that this child decides to circle the block on his own. His father is waiting, smiling—anticipating their reunion. But the child gets to fantasizing while he rides, as children often do. This particular boy is willful, and instead of acknowledging his father's sacrifice in providing the bicycle and teaching him how to use it, he starts to think of another explanation.

"This bicycle came into being through my abdominal exertion. I don't even have a father. In actuality, what happened," he theorizes, "is that I defecated as a baby and my feces were petrified through interaction with the elements, and sundry meteorological phenomena. Then I defecated again, and they were petrified again. And, quite by chance, and by the movement of my legs as I tried to crawl away from my stink, this thing that we now call a bicycle, came into being underneath me."

"How else could this have come to be," he infers, "than through the production of my ass? After all, I'm sitting on it! It is only poetic that something of such utility is a derivative of that bodily function that pleases me the most."

While the boy is still within his scatological daydream he is suddenly confronted by his father, smiling proudly at him and the bicycle he has provided.

The boy looks up and says, "What the hell are you doing here?! This bicycle is my shit!"

Now, children do not have a conception of sexual pleasure. Their greatest pleasures are found in eating candy[778] and having a good bowel movement. Therefore, I have constructed the allegory such that the boy's bicycle fantasy is aligned to the excretory function.

Human adults, however, know very well the pleasures of sex. Is it, then, not suggestive that the Rationalists' evolutionary fantasy is centralized upon the reproductive function? The willful boy insists that he is building bicycles by soiling his diapers—the impenitent man insists that he is advancing the species by spreading his seed around town. Both grasp at straw arguments to justify themselves.

One of the great things about being a Christian are that we do not have to self-justify. We have been spiritually washed.

> *Baptism does not mean we wash our bodies clean. It*
> *means we are saved from the punishment of sin and go*
> *to God in prayer with a heart that says we are right.*
> *[1 Peter 3:21 NLV]*

Have you been following me in this quest for a link between sexual vulgarity and evolutionary absurdity?

In case you haven't, I will be plain in my conclusion: evolutionary theory is nothing more than a gussied-up attempt to justify one's plentiful ejaculate without the spiritually-cleansing waters of Christian baptism.

Ezekiel 28:2 [NIV]
In the pride of your heart you say, "I am a god in the heart of the seas." But
you are a man and not a god, though you think you are as wise as a god.

94. The Pathetic Character

In late AD 1999, there were many retrospectives on the twentieth century. One of them was on a political talking-heads television program, where the question was posed: "What has mankind learned over the last one hundred years?" One person on the panel, a liberal political pundit, cockily pronounced, "Since the human race did not destroy itself with nuclear weapons when the two superpowers had the opportunity to do so, we can be assured that it will never destroy itself. We came so close to the zero-hour during the Cold War, but calmer heads prevailed and it was never done. Therefore, it will never be done in the future."

Upon hearing this I leapt forward in my chair and exclaimed, "What a moron!"

Insanity is commonly defined as doing the same thing over and over while expecting a different result. I agree. But I offer this addendum: moronity is not expecting a result that has never been observed before.

Is there any more ignorant assumption than that the things that have 'always' been will 'always continue' to be? Is that not the premise of animal, rather than human, behavior?[779]

The male dog lifts his leg toward a wire fence because he deposits his scent wherever he pleases and has never before encountered a problem. Then one day the farmer attaches an automobile battery to electrify the fence and the dog yelps in pain and bewilderment.

The male human being [usually] looks upon the wire before unzipping and says to himself, "I wonder if that thing has finally been activated—better turn around and not try my luck."

In the same way, animals do not expect that there may be an end to the world that they know. But men that use their reasoning ability say, "Just because the sun comes up every day, it doesn't necessarily mean that it will come up again tomorrow. The things that appear to be most reliable may have a limit of which I am unaware—better seek God and be on the safe side."

~~~~~~~~~~~~~~~~~~~~~~~

Picture, if you will, the Darwinian scientist in all his glory, strolling through a virgin forest. Perhaps it is a piece of land that has been preserved by the Nature Conservancy partially through his own largesse. He folds his hands and looks upon the flora and the fauna with a benign smile, as an artist looks over his canvas. In the Darwinian's mind, either in the front or in the back, is the prideful thought, "I am the master of these things. I am the apex of nature. I am lord over all I survey. What an unlikely series of trial-and-error evolutionary accidents produced all these species, and then produced me to be here, now, understanding it all. And yet here I stand. I am great, for I exist, and comprehend the system of nature."

Then he develops a wasting disease and dies a gaunt shadow of his former self. Then the worms that he was admiring the previous season feast upon his flesh.

How could a people so vulnerable to the whims of nature be so arrogant toward her Creator? Watching the activities and machinations of unrepentant men, one gets the impression of a pathetic character in a movie that boasts and blusters until he realizes that the person that he is strutting before is his very executioner. And then, upon the executioner's revelation of his identity and intention, the pathetic character cries pitifully and asks for mercy. He says that he is sorry and would never act in an offensive manner again. When the executioner puts his sword back in its sheath, and appears to be off-guard, the pathetic character jumps him. The moment that the pathetic character thinks he has the upper hand and will be able to beat the executioner to death, he starts talking trash again. But the executioner shrugs him off, the way a man brushes off a fly. The pathetic character realizes that the whole thing was a ruse to prove his sincerity. Once again, he falls to his knees and pleads for forgiveness.

Dear reader, the life-stories of unbelieving men are nothing more than infinite iterations of this pathetic character scene.

> *Those who cling to worthless idols forfeit the grace*
> *that could be theirs. [Jonah 2:8 NIV]*

God waits until it is a cosmic certainty that any given pathetic character is devoid of contrition. Then He administers justice upon him.

> *Since they show no regard for the works of the Lord*
> *and what his hands have done, he will tear them down*
> *and never build them up again. [Psalm 28:5 NIV]*

But the wise and prudent man is the one that stays eternally penitent even when he feels healthy, prosperous, and secure. He does as his Master wishes in all seasons, and in all circumstances. And when he fails, he trusts that his eternally penitent heart shall be forgiven. Then God showers mercy upon him.

Proverbs 29:9 [CEV]
Be wise and don't sue a fool. You won't get satisfaction, because all the fool
will do is sneer and shout.

95. On the Futility of Debates

I was hopelessly lost four weeks into an elective course in biological ocean-ography. I went to see the professor, a forty-five year old, resentful, chrome-dome. His office was in the basement of a dank old federal building. It smelled like the moldy potato sacks in my uncle's barn.

I had excelled at every biology course I had previously taken, and was flummoxed by the 'D' that I received on the professor's first exam. He suggested that I had not previously had a professor as knowledgeable and challenging as himself. He then asked about my undergraduate background (which was in engineering, not biology), and missed no opportunity to be dismissive.

I couldn't understand a thing that came out of his mouth concerning science, and he was quite good at making me feel small. As he spoke, I actually considered putting myself into his hands as my graduate advisor. "He must have something to offer if he is this much smarter than me," I thought.

Just then his telephone rang. He answered the call without excusing himself from our conversation. I was a plebe graduate student, after all.

He took his time on the telephone, so I squeaked out of my low chair and perused his office walls. There were his credentials and honors, of course, and lots of framed photographs of him on ships and in laboratories. In the center of the display was a signed and notarized legal contract with his name in calligraphy. It was from the Church of Satan. He had sold his soul to the devil for 25¢.

He got off the phone and said, "Where were we? Ah, yes, we were discussing the many ways in which you are not a good student."

I said, "You've convinced me. I'm just not at your level. I'll drop the course."

The sarcasm of my *bon mot* was lost on him, but I did not care. I marched directly to the registrar's office and freed myself of the fool. I am so proud of the 'W' (for withdrawal) from that course that is on my permanent transcript. It is a badge of honor.

'W' for winner; 'W' for wise; 'W' for won't give opportunity to the devil.

~~~~~~~~~~~~~~~~~~~~~~~

That fellow did not want to teach me science; he was looking for a lapdog—a bootlicker—a disciple. But a person that denies the existence of God has precisely nothing to offer in the role of mentor.

> *A fool finds no pleasure in understanding but delights*
> *in airing his own opinions. [Proverbs 18:2 NIV]*

If an atheist wants to teach me biological oceanography, or fly-fishing for that matter, I will listen. He will have my attention until he starts to speak of how the trout evolved by an accident of nature to eat the mayfly, which simultaneously evolved by a different, serendipitous, accident of nature. Then I will thank him for his time, and teach myself the rest of fly-fishing from a book. I will not waste my time by engaging him.

Herein lies a fundamental problem with debates: if they are framed incorrectly, they are conveyors of untruth rather than truth.

Let's say, for example, that there are two fiercely opposed opinions on the sun's average surface temperature. The majority of astrophysicists say that it is 10,000°F, but a minority believe it to be 9,000°F. A moderator asks the two sides to debate. He invites one traditional astronomer to explain why ten thousand is the correct number; he invites one minority astronomer to explain why nine thousand is the correct number. But he is unable to find a 9,000°F astronomer to appear because they are not confident enough in their data. Unwilling to have the debate forfeited, the moderator locates an astrologist to appear with the astronomer. The astronomer presents scientific evidence, but the astrologist matter-of-factly counters, "The exact temperature of the sun is unknown and will always be unknown. However, I and my star-gazing colleagues believe that it is not so hot as 10,000°F; it is colder than that. We should move beyond the old notion that the sun is hot. There are, in fact, many alternate ways to view the sun. It is a large and gaseous sphere, for example, like Jupiter—which has a temperature near absolute zero. The sun has many other cold-planet-like attributes, such as having smaller, planetary, satellites. The sun may thus be said to be cold as easily as it may be said to be hot."

The astronomer tries to rebut, but it is impossible to do so in a polite manner without giving credence to his debating opponent and providing him with another angle from which to mock the truth. The astronomer gets frustrated, and says that the forum is unprofitable, and leaves. The astrologist, however, makes a big splash in the media with his pronouncement "… the sun may be said to be cold …"

Now, the public knows next-to-nothing about astronomy. Most of them have never taken any college course, let alone astrophysics. They become aware that there is some controversy on the issue of the sun's average surface temperature. They know in their hearts that the sun is terribly hot, and they would never travel on a space voyage to the surface of the sun, but they still find the astrologist intriguing on some level. They can identify with his jargon because of the ubiquity of astrological horoscopes, and his audacity has an underdog allure. They also know from experience that the truth often lies somewhere in between two arguing parties (again, provided the argument is framed properly). A subsequent poll finds the plurality of public opinion to be that the sun's surface temperature is 4,770.2°F—halfway between 10,000°F and absolute zero (i.e., -459.67°F). That's still hot, but by agreeing to a debate with an astrologist, the astronomer succeeded only in cementing a lie in the peoples' imagination (i.e., that the temperature is less than half of what it actually is).

~~~~~~~~~~~~~~~~~~~~~~~~

It is of little consequence what people think about the surface of the sun. No one is going to visit there. But what each individual believes about God is highly consequential: it determines the fate of his or her soul. You must believe the truth about Him in this life in order to have eternal communion with Him.

God exists. He is eternal, omnipotent, omniscient, omnipresent, and all-loving. To reject these facts is scientific quackery. To debate them is futile. To sell your belief in them to the devil for two bits of American currency is damnatory arrogance.

Daniel 2:45 [TNIV]
The great God has shown the king what will take place in the future. The dream is true and the interpretation is trustworthy.

96. Against Dream Interpretation

In the second year of his reign, King Nebuchadnezzar of Babylon had a nightmare that interrupted his sleeping habits. The king summoned the wise men of his far-flung empire to tell him the meaning.

The wise men told him that his request would not be a problem. They asked him what the dream was about, and promised a proper interpretation.

The king immediately replied,

> *No! I have made up my mind. If you don't tell me both the dream and its meaning, you will be chopped to*

pieces and your houses will be torn down. However,
if you do tell me both the dream and its meaning, you
will be greatly rewarded and highly honored. Now
tell me the dream and explain what it means. [Daniel
2:5–6 CEV]

They begged him to tell them the particulars of the dream, but he suspected that they were specifically tailoring their interpretations to fit the preconceived purpose of pleasing him. He was determined to get sure proof of their veracity.

I can see through your trick! You are trying to stall for
time because you know I am serious about what I said.
If you don't tell me the dream, you will be condemned.
You have conspired to tell me lies in hopes that some-
thing will change. But tell me the dream, and then I
will know that you can tell me what it means. [Daniel
2:8–9 NLT]

The wise men told him that he wasn't being reasonable by expecting them to read his mind, so he gave orders to have them all rounded up for execution. The Prophet Daniel was not at the royal court that day. When officers came to roust him, he requested time to come up with the correct answer to the mystery.

Daniel and his three friends prayed to the God of Israel for mercy, and that night the mystery was revealed to him in a vision.

The dream was of a gold, silver, bronze, and iron statue that represented the succession of world empires from Babylonian, to Medo–Persian, to Grecian, to Roman. Daniel correctly interpreted the dream, including the statue's feet of iron and clay which indicated that the Roman Empire would fall because the,

... people will be a mixture and will not remain
united ... [Daniel 2:43 TNIV]

~~~~~~~~~~~~~~~~~~~~~~~

I am often appalled when I read the science section of the newspaper. One recent article referenced a study about the brightly-colored poison frogs that are found in the jungles of both Africa and South America. These amphibians feast upon ants, and sequester the ant's alkaloid toxin in their skin sacs. The study found that the frogs on both continents developed the defensive weapons of toxin and color-warning in their skin independently from each other—without a common poisonous ancestor.

This was upheld as an example of 'evolutionary convergence,' where two different species in different parts of the world are confronted with the same set of challenges/opportunities in their ecosystem, and end up appearing very much alike, although they are not closely related. The end result in both cases was the advantageous ability of poison frogs to forage in open daylight, without fear of predation.

The scientists inferred that if you put a bland-colored, non-poisonous, ancestor frog in a jungle with alkaloid ants, its descendants would mutate, and eventually adapt to their surroundings by developing flamboyant skin pigments and toxins. One author noted,

> *Sometimes the resemblance really is striking. You'll see two unrelated species of frog, one Madagascan, one [Columbian], and they'll be almost the same size and shape, they'll move in a similar style, and they'll have the same vivid markings in virtually the same place on the body.*[780]

The newspaper reporter said that evolutionists see convergence as a foundational principle that shows that,

> *... often there is one right tool for the job, and that selective pressures will reinvent the bio-utensil whenever the need arises—[and this] exemplifies just how non-random and ostensibly purposeful natural selection can be, **and how readily it may be mistaken for evidence of supernatural "design."***[781]

Umh ... Interesting ... Hummingbirds are the only feathered animal that can hover in place, and deliberately fly vertically and backwards. Some species flap their wings eighty times per second, and their heart rate can exceed one thousand beats per minute.[782] These specializations make it possible for them to maintain position while drinking nectar from oblique-angled flower blossoms. They also have long beaks to penetrate the deep throats of certain flowers—making them important pollinators.

Yet they are only native to North and South America.[783] There are similar flowers in Africa, and all around the world, but hummingbirds are not to be found there. Nevertheless, Rationalists tout the unique speciation of hummingbirds within the ecological niches of the Americas as prime examples of natural selection at work.

You see, no matter what the Rationalist sees in biological nature, he rationalizes it (hence the name) as evolution. If the same type of animals develop independently on different continents, it proves evolution; if a unique animal is found on only one continent, it proves evolution. To them, anything that exists is brilliantly inferred to deconstruct the design feats of God Almighty.[784]

Francis Bacon (AD 1561–AD 1626) cautioned us that,

> *... human understanding is of its own nature prone to suppose the existence of more order and regularity in the world than it finds. And though there be many things which are singular and unmatched, yet it devises for them parallels and conjugates and relatives which do not exist.*[785]

Before Bacon's day, all celestial bodies were thought to move in perfect circles. This was, in time, shown to be untrue. Charles Darwin, in his day, believed that mammalian cells were simply building blocks, filled with an amalgamation of plasma, and stacked on each other. Now we know that cells are unspeakably complicated. The theory of plate tectonics, the theory of the infectious cause of stomach ulcers, the latest theories concerning the peopling of the western hemisphere, are all now radically different from what was thought to have been scientifically 'proven' just a few decades ago.

Those that initially propose to upset the Rationalist orthodoxy are invariably savaged by other scientists. Later, when their findings are brought into orthodoxy, they are lionized. Maddeningly, these contradictions are touted as a sign of enlightenment. Again, the noted atheistic philosopher, Dr. Daniel Dennett, has complained,

> *... where are the examples of religious orthodoxy being simply abandoned in the face of irresistible evidence? Again and again in science, yesterday's heresies have become today's new orthodoxies. No religion exhibits that pattern in its history.*[786]

Where indeed? Rationalists are willing to accept lies as scientific proofs as long as those lies bolster their ambivalence and hostility toward their Creator. They are willing to do so until more ingenious lies are conjured. Yet irresistible evidence for a transcendent God is presented to the Rationalists' senses at every moment of their lives.

> *The heavens declare the glory of God; the skies proclaim the work of his hands. [Psalm 19:1 TNIV]*

Science is still chock-full of untenable 'parallels, conjugates, and relatives' that are employed and defended as stop-gap-measures to avoid saying 'God made it so.' They are employed and defended until new discoveries are made—then they are dumped. This is called scientific progress.

Evolutionary theory is simply the most obnoxious of the stop-gap-measures.

> *Where is the wise man? Where is the scholar? Where is*
> *the philosopher of this age? Has not God made foolish*
> *the wisdom of the world? [1 Corinthians 1:20 NIV]*

Evolution is a faux science—standardless and irreproducible—like Freudian dream interpretation. The 'evidence' for it is either inferential (i.e., based on a sequential series of fossils), or associative (e.g., the presence of angled flowers and hummingbirds in the same ecosystem implies that they must have evolved together). Whichever the case, the Rationalist invariably assumes the dream to mean what he wants it to mean. You cannot disprove him because no actual and reproducible experiments can ever be performed.

A neat trick would be for the evolutionist to gather every manner of physical and chemical information on a hypothetical ecosystem (e.g., soil pH, mean temperature, annual rainfall, percent cloud cover, etc.), and then predict all the living species that will be found there. Somehow, for all their cocksurety, Evolutionists have never volunteered to test their dream interpretation theory against nature in that way. There is no such thing as a predictive theory of biological speciation.

A true scientist puts forth a hypothesis, and then puts it to the test with statistical analysis. For example, our knowledge of the tidal cycles relative to the motion of the moon and sun is science. They can be correlated exactly, and that prediction can be tested into the future with complete accuracy. It is not solely based upon an association of past events.

Any idiot can look at some aspect of the natural world and then conjure up an imaginative theory as to how it came to be. I once heard a limnology professor postulate that the presence of the exact same species of African cichlid fish in two lakes that were a hundred miles apart was attributable to volcanic activity. He said that an eruption under one lake had catapulted its fish into the stratosphere, and splashed them into the other lake where they found a home and reproduced. He was perfectly serious; this was his 'scientific' explanation that justified his underlying belief in evolution. It also justified his research trips to Africa on grant money. I knew at that moment that I was in the presence of a charlatan.

> *How long will this continue in the hearts of these lying prophets, who prophesy the delusions of their own minds?* **They think the dreams they tell one another will make my people forget my name** *... [Jeremiah 23:26–27 NIV]*

So please, if you can explain through evolutionary dream interpretation how the life cycle of the Monarch butterfly has come to be, I don't want to hear it.

In my wildest imagination I cannot see how evolutionary theory could account for the metamorphoses from caterpillar to butterfly. But even if it could, the lifespan of the Monarch is much shorter than the time that it takes to annually migrate from a small forest in central Mexico throughout North America, and back again. All summer long the butterflies are laying eggs and dying in every corner of the United States and southern Canada. Yet the generation alive at the end of summer somehow finds its way to their great grandparents' winter residence in Mexico.[787] Perhaps you'd like to re-think the extent to which natural selection and survival of the fittest can demystify God's handiwork.

My explanation for Monarch butterflies is simple: God wanted to show us an analogy about the afterlife. The bulbous, lumbering, larva is akin to our lives on this earth. The disgusting pupa and cocoon are akin to physical death and placement in a coffin. This is why the Apostle Paul speaks of dead people as having,

> *... fallen asleep. [1 Corinthians 15:6 NKJV]*

But the emergence of the brilliant imago from the cocoon is akin to what will happen to a believing person when he or she will be given a new body at the Second Coming.

> *... let me reveal to you a wonderful secret ... we will all be transformed! [1 Corinthians 15:51 NLT]*

Christ will make us into something as different from a caterpillar as is a beautiful, free, butterfly. The caterpillar lives only on the plant on which it was born, as we live only on planet Earth. But when we shall be given wings, we will fly to the ends of the universe and not lose our way.

> *Even youths grow tired and weary, and young men stumble and fall; but those who hope in the Lord will renew their strength. They will soar on wings like eagles; [Isaiah 40:30–31 NIV]*

Figure 5. God's Foreshadowing of Christians' Resurrected Bodies

One of several hundred Monarch butterflies in a field on the coast of Maine in mid–September. They had just emerged from their cocoons, and immediately headed south toward a small forest in central Mexico. Their brains are the size of a grain of sand and they are several generations removed from the butterflies that came forth from Mexico. Did chance teach them the way to their ancestral winter home? Or did God make these creatures to illustrate something about the afterlife? Photograph by J. Carroll. Used by permission.

2 Timothy 4:3–4 [ESV]
*... the time is coming when people will not endure sound teaching, but hav-
ing itching ears they will accumulate for themselves teachers to suit their own
passions, and will turn away from listening to the truth and wander off into
myths.*

97. Against Pantheistic Myths

In order for the Rationalists' evolutionary religion to be true, it must explain all
the traits and behaviors in living things, but it explains precious few of them.

I recently viewed a program on the Public Broadcasting Service about
baby animals. They showed newborn foxes, seals, bears, and horses. The
matronly-sounding narrator said,

> *There's a visual bond, too—a pattern found in young-
> sters of many species that evokes a nurturing response.
> Big heads, big eyes, little noses—the visual stamp we
> call cute is etched in our genes ... Even creatures quite
> unlike us have that unmistakable appeal. But for all
> the oo-ing and ahh-ing, cuteness is actually a deadly
> serious business. It's no coincidence that the cutest
> young are often the ones most dependent on parental
> care. **Evolution has been perfecting infants for mil-
> lions of years for the sole purpose of making mom
> go that extra mile to keep baby alive ...** [788]*

Think about that assertion for just a moment. That is not science, my
dear reader; it is a pantheistic myth!

Are we to believe that eons ago most baby animals were ugly, and the
parent animals either killed them or neglected them, but preserved the occa-
sional cute newborn—preserved them to the extent that the genes for button
noses and doe eyes were conserved, and all newborns eventually became cute?

That is precisely what we are asked to believe under evolutionary theory. But, the problem is that we never observe animals in nature killing their
offspring based upon their looks. And furthermore a good-many dependent
animals are grotesquely ugly when they are born. Have you ever seen a baby
squirrel?

In fact, now that we can look inside a woman's womb, evolutionary
theory would lead us to conclude that human fetuses will change from looking
like space aliens to looking like baby seals. Then their mothers would be less
likely to abort them, you see ...

The narrator of the public television program actually provided an unknowing service. In making the woefully incorrect statement about the cause of cuteness in baby animals, she let out the house secret of evolutionary theory: in order for it to be correct, it must explain every trait in every species—including my twenty month old goddaughter's impeccable comedic timing. Obviously, it does not.

One does not have to think about one's experiences in the natural world for long before it becomes obvious that forces other than Darwin's pantheistic myth of natural selection are at work.

In AD 1869 the European gypsy moth was introduced to a laboratory near Boston in an attempt to breed it with the silkworm. These non-native pests spread over the region until thirteen million acres of deciduous forest were defoliated in the spring of AD 1981.[789] People in the northeastern United States were panicked at that time, for fear that they would lose their favorite shade trees. They scraped the gypsy moth's fuzzy egg sacks off their trees and put petroleum jelly around the trunks so that the caterpillars would get stuck when they tried to climb up them. You can still see the petroleum jelly rings on the trees today.

That spring, I went for a hike in the Berkshire Mountains; the forest resounded with the sound of billions of caterpillars chomping on young oak and maple leaves. They would sun themselves by hanging from silk in the morning and, as I would walk to class, they would get in my hair and leave a rash on my skin. I drove to eastern Connecticut in June of that year, and all the trees were denuded—as though it were March.

It seemed like the end of the world. According to Darwin's simple predator/prey model, only a few trees that had a natural resistance would survive the infestation; they would have to give seed to repopulate the trees that did not have the genetic mutation to withstand co-existence with gypsy moths. It would take a millennium to recover from this catastrophe. That is precisely what happened when a blight killed billions of American Chestnut trees seventy years before.

But a tremendous thing happened with this particular pestilence: by late June the gypsy moth population had collapsed, and the trees re-budded. The new leaves were not eaten. And the next year those same trees had only a few gypsy moths. Nowadays I have trouble finding gypsy moth egg sacks in the early springtime. It was a one-season correction.

How did this happen? At the time, a botanist posited the pantheistic myth that the trees had chemically communicated with each other via their root systems on how to produce gypsy moth toxin in their sap. I found this implausible when I heard it. If it were true, then every tree that was isolated in a hayfield would have been doomed.

I don't know how God saved the great deciduous forests of the northeastern United States. But one thing is for certain: it was not by evolution, otherwise you'd have a hard time finding trees that are more than twenty-five years old.

Would you excuse me for a moment? I must take a break from writing to rake the leaves that have fallen from the two hundred year old oak in my backyard.

~~~~~~~~~~~~~~~~~~~~~~~~

Ah, there's nothing like some brisk yard work in the fall!

Let us again turn to the issue of proof: in order for the Rationalists' evolutionary religion to be true, species must be able to morph into entirely different species. There is no direct evidence for this.

Evolutionary theorists tell us that the reason that we do not observe species changing radically is that we live within a short chunk of evolutionary time. But they tell us that there is still proof that evolution is occurring today. They often point to the human immunodeficiency virus [HIV] for evidence. It has developed drug resistance as the fight against Acquired Immune Deficiency Syndrome [AIDS] has progressed.

Now, we know that the HIV virus replicates every twenty-four hours in the human body, and some people have been living with the disease and taking protease inhibitor drugs for years. If this went on for fifteen years, that would be about 5,500 virus 'generations.' This translates to about 110,000 human years, assuming humans reproduce every twenty years.

Don't you think that this is long enough for HIV to not just gain drug resistance, but to become something other than a virus? After all this time, it is still just a virus. It has not become a bacterium, or a fungus, or a protozoan, or anything else. It has not sprouted wings and flown out the nostril of an AIDS patient who is taking drugs that it does not like.

But evolutionists would have us believe (based upon the drug resistance, and the inferences they make from fossils) that things that do not have wings develop them through a series of mutations that are compounded by natural selection. Their religion is an affront to objectivism and has no more place among the legitimate sciences than does Freudianism.

~~~~~~~~~~~~~~~~~~~~~~

Allow me to take a recess from my exegesis against Pantheism and Rationalism in order to share with you a joy that I have recently discovered: for the last few months, I've been driving through the mountains of central Pennsylvania on business (Section 10). As I pass the Appalachian bedrock through which the highway cuts, the following thoughts have come into my mind: God made these magnificent rock formations in order for me to look upon them. They are not here by accident; I am not here by accident. God went through the trouble of making both the earth and me. He granted the English colonists victory in the French and Indian War; then He enabled people to make automobiles, and dynamite, and roads. He saw to it that I could drive, and He set me upon this road this year, and He made my eyes to glance at the cut-outs of tilted and whirled metamorphic rock. He did this so that I could, in turn, say, "Wow. Thanks, Jesus. That's so-o-o-o beautiful."

> *Fear God and give him glory, because the hour of his judgment has come. Worship him who made the heavens, the earth, the sea and the springs of water. [Revelation 14:7 NIV]*

Likewise, the baby horses and seals and bears are not cute as a result of evolutionary forces that stimulated the parent animals to care for cute off-spring. They are cute because God wanted me to look at them, and say, "Oh! That's so-o-o-o cute. Praise Father, Son, and Holy Spirit for making such lovely creatures."

The earth is God's garden, given for me. The entire universe has been given to me.

> *Now the Lord God had planted a garden in the east, in Eden; and there he put the man he had formed. And the Lord God made all kinds of trees grow out of the ground—trees that were pleasing to the eye and good for food. [Genesis 2:8–9 NIV]*

Nothing is too good or too much trouble for His children. In fewer than thirty years, I will be exploring every corner of His Creation in an incorruptible body. I am a child of privilege, and all these years I did not even realize it.

> *He that spared not his own Son, but delivered him up for us all, how shall he not with him also freely give us all things? [Romans 8:32 KJV]*

How happy—how overwhelmed with joy I am to begin to discover the fullness of what my Heavenly Father has in store for me. Words are not enough for me to express my gratitude for this undeserved gift.

I love Him. That is the crux of the matter. I love Him because He loved me when He did not have to love me. It matters not to me how few persons in the world will heed the Lord Jesus. I will trust and obey because I love Him.

> *May you have power with all God's people to understand Christ's love. May you know how wide and long and high and deep it is ... Then you will be filled with everything God has for you. [Ephesians 3:18–19 NIrV]*

Do you see the difference in outlook that such a mindset causes? A Rationalist feels that his existence is insignificantly meaningless in the great scheme of things. At the same time, his very against-all-odds presence in the world makes him prideful. It is the serendipitous pride of a lottery jackpot winner. He is driven to justify himself with 'good works' and to leave a legacy on the face of the earth. In so doing he strikes a holier-than-thou pose, and preaches to others about being environmentally-conscious (Section 94).

The Christian feels his existence is a planned birth (or adoption) into a royal household. He is humbled by his unworthiness to receive such an inheritance. He is overwhelmed with gratitude as he tries to come to terms with his Father's unfathomable generosity. He knows that he can never do anything to repay God, so he is just devoted and thankful. He takes on Christ's humility, and spreads the Gospel message. His legacy is to love God and to be about God's business.

Proverbs 9:10 [NKJV]
The fear of the Lord is the beginning of wisdom, and the knowledge of the Holy One is understanding.

98. The Word of Knowledge

If a Rationalist, especially an evolutionary zealot, is reading this, I predict that he is fuming over my 'misrepresentation' of his orthodoxy. If I were giving a lecture, he might interrupt me, or at least challenge me during the question-and-answer period. But how could he say one critical word without demolishing his argument for evolution? As a believer in evolution, he would have to accept my arguments against it as being valid in their own right.

When Dr. Jane Goodall began to observe the chimpanzees of the Gombe Stream National Park in Tanzania, she had expected to find a society of noble savages. Instead, she found that they engage in gang wars, murder by dismemberment, and even cannibalism.[790] Nevertheless, she did not interfere or make moral judgments on their various behaviors. As a dedicated and capable behavioral scientist, she just observed and documented.

If evolutionary biology is true, then I, as a biological organism, am a product of it as much as my cousin, the chimpanzee. I have been produced as a result of innumerable fertile unions of individuals that came together under the paradigm of natural selection.[791] Some of these matings were between humans; some were between pre–human man/apes; some were between lower life forms that lived in slimy pools of water. My rational mind is nothing more than the composite product of creatures that competed with each other for food, shelter, and, most recently, tax loopholes. There can be no question of my having freewill, or of my being either right or wrong, or of my being either a saint or a charlatan, because my thoughts are under the constraints of my evolutionary inheritance.[792]

So a pure evolutionist would not indict me as a liar or a kook. He would have no moral fervor whatsoever—even if all my readers are converted away from evolutionism. Instead, he would sit back and take notes on my, and your, behavior. He would act as a detached, dispassionate, scientist, and postulate that survival-of-the-fittest was at work in the bookstores. Perhaps he would hypothesize that I am preening on these pages because I hope to copulate with the ovulating females that come to my book signings. In that way they would carry on my seed so that my offspring would grow up to become even stronger anti-evolutionists. Or perhaps my goal is to impress the male members of the audience with my intellectual prowess and make them subservient to me.

In any case, the one thing that a pure evolutionist would not do, if he remembered his evolutionary theory out-of-school, would be to question my veracity.[793] Because for those that do not accept the necessity of a transcendent God as a prerequisite for life, there can be no such thing as truth. There just is what there is; and that, by definition, is evolution; and evolution is what they believe in. **So they must shut-up and accept what I say.**

In this way, the circular logic of Rationalism refutes itself for, as J.B.S. Haldane (AD 1892–AD 1964) noted,

> *If my mental processes are determined wholly by the motions of atoms in my brain, I have no reason to suppose that my beliefs are true ... and hence I have no reason for supposing my brain to be composed of atoms.*[794]

So, likewise, if Charles Darwin's ability to formulate and publish *The Origin of the Species* is properly represented by the Modernist icon of apes transitioning into *Homo sapiens* along an evolutionary continuum, then we have no reason to believe that the words that came out of Darwin's head are any more enlightened than the sticky tongue that shoots out of a frog's head … and hence we have no reason to believe that human beings and apes evolved from a common ancestor.[795]

I hope that I have demonstrated to your satisfaction that the phenomenon of human reason cannot be accounted for by the theory of evolution. But please don't wait for me to offer an alternative scientific explanation.

I have no idea how even single-celled life originated on this planet. Scientists have not yet been able to create living things in the laboratory from inert things. They can recreate the proverbial primordial ooze, and zap it with radiation, all they want—all they get is hot ooze.

That being the case, I certainly have no scientific explanation about how human minds came into being. But this much is obvious: in order for anything that anyone says to be either truthful or untruthful, human reason must not be a derivative phenomena brought about gradually by environmental factors.[796] Rather, it must have its origin in something that stands outside of nature and outside of time.[797] That can only be the eternal God. Human reason must be kindled by a transcendent God, or it loses its own credentials.[798]

The Apostle John was telling us this when he wrote of the God-man, Jesus Christ,

> *In the beginning was the Word, and the Word was with God, and the Word was God. He was with God in the beginning. Through him all things were made; without him nothing was made that has been made. [John 1:1–3 NIV]*

The word, 'Word,' here is *Logos* in the Greek language. It means logical, true, reasoned knowledge. We get the English word 'logic' from *logos*, as well as the suffix, '–ology,' meaning 'the study of.'

This verse may, therefore, be paraphrased:

> *In the beginning was that which makes it possible for human beings to understand the truth, and that which makes it possible for human beings to understand the truth was with God, and that which makes it possible for human beings to understand the truth was God. He was with God in the beginning. Through him all*

*things were made; without him nothing was made that
has been made.*

I pray that you would swear-off the false prophecy of Rationalism, and come to know the Word of Knowledge that makes it possible for human beings to understand the truth.

John 18:37 [NKJV]
For this cause I was born, and for this cause I have come into the world, that I should bear witness to the truth. Everyone who is of the truth hears My voice.

99. The Ultimate Because

Even if Rationalists turn a blind eye to all the evidence for God in every aspect of Creation, there is still yet another great evidence that they must ignore: wondrous miracles.

If you think you have never seen a miracle in your life, you should stifle your predisposition to explain everything causally. This is a uniquely human trait. We wish to know the 'why' of things, just as if the knowledge of the motivational cause explains away the meaning of the thing being observed. We often say in refutation, "He is in favor of public works projects *because* he is a state contractor" or "She is against yogurt consumption *because* she is lactose intolerant."[799]

Likewise, in science, the tendency is to think that various explanations for natural phenomena lead us closer to demystifying God's miraculous Creation.[800] For example, scientists recently discovered the flight mechanism of honeybees. They pronounced that this 'put to rest' the suggestion that a Supreme Being must be responsible for the complexity of bee flight.[801]

Significantly, the scientists only accounted for the aerodynamics of bee flight; they did not 'put to rest' the mystery of how to manufacture a living bee out of a complete vacuum, as God did at Creation.

The Bible foretold that people would be made proud through scientific discovery:

> When God hides a matter, he gets glory. When kings
> figure out a matter, they get glory. [Proverbs 25:2
> NIrV]

Therefore, God predicted that He would perform completely inexplicable miracles to confound the worldly wise:

> *... once again I will do things that shock and amaze*
> *them, and I will destroy the wisdom of those who claim*
> *to know and understand. [Isaiah 29:14 CEV]*

Belief in miracles is not due to ignorance, nor are miracles undocumented. A recent national survey has found that three quarters of physicians believe in miracles; two thirds believe that the Bible is either inspired by God, or written by God; and fifty-five percent say they have witnessed miraculous results in their patients.[802]

The fact is that supernatural miracles do occur all the time in the natural world—in the very light of day. And they invariably occur upon the invocation of the Triune God (as opposed to the Islamic, Judaic, Hindu, or pantheistic gods).[803] Yet Rationalism does not—cannot—account for these miracles.

In the early AD 1980's there was a nationally-broadcast television program called *That's Incredible!* One week they showed a man that had lost an eyeball in a childhood accident. What was incredible about this man was that he was able to read through that very eye socket. The producers of the television program proved this by plastering and wrapping his remaining eye, and then handing him a randomly-selected book off a shelf in a library, and pointing to a random passage. He read every word.

The man explained that an old woman had prayed over his plastic prosthetic eye in the name of Jesus Christ of Nazareth, and after that he could see through it. His ophthalmologist was dumbfounded.

There is no rational 'because' explanation for this event. The man's ability to read through his non-existent eyeball is impossible without a supernatural miracle. But if you accept even one supernatural miracle, how can you then say that the miracle of a Six Day (or six minute) Creation is too much for God to handle? Or how can you say that Jesus Christ cannot return from the sky to put an end to this earth at any moment?

He can do whatever He wants. He is God. He is the Ultimate Because.

> *You are the God who performs miracles; you dis-*
> *play your power among the peoples. [Psalms 77:14*
> *TNIV]*

My three year old godson knows this very well. I was visiting with him last week, and he asked me a question about some aspect of the physical world. I answered the question, and he immediately asked a follow-up, 'Why?' I answered in more detail, and he immediately follow-up again with, 'Why?' Children like to do this.

I was on to him, so I borrowed my third answer from the Khoja (Section 89), "Because God made it that way." The boy accepted that answer. But 'belief in science' is the game of shaking off that answer and replacing it with endless iterations of cause-and-effect explanations—even if you have to lie, as in the case with biological evolution.

Open your eyes—open your eyes and stop believing that the calloused cause-and-effect explanations of science, whether legitimate or bogus, will ever bring us any closer to explaining human existence. The ultimate 'because' is always an unknowable, supernatural, invasion of nature by God Almighty.[804]

We are alive because God chose to become a man through a wondrous miracle in the virgin Mary; we are alive because God is love.

Luke 21:11 [NKJV]
And there will be great earthquakes in various places, and famines and pestilences;

100. The Thirty Year Warning

In AD 1994 I attended a Christian conference where the speaker was a spunky old Scotsman from a Bible college. In the middle of his lecture he referenced this section's verse heading. He looked up from his notes, and spoke extemporaneously.

"By the way," he said, "whenever an earthquake occurs in our modern age—like the one in Northridge, California this year, people ask silly questions. They say, 'Do you think God is trying to tell us something? Is it a sign of some sort? Could there be any meaning behind it?' The answer to those questions is an emphatic 'Yes!' God is always trying to tell us something, and the message is always the same. He's saying, 'Repent! The end of all things is near!'"

He continued, "Whenever earthquakes are mentioned in the Bible, they are always associated with God's hand. The shifting of tectonic plates are no accident of geology—they are directed. Pay attention when they happen. God is speaking through them. And that very same divine message is given when we hear of people dying. God wants to get it through our thick skulls that our lives, and this whole world, are going to pass away soon."

A few months later I was at a business buffet that was completely unrelated to the Christian conference, and I overheard a lady mention the Scotsman's name. I asked what she was talking about.

"Oh, a professor from the UK," she said sadly. "He was a great guy. He just died of a massive heart attack. The Good Lord took him home."

~~~~~~~~~~~~~~~~~~~~~~~~~

The chances of a random annual event happening on one particular day of the year is obviously one in three hundred and sixty-five. That's the chance, for example, that the largest tarpon caught in Florida waters during AD 2005 will fall on Independence Day (assuming equal fishing pressure and equal fish activity all year long).

The chances of two such random annual events (e.g., largest and second largest tarpon catch) happening on two particular days of any given year (e.g., Independence Day and Labor Day) are one in three hundred and sixty-five *squared*, or one in 133,225.

In the twelve months between mid AD 2004 and mid AD 2005, there were two enormous earthquakes off the coast of northwest Sumatra. The first earthquake had the longest duration ever recorded (nearly ten minutes), and the second largest magnitude ever recorded (9.2 on the Richter scale). The earthquake together with the resulting tsunamis left 230,000 people dead.[805] It occurred on the day after Christmas.[xliv]

> ... *the nations will be in turmoil, perplexed by the*
> *roaring seas and strange tides. [Luke 21:25 NLT]*

The second earthquake had a magnitude of 8.7 on the Richter scale—making it the seventh largest earthquake in the preceding one hundred years. It was too large to be considered an aftershock, and was called a 'triggered earthquake' by seismologists. It left 1,300 people dead, and occurred on the day after Easter.[806]

The chances that these two events would fall on the days following the two greatest holidays on the Christian calendar are one in 133,225. I believe the earthquakes were Providence's thirty year warning to planet Earth. This whole world is going to pass away that soon.

> ... *a loud voice came out of the temple of heaven, from*
> *the throne, saying, "It is done!" And there ... was a*
> *great earthquake, such a mighty and great earthquake*
> *as had not occurred since men were on the earth.*
> *[Revelation 16:17–18 NKJV]*

---

xliv   Amazingly, this was one year, almost to the hour, after the Bam, Iran earthquake that killed 30,000 people.

~~~~~~~~~~~~~~~~~~~~~~~

On March 27, AD 1964, Providence gave a seventy year warning to planet Earth: The most powerful earthquake in North American history occurred in Prince William Sound, Alaska the day after the Christian holiday of Maundy Thursday (i.e., on Good Friday). The magnitude was 9.2; one hundred and thirty-one people perished.

~~~~~~~~~~~~~~~~~~~~~~~

At the time of the Indian Ocean earthquake and tsunami, a teenaged friend asked me if this was a sign of the end of the world. By that time in my life, I knew better than to say that it was merely a random geologic event. I answered, "Yes. It is a sign from our great and mighty Creator that the end is coming soon. It is important that people repent and be prepared for it."

The boy that asked the question was satisfied, but a boy standing next to him scoffed. I said, "Oh, you're saying to yourself that terrible earthquakes happen all the time—in previous centuries, as well as now?"

He nodded.

"They sure do," I confirmed. "They happen in so-called Christian nations, as well as in Muslim nations like this one in Indonesia. They are all miraculous signs of the Second Coming of Christ and the end of the world. Every day after the Creation of the world is a day closer to the end of the world. And the time between the Ascension of Christ and the Second Coming of Christ is known in the Bible as the End Times. Everything that happens during this Messianic Era—whether common or extraordinary—is a sign of His imminent return."

1 John 1:4 [TNIV]
We write this to make our joy complete.

101. The Dearth of Writing

I have a friend that obtained a doctoral degree in Victorian British history. I once asked him why he chose to study the reign of Victoria (AD 1819–AD 1901). If he so admired British Regina, why had he not written a dissertation about Queen Anne (AD 1665–AD 1714) or Queen Elizabeth I (AD 1533–AD 1603)?

He told me that one of the problems that historians run into are a lack of primary sources. The further back your specialization, the greater the dearth of written material. People that study the history of ancient civilizations are in quite a pickle. They have a minuscule written record to comment upon.

I relate this story to illustrate a remarkable, but invariably glossed-over point: precious little was ever written down before 1500 BC; and virtually nothing was written down before 3000 BC.

The first 'writings' are those of the Sumerian civilization of southern Mesopotamia. It is a pre–cuneiform system that dates to 3500 BC.[807] Proto–hieroglyphs have been found in Egypt from ~ 3300 BC, but the first full sentence is from the tomb of a pharaoh that died in ~ 2700 BC.[808] That is about the same time that the oldest pyramid was built. Chinese scripting originated around 1200 BC—roughly the same period that the Greeks and Hittites started writing. In the New World, the Zapotecs of southern Mexico wrote on stone blocks no earlier than 500 BC.

The greatest treasure-trove of ancient writing comes from the city of Ebla in northern Syria. An archive of more than 20,000 cuneiform tablets was found there dating from approximately 2250 BC.[809] These provide intriguing details of daily life and commerce in both a Sumerian and Semitic language. Around that same time the city of Lothal in the Indus Valley was founded, and the world's first trading dock was built there.[810]

Now, we know that language and communication are central to human nature. We have seen twins that make up their own unique language while they are toddlers. No human beings have ever been found that do not form a community, and speak with each other over meals, and build things. It is also a fact that the cuneiforms and hieroglyphs of the Middle East, Far East, and New World all developed independently from each other within a period of three thousand years. Why, then, is there a total absence of written records from *Homo sapiens* that supposedly lived hundreds of thousands of years ago?

We are told that the oldest *Homo sapiens* fossil is at least 130,000 years old.[811] Paleoanthropologists universally agree that humans have existed with the same DNA and mental capacity as ourselves for over 200,000 years.[812] The latest archaeological research even shows evidence of human activity in Europe from as long as 700,000 years ago.[813] [And we are not supposed to laugh at this absurd assertion? Is it not *prima facie* evidence that their dating techniques are flawed?]

Don't you find it odd that these one-hundred-percent genetically-human people only left behind cave wall paintings and crude stone and bone tools for ~ 194,500 of the 200,000 years, and then suddenly started writing and building cities ~ 5,500 years ago? What were they doing for all those tens of thousands of years beforehand? Was it something in the water that made the isolated civilizations around the globe simultaneously become inventive within the biblical time frame—after living in illiteracy and intellectual dormancy for eons?

It's no use saying that it took 194,500 years for man to become intelligent enough to write things down—they were as human and as intelligent as you and me!

Take, for example, the temple complexes, celestial calendars, and detailed annals from the Mayan civilization that rose and fell between 600 BC and AD 900. Their story is an impressive, if bloody, historical fact. But if the Maya are representative of what would happen to a people that are kept in a proverbial ant farm in the jungle, then why has that cycle not repeated itself a hundred-times-over throughout the supposed age of the humans? Where are the equivalent ruins from the civilizations that rose and fell between, say, 151500 BC and 150000 BC? What about those that rose and fell between 101500 BC and 100000 BC? What about between 51500 BC and 50000 BC?

There are no cities and no writings. Absolutely none. There are only the scant remains of campsites and caves dwellings.

Think of it: we do not know the name of even one person that was [supposedly] alive more than six thousand years ago.

Do the paleoanthropologists take us for fools?

Genesis 1:27–28 [NKJV]
God created man in His own image; in the image of God He created him; male and female He created them. Then God blessed them, and God said to them, "Be fruitful and multiply; fill the earth and subdue it; have dominion over the fish of the sea, over the birds of the air, and over every living thing that moves on the earth."

102. Against Anthropomorphism and Zoomorphism

Timothy Treadwell (born Timothy William Dexter; AD 1957–AD 2003) was a failed actor, a recovering opiate addict, and a self-described eco-warrior. After a whimsical motorcycle ride from southern California to Alaska, he took upon himself the cause of the brown bears—the largest land predators in the world. He had no formal training as a wildlife biologist, but he was a pioneer in the ephemeral belief that men and bears could live together in harmony. Mr. Treadwell and his supporters theorized that a progression of understanding about the reliability of bear behavior could benefit bears—just as it was eventually deemed safe for people to scuba dive alongside orcas.

Mr. Treadwell took great risks to prove that bears are not the ferocious beasts depicted in hunting magazines. For thirteen summers he went to the Katmai National Park to film himself inching up to them and chanting, "I love you ... I love you ..." He spoke to them in a high-pitched, sing-song, voice that he believed calmed them. The more success he had, the more invulnerable, and bear-like, he felt. He boasted,

> *I will protect them, I will die for them, but I will not die*
> *at their claws and paws. I will fight, I will be strong.*
> *I'll be one of them.*[814]

His AD 1997 book, *Among Grizzlies*, brought Treadwell the fame that had eluded him fifteen years beforehand when he had auditioned for roles in Hollywood situation comedies. For several years after his book was published, he appeared in television interviews, and traveled the country giving slideshows to schoolchildren. He became a *cause célèbre*, and two hikers were killed by bears in Glacier National Park trying to emulate his technique.

Mr. Treadwell maintained that his presence in Katmai deterred bear shootings, but sport hunting is illegal in the park, and rangers never reported there being any poaching. A majority of bear cubs are killed by male bears every year; sometimes adult bears are also killed and eaten by larger, more powerful, bears. Mr. Treadwell found ways to blame mankind and God for bear cannibalism. During a drought that dried up the salmon run, he ranted,

> *I want rain. I want, if there's a God, to kick some ass*
> *down here. Let's have some water! Jesus boy! Let's*
> *have some water! Christ man, or Allah, or Hindu*
> *floaty thing! Let's have some [expletive] water for*
> *these animals!*[815]

He considered the bears to be his personal furry friends; he gave them inane names like, Aunt Melissa, Booble, Mr. Chocolate, Freckles, and Cupcake. He maintained that he was able to get "deep within the brown bear culture." When Katmai National Park zoologists warned that his behavior was dangerous, he famously said, "I would be honored to end up in bear scat."[816]

During his final field season, he purposely situated his tent in a heavily trafficked bear trail that he called 'The Grizzly Maze.' He stayed there with his girlfriend until the salmon run had tapered off, and during a year in which there had been a poor berry crop. From his tent, on September 14, AD 2003, he wrote an obsequious letter to his primary benefactor in Colorado:

> *Hello! I am writing you a last letter for the journey ...*
>
> *My transformation [is] complete—[I'm] a fully accepted wild animal—[I'm a] brother to these bears. I run free among them—with absolute love and respect for all the animals. I am kind and viciously tough.*
>
> *People—especially the bear experts of Alaska—believe this cannot be done. Some even bet on my death. They are sure you must have some sort of weapon for defense—pepper spray at the least, an electric fence a must. And you cannot hope to make it in a flimsy tent under thick cover among one of Earth's largest gatherings of giant brown grizzly bears.*
>
> *People who knowingly enter bear habitat with pepper spray, guns, and electric fences are committing a crime to the animals [sic]. They begin with the accepted idea of bringing instruments of pain to the animals. If they are that fearful, then they have no place in the land of this perfect animal.*
>
> *Could I look at [the cubs] Dixon, Lilly, and their mother, Melissa, and tell them that I love them, that I will care for them, with a can of mace in my pocket? Does the fox or vole get zapped by the wicked sting of an electric fence for being curious?*
>
> *This wilderness—the Grizzly Maze—had big problems not too many years ago. People who came to kill the animals [sic]. I was threatened with death. One group promising to stuff me alive in a crab pot and submerge it in the icy sea [sic].*
>
> *They are gone now. The Maze returned to the animals.*
>
> *You made this possible. I am a miserable fundraiser. Without you these animals would have been left without any care. Care that I can offer them without any displacement or disrespect [sic]. I even erase my footprints.*

... You got me here for so many years. I will always remember and be thankful ... I will tell [the bears] of your kindness and generosity. Animals are alive because of you. Myself included.[817]

Three weeks later—less than a day before they were to be airlifted out—Mr. Treadwell and his girlfriend were mauled and eaten. An old male bear was found sitting on what was left of their corpses. It had rotten teeth and had not put on enough fat for winter.

Mr. Treadwell's last words were recorded by the video camera that he switched on before leaving his tent to confront the old bear. He yelled to his girlfriend, "Get out here! I'm getting killed!" and finally, "Hit the bear [with a frying pan]!"

~~~~~~~~~~~~~~~~~~~~~~~~~

Werner Herzog, the German filmmaker, made a documentary about Timothy Treadwell after his horrific death. He narrated,

... what haunts me is that in all the faces of all the bears that Treadwell ever filmed, I discover no kinship, no understanding, no mercy. I see only the overwhelming indifference of nature. To me, there is no such thing as a secret world of the bears. And this blank stare speaks only of a half-bored interest in food. But for Timothy Treadwell, this bear was a friend, a savior.[818]

The Timothy Treadwell story demonstrates the folly of anthropomorphizing animals. He mistook dangerous giant predators for people in bear suits.

His story also demonstrates the flipside of anthropomorphism: zoomorphizing human beings into animals. Mr. Treadwell thought of himself as a bear; he wanted to know them and to be accepted into their society. Sometimes he grunted and moved like a bear when he dealt with other humans.

But a bear is a bear, and a human is a human. The bears do not have a society, and they can never be reasoned with. No amount of baby talk will acculturate them to any standard of civilized behavior. Disney movies aside, they are not capable of intimate kinship with human beings. The same may be said for dolphins, apes, horses, and even companion animals like dogs.

The difference is that God did not make animals in His image—they do not have souls. Humans were never meant to be one with nature; we were created to be lords over all the soulless creatures of nature (Genesis 1:26).

If you believe the fantasy that humans and apes share a common ancestor, you practice a subtle variant of anthropomorphism. That is what Darwin's ape-to-man progression is all about. Treadwell simply had the lunacy to put the theory of evolution to the test by visiting his bearish cousins. He would have gotten away with it if he had not overstayed his welcome by one crucial day.

Also, if you believe the fantasy that *Homo sapiens*, with the exact same DNA as you and me, existed as grunting cavemen for 200,000 years, you practice a form of zoomorphism.

In either case, you cannot be intellectually consistent and simultaneously believe that God became a human being just 2,000 years ago in accordance with the Old Testament prophecies. Therefore, you are one that uses science to prop-up the Antichrist's rejection of God's message of salvation. Therefore, you are part of the False Prophet of Revelation.

~~~~~~~~~~~~~~~~~~~~~~~

The anthropomorphic implications of evolution are exceedingly racist. It is shameful how widely-held these beliefs are on supposedly hypersensitive college campuses.

The Bible tells us that all modern people trace their paternal lineage to Noah, who lived fewer than five thousand years ago in the Armenian highlands.

> *All flesh is not the same flesh, but there is one kind of*
> *flesh of men, another flesh of animals, another of fish,*
> *and another of birds. [1 Corinthians 15:39 NKJV]*

But the evolutionists insist that humans broke off from apes about five million years ago somewhere in the Horn of Africa. They say that we moved across the face of the earth from that cradle, and adapted to the climate and terrain wherever we went. Does that not imply that today's natives of East Africa are the least changed from our common, sub-human, ancestors?

You Rationalists needn't fake indignation at my astringent question. Whether I say it or not, you're not fooling anyone: if you believe in evolution, you believe that Black people are a tiny bit more monkey-like than everybody else. You see an association between their skin-tone, flat noses, and sweat glands, and those of the gorilla. In your heart-of-hearts you are repulsed by the reminder that you see in Black people of what your ancestors once were.

You find it disconcerting. Moreover, the guilt over your undeserved status as a superior being leads you to patronize them. Like the Deist, Thomas Jefferson (AD 1743–AD 1826), who thought Negro women could only be found attractive by male orangutans,[819] and like all good Liberals after him, you are a filthy racist.

I, on the other hand, see the differences between the races as only artifacts of the sinful world. This includes my very own olive skin, Roman nose, and brillo-textured beard. As a Christian, I believe that all people were created in the image of God Almighty. I believe we are all fallen creatures. I believe that after the Tower of Babel, people went in different directions, and the peculiarities of their family lines became accentuated into races and nation-groups.

> *That is why it was called Babel—because there the Lord confused the language of the whole world. From there the Lord scattered them over the face of the whole earth. [Genesis 11:9 NIV]*

Each race of people has inherited the nominal trait differences of their completely-human common ancestor, Noah, from just a few hundred generations ago.

> *From these three sons of Noah came all the people who now populate the earth. [Genesis 9:19 NLT]*

And Noah was a descendant of Adam, who was created all-at-once by God Almighty out of the elements.

> *From one man he made every nation of men, that they should inhabit the whole earth; and he determined the times set for them and the exact places where they should live. **God did this so that men would seek him** and perhaps reach out for him and find him, though he is not far from each one of us. [Acts 17:26–27 NIV]*

It is, therefore, my working hypothesis that black Africans have the racial features that they do, and white Europeans have the racial features that they do, for no other reason than that God directed certain husband and wife pairs to certain places. This separation occurred in modern-day Iraq in 2144 BC,[820] and the family traits became accentuated over a few generations. The devil has used that demographic coincidence to fool Rationalists into drawing a [false] scientific inference. Where they see an association between human beings and apes, I see a poorly-contrived charade.

I believe this because Holy Scripture testifies that all are equal in God's eyes, and that each human being is afforded an opportunity that is not available to any derivative of an animal.

> For as many as are led by the Spirit of God, these are
> sons of God. [Romans 8:14 NKJV]

We are sons of God based upon faith, not the sons of apes based upon chance! No ancestor of any human being that has ever lived is the least bit closer to a soulless animal than any other human being.

Therefore, if I were living in the Sudan today, I would eagerly seek out my black Christian brothers in the south, and avoid like the plague the lighter-skinned Muslims of the north. My physical appearance is much more like the Arab Muslims of northern Sudan, but what do I care about that? I want to live among Christians! Please, African brothers, take me into your community and shelter me from the Antichrist Beast!

O the joy to be a Christian. Sweet-freedom from race-obsession. Thank you, Lord Christ!

~~~~~~~~~~~~~~~~~~~~~~~~

The zoomorphic implications of evolution are more subtly racist than the anthropomorphic implications, but just as disturbing. Zoomorphism implies that [what are ostensibly] fully-evolved people may become sub-human based upon their acculturation or upbringing.

It is not uncommon to hear Rationalists (or Liberals) say that we in the United States must not 'force' our way of life upon other peoples. I grew up during the Cold War hearing Liberals confidently pronounce that the people behind the Iron Curtain did not want to be free. Their theory was that the people living in communist countries had their own, innate, economic and political system, and we had our system—theirs was right for them; ours was right for us. And, all the more so today, Liberals say that it is wrong to force freedom onto the Muslim peoples. We are told that they do not want to have the franchise to vote for their laws and their leaders.

In order for this to be true, they must be a different type of creature than we are—their childhood environment must have changed them to the point where they are human in a different way than we are human.

This is, of course, malarkey. It is so easily disproved that I hesitate to proceed with any argument against it ...

> Why are you doing this? We are humans just like you.
> Please give up all this foolishness. Turn to the living

> *God, who made the sky, the earth, the sea, and every-*
> *thing in them. [Acts 14:15 CEV]*

How could it ever be that West Germans wanted to own Mercedes, while East Germans were satisfied with Ladas? How could Puerto Ricans want to vote for their leadership, while Cubans eternally love Fidel? How could Taiwanese enjoy public dissent, while Mainland Chinese march in lock-step for Mao? How could Lebanese Arab women want to wear bikinis on Mediterranean beaches, while Saudi Arab women want to wear burqas and be under house arrest?

In marked contrast, Christians believe that all people—regardless of the oppression of their family and society—regardless of their salvation-state—yearn to be free.

I once saw a wildlife program in which a female of a fish-eating spe-cies of duck snuck into the nest of an algae-eating species of duck and lay an egg there. Ornithologists call this behavior 'egg parasitism.' All the eggs in the nest hatched around the same time, and they were all led out of the nest by their mother/foster mother to swim and forage.

The ducklings that were the adult duck's true offspring followed her, and mimicked her behavior by skimming the surface for algae. But the one duckling that was of another species could not help itself but to dive for min-nows to eat. It would come back up to the surface, and try to get back in-line with the brood, but then it would feel the impulse to dive again. Within an hour it became distracted by its instinct to the point where it wandered away permanently.

I was at a wholesale warehouse the other day, and I turned into an aisle in which there was a young family of human beings. The parents were looking at frozen food, and their two year old boy was at the opposite side of the aisle looking at bulk-packaged macaroni and cheese. I watched as the boy grabbed a box that was almost as big as he was, and wrestled it into the lower level of his parent's shopping cart. This took him some time and he almost fell twice while managing the task. When he finished, he dusted off his hands and said to himself in exultation, "I did it!"

His parents turned around to see what it was that he had done. His father said, "Good job, Douglas! But I already have one of those in the cart."

The boy looked up at him as if to say, "Why not two?"

His father said, "You're right. Two is better than one."

The little boy's behavior tells us several key things about human beings: his mother had obviously made macaroni and cheese for him before. He obviously liked it. He saw it on the shelf, and made the association, "If I put this in the cart, Mom will buy it and make it for me again." His tiny two year old brain, fed by tiny amounts of two year old testosterone, led him to work toward a goal—a goal that he desired to accomplish by himself. When he had successfully completed his task, he communicated satisfaction on a job well done.

Humans purchase, warehouse, and prepare food—procedures that require intellect. Fish-eating ducks dive for fish. Grizzly bears tear flesh from bone by chomping down and then waving their head with their massive neck muscles.

It does not matter how these creatures are raised. Each acts according to its instinct.[xlv]

~~~~~~~~~~~~~~~~~~~~~~~

As we have discussed, in order for the theory of human evolution to be true, fully-evolved *Homo sapiens* had to have been alive on earth for two hundred thousand years. And, as we have also discussed, there are no writings, no evidence of clay-baking or metal smelting, and no complex architectural ruins from before the biblical period. Therefore, evolution requires that it is possible for humans to exist—virtually indefinitely—without forming historical civilizations. Evolution necessitates that human beings, for ten thousand generations in a row, possessed dormant, vestigial, brains that did not feel the desire to innovate a civilization any more than the brains of the animal beasts around them.

Anyone that has seen what happens to an unemployed man knows that this simply cannot be true. Anyone that has seen what happens to a woman when she is denied a committed relationship with her husband knows the same thing. The human male is driven by his very nature to be creative and industrious; the human female is driven to be desirable to a man so that she can carry his children and nurture a family.

It's like swimming to a duck.

---

xlv   Remember, there are many different species of duck and bear—each has a different natural instinct. But there is only one species of human. All *Homo sapiens* have the same natural instinct, as well as the free will to deal with it.

Luke 11:24–26 [NIV]
When an evil spirit comes out of a man, it goes through arid places seeking rest and does not find it. Then it says, 'I will return to the house I left.' When it arrives, it finds the house swept clean and put in order. Then it goes and takes seven other spirits more wicked than itself, and they go in and live there. And the final condition of that man is worse than the first.

103. The Singularity of Demonism

When I was a teenager, I worked at a filling station that was a hangout for the local hippies. The owner let them work on their cars in one of the garage ports and smoke marijuana behind the building. Most of the guys were in their mid–twenties. The town's high school was next to the filling station. One of the motorcycling hippies took up with a spirited freshman girl that liked to, ahem, go for fast rides on his hog.

Another of the hippies had cleaned himself up and gone to law school. When he saw his friend pull in with a fifteen year old girl on the bike, he took him aside and said, "As an officer of the court, it is my duty to tell you that what you're doing is statutory rape; the age-of-consent in this state is sixteen."

The motorcycling hippie said, "Hey, she may be fifteen, but she can [expletive] like she's ninety!" By saying this he did not mean to imply that she was decrepit—he meant that she partook in sex with the enthusiasm and plea-sure-giving skill of a woman that had seventy-five year's of orgasmic experi-ence. To clarify, he imitated her by scissoring his arms up and down, pivoting his hips, and rolling his eyes, "Woo-hoo!"

~~~~~~~~~~~~~~~~~~~~~

Futurist Ray Kurzweil has written that within one or two decades the compu-tational power of the average personal computer is going to exceed that of the human brain. Kurzweil foresees nanotechnology, biotechnology, and robotics merging to the point where the distinction between computers and humans will be blurred. He suggests that exponential increases in technology will soon result in tiny robots that can be injected into the human body to reverse the aging process. Eventually, a person will be able to download the contents of his or her mind into a machine, and thus live forever—as software—in a dis-embodied state.[821]

He's quite serious about it. One of his books is subtitled, *Live Long Enough to Live Forever.* Kurzweil is sixty years of age and takes a daily regi-men of over one hundred dietary supplement pills to stay healthy.[822] He is also an advocate of drinking alkaline water and of meditation. He thinks that if he can keep his body going for just another few decades, he will be one of the first human beings to achieve immortality.

Where does the sovereign, preexistent, God fit into all of this? According to Kurzweil, nowhere. He begins his most seminal work with these words:

> Our story begins perhaps 15 billion years ago. No conscious life existed to appreciate the birth of our Universe at that time, but we appreciate it now ... we could say that any Universe that fails to evolve conscious life to apprehend its existence never existed in the first place ... [823]

Kurzweil maintains that the Big Bang was a retroactive event—that it is somehow validated by our ability to now understand it. And he says that when all of the inanimate matter in the universe is someday utilized for computing power, then a god-like-being will come into existence through human endeavor.[824] You will see, then, how imperative it is that he and others be transformed into beings of limitless intelligence, comprehension, memory, endurance, and pleasures: the very existence of God and the universe is dependent upon the continuance of evolutionary progress.

He calls the advent of the epoch of unconstrained human capacity, 'The Singularity.' Our species will not quite be recognizable as human upon achieving singularity—the expansion of scientific knowledge will result in our becoming like gods.

You may be surprised to learn that I believe that much of Kurzweil's fantastic vision is possible within our lifetimes. It is already possible to move and click a computer mouse with brainwaves that are transmitted outside the skull. It's only a matter of time before tiny computers are implanted into us, or we are implanted into them.

~~~~~~~~~~~~~~~~~~~~~~

God's concern has always been to prevent us from living forever in a state of sin. That is part of the definition of Hell, and Jesus ultimately died to save the remnant (i.e., Christians) from it. But even at the beginning—immediately after the fall of man—God expelled Adam and Eve from the Garden of Eden to keep them from making their horrendous mistake permanent. He said,

> The man has now become like one of us, knowing good and evil. He must not be allowed to reach out his

hand and take also from the tree of life and eat, and
live forever. [Genesis 3:22 NIV]

And later, when God watched human beings building the Tower of Babel, He said,

These people are working together because they all
speak the same language. This is just the beginning.
Soon they will be able to do anything they want.
[Genesis 11:6 CEV]

God needed to retard our technological progress in order to deter us from learning how to live forever in our fallen state.

I will cancel the bargain you made to cheat death, and
I will overturn your deal to dodge the grave. [Isaiah
28:18 NLT]

It's not because He is afraid of us. God always acts out of love. He needed to afford time for His rescue plan to be accomplished. He decided to confuse our language because He knew that nothing would be impossible for people if they cooperated with each other.

However, today the universal language of science and business is English. And our hunt for the tree of life (i.e., unending rejuvenation through science) is progressing exponentially. Left to our own devices, humans will most definitely attempt to back-up our memories and personalities in the same way that we back-up our computer files. Then, if we can remake our physical selves through cloning technology, there will be no stopping the public demand to upload our minds into fresh bodies—just as there is no stopping embryonic stem cell research today.

Under this scenario, spare clones would not simply be kept in case of accident, or after ninety years of life; every forty year old with a touch of rheumatism would be willing to pay a premium to become a teenager again. In fact, people would have no care for their bodies, and would discard them the way that one does an outdated personal computer.

I am reminded of the legendary guitarist and infamous drug addict, Keith Richards. He once overdosed on heroin and had to have all his blood exchanged with fresh blood at a clinic in Switzerland. The procedure was obscenely expensive, but it saved his life and he walked out feeling great.[825] Soon thereafter, he was injecting heroin into his veins again. When asked why he would go back to such a dangerous narcotic after his close call with death, he apocryphally said, "Now that I know how easy it is to detox, I'm not worried. I can afford a blood exchange whenever it becomes necessary."

With the same reasoning, unbelieving people's penchant would be toward perpetually recycling themselves between the ages of fifteen and twenty-five. All the money that the public devotes to apothecaries and plastic surgeries would naturally be re-channeled to exchange their birth bodies with a more youthful, healthy, and attractive body—or even bodies of the opposite sex.

Science has already decoded the human genome. Customizing it will soon become a triviality. But the French have a saying:

> *There is nothing meritorious about looking good at*
> *the age of sixteen.*

One thing that I learned by watching my many great aunts grow old and die is that unbelieving people do not get better with age—they only get more insidious. My great aunts all lived into their nineties and, to their dying days, their interests were directed toward the vanities of family politics and trying to ruin other people's lives. But they all ended up in the ground because, up to the present time, there has been no stopping the aging process.

Now, I want you to imagine the mind of a ninety year old woman with no fear of God superimposed into the blank brain of a beautiful and healthy fifteen year old clone girl. Imagine her waking up in the hospital after the procedure. She gets out of bed and walks over to her old, now dead, body laying on a slab, and looks in revulsion at its flat, sagging, breasts. Then she finds a full-length mirror, slips off her hospital gown, and examines every square inch of her pert virginal body. Finding everything to her satisfaction, she smirks wickedly, throws on an overcoat, and runs out of the hospital barefooted.

Eeek! My skin is crawling with the thought of the havoc that she would wreak!

~~~~~~~~~~~~~~~~~~~~~~~~

Kurzweil's ideal of unending health, limitless vigor, and unconstrained potential is appealing until one realizes that in order to achieve it we would be reduced to spiritual forces, possessing unsuspecting hosts—in a word, demons.

That is precisely what evil spirits are: powerful, bodiless, forces in search of a pod to call home. Demons claim a host as their home, and then they parasitically destroy that home. They think that by perpetually reincarnating themselves, they will eventually usurp God. Because they are spirits, they cannot be killed—only confined.

Fortunately for Christians, a potential host's mind cannot be occupied by demons unless it is amenable to a hostile takeover. Therefore, the Apostle Paul advised us,

> *Put on the full armor of God so that you can take your stand against the devil's schemes. For our struggle is not against flesh and blood, but against the rulers, against the authorities, against the powers of this dark world and against the spiritual forces of evil ...*
> *[Ephesians 6:11–12 NIV]*

I have done this—or, rather, this has been done in me. As a result, my mind is in no way a suitable place for demons to reside. My cerebral synapses have been trained, and retrained, by the Word of God to be hostile to the deceits of the False Prophet. And if reading my book is repugnant to someone with the Rationalist mindset, how much more repugnant would it be for the evil spirits that inhabit such people to set up new residence inside my cranium?

On the other hand, he whose hope is set against the idea that God became a man in Jesus is quite susceptible to demon possession, even before Kurzweil's Singularity Epoch is ever achieved by mankind.

~~~~~~~~~~~~~~~~~~~~~~~~

I, myself, cannot envision a viable Christianity coexisting alongside the scientific advances outlined in this section. It is fundamentally at odds with God's purpose that we should be able to rejuvenate our bodies and live forever in our fallen state. In western society, people already feel that there is no accountability to God—but under Kurzweil's scenario there would be no stopping that penchant. Then science really would have provided a reasonable facsimile of eternal life (Genesis 3:22; 11:6), and the Christian message would be entirely eclipsed, and the door to the Church would collapse.

God will not allow this to happen. Jesus' claim to Lordship is at stake.

> *It is time for you to act, Lord; your law is being broken. [Psalm 119:126 TNIV]*

Christ is alive, and He will come again within this generation to validate the Gospel message. He is only waiting a few more years for our sake.

> *Don't forget that the Lord is patient because he wants people to be saved. [2 Peter 3:15 CEV]*

When the elapse of time no longer results in souls being gained for eternal life, God will end time forever.

Luke 19:11–27 [NIV]
... [Jesus] went on to tell them a parable, because he was near Jerusalem and the people thought that the kingdom of God was going to appear at once. He said: "A man of noble birth went to a distant country to have himself appointed king and then to return. So he called ten of his servants and gave them ten minas. 'Put this money to work,' he said, 'until I come back.'
But his subjects hated him and sent a delegation after him to say, 'We don't want this man to be our king.'
He was made king, however, and returned home. Then he sent for the servants to whom he had given the money, in order to find out what they had gained with it.
The first one came and said, 'Sir, your mina has earned ten more.'
'Well done, my good servant!' his master replied. 'Because you have been trustworthy in a very small matter, take charge of ten cities.'
The second came and said, 'Sir, your mina has earned five more.'
His master answered, 'You take charge of five cities.'
Then another servant came and said, 'Sir, here is your mina; I have kept it laid away in a piece of cloth. I was afraid of you, because you are a hard man. You take out what you did not put in and reap what you did not sow.'
His master replied, 'I will judge you by your own words, you wicked servant! You knew, did you, that I am a hard man, taking out what I did not put in, and reaping what I did not sow? Why then didn't you put my money on deposit, so that when I came back, I could have collected it with interest?'
Then he said to those standing by, 'Take his mina away from him and give it to the one who has ten minas.'
'Sir,' they said, 'he already has ten!'
He replied, 'I tell you that to everyone who has, more will be given, but as for the one who has nothing, even what he has will be taken away. But those enemies of mine who did not want me to be king over them—bring them here and kill them in front of me.'"

104. Unconscionable

This parable is so meaningful to me. It is my favorite of all Christ's parables. In this story, Jesus brilliantly satirized the true state-of-affairs in the world.

I read it to an unbelieving friend once, and he shook his head with frustration and disgust and said, "Chris, I have no idea what the point of that story was!"

I think I can expound upon it to the point of clarification for even the most dense Rationalist ...

~~~~~~~~~~~~~~~~~~~~~~~~

I was thirty-two years old while finishing the last of my graduate degrees. My advisor during that period was a brilliant young scientist, and an unbeliever in Christ. He was only five years my senior. In fact, he had been finishing his doctorate at the university when I began my studies there. We had been acquainted with each other since that time, and I felt comfortable speaking with him as an equal.

By that time I had begun to see the light concerning academic claptrap. So my antennae were raised when he began to impress upon me the vital importance of publishing the results of my graduate research. It was part of the routine, self-serving, spiel that professors tell wide-eyed graduate students. Like every good con artist, he never mentioned how it would affect his bottom line: the advisor's name appears on the article, and that would help him achieve tenure.

"Why is it important to publish?" I asked in mock innocence. "After all, I don't plan to make a career for myself in research."

"Well," he started, "what a shameful waste it would be for you to do all that work and then allow it to just gather dust as a bound thesis in our departmental library. You have a gift, and your work should be in the libraries of every major university in the world. The only way to be assured of that is to publish it in a peer-reviewed journal. That is how science progresses. In my opinion, every master's degree should result in at least one peer-reviewed paper, and every doctorate should result in at least two."

"Umh. I see. But journal publication is not required of me, right? I mean, I am going to get the degree whether science progresses or not. All I want is the degree, so it won't affect me either way."

He furrowed his brow, "You must remember that your education has not been free."

"Certainly not," I chirped up. "I paid tuition and expended several years of my life for this crap." I was really enjoying the exchange.

"But tuition doesn't begin to cover the cost of an education," he pleaded. "This is a public institution. The people of New York heavily subsidize what goes on here. And your research was sponsored by a federal grant—courtesy of the American people. It would be absolutely unconscionable for you not to give something back."

"I am going to give something back. I'm going to get a job and pay taxes, and get married and have babies. How's that?"

"Insufficient! You have to be a participant in working toward the goal."

"The goal?" I said incredulously. That was a new wrinkle in the argument. I must have missed an editorial in *The Chronicle of Higher Education*.

I crossed my arms and waved him on, "Okay, I'm intrigued. Tell me about the goal."

He leaned back in his chair, clenched his pipe in his teeth, and spun a yarn that I have since heard many times from other eggheads. "It is the dream of every scientist to eventually become irrelevant. We all want to become fossilized dinosaurs, because we know that that is the only way that science can advance. We will consider ourselves successful if students fifty years from now—even twenty-five years from now—will say of us, 'What Mickey Mouse stuff they were involved in back then. How could they ever have thought it to be cutting-edge?' Then our satisfaction will be in that we laid the foundation for the glories that came after us."

"I wonder, are you an assistant professor in the College of Science, or a recruiter for a New Age cult?"

"See, Chris, your problem is that you are a natural skeptic. Skepticism has its place in science, but one must also be appreciative. Do you have any idea how fortunate you and I are to be living in this place, at this time in history?

"In David Dinkins' New York City?!" I exclaimed. "I'm counting the days until I can get away and move back Upstate."

"What a waste!" he said. "Think about it: the brightest minds in the world are concentrated right here in Manhattan, and are engaged everyday in the business of sharing ideas. All of today's great university towns are like ancient Athens during the time of the Stoics. But we have it even better: We are at the very cusp of the empirical revolution that Aristotle sought. We are in the process of discovering the very truths of the universe."

His inflated sense of self-importance shocked me. He actually believed that the metaphysical waters were getting clearer with each new journal publication. I blinked at him and thought, 'How can I extricate myself from this conversation without forever being cast as an infidel?'

I looked at my watch, "Hey, uhhh, me and the other Stoics back in the lab are ready for lunch. You wanna get some tacos??"

~~~~~~~~~~~~~~~~~~~~~~~

Solomon noted,

> What has been will be again, what has been done will
> be done again; there is nothing new under the sun.
> [Ecclesiastes 1:9 TNIV]

So it is of little surprise that in AD 51[826] the Apostle Paul ran into my advisor's mentality during a missionary trip to Athens, Greece, of all places.

> A group of Epicurean and **Stoic philosophers began
> to debate with him.** Some of them asked, "What is this
> babbler trying to say?" Others remarked, "He seems
> to be advocating foreign gods." They said this because
> Paul was preaching the good news about Jesus and
> the resurrection. [Acts 17:18 TNIV]

The part of the encounter with my advisor that made the greatest impression upon me was his comment, "It would be absolutely unconscionable not to give something back." I knew there was a point to be made about that, but it did not come to me at first. Weeks later I came across the parable in this section's heading during my daily Bible reading, and had an epiphany: my advisor will someday be called to account by his own words.

> I tell you, on the day of judgment people will give
> account for every careless word they speak, for by
> your words you will be justified, and by your words
> you will be condemned. [Matthew 12:36–37 ESV]

Do we not owe God more than a graduate student owes the taxpayers of New York? In what way was my advisor giving something back to God, who gave him life and reasoning ability? In what way was his own skepticism concerning God's omnipotence counterbalanced with appreciation for God's love and sustenance?

God is going to ask every human being what they have done with what He has given them. If your answer is, "I participated in the goal of advancing science," you will surely be rejected from everlasting life. The same goes for any other worldly objective. The only possible satisfactory answer is, "I participated in the goal of advancing Christ's Kingdom." That will be sufficient, even if your participation is limited to only believing the truth with the final beat of your heart.

But imagine somebody that has devoted not a dime of money, not a moment's serious thought, not a drop of sweat-equity, into Christ's Kingdom. Image somebody that has expended their life in direct opposition to Him—trying to expunge Christ's name from the public forum.

> *Many people live like enemies of the cross of Christ
> ... In the end, they will be destroyed. [Philippians
> 3:18–19 NCV]*

What will be their reaction when they see Him coming upon the clouds in glory?

> *... the Lord Jesus will be revealed from heaven with
> His mighty angels in flaming fire, dealing out retribu-
> tion to those who do not know God ... [2 Thessalonians
> 1:7–8 NASB]*

On that day, will the scientists continue to pontificate about lofty humanistic goals, or will they shit their pants and wail like babies?

Romans 8:28 [NLT]
God causes everything to work together for the good of those who love God and are called according to his purpose for them.

105. For the Good of Those Who Love God

A month after I commenced work on my doctoral research project, my advisor abruptly went on a two year sabbatical to the Marquises Islands. [This was a different fellow and a different degree than the one that I mentioned in the previous section.] He said it was a once-in-a-lifetime opportunity for him to study an obscure species of South Pacific snail. He left me with a budget of five thousand dollars for the research proposal that I had just drawn up, and told me that he looked forward to reading the dissertation when he returned.

The central part of my laboratory apparatus was to be a series of thousand gallon polyethylene tanks. They were crucial in order for the experiment to proceed. But it was not until after my advisor left the country that I priced all the components in my schematic. The tanks were going to eat up the entire budget! I had just barely enough money to do the work *not including the cost of the tanks*.

My advisor had not left a telephone number in the Marquises, and there was no e-mail in those days. Besides, he was not the type to commiserate. He would have just told me to scrap my plans and do something else. But I had dreamt of pursuing this line of research for years, and could not bring myself to give it up. I decided to borrow the extra five thousand dollars on my credit cards and do the project anyway.

I called my best friend to bounce the idea off him before proceeding. His wife answered and told me that he was not at home. I asked her to have him give me a call. She said, "Is everything okay with you, Chris? You don't seem quite yourself." She's a delightful woman.

I told her that I had been spinning my wheels for a couple days trying to figure out how to procure the necessary equipment for my experiment on a limited budget.

"Have you taken it to the Lord in prayer?" she asked.

I had not. She told me not to fret, and that she was going to pray about it the moment that we got off the phone. She told me to pray, too, and to wait for an answer.

I prayed, and then decided to go for a walk. I cut through the university's machine shop on the way out, and the machinist, a dour old New England Yankee, said, "What's on your mind, Chris? Something's eating at you—I can tell."

I was taken aback by his comment because he was not usually the type to speak proactively. I told him the same thing that I had told my friend's wife, and he asked, "What kind of equipment?"

I told him, and he scratched his chin, "Tanks, you say? You mean big, white, plastic tanks?"

"Yes. Exactly."

He looked up at the ceiling, paused, and then nodded, "Yehs-suh, by Jesus.[xlvi] I know where you can get them tanks."

I stared at him blankly. He explained that one of the professors in another department had conducted a precipitation experiment ten years before on a nearby mountain, and had left the tanks there when he finished. The National Forest Service was pressing him to remove his contraption, and I'd be doing him a favor if I took them off his hands.

I called the professor and he gladly offered me all the tanks if I'd clean up the site. But there was a problem: spring rains were upon us, and the road up the mountain was impassible due to mud. It wasn't much of a road to begin with, actually. The professor had cut some trees and dragged the tanks up with a crawler. The trail had become choked with brush and fallen trees in the intervening years. I was going to have to wait until the summer and re-cut it before I could take possession of the equipment. I started pricing chainsaws and crawler rentals, and planning on a four month delay in my research.

A few days later I again telephoned my best friend to whine. Again, he was not home and his wife answered. She again suggested that we both pray.

---

xlvi   A common expression of affirmation among old-time New Englanders.

Afterward I sought out the dour old Yankee. "I really appreciate your putting me on to the precipitation tanks, but it's going to cost a thousand dollars to get them off the mountain; and the time delay makes it almost not worth it. I wish someone would just fly them down for me."

He scratched his chin, "Fly them down, you say? You mean with a helicopter and a net?"

"Yeah ... I guess that'd be the way to do it."

He looked up at the ceiling, paused, and then nodded, "Yehs-suh, by Jesus. I know someone that'll fly them tanks down for you."

My mouth fell open as he pointed to an undergraduate student working on a lathe at the other end of the machine shop. "You see that fellah? He flies helicopters for the National Guard. He was telling me this morning about how his troop is in need of a good training exercise. Your project would probably be up their alley, since they are part of the Mountaineering Division."

The distance from the National Guard base to the mountain was just within range for the helicopter's fuel radius. The tanks were in my lab and full of solution within two weeks.

The entire operation cost me fifty dollars: I bought the National Guardsmen a case of beer and a fruit basket.

~~~~~~~~~~~~~~~~~~~~~~~

I think we can all agree that God is a busy guy. He has the cosmos to run, after all.

> *From the very beginning, God has been in control*
> *of all the world. If God took back the breath that he*
> *breathed into us, we humans would die and return to*
> *the soil. [Job 34:13–15 CEV]*

Who am I that He should take an interest in my goofy research project?

Nobody could blame Him if His answer to me and my friend's prayer was, "Listen, it's really very touching of you to ask Me about every triviality that passes through your mind, but I've got my hands full trying to keep the sun and the earth in perfect alignment so that you don't all get vaporized tomorrow. So just take your piddling issues to someone who cares—or better yet, get a real job, and stop playing scientist."

I would have been tempted to respond in such a way because my organizational capabilities and my love is limited. But God never says that. He always cares for us. He cares about things that are trivialities in the cosmic scheme of things.

Any loving parent can identify with this: a substantial amount of care-giving effort goes into things that are quite important to children, but quite trivial to adults. The Bible says,

> *Don't be deceived, my dear brothers. Every good*
> *and perfect gift is from above, coming down from the*
> *Father of the heavenly lights, who does not change*
> *like shifting shadows. [James 1:16–17 NIV]*

Do you understand? Can you come to terms with this? God did not have to help me. *He chose to help me.* His loving interest in my welfare is boundless.

The God of the universe—that Infinite Mind—is your Heavenly Father. He is deeply concerned with your problem, whatever it is. Jesus Christ has committed Himself to arrange all the chaos and interrelated coincidences of this world for your salvation and sanctification. In a mysterious and mostly inexplicable way, God incorporates everyday happenstance—both good and bad—into His plan for His children. It takes faith to believe this because we only see glimpses of His providential genius.

> *No one can comprehend what goes on under the sun.*
> *Despite all his efforts to search it out, man cannot*
> *discover its meaning. Even if a wise man claims he*
> *knows, he cannot really comprehend it. [Ecclesiastes*
> *8:17 NIV]*

But be assured,

> *... the Lord knows how to rescue godly men from tri-*
> *als ... [2 Peter 2:9 NIV]*

This is the love with which your God has loved you—infinite. It is the kind of love that brings a grown man to the point of tears every time he contemplates it.

Will you believe in God and live? Or will you disbelieve and die?

Romans 9:22–24 [NIV]
What if God, choosing to show his wrath and make his power known, bore with great patience the objects of his wrath—prepared for destruction? What if he did this to make the riches of his glory known to the objects of his mercy, whom

he prepared in advance for glory—even us, whom he also called, not only from the Jews but also from the Gentiles?

106. For the Destruction of the Objects of His Wrath

The American novelist and lesbian, Willa Cather (AD 1873–AD 1947) said,

> *The end is nothing; the road is all.*[827]

I like this saying because it is so exquisitely incorrect. The opposite is true, actually: the road-of-life that you have walked is utterly inconsequential as long as your soul's heavenly end-state is secure.

If you think about Mr. Treadwell's horrific mauling, you will quickly see the folly of living for the road. The road is finite—in Mr. Treadwell's case, thirteen short Alaskan summers—but an end in which one is separated from God is eternal.

In this way, Hell may be reasonably described as an infinite road of regret; and Heaven may be described as a destination of eternal exultation.

Any person is free to ensure a positive end-state for his or her soul by believing that God became a man in Jesus Christ. God is eager for us to believe this—He wants each of us to be a member of the Christian nation (i.e., the Church, or the invisible, indivisible, body of Christian believers). But He has left us with free will. Everyone can choose for himself or herself whether to become part of the Israel of God.

You may wonder, then, if God is omniscient, and if He knows who are the ones that will ultimately choose the way of death, why He puts up with their evildoing. Sometimes they live to an old age, and cause a lot of trouble for God's Own People.

He allows it for the Christians' sake. For the short while that the wicked have life, they exist that we, the True Israel, might be saved and sanctified in Christ Jesus. In this sense we are all in God's employ—both Christian people, and non-Christian people. Whether we know it or not, we are all interwoven into His plan.

> *... for all things are your servants. [Psalm 119:91 ESV]*

Thus, God allowed Judas to betray Jesus so that He could save the Chosen People that would trust in His name (i.e., the Christians). It is no credit to Judas that he was an integral part of God's plan. Judas did not intend to be used for good—quite the contrary! But God, in His sovereignty, decided to use him for a key role in Good Friday. Judas was going to die anyway, so he might as well have been useful for God's greater purpose, you see.

> *The Lord works out everything for his own ends—even*
> *the wicked for a day of disaster. [Proverbs 16:4 NIV]*

Think of a fisherman that catches some trash fish. Nobody will eat those species of fish, but the fisherman keeps them anyway. When he returns to shore he spreads their flopping carcasses into a furrow and plants kernels of corn above them. "If they can be of no direct profit to me," he reasons, "they might as well be made into fertilizer for the crop."

> *The angel swung his sickle on the earth, gathered its*
> *grapes and threw them into the great winepress of*
> *God's wrath. [Revelation 14:19 TNIV]*

You'll see now that this sinful world may be likened to a scaffolding that was temporarily put into place to build a great cathedral. The cathedral is God's Church—begun at Pentecost—reigning for a thousand years (Revelation 20:4) through faithful adherence to the three Ecumenical Creeds (i.e., the Apostles', Athanasian, and Nicene with the inclusion of the Filioque). Once Jesus returns for the completed Church, there will no longer be any use for the scaffolding. It will be disassembled and burned.

> *Has not the Lord Almighty determined that the peo-*
> *ple's labor is only fuel for the fire, that the nations*
> *exhaust themselves for nothing? For the earth will be*
> *filled with the knowledge of the glory of the Lord, as*
> *the waters cover the sea. [Habakkuk 2:13–14 NIV]*

God has made the entire universe for His Chosen People, the Christians; He arranges every particular of this life for our ultimate good. Those unprofitable souls that reject God's plan of salvation are used, in His power and in His wrath, for the good of those profitable souls that accept His plan of salvation. Do not despise Him; it is your own choice whether you are a profitable soul or not. God is doing everything possible to save everyone that can be saved.

> *Prove by the way you live that you have repented of*
> *your sins and turned to God ... Even now the ax of*
> *God's judgment is poised, ready to sever the roots of*
> *the trees. Yes, every tree that does not produce good*
> *fruit will be chopped down and thrown into the fire.*
> *[Luke 3:8–9 NLT]*

He will not stop until the Church is complete through the overspreading of His Word. It is nearly complete. There will soon be no more purpose for those that do not turn to God and believe.

> *His winnowing fork is in his hand, to clear his threshing floor and to gather the wheat into his barn, but the chaff he will burn with unquenchable fire. [Luke 3:17 ESV]*

Then will come our Savior from the sky—making order out of chaos—bringing meaning out of insignificance—erasing sixty centuries of pain in a single stroke for those who know Him, and administering eternal justice upon those He does not know.

Isaiah 32:8 [NIV]
... the noble man makes noble plans, and by noble deeds he stands.

107. Noble Deeds

I spent the weekend before Tuesday, September 11, AD 2001, at a cabin in Quebec with a group of college friends and their wives. We ate barbeque, drank beer, and talked about our lives. I was unemployed at the time and everyone there was concerned about what I would do next with my career.

I came home and wrote a thank you card to the host and hostess on the evening of Monday, September 10th. I added this postscript to the card:

> *P.S. – I've been listening to books-on-tape, and recently rented The New Testament. I noticed a lot of things listening to it that had escaped me in my Bible readings. I'd been thinking about getting another degree (if I can't find a good job), but maybe I'll just get any job I can and study the Bible instead.*

I did not appreciate it at the time, but God took my postscript as a written contract. He decided to tutor me in a program of study that was more important than any college degree or any prestigious job.

Providence arranged world events such that my lessons began the very next morning. God wanted me to turn on the television and watch a profound occurrence, but I was late to His class because of my exhaustion from the three days away.

As I exited the shower, my father shouted from his upstairs apartment, "Hey, Chris! Two planes just crashed into the Twin Towers in New York!" I sat down with nothing but a towel around my waist and saw Babylon the Great fall in one hour (Section 35). The strange thing is that I immediately knew what I was witnessing. After the second building fell, I turned down the volume on the television and read Revelation 18 aloud and wept.

Shortly after that I got a job that did not occupy all my little grey cells, and began to study the Bible in depth. The book that you are reading is the unplanned result of that four year program.

God is faithful to a commitment to study His Word, you see, and He began to show me what it all meant.

~~~~~~~~~~~~~~~~~~~~~~~

Throughout my life I had felt as though time was limited—that I must get on to the core of the matter—that I must not waste my talents. I suffered with a discontentment with what I knew—a restless desire for knowledge—a pained yearning for a more worthy and gratifying subject. But no matter what field of science I studied—what professional endeavor I put my hand to—what part of the country I lived in—I always came away shrugging my shoulders and saying, "Is that all there is to it? How utterly unfulfilling."

I was on a quest for ultimate truth. I stayed in school for so long that I came to realize that my professors were nitwits, and I would be better off with books. But, after such striving, which book to focus upon?

Jesus told one of his friends that was overwhelmed with the cares of this life,

> *Martha, Martha, you are anxious and troubled about*
> *many things, but one thing is necessary. [Luke 10:41–*
> *42 ESV]*

So I turned my attention over to the one thing that is necessary: the Word of God. I read the Bible, and books about the Bible. I gave the firstfruits of my humble income for the Lord's work. I refused to enter the Church of the Emasculated Christ for worship (Section 77). And because I enjoy sleeping, I decided to get up early one day per week in order to be of service to Jesus' people.

> *Religion that God our Father accepts as pure and*
> *faultless is this: to look after orphans and widows in*
> *their distress and to keep oneself from being polluted*
> *by the world. [James 1:27 NIV]*

I did all this gladly.

> ... *God loves a cheerful giver.* [*2 Corinthians 9:7 NKJV*]

Thus, while many others were advancing their careers and earning gobs of money, it was given to me to know the mystery of the ages. I, in turn, now give that knowledge to you.

~~~~~~~~~~~~~~~~~~~~~~~~

Perhaps some of you are saying of me as the Roman governor said to the polymathic Apostle Paul,

> *You're out of your mind, Paul! Too much study is driving you mad!* [*Acts 26:24 HCSB*]

But my Christian brothers and sisters do not think so. I have shown this manuscript to some of them for initial review; their response has been effusive.

"Do you realize what you have produced?!" one exclaimed. "You have cracked the code! You have found the answer to what every Christian since the first century has pondered."

My proof-readers say that my book has positively affected their perspective in a way that they have not experienced before. If you also find it so, I am gladdened. That was my intention. I wanted to bolster faith in Christ in advance of the inevitable end of all things; I wanted to encourage steadfast devotion to the orthodoxy of the three Ecumenical Creeds before we see Christ in the sky.

> *... let us encourage one another—and all the more as you see the Day approaching.* [*Hebrews 10:25 NIV*]

As for me, dear Christian reader, there is no need to offer thanks. This guy that I have been writing about—Jesus of Nazareth—*He gave up His life for me.*

> *This Jesus I am proclaiming to you is the Messiah ...* [*Acts 17:3 TNIV*]

A labor for Him is its own reward.

So it is that I have been just as blessed in writing this work—blessed with a peace that had previously eluded me.

Psalm 118:17 [NKJV]
I shall not die, but live, and declare the works of the Lord.

108. The Miracle of Not Dying

It has always struck me that when the God-man, Jesus, taught us to pray, He began with one praise:

> *... hallowed be thy name. [Matthew 6:9 KJV]*

And He ended with three praises:

> *For thine is the kingdom, and the power, and the glory ... [Matthew 6:13 KJV]*

It may be that this signifies that there is one God in three Persons—Father, Son, and Holy Spirit.

In any case, those that have eternal life know that we live:

- in the name of Jesus;
- through the kingdom of Jesus;
- by the power of Jesus;
- and for the glory of Jesus.

We praise God for victory over death when we pray the Lord's Prayer; we believe that we shall come back from the dead because Jesus Christ rose from the grave on Easter morning.

~~~~~~~~~~~~~~~~~~~~~~

I once witnessed a dying man come back to life.

My father slipped backwards while working in his garden, hit a pointed stone, and suffered a severe brain injury one sunny day. It was a shock to his loved ones, but we were ready from the beginning to let the Lord take him to eternal life. The Bible says,

> *If we live, we live to the Lord; and if we die, we die to the Lord. So, whether we live or die, we belong to the Lord. [Romans 14:8 TNIV]*

However, a few things happened concurrent with this incident that made us hope that the injury might not lead to death: my mother had been scheduled to help her friends pack for their relocation to California on the day after he fell. The friends are two elderly, unmarried, sisters. They live very much like cloistered nuns—praying and reading the Bible all the time. My mother asked a third party to call the sisters to postpone the packing, but they were only told that my father was seeing the doctor and needed some assistance.

Two days passed. The situation looked horribly bleak. I came home from the hospital and shut myself in my bedroom to mourn, and to await the inevitable telephone call.

Suddenly, something got into me. I couldn't sit still. I had to drive to the old ladies' house and tell them what had happened. When I arrived the older sister answered the door and greeted me by my childhood name, "O Chrisy! We have been praying for you non-stop since we heard that something was wrong with your father. The Spirit has told us that it is serious. But we did not want to call and bother anyone. We have only prayed and prayed. Now tell us everything and do not leave us in suspense any longer."

The younger sister is hard-of-hearing and did not know that the door-bell had rung, but when she heard her sister talking, she came out of her room. She saw me and immediately raised her hands and face toward Heaven in a victory salute, "All praise, glory, and honor be to our Heavenly Father! It is a sign from the Holy Spirit! Christian has appeared!"

Then she turned to me and explained, "I was just at my bed praying that Jesus would send somebody to tell us the news about your father. And when I finished the prayer, I heard a noise. I came out, and here you are! Now tell us, Christian! Tell us the truth!"

I looked at the floor and spoke softly, "It is very bad news. Very bad. He fell and suffered major head trauma. A third of his brain is now a soupy mixture of blood and bits of brain matter. It is destroyed—I have seen the scans with my own eyes. The doctors are amazed that the internal hemorrhage stopped during the first night, and that he has survived these three days. But now his bruised brain tissue has swollen against the inside of the skull, and he is in death throes ..." My voice cracked, "Today he is definitely dying."

The younger sister stomped her foot and yelled an oracle at me, "He is not dying! Our Lord Jesus has not sent you here at this moment that I was praying so that we could comfort you on his death! Your father shall not die, but live, and declare the works of the Lord!"

My eyes filled up, "But the doctors say that the intercranial pressure is too high, and his heart is not able to deliver oxygen to the brain. The doctors say that a man cannot live even a few hours with this level of pressure. It has already been too long now. Whatever brain he had left is gone. The doctors say that even if he does somehow live through it, he will never get out of bed again. And they assured me that he has forever lost the ability to speak or to understand anything."

As I was reciting the litany of doom, the old woman peered into my pupils intensely. It was as though she were looking down a deep and endless wellspring. After I finished, she calmly spoke into the well, "The doctors do not know what my Jesus knows."

Then her eyes flared, and she raised her voice to a crescendo, "Our God is great, and now He will heal him! God is going to heal him completely! Your father shall not die, but live, and declare the works of the Lord!" Her voice was so strong that her entire body shook as she spoke.

I tried to talk sense one last time, "But, you haven't seen him ... You don't know how bad it is ... He is in an irreversible coma. His breathing is labored and irregular, like that of a dying ma—"

"Stop saying that!" she snapped. Without breaking her gaze upon me, she rocketed her right index finger toward Heaven and proclaimed, "In the name of the Living God, your father shall not die, but live, and declare the works of the Lord! Believe it! Confess it!"

I fell to my knees and burst into tears. The two old women joined me on their knees and hugged me. The three of us prayed.

We prayed in the name of Jesus; we prayed through the kingdom of Jesus; we prayed by the power of Jesus; we prayed for the glory of Jesus.

> *For where two or three are gathered together in My name, I am there in the midst of them. [Matthew 18:20 NKJV]*

Then a curious thing happened: after two more weeks of being a hair's-breadth away from death ... he lived.

~~~~~~~~~~~~~~~~~~~~~~~

Soon interns at hospitals throughout New York were speaking about my mother. They were saying that some praying-woman had ambulanced her as-good-as-dead husband to the emergency room, and he had miraculously survived.

My father's neurologist was befuddled, but unmoved. The last time I saw him, he blandly said, "Well, you got what you wanted. He lived through it, but he'll never recover."

I smiled and gibed him, "Aren't you the one that told me that he would bleed to death within twelve hours of the accident?"

He shrugged his shoulders, "It was a one-in-a-million."

"And then a couple days after that you again said that he would die before morning because his intercranial pressure was off-the-chart. I suppose his living through that was another one-in-a-million?"

He glared at me.

"Have I told you that I work in the field of biostatistics?" I asked.

"What does that have to do with it?"

"If a one-in-a-million happens two consecutive times, then it collectively becomes a one-in-a-trillion. This Jesus that we've been praying to has been able to do something that you've never seen before—something for which medical science cannot account."

"That's a very nice sentiment, but the reality is that we've ended up with a vegetative patient, and that's no way for a human being to live. Within a year's time you are going to have to make an excruciating decision: you're going to have to decide whether to pull his feeding tube and let him starve to death, or to feed him indefinitely and let him die from bed sores."

At that moment my father opened his eyes and surveyed the room. "Look!" I pointed.

The neurologist waved his left hand dismissively, "Sometimes they open their eyes. It doesn't mean anything. He can't understand us. He isn't even awake, really. He'll close his eyes again in a moment."

I protested, "But when we put his grandson on the bed, he sobs, and when we take the baby away and tell him that everything is going to be alright, he calms down."

The neurologist wagged his head, "Your religion is making you imagine things. It's a gag reflex attributable to the baby leaning on the patient's chest. The brain scans don't lie; he's not coming back."

I raised my eyebrows, "Are you sure?"

It then became apparent that he was resentful because we had not allowed him to perform a costly brain surgery on the day of the accident. My father had excellent insurance coverage, but without the surgery his presence in the hospital was a net loss for them. He said, "If you had let me take out the useless brain matter on the first day, I could have cauterized the wound and stopped the bleeding."

"But the bleeding stopped by itself that night, remember?"

"Yes … True … But chances are that it would not have stopped."

I clenched my jaw and bared my teeth at him.

He stammered, "Well, anyway, my point is that if I had performed the surgery there would have been enough void space inside his cranium to accommodate the subsequent swelling."

"Void space?!"

"Yes," said the neurologist. "Then he might have stood a chance of at least waking up."

His motivation was transparent, and after three weeks of wrangling with him for proper care I was sick of him, "Let me explain something to you, Dr. Frankenstein: We are Christians. We believe in honoring our mother and father. God has forbidden that we should ever acquiesce to lobotomizing our own father. We wanted you to do everything for him short of invading his brain for no good reason."

"It would not have been a lobotomy," he said. "There is not a neurosurgeon in this country that would remove viable brain tissue in this day-and-age."

"But it is ethical to remove non-viable brain tissue?"

"Of course! We're talking about saving people from certain death here."

"Who's to say what is viable and what is not?" I asked.

"I am."

"You're very sure of your surgical abilities," I noted.

"I am who I am."

"Umh. Are you one hundred percent certain that every juicy morsel of brain matter that your suction tube would have removed—" I made slurping noises with my mouth, "—would have been completely useless, non-viable, brain tissue?"

"There is no such thing as one hundred percent surety in medicine. There are only probabilities," he said.

"I see. We didn't opt for surgery, and the probability is that the damage is done, both to the patient's brain and to the hospital's budget. Is that it?"

With that he frowned and began to leave the room.

I talked after him, "Tell me your medical opinion now: what is the probability that your patient will be able to confess Christ and receive Holy Communion with his own hands again?"

He paused in the doorway and, without looking back, said disdainfully, "One-in-a-million."

We decided that my father's life was not safe there. During his time in intensive care, we had to ask my father's friend in the governor's office to call the president of the hospital and 'encourage' them to continue his anti-swelling medication. And a few hours before the above encounter I discovered that the nursing staff had 'forgotten' to give him water over the Labor Day weekend.

We took him to another hospital, and after nine months we brought him home. Now he can get out of bed by himself. And he can feed himself. And he can speak, and understand speech. *And He confesses Christ when He eats the body and drinks the blood of his Risen Lord.*

Name. Kingdom. Power. Glory. Believe it! Confess it!

~~~~~~~~~~~~~~~~~~~~~~~~~

Jesus taught us,

> *The work of God is this: to believe in the one he has*
> *sent. [John 6:29 TNIV]*

Therefore another way to say, "I shall not die, but live, and declare *the works of the Lord*," is "I shall not die, but live, and declare *belief in the resurrection of Christ.*"

Metaphysically-speaking, the only justification for the continuance of human life is:

- to declare belief in the name—the name of Jesus,
- and to declare belief through the kingdom—the kingdom of Jesus,
- and to declare belief by the power—the power of Jesus,
- and to declare belief for the glory—the glory of Jesus.

God has redeemed our lives for this very purpose, for,

> *It is not the dead who praise the Lord, those who go*
> *down to silence; it is we who extol the Lord, both now*
> *and forevermore. [Psalm 115:17–18 NIV]*

He loves us and wants us to live and praise Him forever.

Brothers and sisters in Christ, this book is finished. The miracle of not dying is reserved for the People of the Living God, the Christians. Jesus is returning between the years AD 2033 and AD 2039 to remake all things and to give you eternal life. There is no power in Heaven, or on earth, or under the earth, that can put His purpose asunder.

> *These words are trustworthy and true. The Lord, the*
> *God of the spirits of the prophets, sent his angel to*
> *show his servants the things that must soon take place.*
> *[Revelation 22:6 NIV]*

May God grant us grace, so that …

- in the matchless name of Jesus,
- and through the coming of the beneficent kingdom of Jesus,
- and by the awesome power of Jesus,

■   and for the glory—the everlasting glory—of Jesus
    Christ of Nazareth,

… we might each say, along with the Psalmist,

*I shall not die, but live, and declare the works of the
Lord.*

Amen.

Daniel 3:16–18 [NIV]
O Nebuchadnezzar, we do not need to defend ourselves before you in this mat-
ter. If we are thrown into the blazing furnace, the God we serve is able to save
us from it, and he will rescue us from your hand, O king. But even if he does
not, we want you to know, O king, that we will not serve your gods or worship
the image of gold you have set up.

Epilogue

I have been sternly warned by some of the persons closest to me that publishing this book shall cost me my life. They say that every Muslim and Jew, every
Eastern Orthodox and Oriental Orthodox, every Rationalist, Über-Baptist, and
Mainline Protestant in the entire world will sincerely wish me dead for what I
have written.

More than that, some of the persons closest to me think that the entire
thesis of this book is preposterous. They say that far from being God's man
for this time, I am confused, delusional, and obsessed with a series of inconse-
quentialities. They say that while I might, incidentally, spread some truth about
God through this book, I will only do so in a manner that will alienate people
and cause strife. They say that I have gone out of my way to insult people, and
that I will end up no better than Mr. Treadwell (see Section 102), who lost his
life to bearish cousins and was proven to be a fool.

How shall I reply to this? It is best to use Christ's own words:

> *Blessed are you when men hate you, when they exclude*
> *you and insult you and reject your name as evil,*
> *because of the Son of Man. Rejoice in that day and*
> *leap for joy, because great is your reward in heaven.*
> *[Luke 6:22–23 NIV]*

I am very well aware that the only people that will be enthusiastic
about my life's work are those that love the Lord Jesus more than they love the
trappings of this world.

> *I am a friend to all who fear you, to all who follow your*
> *precepts ... May those who fear you rejoice when they*
> *see me, for I have put my hope in your word. [Psalm*
> *119:63,74 NIV]*

The rest—those who are not busying themselves building treasure in
Heaven—will be infuriated.

> *O Lord, by your hand save me from such men, from*
> *men of this world whose reward is in this life. [Psalm*
> *17:14 NIV]*

Mr. Treadwell was not a fool because he died young. Left to their own devices, everyone would eventually die—whether young or old. He was, rather, a fool because he died without faith in the God-man, and for a cause that was against the purposes of the God-man.

But the Lord Jesus has promised,

> *If you cling to your life, you will lose it; but if you give*
> *up your life for me, you will find it. [Matthew 10:39*
> *NLT]*

You are never as secure as when you make yourself vulnerable for Jesus Christ; you are never as rich as when you make a free-will offering unto Him.

> *With a freewill offering I will sacrifice to you; I will*
> *give thanks to your name, O Lord, for it is good. For*
> *he has delivered me from every trouble, and my eye*
> *has looked in triumph on my enemies. [Psalm 54:6–7*
> *ESV]*

Though I have a morbid fear of the public spotlight, and it is in my nature to avoid conflict, the Holy Spirit has emboldened me to proclaim God's message.

> *... I am filled with power—with the Spirit of the Lord.*
> *I am filled with justice and strength to boldly declare*
> *Israel's sin and rebellion. [Micah 3:8 NLT]*

By this power I have warned people that the theater of life is closing—much as the vacationing schoolgirl warned the beachgoers in Thailand (see Section 14).

> *I do not hide your righteousness in my heart; I speak*
> *of your faithfulness and salvation. I do not conceal*
> *your love and your truth from the great assembly.*
> *[Psalm 40:10 NIV]*

It would have been easier to run away and watch from a distance, but sounding the alarm was the right thing to do.

> *For Zion's sake I will not keep silent ... [Isaiah 62:1*
> *TNIV]*

I will not regret my work unless the seven year time-window that I put forth (i.e., the beginning of AD 2033 to the end of AD 2039) comes-and-goes without Jesus Christ returning from the sky. That is a metaphysical impossibility. God promised a blessed rest for His Chosen People (i.e., the Christians) after the sixth day, and it is written,

> *Thy word is truth. [John 17:17 KJV]*

So I await the close of the sixth millennium, and the dawn of a new Heaven and new Earth (Section 48).

> *... based on His promise, we wait for new heavens and a new earth, where righteousness will dwell. [2 Peter 3:13 HCSB]*

As for the duration of my earthly life, it will be whatever my Lord decides it to be.

> *As no one has power over the wind to contain it, so no one has power over the time of their death. [Ecclesiastes 8:8 TNIV]*

Although nobody knows the exact course of his or her future, one can do no better than to faithfully serve God. I have done that, and I will continue to do that. I know that Christ will save me from every danger and rescue me from every evil design. *But even if He does not,* I want you to know that I will not serve the gods of this world: I will not worship the abominable image of gold that has been set up on the Temple Mount in Jerusalem (i.e., the Cult of Muhammad); and I will not heed the false prophecies about the ultimate parameters of the physical world (i.e., the Cult of Science). Neither will the remainder of God's Chosen People, the Christians.

> *The godly people in the land are my true heroes! [Psalm 16:3 NLT]*

We will read the Bible, and spread the Good News of Jesus Christ through all available means, and wait patiently for His Second Coming. I have hope that I shall live to a healthy old age and, during the fourth decade of this century, look up to see my Lord's glorious return with the same eyes that are looking upon this page as I write.

> *I believe that I shall look upon the goodness of the Lord in the land of the living! [Psalm 27:13 ESV]*

Should my Good Friend, Jesus, take me into His kingdom before that, do not shed one tear for me. Under such a turn of events, I will have lost nothing: I'll still be welcomed by Him—only sooner.

I know that my Redeemer lives. In the end he will stand on the earth. After my skin has been destroyed, in my body I'll still see God. I myself will see him with my own eyes. I'll see him, and he won't be a stranger to me. [Job 19:25–27 NIrV]

Whatever the case, it is my fervent prayer that I shall also see you, the reader of this book, there among Christ's Elect.

Appendix I. How to Think Outside the Box

In order to solve the Nine-Dot Problem (Section 3) with only four contiguous lines, your pencil must extend beyond the boundaries of the box that the dots form. If you don't break the paradigm, there is no solution.

Figure 6. The Nine-Dot Solution

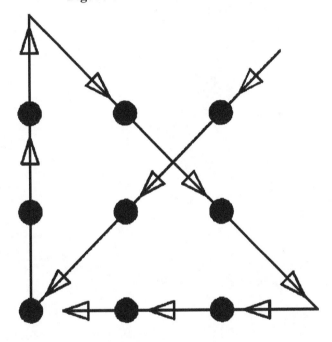

Likewise, if you don't think outside the box of this world, you will never understand the meaning of life. Hint: heed the title of this book.

See the Holy Bible for the solution to the problem of life.

Appendix II. Glossary

Abaptist—An epithet that I have coined for heterodox Reformed Evangelical Protestants for whom infant baptism has been deferred, and who then neglect to get baptized in adulthood because they consider themselves already saved by means of praying the sinner's prayer (see bottom of Section 2) at an altar call. They think of baptism as a symbolic, take-it-or-leave-it, statement of faith, rather than a mechanism by which God bestows His grace upon us (i.e., a sacrament). Every breath they take is a deliberate rebellion against Christ's Great Commission (Matthew 28:19–20; Section 18).

Abomination that Causes Desolation—The establishment of Ali's dream of an Islamic religion, symbolized by the Antichrist inscriptions on the gilded Dome of the Rock. Also symbolized by the Antichrist currency reforms completed by Caliph Abd al-Malik in AD 699—*exactly* six hundred and sixty-six years after the dispersal of the Pentecostal Church from Jerusalem (Revelation 13:18; Section 22), and *exactly* twelve hundred and ninety years after the taking away of the perpetual sacrifice from the First Temple (Daniel 12:11; Section 46). See Temple (false third); also see Mark of the Beast—Could Not Buy or Sell.

al-Malik, Abd—The seventh major caliph, and seventh head of the Seven-Headed Sea Beast (Revelation 13:1). He built the Dome of the Rock between AD 692–AD 699, *exactly* six hundred and sixty-six years after Christ's earthly ministry (Revelation 13:18), and instituted Islam with his inscriptions on it (Daniel 12:11), and with his issuance of an Islamic currency (Revelation 13:16–17; Sections 22–24).

Alawite—An offshoot sect of Shi'a Islam that most Muslims consider outside the bounds of the Islamic religion. They are ultra-devoted to Ali, and were sent by him into his enemy Muawiyah's territory in Syria. They remained in Syria as an oppressed minority until the 'Corrective Revolution' of AD 1970 brought the secular Alawite, Hafez al-Assad, to power (Section 68).

Ali—Ali ibn Abi Talib, the cousin, step-son, and son-in-law of the Prophet Muhammad. He was the first male convert to Muhammad's teachings, and was an early warrior for Muhammad's struggle. He became the fourth caliph and head of the Shi'a branch of Islam. He is both the Son of Perdition (2 Thessalonians 2:3), and the [fourth] head of the Seven-Headed Sea Beast (Revelation 13:1) that was mortally wounded and symbolically healed (Revelation 13:3). His assassination occurred *exactly* six hundred and sixty-six years after Christ's Incarnation—giving birth to Islam as we know it (Revelation 13:18; Sections 22–23).

Allah—The devil (as when the word is used in the Qur'an) who gave the Antichrist Beast of Islam its power (Revelation 12:2–4; Section 21). See Dragon, Serpent, and Termagant.

American Dichotomy—The two incongruous eschatological roles of the United States; it is both the Great Eagle that protected the Church, and the Great Harlot that polluted the world's morals. As evidenced in the Culture Wars (Revelation 12:14, 17:1–3; Zechariah 5:5–11; Sections 28, 31–32, 34–35). See Wilderness (positive meaning) and Wilderness (negative meaning).

Anabaptist—A number of heterodox Reformed Protestant sects that believe that a person must be baptized as an adult after the 'age of accountability'— usually by immersion. They are non-creedal, and are particularly susceptible to the deceptions of Dispensational Premillennialism and the antichrist teachings of 'Christian' Zionists (Section 27).

Anti-Chalcedonian—Both the Nestorian and Oriental Orthodox (Monophysite) churches that do not accept that Jesus Christ was one undivided Person, but with the separate nature/will of God and the separate nature/will of man. They do not accept that the Christ was subject to sin, or that He suffered indignities that were against His [human] will. They fell away from Christian orthodoxy after the third and fourth ecumenical councils, respectively (2 Thessalonians 2:3; Sections 62, 68).

Antichrist—Any human being or institution that denies that Jesus is the God-man (2 John 7; Sections 15–16), but especially the Antichrist Beast of Islam (or the Cult of Muhammad) that Caliph Ali initiated and Caliph al-Malik institutionalized (Sections 20–23).

Anti-Filioqueanism—An epithet I have coined for the Eastern Orthodox and Oriental Orthodox churches that do not accept that the Holy Spirit proceeds from both the Father and the Son (as is clearly taught in John 16:7, 20:22). The Eastern Orthodox objected to the insertion of the Filioque into the Nicene Creed by the western Church; they built a false doctrine around this stance, and fell away from Christian orthodoxy in the eleventh century—immediately before the Seljuk Turks' conquest of Greek and Armenian Anatolia (2 Thessalonians 2:3; Section 69).

Arianism—The antichrist heresy that taught that Christ was not true God, but that He and the Holy Spirit were created by God the Father—an assault upon the doctrine of the Trinity. Condemned by the first two ecumenical councils in AD 325 and AD 381. The Nicene Creed was formulated to combat Arianism. The heresy was founded and named after Arius of Alexandria, who died of an abdominal hemorrhage while sitting on a Constantinopolitan public toilet in AD 336 (Sections 61, Tables 11 and 12).

Ataturk, Mustafa Kemal—Ruthless Ottoman general, alcoholic, and sexual deviant; founder and dictator of the Republic of Turkey from AD 1923 to AD 1938. God used him to end the power of the Caliphate through the AD 1921 Turkish Constitution—one thousand two hundred and sixty years after the inception of the Muslim religion in AD 661 (Revelation 12:6, 13:5; Section 30).

Athanasius—Patriarch of Alexandria and tireless champion of Nicene Christianity. Opponent of Arius' Anti-Trinitarian heresy. The Athanasian Creed is named in honor of him (Sections 18, 61).

Babaiism—An epithet that I have coined for the false christological formula whereby Christ is said to be one Person, but with two souls (or essences), two wills, and two natures. Put forward by Babai the Great, who had a lasting effect upon the Assyrian Church of the East. This doctrine is condemned by all other Christian churches, but is especially noxious to the Syriac Orthodox Church, which is Monophysite (Sections 62, Table 12).

Babylon the Great—The Twin Towers of the World Trade Center in New York City (Revelation 18; Section 35).

> **Fall of**—The attacks by the Antichrist Beast of Islam in AD 2001 (Revelation 18:2).
> **Never Shine Again**—Indication that the Twin Towers would be damaged beyond repair (Revelation 18:21–23).
> **One Day (plagues will overtake her)**—September 11, AD 2001 (Revelation 18:8).
> **One Hour (brought to ruin in)**—The time between the attacks and the collapse of the World Trade Center towers in New York City—one

hundred and two minutes for the North Tower, and the fifty-six minutes for the South Tower (Revelation 17:12, 18:10,19).

Baptism (Holy)—A Christian ceremony in which an ordained minister of the Word (i.e., a priest) applies water (either by sprinkling, pouring, or immersion) onto a prospective Christian in the name of the Father, and of the Son, and of the Holy Spirit. This may be done at the person's request, or at his or her legal guardian's request. Holy Baptism mysteriously results in the forgiveness of the individual's sins, and in he or she gaining trust in the Lord Jesus (Mark 16:16; John 3:5; 1 Peter 3:21). It is a means by which God bestows His grace (i.e., a sacrament). At the same time it does not necessarily guarantee salvation—if the baptized person later chooses to reject the Christian faith that they mysteriously received at Holy Baptism, he or she will surely go to Hell. The ceremony is usually performed in infancy (for the forgiveness of the child's original sin), but may also be done later for those that were not raised in orthodox Christian households (Matthew 28:19; Section 18).

Bear—Represents the Medo–Persian Empire (539 BC–334 BC; Daniel 7:5; Section 19).

Beast (from the land)—Islam as sustained by the Oghuz Turks. These people originated from the Atlai Mountains in the land mass of Central Asia (Revelation 13:11; Section 25).

>**Two Horns**—The Seljuk Empire (AD 1055–AD 1327) and Ottoman Empire (AD 1299–AD 1922).
>
>**Exercised All the Authority (of the first beast on his behalf)**— Refers to the Turks' assumption of the Caliphate, and reinvigoration of Islam during and after the Crusades (Revelation 13:12).
>
>**Fire to Come Down**—Symbolizes the Turks' early use of gunpowder (Revelation 13:13).
>
>**Image (that could speak in honor of the Beast)**—The minarets built by the Turks, from whence the Muslim call to prayer proceeds five times per day, everyday (Revelation 13:14–15).

Beast (from the sea)—The religion of Islam, as established by the seventh century Arabs. They originated from the Mediterranean/Red Sea region (Revelation 13:1; Section 20).

>**Seven Heads**—The first seven major Caliphs of the Arab Empire. They ruled between the time of Muhammad's death in AD 632 and

the sending forth of Islamic orthodoxy from Jerusalem in AD 699 (Revelation 13:1).

Name of Blasphemy (upon the seven heads)—'Muhammad' who rejected the Trinity, the Incarnation, and the Easter-Resurrection. He taught that Jesus was a messenger, or prophet, or apostle, or slave of Allah, rather than the Son of God. He is praised five times per day by every pious Muslim as "the Prophet of God" (Revelation 13:1,6).

Mark of—See Mark of the Beast.

Number of—See Number of the Beast.

Ten Horns—The lands that Muslims conquered and held, including Syrio–Phoenicia, Palestine–Transjordania, Mesopotamia, Egypt, Cyrene, Persia, Armenia, Carthage–Tripolitania, Mauretania–Numidia, and eventually the entirety of Asia Minor (Revelation 13:1).

Eyes of a Man—Reference to the large number of Muslims, and to their covetousness and lawlessness (Daniel 7:8).

Healing of Deadly Wound—Arab Empire's institutionalization (between AD 692 to AD 699) of the martyred Ali's dream of a new world religion to challenge Christianity (Revelation 13:3; Section 22).

Change Set Times—The introduction of the Hijra calendar upon the Arabs' conquest of Palestine in AD 638. In this dating system, the first year was changed from Christ's birth to the Hijra (or the flight of Muhammad from Mecca to Medina) in AD 622 (Daniel 7:25; Section 29).

Change Set Laws—The Qur'anic and extra–Qur'anic laws that the Muslims have imposed upon their subjects (Daniel 7:25; Section 29).

Beast (scarlet)—The Scarlet Beast itself represents the recurrence of lawlessness and terrorism, which were the roots of the kingdoms represented by the seven heads before they became established powers. This anarchy will become more prevalent during the Tribulation (Revelation 17:8,11; Sections 34–37).

Heads of Beast (that have fallen)—Five great worldly empires that tried to quench God's plan for salvation: ancient Egypt, Assyria, Babylonia, Medo–Persia, and Greece (Revelation 17:10).

Head of Beast (that is)—The Roman Empire that crucified the Savior (Revelation 17:10).

Head of Beast (that has not yet come)—The Caliphate of the Arab Empire (and later the Ottoman Empire) that opposed the saints (Revelation 17:10).

Little While (that the last head remained)—One thousand two hundred and sixty years of the post–Ali Caliphate (Revelation 17:10, 13:5).

Ten Horns of Beast—Socialist political and cultural forces in the United States (e.g., the mainstream news media, Hollywood, American Civil Liberties Union, academia, Democratic Party, National Abortion Rights Action League, teachers' unions, Public Broadcasting Service, etc.). Those that would make a pact with the devil before agreeing to live at peace with the Word of God (Revelation 17:12).

War with the Lamb—Culture Wars waged in the United States since ~ AD 1960 (Revelation 17:14).

Hatred of the Great Harlot (by the Beast and its ten horns)—The Anti-Americanism and self-destructive tendencies of the socialist political and cultural forces in the United States (Revelation 17:16).

Agreeing to Give the Beast their Power to Rule—The vulnerable position in which the socialist political and cultural forces left the United States' defenses—especially during the Clinton Administration (Revelation 17:17).

One Hour of Authority (along with the Beast)—Symbolic time that the ten horns reigned with the Scarlet Beast during the attacks of September 11, AD 2001—one hundred and two minutes for the North Tower and the fifty-six minutes for the South Tower (Revelation 17:12).

Will Ascend Out of the Bottomless Pit—The rise of terrorist anarchy and chaos in the last days (Revelation 17:8).

Beast (terrifying and frightening)—Represents the Roman Empire (27 BC–AD 1453; Daniel 7:7; Section 19).

Benz, Karl—Inventor of the automobile in AD 1886, and father of the age of automated transportation. His invention is called 'locusts' by the Apostle John (Revelation 9:3; Section 49).

Byzantine Empire—A name coined by a German historian in the nineteenth century to describe the Eastern Roman Empire between AD 476 and AD 1453. The word 'Byzantine' would have been unknown to the rulers and citizens of the Eastern Roman Empire. They thought of themselves as the intact portion of the Roman Empire (Daniel 7:7; Section 19). Synonymous with 'Beast (terrifying and frightening).'

Caliphate—The kingdoms of the one hundred successors of Muhammad that ruled the Arab and Ottoman Empires from AD 632 to AD 1921 (Revelation 13:5,12; Sections 20, 30).

Chalcedonianism—The correct Christology whereby Jesus is said to have two natures (i.e., fully divine and fully man) and two wills (i.e., fully divine and fully human) in one undivided Person and one undivided Soul (or essence). Affirmed at the fourth ecumenical council in AD 451, and reaffirmed at the fifth ecumenical council in AD 553 and the sixth ecumenical council in AD 680. Accepted by the Roman Catholics, Protestants, and Eastern Orthodox; rejected by heretical churches of the Oriental Orthodox (Monophysite) Communion, as well as the few remaining Nestorians (Sections 62, 67).

Chosen People—Creedal Christians; anyone that trusts that God loves us enough to have become a man in Jesus of Nazareth. Also, known as the True Israel, Spiritual Israel, Children of Israel, Israel of God, Remnant, Children of Promise, Apple of God's Eye, the Head and Not the Tail, an Acceptable People, a Blessed People, God's Children, People of the New Name, People of God, Elect, and the Church (Galatians 3:7, 3:29, Ephesians 3:6; Sections 28, 56). See Christian, Christian Church, Israel (of God), Protestant (Confessional), Roman Catholic, Temple (true third), Two Witnesses, Woman (clothed with the sun), and Yahwism.

Christian—Any person that entrusts his or her soul to the care of Jesus Christ, the God-man, and is baptized with water in the name of the Father, and of the Son, and of the Holy Spirit (Mark 16:16; Section 17). This is the new name of the People of God (Isaiah 56:5; Isaiah 62:2; Isaiah 65:15; Acts 11:26; Section 56). See Chosen People, Christian Church, Israel (of God), Protestant (Confessional), Roman Catholic, Temple (true third), Two Witnesses, Woman (clothed with the sun), and Yahwism.

Christian Church—The invisible, indivisible, Body of Christian believers that accepts and confesses the three Ecumenical Creeds (with the Filioque). The Bride of Christ (Ephesians 5:23,31–32; Revelation 21:2; Sections 18, 28, 56). See Chosen People, Christian, Israel (of God), Protestant (Confessional), Roman Catholic, Temple (true third), Two Witnesses, Woman (clothed with the sun), and Yahwism.

'Christian' Zionism—An antichrist cult that maintains that ethnic or 'natural' Jews do not need to accept Jesus Christ into their hearts in order to be temporally or eternally blessed because God favors them above the rest of humanity (Galatians 4:17; Jude 4; Sections 27, 53). See Dispensationalism, Premillenialism, and Über-Baptist.

Christology—The particulars of how God became a man in Jesus, best explained in the Athanasian Creed. Accepting the proper Christology (i.e., Chalcedonian and Filioquean) is vitally important to individuals and nations (Sections 18, 61–69).

Church of the Emasculated Christ—See Protestant (Mainline) and Seven Sisters (Section 77).

Church of the Holy Sepulchre—A church built over the sight of Christ's empty tomb in Jerusalem. Construction was begun by Emperor Constantine in AD 336. The building was partly burned by a Muslim mob in AD 966, and completely destroyed by Caliph al-Hakim in AD 1009—an act of vandalism that precipitated the Crusades (Section 71).

Confirm a Covenant (with many)—An angelic prophecy made in 539 BC that the Messiah's earthly ministry would be to a large number of Jews and would last for three and a half years—beginning with His anointing in AD 26 (Luke 3:21–22). At the end of this period He would, "... put an end to sacrifice and offering ..." [Daniel 9:27 NIV] through the institution of Holy Communion (Matthew 26:26–28) and the sacrifice of Himself as the Lamb of God (Matthew 27:50). Afterward, the resurrected Messiah would protect His Christian Church in Jerusalem for another three and a half years. This seven year period ended with the stoning of St. Stephen in AD 33 (Acts 8:1,4; Sections 26–27).

Creeds (three proper, Christian, Ecumenical)—The Apostles', Athanasian, and Nicene (with inclusion of the Filioque) Creeds that define the Christian religion (1 Timothy 4:16; Titus 2:1; Section 18).

Culture Wars—The relentless struggle by Liberals since ~ AD 1960 to oppose the Gospel, and to wrest control of the American national identity from the Christian Church. Waged through judicial activism, feminism, hedonism, liberal media bias, and the cult of science (2 Timothy 3:1–5; Revelation 12:15; 17:14; Sections 32, 34, 37). See American Dichotomy.

Dispensationalism—The heretical belief that God deals with different groups of human beings by different methods (or economies) during different periods (or dispensations) of human history. They maintain that the Bible shows God testing and making covenants with these groups during seven distinct dispensations (e.g., Patriarchal, Mosaic, Church, etc.). They say that these groups received different promises from God. The covenants are racially-based, rather than contiguous to all God-fearing believers throughout the ages. They therefore make a strong differentiation between the Israel of God in the Old Testament and the Church of God in the New Testament. Today's Jews are [supposedly] irrevocably entitled and destined to receive the promises that God [supposedly] made to Abraham on their behalf. The Jews are said to enjoy God's protection regardless of their response to Christ's Gospel, and to have a separate, favored, prophetic track as His [supposed] Chosen People. The fulfillment of God's promises to them will [supposedly] occur after the close of the 'provisional,' Church, era—during Christ's [supposed] thousand year bodily rule from this earth's Jerusalem. In this way, Dispensationalism is a form of Premillennialism that views the Christian Church as a 'parenthesis' in God's larger plan for the Jewish race. [In contrast to this disjointed view of God's dealings with men, I provide a harmonious layout of Biblical history in Section 70, as well as a systematic defense of God's racial impartiality in Sections 53–57, 102.] The Dispensationalists clearly have an inferiority complex when comparing their spiritual state to that of ethnic or 'natural' Jews, and as a consequence, their eschatology is full of red herrings: They eagerly anticipate a 'rapture' of all Christians seven years before the Second Coming of Christ. This is said to be followed by a mass conversion of Jews to Christianity and an intense persecution of that new, post–rapture, Church. Dispensationalist-thought is fueled by their misinterpretation of the last 'week' in the Daniel 9:20–27 prophecy. Dispensationalism was introduced by the Anglo–Irish evangelist, John Darby, and popularized with the publication of the Scofield Reference Bible in AD 1909. The doctrine's homebase is a denomination called the Plymouth Brethren, but its basic tenets are widely held among Anabaptist sects, and are fashionable among American Evangelicals and ostensibly non-denominational churches. Dispensationalists view the twentieth century establishment of a Jewish state in Palestine as divine validation of their message. They believe that it is every Christian's duty to work toward complete Jewish restoration—including the construction of a new Jewish Temple in place of the Dome of the Rock (Sections 27, 53–54). See 'Christian' Zionism, Premillennialism, and Über-Baptist.

Dome of the Rock—The earliest Muslim religious shrine. Built between AD 692 and AD 699 on the Temple Mount in Jerusalem. It is not a mosque, but a monument to Islam's triumph over eastern Christendom. Its interior and exterior arcade inscriptions constitute the 'Abomination that Causes Desolation' (Daniel 12:11; Sections 22, 46). See Temple (false third).

Dragon—The devil, known by many non-Trinitarian names including 'Allah'—as when 'Allah' is used in the Qur'an, but not when it is used in the Arabic Christian Bible (1 Corinthians 10:20–21; Revelation 12:3; Section 21). See Allah, Serpent, and Termagant.

>**Persecuted the Woman, and War with Her Offspring**—Worldwide persecution of Christians currently taking place (Revelation 12:13,17; Section 32).

>**Spewed Out of His Mouth (like a flood)**—The myriad of lies that collectively work to keep people from coming to a knowledge of God, and that distort objective truth—especially during the Culture Wars (Revelation 12:15–16; Section 32).

Eastern Orthodox—A heterodox branch of Christianity that, although Chalcedonian, refuses to accept and profess that the Holy Spirit proceeds from both the Father and the Son. These churches are against the inclusion of the Filioque in the Nicene Creed. They incorrectly conceptualize the Persons of the Holy Trinity as being in a hierarchical relationship, and they imagine that human beings go through a process of 'deification' during their Christian walk (as opposed to the correct view of sanctification). They include the national churches in Greece, Bulgaria, Serbia, Romania, Georgia, Russia, Belarus, and Ukraine (Section 69).

Eastern Roman Empire—Begun when Emperor Diocletian split the Roman Empire into two parts to make it more manageable. It was the sole remaining part of the Roman Empire after the deposition of Romulus Augustus from Rome and the dissolution of the Western Roman Empire in AD 476. The Eastern Roman Empire's capital of Constantinople was known as 'New Rome.' It was finally conquered by the Ottomans (i.e., the second horn of the Land Beast) in AD 1453—thus extinguishing the Roman Empire (Daniel 7:7–8; Sections

19, 41). Synonymous with 'Beast (terrifying and frightening).' See Byzantine Empire.

Ecumenical Councils—A series of early councils held by Christian bishops from around the world in which Christian orthodoxy was established. The seven ecumenical councils were: the First Council of Nicaea in AD 325; the First Council of Constantinople in AD 381; the Council of Ephesus in AD 431; the Council of Chalcedon in AD 451; the Second Council of Constantinople in AD 553; the Third Council of Constantinople in AD 680; the Second Council of Nicaea in AD 787 (Table 11).

Edict of Milan—Law removing penalties for professing Christians in the Roman Empire. Issued by Emperor Constantine in AD 313 (Section 61).

End Times—The period between the Ascension of Christ and the Second Coming of Christ (1 John 2:18). The final two thousand years of the six thousand year world history (Sections 15, 27). The 'Encore' and 'Finale' of the Divine Idiom (Section 70).

Eschatology—The branch of theology that is concerned with the Second Coming of Christ and the end of the world. In this book I espouse a new, date-specific, formulation of Postmillennialism (see Foreword and Sections 37–38, 71).

Falling Away—The Nestorian (AD 428–AD 431), Monophysite (AD 451–AD 728), and Anti-Filioquean (AD 589–AD 1054) schisms of the eastern churches from Christian orthodoxy. Subsequent to the arrival of these heresies, there was a forced conversion of many of their adherents to the Son of Perdition's religion, Islam (2 Thessalonians 2:3; Sections 62–69).

False Prophet—Rationalism, or Naturalism, or Liberalism, or Modernism, or Evolutionism. Any human being or institution that believes that scientific discovery leads to metaphysical truth. The secular Anti-Christian forces of the Cult of Science (Mark 13:22; 1 Timothy 6:20–21; Revelation 16:3; 19:20; Section 87).

Filioque—Latin for 'and the Son'—especially when included in the Nicene Creed clause about the procession of the Holy Spirit (John 16:7; Section 18).

Filioqueanism—A moniker I have coined for the biblically-correct belief that the Holy Spirit proceeds from God the Father *and* God the Son (John 20:22). The proclamation of this truth by adding 'and the Son' into the Nicene Creed, just as it is in the Athanasian Creed. Begun in AD 589 at the Council of Toledo and accepted by the Roman Catholic Church in AD 1014 (Section 69).

Forty-Two Months—The prophesied time during which the post–Ali Islamic Caliphate will control Jerusalem (Revelation 11:2) and flaunt their blasphemous authority (Revelation 13:5; Section 33). Faithful Christians bore witness against the Caliphate during forty-two periods of thirty years each, or the 1,260 years between the conception of the Beast of Islam (with Ali's assassination in AD 661), and the Caliphate's permanent loss of power (with the Turkish constitution of AD 1921). See Two Witnesses and 'One Thousand Two Hundred and Sixty Days (years).'

Gnosticism—A first and second century antichrist heresy in which all matter was thought to be evil. The Docetic variant of Gnosticism taught that Christ only appeared to become a man, and only appeared to suffer and die—an assault upon the Incarnation. The Gnostics maintained that salvation came not from faith in the Resurrected Christ, but from escaping the confines of our physical bodies through a special spiritual knowledge (as in Buddhism). The Apostles' Creed was designed to combat Gnosticism (Sections 18, Table 12).

Gog and Magog—Symbolizes all the nations that will join together to attack God's people during the Tribulation (Revelation 20:7–10). Before the battle can even begin, this evil infantry will be stopped by a holocaust (probably a nuclear missile) from the sky (Revelation 9:14–19; Sections 72, 74).

Great Eagle—The United States of America in its role as the refuge for the Christian Church during the Cold War. A reference to the US national symbol during the great immigration wave of Christian peoples that ended with the Emergency Quota Act of AD 1921 (Revelation 12:14; Section 31).

Great Harlot—The United States of America in its role as the corruptor of the world's culture and spreader of Rationalism. Specifically, the liberal American culture that is headquartered in New York City (Zechariah 5:5–11; Revelation 17:18; Section 34).

> **Sits on Many Waters**—New York Harbor where immigrants from around the world arrived (Revelation 17:1,15).

Wine of Her Fornication (earth made drunk with)—The export of American music, movies, and moral degradation (Revelation 17:2).

Arrayed in Purple and Scarlet—Representative of western prosperity (Revelation 17:4).

Drunk With the Blood of the Saints—An acknowledgement that the prosperity that allowed the Great Harlot to live in debauchery was the spiritual result of the sacrifice of martyred Christian saints (Revelation 17:6).

Riding (upon the Scarlet Beast)—Represents how modern American Liberalism is riding upon the antichrist legacies of ancient Egypt, Assyria, Babylonia, Medo–Persia, Greece, Rome, and the Caliphate. These are the seven heads of the Scarlet Beast that have a historic hostility toward God's salvation plan (Revelation 17:7–11).

Gutenberg, Johannes—Inventor of the printing press and first mass-printer of the Bible. His initial work on the Word of God is the same amount of time after Christ's birth as Moses' initial work on the Word of God is before Christ's birth (i.e., 1456 years; Section 70).

Hadith—The extra–Qur'anic reports of the sayings of Muhammad (Section 73).

Hajj—The annual pilgrimage of Muslims to Mecca. One of the five pillars of Islam (Section 82).

Henry II—The Saxon Holy Roman Emperor that asked that the Nicene Creed be recited with the inclusion of the Filioque during his coronation Mass in AD 1014. The Pope obliged him. This was the first time that the Roman Catholic Church officially endorsed the Filioque. It led to the Great Schism of AD 1054, but also ushered in the Millennial rule of the saints with Christ (Revelation 20:4; Section 69).

Heraclius—The seventh century Eastern Roman Emperor whose incompetent hundred year dynasty paved the way for the Antichrist Beast of Islam (Sections 63–65).

Hijra—The flight of Muhammad from Mecca to Medina in AD 622. Marks the beginning of the Islamic calendar (Section 29).

Iconoclasm—A heresy that prohibits images of Jesus Christ on the grounds that they are idolatrous—an often-employed trick of the devil to deny the historical reality of the Incarnation. When the Eastern Roman Empire issued coins with a full-face image of Christ, the Arab Caliphate took iconoclastic offence and began to mint an Antichrist-inscribed currency (in AD 692). This occurred *exactly* six hundred and sixty-six years after the commencement of Christ's ministry (Sections 22–23). Iconoclasm was condemned at the seventh ecumenical council (Table 11), which held that such images are useful objects of adoration (but not worship). See Triumph of Orthodoxy.

Incarnation—The miraculous phenomenon in 6 BC whereby the eternal and omnipotent Person of the Holy Trinity, God the Son, became a male human being inside the womb of the blessed virgin Mary (Luke 1:30–35). God took humanity into Himself at that moment. One divino-human Person with one divino-human Soul was born as Jesus Christ (Table 12). He had the separate nature of God and the separate nature of man; He also had the separate will of God and the separate will of man. He was subject to sin, tempted as a man is tempted, and destined to three days of decay. Yet He had no sin and was raised from the dead on the third day (Sections 23, 67).

Islamism—The Antichrist religion of the Son of Perdition, Ali. It is the Beast of Revelation 13, as well as the boastful horn of Daniel 7. Islam's two main branches are the Shi'a and Sunni—the sempiternal enemies of Christianity. They emphatically reject the Crucifixion, Resurrection, and the Messiahship of Jesus of Nazareth (Section 19–23). See Beast (from the sea), Beast (from the land), and Abomination that Causes Desolation.

Israel (of God)—Any human being or group of human beings that trust that God became a man according to the Old Testament prophecies. Today's Creedal Christians, about whom God made the promise to Abraham (Genesis 13:14–17; Galatians 3:29; Sections 28, 56). See Chosen People, Christian, Christian Church, Protestant (Confessional), Roman Catholic, Temple (true third), Two Witnesses, Woman (clothed with the sun), and Yahwism.

Israel (modern State of)—A secular parliamentary democracy in the eastern Mediterranean that is almost entirely populated by non-Christians. Many of its citizens are descended from Jesus' near-kin, but this is of absolutely no spiritual benefit or eschatological significance (Section 54).

Jew (as ethnicity)—An ethno-religious group largely descended from the patriarch Jacob. Approximately fourteen million in number—residing mostly in the United States and the State of Israel—of whom ~ ninety-nine percent are not of the Christian faith (John 1:11; Ezekiel 22:18). A people that God loves as much as He loves every other people, but not more (Hosea 1:10; Isaiah 19:25, 56:3; John 1:12; Section 53–55).

Jew (as Old Testament religious title)—The old name for the Israel of God, or the old name for the pre–Christ Church that trusted that God would become a man in accordance with Old Testament prophecy (Isaiah 65:15; Zechariah 8:23; Section 56). See Yahwism.

Judaism (Rabbinic)—A group of antichrist sects that adhere (to varying degrees) to Jewish religious customs, but that specifically reject the messiah-ship of Jesus of Nazareth (Revelation 2:9, 3:9). It is not to be confused with Yahwism—the pre–Christ religion of the Old Testament (Section 54).

Karbala (Battle of)—The quixotic campaign by Ali's second son and heir, Husayn, to gain control of the Arab Empire in AD 680. He and his seventy-one followers were slaughtered by a Sunni force of four thousand led by Caliph Yazid. The event is remembered each year by Shi'a through self-flagellation on the Day of Ashura (Section 22).

Kharijite—An offshoot sect of Sunni Islam. Its members assassinated Caliph Ali and attempted to assassinate his rival and successor, Muawiyah. They are ultra-devoted to the Qur'an and believe in killing infidels with impunity. At the end of the seventh century they rebelled against Caliph al-Malik in Iraq and were crushed. A dormant branch of the Kharijites form the majority in the modern Sultanate of Oman (Section 68).

Khoja, Nasr-ed-Din—A wiseman and jester in the court of Tamerlane. He lived southwest of modern Ankara, Turkey. His name means 'Master' or 'Teacher' (Section 89).

Knowledge Shall Increase—A prophecy that the end of the world would come shortly after the advent of the Information Revolution (Daniel 12:4; Section 88).

Leopard—Represents the Grecian Empire (334 BC–30 BC) begun by Alexander the Great (Daniel 7:6; Section 19).

Levant—An imprecise geographic area, roughly south of the Taurus Mountains, north of the Red Sea, east of northern Egypt, and west of the Arabian Desert and Euphrates River. Encompasses modern Lebanon, Syria, Israel, West Bank, Jordan, and the Sinai (Section 40).

Lion—Represents the Babylonian Empire (626 BC–539 BC; Daniel 7:4; Section 19).

Little Horn—The Caliphate, or Arab Muslim Empire (and later the Seljuk and Ottoman Empires). The historical dates are AD 632–AD 1924, but the effective dates for Islamic religious rule are the one thousand two hundred and sixty years between AD 661–AD 1921 (Daniel 7:8; Revelation 11:2–3, 12:6, 13:5; Section 19–20). Synonymous with the 'Beast (from the sea)', and later the 'Beast (from the land)'.
> **Uprooted Three Horns**—The lands and cultures of the Babylonian Empire, Medo–Persian Empire, and Grecian Empire that the Muslims overran (Daniel 7:20,24–25).

Locusts—Automated transportation, especially the automobile powered by the internal combustion engine (Revelation 9:3; Sections 49–50).
> **Bottomless Pit**—Oil wells (Revelation 9:2).
> **Sun Darkened**—Smog (Revelation 9:2).
> **Torment (of those without the seal of God)**—Spiritually-deleterious effect of oil wealth upon Muslims (Revelation 9:4–5).
> **Seeking Death**—Desire of Islamists from oil-rich nations to die in jihad (Revelation 9:6).
> **Faces of Men**—Automobile headlights and grills that look like eyes and teeth (Revelation 9:7).
> **Power to Hurt Men for Five Months**—Age of the internal combustion engine from Benz' patent in AD 1886 to AD 2036 (Revelation 9:5,10).

Mahdi—The prophesied redeemer of Islam, or the 'Muslim Messiah.' The word means 'the [Rightly] Guided One,' and is not mentioned in the Qur'an, but is mentioned in the Hadith. The Muslims believe that the Mahdi will appear shortly before the Judgment Day. They do not say that the Mahdi is the Son of God, but that he will come to rescue them from their troubles and institute Islam across the world. The Shi'a think that the Mahdi is the historic figure, Muhammad al-Mahdi—the boy that was of the twelfth generation from Muhammad (through Ali), and disappeared after his father's funeral in Samarra, Iraq (Section 73).

Many Shall Run to and fro—A prophecy that the end of the world would come shortly after the advent of intercontinental air travel (Daniel 12:4; Section 88).

Manzikert (Battle of)—A pivotal battle in AD 1071 where the incipient Seljuk Empire (i.e., the first horn of the Land Beast) soundly defeated a larger force from the Eastern Roman Empire. Resulted in the permanent loss of Christian sovereignty over Anatolia; this catastrophe was the spiritual consequence of the Greek's Anti-Filioquean schism (Luke 7:23; Sections 68, 71).

Manzikert (Synod of)—A local council of Armenian Apostolic and Syriac Orthodox bishops in AD 728 which denounced Pope Leo I and Chalcedonianism, and formally embraced the Monophysite heresy. Their canon that Christ's body was "… neither subject to sin nor destined to decay," was fundamentally sacrilegious (Matthew 16:21–23). The synod solidified the Oriental Orthodox Communion, but had the spiritual consequence of their near-annihilation by the Antichrist Beast of Islam (Isaiah 42:24–25; Hosea 13:16; Section 67).

Mark of the Beast—A rug burn on one's forehead and/or rug calluses on one's right hand from the observance of Muslim call to prayer (Revelation 13:16; Section 24).

> **Could Not Buy or Sell**—The Dhimmi religious caste system in Muslim lands whereby there is an economic disincentive to remain a non-Muslim. First begun with the [Iconoclastic] Islamic currency reforms of AD 692–AD 699 (Revelation 13:17).

Martel, Charles—The French leader whom God used to save western Christendom from being overrun by Muslims at the Battle of Tours in AD 732. His fur-clad rabble were the only armed force between the Antichrist Beast of Islam and the Church that the Apostle Peter founded in Rome (Matthew 16:18; Section 69).

Mashdots, Mesrop—Inventor of the Armenian alphabet in AD 405, born in Hatsekats, Province of Manzikert. His aim was to spread Christianity. The new alphabet resulted in an Armenian translation of the Bible by AD 434 (Section 67). *Exactly* six hundred and sixty six years after the completion of his work on the alphabet the Seljuk Turks conquered Anatolia at the Battle of Manzikert (Revelation 13:18; Table 15).

Meaning of Life—To glorify and enjoy the Triune God (1 Corinthians 10:31); to declare faith in the Resurrection of Jesus Christ (John 6:29; Section 108).

Millennium—The sixth, and final, millennium in human history, approximately from AD 1014 to AD 2014. During this time, the devil has been bound (Revelation 20:2), the Beast of Islam has been on the defensive, and the Church has grown with three proper Ecumenical Creeds. The devil will be released for the last twenty years of history and there will be havoc during the Tribulation—especially in the Middle East and in Muslim countries (Revelation 20:3–4; Sections 69, 71).

Monophysitism—The false christological formula whereby Christ is said to have only one divino-human nature and only one divino-human will. Held by the heretical Oriental Orthodox churches, though they prefer the term 'Miaphysitism.' Condemned by the fourth, fifth, and sixth ecumenical councils. This doctrine was the spiritual precursor of Sunni Islam (Sections 62, 66–68).

Monotheism—Any of a number of antichrist sects that professes one God, but not three Persons, and not the Incarnation. The true religion of the Holy Bible is *Nicene Trinitarian* Monotheism (Sections 21, 54).

Monothelitism—The false christological formula whereby Christ is said to have two natures (i.e., fully God and fully man), but only one divino-human will. Emperor Heraclius' Monothelite initiative immediately preceded the advent of the Arab Empire. This heresy was condemned by the sixth ecumenical council in AD 680, but was the doctrine of the Maronite Christians of Lebanon from the seventh century until the Crusades (Sections 64–66, 71).

Muawiyah—The notorious fifth caliph who fought against Caliph Ali during the first Muslim civil war and assumed control of the empire after Ali's assassination. Reviled by the Shi'a; reluctantly accepted by the Sunni (Section 22).

Nestorianism—The false christological formula whereby Christ is said to be two persons with two souls (or essences), two wills, and two natures—essentially a dual personality. Dates to AD 428. Condemned by the third ecumenical council in AD 431. A variation of this heresy was held in the Assyrian Church of the East until AD 1994. Now held only by the tiny breakaway Ancient Church of the East. This doctrine was the spiritual precursor of Shi'a Islam (Sections 62, 67–68).

Nicene Formulation—The true Christian faith affirmed at the first two ecumenical councils, and promulgated by the Nicene Creed (Section 18). See Trinitarianism.

Number of the Beast—A series of six-hundred-and-sixty-six-year timelines throughout history in which the devil sought to counteract God's plan for salvation by establishing his religion of Islam and persecuting God's people—especially the time between Christ's incarnation/ministry, and the assassination of Ali/Dome of the Rock project (Revelation 13:18; Sections 23, 83).

One Thousand Three Hundred and Thirty-Five Days (years)—The prophesied time between the gilding of the Dome of the Rock/promulgation of Islamic orthodoxy in AD 699, and the Second Coming of Christ/end of the world in AD 2034 (Daniel 12:12; Section 46).

One Thousand Two Hundred and Ninety Days (years)—The prophesied time between the taking away of perpetual sacrifices in the Second Temple in 592 BC, and the gilding of the Dome of the Rock/promulgation of Islamic orthodoxy in AD 699 (Daniel 12:11; Section 46).

One Thousand Two Hundred and Sixty Days (years)—The prophesied time between the conception of the Beast of Islam with Ali's assassination in AD 661, and the Caliphate's loss of power with the Turkish constitution of AD 1921. During this period Creedal Christians prophesied in sackcloth (Revelation 11:3) and moved into the wilderness of Europe, the Americas, and Oceania for protection (Revelation 12:6; Section 30). See Forty-Two Months, and Two Witnesses.

Oriental Orthodox—A heterodox branch of Christianity that refuses to accept that Jesus Christ had two separate natures and two separate wills within one undivided Person. Includes Armenian Apostolic, Egyptian Copt, Ethiopian

Tewahedo, Eritrean Tewahdo, Malankara Orthodox, and Syriac Orthodox (Sections 62, 66–68). See Monophysite.

Pentecostalism—An Anabaptist movement where special emphasis is placed on the baptism of the Holy Spirit and speaking in tongues (as in the Pentecost of Acts 2:1–4). They are non-creedal, and are especially susceptible to Anti-Trinitarian 'Oneness' cultism (Section 18). See Sabellianism.

Premillennialism—The heretical belief that the thousand year reign of Christ, known as the Millennium, will be *after* His Second Coming. They teach the following eschatological sequence: (1) Christians will be 'raptured' to heaven, (2) there will be a mass conversion of new Christians—most notably the Jews within the State of Israel, (3) an Antichrist personality will arise from within the European Union, and there will be an intense period of tribulation, (4) the State of Israel will be attacked by the Antichrist and his allies, (5) Christ will return to rule from the present earth's city of Jerusalem, and He will throw Satan into a pit, (6) after a thousand years, Satan will be released from the pit and will gather an army to attack Christ in Jerusalem, (7) fire will come down from Heaven, Satan will be defeated and vanquished to eternal Hell, (8) there will be the Judgment Day. The Premillennialists' obsession with the Jews puts them in danger of falling into the Antichrist cult of 'Christian' Zionism (Sections 27, 53–54). Also, see Dispensationalism and Über-Baptist.

Protestant (Confessional)—The various biblical denomination and churches that have remained faithful to the Gospel message of God becoming a man. The Israel of God that is Chalcedonian, Filioquean, and in all other indispensable respects Christ-centered and Bible-based (Sections 28, 33, 81). See Chosen People, Christian, Christian Church, Israel (of God), Temple (true third), Two Witnesses, Woman (clothed with the sun), and Yahwism.

Protestant (Mainline)—Heretical liberal churches that have many ordained ministers and communicant members that deny the divinity and/or the manhood of Jesus. Especially, but not limited to, the Seven Sister denominations (1 Timothy 4:1; Section 77).

Rapture—The false teaching of Dispensational Premillennialists that Christian believers will be caught up to Heaven seven years before the Second Coming of Christ. The Bible actually teaches that at the Second Coming the dead in Christ will arise with incorruptible bodies, and then the living Christian believers will also receive incorruptible bodies. On that day all Christians will be taken to Heaven by the Lord Jesus—not seven years before (1 Thessalonians 4:16–17; Sections 27, 52).

Replacement Theology—The idea that God's covenant has shifted from Jews to Christians (also known as Supersessionism). This is not correct: in point of fact, there never was a covenant with Jews *per se*. There was, rather, a covenant with persons (mostly Jews) that believed that God would become a man. And now that God has become a man, that very same covenant resides with persons (mostly non-Jews) that believe that God did become a man. Both groups make up one Chosen People—a Communion of Saints throughout human history—known as the Israel of God (Psalm 87:4–5; Isaiah 19:25; Galatians 3:14; Section 56).

Roman Catholic—A Christian denomination that is steadfastly Chalcedonian and Filioquean, but is entrenched in several doctrinal errors, as reflected in the canons of the Council of Trent (Romans 3:28; Sections 28, 33, 81). See Chosen People, Christian, Christian Church, Israel (of God), Temple (true third), Two Witnesses, Woman (clothed with the sun), and Yahwism.

Sabbath Rest—The weekly worship service after six days of toil—a foreshadowing of the rest that believers will enjoy in Heaven after six millennia of human toil on earth (Hebrews 4:9; Section 48).

Sabellianism—A third century antichrist heresy that held that the Heavenly Father, the Resurrected Son, and the Holy Spirit are different manifestations of the one true God. It rejected three distinct Persons in a single Godhead, and therefore was definitely not a saving faith. Currently practiced by 'Oneness Pentecostal' cults (Section 18).

Sealed (words)—A prediction by the pre-incarnate Christ that the prophecies concerning His Second Coming would remain a mystery "until the time of the end"—early AD 2004 when it was revealed to the author of this book. Christians around the world will soon realize (both from this book, and by other means) that Christ's return is imminent (Daniel 12:9; Sections 38, 51).

Second Coming—The bodily return of Jesus Christ from the sky on a specific calendar date sometime between AD 2033 and AD 2039 (Matthew 24:30–31; Sections 7, 39, 52).

Serpent—The devil (Revelation 12:3; Section 21). See Allah, Dragon, and Termagant.

Seven Sisters—The major heretical, liberal, Protestant denominations within the Unites States: United Methodist Church, Evangelical Lutheran Church in America, Presbyterian Church USA, Episcopal Church USA, American Baptist Church USA, United Church of Christ, Disciples of Christ, (2 Peter 2:1–2; Section 77). See Protestant (Mainline).

Scatter the Power—The dispersal of the Bible and the Gospel message to all nations—the one and only specific requirement for Jesus Christ's return (Daniel 12:7; Matthew 24:14; Section 45).

Shi'a—The second largest branch of Islam which venerates Caliph/Imam Ali. Also known as 'Twelvers' for their belief that the divinely-appointed Imams were those in the twelve generations after Muhammad—from Caliph Ali to the Mahdi. The spiritual consequence of the Nestorian heresy of the ancient Assyrian Church of the East (2 Thessalonians 2:3–4; Revelation 13:1,5; Sections 22–23, 67–68, 73).

Signs and Wonders to Deceive—The demonic allure of antichrist religiosity and antichrist secularism that has cost many ostensibly Christian people their souls (Mark 13:22; Section 86). See Unholy Alliance.

Son of Perdition—Ali, the prototypical Antichrist, who emerged after the 'falling away' from Christian orthodoxy of the Nestorians and the Monophysites (2 Thessalonians 2:3). He and his followers shouted "Ali Akbar!"—putting himself in the place of God in men's hearts (2 Thessalonians 2:4). He received a mortal head wound by a poison-tipped spear *exactly* six hundred and sixty-six years after the Incarnation. It took him three days to die. His dream of a new world religion was resurrected thirty-eight years after his death, and *exactly* six hundred and sixty-six years after the spreading forth of Christ's Gospel from Jerusalem (Revelation 13:3; Sections 15, 22).

Sophronius—Patriarch of Jerusalem in AD 637, when it was surrendered to the Arabs. As he escorted Caliph Umar, and Ali, through the Church of the Holy Sepulchre he muttered, "The abomination of desolation is in the holy place" (Daniel 12:11; Section 22).

Sunni—The largest branch of Islam. The spiritual consequence of the Monophysite heresy of the Oriental Orthodox churches (2 Thessalonians 2:3–4; Revelation 13:1,5; Sections 22–23, 67–68, 73).

Tamerlane—Turco–Mongol warlord and founder of the Timurid dynasty. His empire stretched from modern Turkey to the border of China at the time of his death in AD 1405. He claimed to be a descendant of Ali and was especially severe toward the Nestorian Assyrians (Sections 67, 89).

Temple (first)—Built by Solomon and the Israelites in Jerusalem on the spot chosen by God (1 Chronicles 22:1). Plundered in 597 BC (2 Kings 24:13) and destroyed in 586 BC (2 Kings 25:9) by the Babylonians (Sections 26–27, 46).

Temple (second)—Built by Zerubbabel and the Jews on the Temple Mount in Jerusalem. Completed seventy years after Solomon's Temple was destroyed (foretold in Jeremiah 25:11–12). Expanded and remodeled by Herod the Great. Destroyed in AD 70 by the Romans (Luke 21:6; Sections 23, 26–27).

Temple (false third)—The golden Dome of the Rock. Construction was begun by Caliph al-Malik on the Temple Mount in AD 692, and it was completed and gilded in AD 699—*exactly* six hundred and sixty years after Christ's anointing, and His sending forth of the Church of Pentecost (Daniel 12:11; Sections 22–23, 46). See Abomination that Causes Desolation.

Temple (true third)—The Body of the Risen Christ and His Bride, the Christian Church, both arising from Jerusalem in AD 30 (John 2:19–21; Ephesians 5:23; Acts 8:1,4; Sections 28, 39). See Chosen People, Christian, Christian Church, Israel (of God), Protestant (Confessional), Roman Catholic, Two Witnesses, Woman (clothed with the sun), and Yahwism.

Termagant—A Medieval European epithet for the non-Triune god worshiped by Muslims (1 Corinthians 10:20–21; 1 John 2:23, Revelation 13:2,4; Section 21). See Allah, Dragon, and Serpent.

Time, Times, and Half a Time (nourishing of the woman)—The seventy years between the establishment of the Union of Soviet Socialist Republics in AD 1922, and the dissolution of the Red Army in AD 1992. The Church was kept safe by God and the United States during this "time, times, and half a time" or three and a half times of Revelation 12:14. The word 'time' here is a reflection of the twenty years that Jacob spent in Laban's house, protected from Esau's fury (Genesis 27–32; Section 31).

Time, Times, and Half a Time (saints given into the hand of the little horn)—The fourteen hundred years between the Battle of Yarmuk in AD 636, and the Second Coming of Christ in AD 2036. The eastern portion of the Church was oppressed by Islam during this "time, times, and half a time" or three and a half times of Daniel 7:25. The word 'time' here is a reflection of the four hundred years that the people of Israel lived as strangers in Canaan, and later as slaves in Goshen, Egypt (Genesis 15:13; Section 40).

Time, Times, and Half a Time (scatter power of the holy people)—The three and a half thousand years between the time of the first writing of the Bible in 1462 BC, and the Second Coming of Christ in AD 2039. The 'power of the holy people' is the Word of God (Isaiah 55:11; Hebrews 4:12). The powerful good news about God's love was scattered throughout the world during this "time, times, and half a time" or three and a half times of Daniel 12:7. The word 'time' here is a reflection of the Millennium, or thousand year reign of Christ and the saints (Revelation 20:3–4; Section 45).

Toledo (Council of)—An Iberian local council of orthodox Christian bishops in Toledo, Spain in AD 589. It was commissioned by the Visigoth King, Reccared, who was converted from Arianism to Trinitarianism by Bishop Leander of Seville. One of the canons of the council added the Filioque to the Nicene Creed, and required it to be recited at Holy Communion (Section 69).

Tome of Leo—A brilliant encyclical written by Pope Leo the Great in AD 449 against the emerging Monophysite heresy. It was accepted by the fourth ecumenical council in AD 451, but condemned by the Armenians and Syriacs at their heretical Synod of Manzikert in AD 728 (Section 67).

Tours (Battle of)—Where Charles "The Hammer" Martel's French peasant infantry defeated an armored Muslim cavalry in AD 732. Perhaps the single most important battle in history. It stopped the Muslim incursion into Western Europe and began the process of expelling them from the Iberian peninsula (Matthew 16:18; Section 69).

Trent (Council of)—The Roman Catholic answer to the Protestant Reformation—also known as the 'Counter-Reformation,' held from AD 1545 to AD 1563. Interrupted several times by outbreaks of the plague and war. Its legacy was to leave the Catholics entrenched in several doctrinal errors, and to add the deuterocanonical books to their Old Testament (Section 81).

Tribulation—An intense period of natural disasters, chaos, and war, ten to twenty years before the Second Coming of Christ and the end of the world (Revelation 7:14). Perhaps punctuated by a meteoric impact (Matthew 24:29–30) and resulting firestorm (2 Peter 3:7–12). The havoc will be brought about by the brief release of the devil at the close of the sixth millennium (Revelation 20:7; Sections 52, 72).

Trinitarianism—Synonymous with Christianity. The belief that the One and Only God exists in three Persons: Father, Son, and Holy Spirit (Ephesians 1:3,17; Section 18). Taught throughout the Bible, affirmed by the First Council of Nicaea in AD 325, and reaffirmed by the First Council of Constantinople in AD 381 (Section 61). See Nicene Formulation.

Triumph of Orthodoxy—An annual Eastern Orthodox celebration of the seventh (and last) ecumenical council in AD 787. The council condemned Iconoclasm, a christological heresy which held that images of the Savior were idolatrous and Anti-Chalcedonian. The council found that adoring (but not worshiping) paintings, tapestries, and statues of Jesus Christ was to be encouraged because it was a reminder that God had become human flesh. The council marked the successful end of hundreds of years of christological debate. This triumph of the Christian religion occurred *exactly* six hundred and sixty-six years before the fall of Constantinople to the Antichrist Beast of Islam (Section 83).

Two Witnesses—Faithful Roman Catholic and Confessional Protestant believers that walked in the power of the Holy Spirit during the 1,260 year reign of the post–Ali Caliphate (Revelation 11:3–6). They spoke the truth about God becoming a man as they recited the three Ecumenical Creeds. See Chosen People, Christian, Christian Church, Israel (of God), Protestant (Confessional), Roman Catholic, Temple (true third), Woman (clothed with the sun), and Yahwism. Near the time when the Gospel is preached to all nations a group of these Creedal Christians will spread the Gospel in Jerusalem (or possibly Rome or Istanbul), and will be massacred. Then, immediately before the

Second Coming of Christ, they will be resurrected from the dead before video cameras (Revelation 11:7–12; Section 33).

Über-Baptist—An epithet that I have coined for Anabaptists that have confused Dispensational Premillennialism for the Gospel of Jesus. Some of them have even given up Christianity for the antichrist cult of 'Christian' Zionism (Sections 27, 53).

Unholy Alliance—The commonality-of-purpose (i.e., to damn human souls) between the Antichrist Beast and the False Prophet. The Beast represents *religious* Anti-Christian forces, or Islamism, or the Cult of Muhammad. The False Prophet represents *secular* Anti-Christian forces, or Rationalism, or the Cult of Science (Mark 13:22; Revelation 16:13; 17:13; Sections 34, 86).

Unholy Trinity—The devil (i.e., Allah), the Beast (i.e., Islam), and the False Prophet (i.e., Rationalism). Their fate is eternal Hell (Revelation 20:10; Section 87).

Wilderness (negative meaning)—The place of the Great Harlot and Babylon the Great that pollutes the world's cultures. The western world, but especially the United States and New York City (Revelation 17:3; Zechariah 5:5–11; Sections 34–35).

Wilderness (positive meaning)—The place where the Church was taken for protection and nourishment. Generally speaking, Central and Western Europe, North and South America, Australia, and New Zealand—but especially the United States of America where there is a constitutional guarantee of freedom of religion (Revelation 12:6,14; Sections 28, 31). See Great Eagle.

Woman (clothed with the sun)—The People of God both before and after the time of Christ (i.e., the Israel of God or the Christian Church). All humans that have lived and died trusting that God loves us enough to become a man and rescue us (Revelation 12:1–2; Section 28). See Chosen People, Christian, Christian Church, Israel (of God), Protestant (Confessional), Roman Catholic, Temple (true third), Two Witnesses, and Yahwism.

> **Earth (that helped the woman)**—The firm ground of solid facts that reinforces Biblical truth and the Gospel message (Revelation 12:16; Section 32).

Labor and Pain—The long wait of the People of God for their Savior, Jesus (Revelation 12:2).

Yahwism—The godly pre–Christ religion of the Old Testament period that professed that God would become a man according to Jewish prophecy (Zechariah 8:23). It is not to be confused with those religious Jews that rejected Jesus Christ after His anointing in AD 26, nor those that developed Rabbinic Judaism after the destruction of the Second Temple in AD 70 (Section 54). See Chosen People, Christian, Christian Church, Israel (of God), Protestant (Confessional), Roman Catholic, Temple (true third), Two Witnesses, and Woman (clothed with the sun); also see Jew (as Old Testament religious title).

Yarmuk (Battle of)—A pivotal battle in AD 636 where the incipient Arab Empire (i.e., the Sea Beast) soundly defeated a larger force from the Eastern Roman Empire due to defections by Arab Monophysite soldiers. The destruction of Emperor Heraclius' army resulted in the surrender of Jerusalem the next year, and the permanent loss of Christian sovereignty over the Levant; this catastrophe was the spiritual consequence of Heraclius' Monothelite initiative (Revelation 11:2; Section 65).

Appendix III. List of Eschatological Timelines

Name	Period	Description
Sabbath	six days in 3976 BC, or AD 28, or AD 30, or any given week	An algebraic foreshadowing (~ 1:365,000 ratio) of the six thousand and ten year period between the beginning of man's toil on earth in 3975 BC to the promised rest in Heaven in AD 2036 (Hebrews 4:9–10). Evident in the Six Day Creation (Genesis 2:2–3; Exodus 31:17), Transfiguration Week (Matthew 17:1–2), Holy Week (Mark 16:1–6), and any given work-week/sunrise-Sabbath-worship (Matthew 12:8; Acts 13:27; 1 Corinthians 11:26). See Section 48.
Noahic	2919 BC to 2318 BC	The six hundred and one year period from the birth of Noah in 2919 BC to the time when Noah worshipped God after leaving the ark in 2318 BC (Genesis 8:20). An algebraic foreshadowing (1:10 ratio) of the 6,010 year period between the Creation of Adam in 3976 BC and the Church's worship of Christ upon entering the new Heaven and Earth in AD 2035 (Revelation 7:9–10; Luke 17:26–27). See Section 47.
Purim	1908 BC to 473 BC	The 1,435 year period between God's promise that the Christ would be born through Abraham in 1908 BC to the exaltation of Mordecai after Purim in 473 BC (Esther 10:3). An exact parallel to the period between the birth of the Son of Perdition, Ali, in AD 599 and the deliverance and exaltation of God's People at the Second Coming in AD 2034. See Section 44.
Mosaic	1543 BC to 1422 BC	The one hundred and twenty year period from the birth of Moses in 1543 BC to the entrance of the children of Israel into the Promised Land under Joshua in 1422.9 BC. An algebraic foreshadowing (1:50 ratio) of the time between the Creation of Adam in 3976 BC and the Christians' entry into the Promised Land of Heaven under Jesus in AD 2036 (Joshua 3:5–17; Mark 12:26–27). See Section 43.
Divine Idiom	1462 BC to AD 1451	The two 1,456 year periods bracketing the Incarnation of the Word of God in 6 BC. The periods begin with Moses' recording of the Word of God in 1462 BC, and end with Gutenberg's printing of the Word of God in AD 1451. See Section 70.
Scatter	1462 BC to AD 2039	The three and a half thousand year period between the first recording of a piece of scripture by Moses in 1462 BC and the complete dissemination of the Word of God to the nations in AD 2039 (Daniel 12:7). See Section 45.

Appendix III. List of Eschatological Timelines *(cont.)*

Name	Period	Description
Jonahic	1076 BC to 612 BC	The 464 year period between the founding of the Assyrian Empire by King Tiglath-Pileser in 1076 BC and the destruction of their capital, Nineveh, by the Babylonians in 612 BC. An algebraic foreshadowing (1:13 ratio) of the period between the fall of man in 3975 BC and the Judgment Day in AD 2035; the 464 year period is punctuated by the prophethood of Jonah in 767 BC—a type for Christ in AD 28 (Matthew 12:39–41). See Section 42.
Abomination	592 BC to AD 2034	The 2,625 year period between the departing of the presence of the Lord from Solomon's Temple (and the taking away of the sacrifice) in 592 BC and the blessed return of Christ in AD 2034 (Daniel 12:11–12). Twelve hundred and ninety years into this period the 'Abomination that Causes Desolation' was set up in the form of the gold-gilded Dome of the Rock (exactly as predicted in Daniel 12:11). See Section 46.
Conquest	586 BC to AD 1453	The 2,038 year period between the conquest of Jerusalem by the Babylonians (the first beast—Daniel 7:4) in 586 BC and the conquest of Constantinople by the Caliphate (the 'fifth beast' or little horn—Daniel 7:8) in AD 1453. Both cities were centers for people that believed in the promise that God would become a man. An exact parallel for the period between Jesus' joyous incarnation in 6 BC and Jesus' glorious return to dispatch evil and rescue His people at the Second Coming in AD 2033 (Ezekiel 35:10–13; Obadiah 18; Isaiah 34:8; Revelation 6:2). See Section 41.
First Coming of Christ	458 BC to AD 33	The 490 year period described by the Angel Gabriel to the Prophet Daniel in 539 BC (Daniel 9:24–27). It is divided into four sub-periods beginning in 458 BC: 49 years until the Jews would finish rebuilding the walls, fortifications, and streets of Jerusalem; 434 more years until the Messiah would be anointed and revealed (when Christ was baptized in AD 26; Matthew 3:16–17), and rejected by his people in Nazareth (Luke 4:28–29); three and a half more years until the Messiah would be made desolate and would put an end to Jewish temple sacrifice (when Christ was crucified in AD 30; Matthew 27:50–51); and a final three and a half years during which the ascended Messiah would confirm His New Covenant with the Church of Pentecost in Jerusalem (Acts 6:7; 8:1,4). The last seven years of this prophecy are misinterpreted by Dispensationalists to be the timeline of the Antichrist's unveiling. See Sections 26–27.

Appendix III. List of Eschatological Timelines *(cont.)*

Name	Period	Description
Number of the Beast	6 BC to AD 661	The six hundred and sixty-six year period from the Incarnation of the Son of God in 6 BC to the formulation of the two branches of Islam with the assassination of the Son of Perdition, Ali, in AD 661. It was the devil's answer to God's salvation plan, and a reflection of the fact that Christ's anointing occurred exactly 66.6% of the way through man's toil on earth. The Number of the Beast occurs numerous other times throughout history (Revelation 13:18). See Sections 23, 83.
Handover	AD 636 to AD 2036	The fourteen hundred year period between the beginning of the handover of eastern Christians to the Beast of Islam (at the Battle of Yarmuk in AD 636) and their rescue at the Second Coming in AD 2036 (Daniel 7:23–25). The "time and times and half a time" refers to a 3.5 multiple of the 400 years that the Children of Promise were oppressed as strangers in Canaan and slaves in Goshen, Egypt (1862 BC to 1462 BC; Genesis 15:13). See Section 40.
Nourishment of the Woman	AD 661 to AD 1921	The 1,260 year retreat of the people of God from the eastern Christian lands into the wilderness of the west. It began with Ali's assassination (and the inception of the Shi'a and Sunni branches of Islam in AD 661), and ended with Ataturk's rise to power (and the permanent loss of the Caliph's power with the Turkish Constitution of AD 1921). Soon after, the Sultan was deposed and the Caliphate was abolished (Revelation 11:2–3, 12:6, 13:5). See Sections 30, 33.
Millennial	AD 1014 to AD 2014	The thousand year reign of the saints with Christ. It began in AD 1014 when the western Church formally adopted the Filioque clause into the Nicene Creed, thus equipping itself with the true message of Christian faith that God desired to be disseminated throughout the world. The initiation of the Millennium was punctuated by an earthquake in Jerusalem in AD 1016 in which the Dome of the Rock (whose gilding and inscriptions symbolize the 'Abomination that Causes Desolation' of Daniel 12:11) was partially destroyed. The earthquake came seven years after the destruction of the Church of the Holy Sepulchre and the desecration of the Lord's empty tomb in AD 1009. That act of vandalism was the high-water mark of the Antichrist Beast of Arab Islam; afterward its influence began to decline with the Crusades and the arrival of the Oghuz Turks. The Millennium will end in AD 2014, with the release of the devil and the commencement of the Tribulation (Revelation 20:1–5). See Section 71.

Appendix III. List of Eschatological Timelines *(cont.)*

Name	Period	Description
Thousand Year Warning	AD 1016 to AD 2016	The thousand year period between the AD 1016 Jerusalem earthquake which partially destroyed the Dome of the Rock and the beginning of the Tribulation in AD 2016 (Luke 21:11). See Section 71.
Locust	AD 1886 to AD 2036	The one hundred and fifty year period between the patenting of the first gasoline-powered motorcar in AD 1886 and the end of the power of automobiles over people's lives (through the Second Coming) in AD 2036 (Revelation 9:5,10). See Section 49.
Great Eagle	AD 1922 to AD 1992	The seventy year period during which the Church was nourished by the Great Eagle of the United States and protected from Soviet tyranny. Preceded by the immigration wave of Christian peoples in the early twentieth century. Begun with the formal establishment of the USSR in AD 1922; ended with the dissolution of the Red Army in AD 1992 (Revelation 12:13–14). A reflection of the time from the destruction of the First Temple to the dedication of the Second Temple (from 586 BC to 516 BC; Daniel 9:2). The "time and times and half a time" refers to a 3.5 multiple of the period when Jacob was protected from Esau by his Uncle Laban (from 1736 BC to 1716 BC; Genesis 31:38). See Section 31.
Seventy Year Warning	AD 1964 to AD 2034	The seventy year period between the Good Friday Alaskan earthquake of AD 1964 and the Second Coming of Christ in AD 2034 (Luke 21:11). See Section 100.
Forty Year Warning	AD 1994 to AD 2034	The forty year period between the Shoemaker-Levy Comet impact on Jupiter in AD 1994 and the Second Coming of Christ in AD 2034 (Luke 21:11). See Section 52.
Thirty Year Warning	AD 2005 to AD 2035	The thirty year period between the two enormous Indian Ocean earthquakes in AD 2004 – AD 2005 and the Second Coming of Christ in AD 2034 – AD 2035 (Luke 21:11). The first earthquake occurred on the day after Christmas; the second earthquake occurred on the day after Easter. See Section 100.
Fall of Babylon the Great	Sept. 11, AD 2001	The 'one hour' that it took for the Twin Towers of the World Trade Center to collapse in New York City. The exact time was one hundred and two minutes for the North Tower, and the fifty-six minutes for the South Tower (Revelation 17:12; 18:10,17). See Section 35.

Appendix IV. Notable Years in God's Dealings with Mankind

3976 BC	Creation of the Universe (Genesis 2:1–2; Section 91).
3975 BC	Fall of Man through Eve and Adam's sin (Genesis 3:6). Promise of Christ's reign through Eve (Genesis 3:15; Section 83).
3740 BC	Purification of the pre–Christian Church through calling upon the name of the Lord (Genesis 4:26; Section 70).
2988 BC	Promise of Christ's reign through Enoch being taken to Heaven without dying (Genesis 5:24; Hebrews 11:5; Sections 67, 70).
2919 BC	Noah is born (Genesis 5:28–29; Section 47).
2419 BC	Purification of the pre–Christian Church though Noah's ark project (Genesis 6:13–14; Section 70).
2319 BC	Floodwaters unleashed (Genesis 7:11; Section 47).
2318 BC	Noah leaves ark and worships God in the post-flood world (Genesis 8:20; Section 47).
2250 BC	The earliest known library established in Ebla, Syria (Section 101).
2144 BC	Languages are confused at the Tower of Babel (Genesis 11:7–9; Section 102).
1908 BC	Abraham leaves his home in Ur of Chaldea and begins his journey to Canaan (Genesis 12:1; Section 43). Christ's reign is promised by God through Abrahamic Covenant (Genesis 12:3; Section 70).
1892 BC	Abraham buries his father in Haran (Genesis 11:32) and arrives in Canaan (Genesis 12:4–5). Marks the beginning of the 430 years of the Children of Promise in Egypt and Canaan (Exodus 12:40–41; Section 40).
1883 BC	God makes a covenant with Abraham (Genesis 15:18; Section 44).
1862 BC	Persecution of Isaac by Ishmael (Genesis 21:9). Marks the beginning of the four hundred years of oppression in Egypt and Canaan (Genesis 15:13; Section 40).
1846 BC	Abraham offers Isaac on the Temple Mount of the future Jerusalem (Genesis 22:10; Section 44).
1808 BC	Jacob (the future Israel) is born to Isaac and Rebekah (Genesis 25:26; Section 44).
1736 BC	Jacob flees Esau's wrath. Lives with his Uncle Laban (Genesis 29:13–14; Section 31).
1716 BC	Jacob returns to Canaan (Genesis 31:17–18). God renames him Israel because he does not ignore God, but contends with Him (Genesis 32:28; Section 31).
1715 BC	Judah marries a Canaanite woman (Genesis 38:2; Section 53).
1543 BC	Moses is born (Exodus 2:2; Section 43).
1541 BC	Moses is weaned and given to Pharaoh's daughter (Exodus 2:10; Section 43).
1501 BC	Moses kills an Egyptian slave master, and flees to Midian (Exodus 2:12–15; Section 43).
1463 BC	Moses called by God at the Burning Bush (Genesis 3:2–6) and returns to Egypt (Exodus 7:6–7; Section 43).

Appendix IV. Notable Years in God's Dealings with Mankind *(cont.)*

1462 BC	Pharaoh tries to destroy Moses and his flock of Israel's children (Exodus 14:9). Purification of the pre–Christian Church through Exodus from Egypt via the Red Sea (Exodus 14:21–22; Section 70). Ten Commandments given by God and recorded on parchment by Moses (Exodus 20:1–17; Section 45).
1423 BC	Moses looks upon the Promised Land of Canaan (Deuteronomy 34:4) and then dies (Deuteronomy 34:5; Section 43).
1422 BC	Joshua leads the children of Israel into the Promised Land (Joshua 3:17; Section 43).
1076 BC	King Tiglath-Pileser, founder of the Assyrian Empire, reaches the zenith of his power and then dies (Section 42).
1014 BC	Promise of Christ's reign through line of David (2 Samuel 7:11–16; Section 70).
868 BC	Elijah taken to heaven without dying (2 Kings 2:11; Section 67).
767 BC	Jonah warns the Ninevites of impending judgment (Jonah 3:4). They repent and are saved (Jonah 3:5; Luke 11:32; Section 42).
721 BC	Kingdom of Israel conquered by Assyrians. Ten tribes carried into oblivion (2 Kings 17:6; Section 42).
712 BC	Isaiah prophesies that the True Israel will be called by a new name (i.e., 'Christian'; Isaiah 56:5; Isaiah 62:2; Isaiah 65:15; fulfilled in Acts 11:26; Section 56).
704 BC	Assyrian king taunts God and King Hezekiah of Judah (Isaiah 37:10–11; Section 63).
701 BC	King of Assyria tries to destroy Judah, but God smites his army (2 Kings 19:35; Section 63).
612 BC	Nineveh falls to the Babylonians and is destroyed (Isaiah 10:12; Section 42).
605 BC	Prophet Daniel deported to Babylon (Daniel 1:3,6; Section 46).
597 BC	Jerusalem conquered by the army of King Nebuchadnezzar. Treasures of the First Temple plundered. Judah forced to pay tribute to Babylon (2 Chronicles 36:10; 2 Kings 24:13; Section 83).
592 BC	The presence of the Lord departs from the First Temple (Ezekiel 10:4,18), and daily sacrifices stop (referred to in Daniel 12:11; Section 46).
588 BC	Jews revolt against Babylonian domination.
586 BC	Jerusalem is re-conquered by the army of Babylonian King Nebuchadnezzar, and the First Temple is destroyed (2 Kings 25:8–10). King of Judah blinded and his heirs killed (2 Kings 25:7). High Priest is killed and the Jews are exiled (Jeremiah 52:24–27; Section 41).
539 BC	Babylonians defeated by Medo–Persians (Daniel 5:30–31; Section 19). Jews are allowed to return to Jerusalem and begin rebuilding their temple (Ezra 5:13). Timeline for First Coming of the Messiah given to the Prophet Daniel by the Angel Gabriel (Daniel 9:20–27; Section 26–27).
521 BC	The Jews' enemies around Jerusalem become alarmed by their determination to return and reestablish the city (Ezra 4:1–5; 5:3–4; Section 44).
516 BC	The Jews dedicate the Second Temple in Jerusalem (Ezra 6:16; foretold in Jeremiah 25:11–12; Section 44). Purification of pre–Christian Church through exilic restoration (Ezra 6:20–21; Section 70).

Appendix IV. Notable Years in God's Dealings with Mankind *(cont.)*

485 BC	Xerxes becomes king of Medo–Persian Empire (Esther 1:1–2; Section 44).
479 BC	Esther becomes Xerxes' queen (Esther 2:17; Section 44).
474 BC	King Xerxes gives order to extirpate all the Jewish believers throughout his empire (Esther 3:11). He later reverses the order at the request of Queen Esther, and the Jews triumph over their enemies at Purim (Esther 9:1–2; Section 44).
473 BC	Mordecai is exalted to Prime Minister of the Medo–Persian Empire by the order of King Xerxes (Esther 10:3; Section 44).
458 BC	Call put forth from Medo–Persian King Artaxerxes for the walls, fortifications, and streets of Jerusalem to be rebuilt (Ezra 8:36; Section 26).
445 BC	Enemies of the Jews tear down their recent work on the walls of Jerusalem (Nehemiah 1:3; Ezra 4:7–23; Section 26).
432 BC	Nehemiah decries the Jews' intermarriage with enemies of Israel (Nehemiah 13:23–25; Section 53).
409 BC	Rebuilding of Jerusalem is completed despite opposition (foretold in Daniel 9:25). Enemies of Jews are vexed (Nehemiah 6:15–16; Sections 26–27).
334 BC	Greeks defeat Medo–Persians (foretold in Daniel 7:6; Section 19).
168 BC	Seleucid ruler desecrates the Second Temple by sacrificing a pig to Zeus upon the altar (foretold in Daniel 11:31). He massacres many Jews in Jerusalem (foretold in Daniel 11:33; Section 34).
63 BC	Roman Republic annexes Judea.
27 BC	Roman Empire founded (foretold in Daniel 7:7; Section 19).
6 BC	God becomes incarnate in the womb of the blessed virgin Mary by the overshadowing of the Holy Spirit (Luke 1:35; Sections 23, 39).
AD 26	Jesus Christ is baptized in the River Jordan; the Father, the Holy Spirit, and John the Baptist testify of His Lordship (Matthew 3:13–17). Christ's ministry begins, and He is rejected in Nazareth (Luke 4:29; Sections 23). He begins to "confirm a covenant with many" for seven years (Daniel 9:27; Sections 26–27).
AD 28	Jesus teaches that Jonah's time inside the fish would be analogous to His own time inside the tomb (Luke 11:29–30; Section 42).
AD 30	Jesus Christ is crucified, buried, and resurrected (Section 83). With this he puts an end to Jewish temple sacrifices and offerings (Daniel 9:27; Sections 26–27), and conquers sin, death, and every power of the devil. Proof of His New Body is shown for forty days. Beginning of the 'End Times' — which lasts until the Second Coming. Promise of Christ's reign through the Ascension (Acts 1:11; Section 70).
AD 33	The Deacon Stephen becomes first Christian martyr (Acts 7:54–60). This ends the seven years during which the Messiah was to "confirm a covenant with many" (Daniel 9:27; Sections 26–27). Christ's early Church is dispersed from Jerusalem and begins to spread the Gospel (Acts 8:1,4).
AD 43	The term 'Christian' is first used to describe believers in Antioch (Acts 11:26; Section 56). This is the new name of the True Israel, and it replaces the old name of 'Jew' (foretold in Isaiah 56:5; Isaiah 62:2; Isaiah 65:15).
AD 51	The Apostle Paul debates Epicurean and Stoic philosophers in Athens, Greece (Section 104).

Appendix IV. Notable Years in God's Dealings with Mankind *(cont.)*

AD 53	The Apostle Paul writes that before the Second Coming of Christ, a 'falling away' from the faith (i.e., Anti-Chalcedonianism and Anti-Filioqueanism) must occur, and the 'Son of Perdition' (i.e., Ali) must first be revealed (2 Thessalonians 2:1–4; Section 15).
AD 70	Because of the Jews' rejection of the Messiah, Jerusalem is conquered and the Second Temple is destroyed by the Legions of Roman General Titus (foretold in Daniel 9:26). The Jews within Jerusalem are slaughtered, but the Judean Christians heeded prophecy and previously fled to the Transjordanian mountains (Daniel 11:41; Luke 21:20–22; Section 26).
AD 96	The Apostle John completes the writing of the Bible with the Book of Revelation (Section 45).
AD 286	Emperor Diocletian splits the Roman Empire into eastern and western halves to make it more manageable (Section 19).
AD 300	Final and most severe Roman persecution of the Church initiated by Emperor Diocletian (Section 71).
AD 301	Countries of Armenia and San Marino are Christianized (Section 71).
AD 313	Edict of Milan issued by Emperor Constantine, removing penalties for professing Christians (Section 61).
AD 325	First ecumenical council held in Nicaea. Arianism is overwhelmingly rejected by the Christian Church. Nicene Creed drafted (Section 61).
AD 336	Construction begun on the Church of the Holy Sepulchre (Section 71). The heretic Arius dies on a public toilet in Constantinople the day before he is to be served communion (Section 61).
AD 337	Emperor Constantine dies (Section 61).
AD 381	Second ecumenical council held in Constantinople; Nicene Creed finalized with addition of the Holy Spirit clause (Section 61).
AD 405	Mesrop Mashdots invents the Armenian alphabet for the purpose of spreading Christianity. The Bible is soon translated into the new Armenian script (Section 67).
AD 428	Heresy of Nestorianism emerges (Section 62).
AD 431	Third ecumenical council held in Ephesus denounces Nestorianism. Assyrian Church of the East splits from the rest of Christianity (Section 62).
AD 449	Pope Leo the Great writes the Tome of Leo which correctly argues that Jesus Christ was one undivided Person with two separate natures. Foundational document of Chalcedonianism (Section 67).
AD 451	Christian Armenians fail to receive military assistance from the Eastern Roman Empire and lose the Battle of Avarayr to Zoroastrian Persians (Section 62). Fourth ecumenical council held in Chalcedon. Monophysitism repudiated by the Christian Church (Section 62). Armenians Apostolics, Egyptian Copts, and Syriac Orthodox do not accept the findings of the council and eventually unite with each other under the heretical Oriental Orthodox Communion (Section 67).
AD 476	Western Roman Empire ends with the deposition of Romulus Augustus. From this time until AD 1453, the Eastern Roman Empire represents the extant part of the Roman Empire (Daniel 7:7; Section 19).
AD 553	Fifth ecumenical council held in Constantinople denounces Monophysitism a second time (Section 63).

Appendix IV. Notable Years in God's Dealings with Mankind *(cont.)*

AD 570	Muhammad is born (Sections 18, 22).
AD 589	Goths of Spain converted from Arianism to Christianity. Council of Toledo is held in which the Nicene Creed is unofficially amended to include the Filioque. Marks the completion of the writing of the three Ecumenical Creeds (with the Filioque). Over half the Christian Church rejects the orthodox faith of the three Ecumenical Creeds (with Filioque) and 'fall away' (foretold in 2 Thessalonians 2:3; Section 69).
AD 599	Son of Perdition, Ali, is born (2 Thessalonians 2:3–4); six years later he is brought into Muhammad's home (Sections 18, 22).
AD 602	Emperor Maurice and his heirs are killed by mutinous troops. Phocas proclaims himself Eastern Roman emperor (Section 63).
AD 610	Heraclius enters Constantinople without resistance, kills Phocas, and becomes Eastern Roman emperor by acclamation (Section 63).
AD 614	Sassanid Persians conquer Jerusalem after stiff resistance. Slaughter of Christians in the city. Persians desecrate Church of the Holy Sepulchre, and steal the relic of the True Cross (Section 63).
AD 620	Maximus the Confessor flees to Carthage because of the Sassanid Persian encroachment into Asia Minor. There he meets the Eastern Roman general, Peter of Numidia, and gains his trust (Section 64).
AD 621	Heraclius invades behind Persian lines and begins re-conquest of Eastern Roman Empire territory (Section 63).
AD 622	Hijra or flight of Muhammad from Mecca to Medina. First year of the Muslim calendar (Section 29).
AD 624	Muhammad wins the Battle of Badr—the turning point for his eventual conquest of Mecca. Ali is commended for bravery and granted Muhammad's daughter's hand in marriage (Section 22).
AD 628	Heraclius completes re-conquest of Eastern Roman Empire territory from Sassanid Persians. Sassanid Emperor killed by his son, and the Persian Empire falls into chaos (Section 63).
AD 629	Emperor Heraclius carries the relic of the True Cross into Jerusalem on his back. It is the second and last time a reigning Roman Emperor visits Jerusalem (Section 64).
AD 630	Heraclius forces the Monothelite heresy upon the Eastern Roman Empire. Muhammad captures Mecca. Muawiyah accepts Muhammad's religious views in order to save his life, and quickly advances in position (Section 22).
AD 632	Heraclius orders Jews of Eastern Roman Empire to be forcibly baptized. Earthquake in Palestine. Sword-shaped comet travels south to north over Levant. Muhammad dies; Abu Bakr becomes first Caliph of the Arab Empire. Maximus the Confessor writes of desert barbarians (i.e., Arab Bedouins) laying waste to parts of the southern Levant (Section 64).
AD 634	Maximus the Confessor raises alarms about Heraclius' Monothelite heresy. A synod is convoked in Cyprus to debate the emperor's christological formulation (Section 64). Abu Bakr dies and Umar becomes second Caliph of the Arab Empire.
AD 635	Nestorians reach China with their heretical Christology on the eve of the Arab conquest of their homeland in Babylon and Persia (Section 62).

Appendix IV. Notable Years in God's Dealings with Mankind (*cont.*)

AD 636	Battle of Yarmuk in which the army of the Eastern Roman Empire is crushed by the emergent Arab Empire (Section 65).
AD 637	Jerusalem surrendered to the Arabs. Caliph Umar and future-Caliph Ali are present for the handover. Patriarch Sophronius correctly identifies the new masters of the holy city, saying, "The abomination of desolation is in the holy place" (a quote from Daniel 12:11; Section 22).
AD 638	Arabs conquer Palestine. Introduction of the Hijra lunar calendar which starts with the flight of Muhammad from Mecca to Medina in AD 622 (Daniel 7:25; Section 29).
AD 641	Emperor Heraclius dies. Monophysite Copts of Egypt celebrate (Section 65).
AD 644	Umar dies, and Uthman becomes third Caliph of the Arab Empire.
AD 649	Lateran council in Rome denounces Monothelitism (Section 65).
AD 653	Pope Martin kidnapped from Rome and brought to Constantinople for trial (Section 65).
AD 654	A Jewish admirer of Ali begins to preach that Ali was the only legitimate successor of Muhammad. He travels west from Iraq spreading his message (Section 22).
AD 655	Pope Martin tortured, exiled, and killed for opposing Monothelitism (Section 65).
AD 656	Uthman pressured to resign as Caliph. He refuses and is killed by a mob. Ali becomes fourth caliph of the Arab Empire, and allows Uthman's assassins to evade justice (Section 22).
AD 657	Muawiyah suspects Ali in the death of his uncle, Uthman. He seizes control of Egypt. Ali is challenged during the first Islamic civil war at the Battle of Siffin (Section 22).
AD 661	Formulation of separate Arab religion inside the head of Caliph Ali (2 Thessalonians 2:3). He cries out, "By the Lord of the Kaaba, I have succeeded!" as he is struck by a poison-tipped spear. Ali's rival, Muawiyah, becomes fifth caliph of the Arab Empire. He is hostile to Ali's dream of a new world religion, and ambivalent toward Muhammad's legacy. The Shi'a and Sunni branches of Islam are born—six hundred and sixty-six years after Christ's Incarnation (Revelation 13:18; Section 22).
AD 662	Maximus the Confessor brought to trial, mutilated, exiled, and killed for opposing Monothelitism (Section 65).
AD 670	Ali's first son, Hasan, (who had renounced any claim to the Caliphate and retired to Medina) is poisoned by one of his wives at the instigation of Caliph Muawiyah (Section 22).
AD 680	Sixth ecumenical council held in Constantinople denounces Monothelitism and affirms Chalcedonianism for a third time (Section 65). Muawiyah dies and his son Yazid becomes the sixth caliph of the Arab Empire. Ali's second son, Husayn, tries to take over the Arab Empire with seventy-one followers. They are massacred at the Battle of Karbala (Section 22).
AD 683	Caliph Yazid dies unexpectedly, creating a struggle for control of the Arab Empire (Section 20).

Appendix IV. Notable Years in God's Dealings with Mankind *(cont.)*

AD 685	After a year and a half power struggle, Abd al-Malik becomes seventh major caliph of the seventh century. These represent the seven heads of the Antichrist Beast (Revelation 13:1). Abd al-Malik spends the next seven years consolidating power within the Arab Empire (Section 22). Heraclius' great-great grandson, Justinian II, becomes Eastern Roman Emperor (Section 65).
AD 692	Caliph al-Malik secures full control of the Arab Empire by putting down rebellions in Iraq and Mecca, and by defeating the Eastern Roman Empire at the Battle of Sebastopolis. He introduces the first Islamic monetary system, begins construction on the Dome of the Rock, and dictates its Antichrist inscriptions. The Christians of Jerusalem revolt, are crushed, and part of the city is destroyed (Section 22). Caliph al-Malik resurrects Ali's dream of a new world religion by deleting the cross from coinage, and imprinting "Muhammad is the Messenger of God." Beginning of the Cult of Muhammad—six hundred and sixty-six years after Christ's baptism (Revelation 13:18; Section 23).
AD 695	Justinian II is deposed as Emperor and his nose is cut off. Beginning of ten year period of political instability in Eastern Roman Empire (Section 65).
AD 696	Mid–point of Dome of the Rock construction. Gold coin issued that denies the Trinity, the Incarnation, and that calls for the new Anti-Trinitarian religion to prevail over all other religions. Marks the institutionalization of the Antichrist Islamic religion—six hundred and sixty-six years after Christ's resurrection from the dead (Revelation 13:18; Section 23).
AD 699	Likely year that the Dome of the Rock is completed and gilded—seven years after the beginning of construction. Islamic monetary system is finalized. Marks the setting up of the 'abomination that causes desolation' (Daniel 12:11), and the sending forth of Islamic orthodoxy from Jerusalem—six hundred and sixty-six years after the Christian Church went forth from Jerusalem (Revelation 13:18; Section 23).
AD 705	Justinian II regains the throne of the Eastern Roman Empire and institutes purges (Section 65). Seventh major caliph, al-Malik, dies.
AD 711	Heraclian Dynasty in Eastern Roman Empire ends when Justinian II and his heir are killed (Section 65).
AD 728	Synod of Manzikert [incorrectly] denounces the Tome of Leo, and entrenches the Armenian Apostolic Church and the Syriac Orthodox Church in the Monophysite heresy. This permanently unites them with the Egyptian Copts, but divides them from the Greeks and Romans, as well as the Georgian Orthodox Church, which rejects Monophysitism and becomes Chalcedonian at this time (Section 67).
AD 732	Charles 'The Hammer' Martel decisively defeats a superior number of Muslims at the Battle of Tours, and halts the Muslim incursion into Western Europe through Iberia—sparing Rome from the Antichrist Beast of Islam (Revelation 12:6; foretold in Matthew 16:18; Section 69).
~ AD 760	Qur'an is finalized—nearly every early draft is destroyed to cover-up the fact that it is an edited work (Section 82).

Appendix IV. Notable Years in God's Dealings with Mankind *(cont.)*

AD 787	Seventh ecumenical council condemns the christological heresy of Iconoclasm. The council affirms that the adoration of images of Jesus are edifying in that they remind Christian worshipers of His dual nature in the miraculous Incarnation. Celebrated as the 'Triumph of Orthodoxy' by the Eastern Orthodox Church (Section 83).
AD 800	Charlemagne re-establishes a semblance of the Western Roman Empire by founding the Holy Roman Empire (Section 69).
AD 868	Twelfth Imam, Muhammad al-Mahdi, is born. Believed by the Shi'a to be the promised redeemer of their faith (Section 73).
AD 873	Muhammad al-Mahdi is said by the Shi'a to have gone into occultation until the end of the world (Section 73).
AD 966	Church of the Holy Sepulchre is partially burned by a Muslim mob (Section 71).
AD 995	Emperor Basil II re-conquers most of Syria from the Arabs (Section 65). The Eastern Roman Empire holds the territory until the Seljuk invasion.
AD 1009	Caliph al-Hakim completely destroys the Church of the Holy Sepulchre, and desecrates the tomb of Christ. The high-water mark for Islam (Section 71).
AD 1014	The Filioque is recited for the first time in Rome at the coronation of the Holy Roman Emperor Henry II (Section 69). The western Church confesses the orthodox Christian faith, and the Millennium begins. Devil is bound for one thousand years (Revelation 20:2), and the saints in Heaven reign with Christ. The Antichrist Beast of Arab Islam begins to decline (Section 71). Promise of Christ's reign in three proper Ecumenical Creeds (Revelation 20:4; Section 70).
AD 1016	Earthquake in Jerusalem partially destroys the Dome of the Rock. Providence's thousand year warning of the coming Tribulation (Revelation 20:7; Section 71).
AD 1048	The Caliph allows a chapel to be built over the Holy Sepulchre, but pilgrimage is restricted (Section 71).
AD 1054	The 'Great Schism' in which the Eastern Orthodox broke off from the orthodox Christian faith—largely over the inclusion of the Filioque in the Nicene Creed (Section 69).
AD 1055	The Oghuz Turks conquer Baghdad and the Seljuk Empire begins. Represents first horn of Land Beast (Revelation 13:11; Section 71).
AD 1071	Eastern Roman Empire loses the Battle of Manzikert to a smaller Seljuk force. Seljuk Empire overruns Anatolia, and permanently establishes Islam there (Section 71).
AD 1072	First Seljuk mosque in Anatolia is constructed in the Armenian capital of Ani. It prominently displays the Turks' introduction of the minaret for the Antichrist's call to prayer (Revelation 13:15; Section 25).
AD 1095	After an appeal for help from the Eastern Roman Emperor, the Pope calls for the first Crusade (Section 71).
AD 1099	Jerusalem is conquered by the Crusaders under Godfrey of Bouillon. Maronite Christians of Lebanon abandon Monothelitism and reestablish communion with Rome (Section 71).

Appendix IV. Notable Years in God's Dealings with Mankind *(cont.)*

AD 1187	Crusaders surrender Jerusalem to Kurdish Muslim, Saladin. Treaty established that allows Christian pilgrimage (Section 71).
AD 1299	Ottoman Empire begins. Represents second horn of land beast (Revelation 13:11; Section 25).
AD 1451	Johannes Gutenberg begins printing pages of the Latin Vulgate Bible on movable type (Section 70).
AD 1453	Constantinople falls to the Ottoman Turks—last remnant of the Roman Empire is extinguished by the 'little horn' of the Caliphate (Daniel 7:8; Sections 19, 41).
AD 1455	Gutenberg sells the first copy of the printed Latin Vulgate Bible (Section 70).
AD 1492	King and Queen of Spain are victorious against the Muslim stronghold of Granada, and finally expel the Moors and Jews from the Iberian peninsula (Matthew 16:18). Columbus discovers America—a vast wilderness that has been reserved by God to harbor the Christian Church (Revelation 12:14; Section 71).
AD 1494	Shah Ismail comes to power in northwest Iran. Claims to be the Mahdi or 'Hidden Imam.' Forces Iranians to convert to Shi'aism (Section 73).
AD 1514	Battle of Chaldiran in which Iranians are slaughtered by Turkish firearms despite their faith in the Mahdi (Section 73).
AD 1517	Martin Luther launches the Reformation of the Church by posting ninety-five theses (Section 70).
AD 1523	Martin Luther introduces a new order of Christian worship (Section 41).
AD 1529	Ottoman Turks advance on Vienna (Section 71).
AD 1530	Augsburg Confession presented to Holy Roman Emperor Charles V. Purification of Christian Church through Reformation (Revelation 12:6; Section 70).
AD 1532	Ottoman Turks advance on Vienna for a second time. Holy Roman Emperor, Charles V, enters into a temporary peace with the Schmalkald League of Lutheran princes and defeats the Turks (Revelation 12:6; foretold in Matthew 16:18; Section 71).
AD 1552	Chaldean Catholic Church comes under Vatican oversight—lessening the numbers and influence of the Nestorian church (Section 67).
AD 1563	End of the eighteen year long Council of Trent. Roman Catholics, in their 'Counter Reformation,' officially and finally reject Luther's Reformation of the Church (Section 81).
AD 1571	Ottoman fleet obliterated by the fleet of the Holy League at the Battle of Lepanto. Last major naval battle involving rowing vessels (Matthew 16:18; Section 71).
AD 1620	Pilgrim Fathers form a permanent colony in Plymouth, Massachusetts, and claim the vast wilderness of the future United States for Christ (Revelation 12:14; Section 59).
AD 1803	The United States, in its first act of war since becoming a sovereign nation, bombards and blockades the Muslim Barbary Coast pirates (Section 71).
AD 1817	King Friedrich Wilhelm III forces the Lutheran and Reformed churches of Potsdam into the 'Evangelical Christian Church,' and mandates an open communion policy. Beginning of the Prussian Union (Section 59).

Appendix IV. Notable Years in God's Dealings with Mankind *(cont.)*

AD 1827	Turkish fleet defeated at the Battle of Navarino in the War of Greek Independence. Last major naval battle involving sailing vessels (Section 71).
AD 1832	Dispensational Premillennialism introduced by John Darby (Section 27).
AD 1834	Heinrich Heine issues a prophetic warning about de-Christianization in Germany (Section 59).
AD 1838	'Old Lutherans' begin leaving Prussia for the wilderness of the New World in protest of the Prussian Union (Revelation 12:14; Section 59).
AD 1867	Czar Alexander II sells Alaska to the United States, preserving all of the wilderness of North and South America for Chalcedonian and Filioquean Christian believers (Revelation 12:14; Section 37).
AD 1886	Karl Benz patents the automobile (Revelation 9:1–10; Section 49).
AD 1909	Scofield Reference Bible published, making Dispensationalism the standard eschatology within the American Evangelical movement—especially in Baptist, Pentecostal, and non-denominational churches (Section 27).
AD 1911	The first-ever aerial bomb is dropped upon Ottoman troops in Libya during the Italo–Turkish War. Beginning of eleven years of war for Turkey (Section 71).
AD 1915	Beginning of the genocides against the Armenian, Greek, and Syriac Christians by the Ottoman Turks (Zechariah 7:13–14). The final, horrific, gasp of the Caliphate, as it tries to impose Islam on eastern Christians (Sections 36, 67).
AD 1920	Bolsheviks emerge victorious in the Russian Civil War. Turkish parliament meets for the first time.
AD 1921	President Warren Harding signs a joint congressional resolution that formally ends the First World War for the United States. Arab lands are colonized by the United Kingdom and France. Turkish parliament ratifies a new constitution, stripping the Caliphate of all power (Revelation 11:2, 12:6, 13:5; Section 30). Great immigration wave of the Christian Church to the United States symbolically ends with the Emergency Quota Act (Revelation 12:14; Section 31).
AD 1922	War in Heaven (Revelation 12:7). The one hundredth caliph, Sultan Mehmed VI, deposed. Sultanate and Ottoman Empire are ended. Smyrna is burned under the command of General Kemal Ataturk, and Greeks are expelled from Asia Minor. End of large-scale massacre of Christians in Anatolia (Sections 30, 36). Union of Soviet Socialist Republics is established (Revelation 12:13; Sections 13, 31).
AD 1923	Republic of Turkey declared; Ataturk becomes its first president (Section 30).
AD 1924	Republic of Turkey officially abolishes Caliphate and exiles all members of the Ottoman dynasty (Section 30).
AD 1949	Sayyid Qutb inspired to become the intellectual father of modern Islamic fundamentalism at a Mainline Protestant church dance (Revelation 17:13; Section 86).
AD 1959	Patriarch of Alexandria grants Ethiopian Monophysites their own patriarchy (Section 62).

Appendix IV. Notable Years in God's Dealings with Mankind *(cont.)*

AD 1960	Unofficial start of the Culture Wars in the United States (Revelation 12:15; Section 34).
AD 1964	On Good Friday a 9.2 earthquake strikes off Alaska. Providence's seventy year warning of the end of the world (Section 100).
AD 1970	Secular Alawites come to power in Syria, aligning this Sunni-majority country with the interests of the Shi'a majorities in Iraq and Iran (Section 68).
AD 1972	Rough drafts of the Qur'an are discovered in a loft in the Sana'a Mosque in Yemen. They pre-date all other copies, and have small but significant variances with the universal version. This proves that the Qur'an is an edited work, and that it was not written all at once by those that personally knew Muhammad. It demolishes Islam's claim that there is an exact copy of the universal version of the Qur'an in heaven (Section 82).
AD 1979	Fundamentalist Shi'a gain control of Iran (Section 73).
AD 1991	As the Soviet Union disintegrates, the United States goes to war in the Persian Gulf and stations troops in Saudi Arabia. This fuels Islamic terrorism (Sections 9, 37, 44). Soviet flag lowered from Kremlin on December 31st (Revelation 12:14; Section 13).
AD 1992	Red Army of the Soviet Union dissolves; its nuclear missiles are redirected to no longer target United States cities. Liberal Anti-Christian political forces gain control of the Presidency, Senate, and House of Representatives of the United States and allow a worldwide terror network to develop (Revelation 17:12–13; Section 37). Period of Christian persecution begins (Revelation 12:17; Section 32).
AD 1993	Ethiopian Patriarch grants the Eritrean Monophysites autocephaly. Five years later their archbishop becomes a patriarch (Section 62). Introduction of the Internet and symbolic beginning of the Information Revolution (Daniel 12:4; Section 88).
AD 1994	Assyrian Church of the East signs a Common Christological Declaration with the Roman Catholic Church, leaving only the small Ancient Church of the East under the Nestorian heresy (Section 67). Shoemaker-Levy Comet strikes Jupiter. Providence's forty year warning of the end of the world (Luke 21:11,25; Section 52).
AD 2001	Fall of 'Babylon the Great' during the attacks of September 11th (Revelation 18; Section 35).
AD 2004	The author of this book receives the eschatological revelation (Section 14). A 9.2 magnitude earthquake strikes off Sumatra and generates Indian Ocean tsunamis on the day after Christmas. Providence's thirty year warning of the end of the world (Luke 21:11,25; Section 100).
AD 2005	An 8.7 magnitude earthquake strikes off Sumatra on the day after Easter. Providence's second thirty year warning of the end of the world (Luke 21:11,25; Section 100). United Church of Christ becomes the first major Christian denomination to officially endorse homosexual marriage by an eighty percent margin (1 Timothy 4:1–3). The same synod rejects a resolution to require ordained clergy to profess the Lordship of Jesus Christ (2 Peter 2:1; Section 77). President of Iran prays for Allah to reveal the Mahdi in a speech before the United Nations General Assembly (Section 73).

Appendix IV. Notable Years in God's Dealings with Mankind *(cont.)*

AD 2006	This book is written and its timeline is miraculously affirmed by a chance encounter (Section 51). Suicide bomb blast on February 22nd at the al-Askari Mosque in Samarra, Iraq from where the Mahdi is said to have disappeared. Sectarian violence between Shi'a and Sunni Arabs claims thirty-five thousand lives (Sections 68, 73). Episcopal Church convention refuses to affirm that Jesus is the only route to salvation (2 Peter 2:1; Section 77).
AD 2014	One thousand years after the Christian Church first officially adopted three proper Ecumenical Creeds (i.e., Apostles', Athanasian, and Nicene with Filioque). End of the thousand year reign of the saints with Christ, or the Millennium (Revelation 20:7). Unofficial end of the sixth millennium, and possible beginning of the Tribulation (see Millennial Timeline – Section 71).
AD 2016	The thousand year anniversary of the AD 1016 earthquake in Jerusalem, and possible beginning of the Tribulation (Section 71).
AD 2025	Six thousand years after the creation of the world. Official end of sixth millennium of human history. The devil has been released and the Tribulation is occurring (Revelation 20:2–3,7). Next ten years are eschatologically-equivalent to the earliest moments of Easter morning when Christ rose from the dead (Section 48).
AD 2026	Six thousand years since the fall of man (Section 48).
AD 2029	The asteroid Apophis will pass very near planet Earth (Matthew 24:30; Section 52).
AD 2032	Christians around the world will anticipate the imminent return of Christ (Luke 21:28; 1 Thessalonians 5:4–6; foreshadowed in Deuteronomy 34:4; Sections 38–39, 43).
AD 2033	Christians delivered from the Antichrist Beast of Islam (Sections 44, 51). A possible year for Christ's return, and the promise of Christ's reign to be fulfilled (see Conquest Timeline – Section 41).
AD 2034	A possible year for Christ's return, and the promise of Christ's reign to be fulfilled (see Purim Timeline – Section 44; Abomination Timeline – Section 46).
AD 2035	A possible year for Christ's return, and the promise of Christ's reign to be fulfilled (see Jonahic Timeline – Section 42; Noahic Timeline – Section 47).
AD 2036	The asteroid Apophis will menace planet Earth a second time on Easter Sunday, April 13th (2 Peter 3:10; Section 52). A possible year for Christ's return, and the promise of Christ's reign to be fulfilled (see Handover Timeline – Section 40; Mosaic Timeline – Section 43; Sabbath Timeline – Section 48; Locust Timeline – Section 49).
AD 2039	Latest possible year for Christ's return, and the promise of Christ's reign to be fulfilled (see Scatter Timeline – Section 45).
AD 2040	A calendar year that will never occur (Section 32).

Appendix V. Bible Translations Cited

ASV   –   American Standard Version, public domain.

CEV™   –   Contemporary English Version™, used by permission of American Bible Society. See copyright page.

ESV®   –   English Standard Version®, used by permission of Crossway Bibles, a division of Good News Publishers. See copyright page.

HCSB®   –   Holman Christian Standard Bible®, used by permission of Holman Bible Publishers, a division of B&H Publishing Group. See copyright page.

KJV   –   King James Version, public domain.

NASB®   –   New American Standard Bible®, used by permission of The Lockman Foundation. See copyright page.

NCV®   –   New Century Version®, used by permission of Thomas Nelson, Inc. See copyright page.

NIrV®   –   New International Reader's Version®, used by permission of Zondervan. See copyright page.

NIV®   –   New International Version®, used by permission of Zondervan. See copyright page.

NKJV®   –   New King James Version®, used by permission of Thomas Nelson, Inc. See copyright page.

NLT®   –   New Living Translation®, used by permission of Tyndale House Publishers, Inc. See copyright page.

NLV™   –   New Life Version™, used by permission of Christian Literature International. See copyright page.

TNIV®   –   Today's New International Version®, used by permission of Zondervan. See copyright page.

YLT   –   Young's Literal Translation, public domain.

Bibliographic Citations

[1] Adapted from Mitchell, H.B. 1996. <u>Roots of Wisdom</u>, Wadsworth Publishing, Belmont, CA, p. 243

[2] Lewis, C.S. 2001. <u>Mere Christianity</u>, HarperCollins Publishers, New York, NY, p. 42

[3] As quoted in Lewis, C.S. 2001. <u>Miracles: A Preliminary Study</u>, HarperCollins Publishers, New York, NY, p. 61

[4] This line-of-thought is derived from Lewis, <u>Miracles: A Preliminary Study</u>, pp. 63–65

[5] Paraphrased from memory of his television commentary, Groeschel, B. 2000? <u>Sunday Night Live with Fr. Benedict Groeschel</u>, Eternal Word Television Network, Irondale, AL

[6] This line-of-thought is derived from Lewis, <u>Miracles: A Preliminary Study</u>, pp. 101, 157

[7] _____, May 20, 2003. <u>Matrix maker rejects crime links</u>, In BBC News, Entertainment, Film. Retrieved December 26, 2006 from, http://news.bbc.co.uk/1/hi/entertainment/film/3042577.stm

[8] Lewis, <u>Miracles: A Preliminary Study</u>, pp. 157–158.

[9] _____, 2006. <u>Kim Il-sung</u>, In Wikipedia. Retrieved December 15, 2006 from, http://en.wikipedia.org/wiki/Kim_Il-sung

[10] _____, 2006. <u>Juche</u>, In Wikipedia. Retrieved December 15, 2006 from, http://en.wikipedia.org/wiki/Juche

[11] _____, 2006. <u>Korea, North</u>, In The World Factbook online. Retrieved December 1, 2006 from, https://www.cia.gov/cia/publications/factbook/geos/kn.html

[12] _____, 2006. <u>Kim Jong Il</u>, In Wikipedia. Retrieved December 15, 2006 from, http://en.wikipedia.org/wiki/Kim_Jong_Il

[13] Hawk, D., Author and Lead Researcher. November 2005. <u>Thank You Father Kim Il Sung: Eyewitness Accounts of Severe Violations of Freedom of Thought, Conscience, and Religion in North Korea</u>, U.S. Commission on International Religious Freedom, pp. 50–51, Retrieved December 26, 2006, from http://www.uscirf.gov/countries/region/east_asia/northkorea/NKwitnesses.pdf; and also _____, 2001–2003. <u>The Bible League Newsletter</u>, The Bible League, Chicago, IL

[14] This line-of-thought is derived from Lewis, <u>Miracles: A Preliminary Study</u>, p. 46

[15] This line-of-thought is derived from Lewis, <u>Miracles: A Preliminary Study</u>, pp. 1–4

[16] Reese, E. 1977. <u>The Reese Chronological Bible</u>, Bethany House, Minneapolis, MN, p. 1415

[17] Stowe, H.B. 1852. <u>Uncle Tom's Cabin</u>, Chapter 40, In Online-Literature.com (public domain). Retrieved December 20, 2006 from, http://www.online-literature.com/stowe/uncletom/

¹⁸ Ibid.

¹⁹ Ibid.

²⁰ Wallace, S. August 2003. <u>Hidden Tribes of the Amazon</u>, National Geographic Magazine, National Geographic Society, Washington, DC, pp. 3–27

²¹ Misra, N. January 4, 2005. <u>Stone Age cultures survive tsunami waves</u>, Associated Press, In MSNBC.com; Retrieved December 21, 2006 from, http://www.msnbc.msn.com/id/6786476/

²² For related peer-reviewed research see, Povinelli, D.J. December, 1987. <u>Monkeys, apes, mirrors and minds: The evolution of self-awareness in primates</u>, Human Evolution, Vol. 2, No. 6, pp. 493–509

²³ _____, 2007. <u>Bouncers</u>, In United Church of Christ online. Retrieved May 19, 2007 from, http://www.stillspeaking.com/media/index.html

²⁴ Reese, p. 1599

²⁵ _____, January 20, 2007. <u>Chavez says Castro fighting for his life</u>, In United Press International online. Retrieved January 21, 2007 from, http://www.upi.com/NewsTrack/view.php?StoryID=20070120-065605-8730r

²⁶ _____, 2006. <u>The Station nightclub fire</u>, In Wikipedia. Retrieved December 16, 2006 from, http://en.wikipedia.org/wiki/The_Station_nightclub_fire

²⁷ _____, 2006. <u>Tilly Smith</u>, In Wikipedia. Retrieved December 16, 2006 from, http://en.wikipedia.org/wiki/Tilly_Smith

²⁸ This line-of-thought is derived from Lewis, <u>Miracles: A Preliminary Study</u>, p. 40

²⁹ Reese, p. 1454

³⁰ Walther, C.F.W. 1986. <u>The Proper Distinction Between Law and Gospel</u>, Concordia Publishing House, St. Louis, MO, p. 148

³¹ This line-of-thought is derived from Lewis, <u>Miracles: A Preliminary Study</u>, p. 188

³² Adapted from _____, 2006. <u>Lutheran Service Book</u>, Concordia Publishing House, St. Louis, MO, pp. 319–320

³³ _____, 2006. <u>Athanasian Creed</u>, In Wikipedia. Retrieved December 16, 2006 from, http://en.wikipedia.org/wiki/Athanasian_Creed

³⁴ _____, 2006. <u>Athanasian Creed</u>. In Encyclopedia Britannica online. Retrieved December 16, 2006 from, http://www.britannica.com/eb/article-9010055; and also _____, 2006. <u>The Athanasian Creed</u>, In Catholic Encyclopedia online. Retrieved December 16, 2006 from, http://www.newadvent.org/cathen/02033b.htm

³⁵ Adapted from _____, 2006. <u>Lutheran Service Book</u>, Concordia Publishing House, St. Louis, MO, pp. 319–320

³⁶ _____, 2006. <u>Sabellianism</u>, In Wikipedia. Retrieved December 16, 2006 from, http://en.wikipedia.org/wiki/Sabellianism

³⁷ The largest non-Trinitarian Pentecostal cult is the United Pentecostal Church International. Their Antichrist doctrine is summarize at _____, 2006. <u>Oneness</u>

of God, In United Pentecostal Church International online. Retrieved December 17, 2006 from, http://www.upci.org/about.asp#oneness

[38] _____, 2006. Lutheran Service Book, Concordia Publishing House, St. Louis, MO, p. 206

[39] _____, 2006. Filioque clause: Further East-West controversy, In Wikipedia. Retrieved December 10, 2006 from, http://en.wikipedia.org/wiki/Filioque_ clause#Further_East-West_controversy; and also _____, 2006. Credo, In Wikipedia. Retrieved December 15, 2006 from, http://en.wikipedia. org/wiki/Credo

[40] _____, 2006. Anne Hutchinson, In Wikipedia. Retrieved December 16, 2006 from, http://en.wikipedia.org/wiki/Anne_Hutchinson

[41] _____, 2006. Lutheran Service Book, Concordia Publishing House, St. Louis, MO, p. 207

[42] _____, 2006. Athanasian Creed, In Wikipedia. Retrieved December 16, 2006 from, http://en.wikipedia.org/wiki/Athanasian_Creed

[43] _____, 2006. Diocletian, In Encyclopedia Britannica online. Retrieved December 17, 2006 from, http://www.britannica.com/eb/article-1830

[44] _____, 2006. Romulus Augustulus, In Encyclopedia Britannica online. Retrieved December 17, 2006 from, http://www.britannica.com/eb/article-9083870

[45] Runciman, S. 1965. The Fall of Constantinople, 1453, Cambridge University Press, Cambridge, UK. 256 pp.

[46] Durant, W. 1950. The Story of Civilization: The Age of Faith, Vol. IV, Simon and Schuster, New York, NY, p. 190

[47] Nevo, Y.D., Koren, J. 2003. Crossroads to Islam: The Origins of the Arab Religion and the Arab State, Prometheus Books, Amherst, NY, Part III, The Arab Religion, pp. 170–354

[48] Kaegi, W.E. 1992. Byzantium and the early Islamic conquests, Cambridge University Press, New York, NY, pp. 133–134

[49] Nevo and Koren, pp. 216–217

[50] Durant, pp. 190, 220–223

[51] Nevo and Koren, pp. 271–274, 326

[52] Reese, p. 1579

[53] Durant, Vol. IV, p. 190

[54] _____, 2006. Abu Bakr, In Encyclopedia Britannica online. Retrieved December 27, 2006 from, http://www.britannica.com/eb/article-9003420

[55] _____, 2006. Umar I, In Encyclopedia Britannica online. Retrieved December 27, 2006 from, http://www.britannica.com/eb/article-9074188

[56] _____, 2006. Uthman ibn 'Affan, In Encyclopedia Britannica online. Retrieved December 27, 2006 from, http://www.britannica.com/eb/article-9074557

[57] _____, 2006. <u>Ali</u>, In Encyclopedia Britannica online. Retrieved December 27, 2006 from, http://www.britannica.com/eb/article-9005712

[58] _____, 2006. <u>Mu'awiyah I</u>, In Encyclopedia Britannica online. Retrieved December 27, 2006 from, http://www.britannica.com/eb/article-9054113

[59] _____, 2006. <u>Yazid I</u>, In Encyclopedia Britannica online. Retrieved December 27, 2006 from, http://www.britannica.com/eb/article-9077878

[60] _____, 2006. <u>Abd al-Malik</u>, In Encyclopedia Britannica online. Retrieved December 27, 2006 from, http://www.britannica.com/eb/article-9003265

[61] _____, 2006. <u>Mehmed VI</u>, In Wikipedia. Retrieved December 17, 2006 from, http://en.wikipedia.org/wiki/Mehmed_VI

[62] _____, September 18, 2006. <u>Al Qaeda threat over pope speech</u>, In CNN online. Retrieved December 15, 2006 from, http://www.cnn.com/2006/WORLD/europe/09/17/pope.islam/index.html

[63] Nevo and Koren, pp. 264–265

[64] Qur'an Sura 3.144

[65] Qur'an Sura 5.75

[66] Trifkovic, S. 2002. <u>The Sword of the Prophet: Islam, history, theology, impact on the world</u>, Regina Orthodox Press, Boston, MA, p. 161

[67] Runciman, p. 79

[68] Durant, Vol. IV, p. 190

[69] _____, 2006. <u>The Bouyeri Trial</u>, In CrimeLibrary.com; Retrieved December 17, 2006 from, http://www.crimelibrary.com/notorious_murders/famous/theo_van_gogh/12.html

[70] Rennie, D. July 13, 2005. <u>I'd do it all again, says film-maker's killer</u>, In The Telegraph online. Retrieved December 17, 2006 from, http://www.telegraph.co.uk/news/main.jhtml?xml=/news/2005/07/13/wbouy13.xml

[71] Tolan, J.V. 2002. <u>Saracens: Islam in the Medieval European Imagination</u>, Columbia University Press, New York, NY, p. 51

[72] Durant, Vol. IV, p. 164; and also Muir, W. 1878. <u>The Life of Mahomet</u>, Smith, Elder, and Company, London, UK, pp. 32, 42, 61, 259

[73] Muir, p. 144

[74] _____, 2006. <u>Battle of Badr</u>, In Wikipedia. Retrieved December 18, 2006 from, http://en.wikipedia.org/wiki/Battle_of_Badr

[75] Muir, pp. 321, 390, 451, 477–478

[76] _____, 2006. <u>Ali: Ali in Medina</u>, In Wikipedia. Retrieved December 18, 2006 from http://en.wikipedia.org/wiki/Ali#Ali_in_Medina

[77] Hooker, R. 1996. <u>Shi'a: The Safavids</u>, In World Civilizations online. Retrieved December 18, 2006 from, http://www.wsu.edu/~dee/TEXT/111/unit6pt2.rtf

[78] Durant, Vol. IV, p. 191

[79] _____, 2006. 1ˢᵗ Holy Imam, In Islamic Institute of New York online. Retrieved December 18, 2006 from, http://iiny.org/1stImam.htm

[80] _____, 2006. Battle of Bassorah, In Wikipedia. Retrieved December 18, 2006 from, http://en.wikipedia.org/wiki/Battle_of_Bassorah; and also _____, 2006. Battle of Siffin, In Wikipedia. Retrieved December 18, 2006 from, http://en.wikipedia.org/wiki/Battle_of_Siffin

[81] Durant, Vol. IV, pp. 191–192

[82] Crone, P. August 31, 2006. What do we actually know about Mohammed?, In OpenDemocracy.net; Retrieved November 29, 2006 from, http://www.opendemocracy.net/faith-europe_islam/mohammed_3866.jsp

[83] Durant, Vol. IV, p. 192

[84] Hooker, R. 1996. Shi'a: The Safavids, In World Civilizations online. Retrieved December 18, 2006 from, http://www.wsu.edu/~dee/TEXT/111/unit6pt2.rtf

[85] _____, 2006. Mu'awiyah I, In Encyclopedia Britannica online. Retrieved December 18, 2006 from, http://www.britannica.com/eb/article-5053/Muawiyah-I

[86] _____, 2006. Muawiyah I, In Wikipedia. Retrieved December 18, 2006 from, http://en.wikipedia.org/wiki/Muawiyah_I

[87] Ibid.

[88] Durant, Vol. IV, p. 192

[89] _____, 2006. Leon Trotsky, In Wikipedia. Retrieved December 17, 2006 from, http://en.wikipedia.org/wiki/Leon_Trotsky

[90] _____, 2006. Ali the Warrior, In Wikipedia. Retrieved December 17, 2006 from, http://en.wikipedia.org/wiki/Ali_the_Warrior

[91] _____, 2006. Wadi-us-Salaam, In Wikipedia. Retrieved December 17, 2006 from, http://en.wikipedia.org/wiki/Wadi-us-Salaam

[92] Shadid, A. 2007. Across Arab World, a Widening Rift, In Washington Post online. Retrieved February 12, 2007 from, http://www.washingtonpost.com/wp-dyn/content/article/2007/02/11/AR2007021101328_3.html

[93] Durant, Vol. IV, p. 193

[94] _____, 2006. Day of Ashura, In Wikipedia. Retrieved December 17, 2006 from, http://en.wikipedia.org/wiki/Day_of_Ashura

[95] _____, 2006. Ali, In Wikipedia. Retrieved December 17, 2006 from, http://en.wikipedia.org/wiki/Ali

[96] _____, 2006. Abd-Allah ibn al-Zubayr, In Wikipedia. Retrieved December 17, 2006 from, http://en.wikipedia.org/wiki/Abd-Allah_ibn_al-Zubayr

[97] _____, 2006. Al-Hajjaj bin Yousef, In Wikipedia. Retrieved December 17, 2006 from, http://en.wikipedia.org/wiki/Al-Hajjaj_bin_Yousef

[98] Blair, S.S. 1992. What is the Date of the Dome of the Rock?, in Raby, J., Johns, J., Editors. Bayt al-Maqdis, Abd al-Malik's Jerusalem, Part One, Oxford

Studies in Islamic Art, Vol. IX, Oxford University Press, Oxford, UK, pp. 59, 84

[99] _____, 2006. Abd al-Malik, In Wikipedia. Retrieved December 23, 2006 from, http://en.wikipedia.org/wiki/Abd_al-Malik

[100] Blair, pp. 59, 84

[101] _____, 2006. Battle of Sevastapol (692), In Wikipedia. Retrieved December 23, 2006 from, http://en.wikipedia.org/wiki/Battle_of_Sevastapol_%28692%29

[102] Blair, pp. 69–70

[103] _____, 2006. Iconoclasm (Byzantine), In Wikipedia. Retrieved December 23, 2006 from, http://en.wikipedia.org/wiki/Iconoclasm_%28Byzantine%29

[104] Nevo and Koren, p. 287

[105] Blair, p. 84

[106] Blair, pp. 63, 85

[107] Blair, p. 68, suggests that the Dome of the Rock and Aqsa Mosque building projects lasted from AD 692 to AD 702

[108] Nevo and Koren, p. 163; and also Blair, p. 67

[109] Nevo and Koren, p. 326

[110] Nevo and Koren, p. 275

[111] Blair, pp. 67–69

[112] What eventually became Qur'an Sura 48.29 ("Muhammad is the Messenger of God") was inscribed on al-Malik's first Islamic coins in AD 692; see Nevo and Koren, pp. 266–267; and also Blair, pp. 65–66

[113] Nevo and Koren, pp. 326–331

[114] Nevo and Koren, pp. 255–256

[115] _____, 2006. Abd al-Malik, In Wikipedia. Retrieved December 23, 2006 from, http://en.wikipedia.org/wiki/Abd_al-Malik

[116] _____, 2006. Ali, In Wikipedia. Retrieved December 17, 2006 from, http://en.wikipedia.org/wiki/Ali

[117] _____, 2006. Ali, In Encyclopedia Britannica online. Retrieved December 17, 2006 from, http://www.britannica.com/eb/article-9005712

[118] Blair, pp. 67–69, 84

[119] Reese, p. 1254

[120] Reese, p. 1262, dates this event at AD 25, not AD 26. However, Hoerber, R.G., General Editor, 1984. Concordia Study Bible, p. 1488, dates this event at AD 26.

[121] Blair, pp. 67–69, 84

[122] Blair, pp. 60–63, 67, 84–85; and also Elad, A. Why did 'Abd al-Malik Build the Dome of the Rock? A Re-Examination of the Muslim Sources, in Raby, J., Johns, J., Editors. 1992. Bayt al-Maqdis, Abd al-Malik's Jerusalem,

Part One, Oxford Studies in Islamic Art, Vol. IX, Oxford University Press, Oxford, UK, p. 37

123 Reese, p. 1262, dates this event at AD 25, not AD 26. However, Hoerber, p. 1488, dates this event at AD 26.

124 Reese, pp. 1424–1427, dates this event at AD 35, not AD 33; Iwas dates this event at ~ AD 34 in Iwas, Z. 1983. The Syrian Orthodox Church of Antioch At A Glance, In the Syriac Orthodox Resources online. Retrieved December 27, 2006 from, http://sor.cua.edu/Pub/PZakka1/SOCAtAGlance.html

125 Kaegi, W.E. 2003. Heraclius, Emperor of Byzantium, Cambridge University Press, New York, NY, p. 303

126 _____, 2006. Umar: Umar's Reign as a caliph, In Wikipedia. Retrieved December 3, 2006 from, http://en.wikipedia.org/wiki/Umar#Umar.27s_Reign_as_a_caliph

127 Gibbon, E. 1782. The History of the Decline and Fall of the Roman Empire, Vol. 5, Chapter LI (In The East), Part II (Invasion of Syria), Conquest of Jerusalem, A.D. 637. In Christian Classics Ethereal Library online. Retrieved December 18, 2006 from, http://www.ccel.org/ccel/gibbon/decline/volume2/chap512.htm

128 Ibid.

129 Nevo and Koren, pp. 195–199, 242–245

130 Nevo and Koren, pp. 114–115, 212–213

131 Gibbon, E. 1782. The History of the Decline and Fall of the Roman Empire, Vol. 5, Chapter LI (In The East), Part II (Invasion of Syria), Conquest of Jerusalem, A.D. 637. In Christian Classics Ethereal Library online. Retrieved December 18, 2006 from, http://www.ccel.org/ccel/gibbon/decline/volume2/chap512.htm

132 _____, 2006. Ali Akbar ibn Hussain, In Wikipedia. Retrieved December 3, 2006 from, http://en.wikipedia.org/wiki/Ali_Akbar_ibn_Hussain

133 _____, 2006. Adhan, In Wikipedia. Retrieved December 3, 2006 from, http://en.wikipedia.org/wiki/Adhan

134 Hooker, R. 1996. Shi'a: The Safavids, In World Civilizations online. Retrieved December 18, 2006 from, http://www.wsu.edu/~dee/TEXT/111/unit6pt2.rtf

135 _____, 2006. Justinian II, In Encyclopedia Britannica online. Retrieved December 18, 2006 from, http://www.britannica.com/eb/article-9044215

136 Blair, pp. 60–63, 67, 84–87; and also Elad, p. 37; and also Nevo and Koren, p. 163

137 I have never seen this piece of history published. It comes from Christian people that lived among the Shi'a for fifty years, and repeated the Shi'a oral tradition to me.

138 Reese, pp. 1424–1427, dates this event at AD 35, not AD 33; Iwas dates this event at ~ AD 34.

[139] Maier, P.L., Translator and Editor. 1994. <u>Josephus: The Essential Works</u>, Kregel Publications, Grand Rapids, MI, pp. 371–372

[140] Nat, A.V., Translator. 2001. <u>Saint Adamnan, Abbot of Iona, Regarding the Holy Places, from the Account of Arculf, Bishop of Gaul, in Three Books</u>. In Early Accounts of the Temple of Jerusalem online. Retrieved December 23, 2006 from, http://homepages.luc.edu/~avande1/jerusalem/sources/arculf.htm

[141] Blair, pp. 67–69, 84

[142] _____, 2006. <u>Abd al-Malik</u>, In Wikipedia. Retrieved December 23, 2006 from, http://en.wikipedia.org/wiki/Abd_al-Malik

[143] Blair, pp. 60–63, 67, 84–87; and also Nevo and Koren, p. 163

[144] Elad, p. 37

[145] _____, 2006. <u>Abd al-Malik</u>, In Wikipedia. Retrieved December 23, 2006 from, http://en.wikipedia.org/wiki/Abd_al-Malik

[146] What eventually became Qur'an Sura 48.29 ("Muhammad is the Messenger of God") was inscribed on al-Malik's first Islamic coins in AD 692; see Nevo and Koren, pp. 266–267; and also Blair, pp. 65–66; Also, what eventually became Qur'an Sura 48.28 ("He sent His messenger with guidance and the religion of truth, that he may cause it to prevail over all [other] religions") was inscribed on al-Malik's coins in AD 696; they also said, "There is no god but God alone, without partner"; see Nevo and Koren, pp. 163, 331; and also Blair, pp. 67–69

[147] Molnar, M.R. 1999. <u>The Star of Bethlehem: The Legacy of the Magi</u>, Rutgers University Press, Piscataway, NJ

[148] Reese, p. 1254

[149] Ibid.

[150] _____, 2006. <u>Ali</u>, In Encyclopedia Britannica online. Retrieved December 27, 2006 from, http://www.britannica.com/eb/article-9005712

[151] Reese, p. 1262, dates this event at AD 25, not AD 26. However, Hoerber, p. 1488, dates this event at AD 26.

[152] What eventually became Qur'an Sura 48.29 ("Muhammad is the Messenger of God") was inscribed on al-Malik's first Islamic coins in AD 692; see Nevo and Koren, pp. 266–267; and also Blair, pp. 65–66, 84; and also _____, 2006. <u>Abd al-Malik</u>, In Wikipedia. Retrieved December 21, 2006 from, http://en.wikipedia.org/wiki/Abd_al-Malik

[153] Reese, p. 1406, dates this event at AD 29, not AD 30. However, Hoerber, p. 1490, dates this event at AD 30.

[154] What eventually became Qur'an Sura 48.28 ("He sent His messenger with guidance and the religion of truth, that he may cause it to prevail over all [other] religions") was inscribed on al-Malik's coins in AD 696; they also said,

"There is no god but God alone, without partner"; see Nevo and Koren, pp. 266–267, 331; and also Blair, pp. 67–69

[155] Reese, pp. 1424–1427, dates this event at AD 35, not AD 33; Iwas dates this event at ~ AD 34.

[156] Blair, pp. 60–63, 67, 84–87; and also Elad, p. 37; and also Nevo and Koren, p. 163

[157] Some Medieval Christians asserted that Muhammad was the Antichrist because [they maintained] he had died in AD 666; however, the commonly-held date for Muhammad's death is actually AD 632. These Medieval Christians also did not know that the Gregorian calendar is five years late, and that it was actually Ali that died six hundred and sixty-six years later (in AD 661); this event gave birth to Shi'a and Sunni Islam; see _____, 2006. Medieval Christian view of Muhammad, In Wikipedia. Retrieved December 21, 2006 from, http://en.wikipedia.org/wiki/Medieval_Christian_view_of_Muhammad

[158] Reese, p. 1146

[159] _____, 2006. Hamidian massacres, In Wikipedia. Retrieved December 21, 2006 from, http://en.wikipedia.org/wiki/Hamidian_massacres

[160] Gibbon, E. 1782. The History of the Decline and Fall of the Roman Empire, Vol. 5, Chapter LI (In The East), Part II (Invasion of Syria), Conquest of Jerusalem, A.D. 637. In Christian Classics Ethereal Library online. Retrieved December 18, 2006 from, http://www.ccel.org/ccel/gibbon/decline/volume2/chap512.htm

[161] _____, 2006. Khomeini's Islamic Leadership, In Wikipedia. Retrieved December 21, 2006 from, http://en.wikipedia.org/wiki/Khomeini's_Islamic_leadership

[162] Qur'an Sura 48.29

[163] _____, 2006. Oghuz Turks: Origins, In Wikipedia. Retrieved December 27, 2006 from, http://en.wikipedia.org/wiki/Oghuz_Turks#Origins

[164] _____, 2006. Ottoman Empire, In Encyclopedia Britannica online. Retrieved December 27, 2006 from, http://www.britannica.com/eb/article-44375; and also _____, 2006. Seljuq, In Encyclopedia Britannica online. Retrieved December 27, 2006 from, http://www.britannica.com/eb/article-9066688

[165] Runciman, p. 78

[166] _____, 2006. Caliph: Ottoman, In Wikipedia. Retrieved December 3, 2006 from, http://en.wikipedia.org/wiki/Caliph#Ottomans

[167] _____, 2006. Suleiman the Magnificent, In Wikipedia. Retrieved December 3, 2006 from, http://en.wikipedia.org/wiki/Suleiman_the_Magnificent

[168] Gottheil, R.J.H. 1910. The Origin and History of the Minaret, Journal of the American Oriental Society, Vol. 30, No. 2, p. 132

[169] Bloom, J. 1989. Minaret: Symbol of Islam, Oxford Studies in Islamic Art, Vol. VII, Oxford University Press, Oxford, UK, pp. 9, 21, 36–37

[170] Bloom, pp. 151–153

[171] Gottheil, p. 132

[172] Gottheil, p. 135; and also Bloom, p. 175

[173] Gottheil, p. 133

[174] Bloom, p. 147

[175] As quoted in Bloom, p. 149

[176] Bloom, pp. 7, 151, 164–165

[177] Bloom, p. 150

[178] Gottheil, pp. 137–138

[179] Bloom, p. 165

[180] Bloom, p. 36

[181] Bloom, p. 7

[182] Gottheil, pp. 139–140, 151; and also Bloom, p. 7

[183] Bloom, pp. 155–156; and also Gottheil, p. 151

[184] Bloom, p. 157

[185] Bloom, p. 175

[186] Bloom, pp. 157, 166

[187] Bloom, p. 151

[188] Reese, pp. 1089, 1191

[189] Reese, p. 1158

[190] Reese, p. 1213

[191] Kaiser, W.C, Garrett, D., Editors. 2006. <u>Archaeological Study Bible</u>, Zondervan, Grand Rapids, MI, pp. 674–675, footnote 4:6–24

[192] Reese, p. 1224, dates the completion of the rebuilding of Jerusalem to 444 BC, not 409 BC; but on p. 1244 he dates the writing of the Book of Nehemiah between 415 BC–405 BC; and also Kaiser and Garrett, p. 699, dates Nehemiah's return at 433 BC to 432 BC—implying that the rebuilding was completed after 432 BC.

[193] Reese, p. 1262, dates this event at AD 25, not AD 26. However, Hoerber, p. 1488, dates this event at AD 26.

[194] Reese, pp. 1270–1271

[195] Maier, pp. 368–378

[196] Hoerber, p. 1613, footnote 5:1

[197] Reese, p. 1406, dates this event at AD 29, not AD 30. However, Hoerber, p. 1490, dates this event at AD 30.

[198] Reese, p. 1262, dates this event at AD 25, not AD 26. However, Hoerber, p. 1488, dates this event at AD 26.

[199] Reese, pp. 1424–1427, dates this event at AD 35, not AD 33; Iwas dates this event at ~ AD 34.

[200] Hoerber, pp. 1301–1302

[201] Green, J.P., General Editor and Translator. 1985. The Interlinear Bible. Volume III: Psalm 56–Malachi, Hendrickson Publishers, Peabody, MA, p. 2066

[202] _____, 2006. John Nelson Darby, In Wikipedia. Retrieved December 22, 2006 from, http://en.wikipedia.org/wiki/John_Nelson_Darby; and also _____, 2006. Plymouth Brethren, In Wikipedia. Retrieved December 22, 2006 from, http://en.wikipedia.org/wiki/Plymouth_Brethren

[203] _____, 2006. Dispensationalism: North America, In Wikipedia. Retrieved December 1, 2006 from, http://en.wikipedia. org/wiki/Dispensationalism#North_America

[204] Ironside, H.A. 1919. Lectures on the Revelation, Loizeaux Brothers, Bible Truth Depot, New York, NY, p. 249; and also _____, 2006. Dispensationalism: The identity of the Antichrist, In Wikipedia. Retrieved December 1, 2006 from, http://en.wikipedia.org/wiki/Dispensationalism#The_identity_of_the_Antichrist

[205] _____, 2006. Rapture, In Wikipedia. Retrieved December 22, 2006 from, http://en.wikipedia.org/wiki/Rapture

[206] Reese, p. 1159

[207] Reese, p. 1213

[208] Reese, p. 1224, dates this event at 444 BC, not 409 BC; but on p. 1244 he dates the writing of the Book of Nehemiah between 415 BC–405 BC.

[209] Reese, p. 1262, dates this event at AD 25, not AD 26. However, Hoerber, p. 1488, dates this event at AD 26.

[210] Reese, p. 1406, dates this event at AD 29, not AD 30. However, Hoerber, p. 1490, dates this event at AD 30.

[211] Reese, pp. 1424–1427, dates this event at AD 35, not AD 33; Iwas dates this event at ~ AD 34.

[212] Reese, p. 1213

[213] Reese, p. 1224, dates this event at 444 BC, not 409 BC; but on p. 1244 he dates the writing of the Book of Nehemiah between 415 BC–405 BC.

[214] Reese, p. 1262, dates this event at AD 25, not AD 26. However, Hoerber, p. 1488, dates this event at AD 26.

[215] _____, 2006. Harry A. Ironside, In Wikipedia. Retrieved December 1, 2006 from, http://en.wikipedia.org/wiki/Harry_A._Ironside

[216] Ironside, pp. 108–110 (public domain)

[217] Hubers, J. 2004. Christian Zionism: A Historical Analysis and Critique, 21 pp. In Reformed Church in America online. Retrieved December 22, 2006 from, http://images.rca.org/docs/synod/ChristianZionism.pdf

[218] This story was related to me by a computer consultant who automated the evangelist's postal solicitations.

[219] Reese, p. 1406, dates this event at AD 29, not AD 30. However, Hoerber, p. 1490, dates this event at AD 30.

[220] Johnson, P. 1999. A History of the American People, Harper Perennial, London, UK, p. 40

[221] Reese, pp. 67, 571

[222] Reese, pp. 571, 1363

[223] Some Muslims place the Hijra at AD 624–625, rather than AD 622: Crone, P. August 31, 2006. What do we actually know about Mohammed?, In OpenDemocracy.net; Retrieved November 29, 2006 from, http://www. opendemocracy.net/faith-europe_islam/mohammed_3866.jsp

[224] _____, 2006. Islamic calendar, In Wikipedia. Retrieved December 22, 2006 from, http://en.wikipedia.org/wiki/Islamic_calendar

[225] _____, 2006. Hijra (Islam), In Wikipedia. Retrieved December 22, 2006 from, http://en.wikipedia.org/wiki/Hijra_%28Islam%29

[226] _____, 2006. Islamic calendar, In Wikipedia. Retrieved December 22, 2006 from, http://en.wikipedia.org/wiki/Islamic_calendar

[227] Crone, P. August 31, 2006. What do we actually know about Mohammed?, In OpenDemocracy.net; Retrieved November 29, 2006 from, http://www. opendemocracy.net/faith-europe_islam/mohammed_3866.jsp

[228] Qur'an Sura 24:58 says, "O you who believe! Let those whom your right hands possess and those who are underage ask leave of you three times: before the morning prayer, and when you put off your clothes in the midday heat, and after the evening prayer; these are three times of privacy for you; at other times it is not a sin for you, nor for them, to go around visiting each other; thus does Allah make clear to you His communications, and Allah is all-knowing and wise."

[229] _____, 2006. Treaty of Berlin, 1921, In Wikipedia. Retrieved December 5, 2006 from, http://en.wikipedia.org/wiki/Treaty_of_Berlin%2C_1921

[230] _____, 2006. Grand National Assembly of Turkey, In Wikipedia. Retrieved December 5, 2006 from, http://en.wikipedia.org/wiki/Grand_National_ Assembly_of_Turkey; and also _____, 2006. Turkish Constitution of 1921, In Wikipedia. Retrieved December 23, 2006 from, http://en.wikipedia. org/wiki/Turkish_Constitution_of_1921

[231] _____, 2006. League of Nations mandate, In Wikipedia. Retrieved December 5, 2006 from, http://en.wikipedia.org/wiki/League_of_Nations_mandate

[232] _____, 2006. Mehmed VI, In Wikipedia. Retrieved December 22, 2006 from, http:// en.wikipedia.org/wiki/Mehmed_VI

[233] _____, 2006. Abdul Mejid II, In Wikipedia. Retrieved December 22, 2006 from, http://en.wikipedia.org/wiki/Abdul_Mejid_II

234 _____, 2006. <u>Battle of Dumlupinar</u>, In Wikipedia. Retrieved December 22, 2006 from, http://en.wikipedia.org/wiki/Battle_of_Dumlup%C4%B1nar

235 _____, 2006. <u>Great Fire of Smyrna</u>, In Wikipedia. Retrieved December 22, 2006 from, http://en.wikipedia.org/wiki/Great_Fire_of_Smyrna

236 _____, 2006. <u>Chrysostomos of Smyrna</u>, In Wikipedia. Retrieved December 22, 2006 from, http://en.wikipedia.org/wiki/Chrysostomos_of_Smyrna

237 _____, 2006. <u>Kamal Ataturk</u>, In BeautifulIslam.net; Retrieved December 22, 2006 from, http://www.beautifulislam.net/articles/kamal_ataturk.htm

238 _____, 2006. <u>Treaty of Sevres</u>, In Wikipedia. Retrieved December 22, 2006 from, http://en.wikipedia.org/wiki/Treaty_of_S%C3%A8vres

239 _____, 2006. <u>Population exchange between Greece and Turkey</u>, In Wikipedia. Retrieved December 22, 2006 from, http://en.wikipedia. org/wiki/Population_exchange_between_Greece_and_Turkey

240 _____, 2006. <u>Mustafa Kemal Ataturk</u>, In Wikipedia. Retrieved December 22, 2006 from, http://en.wikipedia.org/wiki/Mustafa_Kemal_Atat%C3%BCrk

241 _____, 2006. <u>Kazim Karabekir</u>, In Wikipedia. Retrieved December 22, 2006 from, http://en.wikipedia.org/wiki/Kaz%C4%B1m_Karabekir

242 As quoted in Yilmaz OZ. 1982. <u>Quotations from Mustafa Kemal Ataturk</u>, Pamphlet, Ministry of Foreign Affairs, Republic of Turkey

243 _____, 2006. <u>Kamal Ataturk</u>, In BeautifulIslam.net; Retrieved December 22, 2006 from, http://www.beautifulislam.net/articles/kamal_ataturk.htm; and also _____, 2006. <u>Adhan: The Adhan in the Republic of Turkey</u>, In Wikipedia. Retrieved December 22, 2006 from, http://en.wikipedia. org/wiki/Adhan#The_Adhan_in_the_Republic_of_Turkey

244 As quoted in Armstrong, H.C. 1972. <u>Grey Wolf, Mustafa Kemal: An Intimate Study of a Dictator</u>, Beaufort Books, New York, NY, 352 pp.

245 Ibid.

246 As quoted in _____, 2006. <u>Mustafa Kemal Ataturk</u>, In Wikipedia. Retrieved December 22, 2006 from, http://en.wikipedia.org/wiki/Mustafa_Kemal_Atat%C3%BCrk

247 As quoted in _____, February 2, 2007. <u>Scandal tails death of Turkey journalist</u>, In Yahoo News online. Retrieved February 3, 2007 from, http://news.yahoo. com/s/ap/20070202/ap_on_re_mi_ea/turkey_journalist_killed

248 As quoted in Mango, A. 2000. <u>Ataturk: The Biography of the Founder of Modern Turkey</u>, Overlook Hardcover, London, UK, 539 pp.

249 As quoted in Yilmaz OZ. 1982. <u>Quotations from Mustafa Kemal Ataturk</u>, Pamphlet, Ministry of Foreign Affairs, Republic of Turkey

250 As quoted in As quoted in <u>Mustafa Kemal Ataturk (1881–1938)</u>, In The Quotations Page online. Retrieved December 22, 2006 from, http://www. quotationspage.com/quotes/Mustafa_Kemal_Ataturk/

[251] As quoted in Sansal, B., 2006. <u>Ataturk quotes and speeches</u>, In All About Turkey online. Retrieved December 22, 2006 from, http://www.allaboutturkey. com/ata_speech.htm

[252] As quoted in Yilmaz OZ. 1982. <u>Quotations from Mustafa Kemal Ataturk</u>, Pamphlet, Ministry of Foreign Affairs, Republic of Turkey

[253] As quoted in Sansal, B., 2006. <u>Ataturk quotes and speeches</u>, In All About Turkey online. Retrieved December 22, 2006 from, http://www.allaboutturkey. com/ata_speech.htm

[254] Gabor, Z.Z. 1991. <u>One Lifetime is Not Enough</u>. Delacorte Press, New York, NY, pp. 19–21

[255] _____, 2006. <u>Mustafa Kemal Ataturk: Family and personal life</u>, In Wikipedia. Retrieved December 22, 2006 from, http://en.wikipedia. org/wiki/Ataturk#Family_and_personal_life

[256] Gabor, p. 14

[257] Gabor, pp. 25–26

[258] Gabor, p. 26

[259] As quoted in <u>Christianity</u>, In Wikiquote, Retrieved December 22, 2006 from, http:// en.wikiquote.org/wiki/Christianity

[260] Ibid.

[261] As quoted in Gingrich, N. 2006. <u>Rediscovering God in America</u>, Integrity Publishers, Franklin, TN, p. 19

[262] _____, February 21 2004. <u>Sabiha Gokchen or Hatun Sebilciyan?</u>, In Turks US Daily News online. Retrieved December 20, 2006 from, http://www.turks.us/artic le~story~2004022108031549.htm

[263] _____, 2006. <u>Caliphate: End of Caliphate, 1924</u>, In Wikipedia. Retrieved December 22, 2006 from, http://en.wikipedia. org/wiki/Caliphate#End_of_Caliphate.2C_1924

[264] _____, August 1, 2006. <u>Al-Zawahiri urges attacks on Israel</u>, In alJazeera. net; Retrieved December 22, 2006 from, http://english.aljazeera. net/News/archive/archive?ArchiveId=24769

[265] _____, 2006. <u>Mehmed VI</u>, In Wikipedia. Retrieved December 3, 2006 from, http:// en.wikipedia.org/wiki/Mehmed_VI

[266] _____, 2006. <u>Soviet Union</u>, In Wikipedia. Retrieved December 3, 2006 from, http:// en.wikipedia.org/wiki/Soviet_Union

[267] _____, 2006. <u>Red Army</u>, In Wikipedia. Retrieved December 3, 2006 from, http:// en.wikipedia.org/wiki/Red_Army

[268] _____, 2006. <u>Emergency Quota Act</u>, In Wikipedia. Retrieved December 19, 2006 from, http://en.wikipedia.org/wiki/Emergency_Quota_Act

[269] Reese, p. 81

[270] Reese, p. 88

271 _____, 2006. Long Island, Battle of, In Encyclopedia Britannica online. Retrieved December 19, 2006 from, http://www.britannica.com/eb/article-9048858

272 As quoted in Christianity, In Wikiquote, Retrieved December 26, 2006 from, http://en.wikiquote.org/wiki/Christianity

273 As quoted in Calvin Coolidge (1872–1933), In The Quotations Page online. Retrieved December 26, 2006 from, http://www.quotationspage.com/quotes/Calvin_Coolidge/

274 _____, 2006. Spontaneous human combustion, In Wikipedia. Retrieved December 26, 2006 from, http://en.wikipedia.org/wiki/Spontaneous_human_combustion

275 Palfreman, J. October 19, 1993. Prisoners of Silence, Frontline, In Public Broadcasting Service online. Retrieved December 26, 2006 from, http://www.pbs.org/wgbh/pages/frontline/programs/transcripts/1202.html

276 Fitzpatrick, S. November 09, 2006. Beheaded girls were Ramadan 'trophies', In The Australian online. Retrieved December 26, 2006 from, http://www.theaustralian.news.com.au/story/0,20867,20726085-2703,00.html

277 _____, 2006. Graham Staines, In Wikipedia. Retrieved December 26, 2006 from, http://en.wikipedia.org/wiki/Graham_Staines

278 _____, 1997. Religious Minorities, In Human Rights Watch online. New York, NY. Retrieved December 26, 2006 from, http://www.hrw.org/reports/1997/iran/Iran-05.htm

279 Grip, L. August 1, 2004. No Free Speech in Preaching, In Christianity Today online. Retrieved December 26, 2006 from, http://www.ctlibrary.com/ct/2004/augustweb-only/8-9-12.0.html

280 Moore, A. September 17, 2003. 'Bible as hate speech' bill nearing vote, In WorldNetDaily online. Retrieved December 26, 2006 from, http://www.worldnetdaily.com/news/article.asp?ARTICLE_ID=34639

281 _____, 2006. Treaty of Berlin, 1921, In Wikipedia. Retrieved December 23, 2006 from, http://en.wikipedia.org/wiki/Treaty_of_Berlin%2C_1921

282 _____, 2006. League of Nations mandate, In Wikipedia. Retrieved December 23, 2006 from, http://en.wikipedia.org/wiki/League_of_Nations_mandate

283 _____, 2006. Turkish Constitution of 1921, In Wikipedia. Retrieved December 23, 2006 from, http://en.wikipedia.org/wiki/Turkish_Constitution_of_1921; and also _____, 2006. Grand National Assembly of Turkey, In Wikipedia. Retrieved December 5, 2006 from, http://en.wikipedia.org/wiki/Grand_National_Assembly_of_Turkey

284 _____, 2006. Mehmed VI, In Wikipedia. Retrieved December 5, 2006 from, http://en.wikipedia.org/wiki/Mehmed_VI

285 _____, 2006. Abdul Mejid II, In Wikipedia. Retrieved December 5, 2006 from, http://en.wikipedia.org/wiki/Abdul_Mejid_II

286 Hoerber, p. 931, footnote 137:7

[287] Reese, p. 139

[288] Reese, pp. 954–955

[289] Reese, pp. 1089–1093

[290] Reese, p. 1202

[291] Reese, p. 1249; foretold in Daniel 11:31–33

[292] _____, 2006. Rome, In Encyclopedia Britannica online. Retrieved December 19, 2006 from, http://www.britannica.com/eb/article-23886

[293] _____, 2006. Culture war, In Wikipedia. Retrieved December 19, 2006 from, http://en.wikipedia.org/wiki/Culture_war

[294] _____, 2006. September 11, 2001 attacks: The attacks, In Wikipedia. Retrieved December 19, 2006 from, http://en.wikipedia.org/wiki/September_11%2C_2001_attacks#The_attacks; and also _____, 2006. World Trade Center: September 11, 2001, In Wikipedia. Retrieved December 19, 2006 from, http://en.wikipedia.org/wiki/World_Trade_Center#September_11.2C_2001

[295] Hoerber, p. 1507, footnote 3:19; and also p. 1558, footnote 6:16; and also p. 1619, footnote 6:71

[296] Schaff, P.S., Wace, H., Editors. 1994. Nicene and Post-Nicene Fathers, Volume 1, Second Series, Eusebius: Church History, Hendrickson Publishers, Peabody, MA, p. 138

[297] _____, 2006. Armenian Genocide, In Wikipedia. Retrieved December 19, 2006 from, http://en.wikipedia.org/wiki/Armenian_Genocide

[298] _____, 2006. Pontic Greek Genocide, In Wikipedia. Retrieved December 19, 2006 from, http://en.wikipedia.org/wiki/Pontic_Greek_Genocide; and also _____, 2006. Great Fire of Smyrna, In Wikipedia. Retrieved December 22, 2006 from, http://en.wikipedia.org/wiki/Great_Fire_of_Smyrna

[299] _____, 2006. Assyrian Genocide, In Wikipedia. Retrieved December 19, 2006 from, http://en.wikipedia.org/wiki/Assyrian_Genocide

[300] _____, 2006. Mehmed VI, In Wikipedia. Retrieved December 19, 2006 from, http://en.wikipedia.org/wiki/Mehmed_VI

[301] _____, 2006. Great Fire of Smyrna, In Wikipedia. Retrieved December 19, 2006 from, http://en.wikipedia.org/wiki/Great_Fire_of_Smyrna

[302] _____, July 2, 2006. Catholic priest knifed in Turkey, In BBC News online. Retrieved December 19, 2006 from, http://news.bbc.co.uk/2/hi/europe/5139408.stm

[303] de Bendern, P., Grove, T. January 19, 2007. Turkish–Armenian editor shot dead in Istanbul, In Reuters AlertNet online. Retrieved January 19, 2007 from, http://www.alertnet.org/thenews/newsdesk/L19386144.htm

[304] _____, 2006. Bible publishing firm murders in Malatya, In Wikipedia. Retrieved June 10, 2007 from, http://en.wikipedia.org/wiki/Bible_publishing_firm_murders_in_Malatya

305 _____, 2006. <u>Ali</u>, In Wikipedia. Retrieved December 19, 2006 from, http://en.wikipedia.org/wiki/Ali

306 Blair, pp. 67–69, 84–87

307 Blair, pp. 60–63, 67, 84–87; and also Elad, p. 37; and also Nevo and Koren, p. 163

308 _____, 2006. <u>Alaska Purchase</u>, In Encyclopedia Britannica online. Retrieved December 19, 2006 from, http://www.britannica.com/eb/article-9005366

309 _____, 1646. <u>The Westminster Confession of Faith</u>, Chapter XXXIII. Of the Last Judgment, In Presbyterian Church in America online. Retrieved December 19, 2006 from, http://www.pcanet.org/general/cof_chapxxxi-xxxiii.htm#chapxxxiii

310 Tolan, p. 43

311 Gibbon, E. 1782. <u>The History of the Decline and Fall of the Roman Empire</u>, Vol. 5, Chapter LI (In The East), Part II (Invasion of Syria), Conquest of Jerusalem, A.D. 637. In Christian Classics Ethereal Library online. Retrieved December 18, 2006 from, http://www.ccel.org/ccel/gibbon/decline/volume2/chap512.htm

312 Tolan, p. 194

313 Runciman, p. 79

314 _____, 2006. <u>Medieval Christian view of Muhammad</u>, In Wikipedia. Retrieved December 19, 2006 from, http://en.wikipedia.org/wiki/Medieval_Christian_view_of_Muhammad

315 Hazlitt, T., Translator. 1997. <u>The Table-Talk of Martin Luther</u>, Of the Antichrist, CCCCXXVI, In The Lutheran Publication Society, Philadelphia, PA. Retrieved December 21, 2006, from http://www.reformed.org/master/index.html?mainframe=/documents/Table_talk/table_talk.html

316 Redeker, R. September 19, 2006. <u>Faced with Islamist intimidations, what should the free world do?</u>, Editorial Section, Le Figaro, Paris, France

317 _____, 1577. <u>Solid Declaration of the Formula of Concord</u>, Solid Declaration VII: The Holy Supper, Parts 100–101, In the Book of Concord online. Retrieved December 19, 2006 from, http://bookofconcord.org/fc-sd.html

318 Reese, p. 1254

319 Reese, p. 1406, dates this event at AD 29, not AD 30. However, Hoerber, p. 1490, dates this event at AD 30.

320 Reese, p. 67

321 Reese, p. 139

322 _____, 2006. <u>Yarmuk River</u>, In Encyclopedia Britannica online. Retrieved December 19, 2006 from, http://www.britannica.com/eb/article-9077844

323 Reese, p. 1089–1093

324 Ibid.

325 Runciman, 256 pp.

[326] Runciman, p. 160

[327] Runciman, p. 79

[328] Reese, pp. 1089–1093

[329] Runciman, 256 pp.

[330] Spitz, L.W., 2001. The Protestant Reformation, 1517–1559, Concordia Publishing House, St. Louis, MO, p. 116

[331] Reese, p. 1254

[332] Reese, pp. 1089–1093

[333] Runciman, 256 pp.

[334] Reese, p. 1191

[335] Spitz, p. 116

[336] Reese, p. 1254

[337] _____, 2006. Tiglath-Pileser I, In Wikipedia. Retrieved December 19, 2006 from, http://en.wikipedia.org/wiki/Tiglath-Pileser_I

[338] _____, 2006. Tiglath-pileser I, In Encyclopedia Britannica online. Retrieved December 19, 2006 from, http://www.britannica.com/eb/article-9072449

[339] Reese, p. 6

[340] Reese, p. 803

[341] Reese, p. 886

[342] Reese, p. 992; foretold in Isaiah 10:12

[343] Reese, p. 1338

[344] _____, 2006. Tiglath-Pileser I, In Wikipedia. Retrieved December 19, 2006 from, http://en.wikipedia.org/wiki/Tiglath-Pileser_I

[345] Reese, p. 803

[346] Reese, p. 992; foretold in Isaiah 10:12

[347] Reese, p. 6

[348] Reese, p. 1338

[349] _____, 2006. Nineveh, In Encyclopedia Britannica online. Retrieved December 19, 2006 from, http://www.britannica.com/eb/article-9055879

[350] Reese, p. 119

[351] Tenney, M., General Editor. 1976. The Zondervan Pictorial Encyclopedia of the Bible, Vol. 5, Zondervan, Grand Rapids, MI, p. 911

[352] Reese, p. 120, dates this event at 1542 BC, not 1541.7 BC.

[353] Reese, p. 121, dates this event at 1502 BC, not 1501.7 BC.

[354] Reese, p. 122

[355] Reese, p. 340

[356] Reese, pp. 340, 348

[357] Hoerber, see essay on 'The Conquest and the Ethical Question of War', pp. 289–290

[358] Reese, p. 119

[359] Reese, p. 3

[360] Reese, p. 121, dates this event at 1502 BC, not 1501.7 BC.

[361] Reese, p. 54, dates this event at 1907 BC, not 1908 BC.

[362] Reese, p. 124

[363] Reese, p. 1406, dates this event at AD 29, not AD 30. However, Hoerber, p. 1490, dates this event at AD 30; also see Hoerber, p. 1566, footnote 9:31, where the Transfigured Jesus uses the Greek word, *exodos*, while speaking with Moses about how His death and resurrection will save God's people from bondage to sin.

[364] Reese, p. 340

[365] Reese, pp. 340, 348

[366] Reese, p. 1406, dates this event at AD 29, not AD 30. However, Hoerber, p. 1490, dates this event at AD 30.

[367] Reese, pp. 1089–1093

[368] Reese, p. 1157

[369] Reese, pp. 1160–1161; and also Kaiser and Garrett, p. 699

[370] Reese, p. 1191

[371] Kaiser and Garrett, p. 676

[372] Kaiser and Garrett, p. 681

[373] Kaiser and Garrett, p. 699

[374] Reese, p. 1183

[375] Reese, p. 1198

[376] Reese, p. 1208

[377] Hoerber, p. 718

[378] Reese, p. 54, dates this event at 1907 BC, not 1908 BC.

[379] _____, 2006. 1st Holy Imam, In Islamic Institute of New York online. Retrieved December 18, 2006 from, http://iiny.org/1stImam.htm

[380] Reese, pp. 58–59, dates this event at 1882 BC, not 1883 BC.

[381] _____, Battle of Badr, In Wikipedia. Retrieved December 19, 2006 from, http://en.wikipedia.org/wiki/Battle_of_Badr

[382] Reese, pp. 67–68, dates this event at 1834 BC, when Isaac was thirty-three years old. He likely came up with the thirty-three year old figure because that is the age that he uses for Christ when He was sacrificed near the same spot. I understand his reasoning, but I think the age for Isaac is unlikely. My eschatological timeline dates this event at 1846 BC, when Isaac was twenty-one years old.

[383] _____, 2006. Ali, In Wikipedia. Retrieved December 19, 2006 from, http://en.wikipedia.org/wiki/Ali

[384] Reese, pp. 73–74, dates this event at 1807 BC, not 1808 BC.

[385] Blair, pp. 60–63, 67, 84–87; and also Elad, p. 37

[386] Reese, p. 1049

[387] _____, 2006. Armenian Genocide, In Wikipedia. Retrieved December 19, 2006 from, http://en.wikipedia.org/wiki/Armenian_Genocide; and also _____, 2006. Pontic Greek Genocide, In Wikipedia. Retrieved December 19, 2006 from, http://en.wikipedia.org/wiki/Pontic_Greek_Genocide; and also _____, 2006. Assyrian Genocide, In Wikipedia. Retrieved December 19, 2006 from, http://en.wikipedia.org/wiki/Assyrian_Genocide

[388] Reese, pp. 1089–1093

[389] _____, 2006. Turkish Constitution of 1921, In Wikipedia. Retrieved December 23, 2006 from, http://en.wikipedia.org/wiki/Turkish_Constitution_of_1921; and also _____, 2006. Great Fire of Smyrna, In Wikipedia. Retrieved December 22, 2006 from, http://en.wikipedia.org/wiki/Great_Fire_of_Smyrna; and also _____, 2006. Soviet Union, In Wikipedia. Retrieved December 19, 2006 from, http://en.wikipedia.org/wiki/Soviet_Union

[390] Reese, p. 1191; and also Ezra 4:1–5; 5:3–4

[391] _____, 2006. Soviet Union, In Wikipedia. Retrieved December 19, 2006 from, http://en.wikipedia.org/wiki/Soviet_Union; and also _____, 2006. World Trade Center bombing: Planning and organization, In Wikipedia. Retrieved December 19, 2006 from, http://en.wikipedia.org/wiki/World_Trade_Center_bombing#Planning_and_organization; and also _____, 2006. Al-Qaeda: Gulf War and start of U.S. enmity, In Wikipedia. Retrieved December 19, 2006 from, http://en.wikipedia.org/wiki/Al-Qaeda#Gulf_War_and_start_of_U.S._enmity

[392] Reese, p. 1208

[393] Reese, p. 1210

[394] Reese, pp. 1424–1427, dates this event at AD 35, not AD 33; Iwas dates this event at ~ AD 34.

[395] Reese, p. 6

[396] Reese, p. 139

[397] Reese, p. 1599

[398] Reese, pp. 1001, 1004

[399] Reese, p. 1093

[400] Reese, p. 1049

[401] Reese, pp. 1089–1093

[402] Reese, p. 1049

[403] Blair, pp. 60–63, 84–85

[404] Elad, p. 37

[405] Paraphrased from Blair, pp. 86–87, and from the translation notes of Nevo and Koren, pp. 415–417

[406] Paraphrased from Blair, p. 86, and from the translation notes of Nevo and Koren, pp. 413, 416

[407] McGee, J.V. 1991. Thru the Bible Commentary Series: Daniel, Thoman Nelson Inc., Nashville, TN, p. 198

[408] Reese, p. 1049

[409] Blair, pp. 60–63, 67, 84–87; and also Elad, p. 37; and also Nevo and Koren, p. 163

[410] Reese, p. 9

[411] Reese, p. 10

[412] Reese, pp. 11–12

[413] Reese, p. 13

[414] Reese, p. 2

[415] Reese, p. 9

[416] Reese, p. 3

[417] Reese, p. 10

[418] _____, 2006. Filioque clause: Further East-West controversy, In Wikipedia. Retrieved December 10, 2006 from, http://en.wikipedia.org/wiki/Filioque_clause#Further_East-West_controversy; and also _____, 2006. Credo, In Wikipedia. Retrieved December 15, 2006 from, http://en.wikipedia.org/wiki/Credo

[419] Reese, pp. 11–12; and also 1 Peter 3:20–21

[420] Reese, p. 13

[421] Reese, p. 5

[422] Brownlie, J., Translator. 1920. Hymns of the Russian Church, R&R Clark, Ltd., Edinburgh, UK, In Hymns and Carols of Christmas online (public domain). Retrieved December 26, 2006 from, http://www.hymnsandcarolsofchristmas.com/Hymns_and_Carols/king_shall_come_when_morning_daw.htm

[423] _____, 2006. Karl Benz, In Wikipedia. Retrieved December 23, 2006 from, http://en.wikipedia.org/wiki/Karl_Benz

[424] _____, 2006. Benz Patent Motorwagen, In Wikipedia. Retrieved December 23, 2006 from, http://en.wikipedia.org/wiki/Benz_Patent_Motorwagen

[425] As quoted in Emerson: Quotes, In Transcendentalists.com; Retrieved December 23, 2006 from, http://www.transcendentalists.com/emerson_quotes.htm

[426] _____, May 29, 2007. Malaysian PM: Muslims 'at crossroads', In CNN online. Retrieved May 30, 2007 from, http://www.cnn.com/2007/WORLD/asiapcf/05/29/malaysia.muslim.ap/; and also Howden, D. June 14, 2007. World oil supplies are set to run out faster than expected, warn scientists, In

The Independent On Sunday online. Retrieved June 14, 2007 from, http://news.independent.co.uk/sci_tech/article2656034.ece

[427] _____, 2006. <u>Mohammed bin Laden</u>, In Wikipedia. Retrieved December 23, 2006 from, http://en.wikipedia.org/wiki/Mohammed_bin_Laden

[428] Seventy percent of the terrorists are Sunni from the oil-rich [southern] Persian Gulf states; the remainder are Shi'a from oil-rich Iran: _____, May 23, 2007. <u>Report: 70 Percent of Insurgents in Iraq Come From Gulf States Via Syria</u>, In FoxNews online. Retrieved May 23, 2007 from, http://www.foxnews.com/story/0,2933,274952,00.html

[429] The words of author Lawrence Wright, as interviewed on the Charlie Rose Show (aired April 6, 2007 on the Public Broadcasting Service), concerning his 2006 book, <u>The Looming Tower: Al-Qaeda and the Road to 9/11</u>, Knopf Publishing, New York, NY, 480 pp.

[430] _____, 2006. <u>99942 Apophis (2004 MN4)</u>. In NASA Near Earth Object Program online. Retrieved December 21, 2006 from, http://neo.jpl.nasa.gov/risk/a99942.html; and also _____, 2006. <u>99942 Apophis</u>, In Wikipedia. Retrieved December 21, 2006 from, http://en.wikipedia.org/wiki/99942_Apophis

[431] Liberties taken from the story as related in Connolly, B., Anderson, P. 1987. <u>First Contact: New Guinea's Highlanders Encounter the Outside World</u>, Viking Penguin, New York, NY, 336 pp.

[432] Hubers, J. 2004. <u>Christian Zionism: A Historical Analysis and Critique</u>, 21 pp. In Reformed Church in America online. Retrieved December 22, 2006 from, http://images.rca.org/docs/synod/ChristianZionism.pdf

[433] _____, 2006. <u>Endogamy</u>, In Wikipedia. Retrieved December 21, 2006 from, http://en.wikipedia.org/wiki/Endogamy

[434] Reese, p. 1243

[435] Reese, p. 92

[436] Hoerber, p. 1642, footnote 18:28

[437] Maier, pp. 371–372

[438] _____, 2006. <u>Israel: People</u>, In The World Factbook online. Retrieved December 23, 2006 from, https://www.cia.gov/cia/publications/factbook/geos/is.html#People

[439] _____, 2006. <u>Michael Dennis Rohan</u>, In Wikipedia. Retrieved December 23, 2006 from, http://en.wikipedia.org/wiki/Michael_Dennis_Rohan

[440] _____, 2006. <u>Turkish Constitution of 1921</u>, In Wikipedia. Retrieved December 23, 2006 from, http://en.wikipedia.org/wiki/Turkish_Constitution_of_1921

[441] Lamb, B., Interviewer. June 13, 2004. <u>C-Span Booknotes, Who Are We? The Challenges to America's National Identity</u>, In BookNotes online. Retrieved November 8, 2006, from http://www.booknotes.org/Transcript/?ProgramID=1784

[442] Mead, F.S., Hill, S.S. 2001. <u>Handbook of Denominations in the United States, 11th Edition</u>, Abingdon Press, Nashville, TN, p. 185

[443] Reese, p. 931

[444] Reese, p. 1434

[445] Maier, pp. 368–378

[446] _____, 2006. <u>Prussian Union (Evangelical Christian Church)</u>, In Wikipedia. Retrieved December 23, 2006 from, http://en.wikipedia.org/wiki/Prussian_Union_%28Evangelical_Christian_Church%29

[447] As quoted in Reinhardt, K.F., 1989. <u>Germany: 2000 Years</u>. Volume II, The Continuum Publishing Company, New York, NY.

[448] _____, 2006. <u>Martin Stephan</u>, In Wikipedia. Retrieved December 23, 2006 from, http://en.wikipedia.org/wiki/Martin_Stephan

[449] Reese, pp. 1424–1427, dates this event at AD 35, not AD 33; Iwas dates this event at ~ AD 34.

[450] _____, 2006. <u>Mayflower Compact</u>, In Wikipedia. Retrieved December 23, 2006 from, http://en.wikipedia.org/wiki/Mayflower_Compact

[451] Reese, pp. 348–393

[452] _____, 2006. <u>The First Council of Nicaea</u>, In Catholic Encyclopedia online. Retrieved December 23, 2006 from, http://www.newadvent.org/cathen/11044a.htm

[453] _____, 2006. <u>Paul of Samosata</u>, In Wikipedia. Retrieved December 30, 2006 from, http://en.wikipedia.org/wiki/Paul_of_Samosata

[454] _____, 2006. <u>Arianism</u>, In Wikipedia. Retrieved December 30, 2006 from, http://en.wikipedia.org/wiki/Arianism

[455] _____, 2006. <u>Arius</u>, In Wikipedia. Retrieved December 30, 2006 from, http://en.wikipedia.org/wiki/Arius

[456] _____, 2006. <u>Athanasius of Alexandria</u>, In Wikipedia. Retrieved December 30, 2006 from, http://en.wikipedia.org/wiki/Athanasius_of_Alexandria

[457] _____, 2006. <u>First Council of Nicaea: Agenda and procedure</u>, In Wikipedia. Retrieved December 30, 2006 from, http://en.wikipedia.org/wiki/First_Council_of_Nicaea#Agenda_and_procedure

[458] _____, 2006. <u>Arius: After the Council of Nicaea</u>, In Wikipedia. Retrieved December 30, 2006 from, http://en.wikipedia.org/wiki/Arius#After_the_Council_of_Nicaea

[459] Schaff and Wace, <u>Volume 2</u>, Second Series, Socrates Scholasticus, pp. 34–35.

[460] Schaff and Wace, <u>Volume 2</u>, Second Series, Sozomen, p. 279.

[461] Schaff and Wace, <u>Volume 2</u>, Second Series, Sozomen, p. 280.

[462] _____, 2006. <u>Macedonius I of Constantinople</u>, In Wikipedia. Retrieved December 30, 2006 from, http://en.wikipedia.org/wiki/Macedonius_I_of_Constantinople

[463] _____, 2006. <u>Ulfilas</u>, In Wikipedia. Retrieved December 30, 2006 from, http://en.wikipedia.org/wiki/Ulfilas

[464] Durant, Vol. IV, p. 62

[465] _____, 2006. First Council of Constantinople, In Wikipedia. Retrieved December 8, 2006 from, http://en.wikipedia.org/wiki/First_Council_of_Constantinople

[466] _____, 2006. Nestorianism, In Wikipedia. Retrieved December 8, 2006 from, http://en.wikipedia.org/wiki/Nestorianism

[467] _____, 2006. Council of Ephesus, In Wikipedia. Retrieved December 8, 2006 from, http://en.wikipedia.org/wiki/Council_of_Ephesus

[468] _____, 2006. Nestorianism, In Wikipedia. Retrieved December 8, 2006 from, http://en.wikipedia.org/wiki/Nestorianism

[469] _____, 2006. Assyrian Church of the East, In Wikipedia. Retrieved December 8, 2006 from, http://en.wikipedia.org/wiki/Assyrian_Church_of_the_East

[470] _____, 2006. Babai the Great, In Wikipedia. Retrieved December 8, 2006 from, http://en.wikipedia.org/wiki/Babai_the_Great

[471] _____, 2006. Assyrian Church of the East: Modern times, In Wikipedia. Retrieved December 8, 2006 from, http://en.wikipedia.org/wiki/Assyrian_Church_of_the_East#Modern_times

[472] Reese, p. 1406, dates this event at AD 29, not AD 30. However, Hoerber, p. 1490, dates this event at AD 30.

[473] _____, 2006. Monophysitism, In Wikipedia. Retrieved December 8, 2006 from, http://en.wikipedia.org/wiki/Monophysitism

[474] Iwas, Z. 1983. The Syrian Orthodox Church of Antioch at a Glance, In the Syriac Orthodox Resources online. Retrieved December 27, 2006 from, http://sor.cua.edu/Pub/PZakka1/SOCAtAGlance.html

[475] _____, 2006. Battle of Avarayr, In Wikipedia. Retrieved December 8, 2006 from, http://en.wikipedia.org/wiki/Battle_of_Avarayr

[476] _____, 2006. Oriental Orthodoxy, In Wikipedia. Retrieved November 30, 2006 from, http://en.wikipedia.org/wiki/Oriental_Orthodoxy

[477] _____, 2006. Miaphysitism, In Wikipedia. Retrieved November 30, 2006 from, http://en.wikipedia.org/wiki/Miaphysitism

[478] _____, 2006. Maurice (emperor), In Wikipedia. Retrieved November 30, 2006 from, http://en.wikipedia.org/wiki/Maurice_%28emperor%29

[479] Durant, Vol. IV, p. 423

[480] Kaegi, Heraclius, Emperor of Byzantium, pp. 50–51; and also _____, 2006. Heraclius, In Wikipedia. Retrieved November 31, 2006 from, http://en.wikipedia.org/wiki/Heraclius

[481] Durant, Vol. IV, p. 147

[482] Reese, p. 951

[483] _____, 2006. Heraclius: War against Persia, In Wikipedia. Retrieved November 30, 2006 from, http://en.wikipedia.org/wiki/Heraclius#War_against_Persia

[484] Durant, Vol. IV, p. 147

[485] Durant, Vol. IV, p.151

[486] Durant, Vol. IV, p.424

[487] Kaegi, <u>Heraclius, Emperor of Byzantium</u>, p. 190

[488] Kaegi, <u>Heraclius, Emperor of Byzantium</u>, p. 215

[489] _____, 2006. <u>Constantinople</u>, In Wikipedia. Retrieved December 30, 2006 from, http://en.wikipedia.org/wiki/Constantinople

[490] Kaegi, <u>Heraclius, Emperor of Byzantium</u>, pp. 30, 194

[491] Kaegi, <u>Heraclius, Emperor of Byzantium</u>, p. 297

[492] Kaegi, <u>Heraclius, Emperor of Byzantium</u>, pp. 205–206; and also Kaegi, <u>Byzantium and the early Islamic conquests</u>, pp. 63–64

[493] Kaegi, <u>Heraclius, Emperor of Byzantium</u>, p. 194

[494] _____, 2006. <u>Phocas</u>, In Wikipedia. Retrieved November 30, 2006 from, http://en.wikipedia.org/wiki/Phocas

[495] Ormanian, M. 1988. <u>The Church of Armenia</u>, St. Vartan Press, New York, NY, p.43

[496] Allen, P., Neil, B. 2002. <u>Maximus the Confessor and His Companions: Documents From Exile</u>, Oxford University Press, Oxford, UK, p. 13

[497] Kaegi, <u>Heraclius, Emperor of Byzantium</u>, p. 213

[498] Kaegi, <u>Heraclius, Emperor of Byzantium</u>, p. 220

[499] Kaegi, <u>Heraclius, Emperor of Byzantium</u>, p. 209

[500] Kaegi, <u>Heraclius, Emperor of Byzantium</u>, p. 214

[501] Kaegi, <u>Heraclius, Emperor of Byzantium</u>, p. 208

[502] Ormanian, p.43

[503] Kaegi, <u>Heraclius, Emperor of Byzantium</u>, pp. 214–215

[504] Kaegi, <u>Heraclius, Emperor of Byzantium</u>, p. 211

[505] Kaegi, <u>Heraclius, Emperor of Byzantium</u>, p. 263

[506] Kaegi, <u>Heraclius, Emperor of Byzantium</u>, p. 216

[507] Kaegi, <u>Heraclius, Emperor of Byzantium</u>, p. 217

[508] Kaegi, <u>Heraclius, Emperor of Byzantium</u>, p. 218

[509] Tolan, p. 194

[510] Runciman, 256 pp.

[511] _____, 2006. <u>St. Maximus of Constantinople</u>, In Catholic Encyclopedia online. Retrieved November 30, 2006 from, http://www.newadvent.org/cathen/10078b.htm

[512] Kaegi, <u>Heraclius, Emperor of Byzantium</u>, pp. 225, 233, 281

[513] Kaegi, <u>Byzantium and the early Islamic conquests</u>, p. 217

[514] Kaegi, <u>Heraclius, Emperor of Byzantium</u>, p. 270

[515] Kaegi, <u>Heraclius, Emperor of Byzantium</u>, p. 271

[516] Durant, Vol. IV, p. 151

[517] Kaegi, <u>Heraclius, Emperor of Byzantium</u>, p. 238

[518] Kaegi, Heraclius, Emperor of Byzantium, pp. 278, 301, 304–305

[519] Kaegi, Heraclius, Emperor of Byzantium, p. 235

[520] Kaegi, Heraclius, Emperor of Byzantium, pp. 195, 201

[521] Kaegi, Heraclius, Emperor of Byzantium, p. 237; and also Kaegi, Byzantium and the early Islamic conquests, pp. 110–111

[522] Kaegi, Heraclius, Emperor of Byzantium, p. 257

[523] Kaegi, Heraclius, Emperor of Byzantium, p. 192

[524] Kaegi, Byzantium and the early Islamic conquests, p. 211

[525] Kaegi, Byzantium and the early Islamic conquests, p. 91

[526] Kaegi, Byzantium and the early Islamic conquests, pp. 129–130

[527] Kaegi, Heraclius, Emperor of Byzantium, pp. 241–243

[528] Kaegi, Heraclius, Emperor of Byzantium, p. 278

[529] Kaegi, Byzantium and the early Islamic conquests, pp. 112–146, 272

[530] Kaegi, Heraclius, Emperor of Byzantium, pp. 244, 295

[531] Kaegi, Heraclius, Emperor of Byzantium, pp. 244–245, 247

[532] Kaegi, Heraclius, Emperor of Byzantium, p. 255; and also Kaegi, Byzantium and the early Islamic conquests, p. 238

[533] Kaegi, Heraclius, Emperor of Byzantium, pp. 252–253

[534] Kaegi, Heraclius, Emperor of Byzantium, p. 249

[535] Kaegi, Heraclius, Emperor of Byzantium, p. 239

[536] Kaegi, Heraclius, Emperor of Byzantium, p. 287

[537] Durant, Vol. IV, p. 218

[538] Kaegi, Heraclius, Emperor of Byzantium, p. 278

[539] Tolan, p. 40

[540] Kaegi, Heraclius, Emperor of Byzantium, p. 207

[541] Kaegi, Heraclius, Emperor of Byzantium, p. 237

[542] Kaegi, Heraclius, Emperor of Byzantium, p. 256

[543] Kaegi, Heraclius, Emperor of Byzantium, p. 258

[544] Kaegi, Heraclius, Emperor of Byzantium, pp. 245, 272, 277

[545] Kaegi, Heraclius, Emperor of Byzantium, p. 255

[546] Kaegi, Heraclius, Emperor of Byzantium, p. 258

[547] Kaegi, Heraclius, Emperor of Byzantium, pp. 272–273

[548] Kaegi, Heraclius, Emperor of Byzantium, pp. 285–286

[549] Kaegi, Heraclius, Emperor of Byzantium, pp. 225, 281

[550] Kaegi, Heraclius, Emperor of Byzantium, p. 233

[551] Kaegi, Byzantium and the early Islamic conquests, p. 217

[552] Kaegi, Heraclius, Emperor of Byzantium, p. 261

553 Kaegi, <u>Heraclius, Emperor of Byzantium</u>, pp. 215, 260

554 Kaegi, <u>Heraclius, Emperor of Byzantium</u>, p. 289

555 Kaegi, <u>Heraclius, Emperor of Byzantium</u>, pp. 247, 288

556 Kaegi, <u>Heraclius, Emperor of Byzantium</u>, p. 262

557 Kaegi, <u>Heraclius, Emperor of Byzantium</u>, p. 263

558 Kaegi, <u>Heraclius, Emperor of Byzantium</u>, p. 294

559 Kaegi, <u>Heraclius, Emperor of Byzantium</u>, p. 238

560 _____, 2006. <u>Heraklonas</u>, In Wikipedia. Retrieved November 30, 2006 from, http://en.wikipedia.org/wiki/Heraklonas

561 Allen and Neil, p. 1

562 Parsch, P. 1953. <u>The Church's Year of Grace</u>, Liturgical Press, Collegeville, MN

563 Allen and Neil, pp. 159–161

564 Allen and Neil, pp. 151–153

565 Allen and Neil, pp. 137, 163

566 _____, 2006. <u>Constans II</u>, In Wikipedia. Retrieved December 19, 2006 from, http://en.wikipedia.org/wiki/Constans_II

567 _____, 2006. <u>Constantine IV</u>, In Wikipedia. Retrieved December 19, 2006 from, http://en.wikipedia.org/wiki/Constantine_IV

568 Blair, pp. 60–63, 67, 84–87; and also Elad, p. 37; and also Nevo and Koren, p. 163

569 _____, 2006. <u>Justinian II</u>, In Wikipedia. Retrieved December 19, 2006 from, http://en.wikipedia.org/wiki/Justinian_II

570 Ormanian, p. 43

571 Allen and Neil, pp. 49–119

572 _____, 1999. <u>Common Declaration Signed by Pope John Paul II and Armenian Catholicos Karekin I</u>, In Eternal Word Television Network online. Irondale, AL. Retrieved December 19, 2006 from, http://www.ewtn.com/library/PAPALDOC/ARMENDEC.HTM

573 Paraphrased from, Schaff and Wace, <u>Volume 12</u>, Second Series, Leo the Great, pp. 40–43; and also Schaff and Wace, <u>Volume 14</u>, Second Series, The Fourth Ecumenical Council, pp. 254–258; and also _____, 2006. <u>The Council of Chalcedon–451 A.D.</u>, In Eternal Word Television Network online. Irondale, AL. Retrieved December 19, 2006 from, http://www.ewtn.com/library/councils/chalcedo.htm

574 Ormanian, p. 46

575 Reese, p. 1441

576 This line-of-thought is derived from Lewis, <u>Miracles: A Preliminary Study</u>, p. 101

577 Reese, p. 1254, dates the Incarnation at 6 BC; Reese, p. 1406, dates the Crucifixion at AD 29, not AD 30. However, Hoerber, p. 1490, dates the Crucifixion at AD 30.

[578] Hoerber, p. 1613, footnote 5:1

[579] This phrasing is derived from Lewis, <u>Miracles: A Preliminary Study</u>, p. 203

[580] This phrasing is derived from Lewis, <u>Miracles: A Preliminary Study</u>, pp. 146, 239

[581] Reese, pp. 1408–1415, dates these events at AD 29, not AD 30.

[582] Ormanian, pp. 44–45

[583] Ormanian, pp. 35, 40–41

[584] _____, 2006. <u>Battle of Manzikert</u>, In Wikipedia. Retrieved December 9, 2006 from, http://en.wikipedia.org/wiki/Battle_of_Manzikert

[585] _____, 2006. <u>Mesrop Mashtots, Saint</u>, In Encyclopedia Britannica online. Retrieved December 9, 2006 from, http://www.britannica.com/eb/article-9052231

[586] Artinian, H., 2000. <u>The Godless and the Infidels: Memoirs of a Rascal Boy During World War I</u>, Writers Club Press, Lincoln, NE, 132 pp.

[587] Paraphrased from Blair, p. 86; and also the translation notes of Nevo and Koren, pp. 413, 416

[588] Ormanian, p. 46

[589] _____, 2006. <u>Timur</u>, In Wikipedia. Retrieved December 9, 2006 from, http://en.wikipedia.org/wiki/Timur

[590] _____, 2006. <u>Chaldean Catholic Church</u>, In Wikipedia. Retrieved December 9, 2006 from, http://en.wikipedia.org/wiki/Chaldean_Catholic_Church

[591] _____, 2006. <u>Common Christological Declaration Between the Catholic Church and the Assyrian Church of the East</u>, In the Vatican online. Retrieved December 9, 2006 from, http://www.vatican.va/roman_curia/pontifical_councils/chrstuni/documents/rc_pc_chrstuni_doc_11111994_assyrian-church_en.html

[592] Paraphrased from, Schaff and Wace, <u>Volume 12</u>, Second Series, Leo the Great, pp. 40–43; and also Schaff and Wace, <u>Volume 14</u>, Second Series, The Fourth Ecumenical Council, pp. 254–258; and also _____, 2006. <u>The Council of Chalcedon–451 A.D.</u>, In Eternal Word Television Network online. Irondale, AL. Retrieved December 19, 2006 from, http://www.ewtn.com/library/councils/chalcedo.htm

[593] Will, G. 2003. <u>The Venting Party</u>, In Jewish World Review online. Retrieved December 9, 2006 from, http://www.jewishworldreview.com/cols/will080703.asp

[594] _____, 2006. <u>Library of Alexandria: Destruction of the Library</u>, In Wikipedia. Retrieved December 9, 2006 from, http://en.wikipedia.org/wiki/Library_of_Alexandria#Destruction_of_the_Library

[595] _____, 2006. <u>Alawite: Religion</u>, In Wikipedia. Retrieved December 9, 2006 from, http://en.wikipedia.org/wiki/Alawite#Religion

[596] _____, 2006. <u>Alawite</u>, In Wikipedia. Retrieved December 9, 2006 from, http://en.wikipedia.org/wiki/Alawite

597 _____, 2006. Ibadi, In Wikipedia. Retrieved December 9, 2006 from, http://en.wikipedia.org/wiki/Ibadi

598 _____, 2006. Kharijites, In Wikipedia. Retrieved December 9, 2006 from, http://en.wikipedia.org/wiki/Kharijites

599 Partlow, J. January 17, 2007. U.N. puts '06 civilian toll at 34,452, Washington Post, In The Arizona Republic online. Retrieved January 18, 2007 from, http://www.azcentral.com/news/articles/0117iraq0117.html

600 _____, 2006. Third Council of Toledo, In Wikipedia. Retrieved December 10, 2006 from, http://en.wikipedia.org/wiki/Third_Council_of_Toledo

601 _____, 2006. Charles Martel: Battle of Tours, In Wikipedia. Retrieved December 10, 2006 from, http://en.wikipedia.org/wiki/Charles_Martel#Battle_of_Tours

602 _____, 2006. Filioque clause: Further East-West controversy, In Wikipedia. Retrieved December 10, 2006 from, http://en.wikipedia.org/wiki/Filioque_clause#Further_East-West_controversy

603 _____, 2006. Credo, In Wikipedia. Retrieved December 15, 2006 from, http://en.wikipedia.org/wiki/Credo

604 Ridenour, F. 2001. So What's the Difference?, Regal Books, Ventura, CA, pp. 60–61

605 As quoted in Benjamin Franklin, In Wikiquote. Retrieved December 10, 2006 from, http://en.wikiquote.org/wiki/Benjamin_Franklin

606 _____, 2006. Soviet Union, In Wikipedia. Retrieved December 10, 2006 from, http://en.wikipedia.org/wiki/Soviet_Union

607 _____, 2006. Battle of Badr, In Wikipedia. Retrieved December 10, 2006 from, http://en.wikipedia.org/wiki/Battle_of_Badr

608 _____, September 7, 2007. Pope makes pilgrimage to Austrian shrine, In USAToday online. Retrieved September 8, 2007 from, http://www.usatoday.com/news/religion/2007-09-07-pope-austria_N.htm

609 This line-of-thought and phrasing is derived from Lewis, Miracles: A Preliminary Study, pp. 201–202

610 Creation took place in 3976 BC; God's promise regarding Eve's offspring occurred immediately after the fall of man in 3975 BC. Reese, pp. 2–6

611 Reese, p. 8

612 Reese, p. 9

613 Reese, p. 10

614 Reese, p. 54, dates this event at 1907 BC, not 1908 BC.

615 Reese, p. 139

616 Reese, p. 510

617 Reese, p. 1191

618 Reese, p. 1406, dates this event at AD 29, not AD 30. However, Hoerber, p. 1490, dates this event at AD 30.

[619] Chalcedonianism became orthodoxy within the Christian church in AD 451; it was emphatically affirmed at the Fifth Ecumenical Council in AD 553. _____, 2006. Second Council of Constantinople, In Wikipedia. Retrieved December 10, 2006 from, http://en.wikipedia. org/wiki/Second_Council_of_Constantinople

[620] _____, 2006. Filioque clause: Further East-West controversy, In Wikipedia. Retrieved December 10, 2006 from, http://en.wikipedia.org/wiki/Filioque_ clause#Further_East-West_controversy; and also _____, 2006. Credo, In Wikipedia. Retrieved December 15, 2006 from, http://en.wikipedia. org/wiki/Credo

[621] Dr. Martin Luther launched the Reformation of the Church in AD 1517; it was codified when the Augsburg Confession was presented to the Holy Roman Emperor by a group of northern German princes in AD 1530. _____, 2006. Augsburg Confession, In Wikipedia. Retrieved December 10, 2006 from, http://en.wikipedia.org/wiki/Augsburg_confession

[622] This phrasing is derived from Lewis, Miracles: A Preliminary Study, p. 201

[623] Hoerber, p. 1613, footnote 5:1

[624] Reese, pp. 1424–1427, dates this event at AD 35, not AD 33; Iwas dates this event at ~ AD 34.

[625] _____, 2006. Church of the Holy Sepulchre, In Wikipedia. Retrieved December 10, 2006 from, http://en.wikipedia.org/wiki/Church_of_the_Holy_Sepulchre

[626] _____, 2006. Diocletian Persecution, In Wikipedia. Retrieved December 11, 2006 from, http://en.wikipedia.org/wiki/Diocletian_Persecution

[627] _____, 2006. Edict of Milan, In Wikipedia. Retrieved December 11, 2006 from, http://en.wikipedia.org/wiki/Edict_of_Milan

[628] _____, 2006. Al-Hakim bi-Amr Allah, In Wikipedia. Retrieved December 11, 2006 from, http://en.wikipedia.org/wiki/Al-Hakim_bi-Amr_Allah

[629] _____, 2006. Church of the Holy Sepulchre, In Wikipedia. Retrieved December 11, 2006 from, http://en.wikipedia.org/wiki/Church_of_the_Holy_Sepulchre

[630] _____, 2006. Battle of Manzikert, In Wikipedia. Retrieved December 11, 2006 from, http://en.wikipedia.org/wiki/Battle_of_Manzikert

[631] _____, 2006. East-West Schism, In Wikipedia. Retrieved December 11, 2006 from, http://en.wikipedia.org/wiki/East-West_Schism

[632] _____, 2006. Seljuq dynasty, In Wikipedia. Retrieved December 11, 2006 from, http://en.wikipedia.org/wiki/Seljuq_dynasty

[633] _____, 2006. Alexios I Komnenos, In Wikipedia. Retrieved December 11, 2006 from, http://en.wikipedia.org/wiki/Alexios_I_Komnenos

[634] _____, 2006. Pope Urban II, In Wikipedia. Retrieved December 11, 2006 from, http://en.wikipedia.org/wiki/Pope_Urban_II

635 _____, 2006. Godfrey of Bouillon, In Wikipedia. Retrieved December 11, 2006 from, http://en.wikipedia.org/wiki/Godfrey_of_Bouillon

636 _____, 2006. 1016, In Wikipedia. Retrieved December 11, 2006 from, http://en.wikipedia.org/wiki/1016

637 _____, 2006. Siege of Jerusalem (1187), In Wikipedia. Retrieved December 11, 2006 from, http://en.wikipedia.org/wiki/Siege_of_Jerusalem_%281187%29

638 _____, 2006. 1492, In Wikipedia. Retrieved December 11, 2006 from, http://en.wikipedia.org/wiki/1492

639 Ibid.

640 Spitz, pp. 120–121.

641 _____, 2006. Battle of Lepanto (1571), In Wikipedia. Retrieved December 12, 2006 from, http://en.wikipedia.org/wiki/Battle_of_Lepanto_%281571%29

642 _____, 2006. Battle of Navarino, In Wikipedia. Retrieved December 12, 2006 from, http://en.wikipedia.org/wiki/Battle_of_Navarino

643 _____, 2006. USS Constitution: History, In Wikipedia. Retrieved December 12, 2006 from, http://en.wikipedia.org/wiki/USS_Constitution#History

644 _____, 2006. Italo-Turkish War, In Wikipedia. Retrieved December 12, 2006 from, http://en.wikipedia.org/wiki/Italo-Turkish_War

645 _____, 2006. League of Nations mandate, In Wikipedia. Retrieved December 5, 2006 from, http://en.wikipedia.org/wiki/League_of_Nations_mandate

646 _____, 2006. Filioque clause: Further East-West controversy, In Wikipedia. Retrieved December 12, 2006 from, http://en.wikipedia.org/wiki/Filioque_clause#Further_East-West_controversy; and also _____, 2006. Credo, In Wikipedia. Retrieved December 15, 2006 from, http://en.wikipedia.org/wiki/Credo

647 _____, 2006. Atomic bombings of Hiroshima and Nagasaki: The bombing, In Wikipedia. Retrieved December 12, 2006 from, http://en.wikipedia.org/wiki/Atomic_bombings_of_Hiroshima_and_Nagasaki#The_bombing

648 _____, 2006. Muhammad al-Mahdi, In Wikipedia. Retrieved December 12, 2006 from, http://en.wikipedia.org/wiki/Muhammad_al-Mahdi

649 _____, 2006. Mahdi: Characteristics of the Mahdi, In Wikipedia. Retrieved December 12, 2006 from, http://en.wikipedia.org/wiki/Mahdi#Characteristics_of_the_Mahdi

650 _____, 2006. Muhammad Ahmad, In Wikipedia. Retrieved December 12, 2006 from, http://en.wikipedia.org/wiki/Muhammad_Ahmad

651 _____, 2006. Ismail I, In Wikipedia. Retrieved December 12, 2006 from, http://en.wikipedia.org/wiki/Ismail_I

652 Hooker, R. 1996. Shi'a: The Safavids, In World Civilizations online. Retrieved December 12, 2006 from, http://www.wsu.edu/~dee/SHIA/SAFAVID.HTM

[653] _____, 2006. <u>Battle of Chaldiran</u>, In Wikipedia. Retrieved December 13, 2006 from, http://en.wikipedia.org/wiki/Battle_of_Chaldiran

[654] _____, 2006. <u>Ismail I</u>, In Wikipedia. Retrieved December 13, 2006 from, http://en.wikipedia.org/wiki/Ismail_I

[655] Durant, Vol. IV, pp. 177–178

[656] Durant, Vol. IV, p. 178

[657] Muir, p. 571

[658] Shadid, A. 2007. <u>Across Arab World, a Widening Rift</u>, In Washington Post online. Retrieved February 12, 2007 from, http://www.washingtonpost.com/wp-dyn/content/article/2007/02/11/AR2007021101328_3.html

[659] Durant, Vol. IV, p. 217

[660] _____, 2006. <u>St. John the Evangelist, III. The Latter Accounts of John</u>, In Catholic Encyclopedia online. Retrieved December 13, 2006 from, http://www.newadvent.org/cathen/08492a.htm#III

[661] Ibid.

[662] _____, 2006. <u>Hasan al-Askari</u>, In Wikipedia. Retrieved December 13, 2006 from, http://en.wikipedia.org/wiki/Hasan_al-Askari

[663] _____, 2006. <u>Muhammad al-Mahdi</u>, In Wikipedia. Retrieved December 13, 2006 from, http://en.wikipedia.org/wiki/Muhammad_al-Mahdi

[664] Hooker, R. 1996. <u>Shi'a: The Safavids</u>, In World Civilizations online. Retrieved December 18, 2006 from, http://www.wsu.edu/~dee/TEXT/111/unit6pt2.rtf

[665] _____, 2006. <u>Mahdi: Shi'a sources</u>, In Wikipedia. Retrieved December 13, 2006 from, http://en.wikipedia.org/wiki/Mahdi#Shi.27a_sources

[666] Ibid.

[667] Ibid.

[668] _____, June 2, 2006. <u>Al-Zarqawi Urges Sunnis to Confront Shiites</u>, Associated Press, In NewsMax.com; Retrieved December 13, 2006 from, http://www.newsmax.com/archives/articles/2006/6/2/91126.shtml

[669] _____, 2006. <u>Al-Askari Mosque</u>, In Wikipedia. Retrieved December 14, 2006 from, http://en.wikipedia.org/wiki/Al-Askari_Mosque

[670] _____, 2006. <u>Mahdaviat</u>, In Wikipedia. Retrieved December 14, 2006 from, http://en.wikipedia.org/wiki/Mahdaviat

[671] Hooker, R. 1996. <u>Husayn</u>, In World Civilizations online. Retrieved December 12, 2006 from, http://www.wsu.edu/~dee/SHIA/HUSAYN.HTM

[672] The words of Professor Bernard Lewis, as quoted in Machlis, D., Lazaroff, T. January 29, 2007. <u>Muslims 'about to take over Europe'</u>, In The Jerusalem Post online. Retrieved January 30, 2007 from, http://www.jpost.com/servlet/Satellite?cid=1167467834546&pagename=JPost/JPArticle/ShowFull

[673] As quoted in Machlis, D., Lazaroff, T. January 29, 2007. Muslims 'about to take over Europe', In The Jerusalem Post online. Retrieved January 30, 2007 from, http://www.jpost.com/servlet/Satellite?cid=1167467834546&pagename=JPost/JPArticle/ShowFull

[674] Nevo and Koren, p. 278

[675] Paraphrased from Blair, pp. 86–87; and also the translation notes of Nevo and Koren, pp. 415–417

[676] Ibid.

[677] Martin, W. 1997. The Kingdom of the Cults, Bethany House Publishers, Minneapolis, MN, p. 220

[678] Ibid.

[679] Martin, pp. 229–230

[680] Martin, p. 238

[681] Trifkovic, p. 64

[682] Martin, pp. 191–192

[683] Karjian, N. 2004. Beyond God as Father, FORUM: The Quarterly Journal of the Armenian Evangelical Union of North America, Vol. 28, No. 1, Fresno, CA

[684] Ibid.

[685] Ibid.

[686] Nimoy, L., Kuspit, D. 2002. Shekhina, Umbrage, New York, NY, 96 pp. In Leonard Nimoy Photography online. Retrieved December 19, 2006 from, http://www.leonardnimoyphotography.com/

[687] Osborne, G., General Editor; Comfort, P., Series Editor. 1997. Life Application Study Bible Commentary: Luke, Tyndale House Publishing, Wheaton, IL, pp. 370–371

[688] Trifkovic, S., pp. 173–174

[689] Paraphrased from Blair, pp. 86–87, and from the translation notes of Nevo and Koren, pp. 415–417

[690] _____, October 31, 2006. Nearly half of Americans uncertain God exists: poll, In Breitbart.com; Retrieved December 19, 2006 from, http://www.breitbart.com/news/2006/10/31/061031235233.s0l4o4wy.html

[691] Chadwick, J. June 15, 2005. Denomination debates declaration of Jesus' divinity, In NewJersey.com; Retrieved December 27, 2006 from, http://www.northjersey.com/page.php?qstr=eXJpcnk3ZjcxN2Y3dnFlZUVFeXkyJmZnYmVsN2Y3dnFlZUVFeXk2NzA4MDkz; and also _____, July 1–July 5, 2005. Come Listen, Go Serve, God is Still Speaking, Minutes, Twenty-Fifth General Synod, Georgia World Congress Center, Atlanta, GA. In the United Church of Christ online. Retrieved December 27, 2006 from, http://www.ucc.org/synod/pdfs/gs25minutes.pdf

[692] Radin, C.A. November 19, 2006. Episcopal split reaches Mass. diocese, Boston Sunday Globe, Boston, MA, pp. A1, B6

[693] The words of Episcopal Presiding Bishop Katharine Jefferts Schori, as quoted in Grossman, C.L. February 4, 2007. Episcopal church's new dawn, In USA Today online. Retrieved February 5, 2007 from http://www.usatoday.com/news/religion/2007-02-04-jefferts-schori-cover_x.htm

[694] Hutchinson, W.R. 1989. Between the Times: The Travail of the Protestant Establishment in America, 1900–1960, Cambridge University Press, New York, NY, 344 pp.

[695] Mead and Hill, p. 239

[696] _____, 2006. ELCA Quick Facts, In the Evangelical Lutheran Church in America online. Retrieved December 19, 2006, from http://www.elca.org/communication/quick.html

[697] _____, 2006. Who We Are, In the Presbyterian Church (USA) online. Retrieved December 19, 2006, from http://www.pcusa.org/navigation/whoweare.htm

[698] Mead and Hill, p. 132; and also Grossman, C.L. February 4, 2007. Episcopal church's new dawn, In USA Today online. Retrieved February 5, 2007 from http://www.usatoday.com/news/religion/2007-02-04-jefferts-schori-cover_x.htm

[699] Mead and Hill, p. 48

[700] Mead and Hill, p. 125

[701] Mead and Hill, p. 107

[702] The words of former Episcopal priest, Rev. S. L. Edwards, as quoted in Nunley, J. June 27, 2002. Controversial Maryland priest renounces ECUSA orders, In the Episcopal Church (USA) online. Retrieved December 12, 2006 from, http://www.episcopalchurch.org/3577_20407_ENG_HTM.htm

[703] Lewis, C.S. 2001. The Great Divorce, HarperCollins, New York, NY, pp. 43–44

[704] These are not her exact words—I've reproduced the quote from memory with poetic license. But she said something that was basically this stupid.

[705] _____, 2006. Council of Trent, In Wikipedia. Retrieved December 19, 2006 from, http://en.wikipedia.org/wiki/Council_of_Trent

[706] Walther, p. 74

[707] Akin, J. 1994. A Primer on Indulgences, In Catholic Answers online. Retrieved December 19, 2006 from, http://www.catholic.com/thisrock/1994/9411fea1.asp

[708] Tolstoy, L. 1869. War and Peace, Book Nine: 1812, Chapter II, In Online-Literature.com (public domain). Retrieved December 19, 2006 from, http://www.online-literature.com/tolstoy/war_and_peace/

[709] _____, 2006. Jamarat Bridge, In Wikipedia. Retrieved December 19, 2006 from, http://en.wikipedia.org/wiki/Jamarat_Bridge

[710] _____, 2006. <u>Salat: The five daily prayers</u>, In Wikipedia. Retrieved December 19, 2006 from, http://en.wikipedia.org/wiki/Salat#The_five_daily_prayers

[711] _____, 2006. <u>Adhan</u>, In Wikipedia. Retrieved December 19, 2006 from, http://en.wikipedia.org/wiki/Adhan

[712] Lester, T. January 1999. <u>What is the Koran?</u>, Atlantic Monthly, p. 45; and also Crone, P. August 31, 2006. <u>What do we actually know about Mohammed?</u>, In OpenDemocracy.net; Retrieved November 29, 2006 from, http://www.opendemocracy.net/faith-europe_islam/mohammed_3866.jsp

[713] _____, 2006. <u>Understanding Islam and the Muslims</u>, Pamphlet, The Embassy of Saudi Arabia, Department of Islamic Affairs, 601 New Hampshire Avenue, NW, Washington, DC

[714] Trifkovic, p. 78

[715] For the Qur'anic apologists' answer to this charge see Saifullah, M.S.M., Karim, E., David, A. 1999. <u>Crucifixion Or 'Crucifiction' In Ancient Egypt?</u>, In Islamic Awareness online. Retrieved December 8, 2006 from, http://www.islamic-awareness.org/Quran/Contrad/External/crucify.html

[716] Nevo and Koren, pp. 266–267

[717] Trifkovic, p. 77

[718] Dawood, N.J., Translator. 2006. <u>The Koran</u>, Penguin Books Ltd., London, UK, p. 1

[719] Ibid.

[720] Crone, P. August 31, 2006. <u>What do we actually know about Mohammed?</u>, In OpenDemocracy.net; Retrieved November 29, 2006 from, http://www.opendemocracy.net/faith-europe_islam/mohammed_3866.jsp

[721] Ibid.

[722] Lester, p. 45

[723] Lester, p. 43

[724] Trifkovic, pp. 81–82

[725] Bingham, H., Interviewer. December 1991. <u>Face to Face with Muhammad Ali</u>, In Reader's Digest online. Retrieved December 20, 2006 from, http://www.rd.com/content/openContent.do?contentId=26496

[726] Reese, p. 2

[727] Reese, p. 5

[728] Reese, p. 1262, dates this event at AD 25, not AD 26. However, Hoerber, p. 1488, dates this event at AD 26.

[729] Reese, p. 6

[730] Reese, p. 1026

[731] Maier, pp. 368–378

[732] Reese, p. 1026

[733] Maier, pp. 368–378

[734] Reese, p. 1254

[735] _____, 2006. Ali, In Encyclopedia Britannica online. Retrieved December 27, 2006 from, http://www.britannica.com/eb/article-9005712

[736] Reese, p. 1262, dates this event at AD 25, not AD 26. However, Hoerber, p. 1488, dates this event at AD 26.

[737] What eventually became Qur'an Sura 48.29 ("Muhammad is the Messenger of God") was inscribed on al-Malik's first Islamic coins in AD 692; see Nevo and Koren, pp. 266–267; and also Blair, pp. 65–66, 84

[738] Reese, p. 1406, dates this event at AD 29, not AD 30. However, Hoerber, p. 1490, dates this event at AD 30.

[739] What eventually became Qur'an Sura 48.28 ("He sent His messenger with guidance and the religion of truth, that he may cause it to prevail over all [other] religions") was inscribed on al-Malik's coins in AD 696; they also said, "There is no god but God alone, without partner"; see Nevo and Koren, pp. 266–267, 331; and also Blair, pp. 67–69

[740] Reese, pp. 1424–1427, dates this event at AD 35, not AD 33; Iwas dates this event at ~ AD 34.

[741] Blair, pp. 60–63, 67, 84–87; and also Elad, p. 37; and also Nevo and Koren, p. 163

[742] Reese, p. 1599

[743] Lester, p. 45; and also Crone, P. August 31, 2006. What do we actually know about Mohammed?, In OpenDemocracy.net; Retrieved November 29, 2006 from, http://www.opendemocracy.net/faith-europe_islam/mohammed_3866.jsp

[744] _____, 2006. Diocletian Persecution, In Wikipedia. Retrieved December 28, 2006 from, http://en.wikipedia.org/wiki/Diocletian_Persecution

[745] _____, 2006. Church of the Holy Sepulchre, In Wikipedia. Retrieved December 28, 2006 from, http://en.wikipedia.org/wiki/Church_of_the_Holy_Sepulchre

[746] This year differential is 673, not 666, but often the date given for the construction of an ancient building is the *terminus a quo* (i.e., the year that the foundation stone was lain). The completion and consecration of the Church of the Holy Sepulchre could have been up to ten years later. See Blair, pp. 62–68, 85

[747] _____, 2006. Al-Hakim bi-Amr Allah, In Wikipedia. Retrieved December 28, 2006 from, http://en.wikipedia.org/wiki/Al-Hakim_bi-Amr_Allah

[748] _____, 2006. Mesrop Mashtots, Saint, In Encyclopedia Britannica online. Retrieved December 14, 2006 from, http://www.britannica.com/eb/article-9052231

[749] _____, 2006. Battle of Manzikert, In Wikipedia. Retrieved December 14, 2006 from, http://en.wikipedia.org/wiki/Battle_of_Manzikert

[750] _____, 2006. Second Council of Nicaea, In Wikipedia. Retrieved December 28, 2006 from, http://en.wikipedia.org/wiki/Second_Council_of_Nicaea; and also _____, 2006. Feast of Orthodoxy, In Wikipedia. Retrieved December 14, 2006 from, http://en.wikipedia.org/wiki/Feast_of_Orthodoxy

[751] Runciman, 256 pp.

[752] _____, January 30, 2007. <u>Two Lovers Stoned to Death in Pakistan</u>, In FoxNews online. Retrieved January 31, 2007 from, http://www.foxnews.com/story/0,2933,248798,00.html; and also _____, January 27, 2007. <u>Harsher penalties fail to stop 'honor killings' in Jordan</u>, In Taipei Times online. Retrieved January 31, 2007 from, http://www.taipeitimes.com/News/world/archives/2007/01/27/2003346560

[753] Miniter, R. July 27, 2005. <u>The Master of Terrorism</u>, In RichardMiniter.com; Retrieved December 14, 2006 from, http://www.richardminiter.com/Archives/osama_bin_laden/index.html

[754] Durant, Vol. IV, pp. 182–183

[755] Lewis, <u>Mere Christianity</u>, p. 103

[756] Brogan, D. June/July 2003. <u>Al Qaeda's Greeley Roots: How the intellectual father of Osama Bin Laden's terrorist network learned to hate America in a tiny Colorado town</u>. In 5280 Denver's Mile-High Magazine online. Retrieved on December 1, 2006 from, http://www.5280.com/issues/2003/0306/feature.php?pageID=269

[757] Ibid.

[758] _____, 2006. <u>Sayyid Qutb</u>, In Wikipedia. Retrieved December 4, 2006 from, http://en.wikipedia.org/wiki/Sayyid_Qutb

[759] Dennett, D.C. 1996. <u>Darwin's Dangerous Idea: Evolution and the Meaning of Life</u>, Simon and Schuster, New York, NY, 592 pp.

[760] As quoted in <u>Daniel Dennett: Darwinian Natural Selection</u>, Evolution Library, In Public Broadcasting Service online. Retrieved November 30, 2006 from, http://www.pbs.org/wgbh/evolution/library/08/1/text_pop/l_081_05.html

[761] _____, 2006. <u>Does evolution prove there is no God?</u>, Evolution Library, The Basics, Frequently Asked Questions about Evolution, In Public Broadcasting Service online. Retrieved November 30, 2006, from http://www.pbs.org/wgbh/evolution/library/faq/cat01.html

[762] This line-of-thought is derived from Lewis, <u>Miracles: A Preliminary Study</u>, pp. 43, 107–108, 130, 149, 173

[763] As quoted in _____, 2001. <u>Understanding Evolution</u>, In Public Broadcasting Service online. Retrieved November 30, 2006 from, http://www.pbs.org/wgbh/evolution/library/08/1/text_pop/l_081_06.html

[764] As quoted in _____, June 15, 2006. <u>Hawking says humans close to finding answers to origin of universe</u>, In BreitBart.com; Retrieved December 14, 2006 from, http://www.breitbart.com/news/2006/06/15/060615121526.oz37mqn8.html

[765] This is evidenced by Osama bin Laden's praise for liberal extremists like Noam Chomsky, and Osama's blather about global warming, etc.: _____, 2007. <u>Bin Laden Urges American to Convert to Islam: Read Transcript</u>, In

WNBC.com; Retrieved September 12, 2007 from http://www.wnbc.com/download/2007/0907/14069356.pdf

[766] _____, 2006. Internet: Creation of the Internet, In Wikipedia. Retrieved December 20, 2006 from, http://en.wikipedia.org/wiki/Internet#Creation_of_the_Internet

[767] Orwell, G. 1945. Animal Farm, Chapter 5, In Online-Literature.com; Retrieved December 20, 2006, from http://www.online-literature.com/orwell/animalfarm/5/

[768] Adapted from Chirol, V., Barnham, H.D. (Translator). 1923. Tales of Nasr-Ed-Din Khoja, C.M.G. Nisbet & Co. Ltd., London, UK. Public domain.

[769] This line-of-thought is derived from Lewis, Miracles: A Preliminary Study, pp. 166–169

[770] Adams, J. January 28, 1817. From the correspondence from John Adams to Professor Nathaniel Gorham, Special Collections, Boston Public Library, Boston, MA

[771] As quoted in Rene Descartes, In Wikipedia. Retrieved December 20, 2006 from, http://en.wikipedia.org/wiki/Rene_Descartes

[772] This line-of-thought is derived from Lewis, Miracles: A Preliminary Study, pp. 21–22, 41–42

[773] _____, 2006. Age of the universe, In Wikipedia. Retrieved December 20, 2006 from, http://en.wikipedia.org/wiki/Age_of_the_universe

[774] _____, 2006. Starlight problem, In Wikipedia. Retrieved December 20, 2006 from, http://en.wikipedia.org/wiki/Starlight_problem

[775] _____, 2006. Omphalos (theology), In Wikipedia. Retrieved December 20, 2006 from, http://en.wikipedia.org/wiki/Omphalos_%28theology%29

[776] _____, 2006. Andy Green, In Wikipedia. Retrieved December 20, 2006 from, http://en.wikipedia.org/wiki/Andy_Green

[777] This line-of-thought is derived from Lewis, Miracles: A Preliminary Study, pp. 30, 165–166

[778] This line-of-thought is derived from Lewis, Miracles: A Preliminary Study, pp. 260–261

[779] This line-of-thought and phrasing is derived from Lewis, Miracles: A Preliminary Study, pp. 30, 165–166

[780] Angier, N. August 9, 2005. Independently, Two Frogs Blaze the Same Venomous Path, New York Times, New York, NY

[781] Ibid.

[782] _____, 2006. Hummingbird, In Wikipedia. Retrieved December 22, 2006 from, http://en.wikipedia.org/wiki/Hummingbird

[783] Ibid.

[784] This line-of-thought is derived from Lewis, Miracles: A Preliminary Study, pp. 79–80

[785] As quoted in Lewis, <u>Miracles: A Preliminary Study</u>, p. 40

[786] As quoted in <u>Daniel Dennett</u>, In Wikiquote. Retrieved December 21, 2006 from, http://en.wikiquote.org/wiki/Daniel_Dennett

[787] _____, 2006. <u>Monarch butterfly</u>, In Wikipedia. Retrieved December 21, 2006 from, http://en.wikipedia.org/wiki/Monarch_butterfly

[788] Lewman, N., Narrator. 2001. <u>Baby Tales</u>, Nature, Malvine Martin Productions, Approximately 60 minutes. The video may be purchased from the Public Broadcasting Service online. Retrieved December 21, 2006 from, http://www.pbs.org/wnet/nature/baby/

[789] _____, 2006. <u>Gypsy moth: North American Introduction</u>, In Wikipedia. Retrieved December 21, 2006 from, http://en.wikipedia.org/wiki/Gypsy_moth#North_American_Introduction

[790] _____, 2006. <u>Gombe Timeline</u>. In JaneGoodall.org; Retrieved December 21, 2006 from, http://www.janegoodall.org/jane/study-corner/chimpanzees/gombe-timeline.asp

[791] This line-of-thought is derived from Lewis, <u>Miracles: A Preliminary Study</u>, p. 161

[792] This line-of-thought is derived from Lewis, <u>Miracles: A Preliminary Study</u>, p. 28

[793] This line-of-thought and phrasing is derived from Lewis, <u>Miracles: A Preliminary Study</u>, p. 57

[794] As quoted in Lewis, <u>Miracles: A Preliminary Study</u>, p. 22

[795] This line-of-thought is derived from Lewis, <u>Miracles: A Preliminary Study</u>, p. 58

[796] This line-of-thought is derived from Lewis, <u>Miracles: A Preliminary Study</u>, pp. 28, 34, 56, 139, 167–168

[797] This line-of-thought and phrasing is derived from Lewis, <u>Miracles: A Preliminary Study</u>, pp. 10–11, 46–47

[798] This phrasing is derived from Lewis, <u>Miracles: A Preliminary Study</u>, pp. 21–22, 44

[799] This line-of-thought and phrasing is derived from Lewis, <u>Miracles: A Preliminary Study</u>, pp. 22–24, 55

[800] Bube, R.H. 1971. <u>The Human Quest: a new look at science and the Christian faith</u>, Word Books, Waco, TX, pp. 110–112

[801] Goudarzi, S. January 11, 2006. <u>Scientists Finally Figure Out How Bees Fly</u>, In FoxNews online. Retrieved December 15, 2006 from, http://www.foxnews.com/story/0,2933,181212,00.html

[802] _____, 2004. <u>Survey of Physicians' Views on Miracles</u>, In The Jewish Theological Seminary online. Retrieved December 21, 2006 from, http://www.jtsa.edu/research/finkelstein/surveys/physicians.shtml

[803] This line-of-thought is derived from Lewis, <u>Miracles: A Preliminary Study</u>, pp. 107–108

[804] This line-of-thought and phrasing is derived from Lewis, <u>Miracles: A Preliminary Study</u>, pp. 48–49, 68, 76, 173

[805] _____, 2006. 2004 Indian Ocean earthquake, In Wikipedia. Retrieved December 21, 2006 from, http://en.wikipedia.org/wiki/2004_Indian_Ocean_earthquake

[806] _____, 2006. 2005 Sumatra earthquake, In Wikipedia. Retrieved December 21, 2006 from, http://en.wikipedia.org/wiki/2005_Sumatra_earthquake

[807] _____, 2006. Cuneiform script, In Wikipedia. Retrieved December 21, 2006 from, http://en.wikipedia.org/wiki/Cuneiform_script

[808] _____, 2006. List of languages by first written accounts, In Wikipedia. Retrieved December 21, 2006 from, http://en.wikipedia. org/wiki/List_of_languages_by_first_written_accounts

[809] _____, 2006. Ebla, In Wikipedia. Retrieved December 21, 2006 from, http://en.wikipedia.org/wiki/Ebla

[810] _____, 2006. Lothal, In Wikipedia. Retrieved December 21, 2006 from, http://en.wikipedia.org/wiki/Lothal

[811] _____, 2006. Human evolution, In Wikipedia. Retrieved December 21, 2006 from, http://en.wikipedia.org/wiki/Human_evolution

[812] _____, 2006. List of human fossils, In Wikipedia. Retrieved December 21, 2006 from, http://en.wikipedia.org/wiki/List_of_human_fossils

[813] _____, December 15, 2005. Evidence of Humans in England 700,000 Years Ago, Associated Press, In FoxNews online. Retrieved December 21, 2006 from, http://www.foxnews.com/story/0,2933,178721,00.html; and also _____, 2006. The first Europeans—one million years ago. In BBC online. Retrieved December 21, 2006 from, http://www.bbc.co.uk/sn/prehistoric_life/human/human_evolution/first_europeans1.shtml

[814] As quoted in _____, 2006. Dream Turns Deadly, In ABC.com; Retrieved December 27, 2006 from, http://abcnews.go.com/Primetime/story?id=1030398&page=2

[815] As quoted in Internet Movie Database online. Retrieved December 27, 2006 from, http://www.imdb.com/title/tt0427312/quotes

[816] As quoted in Medred, C. October 8, 2003. Wildlife author killed, eaten by bears he loved, In Anchorage Daily News online. Retrieved December 27, 2006 from, http://www.adn.com/front/story/4110831p-4127072c.html

[817] _____, January 2004. Some Bet on My Death, In Outside Magazine online. Retrieved December 27, 2006, from http://outside.away.com/outside/news/200401/200401_treadwell_letter.html

[818] As quoted in Internet Movie Database online. Retrieved December 27, 2006 from, http://www.imdb.com/title/tt0427312/quotes

[819] Jefferson was not only a racist, but also a hypocrite. Several years after he wrote this he began a long-term affair with his mulatto slave, Sally Hemings; see Jefferson, T. 1781. Notes on the State of Virginia, Query XIV, In Public Broadcasting Service online. Document Transcript, page 230, Retrieved December 27, 2006, from http://www.pbs.org/jefferson/archives/documents/frame_ih198157.htm; and also _____, 2006. Sally Hemings,

In Wikipedia. Retrieved December 21, 2006 from, http://en.wikipedia. org/wiki/Sally_Hemings

[820] Reese, p. 17

[821] _____, 2006. The Age of Spiritual Machines, In Wikipedia. Retrieved December 21, 2006 from, http://en.wikipedia.org/wiki/The_Age_of_Spiritual_Machines

[822] _____, February 12, 2005. Never Say Die: Live Forever, In Wired online (Associated Press release). Retrieved December 27, 2006 from, http://www.wired. com/medtech/health/news/2005/02/66585

[823] Kurzweil, R., 2000. The Age of Spiritual Machines: When Computers Exceed Human Intelligence, Viking Penguin, New York, NY, p. 9

[824] _____, 2006. The Singularity Is Near, In Wikipedia (see Epoch 6. The Universe Wakes Up). Retrieved December 21, 2006 from, http://en.wikipedia. org/wiki/The_Singularity_Is_Near

[825] The story is an urban legend originating from Sanchez, T. 1996. Up and Down With the Rolling Stones, Da Capo Press, Cambridge, MA, 320 pp. The truth is that he simply had his blood filtered. See _____, 2000. Let It Bleed, In Snopes.com; Retrieved November 29, 2006 from, http://www.snopes.com/ music/artists/richards.htm

[826] Reese, p. 1448

[827] _____, 2006. Willa Cather: Film Maker Interview, American Masters, In Public Broadcasting Service online. Retrieved December 27, 2006 from, http:// www.pbs.org/wnet/americanmasters/database/cather_w_interview.html

978-0-595-43798-6
0-595-43798-2

CPSIA information can be obtained
at www.ICGtesting.com
Printed in the USA
FFHW021556241019
55765541-61622FF